AFRICAN AMERICAN WRITERS

AFRICAN AMERICAN WRITERS

SECOND EDITION

VALERIE SMITH

EDITOR IN CHIEF

VOLUME 2

JUNE JORDAN TO RICHARD WRIGHT

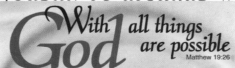
Charles Scribner's Sons

an imprint of the Gale Group
New York • Detroit • San Francisco • London • Boston • Woodbridge, CT

Copyright © 2001 by Charles Scribner's Sons, an imprint of the Gale Group

Charles Scribner's Sons
1633 Broadway
New York, NY 10019

Gale Group
27500 Drake Rd.
Farmington Hills, MI 48331

1 2 3 4 5 6 7 8 9 10

Printed in the United States of America

Library of Congress Cataloging-in-Publication Data

African American Writers / Valerie Smith, editor.   Rev. ed.
    p. cm.
    Includes bibliographical references and index.
    ISBN 0–684–80638-X (set)   ISBN 0–684–80639–8 (vol. 1)   ISBN 0–684–80640–1 (vol. 2)
    1. American literature—Afro-American authors—Dictionaries. 2. Afro-American authors—
Biography—Dictionaries. 3. Afro-Americans in literature—Dictionaries. I. Smith, Valerie, 1956–
PS153.N5 A344   2000
810.9′896073′03   dc21
00–058371

JUNE JORDAN
(1936–   )

CARLA FRECCERO

BEST KNOWN FOR her political poetry, her incisive occasional essays, and in the 1990s as the founder and director of the Poetry for the People project at the University of California at Berkeley, June Jordan is a woman of great professional, artistic, and political breadth. She is an activist, a poet, an essayist, a teacher, a playwright, a composer, a librettist, an urban planner, and an author of children's books. Born in Harlem on 9 July 1936 to Granville and Mildred Jordan, who emigrated to New York City from their home in Jamaica, Jordan began to write poetry at the age of seven, two years after her family moved to a brownstone on Hancock Street in Brooklyn's Bedford-Stuyvesant neighborhood. Much of her early work moves between these four principal coordinates: father, mother, child, and the neighborhood, with all its economic, social, and political significance as "the ghetto."

In Jordan's work, family and location are concentric circles moving outward from a center and inward toward it. In her first collection of essays spanning the period from 1964 to 1980, *Civil Wars* (1981), she describes the process:

You begin with your family and the kids on the block, and next you open your eyes to what you call your people and that leads you into land reform into Black English into Angola leads you back to your own bed where you lie by yourself, wondering if you deserve to be peaceful, or trusted or desired or left to the freedom of your own unfaltering heart. And the scale shrinks to the size of a skull: your own interior cage.

In that same passage she expresses what can be seen as the core principle of her work: the desire to connect individual human experience to the unfolding of history, to forge the link between the political in its largest sense and the personal in its most intimate aspects. "My life," she writes, "seems to be an increasing revelation of the intimate face of universal struggle."

Civil Wars enacts the connection between individual autobiography and history. The essays are arranged in chronological order, each prefaced by the author's explanation both of what was happening in her own life at the time and of the particular political events that provide the occasion or the context for the essay. This work—together with an essay (1985) by Peter Erickson, the scholar she designated as her biographer—provides a biographical portrait of Jordan. *Civil Wars* also documents recent history, as its title suggests. Focusing most specifically on New York City itself, the volume examines the continuing war in the United States against the enfranchisement of the African American. Like *Dry Victories* (1972)—a comparative study of Reconstruction and the civil rights era written for young people and cast as a dialogue between Jerome, a descendant of the Mississippi Senator Charles Caldwell, who, in 1870, along with thirty-four other men, became one of the first African Americans to enter the Mississippi state legislature, and Jerome's friend Kenny, who discusses more current events—*Civil Wars* implicitly compares the civil rights struggles in the South and the North in the 1950s and 1960s with the ongoing struggles of the 1970s in the United States and abroad. The book is also a record of Jordan's career in journalism. Many of the essays were originally written for publications such as the *Nation, Black World, New Republic, First World, Ms., Essence, Seven Days,* and the *New York Times Book Review.*

Early Life

Jordan's early life in Bedford-Stuyvesant as a daughter of poor working parents—her father was a postal clerk, her mother a nurse, and both eventually worked night shifts for slightly more pay—introduced her to the overwhelming odds against which her people struggle and the contradictions produced by those odds. In one moving passage from an essay delivered as the keynote address for a Northwest Regional Conference of the Child Welfare League of America in 1978, "Old Stories: New Lives"—an essay punctuated, like Toni Morrison's *The Bluest Eye* (1970), with a refrain reminiscent of the "Dick and Jane" readers used to indoctrinate children into the white middle-class American dream ("See Valerie. She is five. She is scared. She is white.")—Jordan describes the brutality of her own painful childhood:

> As a child growing up in Bedford-Stuyvesant . . . I did surmise . . . that nobody really liked me or any of the people in my community. . . . And while it would not have helped me, it would not have rescued me, to know that one reason my father beat me to the extent of occasional scar tissue was because he himself felt beaten and he himself felt bullied

and despised by strangers more powerful than he would ever be . . . , is it not apparent to me today, is it not crystalline to all of us, that the pain and the grief, the racist and sexist destruction of our possibilities, the incessant competition, the humiliating uncertainty, impotence, and disappointment of our grownup existence cannot but punish those who are yet weaker than we: our children?

The strength and creativity that were to shape her life also began during her childhood. "I thought it was normal to be involved in a regular family way with something called poetry," she said in an interview with Alexis DeVeaux in *Essence* (April 1981). Her parents, primarily her father, introduced her to poetry, to the Bible, Shakespeare, Edgar Allan Poe, and the dialectical poetry of Paul Laurence Dunbar. "Early on," she writes in the introduction to *Civil Wars,* "the scriptural concept that 'in the beginning was the Word and the Word was with God and the Word was God'—the idea that the word could represent and then deliver into reality what the word symbolized—this possibility of language, of writing, seemed to me magical and basic and irresistible." As for Black English, her uncle Teddy—who lived upstairs—also provided her with inspiration through his storytelling, rescued her from the excesses of her father, and taught June ("small, short . . . a target") to defend herself against neighborhood bullies.

For one year of high school Jordan commuted an hour and twenty minutes to attend Midwood High School, where she was the only African American in a school with a student body of three thousand. Her father then enrolled her in Northfield School for Girls (now Northfield–Mount Hermon), an exclusive prep school in Massachusetts. In the autobiographical essay "Notes of a Barnard Dropout," originally presented in dialogue with Alice Walker at Barnard College on 11 November 1975 and later included in *Civil Wars,* she explains: "I began my life in a completely Black universe, and then for the three years of prep school, found myself completely immersed in a white universe."

June Jordan

And nobody, and not a single course of study at Barnard, ever spoke to issues judged critical, or to possible commitments evaluated as urgent. More specifically, no one ever presented me with a single Black author, poet, historian, personage, or idea, for that matter. Nor was I ever assigned a single woman to study as a thinker, or writer, or poet, or life force. Nothing that I learned, here, lessened my feelings of pain and confusion and bitterness as related to my origins: my street, my family, my friends. Nothing showed me how I might try to alter the political and economic realities underlying our Black condition in white America.

During her twenties, then, she studied the poetry of Margaret Walker, Robert Hayden, and Langston Hughes, who she says were among her favorite writers. In the 1977 essay "Thinking about My Poetry," collected in *Civil Wars*, she says of this time, "I passed through a period of years during which I pretty much refused to read, or hear, any poetry that was not Black."

The Civil Rights Era

In her sophomore year at Barnard, June Jordan met Michael Meyer, a senior at Columbia University. They married a year later, in 1955. In 1958 their son, Christopher David, was born. Jordan touches upon the vagaries of the marital relationship and eventual divorce in numerous poems, but the fullest prose account of their interracial marriage appeared nearly thirty years later in an essay from 1983 titled "Love Is Not the Problem" in *On Call: Political Essays* (1985). Here, too, the political and the personal form a seamless web. She and Meyer met, she says, while he was collecting signatures for an anti-McCarthy petition, and it was his fortitude of purpose on that freezing day that first attracted her. That same year, 1954, the Supreme Court, in *Brown* v. *Board of Education of Topeka*, overturned the "separate but equal" ruling established in the *Plessy* v. *Ferguson* case of 1896 and paved the way for the abolition of racial segregation. Jordan cites the decision as a

The shock of this transfer to an all-white world with its corresponding blindness to and silence about anyone or anything African American and female informed Jordan's period of militancy about the use and promotion of Black English and African American art. As a child, in high school, and again in college, she learned about and studied poets who were usually white and male. "Notes of a Barnard Dropout" describes her experiences at the college, which she began attending in September 1953. She writes, "I hoped that Barnard College—which I attended while living at home, in Brooklyn— I hoped that Barnard College would either give me the connection between the apparently unrelated worlds of white and black, or that this college would enable me to make that connection for myself." The bitterness and sense of betrayal that charge the impassioned, insistent staccato of passages in this essay retrospectively "prefigure," as it were, the committed course her life was to take during and after college:

gloss on her laconic sentence about racial difference: "We were not the same." She meditates on the acts of racial hatred committed in the 1950s and 1960s and on the connection between those acts and the mentality of those who looked askance at this mixed couple, "those two kids," who "quietly did something against the law, against every tradition, against the power arrangements of this country." In the 1981 interview with Alexis De Veaux, she mentions that when she and Meyers traveled together they were often the object of insults and slurs. The essay ends by describing a scene of conflict between wife and husband over Jordan's decision to join a Freedom Ride to Baltimore with her infant son and Meyer's anger at her risking her life and that of her son. Her didactic last paragraph, like an ironic twist in the final couplet of an Elizabethan sonnet, beautifully rewrites this chapter of her life as a political and spiritual parable: "None of this means that any marriage is a great idea or a terrible thing. All I'm saying is that *love* is not the problem."

In 1955, the year she married Meyer, Jordan temporarily interrupted her college career to follow her husband to the University of Chicago, where he pursued graduate studies in anthropology. She attended the same university for a year and returned to Barnard in 1956, leaving the college permanently in February 1957. By 1964, the date of "Testimony," the first essay in *Civil Wars*, she was a working mother living in housing projects in Queens, writing poetry four hours a day, studying architecture at the Donnell Library in Manhattan (where she discovered the work and writings of R. Buckminster Fuller), and pursuing her career as a freelance journalist. It was at this time that she met Malcolm X as well as local and national members of CORE (Congress of Racial Equality, a largely northern organization that in the 1940s initiated the sit-in tactics later used by the Student Nonviolent Coordinating Committee and other organizations in the South), and became involved in Harlem politics.

At the instigation of a friend, Jordan became assistant to Frederick Wiseman, the producer of the film adaptation of a 1959 novel by Warren Miller, *The Cool World* (1964), directed by Shirley Clarke, set in Harlem and "starring," as she puts it, "Black kids from the streets." "Testimony," in which, Jordan writes, "I used cinematic techniques of jump-cuts and juxtaposition," is a written documentary (a "spoken scenario") of the experiences of Hampton Clanton (the boy who played the role of the protagonist, "Duke") and others involved in the process of making the film. The experiences of young African Americans have been a dominant concern of Jordan's life and work, encompassing both the intimate sphere of her life with her son, Christopher, and the public domain of education and welfare. She worked as a research associate and writer for Mobilization for Youth in the year 1965–1966, ran a writing workshop for children in Brooklyn with the Teachers and Writers Collaborative founded by Herb Kohl (which produced the collaborative anthology *The Voice of the Children*, edited by Jordan and Terri Bush, in 1970), and began a college teaching career in 1967 at City College. She has continued to pursue these issues in her poetry, especially her first collection, *Some Changes* (1971), her work as a teacher and theorizer of the principles of Black English, and her children's books, all of which have explicitly political content: *Who Look at Me* (1969), *His Own Where* (1971), *Dry Victories* (1972), *Fannie Lou Hamer* (1972), and *New Life: New Room* (1975).

The year 1964 proved to be a difficult year for Jordan, both personally and in terms of the "up North variations of the racist storm convulsing America," as she calls it in her introduction to her "Letter to Michael" of the same year (in *Civil Wars*). She had taken on full responsibility for supporting herself and Christopher, working as a freelance journalist in New York, while her husband remained in Chicago. In Mississippi that summer three student civil rights workers "disappeared," while in Harlem, a police officer named Thomas Gilligan shot Jimmy Powell, a fifteen-year-old African American boy, for threatening him with a penknife. Rioting ensued in Harlem and, using the fiction of a letter to her husband, Michael, Jordan gives an account of the frightening weekend she spent dodging bullets with her running buddy, Bostic Van Felton, from the cast of *The Cool World*, and assisting Douglas Hitchings, a white psychiatrist, in caring for the wounded. A week after the riot, Michael wrote to tell her he would not return. The only ray of hope in what was otherwise a bitterly bleak time of her life (including extreme financial poverty) was that she was collaborating with Buckminster Fuller on a plan for the architectural redesign of Harlem, commissioned by *Esquire* magazine. Their goal, she explains in an introduction to her letter to Fuller (1964, in *Civil Wars)*, was to "demonstrate the rational feasibility of beautiful and low-cost shelter integral to a comprehensively conceived new community for human beings." The project culminated in disappointment. She concludes her introduction: "When the article appeared in the April 1965 issue of *Esquire*, with the results of our collaboration ascribed entirely to Fuller, the editors referred to it as 'an utopian plan.' These same editors called the piece 'Instant Slum Clearance.' My title had been 'Skyrise for Harlem.' " Yet, as Jordan notes in the foreword to *Civil Wars*, the imaginative exercise saved her life, gave her renewed optimism at a time when she "was filled with hatred for everything and everyone white." In her first published novel, *His Own Where*, she translates these aspirations for architectural redesign into fiction; the protagonist, Buddy, remodels the interior of his house and rearranges the gardens on his block to create community spaces.

In 1966 Mildred Jordan committed suicide, an incident about which June Jordan remained silent until the 1975 essay, "Notes of a Barnard Dropout." Later, in the introduction to *Civil Wars*, "One Way of Beginning This Book," she movingly connects her desire to be an artist to the wish to "vindicate" her mother's "sacrifice" (as she referred to her mother's death in the dedication of the 1977 poetry collection *Things That I Do in the Dark*):

The picture of a spoon, of an elegant, spare utensil as common in its purpose as a spoon, and as lovely and singular in its form as sculpture, utterly transformed my ideas about the possibilities of design in relation to human existence. If my mother had held such a spoon, if I could have given her such a useful piece of beauty, even once, perhaps everything would have been different for her: she who committed suicide, not so many years later.

In "Ah, Momma," the prose poem that appears at the end of the Barnard speech, Jordan comes to terms with the frustrated aspirations of her mother ("you told me, whispering, that once, you wanted to become an artist"), her sacrifice ("in the ugly, spacious kitchen where you never dreamed about what you might do instead"), and the challenge that sacrifice represents for the artist, her daughter ("It was there that I came, humbly, into an angry, an absolute, determination that I would, one day, prove myself to be, in fact, your daughter / Ah, Momma, I am still trying").

The work of mourning for her mother continued through the 1970s. "Ah, Momma" reappears in *Things That I Do in the Dark*, a collection dedicated to her parents that includes selected previously published poems with some new ones. There it follows a series of poems: "One Minus One Minus One" (1976), "For My Mother" (1969), "On the Spirit of Mildred Jordan" (1971), and "Gettin Down to Get Over" (1972). This last poem, dedicated to her mother, is one of Jordan's most powerful poems (particularly as she recites it on the recording produced by Spoken Arts in 1978, also titled *Things That I Do in the Dark)*. Together all of these poems—which first appeared in Jordan's 1974 collection titled *New Days: Poems of Exile and Return*—combine a celebration of African American womanhood reminiscent of the black arts movement's rap-style recitations and a scathing indictment of racism and sexism with a prayer to the mother-muse to "help me / turn the face of history / *to your face.*"

Seven years after the publication of *Things That I Do in the Dark*, in an essay entitled "Many Rivers to Cross"—originally presented as the keynote address at a conference titled "Women and Work" at Barnard in 1981 and later included in *On Call*—she tells the full story of her mother's death in angry, pain-filled, guilt-ridden detail. Again the personal experience becomes a political parable:

> I cherish the mercy and grace of women's work. But I know there is new work that we must undertake as well: that new work will make defeat detestable to us. That new women's work will mean we will not die trying to stand up: we will live that way: standing up.
>
> I came too late to help my mother to her feet.
>
> By way of everlasting thanks to all of the women who have helped me to stay alive I am working never to be late again.

June Jordan's teaching career began in 1967, when Herb Kohl asked her to take his place teaching freshman composition at City College in New York. At that time the English department boasted an illustrious faculty, including Toni Cade Bambara, Addison Gayle Jr., Ray Patterson, Barbara Christian, David Henderson, Adrienne Rich, Audre Lorde, and Mina Shaughnessy. Jordan and others became involved in the minority students' movement to establish an open admissions policy at the college. At the time there were movements at colleges and universities throughout the United States to establish Third World studies, black studies, and Afro-American studies programs. The essay "Black Studies: Bringing Back the Person," published in 1969, in *Civil Wars*, is an initial position paper on a subject that marked a decade of struggle over the adequacy of American higher education to the experience of American people of color and continued to remain a concern for Jordan in the decades that followed. Central to this issue is the situation of speakers of Black English, long penalized in public schools for using "bad" English. Jordan's books for children employ Black English, as do many of her poems and one essay in *On Call* ("White Tuesday," 1984). She dates her commitment to Black English to the period in 1968 when she conducted a writing workshop for children in the Fort Greene neighborhood of Brooklyn (a project reflected in the 1970 anthology *The Voice of the Children*). The workshop took place during the same turbulent period as the calamities that devastated the African American community in 1968: the assassination of Martin Luther King Jr., the Chicago convention, and nationwide riots. She writes in "Thinking about My Poetry": "It was the attempt to carry them [the children at the workshop] through the unspeakably brutal year of 1968, that riveted my heart and mind to the preservation of Black English and to distinctively Black poetry." Two essays in particular eloquently express her affirmation of Black English, "White English/Black English: The Politics of Translation" (1972, in *Civil Wars*) and "Nobody Mean More to Me than You and the Future Life of Willie Jordan" (1985, in *On Call*).

One of the most controversial aspects of her work has been Jordan's use and advocacy of Black English. In 1971, African American parents in Baltimore organized in an effort to ban *His Own Where* for fear that students would be unwilling to master the standard English required for success in white America. The April 1989 issue of the *New Criterion*, a right-wing journal of the arts, published an article by Richard Abowitz, a junior at the University of Wisconsin at Madison (where Jordan taught during the summer of 1988), attacking Jordan for teaching Black English "at a time when students are graduating from college with an increasingly feeble command of the English language." In fact, however, as Jordan points out in her essay "Nobody Mean More to Me," mastery of the dialect has to be learned and is by no means a "natural" written art. She notes that in 1979, "Michigan courts ruled that Black English is, indeed, an identifiably different language system from that of Standard English and that public schools presuming to teach Black children must present these children with teachers and language studies positively oriented to the distinctive language skills these children bring into the classroom."

The 1970s

In 1969 Jordan made her first trip to Mississippi to write an article for the *New York Times Mag-*

azine called "Black Home in Mississippi." The trip was a sort of pilgrimage, for Mississippi had become, since 1964 and the Mississippi Freedom Summer Project, a national symbol of all that the Civil Rights movement had been fighting against. It was there she met Alice Walker, who became her lifelong friend, and the activist Fannie Lou Hamer, whom she visited again in 1971 after the murder of an African American girl, Joetha Collier, by a gang of drunken white teenagers. Subsequent to this second visit she wrote a biography for children, *Fannie Lou Hamer*. It was Hamer, she claims, who stemmed the tide of her hatred for whites with her famous phrase, "Ain' no such a thing as I can hate anybody and hope to see God's face." In late 1969 Buckminster Fuller nominated Jordan for the Prix de Rome in Environmental Design, which she won primarily for her novel intended to introduce children to notions of urban design. *His Own Where* which was published in 1971. She spent the year 1970 at the American Academy in Rome, where her project, as she describes it in the introduction "White English/ Black English," was ostensibly to "transmute this novel into a scenario for a commercial feature film, and to study alternative urban designs for the promotion of flexible, and pacific, communal street life." From Rome, she traveled to the Greek island of Mykonos, where, she continues, she formulated the idea of writing about land reform in Mississippi:

> As I stood on the rock of Mykonos, the horrible absurdity of hunger in Mississippi hit me hard: Here, in Mykonos, the people were surviving with dignity where there were no natural support systems for such survival. There, in Mississippi, Black people were perishing from forced dependency and kwashiorkor [severe malnutrition] while bigtime landowners let arable land lie idle, so they could collect government subsidies!

She cut short her year abroad and returned to New York to complete the manual on land reform. Robert Gottlieb, the publisher who had commissioned a book on Mississippi, refused to accept the manuscript, "More Than Enough."

She translated her project into fiction instead, but the resulting novel, titled "Okay Now" did not achieve publication either.

The early to mid 1970s were mobile and productive years in Jordan's professional life. Upon her return from Rome, she resumed teaching at City College while also joining the faculty at Sarah Lawrence, where she taught from 1971 to 1975, interrupted by a year as visiting professor at Yale (1974–1975). Her first collection of poetry, *Some Changes*, was published in 1971, and her second, *New Days*, in 1974. The first collection reflects the changing foci of Jordan's life, from her parents, to sexual celebration and loss, to children. It also charts national and world events, from violence against African Americans and King's assassination, to the rise of Malcolm X and Black Power, to the Vietnam War. Finally, as Peter Erickson has noted in Callaloo, it also charts the changing influences in the poet's development, from T. S. Eliot, Emily Dickinson, and Shakespeare, to distinctively African American poetry inspired by African American music. Julius Lester praises this poetry in his introduction to the collection, describing it as:

> poetry which speaks to and of the black experience, and the black experience is how blacks experience America and themselves. . . . Her poetry is highly disciplined, highly controlled. It's tight, like the Muddy Waters blues band is tight. There is nothing wasted, and it is impossible to separate what she says from how she says it. . . . She isn't concerned with converting the listener (and her poetry must be listened to, not merely read) to a particular point of view. Her concern is the concern of the poet who is also a musician.

New Days marks the voyage abroad with its series of "Roman poems" in section 2, "Poems of Exile." Section 3, "Poems of Return," combines personal reflections and political poems. The collection is introduced by a section entitled "Conditions for Leaving" that expresses the poet's alienation in a country that wants to eliminate her like "a darkspot on / the underwear of ivory snow" ("May 1, 1970"). The second introductory poem, "On the Twenty-fifth Anniversary of the United Nations: 1970," takes a more lofty tone, expressing the poet's personal poetic and political commitment: "human soul will only listen when / the witness takes a stand." The final poem in this section, bristling with anger and written in Black English, becomes more playful and sassy in its "talking back" tone. "Memo to Daniel Pretty Moynihan" (1969) attacks the U.S. undersecretary of labor's report, *The Negro Family: The Case for National Action* (1965), which claimed to describe the "pathology" of the African American family as a function of its "matriarchal" family structure, promoting a racist myth so powerful it has become enshrined in such liberal "documentaries" as Bill Moyers's video *The Vanishing Family: Crisis in Black America* (1986). Jordan's poem strikes back with "Don't you liberate me / from my female black pathology" and concludes with a counterproposition, "I got a simple proposition / You takeover my position / Clean your own house, babyface." Jordan's alternative vision of the African American woman is expressed in the beautiful "Gettin Down to Get Over," the penultimate poem in the volume, which, Jordan explains in "Thinking about My Poetry," had as its aim "the achievement of a collective voice." The volume ends with "These Poems," which contains the line that became the title of her subsequent major collection, *Things That I Do in the Dark*, which appeared under the general editorship of Toni Morrison. This final poem makes a statement about the purpose of poetry that marks a transition in Jordan's work from the notion of the poet as witness, described in the introductory poems, to the poet as intimate interlocutor in the world:

> These poems
> they are things that I do
> in the dark
> reaching for you
> whoever you are
> and
> are you ready?
>
> These words

> they are stones in the water
> running away
>
> These skeletal lines
> they are desperate arms for my longing and
>   love.
>
> I am a stranger
> learning to worship the strangers
> around me
>
> whoever you are
> whoever I may become.

From the mid to late 1970s Jordan's writing testifies to a broadening of her political and personal horizons. A strong and consistent concern for Africa emerges in her work. In 1973 she organized an all-black emergency task force, Afro-Americans against the Famine in the Sahel, along with Inez Smith Reid, then executive director of the Black Women's Community Development Fund. The instructive but unsuccessful conclusion to the campaign (they had wanted to create an effective African lobby) led to a change in the direction of her mobilizing, away from an emphasis on nationalism and an exclusively African American solidarity. She wrote in her introduction to "Whose Burden?," an essay published in 1974, later collected in the volume *Civil Wars:* "It seemed to be true, like it or not, that skin was not enough: That color is not enough to save your life. Certainly it is quite enough to kill you." "Notes toward a Black Balancing of Love and Hatred" (also written in 1974 and collected in *Civil Wars*) reflects this transition in the way it continually returns to binary oppositions to interrogate and complicate them: black and white, protest and affirmation, Malcolm X and Dr. King, Richard Wright and Zora Neale Hurston, men and women, love and hatred. This essay also marks Jordan's turn to the feminist consciousness that became integral to her visions of struggle and change, as well as to the vision of love she articulates in "Declaration of an Independence I Would Just as Soon Not Have" (1976, in *Civil Wars*).

In "Angola: A Victory and a Promise" (1976, in *Civil Wars*), Jordan turns her attention to southern Africa, which became the subject of many of her essays and poems in the 1970s and the 1980s. The essay celebrates Angola's liberation in 1975 and honors the first president of the People's Republic of Angola, Agostinho Neto, whom she introduces to her American readership by reprinting some of his poetry. Once again, Jordan reveals the didactic intent of many of her essays, giving a miniature history of Angola and introducing the reader to one of its leading poets and politicians. This essay also marks the beginning of her increasing focus on international poets, particularly those engaged in national liberation struggles throughout the world.

Things That I Do in the Dark, published in 1977, represents the bulk of Jordan's work up to that time, for it includes most of her previously published poetry (here the poems are individually dated for the first time) as well as twenty-eight new poems, written between 1973 and 1976. This collection demonstrates—in its organization into divisions titled by lines from poems in section 2 of *Some Changes*—the extent to which her two earlier volumes of poetry are thematically interconnected. There are four principal themes, corresponding to the divisions in the book: family ("For My Own"), love ("Directed by Desire"), struggle ("Against the Still-waters"), and language ("Toward a Personal Semantics"). "Who Look at Me"—an early poem first published as a book in 1969 and illustrated with a series of paintings depicting African American life—begins the collection, and a prose poem, "Fragments from a Parable (of the 1950s)"—written between 1958 and 1973—concludes it. "Fragments from a Parable" recounts Jordan's personal and mythic struggle to escape others' definitions and move toward self-determination, to resist being named and speak for herself. She enacts a struggle *with* words to depict a struggle *about* words, beginning with an epigraph about the power of conversion through the Word: *"Paul was Saul. Saul got on the road and somebody else changed him into somebody else on the road."* A kind of poetic autobiography, the piece traces the genesis of "Her" through to "I am"—"My name is me. I am what you call black."—first in relation to the mother and then, most emphatically in the section on language, more ambivalently in relation to (white) paternal law. The convergence between poetry and the father appears elsewhere. Echoing Sylvia Plath's ambivalence toward both poetic and paternal laws, Jordan writes in "Thinking about My Poetry," "From the age of seven through my mid-twenties, poetry was the inside dictator to whom I more or less simply submitted myself." June's own father died on December 21, 1974, in the year *New Days* was published. "Poem for Granville Ivanhoe Jordan" commemorates his life.

That June Jordan's *Things That I Do in the Dark* represents a kind of milestone in her career is confirmed by her choosing its publication as the moment in which to meditate on her poetic development. In the 1977 essay "Thinking about My Poetry," she attests to her movement from a grandiose notion of a collective voice toward a renewed "ordinariness" and singularity:

> If I could truthfully attend to my own perpetual birth, if I could trace the provocations for my own voice and then trace its reverberations through love, Alaska, whatever, . . . then I could hope to count upon myself to be serving a positive and collective function, without pretending to be more than the one Black woman poet I am, as a matter of fact.

The changes of focus and influence she notes in the essay resonate powerfully in the collection, from "Metarhetoric" (1976), a poem about sexual love between women, to "I Must Become a Menace to My Enemies" (1976), dedicated to Agostinho Neto, a manifesto of self-determination tempered by the self-discipline of Mrs. Hamer's lesson:

> And if I
> if I ever let love go
> because the hatred and the whisperings
> become a phantom dictate I o-

451

bey in lieu of impulse and realities
(the blossoming flamingos of my wild
    mimosa trees)
then let love freeze me
out.

In "Thinking about My Poetry" she extends this transition from victim to agent and concludes with a credo that provides her work of the 1980s with a note of optimism about people's ability to prevail against the odds:

> I have moved from an infantile reception of the universe, as given, into a progressively political self-assertion that is reaching beyond the limitations of a victim mentality. I choose to exist unafraid of my enemies; instead I choose to become an enemy to my enemies. . . . As a woman, as a Black woman, as a Black woman poet and writer, I choose to believe that we, women and Third World peoples, will in fact succeed in saving ourselves, *and* our traditional assassins, from the meaning of their fear and their hatred. Even more deeply, I believe we can save ourselves from the power of our own fear and our own self-hatred.
>
> This is my perspective, and this is my faith.

Another poem worth noting for its uncompromising stance on self-determination and its exemplarity as one of Jordan's poems in which—as she puts it in "Thinking about My Poetry"—"rhythm and political concept [are] merged into a vertical event" is "From *The Talking Back of Miss Valentine Jones*" (1976). Here, in the voice of the persona she adopts for several other poems, Jordan celebrates the victory of the Vietnamese people over "the imperial / big-nose / eagles." This poem, which she also reads on the 1978 album, *Things That I Do in the Dark*, is a decidedly oral event, combining several rhythms and voices in the call-and-response pattern of African American worship. The quiet triumph of the final stanza combines the militant self-determination and love that became the dominant theme of her next collection, *Passion* (1980):

In Africa
in Mozambique
Angola
liberation lifts
the head of the young girl
formerly burdened by laundry
and yams

She
straps the baby to her back
and
she carries her rifle
like she means
means to kill

for the love

for the life
of us all

The 1980s

In 1978 June Jordan joined the faculty at the State University of New York at Stony Brook, where she remained until 1989, when she moved to take a position as professor of Afro-American studies and women's studies at the University of California at Berkeley. Her writings in the 1970s continued to chronicle, journalistically, the numerous acts of violence against African American people. In June and July of 1979 she wrote a play called *The Issue*, about freedom, police violence, and Black life. The essay "In the Valley of the Shadow of Death" (1978, in *Civil Wars*), documents several events with a relentless yet disciplined anger. She describes crimes that went unacknowledged by the law and by the press, from the police's shooting of fifteen-year-old Randolph Evans in Brooklyn in 1977 to the Miami police's beating Arthur MacDuffie to death for a traffic violation in 1980. "Over and over and over again a child is killed by police because he is a Black boy," she writes in her introduction to the essay. "Sometimes it gets to the point that, when my son is around the house and I leave on an errand by myself, when I come back the first thing I do is call, 'Christopher?' I have to know: Is he all right?"

The final essay in *Civil Wars*, a 1980 essay from which the volume gets its name, summarizes the change in Jordan's thinking about struggle. The essay is ostensibly about "politeness," about how "the courtesies of order, of ruly forms pursued from a heart of rage or terror or grief defame the truth of every human crisis." It is about her falling out with Frances Fox Piven, coauthor with Richard Cloward of *Poor Peoples' Movements: Why They Succeed, How They Fail* (1977), over Piven's accusation that Jordan's focus on the assault and murder of Victor Rhodes by Hassidic Jews was anti-Semitic and over Piven's lack of sympathy for the gay rights movement. It is also an essay about the dangerous power of charismatic leaders and the spontaneity of the African American uprising in Miami following the police murder of Arthur MacDuffie. This essay, more than others, elaborates on Jordan's characterization of herself as an anarchist in an interview with Sharon Bray (*WIN* magazine, March 1, 1981). Jordan reworks the relationship between leaders and people and begins to move away from the limitations of so-called "dentity politics. One sentence in particular sets the tone for one of her most moving essays of the 1980s, "Report from the Bahamas" (1982, in *On Call*): "Neither race nor gender provides the final definition of jeopardy or refuge." She finds her meditations confirmed in Piven's book: "In every instance, it has never been *who is the leader* but rather *who are the people*. It has never been *what is the organization* but *what is the crisis*." At the end of the essay Jordan finds herself in a dilemma over whether to maintain the silence between herself and her friend or to "engage once again in talk about tactics of struggle." Finally, in a move that prefigures, as the writing itself practices, the coalition politics of the 1980s, she calls her friend.

Passion: New Poems, 1977–1980 is perhaps June Jordan's best-known collection, both for its exploration of violence—violence against women in particular—and for the beautiful "Alla That's All Right, but," set to music by Sweet Honey in the Rock on their *Good News*

album. Many of the poems can be heard on the Black Box/Watershed recording *For Somebody to Start Singing* (1980), by June Jordan and Bernice Reagon, lead singer of Sweet Honey in the Rock. The volume is prefaced by "For the Sake of a People's Poetry: Walt Whitman and the Rest of Us," which also introduces *On Call*. In it she praises Whitman as the father of the "New World" poets, the African American and Third World poets who are "wild" and "democratic": "What Whitman envisioned we, the people and the poets of the New World, embody. He has been punished for the political meaning of his vision. We are being punished for the moral questions that our very lives provoke." In this essay and elsewhere, Jordan rankles at the difficulty she and other oppositional writers have had getting published in the United States. In the introduction to *On Call*, the sentence "I am learning about American censorship" returns like a refrain, punctuating an essay about the descendants of Walt Whitman, America's dissident poets:

Here, supposedly, we do not have "dissident" poets and writers—unless they are well rewarded runaways from the Soviet Union. Here we know about the poets and writers that major media eagerly allow us to see and consume. And then we do not hear about the other ones. But I am one of them. I am a dissident American poet and writer completely uninterested to run away from my country, my home.

Passion contains one of the most inspiring and heartbreaking war cries of women's and Third World peoples' movements, "Poem about My Rights." Jordan has said on several occasions that this poem was a watershed, "the turning point poem for me, the poem turning me away from my rage or despair towards an analytical, confident, faithful purity and self-love." "I was in such a rage writing that poem," she said in the 1981 *Essence* interview with Alexis DeVeaux, during which she explained that, several months before writing it, she had been raped, and that the poem was a way of comparing all violations of self-determination.

This poem and the entire volume—dedicated to "everybody as scared as I used to be"—represent the culminating point of the emotions that began to be apparent in poems such as "From *The Talking Back of Miss Valentine Jones*" in *Things That I Do in the Dark:*

> I am the history of rape
> I am the history of the rejection of who I
> am
> I am the history of the terrorized
> incarceration of my self
> I am the history of battery assault and
> limitless
> armies against whatever I want to do with
> my mind
> and my body and my soul and
> whether it's about walking out at night
> or whether it's about the love that I feel or
> whether it's about the sanctity of my
> vagina or
> or the sanctity of my leaders or the sanctity
> of each and every desire
> that I know from my personal and
> idiosyncratic
> and indisputably single and singular heart
> I have been raped

"Poem about My Rights" concludes with a powerful refusal and a mustering of strength and self-confidence to expel the enemy. It addresses us directly for the first time and, in doing so, shocks us into an awareness of our own complicity:

> *I am not wrong: Wrong is not my name*
> My name is my own my own my own
> and I can't tell you who the hell set things
> up like this
> but I can tell you that from now on my
> resistance
> my simple and daily and nightly self-
> determination
> may very well cost you your life

In a lighter vein, "A Short Note to My Very Critical and Well-Beloved Friends and Comrades" also expresses Jordan's resistance to being determined by the other, her resolute independence from prevailing orthodoxies either on the right or on the left:

> First they said I was too light
> Then they said I was too dark
> . . . .
> Make up your mind! They said. Are you
> militant
> or sweet? Are you vegetarian or meat? Are
> you straight
> or are you gay?
>
> And I said, Hey! It's not about *my* mind.

In 1985 June Jordan published *Living Room,* a collection of new poems, and *On Call: Political Essays,* her second collection of essays, mostly occasional pieces and presentations that were originally published in such periodicals as the *New York Times* ("South Africa: Bringing It All Back Home," 1981), *Savvy* ("Many Rivers To Cross," 1982), the *Boston Globe* ("The Case for the Real Majority," 1982), *Ms.* ("Report from the Bahamas," 1982), *Dial* ("Love Is Not the Problem," 1983), the *Village Voice* ("Black Folks on Nicaragua: 'Leave Those Folks Alone!'" 1983, and "White Tuesday," 1984), *Essence* ("Nicaragua: Why I Had to Go There," 1984, and "In Our Hands," 1985), and *Sojourner* ("Life after Lebanon," 1985). South Africa, Nicaragua, Lebanon, and Palestine figure prominently in these collections. In the introduction to *On Call,* she reaffirms the autonomy of her perspective and the intimate link she feels between the events of the world and her own individual life:

> Because my politics devolve from my entire real life, and real phone calls and meetings about real horror or triumph happening to other real people, none of it respects or reflects any orthodox anything, any artifice of position or concern. From Phillis Wheatley to Walt Whitman, from Stony Brook to Lebanon, these writings document my political efforts to coherently fathom all of my universe, and to arrive at a moral judgement that will determine my further political conduct. . . . This collection brings together the po-

litical writings that the past four years have caused me to produce.

Jordan, in the late 1980s, connected her struggle for self-determination to the national liberation struggles occurring all over the world. The connection involves poetic endeavor as well:

There is a perspective on poetry that prevails outside the United States, that is to say throughout the First World, and that is: when you are in any serious process of self-determination, you are necessarily preoccupied by concerns for accuracy and telling the truth about yourself in the context of the whole world. Those concerns are, I believe, central to the writing of poetry. . . . When people have been suffering subjugation by others who despise them, when those people decide to rise up and to determine their own lives and to attempt to arrive at some kind of effective control of their destinies, there does concomitantly emerge a preoccupation with language that is intimately related to the creative process that underlies the writing of a poem, and that is, a concern to be accurate and to tell the truth. There is a third concern, and that is to name the universe in your own image.

The Israeli invasion of Lebanon in the summer of 1982 and the massacre of Palestinian refugees in the camps of Sabra and Shatilah later that year haunt the pages of *On Call* and *Living Room,* the latter dedicated, in part, to "the children of Lebanon." In the essay "Problems of Language in a Democratic State" (1982) she uses Homer's tale of the Cyclops Polyphemus, who was duped by Ulysses and therefore unable to name his aggressor, as a parable for the passivity of Americans in the face of state and media doublespeak—in contrast to the four thousand Israelis who protested their state's attempt to misrepresent the invasion of Lebanon and the massacre of Palestinians. In *Living Room,* her anger and shame are acute. "The Beirut Joke-book" attacks the obscenity of the language of the state:

1. June 8, 1982: This is not an invasion.
2. July 9, 1982: This is a ceasefire.
3. July 15, 1982: This is a ceasefire.
4. July 30, 1982: This ceasefire is strained.
5. August 4, 1982: This is not an invasion.

"Apologies to All the People in Lebanon: Dedicated to the 600,000 Palestinian Men, Women, and Children Who Lived in Lebanon from 1948–1983" mourns the ignorance of the "well-meaning" American people:

I didn't know and nobody told me and what
   could I do or say, anyway?

Yes, I did know it was the money I earned
   as a poet that
paid
for the bombs and the planes and the tanks
that they used to massacre your family

But I am not an evil person
The people of my country aren't so bad

You can't expect but so much
from those of us who have to pay taxes and
   watch
American tv

You see my point;

I'm sorry.
I really am sorry.

In the essay "Life after Lebanon" (1984, in *On Call*) she angrily modifies her position in the context of a celebration of women's solidarity and "women who are making over this place of ours into a place of safety for all of us, including white men." She writes, "The problem was not one of misinformation, or ignorance. The problem was that the Lebanese people, in general, and that the Palestinian people, in particular, are not whitemen." The essay concludes with the emergence of "a New Woman" with a defined identity, unlike the struggling "Her" from "Fragments." The privileged spokesperson, in this context, is Etel Adnan, the Lebanese poet and author of the novel *Sitt-Marie Rose* (1982), whom Jordan quotes in her ongoing commitment to introducing international voices to the American literary scene. She also recites, in pedagogical and commemorative fashion, a list of "New Women," as though to supply the missing names, like those missing from history from the minds of women at the conference she refers to in "Problems of Language in a Democratic State," where an attempt to commemorate Black American women of the past five hundred years breaks down.

In 1983 Jordan went to Nicaragua. "It was the most important experience of my adult life," she said in an interview. She was invited there by the poet Roberto Vargas, first secretary of cultural affairs at the Nicaraguan embassy in Washington, D.C. Her attempt to secure a commission for an article met with resistance, except from *Essence* magazine, where her friend Susan Taylor was editor in chief. She wrote "Nicaragua: Why I Had to Go There" (1984) for *Essence*. Like many of Jordan's essays, it is a work of education as well as advocacy, recapitulating briefly the history of the Sandinista overthrow of Anastasio Somoza in 1979 and the subsequent developments in the Nicaraguan revolution. Jordan's urgent concern for the fate of Nicaragua frames the volume *On Call*. The cover of the book is a photograph of Jordan and Francisco Campbell, first secretary of political affairs in the Nicaraguan embassy in Washington, D.C., standing in a recently bombed area of Teotecacinte, about which she writes a poem in *Living Room* ("First Poem from Nicaragua Libre: *Teotecacinte*"). At the back of the book she appends: "What You Can Do about Nicaragua." A series of poems in *Living Room* commemorates the trip as well; the poetry is paired down and sparse, "analytical" as she terms her new style, and informational, as in "From Nicaragua Libre: Photograph of Managua": "The man is not cute. / The man is not ugly. / The man is teaching himself / to read." Or it is sparingly lyrical, as in "Poem for Nicaragua":

> I imagine you among the mountains
> eating early rice
>
> I remember you among the birds
> that do not swallow blood

Upon her return from Nicaragua, June Jordan returned to Stony Brook, where in 1986 she became director of the Poetry Center and the Creative Writing Program. She also continued her work as a dramatist. By 1981 her first full-length drama, *The Issue,* directed by the playwright and poet Ntozake Shange (who is a friend of Jordan's), had been produced as a staged reading by the New York Shakespeare Festival. In 1986, the full-length musical drama, *Bang Bang Uber Alles,* written in collaboration with the American composer Adrienne B. Torf, received its world premiere production at Seven Stages Theater in Atlanta, Georgia, in the face of threats by the Ku Klux Klan (the play deals with Klan violence, among other things). In the year 1987–1988, Jordan became playwright-in-residence for the New Dramatists in New York City and completed another, autobiographical, drama entitled *All These Blessings,* which has had several staged readings.

Jordan's essays from the 1980s testify to a stronger, more aggressively affirmative voice characterizing her political stance. Her arguments generally proceed from autobiographical accounts, narratives of experience that frame a question in personal terms and then expand outward to include factual research on a given subject. Once the context is in place, she uses the occasion of an event or situation to interrogate her own position and, by extension, the reader's. Thus she exposes not only the results of self-criticism, but also its process, as a way of drawing a reader into his or her own self-examination. Most of these essays conclude with a challenge to move beyond the limitations of a particular debate in order to find commonalities of interest and goal. As in the title of the final essay of *On Call,* "Moving beyond the Enemy: Nicaragua and South Africa" (1985), the essays proceed from critique toward affirmation. "There is much more that we must do, besides attempting to checkmate the enemy," she writes. "Let us, at last, emulate the astonishing and aggressive faith of the majority peoples of the world."

Three principal elements, incipiently apparent in her earlier writings, describe June Jordan's work beginning in the mid 1980s: a coherent worldview, a commitment to internationalism, and a sense of the political efficacy of poetry as action in the world. Of the latter, she said in 1989, "In the narrowest sense of being an intellectual in the world, I know that what you do really matters, and what you say and how you say it. All these things have serious international consequence, and it's very sobering and very exciting to me at once."

In 1989 June Jordan published two more works: a book of selected poems from *Things That I Do in the Dark, Passion,* and *Living Room,* entitled *Lyrical Campaigns;* and a collection of selected political essays, *Moving towards Home,* which, with the exception of the final two, were taken from *Civil Wars* and *On Call.* Both books were issued by Virago Press in London, where Jordan enjoys tremendous popularity. *Moving towards Home* takes its title from the final poem of *Living Room* (whose title also comes from this poem), where Jordan links her destiny to that of the Palestinian people:

I was born a Black woman
and now
I am become a Palestinian
against the relentless laughter of evil
there is less and less living room
and where are my loved ones?

It is time to make our way home.

In an unpublished interview, Jordan told a story about this poem that illustrates her sense of the political validity of her poetic production and its place in an international context:

A friend of mine visited the West Bank in the Gaza strip as a representative of MADRE last year in 1988. And she said that when she got into the refugee camps and they found out she was from this country, again and again people wanted to know if she knew June Jordan, because my poem "Moving towards Home" has been translated into Arabic, and all these people over there know this poem by heart. As far as I'm concerned, that's the kind of validation of the usefulness of my work that's beyond anything I've ever dreamed of.

Although she is, and has always been, a distinctively American intellectual, the international dimension of Jordan's work became increasingly more important during the 1980s. Her poetry and essays were translated into Spanish, French, Swedish, German, Arabic, and Japanese, and she experimented with poetic forms and rhythms from other cultural traditions, examples of which appear in *Naming Our Destiny,* also published in 1989. *Naming Our Destiny* includes selections from *Things That I Do in the Dark, Passion,* and *Living Room,* as well as a section entitled "North Star," containing new poems written between 1985 and 1989. Peter Erickson's review of the volume in *Hurricane Alice* focused on Jordan's revision of the canon, strikingly illustrated by "The Female and the Silence of a Man," a radical reconfiguration of William Butler Yeats's "Leda and the Swan," where the erotic encounter between the two is de-eroticized and rewritten as a particularly brutal rape. Erickson points out, however, that in this poem Leda returns not as a victim, but as a newly empowered and retaliatory force in the world. Jordan also defends Phillis Wheatley ("Something Like a Sonnet for Phillis Miracle Wheatley"), whose prominent position in the African American literary canon has often been disputed because of the perceived mimicry of her verses. Borrowing from Wheatley's imagery ("They dressed you with light but you dreamed with the night"), Jordan constructs her both as a vulnerable, sickly slave girl and as a master poet to demonstrate the miraculous improbability of Phillis "Miracle" Wheatley's achievement.

"North Star" also records Jordan's encounter with England, as in the elegant dialogue/argument about nationalism and African identity, "Poem for Mark":

and you said
"Rubbish!" to the notion of a national
identity
and if I answered,
"In my country—"

You would interrupt me, saying,
"You're not serious!"

Here Jordan reexamines the certainties of her "American" identity and embraces a broader concept of "my people," with the final lines:

I knew
whoever the hell "my people"
are
I knew that one of them
is you.

Several poems commemorate both London and Jordan's stay in New Hampshire (at the writer's colony in Peterborough) in the dialect-persona of a woman named DeLiza. Jordan returns to the themes of paternal authority and maternal loss in the final poem of the collection, "War and Memory," which, as Erickson notes, connects the personal father with poetic or canonical fathers, enacting the separation from them and the emergence of a warrior poet whose maternal nurturance she has had to invent.

Erickson classifies Jordan's poems in two categories: political poems and love poems. "The former," he writes, "are public and militant, the latter private and contemplative." He argues that the challenge for the reader is how to move between these modes, how to make sense of both within the context of a single body of work. But it is precisely this combination that marks Jordan as a distinctively African American, a distinctively female and feminist, poet. In both traditions the personal, deeply informed by love—an emotion which, however defined, inspires the desire to live and struggle against all odds—is inextricably intertwined with the political, an understanding of the ways in which institutions and power shape human identity. At the end of the 1980s, Jordan was intent on defining and refining the ways in which these two realms must inform the lives of all people in the future.

"Waiting for a Taxi," an essay from the *Progressive* (June 1989), exemplifies her "new" coherent worldview. She writes, "The issues must configur[e] the politics, and not the identity of people." Originally presented at the Eighth An-

nual Gender Studies Symposium at Lewis and Clark College as "Beyond Gender, Race, and Class," "Waiting for a Taxi" meditates on the limitations of identity politics, rendering more programmatically explicit the poetic and personal politics of "Report from the Bahamas." She proposes an alternative: "political unity and human community based upon concepts that underlie or supercede relatively immutable factors of race, class, and gender: the concept of justice, the concept of equality, the concept of tenderness." She cites successful instances of such coalitions: Jesse Jackson's 1988 presidential campaign, the April 1989 pro-choice march on Washington, as well as events that require broad-based international response, such as the 1989 Exxon oil spill in Alaska's Prince William Sound.

The 1990s

June Jordan migrated to the West Coast in 1991 to take a position as professor of African American Studies at the University of California at Berkeley. That same year she organized a campus-wide Gulf War "teach-in" and also founded the Poetry for the People project, described in her textbook or pedagogical manual as a way to teach poetry and encourage students to write it, to integrate school and life, and to create, as she says, "a foundation for true community: a fearless democratic society." A collection of political essays published in 1998, titled *Affirmative Acts*, charted the political, social, and economic concerns of the 1990s, commenting on events such as the release of the South African antiapartheid activist Nelson Mandela, the war in the Persian Gulf, the Supreme Court confirmation hearing of Clarence Thomas, the police beating of Rodney King in Los Angeles, the war in Bosnia, and the murder trial of O. J. Simpson. Jordan also focuses more frequently than in her earlier writings on the struggle for sexual rights, while continuing to address the need for radical economic and social change in the United States. Alternating between moments of despair and affirmations of the collective energies of communities of struggle, June Jordan's voice, prophetic and practical, impassioned and compassionate, continued at the turn of the century to challenge her readers and inspire them with visions of a more democratic future.

Selected Bibliography

PRIMARY WORKS

POETRY

Who Look at Me. New York: Crowell, 1969.
Some Changes. New York: Dutton, 1971.
New Days: Poems of Exile and Return. New York: Emerson Hall, 1974.
Things That I Do in the Dark: Selected Poetry. New York: Random House, 1977.
Passion: New Poems, 1977–1980. Boston: Beacon, 1980.
Living Room: New Poems. New York and Chicago: Thunder's Mouth, 1985.
Lyrical Campaigns: Selected Poems. London: Virago, 1989.
Naming Our Destiny: New and Selected Poems. New York: Thunder's Mouth, 1989.
Haruko/Love Poetry: New and Selected Love Poems. London: Virago, 1993.
Kissing God Goodbye: Poems 1991–1997. New York: Anchor, 1997.

ESSAYS

Civil Wars. Boston: Beacon, 1981.
On Call: Political Essays. Boston: South End, 1985.
Moving Towards Home: Political Essays. London: Virago, 1989.
Technical Difficulties: African American Notes on the State of the Union. New York: Pantheon, 1992.
Affirmative Acts: Political Essays. New York: Anchor, 1998.
Soldier: A Poet's Childhood. New York: Basic Civitas Books, 2000. (Memoir.)

CHILDREN'S BOOKS

His Own Where. New York: Crowell, 1971.
Dry Victories. New York: Holt, Rinehart, Winston, 1972.
Fannie Lou Hamer. Illustrated by Albert Williams. New York: Crowell, 1972.
New Life: New Room. Illustrated by Ray Cruz. New York: Crowell, 1975.
Kimako's Story. Boston: Houghton Mifflin, 1981.

AUDIO RECORDINGS

Things That I Do in the Dark, and Other Poems. Spoken Arts, 1978.
For Somebody to Start Singing. Black Box/Watershed Foundation, 1980.
I Was Looking at the Ceiling and then I Saw the Sky. Warner-Nonesuch, 1998.

OPERA AND MUSICAL PRODUCTIONS

Bang Bang Uber Alles. Lyrics and libretto by June Jordan, music by Adrienne B. Torf. First production: Atlanta, Ga., Seven Stages Theater, 1986.
I Was Looking at the Ceiling and Then I Saw the Sky. Lyrics and libretto by June Jordan, music by John Adams, directed by Peter Sellars. First production: Berkeley, Calif., Zellerbach Playhouse, 1995.

ANTHOLOGIES

Soulscript: Afro-American Poetry. Edited and with an introduction by June Jordan. Garden City, N.Y.: Doubleday, 1970.
The Voice of the Children. Edited by June Jordan and Terri Bush, with an afterword by Jordan. New York: Holt, Rinehart, Winston, 1970.
June Jordan's Poetry for the People: A Revolutionary Blueprint. Edited by Lauren Muller and the Poetry for the People Collective. New York: Routledge, 1995.

SECONDARY WORKS

BIOGRAPHICAL AND CRITICAL STUDIES

Bambara, Toni Cade. "Chosen Weapons." *Ms.* 10:40–42 (April 1981). (A review of *Civil Wars.*)
Bray, Sharon. "A Poet of the People: Interview with June Jordan." *WIN* magazine, March 1, 1981.
DeVeaux, Alexis. "Creating Soul Food: June Jordan." *Essence* 11, no. 82:138–50 (April 1981).
Erickson, Peter. "June Jordan." In *Dictionary of Literary Biography.* Vol. 38, *Afro-American Writers after 1955: Prose Writers and Dramatists.* Edited by Thadious M. Davis and Trudier Harris. Detroit: Gale Research, 1985. Pp. 146–62.
———. "The Love Poetry of June Jordan." *Callaloo* 9:221–34 (Winter 1986).
———. "Putting Her Life on the Line: The Poetry of June Jordan." *Hurricane Alice: A Feminist Quarterly* 7, nos. 1–2:4–5 (1990).
Freccero, Carla. "June Jordan's *Technical Difficulties.*" *African American Review* 32, no. 3:504–06 (Fall 1998).
Miles, Sara. "This Wheel's on Fire." In *Woman Poet: The East.* Edited by Elaine Dallman et al. Reno, Nev.: Women-in-Literature, 1982.

ADRIENNE KENNEDY
(1931–   )

ELIN DIAMOND

WHEN EIGHT OF Adrienne Kennedy's plays and adaptations were collected and published in 1988, actors, directors, drama scholars, and students of U.S. experimental theater had occasion to rejoice. A modest but well-produced volume by the University of Minnesota Press, *Adrienne Kennedy in One Act* ended the headache of hunting down Kennedy's fiercely original one-acts in long-forgotten journals or out-of-print anthologies. People had photocopied Kennedy's plays so often that they had no idea where the originals were or whether their dog-eared copies were corrected or uncorrected versions. With *In One Act* readers at last found authorized texts of the plays on which Kennedy's reputation rests: *Funnyhouse of a Negro*, which won the coveted Off-Broadway or Obie award in 1964, *The Owl Answers*, first produced in 1965, *A Rat's Mass* (1966), *A Lesson in Dead Language* (1968), and *A Movie Star Has to Star in Black and White* (1976). With their violent, incantatory poetry and metamorphosing characters, their temporal disjunctions, historical references, and cinematic dissolves, Kennedy's early plays made a unique contribution to American avant-garde theater in the 1960s and 1970s. Then, in the late 1980s, she had a second wave of creativity: a brilliant autobiography, *People Who Led to My Plays* (1987); a novel, *Deadly Triplets: A Theatre Mystery and Journal* (1990); and a play cycle, *The*

Alexander Plays (1992), including the powerful *The Ohio State Murders*. In 1995–1996, during an off-Broadway season devoted to old and new Kennedy plays, two world premieres, *June and Jean in Concert* and *Sleep Deprivation Chamber* (the latter written with her son, Adam Kennedy) were each honored with an Obie for Best New American Play of 1996. This outpouring of new work has revived scholarly interest in Adrienne Kennedy's entire oeuvre and in her distinctive, troubling vision of American identity, sexuality, and race in the latter half of the twentieth century.

Early Years

Born in Pittsburgh, Pennsylvania, on September 13, 1931, Adrienne Kennedy, née Hawkins, was raised in middle-class neighborhoods in Cleveland, Ohio, the elder of two children. Her parents, Etta and Cornell Wallace "C. W." Hawkins were educated at Morehouse and Atlanta University, historically black colleges in the South. In Cleveland her father worked as a social worker; her mother, after the children were slightly older, as a teacher. In an interview with Paul Bryant-Jackson and Lois Overbeck, Kennedy remembered the stability of her parents, their friends, their religion, and their community: "There was something about the values of

461

that time. . . . These people were working all the time, . . . were keeping black culture alive. And they were forging ahead financially at the same time." This image of middle-class normalcy is echoed in Kennedy's fond recollection of the integrated, largely immigrant Cleveland school system, where her precocity was noticed and where her mother, who had taught her to read at age three, encouraged her to excel.

Yet these sunny memories of a stable family and academic achievement are belied by others: the numbing racism of a teacher who told her she would never have a writing career, and the sense from earliest childhood that identity was frighteningly fluid and that secrets lodged within persons and events might never be told or fully understood. The glamorous fictional world of movies and movie-magazine celebrity, of which Kennedy was enamored from her teenage years through adulthood, clashed with her increasing awareness of the systemic oppression of African Americans. The presence, in her own and other black families, of mixed-race lineage intensified the contradictory nature of race in American society. These themes would surface continually in Kennedy's oeuvre, from *Funnyhouse of a Negro* (1964) and the other plays of *In One Act* to *The Alexander Plays* in 1992.

As a freshman at Ohio State University (1949–1953), while reveling in her love of literature, Kennedy experienced for the first time racism in the raw, as she and other African American female students were ghettoized onto one floor in one dormitory. Behind the smiles of white students lurked a malevolence that Kennedy addressed specifically in her play *The Ohio State Murders*. She sought refuge in her relationship with her fiancé, Joseph Kennedy, whom she married in 1953 and who, after serving in the Korean War, brought Kennedy and their first child, Joseph Jr., to New York City. While her husband pursued a doctorate in social psychology at Columbia University, Adrienne Kennedy began to work seriously on her writing, taking classes at the New School and the American Theatre Wing. Reading widely and writing daily, Kennedy was surprised by "the strange, fragmented thoughts that poured from my diaries, the violent imagery. Why so violent? I didn't understand." By identifying with other writers, especially Tennessee Williams, James Baldwin, Gwendolyn Brooks, Lillian Hellman, Arthur Miller, Langston Hughes, and Garcia Lorca, Kennedy felt part of a writers' community. Identifying with such film stars as Bette Davis, Dorothy Dandrige, Marlon Brando, and Montgomery Clift, as well as with the characters they played, Kennedy cultivated the power of fantasy. Jazz and painting were also a constant influence: "After I saw [Picasso's] *Guernica* at the Museum of Modern Art, the concept of placing my characters in a dream domain seemed more and more real to me. . . . After seeing [Jackson Pollock's] work . . . , I thought continually of how to write (was it possible?) without a linear narrative."

West Africa, *Funnyhouse of a Negro,* and Other Early Plays

In 1960, when her husband took the family on a 13-month research trip to West Africa and Europe, Kennedy's writing became sharper and more focused. She was living in Accra, the capital of Ghana, as liberation struggles against centuries-long colonial rule were propelling new African nations onto the world stage. Having absorbed the optimism and courage of the U.S. Civil Rights movement, and having lived in New York City in the company of intellectuals who read Frantz Fanon and debated global politics, Kennedy now found herself amid political struggles on the African continent, ones that seemed to be succeeding. Ghana had gained independence in 1956, and the year she arrived the Belgian Congo became Zaire. One its foremost revolutionary leaders, Patrice Lumumba, whose life and work were emblematic of new political possibilities, was on everyone's lips, especially after the shock of his murder not long after Kennedy's arrival.

For Kennedy, the excitement of Africa was political and sentient. She was alternately frightened and energized by the penetrating heat, the beauty of the savannas, the sound of rats in the underbrush, and at night, while she slept under a mosquito net, the sound of owls in the trees of her garden: "In the mornings I would try to find the owls in the trees but could never see them. Yet, at night in the shuttered room under the huge white canopied nets, the owls sounded as if they were in the very center of the room." In the midst of this Kennedy became pregnant with her second child. "And there were difficulties. I had to stay in bed for a week, as I bled. I listened to the owl sounds, afraid." The most important incident in Kennedy's sojourn in Africa was both material and aesthetic. She bought a large African mask from a vendor on the streets of Accra, "a woman with a bird flying through her forehead. . . . [It inspired me to] totally break from realistic-looking characters. I would soon create a character with a shattered, bludgeoned head. And that was his fixed surreal appearance."

Readers of Kennedy's *Funnyhouse of a Negro* and *The Owl Answers* will recognize many of these images in her plays. But no biographical insights can help us imagine the shocking innovation of *Funnyhouse of a Negro* when it was staged in New York in 1964. On a dark stage are features of a young woman's apartment bedroom. But soon ravens fly across the stage, bald heads drop from above, and bludgeoned faces appear—all horrific and, it seems, unexplained. *Funnyhouse of a Negro* summons the audience into fragmented scenes, punctuated by blackouts, between "Negro-Sarah" and four masked or grotesquely made-up characters designated "Herselves"—Queen Victoria, the Duchess of Hapsburg, Patrice Lumumba, and a hunchbacked Jesus—along with two white characters, a Landlady and a boyfriend named Raymond. Like the carnival (funnyhouse) mirrors that return a distorted image of the one who looks into them, Sarah's "self" is presented as unreconciled and unreconcilable embodiments of powerful historical-iconic figures, each of whom in turn shares some version of her own "Negro kinky hair"—hair that is falling out and carried around in red paper bags. When Sarah speaks, we hear of a solitary young woman, alienated from a light-skinned mother and a dark-skinned father, who keeps a statue

of Queen Victoria in her room and writes poetry in imitation of Edith Sitwell. Tormented by her "yellow" skin, Sarah cultivates white friends to keep her "from reflecting too much upon the fact that I am a Negro." When the "selves" speak, they raise the pitch of Sarah's discourse with incantatory references to a mother who was raped by her father, "the blackest one of them all." Although, as Sarah tells us, she bludgeoned her father with an African mask, he "keeps returning. . . . He comes through the jungle to find me." Lost in the depths of a personal nightmare from which she cannot awaken, Sarah announces, "I want not to be."

The genius of the play lies in its ability to give private suffering a wider resonance. Kennedy's drama revives and extends the elements of European surrealist drama of the 1920s and 1930s, which, in protest against realist conventions, experimented with nonsensical language, discordant images, masks, and for the audience, spatial and temporal disorientation. Kennedy, however, puts these devices at the service of a torture that is as historically dense as it is psychically punishing. The female selves, the Duchess of Hapsburg and Queen Victoria, with their white powdered faces and kinky hair, are, in the emotional logic of the play, extensions of her mother; that intimate relation is deepened by their link to royal lineages stained by brutal imperialist adventurism in Africa. The father figures are more contradictory, carrying the double vision of African American liberation that Kennedy inherited from her parents' generation. To put it too simply, some African Americans felt obliged to choose between in Christian values of hard work and self-sacrifice and a pan-Africanism that sought change through political and social contestation. In the 1960s such double vision played out in the tension between the nonviolent strategies of the Civil Rights movement and black nationalist militancy that drew strength from the example of revolutionary leaders such as Patrice Lumumba. Sarah's father is associated with a missionary zeal that sought liberation through Christ.

In *Funnyhouse of a Negro* the Christian position is discredited by a fragment of Jesus' monologue: "I am going to Africa and kill this black man named Patrice Lumumba. Why? Because all my life I believed my Holy Father to be God, but now I know that my father is a black man." Sarah's father, we are told repeatedly, is a "nigger of torment," who hangs himself in a Harlem hotel the day Patrice Lumumba is murdered. The father never appears as such but is internalized and projected as the deformed hunchbacked Jesus, one of Sarah's selves. Later, the selves make the connection explicit: "Forgiveness, Sarah, I know you are a nigger of torment." In the end Sarah, too, hangs herself.

The historical references in *Funnyhouse of a Negro* work on an audience subliminally. In the theater one is riveted and penetrated by the loud knocking, swift light changes, heads dropping, walls falling, and rather horribly, the loud, persistent laughter of the landlady (with the resonant name of Mrs. Conrad) and the "funnyman" Raymond. Significantly, Raymond's story fragments elaborate or contradict Sarah's own. The penultimate scene "in the jungle . . . with RED SUN, FLYING THINGS," shows a now silent Sarah encircled by her selves, who turn distinctly malevolent. They chant lines from previous scenes and taunt her with raucous laughter. After a sudden blackout we see Sarah hanged, hear more laughter, and then Raymond's surprising words: "She was a funny little liar. . . . Her father never hung himself in a Harlem hotel. . . . I know the man. He is a doctor, married to a white whore."

Whom do we believe? Negro-Sarah? Her selves? Raymond? Such questions, the staple of conventional plays that seek to engage audiences with suspenseful plots, are lost in the horror of *Funnyhouse of a Negro*. Exploiting the full resources of the theater, Kennedy hurls us into the dark tunnel of Sarah's life. At the other end we find not the sentimental solace of pity for a poor unfortunate victim but an appalling awareness of the effects of our collective history. Family secrets, so troubling to Sarah, become for the audience nothing less than the daily violence of racism as it is felt through the skin and in the deepest layer of private fantasy. History, for Kennedy, is an emotional landscape. Yet, paradoxically perhaps, this very emotion

produces a clearer sense of history's persistent presence—a presence barely glimpsed in daily living or in conventional theater. Kennedy herself tried to censor the violence of her play's language and conception. After returning from abroad, she showed the manuscript to Edward Albee and the members of his playwriting workshop. When, at Albee's instigation, the play went into production, Kennedy removed the word "nigger" from the script. Albee objected, advising her to be true to her original. Fortunately, Kennedy took that advice.

While *Funnyhouse of a Negro* was moving toward its off-Broadway opening, Kennedy wrote *The Owl Answers* (1965). This time there is no evidence of self-censorship. Kennedy again mined the material of family guilt and trauma to embrace a wider horror, but she was no less inventive in this play. Instead of externalizing the figures who have formed her, as Sarah does in *Funnyhouse of a Negro*, the protagonist Clara transforms before the audience's eyes into various related identities. In *The Owl Answers* every character is also another, and another, defying the logic of simple disguise or double casting. Indeed, Kennedy's play teaches us that singular identity, rather than a given of human existence, is merely a strategy to conceal a much more turbulent psychic process, the tendency to identify with and, in fantasy, to become another. Clara is not Clara but "She who is Clara Passmore who is the Virgin Mary who is the Bastard who is the Owl." Virginal but a bastard, a middle-class English teacher from Savannah, Georgia, but also an owl (we recall the owls that haunted Kennedy's nights in Accra), "She" is tortured by the guilty secret of her own illegitimacy. Yet her mother—"Bastard's Black Mother who is the Reverend's Wife who is Anne Boleyn"—is not simply a token in a tale of race and class exploitation. Although a maid who worked for the rich white man who may have impregnated her, she is also associated with the romantic, indeed heroic victim-image of Anne Boleyn, the beheaded second wife of Henry VIII and mother of Elizabeth I. Similarly, rage toward the father—"Goddam Father who is the Richest White Man in the Town, who is the Dead White Father who is Reverend

Passmore"—is complicated by the European culture he symbolizes and that Sarah adores: the "England . . . of dear Chaucer, Dickens and dearest Shakespeare." As one might expect from Kennedy's distinctive mise-en-scène, some of those adored cultural icons will appear on stage. And yet the most shocking transformations occur in the nonhuman spaces of the drama: the stage directions inform the reader that "the scene is a New York subway is the Tower of London is a Harlem hotel room is St. Peter's. . . . The scene should lurch, lights flash, gates slam." Only one character is given a unitary, if anonymous, identity: "The Negro Man."

While the play unravels with dreamlike swiftness, a story emerges of a bastard daughter of an illicit union, who is adopted by the Reverend Passmore, legitimized as Clara Passmore, but who carries her black mother's color and a passion for the white authors she reads in the Passmore library, and as an adult teaches, as a "plain, pallid" schoolteacher. Cruelly, the glorious fathers of literary history merge with those of Christian myth. God's white dove, associated with Reverend Passmore's preaching (but also the hypocrisy of "passing" as white), presides over the central event of the play: on a fantasized visit to England to attend the funeral of her white father, Clara is refused access to St. Paul's church, where he lies. She is instead imprisoned in the Tower of London, guarded by Shakespeare, Chaucer, and William the Conqueror. The white fathers, having colonized Clara's desire, refuse her white ancestry, her blood connection to their "family":

You are not his ancestor.
Keep her locked there, guard.
Bastard.

As in *Funnyhouse of a Negro*, Christian figures and symbols here play a vivid, ultimately destructive role. As the Tower of London becomes a screeching New York subway car, Clara picks up a The Negro Man and goes with him to a Harlem hotel, where she introduces herself as Mary, addresses him as God, and tries to stab him. Also as in the previous play, the pieces and sites of Clara's identity are irrecon-

cilable, but in *The Owl Answers* gender becomes another layer of meaning and awareness. The ever-transforming Tower (dominant white culture) and Reverend Passmore's High Altar (sacrificial Christianity) are specifically male-dominated edifices against which Clara, the good daughter, measures her being. They also generate the self-loathing projections that destroy her connection to The Negro Man.

Ultimately, Sarah transforms into the screeching owl, symbol of her black mother and her illegitimate origins. As her mother says: "Why be confused? The owl was your beginning, Mary." It is because of her "owl" origin that *The Owl Answers* consistently confuses the words "descendent" and "ancestor": a bastard can be neither. Clara has no legitimacy and finally has no faith. In midplay, Clara tells us, "I belong to God and the owls." But near the end, kneeling to pray, she confesses: "I call God and the Owl answers. It haunts my Tower calling, its feathers are blowing against the cell wall, speckled in the garden on the fig tree, it comes, feathered, great hollow-eyed with yellow skin and yellow eyes, the flying bastard." At the end, as she lies by the burning altar, amid flying feathers and green lights, Clara sprouts owl feathers and blankly utters her last sounds: "Ow . . . oww."

More pointedly than *Funnyhouse of a Negro*, *The Owl Answers* is about betrayal and sexual guilt. A dutiful daughter of Christ and of the secular gods of literature, Clara is full of desire and seeks connection to her sacred objects. Her fathers, Christian and literary, are seductive but ultimately rejecting. Even God's white dove laughs at the spectacle of Clara's suffering. Betrayed by the culture she loves, she is also guilty for loving it. Throughout the play Clara carries notebooks, presumably notes about literature, and continually drops them. Kennedy's stage directions read, "She will pick them up, glance frenziedly at a page, . . . be distracted, place the notebooks in a disorderly pile, drop them again." No less frenzied is the encounter with The Negro Man in the final moments of the play. The owl, a resonant symbol of evil and death in certain African mythologies, claims her at the moment that she acts on, and destroys, "in a gesture of wild weariness," this relationship.

Audiences have had strong reactions to Kennedy's shocking plays. They have become life-long devotees and supporters or have reacted with rage to the unrelentingly personal, familial lens through which complex cultural and political issues are filtered, objectified, and distorted. In 1969 Joseph Papp produced a double bill called *Cities in Bezique,* a title he borrowed from a Kennedy play he did not produce. Instead, the evening consisted of Kennedy's *A Beast Story* and *The Owl Answers,* both directed by Gerald Freedman, one of the playwright's favorite directors. In April 1969 a reviewer, J. Lance Ermatinger, described the audience's response to the evening:

> The witnesses are completely involved, although there is no physical invasion of the audience. Neither black nor white can deny the power of Adrienne Kennedy's fierce poetry. . . . Yet both react with confused anger.
>
> What provokes this anger? I think it is the absence of the doctrinaire in *Bezique.* The White Liberals are offered none of the cliches that bring cold comfort to our day of confrontation. The Black Militants, on the other hand, hear no sizzling slogans. All witness only the story of one human being in a context as richly personal as it is beautifully black.

Kennedy's *A Beast Story* is another family play with echoing allusions to rape, murder, and guilt, but it has none of the emotional reach of *The Owl Answers.* The dialogue is turgid, and Kennedy considered it (the text, not Freedman's apparently stunning production) a failure. Strikingly, however, it extends the transformation motif into new and dangerous territory. In these years Kennedy was creating theatrical bestiaries in which guilt, sexual terror, and barely suppressed rage are signaled by animality. In true surrealist tradition, this animality is naturalized; that is, it becomes part of the logic of the nightmare. *A Beast Story* includes Beast Girl, Beast Woman, Beast Man, and Dead Human, and Kennedy's stage directions note "The

beasts are real people, a black family. At times their speech can be slightly unreal or at times their physical movements can suggest a bestiality, but they are real people." The bestiary aesthetic also holds true for two beautifully crafted plays of the 1960s, *A Lesson in Dead Language* (1968) and *A Rat's Mass* (1966). In both social and cultural exclusion translate into sexual terror and guilt and are, in turn, signaled by the presence of a beast/human.

In *Lesson in Dead Language,* a Latin class is the setting for the transmission of the truth and beauty of western culture. The schoolteacher, a nightmare version of Nellie Rosebaugh, Kennedy's revered Latin teacher, is costumed from the waist up as a White Dog, and Christianity, in the form of enormous statues of Jesus, Joseph, Mary, and the Wise Men, looms intimidatingly over seven little girls, the White Dog's pupils. The girls are dressed in white organdy dresses, white socks, and black shoes, and as they receive their first dictation from the White Dog, "Lesson I bleed." They respond: "The day the white dog died, I started to bleed. Blood came out of me." During the play the girls stand up in the rows between their desks, and the audience sees menstrual stains on the backs of their dresses, stains that grow until the dresses are covered in blood. Although menses is a normal biological development in girls, indeed a sign of life that opposes the dead Latin they are learning, the girls ascribe their blood to individual and collective guilt. They speak in unison to their teacher, whom they also call "Mother": "I killed the white dog and that is why I must bleed for Caesar." The layering of painterly, hermetic language, a characteristic of earlier plays, is in this brief text particularly arresting. We don't understand the meanings or the connections between the white dog, the green grass, a game with lemons, and the growing blood stains, but that is because sexual guilt is not logical. The last line of the play, "Calpurnia dreamed a pinnacle was tumbling down," presages perhaps the fall of the empire that Caesar, Calpurnia's faithless husband, had built over many years. But moments earlier, the girls have performed their own translation: "Since I became a woman, blood comes out of me. I am a pinnacle tumbled down." Female sexuality, signaled by blood, inaugurates a fall from grace into terror and torment.

A Rat's Mass, imagined, like *Lesson in Dead Language,* as a partial bestiary, replays the themes of childhood guilt—here brother-sister incest—and seduction/betrayal by a forceful other, an Italian child called Rosemary. Rosemary is devout in her Catholicism and firm in her belief that she has inherited the glory of Caesar's empire. Amid references to Nazis and bloody battle, the Rat siblings, Fay and Blake, recount a story of a childhood game, engineered by Rosemary, that causes Fay to imagine she is carrying her brother Blake's baby. It seems that their sin, or their guilt for an imagined sin, turns them into beasts. Blake is introduced as Brother Rat—he has a rat's head, a human body, and a tail. Fay has a human head, a rat's belly, and a tail. A processional line of religious icons—Jesus, Joseph, Mary, Wise Men, and a Shepherd—enters, and Sister Rat pleads for atonement. Rosemary, in the garbled talk of children, announces, "I will never atone you," and the Christian figures leave the stage, ignoring the siblings' supplication, until they return as Nazis and shoot them. Rosemary watches, unmoved.

Notwithstanding the violent content of these early plays, the intensity of their images and rhythmic repetitions unencumbered by linear plots and realistic situations have long appealed to performers in other media. Choreographer Jerome Robbins admired *Funnyhouse of a Negro* and commissioned a piece from Kennedy that later developed into *Sun,* a dramatic poem for the murdered Malcolm X that was performed in London's Royal Court theater in 1968. The production of *A Rat's Mass* so appealed to Ellen Stewart, the innovative producer of New York's Cafe LaMama, that she asked Cecil Taylor to write an opera score for the play. It was no doubt on the basis of Kennedy's surrealist imagination that Beatles member John Lennon became interested when she sought to dramatize his nonsense books, *A Spaniard in the Works* and *In His Own Write.* From 1966 to 1969 Kennedy, now a celebrity in her own right, lived in London's Primrose Hill district, supported by a Rockefeller grant and a Guggenheim Fellowship. She relished the friendship of writers Fay Weldon and Adrian Mitchell and the actor Victor Spinetti, not to mention her encounters with the Beatles. In 1969 Kennedy returned to New York, which has remained her constant place of residence. However, beginning in the 1970s, she has held teaching positions as a visiting lecturer or writer-in-residence at Yale, Princeton, Brown, the Universities of California, Berkeley and Davis, Stanford, Rutgers, New York University, and Harvard.

Celebrity and Memory

In the mid 1970s Kennedy developed an old obsession—celebrity—into two of her finest works, the play *A Movie Star Has to Star in Black and White* (1976), and her visual autobiography, *People Who Led to My Plays* (1987). Although eleven years apart, these texts together explore not only the seduction of Hollywood images but the way in which fantasy creates meaning and possibilities among diverse groups in American society. Remembering the casual racism of dormitory life at Ohio State in the early 1950s, Kennedy noted in her autobiography that Marlon Brando in the film version of *Streetcar Named Desire* was "the first movie star . . . that both my white and my Negro friends had loved equally, at a time when we seemed to have little in common except our passion for 'engagements' and engagement rings. And weddings." This memory resonates clearly in *A Movie Star Has to Star in Black and White,* for the family story of Clara, pregnant and a writer, is told not only by characters playing her parents and brother and husband but also by actors who are costumed to look like movie stars in the roles they played in three major Hollywood films— Bette Davis and Paul Henried in *Now, Voyager;* Marlon Brando and Jean Peters in *Viva Zapata!;* and Montgomery Clift and Shelley Winters in *A Place in the Sun.* Three scenes, one from each of the films, are enacted over the course of the play. However, the lines spoken are not those of the movie script but of the script Clara is writing as she wanders from scene to scene.

467

There are many layers of representation here. One senses that Kennedy, a fervent movie fan, is giving play to her desires not only to enter the world of celluloid celebrity but to control it. "Her movie stars speak for her," the stage directions indicate, suggesting the ways in which mass culture stories shape our lives. Yet these movie stars are indeed "her" movie stars. Although exclusively white, they star in black and white—an allusion to film technology during Hollywood's memorable 1940s and to the fact that in the play they speak the words of black Clara's life. This fabulous conception extends even to the family members who play the "supporting roles." Mother, father, and husband "all look like photographs Clara keeps of them."

Yet in the unraveling of Clara's story, there is a powerful tension between stars and supporting characters. While there are no Gothic terrors here, no beasts, rape, murder, or laughing doves, we become absorbed in the details of two periods of Clara's life: the first, the summer of 1955 when she and her husband, Eddie, becoming increasingly estranged, move to New York, and the second, the summer of 1963, as she and her parents, now separated and bitter, gather around the comatose body of her brother, Wally. Only the motif of bleeding, a persistent feature of pregnancy for Kennedy in earlier plays, recurs here, represented in the *Viva Zapata!* scene when Josepha (Jean Peters) bleeds on her wedding sheets and Zapata (Marlon Brando) helps her change them. (This scene does not occur in the movie, another example of Clara's assertiveness in scripting her fantasies.)

At first blush *A Movie Star Has to Star in Black and White* seems to lack the political and historical resonance of earlier Kennedy plays, but this is not really the case. If Clara appears to be consumed by her movie stars, Kennedy gives a very different perspective to Clara's mother:

In our Georgia town the white people lived on one side. It had pavement on the streets and sidewalks and mail was delivered. The Negroes lived on the other side and the roads were dirt and had no sidewalk and you had to go to the Post Office to pick up your mail. . . . A Negro couldn't sit down at the soda fountain in the drug store but had to take his drink out. In the movies at Montefore you had to go in the side and up the stairs and sit in the last four rows.

As "Mother" says these lines, stage directions indicate that she is facing the actors who play movie stars in their seductive black-and-white celluloid simulations. In contradistinction to Clara's rapture, her mother reminds us that the racism embedded in southern institutions was manifest not only in the near-exclusion of African Americans from film roles (other than that of servants) in the great movies of the 1930s and 1940s but at all levels of distribution. For the mother's generation, cinematic pleasure was tainted by the conditions under which films were seen. In the closing seconds of the play, as we witness the murder scene from *A Place in the Sun*, in which the working-class pregnant wife (Shelley Winters) is tipped out of a boat by her ambitious young husband (Montgomery Clift), Clara and her parents learn that Wally will be brain damaged and paralyzed from his injuries in a car accident. "After [the doctor] told us," says Clara, "my mother cried in my arms outside the hospital. . . . She shook so that I thought both of us were going to fall headlong down the steps." The stage directions next read, "Shelley Winters drowns." The mother's near fall parallels the drowning of the fictional character, and we are asked to contemplate the relation of fantasy to the cataclysms of real life. Does Hollywood trivialize our lives? Or do stories produced by the dream factory provide useful scenarios for self-creation beyond the structures provided for us by family and society?

In her autobiography Kennedy clearly subscribes to the latter position. Begun in New York and developed over the course of teaching residencies in California between 1981 and 1987, *People Who Led to My Plays* suggests that identity is not a secure set of familial and cultural traits that an individual carries from childhood to the grave. Rather, identity is imagined as a kind of assemblage of the memories, desires, places, and objects one has experienced over the course of a life. Genetic inheritance plays a part, and powerful parental figures stalk our psyches forever, but Kennedy takes (although she would not say so) a distinctly postmodern approach to the story of a life. Although roughly chronological, the autobiography is not a narrative. There are no foundational principles or events that "determine" her development. Indeed the book contains little self-analysis and comparatively little writing. Instead, *People Who Led To My Plays* is a chronological collage of language, drawings, and photographs, such that Kennedy's "I" appears to the reader to be less a coherent whole than a piece the totality of commodities and images of twentieth-century American culture. The reader encounters a brief topic word or phrase (e.g., "Old Maid Playing Cards," "My Mother," "Orson Welles," "Jesus," "Myself") followed by brief lines of description and often an image from a newspaper, a family snapshot, or a glossy photograph of a movie star such that a teenager might collect. Indeed, Kennedy has kept scrapbooks since childhood and as a teenager addicted to movie magazines, collected all the glossies reprinted here. Significantly, no distinction is made in the style of the entries between fictional and real human beings, or between historical and religious figures, or between races. All are "people mingling in my life, my thoughts and my imagination . . . leading to a strengthening of my writing and a truer expression of it."

It is worth looking closely at parts of one page of the autobiography, keeping in mind that no single page is any more or less representative than another:

Freddy Jamison:
I was still secretly in love with him, but my mother didn't approve of him. I wrote about him in the autograph books I hid under the mattress.

Miss McCreary:
I did well in our journalism class and informed Miss McCreary, our teacher, that I wanted to be a journalist. She said she didn't think, because of my color, that it was realistic for me to pursue that thought.

Louis Jordan, Nat King Cole, Billy Eckstine, Frank Sinatra:
Said romance and joy awaited me.

Elizabeth Taylor (in Jane Eyre):
She was Jane Eyre's best friend, Helen, and as a child died of pneumonia because cruel Mr. Brocklehurst punished her and made her walk in the rain after he had cut off her hair.

My mother and her hair:
When my mother cut her hair I used to beg her to let me keep the strands.

A reader can immediately identify, and identify with, the categories, if not all the details, of Kennedy's "people"—an unapproachable love object, a racist teacher, popular singers who promise the pleasures of adult sexuality, a high-culture figure (Jane Eyre), a popular-culture figure (Elizabeth Taylor), mingled with her mother, and Kennedy's familiar obsession with hair. Indeed, the space between each entry gives readers a place to, as it were, enter their own memories of the past. Despite the absence of a gripping story, the fragmented style of *People Who Led to My Plays* nonetheless creates a smooth join between reader and text.

Scattered across the autobiography are references to themes and ideas from Kennedy's plays. For the young Kennedy, Lon Chaney Jr.'s performance in *The Wolf Man* (1941) epitomized the terror of shape-changing, which ultimately became a unique feature of the mature writer's aesthetic. There are repeated references to her mother's pretty hair, her sayings, her love of movies, and most of all her stories. After the topic line *"People my mother dreamed about,"* the Kennedy persona writes:

In the morning I could hardly wait to hear about them. The stories she told of them were as exciting as the movies of Frankenstein and Dracula that I saw at the Waldorf. . . . There is no doubt that a person talking about the people in his or her dreams became an archetype for people in my monologues, plays and stories.

Such analysis, fulfilling the mission of the title of the autobiography, tantalizing and significant as it is, also leaves much that is untold. Like many postmodern texts, Kennedy's subtly questions the ability of an author to be "authoritative," even about her own life.

In exchange for firm truths, Kennedy provides readers the pleasure of interpretation. For example, on one page of the autobiography is a studio glossy of Fred Astaire and Ginger Rogers caught in a whirling embrace, his tuxedoed leg kicking back, the epitome of grace in motion. On a facing page, directly across from Fred and Ginger, is a reprint of a photograph of Adolph Hitler in jackboots, striding stiffly forward, flanked by grim-faced officers. Kennedy juxtaposes two images of decisive movement, one capturing the rhythm of dance, glamour, and perfect symmetry, the other the drumbeat of military domination. But there is a third image on these pages, a snapshot not of people but of her mother's china cabinet. The entry reads, "There is beauty in order." Dance choreography, military uniforms—these too are about order. What lends order and clarity to the consciousness of the writer, however, is a familiar object that might be found in anyone's home. Yet even as we honor the homely china cabinet, we must acknowledge that it is no more true than the pictures of Hitler or Fred and Ginger. It too is an image reproduced by the publisher for Kennedy's book. In this dazzling and moving collage, no one impression can dominate another or become the definitive basis for understanding.

The 1990s

Kennedy's work in the 1990s produces a similar effect, even as it coalesces around a quasi-autobiographical persona named Suzanne: Suzanne Sand in the novel *Deadly Triplets* (1990) and Suzanne Alexander in a new collection, *The Alexander Plays* (1992), containing *She Talks to Beethoven*, *The Ohio State Murders*,

The Film Club (A Monologue by Suzanne Alexander), and *The Dramatic Circle.* Both the novel and the plays develop material from Kennedy's experiences abroad, especially her long stay in London from 1966 to 1969. Her earlier fascination with untold secrets shaped an entire cultural experience. "Despite the enchantment, there was a subplot in England I couldn't perceive," Kennedy wrote in *A Theatre Journal*, a short appendage to *Deadly Triplets.*

In *Deadly Triplets*, Kennedy's only published novel, a young writer goes to London with her two sons, seeking backers for a play based on John Lennon's nonsense books and seeking as well to unravel a mystery—"the strange demise of my adopted mother years ago in England." As with *People Who Led to My Plays*, autobiographical fragments entwine with fiction; that is, Kennedy's own mystery—her unsuccessful effort to have her version of Lennon's texts produced at the National Theater—is one strand of a Gothic plot about multiple murders and betrayals. (Kennedy's *The Lennon Play: in His Own Write*, coauthored with John Lennon and Victor Spinetti, was eventually published in 1968.) An actor, James Eyre, performing in a play entitled *Deadly Triplets*, falls in love with the writer Suzanne, even as he grows despondent over the difficulty of playing identical characters. James has information about Suzanne's adopted mother, Gina, and about Antonia, Gina's biological daughter, who was jealous when Suzanne was adopted and who has accused Suzanne of being responsible for their mother's death. James's brother, another actor, begins to torment and impersonate James, and finally, James is murdered under mysterious circumstances. At the same time Suzanne discovers that Gina was also murdered—by Antonia. James's murder is "solved," but the death of Gina remains unresolved. Indeed, Suzanne wonders, at the end of the novel, "Is Gina still alive?" The dread and paranoia of *Deadly Triplets* will permeate *The Alexander Plays.*

In Kennedy's imaginative world the dead mingle with the living and faces on Old Maid playing cards can be as compelling and significant as historical figures, fictional characters, or members of her family. In *Funnyhouse of a Negro* the father, although dead, keeps returning, filling the theater with sounds of his horrible knocking. In *The Owl Answers* a subway car is a hotel bedroom or a royal prison, and no identity is safe from incursion. In *The Alexander Plays* the mood is retrospective—narrators step forward and frame the action—yet equally experimental, for in these plays, too, the dead are not quiet. Suzanne Alexander's rooms may not transform into subway cars, but hints of imminent disaster abound: the frightening disappearance of husband, David Alexander, an equally mysterious reunion, the possibility of hidden disease, and everywhere, deaths revealed as murders. Although Suzanne or her sister Alice address the audience as narrators of past events, they are not reliable narrators but rather participant witnesses who convey a sense of overwhelming foreboding. Neither the audience nor they, however, can uncover the subplot. Perhaps the intrusion of onstage storytelling began with the presence of writer-protagonist, Clara, in *A Movie Star Has to Star in Black and White*. In *The Alexander Plays*, however, there is a dizzying amount of textuality. Mingling dramatic enactment with fragments of diaries, radio programming, histories, and biographies, Kennedy's plays of the 1990s range over time and space, moving us from Accra, to Columbus, Ohio, to Washington, D.C., to London.

The Ohio State Murders consolidates the technique of all *The Alexander Plays* most successfully. A "well-known black writer" returns to Ohio State University, where she was a student from 1949 to 1952, to give a talk about the violent imagery in her work. The actor playing the mature Suzanne addresses the audience as though delivering her invited speech. She tells us that when she first arrived at university as a young student, the geography of the campus "made her anxious." Soon we are in the past, following the young Suzanne to her English class, as she reads Thomas Hardy's *Tess of the D'Urbervilles* and falls in love with her teacher, who has the distinctly British name Robert Hampshire. Through the double medium of narration and enactment, we learn that the

young Suzanne, having slept with her teacher, produces twin baby daughters. Robert Hampshire secretly kidnaps and murders the babies and then kills himself. He is never openly charged with the murders; indeed, the university conceals the act to save its reputation. However, Suzanne's life is redeemed by marriage to a sensitive and intelligent black student, David Alexander. These are the "facts" of the story. But we never see the murders or understand them. Instead, through fragments of Hardy's text, references to a book of symbols, and finally, long excerpts from Hampshire's oblique lectures, the two Suzannes create a morbid atmosphere of confusion, paranoia, and despair.

There is a crime scene in *The Ohio State Murders*, but it has nothing to do with cold ravines, bloody knives, or mad professors. The crime scene is the girls' dormitory at Ohio State and the palpable racist hatred the young Suzanne experiences from groups of white girls. This is the real secret of the play, a secret that has no logic and no explanation but that bites into the consciousness of Suzanne Alexander: "I felt such danger from them."

In *The Dramatic Circle*, the last of *The Alexander Plays*, there is danger surrounding Frantz Fanon, the Martiniquan psychiatrist whom David Alexander is researching in Africa. Suzanne and Alice explore their fear over David's disappearance by taking part in a reading of Bram Stoker's *Dracula*, organized by a mysterious English psychiatrist, Dr. Freudenberger. In typical Kennedy fashion, bits of the Stoker text mingle with passages from Fanon's *Wretched of the Earth*, particularly his chapter on "Colonial War and Mental Disorders." For Fanon the violence of colonial oppression produced possibly incurable psychic wounds in the Algerians he treated, and the play draws clear connections between those wounds, Suzanne's nervousness in London, David's premature aging, and the subhuman world Jonathan Harker confronts in Dracula's castle. As Suzanne Alexander's fragmented stories emerge nonlinearly across multiple texts and sites, Kennedy leaves the reader/spectator with a profound sense that racism—doubled, tripled, indeed endlessly repeated and evaded—is the "undead" of Euro-American culture.

Adrienne Kennedy's work made an impressive return to New York City in the mid-1990s. The New York–based Signature Theater Company has a unique policy of devoting an entire season to the production of old and new works by leading living playwrights. In 1995–1996, its Kennedy year, it produced splendid revivals of *Funnyhouse of a Negro, A Movie Star Has to Star in Black and White, The Ohio State Murders,* and *The Dramatic Circle,* as well as world premieres of *June and Jean in Concert* (1996) and *Sleep Deprivation Chamber* (1996), both of which won an Obie for Best New Play. *June and Jean in Concert* draws its materials from Kennedy's autobiography, *People Who Led to My Plays.* As though Kennedy were not satisfied with its book format, however innovative, *June and Jean in Concert* gives three-dimensional existence and sonority to the autobiography's brief references to childhood friends, the twins June and Jean, and various family members, living and dead. Kennedy splits her autobiographical "I" into June and Jean, one of whom dies but returns, like "crazy" Aunt Ella, to circle again around the themes of childhood pleasures, the sadness of (Kennedy's parents') divorce, and Jean's writing career (to which June's ghost contributes). Maintaining the playwright's fascination with celebrity, the play weaves memory fragments into a delicate musical score sung by onstage representations of Paul Robeson, Judy Garland, Nat King Cole, and Frank Sinatra.

In marked tonal contrast, *Sleep Deprivation Chamber,* cowritten with Kennedy's younger son, Adam Kennedy, dramatizes a son's beating by a Virginia policeman, after his car was stopped for a broken taillight. The aggrieved son, Teddy Alexander, is then charged with assaulting the officer, and the phony case goes to trial. Based on a real incident that happened to the Kennedy family, *Sleep Deprivation Chamber* interweaves different spatial zones—a college production of *Hamlet,* directed by Teddy, a hotel room where Suzanne Alexander reads aloud her passionate letters of protest to the governor of Virginia, and a Virginia courtroom where an "Unseen Questioner" interrogates fa-

ther and son and ultimately the police officer, whose testimony is discredited. Across many Kennedy texts, childhood memories of parental optimism about eventual racial equality contrast obliquely with the expression of personal terrors, and these in turn mingle with profound anxiety about the historical intractability of racism. *Sleep Deprivation Chamber* takes a harsher view. The familiar Kennedy dreamscape is cruelly and insistently ruptured by the rhetoric of interrogation, such that, while the play reveals the writer's abiding love for her family, "sleep deprivation" becomes a bitter metaphor for the racial tensions that scarred American society in the 1990s.

Adrienne Kennedy remains one of the United States' most gifted dramatists, the recipient of a Rockefeller grant and a Guggenheim Fellowship in 1967 and the Manhattan Borough Presidents' Award for Excellence in the Arts in 1988. Her work has attracted the talents of visionary directors—among them, Joseph Chaikin, Gerald Freedman, and Michael Kahn—as well as such distinguished performers as Ruby Dee, Mary Alice, Gloria Foster, Billie Allen, Diana Sands, and Robbie McCauley. She has been commissioned to write plays for Jerome Robbins, the Public Theater, The Royal Court, the Mark Taper Forum, and Juilliard. An enthusiastic and inspiring teacher, she has taught at major universities on both coasts. If, as Kennedy remarked somewhat ruefully, her plays appear more frequently on university syllabi than on American stages, their contribution to the development of American drama is undeniable. In the 1960s and 1970s, when American theater was unusually receptive to innovation and change, Adrienne Kennedy's plays demonstrated the need for experimentation unfettered by mainstream taboos. They testified to the clarity, honesty, and power of Kennedy's aesthetic, her capacity to address violent emotion without sentimentality or self-indulgence, and her refusal to deal in theatrical clichés that make the world seem familiar and comfortable to audiences. Kennedy's dramas show us that wearily familiar social problems can give rise to unique stage images and to a dramatic poetry

so powerful that decades after its first soundings, still has the power to seduce and hurt, to
puzzle and inspire.

Selected Bibliography

PRIMARY WORKS

PLAYS

The Lennon Play: In His Own Write. With John Lennon
and Victor Spinetti. London: Cape; New York: Simon
& Schuster, 1968. (Adaptation of the writings of John
Lennon from his *In His Own Write* and *A Spaniard
in the Works.*)
Cities in Bezique. New York: Samuel French, 1969. (In-
cludes *A Beast Story* and *The Owl Answers.* Reprinted in *Kuntu Drama: Plays of the African Continuum.* Edited by Paul Carter Harrison. New York:
Grove Press, 1974.)
"An Evening with Dead Essex." *Theater* 9:66–78
(Spring 1978).
People who Led to my Plays. New York: Knopf, 1986.
Adrienne Kennedy in One Act. Emergent Literatures
series. Minneapolis: University of Minnesota Press,
1988. (Includes *Funnyhouse of a Negro, The Owl Answers, A Lesson in Dead Language, A Rat's Mass,
Sun, A Movie Star Has to Star in Black and White,*
and adaptations of *Electra* and *Orestes.* This is the
definitive edition of the plays. *A Movie Star Has to
Star in Black and White* has been reprinted in *The
Norton Anthology of American Literature,* 3rd ed.
1989.)
The Alexander Plays. Minneapolis: University of Minnesota Press, 1992. (Includes *She Talks to Beethoven,
The Ohio State Murders, The Film Club [A Monologue by Suzanne Alexander],* and *The Dramatic
Circle.*)
Sleep Deprivation Chamber. New York: Theatre Communications Group, 1996.
The Adrienne Kennedy Reader. Minneapolis: Univer-
sity of Minnesota Press, forthcoming. (Will contain
June and Jean in Concert, "The Sisters Etta and
Ella," "Grendel and Grendel's Mother," "Letter to
my Students on my 61st Birthday, by Suzanne Alexander," "A Letter to Flowers," *An Evening With
Dead Essex, Motherhood 2000,* "The Black Columbiad," "Secret Paragraphs about My Brother," "Be-
cause of the King of France," *In One Act,* and *The
Alexander Plays.*)

UNPUBLISHED PLAYS

Pale Blue Flowers, 1955.
Boats, 1969.
Black Children's Day, 1980.
Lancashire Lad, 1980.
Diary of Lights, 1987.

FICTION

"Because of the King of France." *Black Orpheus: A Journal of African and Afro-American Literature* 10:30–
37 (1963). (Under the pseudonym Adrienne Cornell.)
Deadly Triplets: A Theatre Mystery and Journal. Minneapolis: University of Minnesota Press, 1990.

AUTOBIOGRAPHY

People Who Led to My Plays. New York: Knopf, 1997.

SECONDARY WORKS

BIOGRAPHICAL AND CRITICAL STUDIES

Blau, Herbert. *The Eye of Prey: Subversions of the Post-
modern.* Indiana University Press, 1987.
Bryant-Jackson, Paul K., and Louis More Overbeck, eds.
*Intersecting Boundaries: The Theatre of Adrienne
Kennedy.* Minneapolis: University of Minnesota
Press, 1992.
Diamond, Elin. *Unmaking Mimesis.* London and New
York: Routledge, 1997.
Cohn, Rudy. *New American Dramatists, 1960–1980.*
New York: Grove Press, 1982.

INTERVIEWS

Betsko, Kathleen, and Rachel Koenig. "Adrienne Ken-
nedy." In *Interviews with Contemporary Women
Playwrights.* Edited by Kathleen Betsko and Rachel
Koenig. New York: Morrow, Beech Tree Books, 1987.
Pp. 246–58.
Bryant-Jackson, Paul K., and Louis More Overbeck.
"Adrienne Kennedy: An Interview." In *Intersecting
Boundaries: The Theatre of Adrienne Kennedy.* Edited by Paul K. Bryant-Jackson and Louis More Overbeck. Minneapolis: University of Minnesota Press,
1992. Pp. 3–12.
Diamond, Elin. "An Interview with Adrienne Kennedy." *Studies in American Drama 1945–Present*
4:143–57 (1989).
Kennedy, Adrienne, and Margaret B. Wilkerson. "Adrienne Kennedy: Reflections." *City Arts Monthly,* February 1982, p. 39.

JAMAICA KINCAID
(1949 –   )

MARIANNE HIRSCH AND IVY SCHWEITZER

JAMAICA KINCAID IS a writer who has had to invent herself out of contradictory histories. She was born Elaine Potter Richardson on May 25, 1949, on the small Caribbean island of Antigua, a British colony that became an associated, self-governing state of the United Kingdom in 1967 and fully independent in 1981. Kincaid received an education she decribed in an interview with Selyn Cudjoe as "very 'Empire,'" that "only involved civilization up to the British Empire . . . We were taught to read from Shakespeare and Milton when I was five. They were read to us while we sat under a tree." This image of inculcating the Western literary canon in a paradisiacal West Indian dominion describes a central tension in Kincaid's work.

Her stepfather, David Drew, was a carpenter and her mother, Annie Richardson, a tall, strong-willed Dominican woman descended from Carib Indians, kept their small home. Kincaid's stepfather was the dominant male figure in her life, as her relationship with her real father, Roderick Potter, was distant at best. In 1965 Kincaid went to New York to work as an au pair, not to return for twenty years. In 1973, as she began to write, she took a significant step and renamed herself "Jamaica Kincaid," a name she chose because it suggested her West Indian origins, but also, and at the same time, disconnected her from her place of birth and family of origin. She has done all her major writing in the United States, but when she found her voice in the breakthrough story "Girl," written one afternoon in 1978, the source of her inspiration was, as it continues to be, the West Indian world and the maternal influence that shaped her. "You see, I spent all the time I had been away from the West Indies and from my mother building some kind of 'literary monument' to it," she told Cudjoe.

Kincaid maintains that the break with Antigua and her mother was necessary, not just as a bid for independence, but as an act of survival. Although she excelled in school, her mother required her help with a family that was growing beyond its means. When Kincaid was about nine, her mother had three sons in quick succession, pushing the family over the edge. The beautiful, intelligent woman she had adored as an only child became overwhelmed and withdrew from her. It was also at this time that the contradictions of British colonial rule in Antigua became painfully apparent to Kincaid who recalled in her interview with Cudjoe, "When I was nine, I refused to stand up at the refrain 'God Save Our King.' I hated 'Rule Britannia' and I used to say that we weren't Britons, we were slaves." This is a central conjunction in Kincaid's work: the embeddedness of individual and family life in national and colonial history, one serving as a metaphor for the other and illuminating the workings of power.

In New York in the seventies, with the women's movement and sexual revolutions in full swing, Kincaid perceived a freedom around her and in other people that encouraged her to create a new identity for herself as a writer. Yet she accepts neither of these influences in an uncomplicated way. After working for several affluent families, first in Scarsdale and then in New York City, Kincaid studied photography at the New School for Social Research in New York and at Franconia College in New Hampshire. Photography, as a metaphor for representation and power relations, would become an important motif in her later work.

In 1973 Kincaid pitched an idea for a story to *Ingenue* that involved interviewing the feminist leader Gloria Steinem about her life at seventeen, which led to a series of interviews with women about their lives at this crucial age. This early project not only reinforces Kincaid's awareness of the U.S. feminist movement, but it also flags her interest in female adolescent development, a theme present in her earliest writing. After doing several stories and reviews for *Rolling Stone*, Kincaid met the writer George W. S. Trow, who introduced her to William Shawn, long-time editor at the *New Yorker*. Shawn became her mentor and in a very important way, another muse, just as the *New Yorker* became another home. In her 1997 book about her brother's death from AIDS, *My Brother*, Kincaid remarks that "the magazine I wrote for all of my writing life so far was like the place in which I had grown up; it was beautiful, an ideal of some kind, but it had been made vulgar and ugly by the incredibly stupid people who had become attracted to it." And, she adds, "one of the ways I became a writer was by telling my husband's father [William Shawn] things he didn't want me to tell him but was so curious about that he would listen to them anyway." From September 1974, the date of her first unsigned "Talk of the Town" piece, until 1983, Kincaid wrote about 80 such pieces for the magazine, honing her particularly incisive yet poetic style. It was in the *New Yorker* that she also first published many of the stories that were collected in her first three books. In 1979 she married Allen Shawn, the son of William Shawn, a composer and professor of music at Bennington College, in Bennington, Vermont. She converted to Judaism, and gave birth to her daughter Annie in 1985 and to her son Harold in 1988.

Critical Contexts

Kincaid's writing has attracted a large popular audience as well as critical acclaim. In particular, her singular, incantatory style and her treatment of the complex and universal mother-daughter relationship, have captivated readers and impressed critics. Kincaid's writing has its hard edges, however. Her work shows an outward progression from dreamlike, surreal imagery and sharply detailed narratives of adolescent development to angry and courageous meditations on the harsh realities of persistent injustice. But because rage and critique are present in all her work, she, like many other writers of color, has had to negotiate a complex politics of address. The enormous success of Kincaid's early fiction stemmed from what some readers labeled its "universal" appeal, but that description obscures the cultural specificity of its powerful evocations. The noted writer Susan Sontag remarked that at least two of the stories in Kincaid's first collection, "My Mother," and the eponymous "At the Bottom of the River," "seem to me more thrilling than any prose I've read in the last few years by a writer from this continent." But other readers found the unconventional structure of the stories "deliberately" inaccessible. *Annie John* (1985) was widely praised for a "charm" that critics rightly found lacking in Kincaid's third book, *A Small Place* (1988), a long, enraged essay on the effects of colonialism in Antigua. Despite the criticism it received, writing *A Small Place* was a major step forward for Kincaid, who retorted in an interview with Donna Perry, "Really, when people say you're charming you are in deep trouble. I realized in writing that book that the first step to claiming yourself is anger." Her fourth work (and third volume of fiction) *Lucy* (1990) also disappointed some readers precisely because it refused *Annie John*'s more elliptical, inferential critique of ethnocentrism and privilege. Kincaid's later fiction is the most difficult and unsparing, especially *The Autobiography of My Mother*, her first exploration of West Indian culture from an adult perspective. Her most recent pieces about gardening, which appeared in the *New Yorker* in the mid-1990s and are collected under the suggestive title *My Garden (Book):* (1999), continue her exploration of the themes of power, conquest, betrayal and self-betrayal on a personal and historical scale.

Another measure of the difficulty or, conversely, brilliance of Kincaid's work is its resistance to conventional categorization. Her stories and critical essays about her fiction are often included in collections about West Indian, Afro-Caribbean, and African women's literature. But she is also a chronicler of the immigrant experience, compared to writers like Sandra Cisneros. Prominent themes in her work, like the centrality of the mother-daughter bond, link her to women's writing more broadly, and her poignant depiction of the construction and imposition of female gender conventions has contributed to the literature of "girls" and adolescent development. Kincaid reappropriates for women of color the classic coming-of-age story, or bildungsroman, and the formation of the artist tale, or *künstlerroman*, and contributes to the growing genres of women's autobiography and autoethnography. However, Kincaid has expressed resistance to being categorized as either a woman writer or a black writer, explaining that, although she supports the struggle of women writers and regards Toni Morrison as one of the greatest writers of our time, she does not personally identify with the African American women Morrison writes about. Nevertheless, as reported by Emily Listfield, the distinguished scholar of black literature Henry Louis Gates has argued that an important contribution of Kincaid's work is that "she never feels the necessity of claiming the existence of a black world or a female sensibility. She assumes them both." Kincaid's work contributes an incisive interrogation of gender and sexuality to the growing body of colonial, postcolonial, diasporic literature. Kincaid has also con-

Jamaica Kincaid

tributed to the literature of photography, travel, and gardening.

An element that exceeds all of these categorizations is the unforgettable quality of Kincaid's voice, expressed in a prose style so powerful and hypnotic that, for readers like Doris Grumbach, it "results not so much in stories as in states of consciousness," and in the powerful expression of a subconscious emotional landscape. Her style has been characterized as particularly feminine, in its use of strong rhythms and refrains to get beyond the imposed rationality of the "father" and of male-dominated culture. It has also been hailed as specifically African American, as well as postcolonial, in its employment of the rhetorical strategies of repetition, parody, and mimicry. It may be more accurate to say, with the West Indian writer Derek Walcott, that a sentence by Kincaid "heads towards its own contradiction." This style allows her to hold opposing, seemingly incompatible elements suspended within an imaginary textual space. This style may be a response to the world created by her powerful mother, who was a product both of the colonial British values of orderliness and respectability and the traditional West Indian practice of obeah, a transatlantic religion of the African diaspora related to *voudun* (voodoo). In obeah dreams matter, appearances can be deceptive, and spirit moves with fluidity through a multitude of forms. It is a world view defined by the constancy of transformation. Reflecting this sense of shifting, multiple, transparent realities, Kincaid's style becomes a strategy for resisting the binary thinking and opacity of Western thought. Thus, love and hatred, sympathy and rage, loyalty and subversion coexist in her sentences, producing a powerful, complicated, layered verbal texture.

Some critics, such as Moira Ferguson in her essay "Lucy and the Mark of the Colonizer," have called Kincaid's writing "oppositional," a "counterdiscourse to the dominant culture," but that ignores its intense doubleness. To understand Kincaid's approach, we need to recall her education within the British colonial system, which elevated the canonical writers of that tradition, such as Shakespeare and Milton, as well as the rightness of everything English, to the complete devaluation and erasure of native life and culture. Antiguan children, like children in British colonies around the globe, were forced to memorize and recite poems such as Wordsworth's "I Wandered Lonely as a Cloud," although they had never seen a daffodil and perhaps never would. They studied British history and culture, rather than the history and culture of their own conquered nations. Unruly children, as Kincaid came to be, were punished by having to copy over parts of Milton's *Paradise Lost*. Despite this self-denying and disfiguring inculcation, Kincaid acknowledges that the texts of the Western canon shaped her sense of aesthetic cultural value. Furthermore, she recognizes that to reject the canon either for silence, or for some authentically "native" means of expression, is impossible. "It's a two-edged thing," she explained to Perry, "because I wouldn't have known how to write and how to think if I hadn't read those things." Her response is to appropriate the dominant narratives of canonical writers like Shakespeare, Milton, Wordsworth, and Annie John's beloved Charlotte Brontë, and rewrite the texts that were meant to exclude her, using them to express a different, though inextricably related, consciousness.

Merging and Separating: *At the Bottom of the River*

Although Kincaid described her first collection of fiction, *At the Bottom of the River* (1983), as "a very unangry, decent, civilized book" in her interview with Perry, its very refusal of conventional narrative form stages an important rebellion and declaration of creative independence. Two influences at this time shaped Kincaid's ideas about writing. Chris Marker's 1962 French film *La Jetée*, composed of a series of black and white still photographs and a voice-over narration, and the experimental work of the French new novelist Alain Robbe-Grillet freed her from the necessity of straightforward plot development, which from her Antiguan perspective, seemed like the imposition of a false—"civilized"—order upon the welter of experience.

In the ten stories that make up *At the Bottom of the River*, we follow disembodied voices through dreamlike images that evoke psychic landscapes. There is, however, a "plot" to this collection, which concerns a painful struggle between the "you" and the "I" in the process of self-definition. Kincaid wrote the frequently cited first story, "Girl," under the influence of Elizabeth Bishop's extraordinary poem "In the Waiting Room" (1946), which describes the poet's young self coming to consciousness as a gendered subject within history. In Kincaid's arresting one-sentence story, a West Indian mother instructs her daughter about domestic chores and female behavior: "Wash the white clothes on Monday and put them on the stone heap; wash the color clothes on Tuesday and put them on the clothesline to dry . . ." Through repetition and subtle shifts in tone, Kincaid suggests the way maternal instruction becomes condemnation, as if the daughter, whose weak protests barely impede her mother's onslaught, is already a failure—a "slut." Failure is always conceived of in sexual terms, in terms imposed upon West Indian culture by British preconceptions, internalized, then recapitulated, by the colonized mother. In a counterpart story, "The Letter from Home," also one sentence long, the voice of the now fully indoctrinated woman chants woodenly, "I milked the cows, I churned the butter, I stored the cheese, I baked the bread, I brewed the tea, I washed the clothes, I dressed the children . . ." Ironically, the repetition of "I" only reinforces the speaker's lack of subjectivity. At the end, however, she manages to escape from the self-denying domesticity by rejecting what appears to be a stultifying Christian submission: "I saw a man, He was in a shroud, I sat in a rowboat, he whistled sweetly to me, I narrowed my eyes, He beckoned to me, Come now; I turned and rowed away, as if I didn't know what I was doing."

In "Blackness," the experience of self-loss becomes existential, rendering the first person voice unable to "say my own name" or "point to myself and say 'I.' " Kincaid explores the terms of this erasure and the peace it strangely brings in the memorable story, "My Mother," where mother and daughter undergo strange and monstrous metamorphoses into mythic creatures that evoke the depths of their primal struggles. At the end, however, the daughter takes a journey by water and leaves her mother behind, only to be met at her destination by a woman with a "face . . . completely different from what I was used to" (p. 59), whom she nevertheless recognizes as her mother, perhaps an "othermother." In the earlier, uncollected story, "Antigua Crossings," a girl sent by her angry mother to stay with her maternal grandmother in Dominica, finds in her a healing, uncritical strength. This motif will recur when Ma Chess, Annie John's maternal grandmother and an obeah woman, comes from Dominica to rescue Annie from her "long sickness" brought on by the conflicts of adolescent development. In the story "My Mother" the daughter finds in this "complete union" with the othermother a boundariless oneness and peace that is, paradoxically, the precondition of her own self-

definition: "As we walk through the rooms [of my mother's house] we merge and separate, merge and separate; soon we shall enter the final stage of our evolution."

Mother and daughter "live in a bower made from flowers whose petals are imperishable," a primordial garden, like the garden of Eden, the precursor of the many gardens in Kincaid's work. Like all of Kincaid's central images, the garden functions on the individual psychic as well as historical levels. It stands for the pre-oedipal connection and the preconquest Antigua, as well as the "terrain," as Kincaid calls it in the title story of the collection, of her self-possession. This garden is not ruled by an imperious, arbitrary power who renders the human desire for knowledge dangerous and banishes his creations from paradise. Unlike the fallen Adam and Eve, Kincaid's narrator glimpses "at the bottom of the river" a vision of life that counteracts "the knowledge of the presence of death." She sees what the single female being in her visionary garden at the bottom of the river sees: "a world in which the sun and the moon shone at the same time. . . . unmindful of any of the individual needs of existence, and without knowledge of future or past." To imagine nature without history significantly revises the canonical Miltonic story of the fall, while to imagine light, or enlightenment, without binary opposition redefines epistemology. This new vision allows the narrator to emerge from "a pit" into a room that is the space of her writerly self. At the end of this remarkable collection, the narrator evolves from the earlier erasures and names herself, each repetition anchoring her more firmly in her self: "I see some books, I see a chair, I see a table, I see a pen. . . . I claim these things then—mine—and now feel myself grow solid and complete, my name filling up my mouth."

Erasures and Repetitions: *Annie John*

In a series of more clearly interconnected stories, *Annie John* repeats the trajectory of *At the Bottom of the River*, from ecstatic and troubling mother-daughter connections to a liberating aloneness. On the surface, *Annie John* can be read as a "universal" female bildungsroman that traces a girl's growth from the age of ten to seventeen, from the maternal to the symbolic, from the familial to the worldly. But the novel is unmistakably marked by its cultural specificity, which in Kincaid's case is hybrid. Thus the language of maternal attachment is clearly marked by the Caribbean landscape. The rebellion against the child's entrapment in the home is couched in the terms of colonial subjugation as well as the fall from paradise. *Annie John*, moreover, uses photography, a technologized means of perception, as a medium through which to re-envision both familial and colonial structures of power.

Annie John begins by describing the simple daily life of the mother and daughter as a "paradise": they are inseparable, sharing an ecstatic preverbal connectedness as well as transmitting and receiving the traditional feminine roles that make women socially acceptable. Their unbounded connection is extreme: when Annie is too "lazy" to eat her meat, her mother chews up the bits for her and places them in her mouth. They engage in rituals of mutuality: bathing, cooking and cleaning, and the important ritual of airing out the contents of Annie's mother's trunk, which she brought from Dominica and has filled with keepsakes of Annie's young life. Each object becomes the occasion for transmitting family stories and memories from mother to daughter. In an essay Annie writes for school that transfixes her schoolmates and teachers, she finds a language to describe the sensuality, plenitude, safety, and radiance that characterize the lack of differentiation between the young daughter and her all-powerful, protective mother. That language is clearly marked by the characteristics of their island world:

> When we swam around in this way, I would think how much we were like the pictures of sea mammals I had seen, my mother and I, naked in the seawater, my mother sometimes singing to me a song in a French patois I did not yet understand, or sometimes not

saying any thing at all. I would place my ear against her neck, and it was as if I were listening to a giant shell, for all the sounds around me—the sea, the wind, the birds screeching—would seem as if they came from inside her, the way the sounds of the sea are in a seashell.

The shattering of Annie's infantile paradise comes with the realization that her mother also represents social acceptability and containment, including a consent to colonial rule. Connection, however, does not become disconnection, but rather a dark world in which "something I could not name just came over us, and suddenly I had never loved anyone so or hated anyone so." The complicated feelings of early adolescent rebellion propel Annie into a protracted and inexplicable illness, mirrored externally in the three months of torrential rain that floods the island. Annie's first move into the world of adult sexuality—punished rather than supported by her mother who calls her a slut—sends her literally back to bed in a withdrawal that reads like a classic psychoanalytic description of latency, that period between child sexuality and puberty when sexuality is dormant.

During her mysterious illness, Annie confronts the photographs that surround her bed, and suddenly "[loom] up big in front of me." Conventional family pictures, each depicts an institution into which Annie will be inducted as she becomes a social subject. In the pictures she wears a white school uniform, a bridesmaid's dress, a communion dress with shoes that have a decorative cut-out on the side of which her mother disapproves. The last is a picture of her parents. In a dreamlike sequence, Annie sees the photographs grow and shrink, perspire, grow weak with exhaustion. She gets out of bed and washes the photos with soap and water, treating them like babies to be put to bed. The result of Annie's feverish manipulation is that the photos are completely transformed: "None of the people in the wedding picture, except for me, had any face left. In the picture of my mother and father, I had erased them from the waist down. In the picture of me wearing my confirmation dress, I had erased all of myself except for the shoes." We can read Annie's encounter with the photographs as an act of resistance in which she attempts to erase the familial and social scripts that position her as an obedient daughter and acquiescent social subject. In an attempt to confront her ambivalence about adolescent development, Annie reduces the unruly photographs, like herself, back to infancy, in order to have a chance at a different start.

Staring at the ruined images the next morning, she can find in them a more fluid and permeable subjectivity, separate from her parents who have constructed her constraining island world, and fostered by her maternal grandmother, Ma Chess, the mysterious obeah woman who comes from Dominica to nurse her. When she decides to leave the island, Annie, in a gesture both of erasure and repetition, asks her father to build her own trunk. As she settles into her berth at the start of her transatlantic escape from a predetermined future in Antigua, she echoes the erasures she performed on the photos: "I could hear the small waves lap-lapping around the ship. They made an unexpected sound, as if a vessel filled with liquid had been placed on its side and now was slowly emptying out." Annie's departure and survival require releasing the bottled-up pressure of the past, to create empty open spaces in which new narratives can be imagined.

But this departure cannot ultimately disconnect Annie from her mother and her home. "Annie John," after all, is the name of the mother as well as the daughter, and it is also the name of the place in which they live: St Johns. In a further irony, when Annie leaves, she goes to England, the very site of imperial subjection to which her mother both offered an alternative and insisted on assimilating her. Mother and daughter are connected by their shared oscillation between complicity with the colonizers and resistance to imperial self-definition. This complex relationship is brilliantly illustrated in the chapter entitled "Columbus in Chains," where the trope of Milton, an exploration of postcolonial and filial relations to history, and history as both personal

and national modes of self-definition, converge. Annie's school, itself, is a perfect kaleidoscope of mixed cultural messages: the Anglican church bell strikes; the girls have tea and buns; the teachers all have the names of English kings; and Annie is given a copy of *Roman Britain* as a prize. In history class they study from *A History of the West Indies*, yet Annie muses about the legacy of slavery in Antigua and confesses, "sometimes, what with our teachers and our books, it was hard for us to tell on which side we really now belonged—with the masters or the slaves—for it was all history, it was all in the past, and everybody behaved differently now; all of us celebrated Queen Victoria's birthday. . . . But we, the descendants of the slaves, knew quite well what had really happened." Using Old English lettering, which allows her to imitate the very look of the masters' speech, Annie writes in her history book under a picture of an enchained Columbus on his way back to Spain in disgrace the words, " 'The Great Man Can No Longer Just Get Up and Go.' " It is an image in reverse and in miniature, of the Middle Passage—the transporting of millions of enslaved Africans across the Atlantic which was a consequence of Columbus's "discovery." But the phrase is one her mother used as she gloated over the news that her own father, against whom she rebelled when she left Dominica for Antigua, had become an invalid. In Annie's world dependence is the sign of gendered, filial, and colonial subjection. Annie's teacher considers her defamation of "one of the great men in history" as not only "arrogant" but "blasphemous" and punishes Annie's heresy by ordering her "to copy Books I and II of *Paradise Lost*, by John Milton." But in copying the words of Milton's rebellious Satan, the Antiguan youngster heard a bracing rejection of submission and inequality and a passionate call to "repossess [her] native seat" that rings with nascent nationalism. It is important that Annie's mother is the model of her rebellion, a shift that points to an indelible maternal genealogy connected with native culture that does not replicate the colonizer-colonized binary. The book's final irony is that to escape her mother, and to make their separation permanent, Annie leaves for England, the "mother country."

England in Antigua: *A Small Place*

This journey will not be Annie's first encounter with Britain. "When I saw England for the first time, I was a child in school sitting at a desk," writes Kincaid in an angry essay entitled "On Seeing England for the First Time." In her next book, *A Small Place,* Kincaid reverses the encounter with England and the Americas. This second person essay addresses the "North America[n] (or worse, Europe[an])" tourist, pointing out all that may not be visible on the Caribbean island through North American and European eyes. Rejected by Robert Gottlieb, William Shawn's successor at the *New Yorker* as too angry and openly aggressive ("the tourist is an ugly human being . . . the people there do not like you"), *A Small Place* represents a turning point in Kincaid's work, a direct confrontation with the history of colonization and her own claustrophobic entrapment in its legacy: "I met the world through England and if the world wanted to meet me it would have to do so through England," she declares. Yet this legacy has also given her the language with which to express her hybrid position as a daughter of the island and of British language and literary culture: "For isn't it odd that the only language I have in which to speak of this crime is the language of the criminal who committed the crime?"

Kincaid explains how difficult it is to twist that language so as to make it reflect the perspectives both of the criminal and of the victim. At the end of the book, she realizes that it is even more difficult to express the transformation of the victims themselves. We might think that "all masters of every stripe are rubbish, and all slaves of every stripe are noble and exalted; there can be no question about this"; but "once they are no longer slaves, once they are free they are no longer noble and exalted: they are just human beings." These formulaic statements express Kincaid's intense disappoint-

ment with the island under self-rule for which the unrepaired ruins of the Antiguan public library, which she frequented as a child, come to stand as a powerful symbol. Where the book begins as an address to the "ugly tourist," it ends with an equally angry indictment of the corrupt new governments of supposed independence.

Accomplishing Aloneness: *Lucy*

With *Lucy,* Kincaid returns to the semi-autobiographical fictions of her earlier books, this time trenchantly inflected by the anger of *A Small Place.* Lucy has left her own family in the Caribbean. She thinks back on them with anger, refuses to answer their mail, and is unmoved by her father's illness and death. Her story takes shape in relation to the wealthy New York family for whom she works as an au pair. If her perceptions differ radically from theirs, it is because of the divergent power structures distinguishing colonizer from colonized. The individual relations they share are embedded in a larger historical and economic plot. But Lucy is, in many ways, also of their world. Her name announces her hybrid identity: her middle name is Josephine "after my mother's uncle Joseph, because he was rich from money he had made in Cuba in sugar"; her last name, Potter, "must have come from the Englishman who owned my ancestors when they were slaves"; and she adopts other names, "Emily, Charlotte, Jane: they were the names of the authoresses I loved." She claims her own name only when she finds out that her mother named her after Lucifer, a name she associates with the literary canon she has had to study, Genesis, Milton's *Paradise Lost.* The stories of the fallen are also her stories, delineating her rebellious role not outside but marginally within the Western world she comes to inhabit.

That canon can also be fruitfully alienating, leaving Lucy with an anger that fosters her resistance and self-possession. A simple, natural scene, such as her first encounter with daffodils, emerges as a complicated social and political drama, "a scene of conquered and conquests; a scene of brutes masquerading as angels and angels portrayed as brutes." Lucy's employer, Mariah, an affluent, privileged, and unselfconsciously "liberal" American woman, eagerly brings Lucy to the park in spring to see the profusion of daffodils, a scene to which she feels deeply connected. Lucy, her West Indian employee, sees these flowers through her colonial school memory of being forced to learn and recite Wordsworth's poem about daffodils, an experience that encapsulates all the disfiguring impositions of British values that taught the colonized to devalue themselves. Although Mariah genuinely wants friendship with Lucy, Lucy realizes that their pasts and current positions make their experiences of the present radically discontinuous: "nothing could change the fact that where she saw flowers, I saw sorrow and bitterness. The same thing could cause us to shed tears, but those tears would not taste the same." When Mariah and Lucy have dinner on the train on the way to Mariah's childhood summer home, the meal is different for Lucy who cannot help but be aware that "the other people sitting down to eat all looked like Mariah's relatives; the people waiting on them all looked like mine." When Mariah admires the beauty of a plowed field, Lucy is grateful not to have had to do the plowing.

Kincaid's bold move is to decenter Mariah's liberal humanist North American view with its invisible privilege: "Mariah wanted all of us, the children and me, to see things the way she did." Lucy is able to see with distinct clarity the upper middle-class United States family and its deceptive self-representations. She sees that Lewis, Mariah's charming husband, is a cad; that Mariah's best friend will betray her; and that Mariah's belief in liberal causes allows her *not* to see her real complicity in social injustice. At the same time, however, Mariah and Lucy converge in their complicated familial relation: "The times that I loved Mariah it was because she reminded me of my mother. The times that I did not love Mariah it was because she reminded me of my mother." Mariah is another othermother, this time from the privileged class, who helps the young West Indian woman chart her path. Lucy finds many con-

tinuities between her island life and her life in New York: people's smells, the taste of boys' tongues, men who remind her of her father. She explores her sexuality in ways even the allegedly feminist Mariah finds worrisome. While sometimes she watches her hosts from a distance, marveling how anyone could be the way they were, at other times, she finds them to be a lot like herself. But she never forgets her status as a servant, the history that put her there, and the power distinctions that separate them.

When Lucy leaves Mariah and her household, it is like leaving her own mother all over again. At the moment of separation, as in *Annie John*, Kincaid introduces the motif of photography, but this time, Lucy takes the pictures. Her active engagement enables her to modulate attachment and separation, similarity and difference, blindness and insight in unprecedented ways. It is not that her camera enables her to reverse the power relations that distinguish her from her employers, to assert her vision, or her "truth," over theirs. Rather, the camera enables her to *see* differently, to define her own and their perspectives as equally contingent. Photography offers her an instrument of the relativity she experiences as she lives in an alien world. For Lucy, "family" pictures of Mariah and the children are a way of disentangling herself from her own family ties, of loosening those invisible strings, and exploring how family functions. Family, in Kincaid's novel, is the site of desire, longing and nostalgia, and the "millstone around your life's neck." It is the space of a love so strong that one can die from it, and it is the space of pain, betrayal, and tears. Lucy's photographs enable her to express the conflicts and contradictions, the unreadability that shapes her encounter with the United States. And as she wants to master her world, the photographs she takes resist mastery and foreground a continuing indeterminacy and opacity.

Annie John and *Lucy* define a female subject who is multiple, fractured, contradictory. Paradoxically, the relationships that bolster it are constraining and disempowering. These characters find agency at the very sites of contradiction and rupture, between attachment and separation, between the Caribbean island and the United States, between the language of the colonizer and the alternate discourses Lucy envisions in her writing and photographs. Like *Annie John, Lucy* charts affiliations and disaffiliations, and ends with an image of erasure. At least outwardly, Lucy is "alone in the world. It was not a small accomplishment." She writes a line in the journal Mariah has given her as a going-away present, and then washes it away with her tears. It is a line full of desire and longing, embodying the mythologies of the family romance: " 'I wish I could love someone so much that I would die from it.' " This wish defines the intense past with the mother that endangers the self, and voices a longing for future attachments and mutual beholdings so powerful that they can supercede that primal passion. *Lucy* ends with the protagonist as writing subject, unanchored and uprooted, though also open to new possibilities.

Dispossession and Rage: *The Autobiography of My Mother*

The Autobiography of My Mother (1996) begins where *Annie John* and *Lucy* end: with a protagonist who is indeed "alone in the world," but for her it is not an accomplishment; rather, it is the condition into which she is born. This novel takes much further Kincaid's sustained questioning of identity and subjectivity in the context of a history marked by slavery, dispossession, and colonization, inflected by race, gender, and power. In this world, the godlike, imperious mother is absent, and even the gesture of naming has no glimmer of self-creation or self-possession: " 'My name is Xuela Claudette Desvarieux.' This was my mother's name, but I cannot say it was her real name, for in a life like hers, as in mine, what is a real name? My own name is her name, Xuela Claudette, and in the place of the Desvarieux is Richardson, which is my father's name; but who are these people Claudette, Desvarieux and Richardson? To look into it, to look at it, could only fill you with despair; the humiliation could only make you intoxicated with self-hatred."

This novel looks unblinkingly into "these people" and is motivated by the "despair" and "humiliation" it finds there. Xuela's name is not a manifesto of a writer, but the signifier of her history and humiliation, her self-division and self-hatred. The novel's paradoxical title already announces the unrealized subject at its center and prompts us to ask: whose autobiography is this? Can one write someone else's autobiography? Xuela's mother died "at the moment I was born"; mother and daughter share the same name and the same condition of motherlessness, for the mother, too, was an orphan, named and abandoned. Thus, if the daughter's story is also the mother's story that never happened, and if the mother's life resists such telling, then all that is left is the pervasive loss and blight produced by maternal death and daughterly abandonment. This loss is not just personal, but global, for the death of the mother, a Carib Indian, reenacts the genocide of the indigenous populations of the New World. She/they continue to be erased from history. Xuela's abandonment is also the abandonment of Dominica, her home, a place she describes as equally unloved and unloving, equally ungenerative. At the end of the book, Xuela restates the claustrophobic and ultimately ungenerative and self-referential textuality of her story: "This account of my life has been an account of my mother's life as much as it has been an account of mine, and even so, again it is an account of the life of the children I did not have, as it is their account of me."

As a motherless and abandoned child Xuela lacks the love and care that makes us human. She is betrayed by her mother who dies, her father who refuses to raise and love her, the washerwoman who becomes her caretaker but who does not love her, the men who say they love her, the women who are jealous of her. The product of Carib, French, Scottish, and African identities, she is betrayed by place and history as well. She moves through many worlds: school, her father's home and new family, a period of manual labor in which she disguises her gender, her passionate affair with Roland, the rakish stevedore, and finally her affair and marriage to Philip, a British doctor and friend of her father. In all these relationships Xuela remains deeply solipsistic and self-reflexive: "No one observed and beheld me, I observed and beheld myself." But she speaks French, English, and two different patois, and if there is one thing in her world that does not betray her, it is the language that allows her to express her barrenness in lush, fruitful ways.

Unlike Annie John and Lucy, Xuela does not have to free herself from human attachment; her attachments never really happen and thus unattached, she herself never quite becomes a subject in her own right. The only thing she can fall back on is the anger and rage of the dispossessed child she was, and the powerful voice, the haunting language made possible by that rage. Hers is the rage of the colonized female subject shaped by the centuries of dispossession she has inherited: it is rage alone that enables her voice to emerge, even if rage unbalanced by love does not allow subjectivity to evolve. "This account is an account of the person who was never allowed to be and an account of the person I did not allow myself to become," she says. Although the "person" was never allowed to become, the "account" is here. But how can one write in the voice of one who has never become? This disjunction creates the powerfully articulate voice of the novel, and, thus, the novel itself. The paradox of identity is further expressed by the photograph on the book's cover, depicting a woman in traditional West Indian dress. Fragments of this image are repeated at the beginning of each untitled chapter, starting with just the top of her head, and continuing until, in the last chapter the entire image emerges. The illusion of presence and wholeness promoted by the photographic image is undermined by what seems like the ever greater emptiness of the character who concludes by telling us that "Death is the only reality, for it is the only certainty, inevitable to all things." The photograph, the reproduction of an image, rather than the representation of a person, then, underscores the textuality of all representation.

The terrifying emptiness of the protagonist of *Autobiography* and the novel's concomitant textual profusion is best exemplified in the scene in which Xuela explains her categorical refusal ever to become a mother. Paradoxically, she insists that not becoming a mother "would not be the same as never bearing children" and she proceeds to describe in great detail the children she would bear in great abundance and all the different ways she would prevent them from living. The violence of these fantasies is made even more frightening by the exuberance with which they are evoked: "I would cover their bodies with diseases, embellish skins with thinly crusted sores, the sores sometimes oozing a thick pus for which they would thirst, a thirst that could never be quenched. I would condemn them to live in an empty space frozen in the same posture in which they had been born." The power Xuela assumes over her "children" is only the power she has over the words that give birth to her "autobiography" and, thus, to her self. Her only power is the power to speak. "I only wish to know it [the sound of much emptiness] so that I may one day tell myself the story of my existence within it."

Xuela's emptiness mirrors the "spell of history" that enchants all the characters, trapping them within their own profound alienation. Her policeman father, of mixed Scottish and African descent, hates the dark side of himself, but all his money and power cannot disguise the violence and hypocrisy at his core. He represents the "emptiness of conquest"; as both the victor and vanquished, he illustrates the equivalence of the two. Philip, the British doctor who lives in a place he hates and dreams of English gardens, is an heir of imperialism. Xuela's involvement with him continues Kincaid's interest in exploring the inescapable, personal face of ethnocentrism and privilege. His desiccated wife, Moira, finds existential solace in being a proper English lady, which is a "prerequisite for the ability to transgress against another" and produces her "living death." Philip loves Xuela, but what can love mean in this context? Xuela's rejection of generative sexuality frees her to explore the intersection of desire and power, but even that pleasure is compromised by history. With the seductive Dominican stevedore, Roland, Philip's opposite, she finds an oceanic pleasure. "He was unpolished, but he carried himself as if he were precious" and "wanted something beyond ordinary satisfaction," but he, too, is "of people who had never been regarded as people at all." In the end, he can only give Xuela the "seeds" of children she refuses to have. With Philip, a man she declares she does not love, she experiences a powerful desire and "makes him" satisfy her, but only after tying her own hands up with his hemp belt. Xuela's half-sister regards her marriage to Philip, who "was of the conquering class," with awe, as Xuela's "own conquest," as if redemption or justice derives from reversing positions or replicating the domination of one's oppressors. But such a conquest is hollow, and Xuela concludes, like Lucy and Mariah but with a more intense weariness, "we could not both be happy at the same time. Life, History, whatever its name, had made such a thing an impossibility."

The Opposite of Flowering: *My Brother*

The darker side of pleasure and the blighting of selfhood are the theme of Kincaid's wrenching memoir *My Brother*. Called back to Antigua after a twenty-year absence by the news that her youngest brother, Devon, has AIDS, Kincaid meditates on what her life would have been if she had not made the break from her mother and Antigua, renamed herself, and become a writer. As she does what she can to prolong her brother's life, from procuring him medicines unavailable in Antigua, to arranging for treatment and therapy, visiting him and, finally, buying him a bed to die in, Devon continues, like the Antiguans around him, to deny the existence of the disease that is consuming him. Because she "was familiar with the act of saving myself" through writing, Kincaid says she "knew, instinctively, that to understand it, or make any attempt at understanding his dying, and not to die with him, I would write about it" (pp. 195–196). Devon's heedless love affairs, before and after his diagnosis, set off Kincaid's ruminations on her "love affair" with

her mother, who did not let Devon and his brothers separate, so that, in very different ways, their lives have been deformed. Love, sexuality, self-expression, and control become tangled in a tenacious, familiar web. She recalls how the frequent visits of a young male school mate to borrow books they both loved infuriated her mother, who saw it as an excuse for sexual activity. Her rage increased when Kincaid neglected to change the infant Devon's diaper, and so she piled all of her daughter's books outside and burned them. "It would not be so strange," Kincaid concludes, "if I spent the rest of my life trying to bring those books back to my life by writing them again and again until they were perfect, unscathed by fire of any kind."

In a by now familiar structure of analogy, Devon comes to stand for Antigua and its failure to grow up, separate, save itself, know itself, bud and flower. Kincaid's deepest sadness occurs, however, when months after Devon's death, she meets an Antiguan woman at a reading and book signing in Chicago, who tells her that her brother frequented her house, where homosexual men who had no other place to meet each other in Antigua gathered on Sundays. Kincaid mourns that Devon "died without ever understanding or knowing, or being able to let the world in which he lived know, who he was—not a single sense of identity but all the complexities of who he was." His life was "the opposite of . . . a flowering, . . . like the bud that sets but, instead of opening into a flower, turns brown and falls off at your feet." This devastating image, recapitulating the harrowing details of Devon's physical and sexual decline, prompts her to conclude, "I could not have become myself while living among the people I knew best." Through her hypnotic, strategic repetitions, Kincaid builds up a profoundly disturbing picture of her brother's marred life and tragic death. Although he was perceptive, and spoke an engaging, acerbic patois, she knows he would not have been interested in her account of these gruesome details. But William Shawn, Kincaid's father-in-law and mentor, also recently dead, was very interested in the difficult revelations Kincaid made, and so she became a writer, because she found in Shawn the perfect reader.

Asterisks: *My Garden (Book):*

Kincaid's *My Garden (Book):*, brings the gardening metaphors that appear throughout her work to the foreground. The very title of the book makes her primary point about the blurring of physical-imaginary gardens and books: that the labors of gardening and writing are analogous and for her, deeply domestic; that both produce an irritation and discontentment so pleasurable, that it must be shared. And so, despite the book's disarming illustrations by a friend, Jill Fox, the playful subject of gardening is also the occasion of Kincaid's penetrating interrogations. Kincaid only began to garden in Vermont, a forbidding climate with a long winter season in which one must read seed and plant catalogues and imagine ideal, visionary gardens. But Kincaid realizes that to garden for the sheer pleasure of it, as a luxury and also as a liberation, as opposed to gardening as a necessity for sustenance or income, as in Antigua or Africa, positions her within the conquering class. For, what in *Autobiography of My Mother* was the British expatriate Philip's "benign" act of conquest—"obsessively rearranging the landscape"—is here revealed to take place at someone else's expense and thus, to be fully complicit with imperial ideology.

This is made painfully clear in the central chapter, "To Name is to Possess," which examines the history of botanical naturalizing and Linnaean nomenclature as a history of conquest and theft. "The naming of things is so crucial to possession—a spiritual padlock with the key throewn irretrievably away—that it is a murder, an erasing." It is hard not to think of the Miltonic-Adamic function of naming that constitutes the garden of the ephemeral Western paradise which Kincaid's earlier work struggles to reverse. Kincaid realizes that she does not know the flora indigenous to her homeland, Antigua, because most of it has been stolen, naturalized in Europe, renamed, and brought back to the New World as possessions exhibited in botanical gardens. Meditating on the glasshouses in Europe that nurtured precious specimens looted from conquered lands, she concludes wistfully: "I do not mind the glasshouse: I do not mind the botanical garden. This is . . . mostly an admission of defeat: to mind would be completely futile, I cannot do anything about it anyway. I only mind the absence of this admission, this contradiction: perhaps every good thing that stands before us comes at a great cost to someone else."

"This contradiction" drives her extraordinary meditation in the next chapter "In History," as she considers "what should history mean to someone like me?" someone of color, of the conquered class. Reading botanical history, she says: "there is always a moment when I feel like placing as asterisk somewhere in its text and at the end of the official story making my own addition." History comes to feel promethean, like an "open wound, each breath I take in and expel healing and opening the wound again, over and over, or is it a long moment that begins anew each day since 1492?" These profound revelations do not, however, prevent Kincaid from doing "what a God would do," painting with "Memory . . . a gardener's real palette," or seed hunting with nursery owners and botanists in China. Her own books have been like the asterisks she wants to place in the texts of official history, her own additions, the voice and perspective of the unvoiced, named and spiritually murdered, possessed, and naturalized. "I shall never have the garden I have in my mind, but that for me is the joy of it." And so, writing is fueled by the joy of unfulfilled desire, by an imagination fettered by the consciousness of history, by the wounds that demand and resist telling.

Selected Bibliography

PRIMARY WORKS

FICTION

At the Bottom of the River. New York: Farrar, Straus & Giroux, 1983. (*At the Bottom of the River* has been recorded by the Library of Congress Archive of Recorded Poetry and Literature.)

Annie John. Farrar, Straus & Giroux, 1985.

Lucy. Farrar, Straus & Giroux, 1990.

Autobiography of My Mother. Farrar, Straus & Giroux, 1996.

UNCOLLECTED FICTION

"Antigua Crossings: A Deep and Blue Passage on the Carribean Sea." *Rolling Stone* 29: 48–50 (June 1978).

"Ovando." *Conjunctions* 14: 75–83 (1989).

"Song of Roland." *New Yorker*, April 12, 1993, pp. 94–98.

NONFICTION

"Jamaica Kincaid's New York." *Rolling Stone,* October 6, 1977, pp. 71–73.

A Small Place. New York: Farrar, Straus & Giroux, 1988.

Annie, Gwen, Lilly, Pam and Tulip. Illustrations by Eric Fischl. New York: Knopf, in association with the Whitney Museum of American Art, 1989.

"On Seeing England for the First Time." *Harper's,* August 1991, pp. 13–17.

My Brother. Farrar, Straus & Giroux, 1997.

Generations of Women: In Their Own Words. Introduction by Jamaica Kincaid and photographs by Mariana Cook. Chronicle Books, 1998.

My Favorite Plant: Writers and Gardeners on the Plants They Love. Edited and with an introduction by Jamaica Kincaid. Farrar, Straus & Giroux, 1998.

Poetics of Place: Photographs by Lynn Geesaman. Essay by Jamaica Kincaid. Umbrage Editions, 1998.

My Garden (Book):. Illustrations by Jill Fox. Farrar, Straus & Giroux, 1999.

SECONDARY WORKS

BIOGRAPHICAL AND CRITICAL STUDIES

Covi, Giovanna. "Jamaica Kincaid and the Resistance to Canons." In *Out of the Kumbla: Caribbean Women and Literature.* Edited by Carole Boyce Davies and Elaine Savory Fido. Trenton, N.J.: Africa World Press, 1990. Pp. 345–54.

Emery, Mary Lou. "Refiguring the Postcolonial Imagination: Tropes of Visuality in Writing by Rhys, Kincaid, and Cliff." *Tulsa Studies in Women's Literature* 16, no. 2:259–80 (Fall 1997).

Ferguson, Moira. "*Lucy* and the Mark of the Colonizer." *Modern Fiction Studies* 39, no. 2:237–59 (Summer 1993).

———. *Jamaica Kincaid: Where the Land Meets the Body.* Charlottesville: University Press of Virginia, 1994.

Hirsch, Marianne. *Family Frames: Photography, Narrative and Postmemory.* Cambridge, Mass.: Harvard University Press, 1997.

Hodge, Merle. "Caribbean Writers and Caribbean Language: A Study of Jamaica Kincaid's *Annie John.*" In

Winds of Change: The Transforming Voices of Caribbean Women Writers and Scholars. Edited by Adele S. Newson and Linda Strong-Leek. New York: Peter Lang, 1998. Pp. 47–53.

Kanhai, Rosanne. " 'Sensing Designs in History's Muddles': Global Feminism and the Postcolonial Novel." *Modern Language Studies* 26, no. 4:119–30 (Fall 1996).

Simmons, Diane. *Jamaica Kincaid.* New York: Twayne Publishers, 1994.

———. "Coming-of-Age in the Snare of History: Jamaica Kincaid's *The Autobiography of My Mother.* In *The Girl: Constructions of the Girl in Contemporary Fiction by Women.* Edited by Ruth O. Saxton. New York: St. Martin's Press, 1998. Pp. 107–18.

Yang, Ming-tsang. "Vision and Revision in Jamaica Kincaid's 'On Seeing England for the first Time.' " *Studies in Language and Literature* 6:143–52 (October 1994).

REVIEWS

Garis, Leslie. "Through West Indian Eyes." *New York Times Magazine,* October 7, 1990, p. 42.

Grumbach, Doris. Review of *Lucy. Washington Post Book World,* October 7, 1990.

Listfield, Emily. Review of *Lucy. Harper's Bazaar* October 1990, p. 82.

INTERVIEWS

Bonetti, Kay. *Jamaica Kincaid Interview with Kay Bonetti* [sound recording]. Columbia, Mo.: American Audio Prose Library, 1991.

———. "Jamaica Kincaid." *Conversations with American Novelists: The Best Interviews from the Missouri Review and the American Audio Prose Library.* Columbia, Mo.: University of Missouri Press, 1997. Pp. 26–38.

Cudjoe, Selwyn R. "Jamaica Kincaid and the Modernist Project: An Interview." *Callaloo: A Journal of African-American and African Arts and Letters* 12, no. 2:396–411 (Spring 1989).

Ferguson, Moira. "A Lot of Memory: An Interview with Jamaica Kincaid." *The Kenyon Review* 16, no. 1:163–88 (Winter 1994).

Muirhead, Pamela. "An Interview with Jamaica Kincaid." *Clockwork Review: A Journal of the Arts* 9, nos. 1–2:141–54 (1994–1995).

Perry, Donna. "Jamaica Kincaid." *Backtalk: Women Writers Speak Out.* Edited by Donna Perry. New Brunswick, N.J.: Rutgers University Press, 1993. Pp. 127–41.

Vorda, Allan. "I Come from a Place that's Very Unreal: An Interview with Jamaica Kincaid." *Face to Face: Interviews with Contemporary Novelists.* Edited by Allan Vorda and Daniel Stern. Houston: Rice University Press, 1993. Pp. 77–106.

Wachtel, Eleanor. "Eleanor Wachtel with Jamaica Kincaid." *Malahat Review* 116:55–71 (Fall 1996).

YUSEF KOMUNYAKAA
(1947–   )

VINCE GOTERA

WHEN HE WON the 1994 Pulitzer Prize for poetry for *Neon Vernacular: New and Selected Poems,* Yusef Komunyakaa soared into the American consciousness—that is, apart from poetry circles, where he already had a sizable reputation. This became Komunyakaa's banner year: in 1994 he also won the coveted $50,000 Kingsley Tufts Award and the William Faulkner Prize from the Université de Haute Bretagne in Rennes, France. Since then, the international acclaim accompanying these honors has been matched by other prestigious distinctions as well as a plenitude of offers for readings, residencies, collaborations, musical performances, and other opportunities. Despite these head-turning fireworks, Komunyakaa's focus has remained unwaveringly aimed at his writing, blossoming more and more now into the realm of music.

On April 29, 1947, Yusef Komunyakaa was born to James William and Mildred in Bogalusa, Louisiana—a small town seventy miles north of New Orleans near the Mississippi border. He described his birthplace to Susan Conley as "a typical Southern town [with] one paper mill that dominated the place, and a public library that did not admit blacks." Son of a carpenter and eldest of six children, Komunyakaa read the Bible from Genesis to Revelations twice in his youth. In school, he read canonized writers such as Shakespeare or Poe and was only intro-

duced to black literature via a brief high school unit on black history. He was struck then by the poetry of Langston Hughes, Paul Lawrence Dunbar, and Phillis Wheatley. At age sixteen, Komunyakaa was inspired to write when he discovered James Baldwin's *Nobody Knows My Name;* "I read that book about twenty-five times," he recalled. For his graduating high school class, Komunyakaa wrote a long poem that contained some one hundred lines in rhymed quatrains, but for the most part Komunyakaa did not write poems seriously until a decade later.

After graduating in 1965, Komunyakaa traveled through and lived briefly in Puerto Rico and Panama, stopping in Phoenix, Arizona, in 1966, where his mother had moved. Here he worked in the McGraw Edison factory until 1967, assembling air conditioning and cooling units. In 1968, Komunyakaa entered the U.S. Army and became an information specialist. During early 1969, he was sent to Officer Candidate School in infantry but did not complete the training and was transferred back into the information field.

On April 1, 1969, Komunyakaa's daughter Kimberly Ann was born in Phoenix. In that same month, the army sent him to Vietnam, where he served as an editor for a military newspaper, *The Southern Cross,* within the American Division. Stationed at Chu Lai, Komunyakaa was often dispatched as a reporter to frontline areas; as he told William Baer, "Whenever there was any kind of conflict or engagement, I'd be ferried out on a helicopter to the action—to the middle of it—and I had to report, I had to witness." During his year "in country," Komunyakaa kept himself "in contact with [his] innermost feelings" by reading poetry anthologies compiled by such editors as Donald Hall and Dudley Randall. He rotated back to the United States in 1970 and was stationed at Fort Carson, Colorado, until his discharge in 1971. Komunyakaa was awarded a Bronze Star.

During these years Komunyakaa traveled a geographic triangle with points in Colorado, Louisiana, and Arizona, where his daughter lived. He stayed for a short time in Japan also. Through his maternal grandmother, Komunyakaa began excavating the heritage of his grandfather, who had emigrated from the West Indies. Part of this heritage is the poet's own name—an Islamic phrase that translates as "Joseph the Compassionate." In this context Conley wrote, "People have often assumed Komunyakaa's name implies he is Muslim, and during the 1970's, he did nothing to dispel the notion. He was drawn to the religion and read its literature. However, the name was actually brought to America by Komunyakaa's grandfather, a stowaway, on a ship from Trinidad."

In 1973, Komunyakaa enrolled at the University of Colorado in "distributive studies," majoring in English, Sociology, and Psychology. Komunyakaa's mentor and creative writing teacher at CU was Alexander Blackburn, editor of *Writers Forum*. Komunyakaa experimented with short fiction in imitation of James Baldwin and Richard Wright but eventually focused on poetry. Taking on exceptionally high course loads—twenty-four hours in one semester—Komunyakaa completed his bachelor's degree magna cum laude in sociology and English in December 1975.

After staying one more semester at CU, flirting with pursuing a doctorate in psychology, Komunyakaa entered the master's program in creative writing at Colorado State University in 1976. His primary teachers at CSU were Bill Tremblay and Chris Howell, but he was also influenced by Richard Hugo, William Matthews, and Gwendolyn Brooks, all of whom he met personally. He started to publish poems in journals: *Chameleon*, *Leviathan*, and *Greensboro Review*. During both of his years at CSU, he taught composition as an associate instructor.

In 1976, Komunyakaa cofounded with Adam Hammer the journal *Gumbo: A Magazine for the Arts*, which flourished for two years, during which they published such writers as Robert Creeley and James Bertolino. During this time, Paul Dilsaver, editor of the *Rocky Mountain Creative Arts Journal*, invited Komunyakaa to publish in the magazine's poetry series. The result was the limited-edition chapbook *Dedications and Other Dark Horses*, Komunyakaa's first collection.

Dedications and Other Dark Horses

In the opening lines of *Dedications and Other Dark Horses* (1977), "The hard white land— / Missoula, winter's place," from a poem for Richard Hugo, "Returning the Borrowed Road," Komunyakaa anchors his apostrophe in a recognizable setting (as Hugo always did). Although these two lines seem clear and straightforward, knowing the poet is black throws the phrase "hard white land" into stark relief as a grim rehearsal of abuse. Hugo himself appears as an abused figure worn down by life's burdens: "we mistook you / for a man who works / a mile down in the ground." When the Hugo character speaks, however, the speaker is transported to "a lifetime of birds / gone wild with brightness," in stark opposition to the "hard white land." Hugo's ability to supercede "winter's place" with a summer of the imagination invests him with wisdom in the speaker's eyes. Hugo tells the young poet, " 'Get away from the poem, / you're too close,' " and the speaker, taking Hugo's hard-won advice, begins letting each poem "write / itself, [seek] its own new mouth." Thus "Returning the Borrowed Road" is both an *ars poetica* as well as a transaction between artists, an acknowledgment of the

Yusef Komunyakaa

content, between celebratory imagism and everyday blues.

These poems share a keen sense of opposition: "hard white land" vs. "wild with brightness"; "wildfire" vs. "slow knocking." Komunyakaa's fascination with dualism is highlighted by a comment he made to Muna Asali: "Many times that is what we have, beauty and violence side by side. We have been taught to see that as contradiction, but to me, contradiction is a sort of discourse." In this same interview Komunyakaa admits, "In my poetry I desire surprises. Of course, those surprises can hurt. Good and bad—that's what I think life happens to be about." This poetic of surprise born out of dialectical opposition is a stratagem that spans Komunyakaa's entire oeuvre.

In 1978, after completing his M.A. at CSU, Komunyakaa enrolled in the Master of Fine Arts program in creative writing at the University of California, Irvine. Here his mentors included James McMichaels, Howard Moss, Robert Peters, C. K. Williams, and Charles Wright. Komunyakaa also fondly remembers classmates: "There were . . . some wonderful student writers there: Garrett Hongo, Deborah Woodard, Vic Coccimiglio, Debra Thomas, and Virginia Campbell." Komunyakaa's literary and writerly influences at Irvine were eclectic, including Eliot, Pound, the French surrealists, Aimé Césaire, Robert Hayden, Bob Kaufman, and Melvin Tolson, to name a few. He continued to publish poems in such varied venues as *Black American Literature Forum, The Beloit Poetry Journal, West End,* and Ishmael Reed's *Yardbird Reader.* He also served as a writing instructor for UC Irvine's Remedial Composition Program. Then, in quick order, Komunyakaa published another limited-edition collection, *Lost in the Bonewheel Factory,* in 1979 and completed his M.F.A. at UC Irvine the following year with a thesis entitled *Premonitions of the Bread Line.*

master/apprentice relationship. This poem forecasts the overall drive of the collection, focusing on experiment, the exploratory control a young artist wants to apply to craft, to artistic process and its intricate dance with perception.

The poem closest to Komunyakaa's mature style is "The Tongue's." The title carries into the first line: "xeroxed on brainmatter." This bravura language continues throughout the poem, a series of meditations on the idea of a "tongue." The poem's closing, "The tongue labors, / a victrola in the mad mouth-hole / of 3 a.m. sorrow," asserts that the tongue (a metonym for speech, language, art) fumbles vis-à-vis madness and depression. The poem's imagery, though, flies in the face of this interpretation; the lush sensuality of "wildfire," "swish of dry reeds," "savage green of oleander," "slow knocking / in the rusty belly of a radiator" suggests a speaker crazy in love with the fierce sensations beckoning each of us daily. The poem thus establishes a tension between form and

Lost in the Bonewheel Factory

The title of *Lost in the Bonewheel Factory* (1979) is a window into another of Komunyakaa's techniques: surrealism (as pioneered by such French practitioners as André Breton). The engine of surrealism is *juxtaposition*, as one finds in the notorious quasi-definition by the poet Isidore Ducasse (the comte de Lautréamont): surrealism is "the chance encounter of a sewing machine and an umbrella on a dissection table." Komunyakaa's word "bonewheel" is a surrealistic yoking of (seeming) accidentals: organic "bone" and mechanistic "wheel." Clamped together, these two signifiers form an uneasy truce that engenders an intricate, double-voiced signification.

Surrealism prevails throughout the collection. Witness the opening of the prose poem "Pushing In All the Buttons":

> With armloads of lignum vitae kinfolk gape at the paradox; hands frightened over murdered mouths. . . . Syndactyl hands plead like a gypsy guitar.

The phrase "lignum vitae" emerges from a register radically different from that of "kinfolk"—first a rarefied intellectual ambience, then a down-home, perhaps Southern, air. Matching "syndactyl" (fingers welded together) to "gypsy" suggests a volatile mixture but simultaneously invokes the spirit of jazz guitarist Django Reinhardt whose left hand was seared in a fire in his family's gypsy caravan when he was a youth. In poem after poem, Komunyakaa meticulously applies surrealistic juxtaposition, an esthetic related directly to his interest in dualities, as noted above.

If juxtaposition is the procedure of surrealism, *image* is the "building block" and Komunyakaa knew that. He said to William Baer, For me, poetry works best when it's aware of music and formed from a composite of meaningful images." Komunyakaa has asserted in a number of interviews that even from his days as a young poet, he knew that he preferred images to statement in his poetry. Such devotion to image is an indispensable ingredient in a passion for surrealism.

The greatest surrealist influence on Komunyakaa was Aimé Césaire, the celebrated black poet from Martinique. One can discern stylistic affinities between Césaire and Komunyakaa in the ending of "Magique" in Césaire's collection *Soleil cou coupe*:

> vous bêtes qui sifflez sur le visage de cette morte
> la belle once de la luzure et la coquille operculée
> . . . .
> réajustent un dieu noir mal né de son tonnerre

Clayton Eshleman and Annette Smith's translation in *Aimé Césaire: The Collected Poetry* is both eloquent and lyrical:

> you beasts hissing over the face of this dead woman
> the beautiful snow leopard of lust and the operculated shell
> . . . .
> restore a black god feebly born to his thunder

Césaire inventively places "leopard" beside "shell"—a wrenching juxtaposition reminiscent of the art of Salvador Dalí or Marcel Duchamp. Césaire's influence on Komunyakaa is substantial not only because of poetics but also because of thematics: a principal subject of Césaire's is colonialism. Above, the "dead woman" refers to Martinique, the "beasts" are colonialist forces, and the "black god" restored "to his thunder" forecasts the end of colonization. Césaire's trademark style lyricizes the colonial problem in a frequently apocalyptic vein.

In *Lost in the Bonewheel Factory*, a decidedly apocalyptic air floats around such lines and images as "death sits in her skull like a dove" or "Sexual blood cadenza / of the preying mantis." The book also catalogs myriad forms of (anti)colonialism—individual, sexual, cultural, national—in echo of Césaire. Perhaps "bonewheel" represents the tyranny of colonialism, melding the unmeldable, and the collection demonstrates how *lost* we still were in 1979, two decades before the new millennium.

Premonitions of the Bread Line

In a fascinating intertextual gesture, the title of Komunyakaa's M.F.A. thesis, *Premonitions of the Bread Line* (1980), appears in *Lost in the Bonewheel Factory*, in the poem "Following Floorplans"—"All the cruel rooms are identical behind different colored doors: a black cellophane window to the outside, . . . a copy of *Premonitions of the Breadline* on the white shag rug." That the thesis title is adjacent to an allusion to Poe's "Masque of the Red Death" implies that the thesis shares the apocalyptic bent of *Lost in the Bonewheel Factory*.

As in the previous collection, the title of the thesis illuminates another of Komunyakaa's strategies: coupling words of dissimilar etymology and collocation. "Premonition" is "hifalutin" Latinate whereas "bread" is basic Anglo-Saxon. Such syncretic diction is sometimes whimsical but more often revelatory of social injustice, as implied by the phrase "bread line"—a metaphor for poverty and economic inequity. *Premonitions of the Bread Line* is peppered with such neologisms: "earthworm's calligraphy," "paradoxical star," "heart's interrogation," "acknowledgement of thorns," "translucent eggs," "aquamarine postcard," "appendages of light," and so on. In each instance, Komunyakaa yokes mainly monosyllabic English words with multisyllabic terms from Latin or some non-English source. Inevitably, this method deconstructs notions of levels of diction—elite vs. mass, academic vs. pidgin, boardroom vs. working-class, city vs. country.

Komunyakaa's sources for wordplay include not only Césaire but also Afro-modernist *American* poets: "Melvin Tolson," Komunyakaa pointed out, "brings together the street as well as the highly literary into a single poetic context in ways where the two don't even seem to exhibit a division." Komunyakaa (re)creates this in his own style: fusion of words, of *types* of words, of selves. In such fusion we can see Komunyakaa's basic poetics: My work is immersed in Southern idiom, along with an acquired literary language," he said in a 1998 interview with Suzan Sherman. "I'm trying to make both function tonally side by side to create music that doesn't have to achieve an absolute scale of meaning, but more or less to induce a certain feeling." In other words, the *wrong* way to read Komunyakaa is to strain only after paraphrasable meaning; instead one must open oneself to a poem's wash of emotion and sound and how this modulates sense.

After leaving UC Irvine, Komunyakaa garnered a fellowship at the Provincetown Fine Arts Work Center in Massachusetts, where he stayed from October 1980 to May 1981. Komunyakaa described this period to Vince Gotera as "a kind of semi-isolation in which I could very methodically deal with my writing. . . . a place to develop one's own voice [and] to remove layers of facades and superficialities." At Provincetown he was honored to work in conferences with Alan Dugan, whose "satirical edge" (as Komunyakaa puts it) influenced his own work.

For the remainder of 1981, Komunyakaa returned to Bogalusa to live with his grandmother Mary Washington: "going back to a hometown inside my head, to my own psychological territory, but in a different way, from a different perspective." A telling echo of Hugo's notion of a "triggering town," a (re)vitalizing context for the completion of his first major collection, *Copacetic*.

Before *Copacetic* was published, however, Komunyakaa was swept up by a tornado of activity in New Orleans. From 1982 to 1984, he taught as an instructor of composition and literature at the Lakefront campus of the University of New Orleans. He simultaneously worked in the Poets-in-the-Schools program, teaching third through sixth graders. He was also engaged in a major renovation of his house in New Orleans. In 1984, Komunyakaa opened with Ahmos Zu-Bolton a bookstore and coffee house called Copacetic, which became a center for cultural events—readings, plays, music—in New Orleans.

Copacetic

Like the bookstore, *Copacetic* (1984) brings into microscopic and telescopic focus a pervasive Komunyakaa theme: African American identity, leading outward to black culture and history worldwide. Césaire is a model for Komunyakaa not only because of his surrealism but also because of his championing of black causes: it was Césaire who coined the term *Négritude*. Césaire's yoking of opposing images and contradictory emotions is cognate to W. E. B. DuBois' notion of *double consciousness*. As Henry Louis Gates Jr. and others have argued, this mindset, converted into "double-voicedness," has allowed blacks to subvert conventional meaning through coded language. Gates would surely label *Copacetic*, in this regard, a "speakerly text" in its employment of linguistic virtuosity and iconoclasm.

Copacetic is largely couched in colloquial speech and vernacular idiom. The opening poem, "False Leads," begins: "Hey! Mister Bloodhound Boss, / I hear you're looking for Slick Sam. . . . They tell me he's a crack shot." We hear street language, along with folklore and fable. If this utterance is "speakerly" in Gates's sense, we may infer that, if the "Boss" is white, the speaker is using coded language to deliver a veiled threat: "he's a crack shot." Such linguistic performances are tied to black idiomatic practice, such as *signifying*—"I'm a womb-scratcher. / I'm a double-dealer. / I'm the chance you take"—or *testifying,* as in this excerpt from a poem with the word "revival" in its title—"my story is / how deep the heart runs"—and *witnessing:* "I am taken back / to where torture chambers / crank up at midnight."

Komunyakaa's focus on blackness in *Copacetic* centers on New Orleans and radiates outward to the nation ("Alabama," "Chicago," "Newport Beach," to quote locales in the poems) through Puerto Rico and Argentina then ultimately to Africa: both the preslavery *paradiso* implied in "Instructions for Building Straw Huts"—"the door's constructed last, / just wide enough for two lovers"—and the apartheid *inferno* of South Africa, illustrated by the exiling of Harold Rubin for blasphemy— "You carbon-dated the skull / paperweight on the commissioner's desk." Blackness is explored on a grand public stage where history and folk wisdom intersect as well as within the invisible arenas of self: "a tall black man" looking in "the day's mirror" is driven by imagination and the impact of centuries to this vision: "The noose pendulous / over his head, / you can feel him / grow inside you, . . . your feet / in his shoes" An irreducible continuum of identity and responsibility connects past victims to ourselves.

Of course, this emphasis on black experience also appears in previous collections; in *Lost in the Bonewheel Factory*, for example, Komunyakaa's preoccupation with the apocalyptic and (post)colonial is a direct response to Jim Crow policies and northern discrimination.

The book's title is an elusive argot that denotes "everything's all right." For Komunyakaa, *Copacetic* "conjures up a certain jazz-blues feeling. . . . linked to . . . psychological survival." In *Copacetic*, psychological survival is indeed linked to the blues, as we can glimpse in these titles: "Blackmetal Blues," "Untitled Blues," "Jumping Bad Blues," "Borinken Blues," "Woman, I Got the Blues," and "Blues Chant Hoodoo Revival."

Komunyakaa defined the blues as "an existential melancholy based on an acute awareness," echoing Ralph Ellison's notion of a "blues impulse," moving from trauma to affirmation. In "Lost Wax," the opening tercet—"I can't help but think / of bodies spoon-fashion / in the belly of a ship"—is resolved by a gentle closing image—"Two hands folded together / as a drinking cup," moving across centuries from slavery to transcendence.

The book's two sections, "Blackmetal Blues" and "Mojo," roughly approximate the inclination of the blues from loss to lyricism. In the first section we glimpse brutality; in "April Fool's Day" a gangbanger speaks at his own funeral: "They had me laid out in a white / satin casket." In "The Vicious," we see the instruments of contemporary enslavement: "Syringe, stylus, / or pearl-handled stiletto?" We witness unsettling images: "Sizzling irons, initials, / whole families branded," "hanging trees," a "cathedral of ashes." The world as experienced in this opening section is savage and unfeeling.

The second section, "Mojo," plays out affirmation through transcendent imagery: "a lazy rhapsody of shadows / swaying to blue vertigo / & metaphysical funk" or "a floppy existential sky-blue hat." There are tributes here to poets like Victor Hernández Cruz and Bob Kaufman, jazz greats such as Thelonious Monk and Charles Mingus, and private, archetypal heroes like Street Cool Clara. The dialogue between the book's two sections is a recursive conversation between the awareness of brutality and the anodyne of celebration. Ultimately, *Copacetic* is a gumbo of blues and blackness, a manifesto of music and manhood.

In 1985, Komunyakaa met his future wife, Mandy Sayer, who came to New Orleans to begin a career as a professional tap dancer. This was a watershed year: Komunyakaa accepted a one-year visiting professorship at Indiana University in fall 1985, and during Christmas break, he and Sayer were married. (A noted Australian writer who has won the Australian/ Vogel Literary Award, Sayer has published several books, including *Blind Luck*, *The Cross*, *Mood Indigo*, and *Dreamtime Alice*.)

After completing his year in Indiana, Komunyakaa sojourned to Australia. He was readily accepted by the poets' community in Sydney and gave readings in the famed Harold Park Hotel Reading Series and at the Evening Star Hotel Poets' Union. He also briefly associated with the poets Les Murray, Vicki Viidikas, and Gig Ryan and published poetry in the Australian journal *Blue Light Lounge*. During this year in Australia, Komunyakaa became interested as well in Aboriginal issues, such as the ongoing struggle for land rights. Since that visit, Komunyakaa has periodically traveled to Australia.

I Apologize for the Eyes in My Head

I Apologize for the Eyes in My Head (1986) perpetuates the musical tonality of *Copacetic* by extending blues into jazz. In "The Unnatural State of the Unicorn," Komunyakaa repeats phrases and sounds just as a jazz musician weaves musical figures in and out of a solo:

Before embossed limited editions,
before fat artichoke hearts marinated
in rich sauce & served with imported
 wines,
before antics & Agnus Dei,
before the stars in your eyes
mean birth sign or Impression,
I am a man. . . .

The ostinato of "before" highlights other key words by repeating the letter "b": "bleed," "birth sign," "broken teeth," "bars," "birthright," and "branding." The repetition of "i's" and "m's" (especially as coupled in "imported" or "Impression") leads us forward to the phrase "I am a man" as well as backward to the opening: "Introduce me first as a man." The alliteration of "me" with "man" and the assonantal "i's" in "Introduce" and "first" contribute to the improvisational groove, as does the phrase "antics and Agnus Dei," which feels concocted on the spot but anchored by the musicality linking the words. Komunyakaa's language-play culminates in this finale: "Inside my skin, / loving you, I am this space / my body believes in." The return of "i's," "m's," and "b's" in this passage enacts a jazz ensemble's regrouping at the end of a song to reprise the melody.

As with the other themes discussed, jazz as inspiration in Komunyakaa's poetry is not limited exclusively to *I Apologize for the Eyes in My Head*. Indeed, two poems in *Copacetic* are frequently cited as exemplary jazz poems: "Elegy for Thelonious" and "Copacetic Mingus." While the majority of critics admire these two poems, there is an occasional complaint that they lean heavily on external references, listing potentially obscure information such as the title "*Pithecanthropus Erectus*" within the text of "Copacetic Mingus." This viewpoint presumes that a "jazz poem" must emulate the music's internal essence (for example, improvisation, syncopation, performance). Nevertheless, Komunyakaa does achieve such emulation, for example, through onomatopoeia in "Copacetic Mingus": "Up & down, under / & over, every which way— / thump, thump, dada—ah, yes."

A different kind of jazz poem, "I Apologize" is a dramatic monologue spoken under interrogation, a catalog of alibis to guarantee the speaker's safety:

My mind wasn't even there.
Mirage, sir. I didn't see
what I thought I saw.

. . . .

I was in my woman's bedroom
removing her red shoes & dress.

Some readers may infer that buckling this way under pressure results in anomie: "This morning / I can't even remember who I am." This speaker, however, can be seen as a trickster who survives through deflection and indirection, resisting the forces that oppress the individual in our times. This tricksterism, as a jazz stance, recurs throughout the book.

Nevertheless, oppression begets pain. The Thorn Merchant and his coterie hint at this pain: "There are teeth marks / on everything he loves" progresses into "he knows how death waits / in us like a light switch." Despite this command, the Thorn Merchant "moans like a statue / of straw," a victim of his own corrosive power. Titles throughout the book elaborate on this inscape of pain and sometime subtle but ever-present loss: "The Falling-Down Song," "Landscape for the Disappeared," "Making Out with the Dream-Shredding Machine," and "For the Walking Dead."

The contrapuntal antidote is jazz. The opening lines of "I Apologize," for example, are essentially riffs and improvisations on the stance "No comment; no way, Jose." Throughout the book relentless enjambments, sudden fluidities, and emphatic pauses reflect what Komunyakaa described to Robert Kelly as a "jagged tonality" borrowed from Thelonious Monk: "repetition with slight variations, playing with pauses and silences, an unspoken call and response." Here are the opening lines from "The Heart's Graveyard Shift":

I lose faith in my left hand
not because my dog Echo's eloped
with ignis fatuus into pinewoods

or that my limp's unhealed
after 13 years. What can go wrong
goes wrong, & between loves an empty . . .

The jazz effects here involve approximating "playing with pauses and silences" by placing end-stopped lines in tension with the hard enjambments of "eloped / with" and "unhealed / after"—sudden pauses that dramatize the theme of hard luck. That the end-stops and enjambments alternate may suggest "an unspoken call and response." Monk's "repetition with slight variations" can be seen in the consonantal shift from "left" to "eloped" to "limped"—the dance of vowels around the "l," "p/f," and "t/d" that remain constant. The reader's bliss in this poem is not necessarily in the content but in the performance.

For Komunyakaa, jazz offers (re)discovery and imaginative jump starts. Jazz "taught me I could do anything in a poem," Komunyakaa told Robert Kelly. This freedom informs Komunyakaa's writing *and* life: jazz "works like a refrain underneath my life keeping it all together and in focus. . . . Anything is possible. . . . My creative universe is always in a flux." The centering of jazz allows *I Apologize for the Eyes in My Head* to have a double-voiced movement, with layered levels of sarcasm and satire directed against racism and other oppression. *I Apologize for the Eyes in My Head* won the San Francisco Poetry Center Award for the best book of poems published in 1986.

In the fall of 1987, Indiana University hired Komunyakaa in English and Afro-American studies to teach poetry writing as well as black culture and literature. During his nine years there, Komunyakaa felt that in Bloomington he could accomplish and complete work, in contrast with, say, New Orleans and its manifold distractions. As he told Gotera, Indiana afforded Komunyakaa "a psychological space to actually deal with certain things and put them down on paper." This space surely helped Komunyakaa be the prolific writer and editor he has been.

Komunyakaa's poems on the Vietnam War launched him into wider notoriety, particularly after *Dien Cai Dau* appeared in 1988. Wherever he goes to give readings, I can attest from personal observation that often many Vietnam veterans will surface, including some who have never been to a poetry reading before. Preceding such celebrity, however, Komunyakaa ventured a first publishing foray into the subject of the war in *Toys in a Field*, his lesser-known Vietnam War chapbook.

Toys in a Field

Toys in a Field (1986) contains eighteen poems, two-thirds of which reappeared (sometimes in variant versions) in *Dien Cai Dau*. Of the remaining six poems, only four were resurrected in *Neon Vernacular* (1993), in some cases heavily revised. A poem that did not reappear in either of the later collections is the chapbook's opening poem, "Nothing Big," which explores the mind-set of a Vietnam vet driven by flashbacks to the past, to the war, "this hard night . . . shadowing men / back from a firefight." The primal image, a hummingbird whose "rainbow / lands among red / geraniums," mutates in the vet's imagination into "God's little hell-rising / helicopter" and the vet finds himself "back in Danang" and "back at the Blue Dahlia." Inside the flashback, experience is sharper, more jagged: "The sun / shines broken glass on the ground / & triggers dancing lights in my head." We are *not* behind the hospital with William Carlos Williams, where pieces of green glass evoke spring. War and memory rend the vet's universe, and he sees "the sky's flesh wounds." This poem establishes for the entire collection a context of dislocation and collision between two planes: *the 'Nam* and *the World* (back home). *Toys in a Field* dramatizes how the war has never let go of certain individuals, especially among veterans.

Dien Cai Dau

Dien Cai Dau (1988) depicts many more sides of the Vietnam War, not merely the experiences of infantry soldiers or grunts: Hanoi Hannah broadcasting to Americans, Bob Hope and the Gold Diggers entertaining the troops, Donut Dollies, Jody (the generic, folkloric name for civilians who "steal" girlfriends or wives while combat soldiers are away on duty), a Buddhist monk and suicide by fire, Saigon bar girls, prostitutes, a Vietnamese woman who is raped and "turns into mist," Amerasian orphans, Vietnamese sappers and prisoners, boat people, and an American mother in denial. Portraits of *soldiers* are equally varied: not just ordinary grunts but tunnel rats, POWs, "short-timers" (close to rotating home), and veterans in the United States. Some critics interpret *Dien Cai Dau* as a verse novel-of-sorts following a black soldier through Vietnam and the war's aftermath, but this reading limits the book's scope to only (African) American perspectives. That a phrase meaning *crazy* is the book's title hints at the insanity of this particular war for a variety of people—not just the *dien cai dau* soldiers but also their counterparts on all sides.

In the memorable poem " 'You and I Are Disappearing,' " memory plagues the speaker: "a girl still burning / inside my head." An imagistic litany unveils the speaker's unavailing attempts to comprehend (and perhaps purge) his harrowing souvenir:

> She burns like oil on water.
> She burns like a cattail torch
> dipped in gasoline.
> She glows like the fat tip
> of a banker's cigar . . .

The speaker finally falls back on religious conventions to no avail: "She burns like a burning bush / driven by a godawful wind." The word "godawful" may even hint that the speaker feels abandoned by providence in the grip of this memory.

Komunyakaa asserted that " 'You and I Are Disappearing'" was the only jazz poem in *Dien Cai Dau*. Its "rhythm," according to Komunyakaa, "came out of listening to Thelonious Monk." In that same interview with Kelly, Komunyakaa talked about his jazz poems containing not just an "emotional thread" but also "a *tonal* thread. . . . whereby we are able to make leaps not necessarily through logic, but through feeling." The tonal thread of " 'You and I Are

Disappearing'" is the phrase "she burns" and its various completions are improvisations. "She burns" sets up a tone of horror, both remembered and present, as well as mordant curiosity. The ending is guided also by jazz coincidence: "The poem pretty much ended itself when Thelonious ended the record." Jazz can modulate surprise by dictating a poem's boundaries.

Komunyakaa's style in *Dien Cai Dau* differs markedly from his earlier modes. These poems are less flashy, less sensational, more focused on common experience, more reportorial. This style shift is visible in the poem "Losses." Here is a tercet from an earlier version published in the *Indiana Review* in 1987:

> away from car horns & the landscape of
> crooked
> things dancing against a neon backdrop
> redder than backfire or blood

In *Dien Cai Dau* Komunyakaa collapsed this tercet into a single line: "away from car horns & backfire." Gone are the mysterious, surreal, technological; what is left is common language—the daily, ordinary fears of vets hiding out from society. The greater accessibility of language in *Dien Cai Dau* has attracted people who don't generally read poetry, resulting in a wider readership for Komunyakaa.

In "Starlight Scope Myopia" a grunt uses an infrared scope at night to observe Viet Cong loading supplies onto an oxcart. Although "the starlight scope brings / men into killing range," the speaker does not fire; he begins to feel a kinship with the enemy: when one of them laughs, he says, "You want to place a finger / / to his lips & say 'shhhh.' " The kinship starts to move toward brotherhood: "This one, old, bowlegged, / / you feel you could reach out / & take him into your arms." This poem reflects Komunyakaa's own experience: as a reporter and editor of *The Southern Cross* newspaper in Vietnam, he reported news but also wrote a column, "Viet Style," on Vietnamese culture. In fact, he told William Baer he felt "a crucial bond was the concept of the Vietnamese 'peasant.' " Komunyakaa added, "I myself came from a peasant society of mostly field workers.

. . . So I saw the Vietnamese as familiar peasants . . . I could have easily placed many of the individuals I'd grown up with in that same situation—especially the sharecroppers." One wonders if other grunts from rural areas felt similarly.

The play of *light* and *dark* and the action of *seeing* or *not seeing* in "Starlight Scope Myopia" are common topics in the book: a tunnel rat "pushed / by a river of darkness" in a tunnel "moves as if trying to outdo / blind fish"; "Damp smoke & mist halo" five grunts planning to execute a cruel officer by fragging; a Vietnamese woman is raped in "the titanic darkness" of an armored personnel carrier; and there are titles like "Seeing in the Dark" and "Eyeball Television." These image patterns map the difficulty during the war of *seeing* the right thing to do—a moral blindness and ambiguity. For Komunyakaa issues of light and dark are tied to conventional language, as he told Muna Asali: The Western psyche [has] this great fear of darkness, of the unknown. Darkness is negative. In the dictionary all the words that begin with *black* have connotations of death. So, for myself, I've been forced to turn around the definitions that we accept . . . [and] turn language back on itself."

Katarzyna Jakubiak's fascinating argument about these metaphors suggests that simply overturning the conventional connotations of light and dark is not sufficient to achieve the goal Komunyakaa desires, because the value and trustworthiness of seeing are compromised by the war's moral ambiguity. She then posits that Komunyakaa must create a "neon vernacular" to eradicate hierarchical thinking and balance these slippery metaphors. *Dien Cai Dau* may be seen therefore as an important way station in Komunyakaa's quest to create a language of metaphor that will allow reliable moral vision in the light or dark. In an ironic aside, *Dien Cai Dau* won the Dark Room Poetry Prize a year later.

In May 1988, Komunyakaa spent a week with six American poets at the *Centro Inter-*

nazionale Poesia della Metamorfosi in Fano, Italy. A tangible outcome of this trip was that several poems translated into Italian by Cosma Siani were published in Italy. Komunyakaa was subsequently invited by the Writers' Union of Vietnam and the William Joiner Center for the Study of War and Social Consequences in Boston to visit Vietnam in June 1990 with a delegation of Vietnam-veteran writers: Philip Caputo, W. D. Ehrhart, Larry Heinemann, Larry Rottman, and Bruce Weigl. This group traveled from Hanoi to Ho Chi Minh City (formerly Saigon). Komunyakaa brought with him several poems translated into Vietnamese, but he lost them almost immediately to a translator in Hanoi who carried them off and never returned. By this time, Komunyakaa's poetry had been translated into and published in French, German, Italian, and Vietnamese. Komunyakaa also began translating Nguyen Quang Thieu's poems into English; his translation of "The Examples: For My Village's War Widows," was published in the 1998 anthology *Mountain River: Vietnamese Poetry from the Wars, 1948–1993.*

February in Sydney

The title *February in Sydney* (1989) riffs on Dexter Gordon's "April in Paris." In this chapbook Komunyakaa returns to jazz territory but discovers it in the antipodes, in Australia. Poems praise an Aborigine named Wally—"Desert dreamer, telepathic / sleepwalker over shifting sand. . . . where gods / speak through blue-tongue lizards"—and a jazz drummer named Gerry: "You rap sticks . . . & sound travels / through everyone like rings of water. . . . knowing you'll ride hope / till it's nothing but a shiny bone / under heavy light." In a poem merging music and Aboriginal spirit, Komunyakaa honors a didgeridoo artist: "You place your lips to it / like a man who fears the unknown . . . to unearth / sounds of some extinct totem."

The best known of these poems is "Blue Light Lounge Sutra for the Performance Poets at Harold Park Hotel." Often a jazz poem features a refrain as an organizing device like a motif in music. This "sutra" uses such refrains: *"the need gotta be / so deep* words can't / answer simple questions" and *"so deep* fragments of gut / & flesh cling to the song" and *"you gotta get into it / so deep* salt crystalizes on eyelashes" and *"into it into it so deep /* rhythm is pre-memory" (emphasis added). When Komunyakaa performs a poem he seems to relineate it on the spot, a voiced syncopation that creates a groove for that single reading. In this poem, (re)combining refrains allows different stresses and emphases that approximate a jazz soloist's stops and starts. Komunyakaa has added a new dimension to (jazz) poetry: a performance can remake texts momentarily, so that improvisation is neither frozen nor stabilized by being written down.

For Komunyakaa the significance of jazz and poetry extends widely beyond his own work. For years before teaching at Indiana University, Komunyakaa had been compiling an anthology of jazz poems. At IU he invited one of his poetry students, Sascha Feinstein, to be coeditor. Feinstein was eminently qualified, a former jazz saxophonist and bandleader in New York City as well as a fine poet and critic. First out was *The Jazz Poetry Anthology* (1991), followed five years later by *The Second Set.* The third volume is currently in progress and scheduled to appear in 2001.

In 1991, Komunyakaa became a visiting professor at the University of California, Berkeley. He taught literature and poetry writing in the fall and then served as the 1992 Holloway Lecturer the following spring. One of Komunyakaa's memorable experiences from this time was the so-called "firestorm" that raged in the Berkeley hills and razed part of the city. In that same year, *Magic City* appeared, followed in quick succession the following year by *Neon Vernacular.*

Magic City

It's a truism among M.F.A. writing students that first books of poetry focus on childhood. This is not the case for Komunyakaa, who waited until his eighth collection (not counting his M.F.A. thesis) to address childhood predominantly in a single book: *Magic City* (1992). This book (re)visualizes a Bogalusa boyhood, from a five-year-old's memory of "Venus's-flytraps" to a teenager's balling his fists in defiance of a white man who said "Emmett Till had begged for it," to a young man in "Butterfly-Toed Shoes" flirting with a pretty woman who had a dangerous husband. In *Magic City* Komunyakaa lyricizes loss of innocence without unnecessary beautification.

Magic City also circles around love's coexistent gentleness and brutality: a mother who says *"Son, you ain't gonna live long"* to save his life. A mother who rips her red slip to make a kite's tail. A mother whose marriage to a violent husband moves her son to imagine their "dresser mirror [as] a moon / Held prisoner in the house." A mother who escaped and then, upon receiving her estranged husband's letters, may have laughed and burned them, the son imagines. Komunyakaa dramatizes in rapid glimpses his mother's strength and regained dignity.

Other fascinating glimpses in *Magic City* describe Komunyakaa's father, James William. Memories of "Daddy" are both lyrical and violent, full of hard work for both father and son, revealed by titles like "Banking Potatoes," "The Smokehouse," "Gristmill," and "Temples of Smoke." Two poems rehearse the ebb and flow of paternal and filial potency: as his father's go-between, the son writes letters to his escaped mother—for him an elementary act, while the father stands "(W)ith eyes closed & fists balled, / Laboring over a simple word"; in "Omen," the speaker is thirteen when his "Daddy shook" in terror facing a snake, and the boy "popped off its head / & threw it at [his] father's feet"—a demonstration of bravado and reversed mastery.

Komunyakaa's major concern in *Magic City* is *history*—national and regional narratives made relevant through personal experiences. Teenage skirmishes in touch football and pickup basketball fast-forward to face-offs between the Knights of the White Camellia and the Deacons of Defense. Komunyakaa's living inheritance—

his grandfather's "mismatched shoes"—are contextualized by the "piece of blond rope. . . . knotted around a limb" outside the courthouse. In *Magic City*, hanging on to heritage is framed by a heritage of hanging.

Neon Vernacular

The operative device in *Neon Vernacular* (1993) is *collage*, the reconstructive fine art that combines disparate fragments into a cohesive whole. For Komunyakaa, the master of the collage is Romare Bearden. It is no coincidence that Bearden is the cover artist for *Neon Vernacular*. In fact, Komunyakaa collects Bearden collages. The book's title phrase is itself a collage, compiling a visual term ("neon") with an auditory ("vernacular"); in terms of disciplines, a scientific word plus a linguistic one. Vis-à-vis etymologies, the "new" (from the Greek *neos*) and the "old" (from the Latin *vernaculus* for "native"); if we go further back to the root word *verna* for "slave" we end up with the resonant translation "new slavery." Ultimately the book is also a collage of "greatest hits" from previous collections (except *Magic City*).

Several poems from different books are themselves collages: "Passions" from *Lost in the Bonewheel Factory*, "Dreambook Bestiary" and "The Beast & Burden: Seven Improvisations" from *I Apologize for the Eyes in My Head*. Each of these poems is composed of individual, separately titled sections all connected by some tonal or associational thread. If we imagine a musical cognate to these poems, with each section played by different artists simultaneously or apart, we have what amounts to a jam session in written form.

In the opening section of *Neon Vernacular*, new poems continue the autobiographical arc of *Magic City*. "Songs for My Father" brings closure to the father-son dynamics in *Magic City*; at the same time, it uses the collage method of vaguely parallel sections, each of which covers some facet of their relationship, a one-sided conversation the son addresses to the now-dead father. There are pastoral reminders of the father riding the son on his handlebars; remembrances of work, for example, taking turns driving a drill with sledgehammers to make a well; violent moments ("Goddamn you. Goddamn you. / If you hit her again . . ."); and instances of gratitude and love. This moving collage of an elegy ends with the realization, "I never knew / We looked so much like each other," and a strong ending memory: "You were skinny, bony, but strong enough to try / Swaggering through that celestial door." The value of the collage strategy in this poem is that the various sections resemble individual photos in a family album, all held in equal importance.

Komunyakaa provides a variant of the collage poem in the long poem "Changes, or, Reveries at a Window Overlooking a Country Road, with Two Women Talking Blues in the Kitchen." Rather than vertical connections, there are two horizontally paralleled columns; the left column features two female voices (one in italics, the other in roman) and the right column has a speaker delivering a stream-of-consciousness meditation. Here is a brief sample in medias res:

. . . It's a wonder	a shadow in a reverie of robes and crosses.
Women don't stick to him	Oriflamme & Judgment Day . . . undulant waves
Like white on rice.	bring in cries from Sharpeville & Soweto,
It's a fast world	dragging up moans from shark-infested
Out there, honey.	seas as a blood moon rises. A shock

There are several interlocking call-and-response fragments here. First the two women talking are in a naturally accessible call-and-response mode. Second, there is a strange yet effective, one-sided call-and-response exchange between the women and the speaker in reverie—a sort of contrapuntal harmony in which occasional dissonance is the connective. At the same time, there is a sinuous call-and-response within the right column as the speaker talks to himself about history, jazz, and poetry—an on-

going solo, signifying. With such a plenitude of content, form, and delivery, Komunyakaa has invented yet another innovation of jazz poetics in *Neon Vernacular.*

On leave from Indiana University, Komunyakaa visited Australia in 1994, but also traveled through eastern Europe in November 1994. Komunyakaa and writer Jane Smiley toured Russia via the "Corridors of Culture" program sponsored by the U.S. Information Service. That same month, Komunyakaa visited Prague with Arthur Miller, Diane Johnson, and others. To round out this "European" year, *Panache de Bouquets,* a chapbook of Komunyakaa's poems translated into French by Isabelle Cadieux, was published in France by the William Faulkner Foundation.

Komunyakaa's noteworthy awards in 1994—the Pulitzer, Kingsley Tufts, and William Faulkner Prizes— are only part of a long list. Komunyakaa has won literary prizes: two Creative Writing Fellowships from the National Endowment for the Arts, an Award for Literary Excellence from *The Kenyon Review,* the Levinson Prize from *Poetry* magazine, and the Morton Zabel Award from the American Academy of Arts and Letters, to name several. He has been honored for humanitarianism and activism—for example, the Thomas Forcade Award from the William Joiner Center. Komunyakaa has also been honored by two alma mater institutions; he received the UCI Medal—the highest honor given by the University of California, Irvine—and the honorary degree Doctor of Humane Letters from the University of Colorado.

In 1996, Komunyakaa left Indiana to become a visiting professor at Washington University in St. Louis for a year, before beginning a new career phase in 1997 teaching creative writing at Princeton University.

In the late 1990s, Komunyakaa began working more on grafting poetry and music, branching sometimes into performance art. In 1995, *Fire Water Paper: A Vietnam Oratorio* composed by Elliot Goldenthal and featuring some of Komunyakaa's poems set to music, was recorded by the Pacific Symphony Orchestra with renowned cellist Yo-Yo Ma; the next year, the Boston Symphony Orchestra under Seiji Ozawa performed the oratorio, followed by a performance at Carnegie Hall in New York, and then at the Kennedy Center in Washington, D.C.

In December 1995, Komunyakaa performed his poetry with the jazz band of Eddie Gale (a Grammy Award winner) along with two other poets, Genny Lim and Vince Gotera, in a "Poetry and Jazz Concert" sponsored by the San Jose Center for Literary Arts in California. In a similar event in Chicago in 1997, Komunyakaa performed his poems with a jazz ensemble led by John Tchicai, resulting in a CD entitled *Love Notes from the Madhouse* (1998).

Testimony—a libretto based on jazz musician Charlie Parker's life—was aired by the Australian Broadcasting Corporation in 1998, with music composed by Sandy Evans. Komunyakaa also began writing jazz lyrics—for example, the song cycle *Thirteen Kinds of Desire*, written for Pamela Knowles, an Australian singer in Sydney; a CD was released in 2000.

Thieves of Paradise

If *Neon Vernacular* were a funnel that catches the strands of Komunyakaa's work and implodes them, then *Thieves of Paradise* (1998) would be the (re)explosion of those strands. Komunyakaa often works on several collections simultaneously, each one dealing with a single unifying theme. In *Thieves of Paradise*, he convinces all these themes to live within one set of covers.

The first section, "Way Stations," delivers a variety of jewels: an ode to Walt Whitman; further memories à la *Magic City* in "Mumble Peg"; an "Ode to a Drum," in which an African speaker fashions a drum "to drive trouble from the valley," then plays it, ". . . Kadoom. / Kadoom. Kadooom. Ka- / doooom," a direct allusion to Etheridge Knight's "Ilu, the Talking Drum."

Other sections expose a cornucopia of thefts: Australia stolen from paradise's original dwellers; thefts from Vietnam vets and Vietnam (poems on "The Hanoi Market" and the "Buried Light" of the countryside); more expansions of the Thorn Merchant galaxy; more blues and vi-

sual art pieces—a surfeit of poems and forms. There are two long elegies: "Quatrains for Ishi" and "Testimony." Ishi was the last of his tribe of Indians and spent the rest of his days in a museum; the poem recounts his life and death, when "a bear [stands] waving a salmon at the sky," while honoring secrets of tribe and self.

"Testimony," made up of fourteen unrhymed double sonnets, elegizes jazz musician Charlie "Bird" Parker without sentimentalizing him; sufficient attention is paid to his weaknesses—"straitjacket" and "track marks"—as well as to his glorious strengths: "when he'd raise his alto / a tropic sun beamed into the club." Ralph Ellison defined the "jazz impulse" as self-definition and self-assertion in relation to community and tradition; Komunyakaa precisely renders how these interconnections functioned in Charlie Parker's life in this libretto, "Testimony."

The central message of *Thieves of Paradise* is that, even though there *are* thieves, we can each *create* our own paradise. As in all his books, Komunyakaa celebrates the *survivor*—the surrealist artist, the copacetic blues musician, the sarcastic apologist, the Vietnam vet and others profoundly affected by the war, the jazz musician, and Ishi, the last man of his own kind. "Anodyne," the last poem of the book is genuine lyricism: "I love this body, this / solo & ragtime jubilee / behind the left nipple," where the heart survives in its cradle of bone.

In 1999, Komunyakaa was named chancellor of the Academy of American Poets, an important milestone in a scintillating career. He continues to publish groundbreaking work. *Blue Notes: Essays, Interviews, and Commentaries*, a Poets on Poetry volume, was published in 2000. Also a new collection entitled *Talking Dirty to the Gods*, composed of sixteen-line poems that "Africanize" classic texts, (re)inserting what has been omitted in literary history, is forthcoming in late 2000. *Pleasure Dome: New and Collected Poems, 1975–1999* will appear in early 2001.

Poetry in progress includes Komunyakaa's book-length poem *Autobiography of My Alter Ego*, spoken by a white Vietnam vet drifting from town to town across America, and *Re-*

membrances of *Things to Come,* poems that excavate black history, bringing to light African American figures who should be more widely known.

Komunyakaa also continues to work on music projects. He is writing two librettos: *Slip Knot,* concerning the "antics, facades, and forays" of a true-to-life slave/sailor in the late 1700s, and *Shangri-la,* a three-act opera about seven characters in the sex-trade underworld in Thailand. Komunyakaa is also writing more blues and jazz lyrics; one of these ensembles, *Blues Jumped the Rabbit & Ran Him a Solid Mile,* will be released on CD in 2000.

As we survey this extraordinary body of work, we might listen to Komunyakaa on his mentor: "Aimé Césaire . . . says that we are a composite of all our experiences—love, hatred, understanding, misunderstanding—and consequently we rise out of those things like—to use a cliché—a phoenix." Cliché or not, Yusef Komunyakaa, melding so many diverse themes and poetic devices with such breadth and heft, rises into our consciousnesses like fire—not like the girl on fire in " 'You and I Are Disappearing' " but instead like the legendary, mystical bird of fire—of victory—of peace.

Selected Bibliography

PRIMARY WORKS

POETRY

Dedications and Other Dark Horses. Laramie, Wyo.: RMCAJ [Rocky Mountain Creative Arts Journal], 1977.
Lost in the Bonewheel Factory. [Amherst, Mass.]: Lynx House Press, 1979.
Premonitions of the Bread Line. Master's thesis, University of California at Irvine, 1980.
Copacetic. Middletown, Conn.: Wesleyan University Press, 1984.
I Apologize for the Eyes in My Head. Middletown, Conn.: Wesleyan University Press, 1986.
Toys in a Field. New Orleans: Black River Press, 1986.
Dien Cai Dau. Middletown, Conn.: Wesleyan University Press, 1988.
February in Sydney. Matchbook #17. Unionville, Ind.: Matchbooks, 1989.
The Jazz Poetry Anthology. Edited with Sascha Feinstein. Bloomington: Indiana University Press, 1991.
Magic City. Hanover, N.H.: Wesleyan University Press, 1992.
Neon Vernacular: New and Selected Poems. Hanover, N.H.: Wesleyan University Press, 1993.
Panache de Bouquets. Translated by Isabelle Cadieux. Rennes, France: William Faulkner Foundation, Université de Haute Bretagne, 1994.
The Second Set: The Jazz Poetry Anthology, Volume 2. Edited with Sascha Feinstein. Bloomington: Indiana University Press, 1996.
Thieves of Paradise. Hanover, N.H.: Wesleyan University Press, 1998.

JOURNALS EDITED

Coeditor of *Gumbo: A Magazine for the Arts.* Cofounded with Adam Hammer. (1976–1978).
Guest editor of *Ploughshares* 23, no.1 (Spring 1997).

RECORDINGS

Love Notes from the Madhouse. Chicago: 8th Harmonic Breakdown, 1998. (Poetry reading with jazz ensemble led by John Tchicai.)

OTHER WORKS

Blue Notes: Essays, Interviews and Commentaries. Edited by Radiclani Clytus. Poets on Poetry Series. Ann Arbor: University of Michigan Press, 2000.
"The Examples," by Nguyen Quang Thieu. Translated by Yusuf Komunyakaa with the poet. In *Mountain River: Vietnamese Poetry from the Wars, 1948–1993.* Edited by Kevin Bowen, Nguyen Ba Chung, and Bruce Weigl. Amherst, Mass.: University of Massachusetts Press, 1998, p. 225.

SECONDARY WORKS

CRITICAL AND BIOGRAPHICAL STUDIES

Aubert, Alvin. "Rare Instances of Reconciliation." *Epoch* 38, no. 1:67–72 (1989).
———. "Stars and Gunbarrels." *African American Review* 28, no. 4:671–73 (1994).
———. "Yusef Komunyakaa: The Unified Vision—Canonization and Humanity." *African American Review* 27, no. 1:119–23 (Spring 1993). Reprinted in *Contemporary Literary Criticism,* Vol. 94. Detroit: Gale Research, 1997. Pp. 234–346. Also reprinted in *Black Literature Criticism Supplement.* Edited by Jeffrey W. Hunter and Jerry Moore. Detroit: Gale, 1999. Pp. 215–27.
Beidler, Philip D. *Re-Writing America: Vietnam Authors in Their Generation.* Athens: University of Georgia Press, 1991.
Collins, Michael. "Staying Human." *Parnassus: Poetry in Review* 18, no. 2/19, no. 1:126–49 (1993–94). Reprinted in *Contemporary Literary Criticism,* Vol. 94. Detroit: Gale Research, 1997. Pp. 241–49.
Conley, Susan. "About Yusef Komunyakaa." *Ploughshares* 23, no. 1:202–5 (Spring 1997).
Derricotte, Toi. "The Tension Between Memory and Forgetting in the Poetry of Yusef Komunyakaa." *The*

Kenyon Review 15, no. 4:217–22 (Fall 1993). Reprinted in *Contemporary Literary Criticism*, Vol. 94. Detroit: Gale Research, 1997. Pp. 239–41.

Engels, John. "A Cruel Happiness." *New England Review* 16, no. 1:163–69 (1994).

Feinstein, Sascha. *Jazz Poetry: From the 1920s to the Present.* Westport, Conn.: Greenwood Press, 1997.

Finkelstein, Norman. "Like an Unknown Voice Rising Out of Flesh." *The Ohio Review* 52:136–40 (Spring 1994).

Gotera, Vince. "Killer Imagination." *Callaloo* 13, no. 2:364–71 (1990).

———. *Radical Visions: Poetry by Vietnam Veterans.* Athens: University of Georgia Press, 1994.

———. " 'Depending on the Light': Yusef Komunyakaa's *Dien Cai Dau.*" In *America Rediscovered: Critical Essays on Literaure and Film of the Vietnam War.* Edited by Owen W. Gilman Jr. and Lorrie Smith. New York: Garland, 1990. Pp. 282–300. Reprinted in *Contemporary Literary Criticism*, Vol. 94. Detroit: Gale Research, 1997. Pp. 230–34.

Gwynn, R. S. "What the Center Holds." *Hudson Review* 46, no. 4:741–50 (Winter 1994).

Jakubiak, Katarzyna. *Yusef Komunyakaa: Questioning Traditional Metaphors of Light and Darkness.* Master's thesis, University of Northern Iowa, 1999.

Jones, Kirkland C. "Folk Idiom in the Literary Expression of Two African American Authors: Rita Dove and Yusef Komunyakaa." In *Language and Literature in the African American Imagination.* Edited by Carol Aisha Blackshire-Belay. Westport, Conn.: Greenwood Press, 1992.

———. "Yusef Komunyakaa." In *Dictionary of Literary Biography.* Vol. 120, *American Poets Since World War II.* Edited by R. S. Gwynn. Detroit: Gale Research, 1992. Pp. 176–79.

Ringnalda, Don. "Rejecting 'Sweet Geometry': Komunyakaa's *Duende.*" *Journal of American Culture* 16, no. 3 : 21–28 (Fall 1993).

———. *Fighting and Writing the Vietnam War.* Jackson: University Press of Mississippi, 1994.

Stein, Kevin. "Vietnam and the 'Voice Within': Public and Private History in Yusef Komunyakaa's *Dien Cai Dau.*" *Massachusetts Review* 36, no. 4: 541–61. Reprinted as chapter 5 of *Private Poets, Worldly Acts: Public and Private History in Contemporary American Poetry.* Athens: Ohio University Press, 1996. Pp. 90–107.

Waniek, Marilyn Nelson. "The Gender of Grief." *The Southern Review* 29, no. 2:405–19 (Spring 1993). Re-printed in *Contemporary Literary Criticism*, Vol. 94. Detroit: Gale Research, 1997. Pp. 237–38.

Warren, Kenneth. "Harsh Judgment." *American Book Review* 16, no. 2:16, 19 (1994).

"Yusef Komunyakaa." *Contemporary Authors*, Vol. 147. Edited by Kathleen J. Edgar. Detroit: Gale Research, 1995. Pp. 264–66.

"Yusef Komunyakaa." *Black Literature Criticism Supplement.* Edited by Jeffrey W. Hunter and Jerry Moore. Detroit: Gale, 1999. Pp. 214–35.

"Yusef Komunyakaa: *Neon Vernacular: New and Selected Poems.*" *Contemporary Literary Criticism*, Vol. 86. Edited by Christopher Giroux. Detroit: Gale Research, 1995. Pp. 190–94.

INTERVIEWS

Asali, Muna. "An Interview with Yusef Komunyakaa." *New England Review* 16, no. 1:141–47 (1994).

Baer, William. "Still Negotiating with the Images: An Interview with Yusef Komunyakaa." *The Kenyon Review* 20, nos. 3–4:5–20 (Summer–Fall 1998).

Carroll, Rebecca. *Swing Low: Black Men Writing.* New York: Crown Trade Paperbacks, 1995.

Gotera, Vince. " 'Lines of Tempered Steel': An Interview with Yusef Komunyakaa." *Callaloo* 13, no. 2:215–29 (1990). Interview conducted in 1986.

Johnson, Thomas C. "Interview with Yusef Komunyakaa." *Worcester Review* 19:1–2 (1998).

Kelly, Robert. "Jazz and Poetry: A Conversation." Interviewed with William Matthews. *Georgia Review* 46, no. 4:645–61 (1992).

Sherman, Suzan. "Yusef Komunyakaa and Paul Muldoon." *Bomb* 65:74–80 (Fall 1998).

Washington, Dorthy A. "Seeing Surprises: An Interview with Yusef Komunyakaa." *The Black Scholar* 27, no. 1:72–73 (1997).

MUSIC BASED ON THE WORKS OF YUSEF KOMUNYAKAA

Fire Water Paper: A Vietnam Oratorio. (Includes poems from *Dien Cai Dau.*) Composed by Elliot Goldenthal. Pacific Symphony Orchestra, featuring Yo-Yo Ma. Sony, 1996. (CD)

Testimony. (Libretto.) Music by Sandy Evans. Broadcast by Australian Broadcasting Corporation, 1998. (CD)

Thirteen Kinds of Desire. (Lyrics by Yusuf Komunyakaa.) Pamela Knowles, vocalist composer, and producer. Additional music composed by Jann Rutherford, Matt McMahon, and Alister Spence. Cornucopia Productions, 2000. (CD)

NELLA LARSEN
(1891–1964)

JACQUELYN Y. MCLENDON

NELLA LARSEN'S RECENTLY achieved renown rests to a great extent on two published novels, *Quicksand* (1928) and *Passing* (1929), but the life of the woman herself has drawn at least as much critical attention. Two decades after Mary Helen Washington's description of Larsen as the "mystery woman of the Harlem Renaissance" in a 1980 *Ms.* magazine article, and despite the publication of two major biographies, questions about Larsen still go unanswered.

Larsen herself sparked much of the controversy. In Zora Neale Hurston fashion, Larsen told stories to white people who, she said, "would have been keenly disappointed had they discovered that I was not born in the jungles of the Virgin Isles. So I entertained them with quite a few stories of my childhood in the bush, and my reaction to the tom-tom undertone of jazz." She also furnished biographical information to Alfred A. Knopf, her publisher, stating that her black father had died when she was two and that her Danish mother then married a man of her own nationality. In a 1928 interview with Thelma E. Berlack of the *Amsterdam News*, following the publication of *Quicksand*, Larsen gave her age as thirty-five when she was actually thirty-seven. She listed her date of birth as April 13, 1893, on her Guggenheim Fellowship application as well, and Chicago as her birthplace. Over the years, Larsen scholars have challenged the veracity of information she provided to various individuals and organizations.

Charles Larson, author of *Invisible Darkness: Jean Toomer and Nella Larsen* (1993) and Thadious Davis, author of *Nella Larsen: Novelist of the Harlem Renaissance: A Woman's Life Unveiled* (1994), are largely responsible for the numerous corrections and clarifications of the facts of Larsen's life. In an earlier publication, Davis established the year of her birth as 1891, and Charles Larson confirms this date based on school records, employment documents, and Nella's younger sister Anna's birth certificate. Davis traces Larsen's beginnings to Chicago, concluding that she was born Nellie Marie Walker and gradually evolved in name and persona into the writer we now know as Nella Larsen Imes. Charles Larson has remained unconvinced that she was born in Chicago, having obtained information from a close Larsen family friend, Mildred Phillips, that contradicts both the place of birth as Chicago and the nationality of the father as West Indian. He therefore concludes that Larsen "fabricated the story [of a West Indian father] for romantic purposes," that her father was really an African American who probably abandoned Larsen and her mother, Marie or Mary Hanson, when Larsen was very young. According to Phillips, Hanson confided to her that Nella Larsen's father was the African American chauffeur of a family for whom Hanson worked in New York, where Nella was born. Davis states that Phillips' story is not true. Further, she speculates that Hanson's allegedly white husband, Peter Walker, might actually have been a black man who later "passed" as white Peter Larsen; therefore, the man assumed to be Nella Larsen's step-father might instead have been her biological father. While Davis dismisses Phillips' story, she suggests that because Nella was too dark to pass, the family sent her away as a young girl and denied her existence thereafter.

Although her biographers correct much misinformation, they raise—perhaps purposely— as many questions as they answer. George Hutchinson, in "Nella Larsen and the Veil of Race," views these biographies as having "further obscure[d] crucial aspects of their subject's life and achievement." Hutchinson has perhaps done more than any other critic to refute many of the arguments put forth by Larsen's biographers, thereby contributing to the controversy that still surrounds Larsen and her work. For example, both biographers question whether Nella Larsen ever visited Denmark, questioning as well the implied closeness with her Danish kin. Indeed, Charles Larson concludes that "her Denmark years are a total fabrication," and Davis writes, "no records support her claim." Hutchinson provides documentation of a trip to Denmark when Larsen was "six or younger" in the company of her mother and sister on the Scandinavian-American Line, which he notes is the name of the line on which Helga Crane travels from New York to Copenhagen in *Quicksand*. Interestingly, the text of *Quicksand* contains a pointed reference to this real-life event as Helga recalls: "the purser, a man grown old in the service of the Scandinavian-American Line, remembered her as the little dark girl who had crossed with her mother years ago, and so she must sit at his table." Hutchinson adds, "Larsen did go to Denmark after leaving Fisk. She boarded for her return from Copenhagen on the ship *C. F. Tietgen* 14 January 1909." She must have traveled to Denmark some time after the spring of 1908, since records show that she had spent the previous school year, from fall 1907 through spring 1908, at Fisk University's Normal School (the university's high school). The evidence of actual trips to Denmark supports Hutchinson's contention that Larsen's *Quicksand* contains "details (. . . some of which, incidentally, pertain to the city of 1908 but not of 1920) that no American could have picked up without experience."

Hutchinson challenges what he deems Davis' "unsubstantiated hypotheses" that Larsen's father passed for white and that her mother placed her in the Erring Woman's Refuge for Reform. Providing a different perspective on much of the same evidence that both Charles Larson and Davis use—census, employment, and school records as well as Larsen's literary and extraliterary writings—Hutchinson argues that the girl in the refuge was identified as white, which Nella Larsen would not have been; that her birthday was listed as July 1892, when Larsen consistently gave her date of birth as April 13 even when she falsified the year; and that there were "several Nellie Larsons/Larsens liv[ing] in Chicago at the turn of the century," leaving "little reason to believe that the seven-year-old white girl in the Erring Woman's Refuge for Reform was the nine-year-old 'colored' girl who would later become a Harlem Renaissance novelist." Hutchinson's essay easily exceeds the typical scope of a review, presenting significant scholarship that complements and should be read alongside Charles Larson's and Davis' biographies.

Even with additional information about her return from Copenhagen, a period between January 1909 and 1912 remains unaccounted for. Larsen lists herself as "Auditor at University of Copenhagen. 1910–12" on the fellowship application form, but the university has no records to substantiate her claim. The strands pick up in the fall of 1912 when she entered a three-year course at Lincoln Hospital Training School for Nurses in New York. After graduating in 1915, Larsen began a career as a nurse, working for a year at the John A. Andrew Hospital and Training School for Nurses in Tuskegee, Alabama. Upon returning to New York, she worked as a supervising nurse at Lincoln Hos-

Nella Larsen

pital until 1918 and served on the staff of the City Department of Health from 1918–1921. Meanwhile, on May 3, 1919, Larsen married Dr. Elmer Samuel Imes, a physicist who later, in 1930, became head of the department of physics at Fisk University. Although she left nursing in 1921, she would return years later and work as a nurse until her death.

In January 1922 Larsen began employment with the New York Public Library. Critics tend to equate her employment as a librarian with her interest in writing. Neither has it been lost on them that *Quicksand*'s protagonist, Helga Crane, contemplates working as a librarian when she is unemployed in Chicago. Finding herself inadequately trained, however, she takes a job as traveling companion to a "financially comfortable" black woman lecturer named Mrs. Hayes-Rore. Larsen, on the other hand, worked as a librarian for four years. According to the New York Public Library's records, she was in charge of the Children's Room at the Countee Cullen branch and later at the Seward Park branch. In October 1924 she returned to the

Countee Cullen Branch, where she remained until her resignation on January 1, 1926.

To say that critics have been especially interested in solving the mysteries of Larsen's life is not to deny scholarly interest in her as a serious and talented writer. Her novels particularly have become the subjects of numerous dissertations, articles, and chapters in edited collections. Jacquelyn Y. McLendon's *The Politics of Color in the Fiction of Jessie Fauset and Nella Larsen* (1995) presents a full-length critical study of Larsen's novels. It rehearses briefly the well-known facts of Larsen's life and the autobiographical elements of her novels, especially *Quicksand*, for purposes of demonstrating that Larsen's fusion of autobiography and fiction places her in a tradition with black literary foremothers such as Harriet Jacobs (*Incidents in the Life of a Slave Girl*, 1861) and Harriet Wilson (*Our Nig*, 1859). Further, *Politics* explores the feminist and sociopolitical implications of Larsen's narrative choices, challenging interpretations that conflate Larsen's life with her characters' fictional lives, even in an autobiographical novel such as *Quicksand*. It argues that one of Larsen's primary objectives was to represent faithfully her own particular view of black life, and for that reason she wrote from her own milieu. She also responded to precursory depictions of mixed race people by white authors such as T. S. Stribling's protagonist Peter Siner in *Birthright* (1922). In a May 1932 interview with the *Southern Workman*, Jessie Fauset stated that she, Larsen, and Walter White were all "affected" by Stribling's depiction and felt better qualified than white writers to portray the phenomenon of passing and the experience of middle-class blacks in America.

Larsen expressed other motives for writing— particularly that she wanted to be famous. Clearly, she was unwilling to sacrifice everything for fame and fortune, though desirous of both, for she did not want "to be merely the best of a bad lot," as she wrote in a letter to Carl Van Vechten on July 21, 1926. In creating her two novels, she resisted the temptation to succumb to popular demands of white audiences and white publishers for books depicting "Harlem dives, race riots, and abject poverty."

Indeed, the temptation must have been great since Van Vechten's *Nigger Heaven* (1926), a novel about the "primitive" side of black people and the seamier side of black life, immediately sold one hundred thousand copies and was translated into French, Swedish, and Japanese. Claude McKay's similar depiction of black life in *Home to Harlem* (1928) resulted in its becoming the first novel by a black writer to make the best-seller list. Still, her own talent and hard work paid off because *Quicksand* has the distinction of having won the Harmon Foundation's bronze medal for literature in 1928. After the publication of her second novel, *Passing*, Larsen became the first black woman to receive a Guggenheim Foundation Fellowship in creative writing, the funds of which she used in 1930 to travel to Spain to research a third novel. Neither it nor other novels she wrote of working on was ever published.

Short Fiction

Larsen's published fiction consists of three short stories and the two novels. Before these works, she had published "Three Scandinavian Games" and "Danish Fun" in *The Brownies' Book,* a monthly children's publication that ran from January 1920 to December 1921. Published in the June and July 1920 issues, these were games that Larsen said she had learned from Danish children when she was herself a child visiting in Denmark. In 1926, however, with the publication of two short stories, "The Wrong Man" and "Freedom," in *Young's Realistic Stories Magazine* (January and April, respectively), she officially embarked on her very brief career as a fiction writer. These stories, published under the pseudonym Allen Semi, Nella Imes spelled backwards, were proleptic of what was to come in the greater accomplishments of *Quicksand* and *Passing*.

"The Wrong Man," for example, has an ambiguous ending like both her novels. Briefly, it is the story of Julia Romley, whose past comes back to haunt her when Ralph Tyler, whose mistress she had been, appears at a party at her home. Tyler is acquainted with her husband from whom she has kept her past a secret. As in *Passing*, in which a suffocating Irene Redfield tries to give the appearance of calmness at her own party, Julia feels "trapped" and desperately afraid. After arranging a secret meeting with Tyler and pleading for his silence, she realizes he is not the Ralph Tyler of her past and there the story ends. The appearance of a man at her home with the same name as a former lover, but who turns out not to be the former lover, begs credulity and leaves the shocked reader to speculate about whether he really is the wrong man. Secrets, shameful pasts, repressed upper-middle-class black life, suffocating marriages, uncontrollable fear, all surface again and again in Larsen's fiction.

"Freedom" is different only in that it is a story told from a nameless man's point of view. This time it is a man who feels "trapped" by his legal tie to a demanding wife. He eventually abandons her, even wishing for her death. He learns two years later that she has in fact died in childbirth along with the child. To him, her death is like a cruel joke because he believes it is she who "escapes," abandoning him to a life of guilt. He dies like Clare Kendry in *Passing* by falling "to the pavement a hundred feet below," only he commits suicide while Clare seems to be pushed.

"Sanctuary," published in *Forum* magazine in 1930, has received more critical attention than either of the previous stories primarily because of the accusation against Larsen that she plagiarized "Mrs. Adis," by Sheila Kaye-Smith, published in *Century* magazine in 1922. "Sanctuary" is the story of a black woman, Annie Poole, who unwittingly hides her son's killer from the whites who are hunting him. When Jim Hammer comes to her asking for help, neither of them knows that her son has been killed. On the verge of getting caught stealing tires, Hammer had shot into a crowd and had run away, not realizing he had killed Annie's son. The white men who come to Annie Poole's house to inform her of her son's death bring his body with them. As Hammer lay hiding, hearing this news for the first time, "into his frenzied brain came the thought that it would be better for him to get up and go out to them before Annie Poole gave him away." However, he is too afraid to move, and, miraculously, Annie does not give him away. The story ends with her ordering him out of her house, saying, "nevah stop thankin' yo' Jesus he don gib you dat black face," a not so subtle suggestion that race solidarity was more important than individual concerns.

Larsen claims to have gotten the idea for her own story from an old woman patient during her nursing days at Lincoln. However, critics argue that the two stories are so strongly similar as to make coincidence unlikely. Without stating explicitly that Larsen plagiarized, Davis offers a detailed comparison of the two stories based on such factors as theme, storyline, language, characterization, and plot, concluding with the possibilities that "Larsen may well have gambled on no one's recognizing the similarities between her story and the earlier one, especially because of her use of black characters and dialect. Or, she may *not* have considered that using the idea and format would constitute plagiarism." Likewise, Charles Larsen believes that the similarities are too great to be merely coincidental; however, he concludes, "it can only have been an accident of fate—a curse upon her for having a photographic memory."

Beverly Haviland's essay "Passing from Paranoia to Plagiarism: The Abject Authorship of Nella Larsen," takes as a given not only that Larsen plagiarized the story but also that the act and accusation are what ended her career. She states that "The sympathetic reader of her work wants to understand this act of literary suicide because the loss of this talented writer is regrettable." In an essay that fuses Larsen's life with the lives of her characters to such a degree that they are often indistinguishable, Haviland states that her purpose is to raise questions about relationships between authors and their texts, but she especially adds fuel to an already raging fire by arguing that Larsen, in common with Irene Redfield in *Passing,* was paranoid. Citing the shared characteristics of paranoia and plagiarism, she goes on to argue that plagiarism was Larsen's way of taking "revenge against her own loved and hated white mother"

who did not protect Larsen as a child in the way that the black mother in "Sanctuary" "protects even the murderer of her own son because of sentiments of race solidarity."

Novels

Interest in "Sanctuary" notwithstanding, Larsen's short fiction thus far has received minimal critical attention, with Davis' and Charles Larson's books as notable exceptions. *Quicksand* and *Passing* are quite another matter. Contemporary reviews of *Quicksand* were favorable, with both white and black reviewers commenting that it was thoughtful, courageous, articulate, sympathetic, and dignified. Reviews of *Passing* were more mixed: the writing merely "adequate," the ending "engineered" and therefore not convincing. On the other hand, *Passing* was praised for its form and characterization. As stated earlier, both books garnered awards for their author. In light of this initial success, her later obscurity is somewhat puzzling. One explanation may lie in the fact that distance and shifts in attitudes about the definition of a black aesthetic caused a series of negative or, at the very least, ambivalent critiques in the years following the end of the New Negro movement. In light of Richard Wright's criticism in "Blue Print for Negro Writing," for example, and the simultaneity of the Black Power movement's and the Black Arts movement's focus on the struggles of the masses, Larsen's middle- and upper-middle-class characters' struggles were deemed unrepresentative and therefore unimportant.

Although cultural historians such as Nathan Huggins (*Harlem Renaissance,* 1971) and David Levering Lewis (*When Harlem Was in Vogue,* 1981) include Larsen in their comprehensive studies of the period, the current intensity of scholarly attention accorded her texts has occurred chiefly as a result of the archaeological work of scholars such as Barbara Christian, Arthur P. Davis, Hortense Thornton, Anne Shockley, Mary Helen Washington, and Mary Mabel Youman, as well as the revisionist work of Hazel Carby, Ann DuCille, Deborah Mc-Dowell, Jacquelyn McLendon, and Cheryl Wall, to name a few, all of whose work on Larsen is worthy of study for a meaningful exploration of her writing in its historical, cultural, political, and critical contexts.

Quicksand

Early feminist Larsen scholars both lay claim to her and criticize her for alleged unrealistic representations of black women, womanhood, and black life experiences generally. Yet, they provide the initial groundwork for later studies, their own and others', in which Larsen's formal narrative strategies and psychological explorations of her female characters are the main focus. Both novels portray the female protagonists' feelings of alienation and their struggles for autonomy. *Quicksand,* obviously autobiographical though not an autobiography, examines the problems of being biracial in America but with much more complexity than conventional "tragic mulatto" tales. Helga Crane does not suffer persistent and uncontrollable urges of mixed blood, the donée of such tales; she suffers from her memories of an alienated childhood "living among hostile white folks" or trying to fit in with blacks with whom "you [had to] prove your ancestry and connections," otherwise "you didn't belong." After Helga tells Mrs. Hayes-Rore a little of her orphan-like background, "the woman felt that the story, dealing as it did with race intermingling and possibly adultery, was beyond definite discussion." F. James Davis' study of race construction and the "one-drop rule" in America, in *Who Is Black? One Nation's Definition* (1991), confirms the view that "when satisfactory evidence of respectable black parents is lacking, being light-skinned implies illegitimacy."

When *Quicksand* opens, Helga is living in a southern community and teaching at Naxos College, a place she describes as a "big knife with cruelly sharp edges ruthlessly cutting all to a pattern, the white man's pattern." Naxos is an anagram of Saxon, a not-so-subtle indication of its imitation of white society, a place where one had to become "naturalized" in order to fit in: "the pun on the word *naturalized,*" writes McLendon in *Politics,* "points to an irony that pivots on the multiple meaning of and inherent contradictions in a term that derives from *natural* or *naturalis,* meaning 'by birth' or 'according to nature.'" Helga is a rebellious young woman in search of love, happiness, and a sense of belonging, who refuses to become naturalized. Thus, she leaves Naxos and travels to Chicago, an act that begins a recurring pattern of enclosure and escape manifested in her move from Chicago to New York, then to Copenhagen, back to New York, and finally to the "tiny Alabama town" from which she does not escape.

Helga's intense vacillation reflects the tension between personal desire and societal expectation. Believing that she lives in a society that punishes passion, Helga looks for material comfort and the security of a "name" in her relationships. She remembers all too clearly that her mother "in forgetting all but love . . . had forgotten, or perhaps had never known, that some things the world never forgives." She, therefore, had been "flung into poverty, sordidness, and dissipation," had become "sad, cold, and—yes, remote." Helga herself is therefore afraid of passion and realizes too late her love for and sexual attraction to Dr. Robert Anderson, principal of Naxos College.

Men in the novel are also sexually repressed. Robert Anderson is unable to admit or give into his feelings for Helga. His marriage to her friend Anne is "his ascetic protest against the sensuous, the physical," and a denial of "that nameless and to him shameful impulse, that sheer delight, which ran through his nerves at mere proximity to Helga." In showing the inhibitions of the male, as she also does in depicting Helga's former fiancé James Vayle, the white Axel Olsen, and the Reverend Mr. Pleasant Green, Larsen dispels the myth regarding the innate frigidity of the light-skinned female, the opposite of the dark-skinned "loose" woman, and thereby inveighs against the correlation of values with color or "blood." Instead, she suggests that members of this class are imprisoned by their overdependence on rationality.

Sexuality in this novel is closely associated with "primitive" rather than "civilized" behavior. A telling scene takes place in a Harlem nightclub. As Helga observes the dancing pairs "violently twisting their bodies . . . or shaking themselves ecstatically to a thumping of unseen tomtoms," she feels "drugged, lifted, sustained. . . . The essence of life seemed bodily motion." Afterward, Helga "dragged herself back to the present with . . . a shameful certainty that not only had she been in the jungle, but that she had enjoyed it." Black music—blues and jazz—has long been associated with immoral, promiscuous behavior. In this passage, with references to the jungle and tomtoms, and with Helga's self-admonition that she isn't "a jungle creature," it is also the mark of a class and race she needs to escape: "She cloaked herself in a faint disgust . . . and when the time came again for the patrons to dance, she declined." Yet, she is clearly envious of Audrey Denney, a young black woman who dances with Dr. Anderson. Audrey can lose herself in the feeling and dance "with obvious pleasure, her legs, her hips, her back, all swaying gently, swung by that wild music from the heart of the jungle." Of course, Audrey is the subject of gossip because she is a "colored" woman who "goes about with white people," an ironic reversal of Helga's mother's situation but equally frowned upon because of its disregard for proper social attitudes.

A second scene that underscores the connection between the primitive and the erotic is the church revival into which Helga stumbles in her effort to escape her "mortification" and "self-loathing." It is a grotesque mosaic of all the themes and metaphors that converge on the central motif of entrapment. Larsen depicts the inextricability of gender and sexual oppression in a scene in which the women behave like crazed animals, crawling around on their hands and knees while the men watch. The women shout accusingly at Helga to "repent," calling her " 'a scarlet 'oman,' " and a " 'pore los' Jezebel' " even as they themselves behave in ways that cause the scene to take on a "Bacchic vehemence," which Helga likens to a "weird orgy": "Behind her, before her, beside her, frenzied women gesticulated, screamed, wept, and tottered to the praying of the preacher, which had gradually become a cadenced chant." Inevitably, Helga, too, becomes "maddened . . . and with no previous intention began to yell like one insane." The scene symbolizes women's subjugation and the suppression of their natural emotions. They are allowed to express their feelings only under the guise of religious fervor, and Larsen's depiction of the grotesque aspect of this revival indicates the unnaturalness of their actions. It is significant that when Helga seduces Green—a man whose name she can't even remember—she is "half-hypnotized" by her religious experience.

Helga's seduction of the Reverend Mr. Pleasant Green is her response to Anderson's rejection: "The wish to give herself had been so intense that Dr. Anderson's surprising, trivial apology loomed as a direct refusal of the offering." Yet her behavior following Anderson's passionate kiss is not impelled simply by sexual frustration, for along with the "voluptuous visions [that] haunted her" are feelings of anger, bitterness, and powerlessness. She feels "belittled and ridiculed" and, what is more important, she is aware of the acute sense of entrapment that has marked her life since childhood.

Larsen explores sexuality openly and honestly, from the sexually repressed behavior of most of the characters to the freely sensuous behavior of Audrey Denney to the lust Helga feels for Green. Critics tout Zora Neale Hurston's *Their Eyes Were Watching God* as perhaps the first book by and about a black woman that confronts issues of female desire head-on. However, there is not a scene in *Their Eyes* that depicts female desire so graphically as Larsen's depiction of Helga's relations with Green. Even the much-written-about scene under the pear tree, in which Janie has her first sexual experience, is couched in descriptions of nature that obscure the meaning. Larsen, on the other hand, explores lust, which traditionally has been the exclusive privilege of men, as a very real experience of women. In her wish to continue fulfilling her sexual desires, Helga ignores her husband's odor and the "atmosphere of self-satisfaction which poured from him like a leaking pipe" and waits eagerly for "night . . . at the end of every day. Emotional, palpitating, amorous, all that was living in her sprang like rank weeds at the tingling thought of night, with a vitality so strong that it devoured all shoots of reason." Helga's difficulty stems not from her own eroticism, but from society's condemnation of it, which weighs heavily in her choice of the wrong man. As the pattern of behavior that has been her life evolves, one thing remains constant: "Robert Anderson, questioning, purposely detached, affecting, as she realized now, her life in a remarkably cruel degree; for at last she understood clearly how deeply, how passionately, she must have loved him."

Unlike Hurston's Janie, who is able to free herself of oppressive relationships with men, Helga is destined to live, or die, with a husband she eventually despises because she comes to understand her desire too late. Thus, Larsen raises serious questions not only about female eroticism but also about the institution of marriage: "This sacred thing of which parsons and other Christian folk ranted so sanctimoniously, how immoral—according to their own standards—it could be!" When the novel ends, Helga has made a supreme sacrifice for the sake of her children and is about to have her fifth child. This ending forces readers to face the questions Larsen raises concerning marriage, motherhood, gender and sexual oppression, and, generally, the unresolved tension between personal desire and societal expectation.

Although she makes us aware of the difficulties men, especially black men, have confronting many of these same issues, Larsen's particular province is the psychological exploration of the female. She presents Helga's story from the harsh reality of a feminine psychology that at once encompasses and transcends racial concerns. In the end, Helga's struggle is against a conventional, unimaginative society that "tolerated no innovations, no individualisms," a society in which "enthusiasm, spontaneity, if not actually suppressed, were at least openly regretted as unladylike or ungentlemanly qualities." Her struggle is against society-at-large as destroyer of life.

The parallels between Helga Crane's life and Larsen's own background are well known and clearly suggest that Larsen considered her own childhood to have been as unhappy as Helga's. Her comment in the 1928 Berlack interview with the *Amsterdam News* is telling: "I don't see my family much now. It might make it awkward for them, particularly my half-sister." This statement, along with Anna's comment at Larsen's death that she didn't know she had a sister, demonstrate Larsen's first-hand knowledge of the alienation Helga feels; she knew the confusion, frustration, and pain of racial dualism, which goes a long way toward explaining why she focused her attention on these particular aspects of black life.

Passing

Larsen's last novel, *Passing*, continues the themes of the first, but with the added dimension of passing, as the title indicates. Analyses that focus less stringently on thematic concerns and more on Larsen's skillful narrative strategies show *Passing* to be the more rhetorically sophisticated and the more tightly controlled of the two novels. The story centers on two women protagonists, Irene Redfield and Clare Kendry, both confined by the psychological narrowness of black and female life, both driven by desires for security and comfort, and both light-skinned enough to pass. Clare Kendry alone, however, physically abandons her race, marries a white man, eventually becomes dissatisfied with the white world, and dies mysteriously at the novel's end while allegedly trying to reestablish ties to the black race. Clare, then, to some extent embodies the stereotype.

With the characterization of Irene and the juxtaposition of the two women's lives, Larsen revises the tragic mulatto and passing stereotypes. Irene seldom passes physically, but she resorts to other forms of disguise and erasure as her means of escape. She strives to mask any feelings and behavior that appear to be uncivilized or unladylike, measures herself by white standards, and lives in constant imitation of whites, thereby experiencing, as completely as

Nella Larsen receiving the Harmon in 1928.

Clare, a loss of racial and cultural ties. In this way, Larsen postulates that passing is as much a state of mind as a physical act, and the title—in its reference to both Irene's and Clare's actions—becomes a metaphor for psychological passing or escapism. By emphasizing the ironic similarity in Irene's and Clare's situations, Larsen reveals the complexity of their shared experience: they are, in fact, psychological doubles. Larsen heightens her readers' awareness of the two as doubles by using Irene as central intelligence. That is, much of the text surfaces in Irene's mind even though the narrative is told in third person. This device emphasizes Irene's repression and creates, in itself, a kind of disguise. The notion of passing, then, has structural as well as thematic significance.

Contrasting images of appearance versus reality, Larsen satirizes the bourgeois class and finds in it a correlation with the concept of passing. Characteristic of members of this class is their propensity for behaving in ways designed to disguise the truth. Larsen's attention to the trivial details of society life sharpens the images of repression, especially the characters' repressed fear and rage. At one moment the narrative describes Clare, for example, as a woman who "wept attractively" and at another as a woman who might kill her husband if he got in her way. Irene, too, sits "pouring tea properly and nicely," all the while feeling the "impulse to laugh, to scream, to hurl things about. She wanted, suddenly, to shock people, to hurt them, to make them notice her, to be aware of her suffering." Because of the narrative point of view, it is Irene's fear and repressed rage to which readers are drawn as she becomes more and more like Clare, wishing first for the death of Clare's child and then for the death of Clare herself. By the end of the novel, Clare's death and Irene's complicity in it should come as no surprise since fear and repressed anger are stressed throughout, and Irene's subtle destructive acts, paralleling Clare's plunge from an upstairs window, act as foreshadowing.

Clare is attending a party in the company of Irene and Brian when Bellew, her husband, bursts in, accusing her of being a "damned dirty nigger." Irene feels that this discovery threatens her own security, for once free of Bellew, Clare might take up with Irene's husband, Brian, with whom Irene believes she is already having an affair. At the sight of Clare at the window, smiling "as if the whole structure of her life were not lying in fragments before her," Irene "ran across the room, her terror tinged with ferocity, and laid a hand on Clare's bare arm. One thought possessed her. She couldn't have Clare Kendry cast aside by Bellew. She couldn't have her free."

The description of Clare's fall reveals only that "one moment Clare had been there, a vital glowing thing, like a flame of red and gold. The next she was gone." Nothing is clearly stated about her death; therefore, it is a critical commonplace to view it as melodramatic and contradictory. However, both the foreshadowing and the descriptions of Irene's repressed fury—bordering on insanity—are strong suggestions of murder. Other compelling facts are offered as well: Irene tries desperately to convince herself that Clare's fall was "a terrible accident," but she is at the same time panic-stricken that Clare might not be dead, and at the announcement that Clare had died "instantly," a "sob of thankfulness . . . rose in her throat." Finally, Irene is cast as both victimizer and victim so that her complicity in Clare's death may also be symbolic of her need to destroy the Clare within. Passing becomes, then, a metaphor for both symbolical and literal death in its suggestion of the ultimate "crossing over," to borrow from Henry Louis Gates Jr., "in that ironic double sense of 'passing' and 'dying.'" The ending of the novel may appear to be melodramatic, but it is grounded in the reality that violence is a consequence of fear and repression. In suggesting murder as a possible ending, it revises conventional endings of tragic mulatto and passing tales. The issues raised in *Quicksand* regarding motherhood, marriage, sexuality, and the like, are thus carried out in *Passing* to their fatal conclusion.

With the success of these two books, her Bronze Award for Literature from the Harmon Foundation (for *Quicksand*) and Guggenheim Fellowship, the support of many prominent people, and especially her talent, Nella Larsen showed promise of becoming one of the major figures of the Harlem Renaissance. If quantity is not the standard of measurement, then surely she is a major figure. Perhaps the biggest question of all, then, is why, with such talent and success, did Larsen stop writing? The most common speculation is that the accusation of plagiarism devastated her, as did the failure of her marriage. No doubt Larsen was devastated by the accusation. Although *Forum* editors supported her, her integrity had been challenged and the viciousness of gossip ensued. Following on the heels of this ordeal came the trouble in her marriage. In a letter Elmer Imes wrote to Van Vechten in 1930, he states that "early in the year and quite by accident Nella became possessed of information which pointed decidedly to the fact that I was at the time very much interested in another girl." His claim to be unwilling to hurt Larsen seems to have been more a desire to keep the matter quiet and his job intact. Larsen was obviously unable to remain "the sweet little sport . . . and not say anything about it."

Thus, Larsen's trip to Spain to work on her third book was preceded by the unhappy discovery of her husband's affair. The communication between them while she was abroad seems to have had mainly to do with money—he complaining that she was spending too much and she complaining that there was not enough to spend. Larsen remained with Imes for several years after the discovery, behaving, from her perspective, like the "dutiful wife" by joining him in Tennessee and, from his perspective, doing nothing more than "keep[ing] all in an unpleasant stew" when she was present, according to a letter Imes wrote to Van Vechten in June 1932. In July 1933 Larsen sought a divorce in Nashville, Tennessee, because it was inexpensive and discreet. Although the tone of the letter she wrote to her friend Dorothy Peterson about the divorce is glib, the hurt must have cut deep as evidenced by the manner in which she alludes in subsequent letters to Imes' new wife and to his approaching fatherhood. In these same letters, however, she wrote of trying to finish her book, and something of the old intensity and determination is present when she talks of having to revise all but two chapters.

The divorce and the plagiarism accusation certainly might have been contributing factors to Nella's abandoning her writing, but necessity possibly counted more. Blacks were rapidly going out of vogue, for, as Langston Hughes notes in his autobiography *The Big Sea*, "when the crash came in 1929 . . . the white people had much less money to spend on themselves, and practically none to spend on Negroes, for the depression brought everybody down a peg or two. And the Negroes had but few pegs to fall." Larsen did not drop from view immediately, though she spent less time in Harlem. By the late thirties, according to Davis in her *Nella Larsen*, "Nella Larsen became an elusive figure." Following Imes' death from cancer in 1941 (which brought, of course, an end to his alimony payments), she went back to her former occupation of nursing. According to Anne Shockley's 1988 account, she went to work at Bethel Hospital in Brooklyn. In her *Nella Larsen* Davis states, however, that she had no "regular employment" until 1944 when she became a night duty nurse at Gouverneur Hospital on Manhattan's Lower East Side. Larsen remained a nurse until her death on March 30, 1964. She was buried on April 6 in Cypress Hills Cemetery in Brooklyn.

Despite numerous speculations, the reasons Larsen stopped writing remain a mystery like much of her life. That she published no more is indeed a loss to the literary world. Yet her creative achievements, though slight in quantity, are a rich legacy. By insisting that black middle-class society could be both interesting and dramatic, and especially by focusing attention on the psychology of the female, Nella Larsen added a unique and enduring voice to the chorus of Harlem Renaissance writers.

Selected Bibliography

PRIMARY WORKS

FICTION

"The Wrong Man." *Young's Realistic Stories Magazine*, January 1926.

"Freedom." *Young's Realistic Stories Magazine*, April 1926.
Quicksand. New York: Knopf, 1928.
Passing. New York: Knopf, 1929.
"Sanctuary." *Forum* 83:15–18 (January 1930).

OTHER WORKS

"Playtime: Three Scandinavian Games." *The Brownies' Book* 1:191–92 (June 1920).
"Playtime: Danish Fun." *The Brownies' Book* 1:219 (July 1920).
"The Author's Explanation." *Forum* suppl. 4, 38:41–42 (April 1930).

CORRESPONDENCE

Larsen's correspondence is in the James Weldon Johnson Collection in the Beinecke Rare Book and Manuscript Library, Yale University. Selected correspondence is also in the Carl Van Vechten Collection, New York Public Library, Rare Book and Manuscript Division.

SECONDARY WORKS

BIOGRAPHICAL AND CRITICAL STUDIES

Blackmer, Corinne E. "The Veils of the Law: Race and Sexuality in Nella Larsen's *Passing*." *College Literature* 22, no. 3:50–67 (October 1995).

Butler, Judith. "Passing, Queering: Nella Larsen's Psychoanalytic Challenge." In *Female Subjects in Black and White: Race, Psychoanalysis, Feminism*. Edited by Elizabeth Abel, Barbara Christian, and Helene Moglen. Berkeley: University of California Press, 1997.

Clark, William Bedford. "The Letters of Nella Larsen to Carl Van Vechten: A Survey." *Resources for American Literary Study* 8:193–99 (Fall 1978).

Cutter, Martha J. "Sliding Significations: Passing as a Narrative and Textual Strategy in Nella Larsen's Fiction." In *Passing and the Fictions of Identity*. Edited by Eloise K. Ginsberg. Durham: Duke University Press, 1996. Pp. 75–100.

Davis, Arthur. "Nella Larsen." In his *From the Dark Tower: Afro-American Writers, 1900 to 1960*. Washington, D.C.: Howard University Press, 1974. Pp. 94–98.

Davis, F. James. *Who Is Black? One Nation's Definition*. University Park, Penn.: Pennsylvania University Press, 1991.

Davis, Thadious. "Nella Larsen." In *Dictionary of Literary Biography*. Vol. 51, *Afro-American Fiction Writers from the Harlem Renaissance to 1940*. Edited by Trudier Harris and Thadious Davis. Gale Research, 1987. Pp. 182–92.

————. "Nella Larsen's Harlem Aesthetic." In *The Harlem Renaissance: Revaluations*. Edited by Amritjit Singh, William S. Shiver, and Stanley Brodwin. New York: Garland, 1989. Pp. 245–56.

————. *Nella Larsen, Novelist of the Harlem Renaissance: A Woman's Life Unveiled*. Baton Rouge: Louisiana State University Press, 1994.

DuCille, Ann. *The Coupling Convention: Sex, Text, and Tradition in Black Women's Fiction.* New York: Oxford University Press, 1993.

Fuller, Hoyt. Introduction to *Passing.* New York: Collier, 1971. Pp. 11–24.

Gates, Henry Louis, Jr. *Figures in Black: Words, Signs, and the Racial Self.* New York: Oxford University Press, 1987.

Haviland, Beverly. "Passing from Paranoia to Plagiarism: The Abject Authorship of Nella Larsen." *Modern Fiction Studies* 43, no. 2:295–318 (Summer 1997).

Hill, Adelaide Cromwell. Introduction to *Quicksand.* New York: Collier, 1971. Pp. 9–17.

Huggins, Nathan I. *Harlem Renaissance.* New York: Oxford University Press, 1971.

Hughes, Langston. *The Big Sea: An Autobiography.* New York: Hill and Wang, 1940.

Hutchinson, George. "Nella Larsen and the Veil of Race." *American Literary History* 9, no. 2:329–49 (Summer 1997).

Joyce, Joyce Ann. "Nella Larsen's *Passing:* A Reflection of the American Dream." *Western Journal of Black Studies* 7, no. 2:68–73 (1983).

Kellner, Bruce. *The Harlem Renaissance: A Historical Dictionary for the Era.* Westport, Conn.: Greenwood Press, 1984.

Larson, Charles R. *An Intimation of Things Distant: The Collected Fiction of Nella Larsen.* New York: Anchor Books, 1992.

———. *Invisible Darkness: Jean Toomer and Nella Larsen.* Iowa City: University of Iowa Press, 1993.

Lewis, David Levering. *When Harlem Was in Vogue.* New York: Alfred A. Knopf, 1981.

McDowell, Deborah E. Introduction to *Quicksand and Passing.* New Brunswick, N.J.: Rutgers University Press, 1986. Pp. ix–xxxv

McLendon, Jacquelyn Y. "Self-Representation and Art in the Novels of Nella Larsen." In *Redefining Autobiography in Twentieth-Century Women's Fiction: An Essay Collection.* Edited by Janice Morgan and Colette Hall. New York: Garland, 1991. Pp. 149–68.

———. *The Politics of Color in the Fiction of Jessie Fauset and Nella Larsen.* Charlottesville: The University Press of Virginia, 1995.

Ramsey, Priscilla. "Freeze the Day: A Feminist Reading of Nella Larsen's *Quicksand* and *Passing.*" *Afro-Americans in New York Life and History* 9:27–41 (January 1985).

Shockley, Anne Allen. "Nella Marian Larsen Imes." In *Afro-American Women Writers, 1746–1933: An Anthology and Critical Guide.* Boston: G. K. Hall, 1988. Pp. 432–40.

Tate, Claudia. "Nella Larsen's *Passing:* A Problem of Interpretation." *Black American Literature Forum* 14:142–46 (Winter 1980).

———. *Psychoanalysis and Black Novels: Desire and the Protocols of Race.* New York: Oxford University Press, 1998.

Thornton, Hortense E. "Sexism as Quagmire: Nella Larsen's *Quicksand.*" *College Language Association Journal* 16:285–301 (March 1973).

Wall, Cheryl A. "Passing for What? Aspects of Identity in Nella Larsen's Novels." *Black American Literature Forum* 20:97–111 (Spring–Summer 1986).

———. *Women of the Harlem Renaissance.* Bloomington: Indiana University Press, 1995.

Washington, Mary Helen. "Nella Larsen: Mystery Woman of the Harlem Renaissance." *Ms.* 9:44–50 (December 1980).

———, ed. *Invented Lives: Narratives of Black Women, 1860–1960.* Garden City, N.Y.: Anchor, 1987.

Whitlow, Roger. *Black American Literature: A Critical History.* Chicago: Nelson Hall, 1973.

Youman, Mary Mabel. "Nella Larsen's *Passing:* A Study in Irony." *College Language Association Journal* 18:235–41 (December 1974).

BIBLIOGRAPHY

Beemyn, Brett. "A Bibliography of Works by and about Nella Larsen." *African American Review* 26, no. 1:183–88 (Spring 1992).

AUDRE LORDE
(1934–1992)

MARGARET HOMANS

AS A CHILD learning to write, Audre Lorde tells us in her "biomythography," *Zami: A New Spelling of My Name*, she chose to spell her name her own way: Audre instead of Audrey. This insistence on composing her own self-definition characterized her entire writing life. When she introduced herself in speeches or interviews, she often began by naming her many selves: "I am a black feminist lesbian poet" or "a forty-nine-year-old Black lesbian feminist socialist mother of two, including one boy, and a member of an interracial couple." She said, "I am a lesbian woman of Color"; "I stand here now—Black, Lesbian, Feminist"; and "I am a Black Lesbian, and I *am* your sister." She named the pieces of her identity because they are seldom thought to be compatible with each other and because she insisted that, in her, they were. "I learned to speak the truth by accepting many parts of myself and making them serve one another." She insisted on her wholeness, as she created it, as well as on the way in which that wholeness was composed of discrete allegiances.

The different parts of herself connected her to different social groups, not all of whose interests overlapped, and it was her major political project, and her major contribution to social and political thought and to feminist theory, to insist on the need to make connections across social boundaries, while accepting and even celebrating real differences. She described this project as "trying to get people you love mightily to hear and use the ways in which you all are totally different." In every political statement she made, she was as respectful of differences as she was urgent about working together on common causes: "When we join hands across the table of our differences, our diversity gives us great power." The struggle to make these connections she carried out daily both within herself and in social relations, and she saw no division between her internal and her external dialogues. As she put it in a 1988 radio profile,

My work is about difference, my work is about how do we learn to lie down with the different parts of ourselves, so that we can in fact learn to respect and honor the different parts of each other, so that we in fact can learn to use them moving toward something that needs being done, that has never been done before.

In her writing, Lorde mastered a broad range of genres: poetry, autobiography, the political and the personal essay. She spelled her own name, but in many different ways. Like the different parts of her identity and the different worlds she traveled in, although they remained distinct, each genre also interpenetrated the

517

others. In speeches and essays, her identity as poet tended to be subordinate to her lesbianism, her feminism, and her racial identity, yet she wrote a poet's prose. Metaphor and simile often carried much of the burden of her argument, as in the following analogy from her well-known essay "Uses of the Erotic: The Erotic as Power":

> During World War II, we bought sealed plastic packets of white, uncolored margarine, with a tiny, intense pellet of yellow coloring perched like a topaz just inside the clear skin of the bag. We would leave the margarine out for a while to soften, and then we would pinch the little pellet to break it inside the bag, releasing the rich yellowness into the soft pale mass of margarine. Then taking it carefully between our fingers, we would knead it gently back and forth, over and over, until the color had spread throughout the whole pound bag of margarine, thoroughly coloring it.
>
> I find the erotic such a kernel within myself. When released from its intense and constrained pellet, it flows through and colors my life with a kind of energy that heightens and sensitizes and strengthens all my experience. (*Sister Outsider*, p. 57)

Although the analogy compares life to margarine and the erotic to artificial food coloring, it devalues neither life nor the erotic element in life, but rather calls attention to the sheer pleasure of the erotic: like the luxury of yellow coloring, the pleasure of the erotic derives in part from its being wholly unnecessary. Moreover, the passage exemplifies one of the essay's key points: if coloring margarine can become as sensual an experience as Lorde's writing makes it here, then the erotic can enrich the most unexpected parts of life.

While Lorde's prose is often poetic, her poetry, which she began writing at the age of six, maintains continuity with the prose of her journals and political essays. The urban realism of much of her poetry, which continues in some of her recent work, often has the urgency of a news bulletin. Helen Vendler in a September 1975 *New York Times* book review describes certain of Lorde's early poems as "New York reportage," "street photographs" that are "acidic and hard-edged." In a 1979 interview with Adrienne Rich, Lorde comments on the origin of her poem "Power," about the shooting of a black child by a white policeman:

> I was driving in the car and heard the news on the radio that the cop had been acquitted. I was really sickened with fury, and I decided to pull over and just jot some things down in my notebook to enable me to cross town without an accident because I felt so sick and so enraged. And I wrote those lines down— I was just writing, and that poem came out without craft. . . . I didn't feel it was really a poem. (*Sister Outsider*, p. 107)

Elsewhere she describes a period in her life when she had ceased writing poetry, but was still writing in her journal.

> Later the next year, I went back to my journal, and there were these incredible poems that I could almost lift out of the journal; many of them are in *The Black Unicorn*. "Harriet" is one of them; "Sequelae" is another. "The Litany for Survival" is another. These poems were right out of the journal. But I didn't see them as poems prior to that.
>
> "Power" was in the journal too.
> ("My Words Will Be There," pp. 265–266)

Lorde the poet was one with Lorde the political activist: "The question of social protest and art is inseparable for me."

Similar to the aim in her political essays to bring together disparate groups, an important project of Lorde's poetry and her more poetic prose was to bring together in language the disparate worlds in which she dwelled. The multiplicity of her psychic and social identities, what Chinasole terms "creative irreconcilability," emerges not only as a theme but also as an aspect of style. For example, the co-presence of two places—New York and the Caribbean, New York and Africa—can represent the multiplicity of her sense of self. Beginning in *The Black Unicorn* (1978)—perhaps her best-known volume of poetry, which concludes with a glossary of African names and a bibliography—and continuing in *Zami: A New Spelling of My Name* (1982) and the volume of poetry *Our Dead Behind Us* (1986), Lorde made the rich mythography of her ancestral places enliven the bleaker scene of her urban life. The most frequently cited instance of this layering is "125th St. and Abomey," a poem from *The Black Unicorn* whose title summarizes that volume's way of connecting Africa and New York. It begins, disjunctively:

Head bent, walking through snow
I see you Seboulisa

Addressing the Abomey mother goddess from the position of her own psychic cold weather, the poet prays to be given "woman strength" like that of "my warrior sisters / who rode in defense of your queendom." Although the speaker concedes that "half earth and time splits us apart / like struck rock," the poem ends by addressing Seboulisa with a triumphant command that overcomes the split:

see me now
your severed daughter
laughing our name into echo
all the world shall remember.

The volume's title and cover illustration reinforce this sense of double identity. The black unicorn is an intercultural image denoting simultaneously an Africanization of the mythic European animal that signifies both phallic masculinity and female purity (it can be tamed only by virgins), and a Europeanized description of the African agricultural goddess Chi-Wara, who is represented by a one-horned antelope. The volume's title poem uses this cross-cultural figure to dramatize the impossibility of single definitions of the self and to explore the potential for one culture to enhance another. Framing the poem, a series of lines beginning "The black unicorn is . . ." poses the problem of fixed definitions, a problem deriving from European cul-

Audre Lorde

tural imperialism that appropriates everything in its path for its own meanings. The poem explains:

The black unicorn was mistaken
for a shadow
or symbol
and taken
through a cold country
where mist painted mockeries
of my fury.

Kidnapped from Africa, this fierce power of fertility was misrepresented in Renaissance painting and tapestry (perhaps Lorde had in mind the white unicorn depicted in a series of tapestries at the Cloisters in New York). Whereas the European figure divides meaning between the passive, pale virgin and the equally powerless phallic horned animal, the African figure combines

519

the two to generate a mysterious power of growth:

> It is not on her lap where the horn rests
> but deep in her moonpit
> growing.

Revising the virginal "lap" on which the unicorn's horn only "rests" into the single, hermaphroditic figure of the "moonpit" in which the horn grows, Lorde revised the embattled gender divisions of European culture into what she experienced as the wholeness of African religions, and at the same time claimed for women the phallic powers that Europe reserves for men.

Equally striking is the intermingling of West Indian culture with New York life in *Zami*, where the cultural dislocations of being raised by West Indian parents in a New York they never considered home form a major theme throughout. Lorde identified the book's genre as "biomythography," a term that denotes the mingling of the mythic (West Indian/African) with the prosaic (New York) in a passage like the following, from near the end of the book:

> I took a ripe avocado and rolled it between my hands until the skin became a green case for the soft mashed fruit inside, hard pit at the core. *I rose from a kiss in your mouth to nibble a hole in the fruit skin near the navel stalk, squeezed the pale yellow-green fruit juice in thin ritual lines back and forth over and around your coconut-brown belly.*
>
> *The oil and sweat from our bodies kept the fruit liquid, and I massaged it over your thighs and between your breasts until your brownness shone like a light through a veil of the palest green avocado, a mantle of goddess pear that I slowly licked from your skin.*
>
> Then we would have to get up to gather the pits and fruit skins and bag them to put out later for the garbagemen, because if we left them near the bed for any length of time, they would call out the hordes of cockroaches that always waited on the sidelines within the walls of Harlem tenements, par-

ticularly in the smaller older ones under the hill of Morningside Heights.   (p. 251)

As when Lorde named herself "Black, Lesbian, Feminist," it is difficult to say whether the disjunctions or the connections emerge the more vividly in this passage. Simultaneously a non-Western religious ritual involving fertility worship ("mantle of goddess pear") and mystical experience ("your brownness shone like a light"), and an episode of imaginative lovemaking in an ordinary Harlem apartment, the scene both conjoins and contrasts its two worlds. Moreover, the very name of the lover—who is introduced as Kitty, but later identified as Afrekete—signifies the doubling of Lorde's identity between New York and African selves. The partial dedication of *Zami* "To the hands of Afrekete" positions Kitty/Afrekete simultaneously as a woman with great sensual gifts and as the goddess into whose spiritual hands the author commended herself. As with all of Lorde's work at its most remarkable, the writing here embodies Lorde's desire both to celebrate difference and to cross its boundaries, to "join hands across the table of our differences."

The phases of her life that Lorde chose to reveal most frankly to her readers are represented in *Zami* and in the writings on her experience with cancer in *The Cancer Journals* and *A Burst of Light*. She recounts less formally some of her intervening life as a poet in her interview with Adrienne Rich (first published in the feminist quarterly *Signs*, later reprinted in *Sister Outsider*) and in other interviews. Because her personal identity was so important a part of her persona as poet, speaker, and essayist, episodes from her experience appear throughout her writing.

Zami, though fictionalized, recounts her life from her earliest childhood to her mid twenties as a lesbian in New York. Born in Harlem on 18 February 1934, the youngest of three daughters, she grew up in a dislocated household. Her parents—immigrants who expected to return to the West Indies until the Depression ended their hopes—painfully missed their home and continued to speak their own language to each other when they didn't want their English-speaking children to overhear. Early chapters vividly depict episodes of racism, which her strong mother tried to deny; her childhood discovery of the magic of written words and of narrative; and her sensual connection to her mother. Rebelling as a teenager from her parents' strictness, she found community among other outcasts at Hunter High School, one of whom was Diane di Prima, who was later to publish Lorde's first volume of poetry at the Poet's Press in 1968. She lived through the suicide of her best friend and moved out of her parents' home after high school graduation to support herself in isolation in a series of low-paid jobs. An abortion (she did not yet know she was a lesbian), hunger, and loneliness followed. She moved to Connecticut, took a grueling factory job, and had her first lesbian affair.

A trip to Mexico in 1954 confirmed her identity as a lesbian and as a poet. On her return, still not yet twenty, she joined the predominantly white Greenwich Village "gay-girl" scene, and it is her emotional life and her participation in gay culture that form the center of *Zami*'s narrative thereafter, although Lorde also mentions that she went to college, kept writing poetry, and began a series of relatively enjoyable librarian jobs. She was slightly involved with the predominantly male (and, in her experience, homophobic) Harlem Writers Guild during this period, and Langston Hughes asked to see her poetry, yet this world was so distant from, and even hostile to, her Village life that she stayed on its periphery. *Zami* continues her story through the late 1950s, during which time she received the degrees of B.A. from Hunter College (1959) and M.L.S. from the Columbia University School of Library Science (1960).

The next period that Lorde mentioned frequently is the pivotal year 1968. As she relates in her interview with Adrienne Rich, just as her first book of poetry, *The First Cities*, was going to press (a momentous occasion for a writer who had been slow to acknowledge the public value of her poetry), she was invited to serve as poet-in-residence at Tougaloo College, a historically black institution in Mississippi. By this time she was working as head librarian at the Town School in New York, married (al-

though she does not detail the history of this marriage), and raising two children, born in the mid 1960s. Her experience teaching poetry to black students, coinciding as it did with her confirmation as a publishing poet, changed her life, as did the fact that at Tougaloo she met Frances Clayton, the woman who was soon to become her long-term partner. During her six weeks at Tougaloo, Lorde wrote almost all the poems for her second book, *Cables to Rage* (1970), and immediately on her return to New York she began teaching writing in the SEEK program at City College (CUNY) and gave courses on racism at Lehman College and at John Jay College. Of the excitement of teaching in those days she said, "The learning process is something you can incite, literally incite, like a riot."

Her next volume of poetry, *From a Land Where Other People Live,* was nominated for a National Book Award in 1974. Her editor had rejected from the book the lesbian love poem that, when Lorde read it publicly in 1971 and later published it in *Ms.* magazine, marked her self-identification as a lesbian in her poetry. *New York Head Shop and Museum,* which appeared in 1975, included the poem "Black-studies," a reflection on Lorde's experiences as a teacher; it is described by Marilyn Hacker in *Commonweal* as a "contemporary classic." In 1976 a limited edition of *Between Ourselves* appeared, a slim booklet of seven poems later reprinted in *The Black Unicorn.* Up to this point, Lorde's work had been published by small presses such as the Poet's Press in New York and the Broadside Press in Detroit, but in 1976, her National Book Award nomination having brought her a degree of celebrity, W. W. Norton published *Coal.* A collection of new poems and poems from her first two, hard-to-find books, *Coal* appeared with jacket copy by Adrienne Rich, one of Norton's own best-known poets; the back cover also carried an advertisement for one of Rich's books. This association between Lorde and Rich, as Robert Stepto points out, continued in the packaging of *The Black Unicorn,* which appeared in 1978 from Norton with the same text by Rich on the front jacket flap, and in 1981 Rich's interview introduced Lorde to the predominantly white readers of *Signs*. In 1982 Norton brought out *Chosen Poems: Old and New*, a selection of pieces from Lorde's first five books (but excluding *The Black Unicorn*, because of its integrity as a volume) plus seven new poems. Lorde continued to publish poetry with Norton, culminating after her death in the 1997 *Collected Poems of Audre Lorde*, but alternative presses have consistently published her prose.

The Black Unicorn was widely reviewed, as was *Zami*, whose appearance in 1982 expanded Lorde's established reputation as a poet who also wrote prose. *Ms.* began reviewing Lorde regularly in the 1970s; although the *New York Times Book Review* in 1975 carried an article by Helen Vendler on fifteen new books, including Lorde's *New York Head Shop and Museum*, it was not until 1982 that the *New York Times* published reviews of Lorde's work on its own (*Zami* and *The Black Unicorn*). *Essence* began reviewing her work in 1983. The publication of *Sister Outsider* in 1984, including writings from 1976 to 1984, again enlarged Lorde's audience: widely taught in women's studies courses, it has become a feminist classic in large part for its forthright confrontation of the issue of racism within white-dominated United States feminism. In 1985 students at Hunter College, where Lorde became a professor of English in 1980, dedicated the Audre Lorde Women's Poetry Center. Her next poetry volume, *Our Dead Behind Us*, continued the cross-cultural connections between the United States and Africa that began in *The Black Unicorn*. Scholarly articles about Lorde's work began to appear soon after the publication of *The Black Unicorn*. Most of the early articles, like the dissertations that began in the early 1980s to focus on Lorde, consider her briefly among a group of affiliated poets—women writers, black women writers, lesbian writers—but increasingly scholars have studied Lorde individually, not only treating important themes in her work but also analyzing her distinctive craft in both verse and prose. Interviews began appearing in the 1980s, when she also began to be widely sought for lectures and readings by universities and community organizations. Lorde was awarded honorary doc-

torates by Hunter, Oberlin, and Haverford colleges; she earned a Walt Whitman Citation of Merit in 1991 and was named New York State Poet from 1991 to 1993.

Essays in *Sister Outsider* afford some glimpses into Lorde's personal life in the years since the close of *Zami*. During the 1970s and 1980s she traveled to Africa and the Caribbean as well as to Europe and Russia. "Learning from the 60s" and "Man Child: A Black Lesbian Feminist's Response" explore the political contexts and ramifications of her family lives, first "raising two children and a husband in a three-room flat on 149th Street in Harlem" during the height of the civil rights and black power movements, and then, since the early 1970s, raising a son as well as a daughter in a lesbian household.

In 1980 Lorde published *The Cancer Journals*; with this work begins a new phase of autobiographical revelation. (See Jeanne Perreault's excellent reading of this volume as an instance of the feminist generation of self through writing about the body.) In 1978, after an earlier false alarm, Lorde developed breast cancer and underwent a radical mastectomy. Journal entries and essays recount her feelings and views during the long process of diagnosis, hospitalization, and recovery. Excruciatingly vivid is her account of what it meant to combine "postmastectomy woman" with her other identities as black lesbian feminist poet: she shocks hospital staff by refusing to wear a prosthesis, refusing to pretend to an ideal of normality that includes a specified number of breasts. Lorde continues this aspect of her life story in *A Burst of Light*, a prose collection published in 1988. Here a series of journal entries recounts her life with her second bout of cancer, which began in 1984, when she chose to forgo surgery in favor of an alternative, noninvasive treatment. During this period of intermittent remission she taught for three months in Berlin (1984), traveled back and forth to the Caribbean, gave readings in the U.S. Midwest, Australia, and New Zealand (1985), and endured several wintry, lonely weeks at the Lukas Klinic in Switzerland "while my body decides if it will live or die."

A Burst of Light connects Lorde's survival to that of the African women of the global diaspora, about whom she is increasingly concerned. Back in New York, she writes: "Battling racism and battling heterosexism and battling apartheid share the same urgency inside me as battling cancer. . . . Each victory must be applauded, because it is so easy not to battle at all, to just accept and call that acceptance inevitable." While the narrative carries her struggle with cancer and her reflections on its meanings up through August 1987, she continued to face the reality of her illness, to work and to write, and to speak out until her death on November 11, 1992.

The love scene that concludes *Zami*, excerpted above, typifies the layered quality of Lorde's writing, her way of living in many selves and in many places at once. But the scene is also typical in exposing the volatility of the selves and places Lorde holds together. Kitty/ Afrekete's sexual generosity heals Lorde after the painful breakup of her first serious relationship and gives the book an optimistic ending. Generally obliged to choose between the heterosexual black community and the white lesbian community, Lorde's autobiographical speaker represents her discovery of a black lover as a healing integration of divided parts. Although Lorde and her lover meet at lesbian bars in the Village, the affair is always conducted in Kitty's apartment in Harlem (a Harlem that is, as we have seen, intermittently also Africa), a region from which Lorde felt excluded.

Yet the very appearance of healing calls to mind the painful rifts that necessitate it and that (on the basis of Lorde's other writings) will follow it. When she introduced herself with a list of attributes—for example, "I am a black feminist lesbian poet"—it was generally because she expected her audience to find the combination strange, if not offensive. Any one of her selves may have aroused hostility in those who valued only one of the others. One of her statements of identity in *Sister Outsider* concludes in this way: "As a forty-nine-year-old Black lesbian feminist socialist mother of two . . . I usually find myself a part of some group defined as other, deviant, inferior, or just plain wrong." Or again, about her life in the 1960s, "As a Black lesbian mother in an interracial

marriage, there was usually some part of me guaranteed to offend everybody's comfortable prejudices of who I should be." She emphasized that those who found her offensive included those who ought to have been comrades-in-arms. *Zami* details a painful episode in the 1950s when Lorde's straight white woman roommate, whom she had met through activism on behalf of the Rosenbergs, was obliged by her political colleagues to move out when they learned that Lorde was a lesbian, as Lorde's "deviance" would harm the cause.

To be black and lesbian, as she explains in *Zami*, meant being an outsider to the primarily white lesbian community in the Village of the 1950s, where she also had to hide her identity as an ambitious student and poet. To be black and lesbian also meant (and still means) alienating the heterosexual black community that believes that lesbianism spells race suicide and an attack on black manhood. To be black and lesbian is to conform to expectations about neither. As she explains these apparent contradictions in a speech reprinted in *A Burst of Light*, "When I say I am a Black Lesbian, I mean I am a woman whose primary focus of loving, physical as well as emotional, is directed to women. It does not mean I hate men."

Likewise, to be black and a feminist should not have to mean divided loyalties. She tells the same group, "When I say I am a Black feminist, I mean I recognize that my power as well as my primary oppressions come as a result of my Blackness as well as my womanness, and therefore my struggles on both these fronts are inseparable." But in practice her sympathies are sometimes torn. For example, the poem "After-images" (1981) powerfully evokes the clash and the continuities between two "images" from Jackson, Mississippi: the dead, mutilated body of Emmett Till (the black fifteen-year-old murdered for whistling at a white woman) and the figure of a despairing white woman who has just lost everything in a flood. At first, Lorde's feminist sympathies are with the woman: "Tearless and no longer young, she holds / a tattered baby's blanket in her arms" while she tries to speak her despair into a microphone,

Until a man with ham-like hands pulls her
    aside
snarling "She ain't got nothing more to
    say!"
and that lie hangs in his mouth
like a shred of rotting meat.
               (*Chosen Poems*, p. 103)

When Till's story is introduced, however, this provisional solidarity with white womanhood is dissolved by the reminder that a white girl's objection to Till's whistling caused his death. And yet there is no simple opposition here between black (manhood) and white (womanhood), for Lorde compares discarded newspaper photos of Till to "a raped woman's face." In the poem the warped value system of "manhood" is blamed both for Till's act and for his murder. Whistling at a woman, Till was only "testing what he'd been taught was a manly thing to do," and it is "his teachers" who destroy him, "in the name of white womanhood." In this way Lorde removes the blame from the white girl; "white womanhood" is only the pretext for the release of white male racial violence. "In the name of white womanhood" these same men then "celebrated in a whorehouse / the double ritual of white manhood / confirmed." (See Amitai Aviram's excellent discussion of the way the grammar of these lines underscores their meaning.) Women of all races are subject to male oppression, as black men are subject to white men.

Although the white girl has been shown to be a mere pretext, the next stanza both continues to compare Till to a raped woman and to blame the white girl for treasuring her "honor." Coming back to the woman flood victim, the poem identifies the flood as a "muddy judgment," an act of vengeance on whites for the murder of Till. But if it is a "judgment," it is also a confused or misguided one, "muddy." Subsequent lines continue this fine balancing of blame and sympathy, returning both to the white girl's absurd "honor" and to the painful sight of the other white woman silenced by the "man with an executioner's face." In the end, the poem merges the speaker's pain over the two victimizations, the flood victim's and Till's. While Till's fate is the more horrifying, the speaker cannot choose to decide that one "image" compensates for the other.

"Afterimages" graphically demonstrates both the psychic and the social dimensions of Lorde's experience of being caught between groups who should be allies but who are at war. One of the most powerful themes in her prose writings is the necessity for frank recognition of differences among groups and individuals and the necessity for building coalitions across those differences. In "Age, Race, Class and Sex: Women Redefining Difference" (a speech reprinted in *Sister Outsider*) she says: "Certainly there are very real differences between us of race, age, and sex. But it is not those differences between us that are separating us. It is rather our refusal to recognize those differences, and to examine the distortions which result from our misnaming them and their effects upon human behavior and expectation." Rather than tolerating the way in which differences turn into hierarchy, Lorde calls for "the interdependence of mutual (nondominant) differences." But because of the difficulties involved in making this conceptual and political shift, Lorde must painstakingly analyze the "horizontal hostility" or destructive hatred among groups that ought to be allies: black men and black feminists or black lesbians; black women and white women; and, worst of all, black women and black women.

The term "sister outsider" refers in the first instance to Lorde's relation to the lesbian community in the 1950s; she uses the term in *Zami* to describe the ambiguous position of black women there, simultaneously inside and outside its conventions and culture. But in the essays collected in *Sister Outsider*, the phrase comes to denote Lorde's relation to every group of which she was a part. Most of the essays and speeches were written for particular audiences, and in each she addresses the way in which that audience has both sought her out and positioned her as alien and other. The first such essay is "The Transformation of Silence into Language and Action," a paper delivered to the Modern Language Association's "Lesbians and Literature Panel" in December 1977, and her subject is the racism of white women academics. She speaks with unnerving directness: "Perhaps for some of you here today, I am the face of one of your fears." She gives as an example the white woman academic who claims, "I can't possibly teach Black women's writing—their experience is so different from mine," and counters with the question, "How many years have you spent teaching Plato and Shakespeare and Proust?" But she goes on to assert that "the fact that we are here and that I speak these words is an attempt to break that silence and bridge some of those differences between us, for it is not difference which immobilizes us, but silence." "An Open Letter to Mary Daly," on the patronizing characterization of African women in Daly's book *Gyn/Ecology,* adopts the same mixture of admonition and hope, as do passages in the interview with Rich.

Over time Lorde grew more impatient with the white women academics who continue to marginalize women of color at their conferences. At the 1979 Second Sex Conference in New York she read "The Master's Tools Will Never Dismantle the Master's House" at "the only panel . . . where the input of Black feminists and lesbians [was] represented." The title refers to the way in which white women replicate the patriarchal strategy of "keep[ing] the oppressed occupied with the master's concerns." Just as feminists "are still being called upon to stretch across the gap of male ignorance and to educate men as to our existence and our needs," so white women are wasting the time of women of color by requiring from them an education about "our existence, our differences, our relative roles in our joint survival. This is a diversion of energies and a tragic repetition of racist patriarchal thought." "The Uses of Anger: Women Responding to Racism," also delivered at a feminist conference, is likewise fierce in tone, yet, by distinguishing between anger and hatred, similarly seeks to keep open channels of communication.

In two essays addressed to the sexism of black men originally published in *The Black Scholar,* "Scratching the Surface: Some Notes on Barriers to Women and Loving" and "Sexism: An American Disease in Blackface," and, less directly, in "Learning from the 60s" (a talk given at the 1982 Malcolm X Weekend at Har-

vard), Lorde deplores the hostility of black men to women who love or form strong alliances with other black women or who "explore the possibilities of a feminist connection with non-Black women." African women have long traditions of female bonding, and yet "all too often the message comes loud and clear to Black women from Black men: 'I am the only prize worth having and there are not too many of me, and remember, I can always go elsewhere. So if you want me, you'd better stay in your place which is away from one another, or I will call you "lesbian" and wipe you out.' "

Both "Scratching the Surface" and "Sexism" dramatize the starkness and urgency of the problem by evoking the appalling story of Patricia Cowan, a black actress who, auditioning for a part in a play called *Hammer* in Detroit in 1977, was hammered to death by the black male playwright in front of her four-year-old child. Anticipating the rhetorical strategy of "The Master's Tools," Lorde here asks the black man to see that "sexism and woman-hating are critically dysfunctional to his liberation as a Black man because they arise out of the same constellation that engenders racism and homophobia." Like white feminist racism, black sexism only perpetuates one of the techniques by which white patriarchy dominates: "Hopefully, we can learn from the 60s that we cannot afford to do our enemies' work by destroying each other." The point is one made earlier in the poem "Between Ourselves," in which a black man sells the speaker's great-grandmother into slavery; the poem concludes by characterizing this sort of intraracial strife as suicidal, "killing / the other / in ourselves."

After this alternating sequence of addresses to white feminists and black men, *Sister Outsider* turns in its penultimate essay to a yet more vexed locus of "horizontal hostility": that between black women. Partially autobiographical, "Eye to Eye: Black Women, Hatred, and Anger" is perhaps the clearest instance in the volume of the way in which Lorde's negotiations among different groups serve simultaneously as negotiations among her different selves. The essay argues that hatred between black women stems from the self-hatred spawned by racism:

Black women internalize white hatred and then unconsciously inflict it on themselves and on each other. The essay often seems both repetitious and self-contradictory, but it is worth following the turns and twists of its internal logic in some detail in order to uncover the complexity of Lorde's conflicting feelings on this painful subject. Dramatizing this sense of a self at war with itself is a series of carefully controlled mixed metaphors for the self's deepest feelings. At the start of the essay, figures of nets and threads alternate with, and seem to contradict, figures of hot liquids:

> My Black woman's anger is a molten pond at the core of me, my most fiercely guarded secret. I know how much of my life as a powerful feeling woman is laced through with this net of rage. It is an electric thread woven into every emotional tapestry upon which I set the essentials of my life—a boiling hot spring likely to erupt at any point, leaping out of my consciousness like a fire on the landscape. (*Sister Outsider*, p. 145)

In the next few paragraphs anger is a "pool" and a "fire," and black women are "steeped in" sexist racism—a "poisonous seepage." At the same time, extending her mixed metaphor, Lorde follows "the threads of my own rage at Blackwomanness back into the hatred and despisal that embroidered my life with fire long before I knew where that hatred came from." At the end of the passage, the speaker expresses certainty about her identity—"I am who I am"—at the same time that another contrary pair of similes conveys a sense of boundary confusion between one self and another: " . . . acting upon you like a drug or a chisel to remind you of your me-ness, as I discover you in myself."

Although the essay includes incidents illustrating hostility among black women generally (for example, a black woman library clerk rudely ignores Lorde's presence at her desk), it quickly emerges that the real subject of the essay is relations between black mothers and daughters, and specifically Lorde's relation to her own mother. The series of memories illustrating the internalization of white hatred begins with an episode, also described in *Zami*, that occurred on a subway train when Lorde was three. That the narrative begins "I clutch my mother's sleeve" suggests that the story is as much about the mother's failure of protection as it is about the racism itself. As in *Zami*, the essay next describes the mother's strategy of combatting racism by pretending to ignore it. Although Lorde admires her mother's bravery and her dedication to keeping "me alive within an environment where my life was not a high priority," she also notes how her mother's own internalized racism communicated itself to her, as when her "light-skinned" mother called her—darker-skinned than either of her two sisters—" 'full of the devil.' " Her sisters are well-behaved and light, while Audre is mischievous and dark: "Did *bad* mean *Black*?" And she describes how her mother's silences on the topic of racism "taught me isolation, fury, mistrust, self-rejection, and sadness." Immediately counterbalancing these angry words, Lorde again praises her mother, yet she returns once again to her legacy of self-hatred, and with it to the contrary metaphors of the essay's opening: "My mother bore me into life as if etching an angry message into marble. . . . That anger lay like a pool of acid deep inside me, and whenever I felt deeply, I felt it, attaching itself in the strangest places."

Earlier in *Sister Outsider* Lorde celebrates her mother's silences: they gave her poetry. In the interview with Rich, she says she learned from her West Indian mother, who was obliged to speak to her children in a language not her own, the importance of communication "beneath language" and a nonrational way of thinking that she associates with her own poetry. In both "Poetry Is Not a Luxury" and the interview, Lorde identifies "the poet" as "the Black mother within each of us." Following these celebratory passages, the revelation about her mother's destructiveness in "Eye to Eye" comes as a shock, and Lorde attempts to compensate for it. "Eye to Eye" turns next to a series of tales of appalling violence against black mothers and children, placing them in solidarity with each other against the shared enemy, followed by a romanticized history of solidarity among black women in Africa: "We are African women and we know, in our blood's telling, the tenderness with which our foremothers held each other." These assurances, however, produce another turn of the emotional wheel, as Lorde laments the failure to live up to this heritage and narrates a series of stories about the intolerance of black women for each other and the self-hatred that fuels this hostility. The same sequence repeats itself a few pages later, when Lorde presents new evidence of her mother's internalized racism:

My mother taught me to survive at the same time as she taught me to fear my own Blackness. "Don't trust white people because they mean us no good and don't trust anyone darker than you because their hearts are as Black as their faces." (And where did that leave me, the darkest one?) It is painful even now to write it down.

(*Sister Outsider*, p. 165)

This passage is followed by another romanticized account of African women's bonding, and then in turn by an admission that "it had never happened for me."

A number of Lorde's African poems in *The Black Unicorn* and *Our Dead Behind Us* invoke the mythic powers of Dahomean and Yoruba mother goddesses and women warriors. "From the House of Yemanjá" transposing the situation of an all-powerful mother goddess into the speaker's own autobiography, generates something of the same feeling as the passages about mothers in "Eye to Eye." In the poem, the speaker alternates painfully between resenting the mother, "pale as a witch," for the

broken pot
where she hid out a perfect daughter
who was not me

and yearning for her breasts and bed, "hungry / for her eyes." There are two mothers in the poem, "one dark and rich" hidden inside the pale (racist?) one. (See Chinasole's probing discussion of the creative tension between mother and daughter in this poem and others and in *Zami*.) The last stanza begins with an incantatory repetition of the words "Mother I need . . . your blackness now," but the poem ends by turning back to a figure of necessary and perhaps racial separation,

the sharpened edge
where day and night shall meet
and not be
one.

This sense of separation between mother and daughter characterizes much of "Eye to Eye," yet that essay ends with a celebration of mothering and woman bonding, and the final essay in *Sister Outsider* makes restitution to Lorde's mother for the revelation of her betrayals. "Grenada Revisited: An Interim Report," written two months after the United States invasion in 1983, identifies the island as "my mother's birthplace." Lorde goes there in search of " 'home,' for . . . she had always defined it so for me." The essay here echoes the early sections of *Zami*, which poignantly detail the experience of growing up in a household in which "home" is Grenada and especially the mother's life among women there. Identified thus with Lorde's mother, Grenada is also in the essay the object of appalling imperialist aggression, economic as well as military, by a United States unable to tolerate Grenada's independence and economic success under Maurice Bishop. Lorde's mother may have responded to racism by inflicting it on her daughter, subjecting her, as in "Eye to Eye," to a guilt-ridden blame. But here, translated into the national body of Grenada itself, the victim of large-scale colonial aggression, Lorde's mother is idealized and placed beyond the possibility of personal reproach. Horizontal hostility gives way to a reassuring solidarity. As the essay draws to a close, Grenada is explicitly feminized—"I came . . . wanting to know she was still alive"—and once again associated directly with Lorde's mother:

She has [survived]. Grenada is bruised but very much alive. Grenadians are a warm and resilient people (I hear my mother's voice:

527

"Island women make good wives. Whatever happens, they've seen worse"), and they have survived colonizations before.

(*Sister Outsider*, p. 189)

With this ending, the book moves away from its preoccupation with "horizontal hostility," especially its painful manifestation as a mother's racism toward her daughter, toward the safer psychic and social ground of absolute villains and resilient, heroic victims. The ending heals the emotional rifts of earlier essays, but only at the price of invoking a greater pain.

Like *Sister Outsider*, *Zami* ends (as it begins) with Lorde's mother and with the evocation of motherhood enlarged into a mythological principle. After the Kitty/Afrekete episode, an epilogue names the different kinds of mothers who have shaped Lorde's life and writing, including her own mother's women relatives as well as the African mother goddesses who inform her poetry. The last line is a saying from her mother's country: "There it is said that the desire to lie with other women is a drive from the mother's blood." Moreover, as in other texts, *Zami* identifies poetry with the mother. An unnumbered chapter (between 3 and 4) entitled "How I Became a Poet" consists entirely of childhood memories of her mother. Lorde spells her name in various ways, but *Zami* seems to spell her truest and deepest name, for "Zami" means, in her mother's mother-tongue, "women who work together as friends and lovers." Lorde identifies her mother as the origin at once of her work (her poetry) and of her love of women.

Curiously, when Lorde writes that in her mother are the origins of her poetry, she emphasizes not her mother's use of language but her silence. Always negotiating in a foreign tongue, her mother uses language that is outside language, whether spoken or silent: Lorde tells Rich, "My mother had a strange way with words: if one didn't serve her or wasn't strong enough, she'd just make up another word, and then . . . woe betide any of us who forgot it. But I think I got another message from her. . . . that there was a whole powerful world of nonverbal communication and contact between people that was absolutely essential. . . . My mother

would expect me to know things, whether or not she spoke them." In *Zami*, despite her mother's power to evoke the sensual world of Grenada, that "truly private paradise of blugoe and breadfruit hanging from the trees, of nutmeg and lime and sapadilla," the meaning of the word *home* remains for the displaced family somewhere beyond language. Small, distant, and idyllic as Grenada is, there is a still smaller island off of Grenada where her mother spent the summers of her childhood: "She grew up dreaming of Carriacou as someday I was to dream of Grenada." Carriacou, an island so small it appeared in no atlas Lorde could find until she was twenty-six, remains for Lorde both home and center, and yet beyond geography and language: "*Home* was still a sweet place somewhere else which they had not managed to capture yet on paper, nor to throttle and bind up between the pages of a schoolbook." It is only in the language of this place, seemingly outside ordinary language, that Lorde can truly spell her name, for "Zami," as Lorde reveals in the epilogue, is a Carriacou term.

"How I Became a Poet" starts off with her mother's imaginative use of language, "full of picaresque constructions and surreal scenes" and of expressions from "home." But after half a page of examples the chapter turns to a sensual description of childhood intimacies with her mother's body apart from language: having her hair combed and braided while enjoying "the warm mother smell caught between her legs, and the intimacy of our physical touching." The child crawls into her mother's warm bed on Saturday mornings, enjoying her mother's "glycerine-flannel smell" and "the rounded swell of her stomach, silent and inviting touch." She plays with her mother's hot-water bottle and "quiet body," "[f]eeling the smooth deep firmness of her breasts against my shoulders, my pajama'd back, sometimes, more daringly, against my ears and the sides of my cheeks." Language enters the scene only when her mother says it's time to get up. Poetry, here, is linked to the mother's silence—her "quiet body"—more than to her speech.

It is in Lorde's lesbian love poetry that this preference for touch over ordinary speech, this heritage from the mother, lives on most vividly. Although the devaluation of language relative to other forms of expression may seem strange for a poet (nonverbal communication may be essential, but it is not poetry), the "mother's quiet body" surely inhabits the following lines from "Fog Report":

> when I am fingerprinted
> the taste of your thighs
> shows up
> outlined in the ink
> (*Black Unicorn*, p. 70)

Poetry is here the tactile experience of writing, not a record of speech (the mouth is for tasting), and writing becomes a residue of lovemaking. In "Recreation" lovemaking becomes a process of mutual and bodily writing:

> you create me against your thighs
> hilly with images
> moving through our word countries
> my body
> writes into your flesh
> the poem
> you make of me
> (*Black Unicorn*, p. 81)

Writing is distinctly tactile, and poetry a form of bodily pleasure.

The chapter immediately following "How I Became a Poet" in *Zami* depicts what could be called the narrator's first lesbian experience, and the narrative here continues to explore the relation between the lesbian heritage from the mother, silent touch, and poetry. From the silent sensuousness of reveling in her mother's body the five-year-old turns to sensual curiosity about a little girl she meets. Her first impulse is to touch the "delectable creature," her "soft velvet shoulders" and "the soft silky warmth" of her fur muff and pompom, which "made my fingers tingle." Few words are exchanged. The narrator sits Toni on her knee, rocks her (feeling "the creeping warmth of her, slowly spreading all along the front of my body"), and begins to undress her ("Was her bottom going to be real and warm or turn out to be hard rubber, molded

into a little crease like the ultimately disappointing Coca-Cola doll?") when her mother appears and interrupts.

Erotic as it is, this episode is also a scene of artistic creation, even more explicitly so than those in "How I Became a Poet." The chapter begins with the narrator's memories of imagining a little sister to play with, and of making and painting flour-and-water figures that she hoped would come alive. She stresses her desire that such a playmate would be entirely under her control, no longer than the palm of her hand. When she sees the beautiful Toni, "[m]y lifelong dream of a doll-baby come to life had in fact come true." The narrator quickly meditates strategies for keeping her all to herself, and she handles Toni as if she were a toy or a pet, to be manipulated and possessed. The episode reenacts the myth of Pygmalion, a paradigm for male-defined romantic art in which subjectivity belongs to the artist and his beloved creation is only a passive object, under his control.

The episode suggests, frankly and perplexingly, that the erotic and poetic heritage from the "mother's quiet body" differs little from the most traditional forms of objectification and exploitation of women by men. Some of Lorde's early love poetry also betrays this bias. The baffled editor who asked, after reading the explicitly lesbian "Love Poem" (1971), "Are you supposed to be a man?" was perhaps responding to the conventionally gender-marked language in lines such as the following: "And I knew when I entered her I was / high wind in her forests hollow." The "I" is the agent, associated with the wind or breath of life spirit, while the beloved is the passive receptacle, figured as earthly nature. That the partners are lesbian does not alter the conventional male-female roles the figurative language confers on them.

Soon, however, the figurative associations of the two lovers become more reciprocal:

> honey flowed
> from the split cup
> impaled on a lance of tongues
> on the tips of her breasts on her navel
> (*Chosen Poems*, p. 77)

Here, the "cup" and phallic "lance" could belong to either partner, and the "lance" is explicitly the beloved's when it becomes "the tips of her breasts." Even more complexly, "Fog Report" and "Recreation" struggle against the impulse to objectify the beloved, by giving up traditional metaphors of sexual activity and passivity (such as lance and cup) and by making the process of writing and lovemaking intersubjective. In the lines quoted above from "Recreation" ("you create me ... my body writes") each lover makes of the other a poem and each acts upon the other erotically. The poems advance beyond erotic and poetic objectification to value the promise of equality and mutuality between lesbian lovers. Later in *Zami*, in contrast to the episode with Toni, Lorde writes of refusing to choose the role of femme or butch in a lesbian culture that, in the 1950s, demanded such a choice. There is something about the mother's heritage of lesbian touch, as Lorde evokes it, that resists cultural imperatives to relations of domination and subordination.

Lorde's resistance to objectifying others is of course most visible in her writings on difference, in which different places, social groups, or parts of her identity are scrupulously given equal weight and value, invited (with a metaphor of touch) to "join hands" in a relation of "mutual (nondominant) differences" and prohibited from usurping the position of exclusive subjectivity or power. In later poems such as "On My Way Out I Passed Over You and the Verrazano Bridge" Lorde explores the political implications of lesbian love and proposes love between women as a model for coalition-building across differences:

> And I dream of our coming together
> encircled driven
> not only by love
> but by lust for a working tomorrow
> (*Our Dead*, p. 57)

In an interview on lesbian sadomasochism (reprinted in *A Burst of Light*) she says that it "feeds the belief that domination is inevitable and legitimately enjoyable," and she criticizes claims for its legitimacy made on the (for her) inadmissible grounds that "sexuality is separate from living." The stakes are political in love, and love must enact our dreams of cooperation.

Lorde's emphasis on mutuality—poetic, erotic, and political—and her refusal to claim the center were perhaps her most important inheritances from her mother, whose strength and whose expressive touch is represented as deriving from her cultural dislocation. Living in two places at once (and thus nowhere) and speaking two languages (and therefore none), Lorde's mother had a power of resistance in racist New York that came from her having been moved off center, from transferring the values and the language of Carriacou to the hostile streets of New York. And the sheer power of her maternal, bodily presence came from her resolutely continuing the line of her independent Carriacou foremothers in the white- and male-dominated North. Or so it appeared to the young Audre—and so for Lorde the adult writer power came not from commanding the center but from an endless displacement of the center, a multiplication of cross-cultural selves. She refused to objectify others, and she resisted others' definitions of her, whether as good daughter, black, lesbian, poet, teacher, mother, or cancer patient. From the "mother's quiet body" came the multiplicity of her identities and her affiliations. This was her struggle and her gift.

Selected Bibliography

PRIMARY WORKS

POETRY

The First Cities. London: Poet's Press, 1968.
Cables to Rage. London: Paul Bremen, 1970.
From a Land Where Other People Live. Detroit: Broadside Press, 1973.
New York Head Shop and Museum. Detroit: Broadside Press, 1975.
Between Ourselves. Point Reyes, Calif.: Eidolon Editions, 1976.
Coal. New York: Norton, 1976.
The Black Unicorn. New York: Norton, 1978.
Chosen Poems, Old and New. New York: Norton, 1982.
Our Dead Behind Us. New York: Norton, 1986.

The Marvelous Arithmetics of Distance. New York: Norton, 1993.

PROSE, ESSAYS, JOURNALS

The Cancer Journals. Argyle, N.Y.: Spinsters, Ink, 1980.
Zami: A New Spelling of My Name. Trumansburg, N.Y.: Crossing Press, 1982.
Sister Outsider. Trumansburg, N.Y.: Crossing Press, 1984.
"My Words Will Be There." *Black Women Writers (1950–1980): A Critical Evaluation.* Edited by Mari Evans. Garden City, N.Y.: Anchor/Doubleday, 1984. Pp. 261–68.
A Burst of Light. Ithaca, N.Y.: Firebrand Books, 1988.

SPEECHES

"Sisterhood and Survival." Conference keynote address, The Black Women Writer and the Diaspora. *The Black Scholar* 17:5–7, 1988.
"A Question of Survival." Commencement speech, Oberlin College. May 1989. *Gay Community News,* August 13–19, 1989. Pp. 5, 12.

COLLECTED WORKS

"Audre Lorde: A Special Selection." *Callaloo* 14, no. 1:39–95. (Winter 1991).
The Audre Lorde Compendium: Essays, Speeches, and Journals. London: Pandora, 1996.
The Collected Poems of Audre Lorde. New York: Norton, 1997.

SECONDARY WORKS

BIOGRAPHICAL AND CRITICAL STUDIES

Alexander, Elizabeth. " 'Coming Out Blackened and Whole': Fragmentation and Reintegration in Audre Lorde's *Zami* and *The Cancer Journals.*" *American Literary History* 6, no. 4:695–715 (Winter 1994).
Annas, Pamela. "A Poetry of Survival: Unnaming and Renaming in the Poetry of Audre Lorde, Pat Parker, Sylvia Plath, and Adrienne Rich." *Colby Library Quarterly* 18:9–25 (1982).
Avi-ram, Amitai F. "*Apo Koinou* in Audre Lorde and the Moderns: Defining the Differences." *Callaloo* 9, no. 1:193–208 (Winter 1986).
Birkle, Carmen. *Women's Stories of the Looking Glass: Autobiographical Reflections and Self-Representations in the Poetry of Sylvia Plath, Adrienne Rich, and Audre Lorde.* Munich: W. Fink, 1996.
Brooks, Jerome. "In the Name of the Father: The Poetry of Audre Lorde." In *Black Women Writers (1950–1980): A Critical Evaluation.* Edited by Mari Evans. Garden City, N.Y.: Anchor/Doubleday, 1984. Pp. 269–76.
Carlston, Erin G. "*Zami* and the Politics of Plural Identity." In *Sexual Practice/Textual Theory: Lesbian Cultural Criticism.* Edited by Susan J. Wolfe and Julia Penelope. Cambridge, Mass.: Blackwell, 1993. Pp. 226–36.

Carr, Brenda. " 'A Woman Speaks . . . I Am Woman and Not White': Politics of Voice, Tactical Essentialism, and Cultural Intervention in Audre Lorde's Activist Poetics and Practice." In *Race-ing Representation: Voice, History, and Sexuality.* Edited by Kostas Myrsiades and Linda Myrsiades. Lanham, Md.: Rowman & Littlefield, 1998. Pp. 119–40.
Carruthers, Mary J. "The Re-Vision of the Muse: Adrienne Rich, Audre Lorde, Judy Grahn, Olga Broumas." *Hudson Review* 36:293–322 (1983).
Chinosole. "Audre Lorde and Matrilineal Diaspora: 'moving history beyond nightmare into structures for the future . . .' " In *Wild Women in the Whirlwind: Afro-American Culture and the Contemporary Literary Renaissance.* Edited by Joanne M. Braxton and Andrée Nicola McLaughlin. New Brunswick, N.J.: Rutgers University Press, 1990. Pp. 379–94.
Christian, Barbara. "The Dynamics of Difference: Review of Audre Lorde's *Sister Outsider.*" In her *Black Feminist Criticism: Perspectives on Black Women Writers.* New York: Pergamon Press, 1985. Pp. 205–10.
DeHernandez, Jennifer Browdy. "Mothering the Self: Writing the Lesbian Sublime in Audre Lorde's *Zami* and Gloria Anzaldúa's *Borderlands/La Frontera.*" In *Other Sisterhoods: Literary Theory and U.S. Women of Color.* Edited by Sandra Kumamoto Stanley. Urbana: University of Illinois Press, 1998. Pp. 244–62.
Dhairyam, Sagri. " 'Artifacts for Survival': Remapping the Contours of Poetry with Audre Lorde." *Feminist Studies* 18, no. 2:229–56 (Summer 1992).
Gillan, Jennifer. "Relocating and Identity in *Zami: A New Spelling of My Name.*" In *Homemaking: Women Writers and the Politics of Home.* Edited by Catherine Wiley and Fiona R. Barnes. New York: Garland, 1996. Pp. 209–21.
Hull, Gloria T. "Living on the Line: Andre Lorde and *Our Dead Behind U.*" In *Changing Our Own Words: Essays on Criticism, Theory, and Writings by Black Women.* Edited by Cheryl A. Wall. New Brunswick, N.J.: Rutgers University Press, 1989. Pp. 150–72.
Keating, Ana Louise. "(De)Centering the Margins? Identity Politics and Tactical (Re)Naming." In *Other Sisterhoods: Literary Theory and U.S. Women of Color.* Edited by Sandra Kumamoto Stanley. Urbana: University of Illinois Press, 1998. Pp. 23–43.
———. *Women Reading Women Writing: Self-Invention in Paula Gunn Allen, Gloria Anzaldúa, and Audre Lorde.* Philadelphia: Temple University Press, 1996.
Kimmich, Allison. "Writing the Body: From Abject to Subject." *A/B: Auto/Biography Studies* 13, no. 2: 223–34 (Fall 1998).
King, Katie. "Audre Lorde's Lacquered Layerings: The Lesbian Bar as a Site of Literary Production." In *New Lesbian Criticism: Literary and Cultural Readings.* Edited by Sally Munt. New York: Columbia University Press, 1992. Pp. 51–74.
Lauter, Estella. "Re-Visioning Creativity: Audre Lorde's Refiguration of Eros as the Black Mother Within." In

Writing the Woman Artist: Essays on Poetics, Politics, and Portraiture. Edited by Suzanne W. Jones. Philadelphia: University of Pennsylvania Press, 1991. Pp. 398–418.

A Litany for Survival: The Life and Work of Audre Lorde. Videotape. Directed by Ada Gay Griffin and Michelle Parkerson. New York: Third World Newsreel, 1996.

Martin, Joan. "The Unicorn Is Black: Audre Lorde in Retrospect." In *Black Women Writers (1950–1980): A Critical Evaluation.* Edited by Mari Evans. Garden City, N.Y.: Anchor/Doubleday, 1984. Pp. 277–91.

Perreault, Jeanne Martha. *Writing Selves: Contemporary Feminist Autography.* Minneapolis: University of Minnesota Press, 1995.

Provost, Kara. "Becoming Afrekete: The Trickster in the Work of Audre Lorde." *MELUS* 20, no. 4:45–59 (Winter 1995).

Smith, Barbara. "The Truth That Never Hurts: Black Lesbians in Fiction in the 1980s." In *Feminisms: An Anthology of Literary Theory and Criticism.* Edited by Robyn R. Warhol and Diane Price Herndl. New Brunswick, N.J.: Rutgers University Press, 1997. Pp. 784–806.

Thomson, Rosemarie Garland. "Disabled Women as Powerful Women in Petry, Morrison, and Lorde: Revising Black Female Subjectivity." In *The Body and Physical Difference: Discourses of Disability.* Edited by David T. Mitchell and Sharon L. Snyder. Ann Arbor: University of Michigan Press, 1997. Pp. 240–66.

Wilson, Anna. "Rites/Rights of Canonization: Audre Lorde as Icon." In *Women Poets of the Americas: Toward a Pan-American Gathering.* Edited by Jacqueline Vaught Brogan and Cordelia Chávez Candelaria. Notre Dame: University of Notre Dame Press, 1999. Pp. 17–33.

INTERVIEWS

Abod, Jennifer, and Angela Brown. "A Radio Profile of Audre Lorde." Audio tape. Cambridge, Mass.: Profile Productions, 1988.

Bowles, Juliette, ed. *In the Memory and Spirit of Frances, Zora, and Lorraine: Essays and Interviews on Black Women and Writing.* Washington, D.C.: Institute for the Arts and the Humanities, Howard University, 1979. Pp. 11–22.

Hammond, Karla. "Audre Lorde: Interview." *Denver Quarterly* 16:10–27 (Spring 1981).

Rowell, Charles H. "Above the Wind: An Interview with Audre Lorde." *Callaloo* 14, no. 1:83–95 (Winter 1991).

Tate, Claudia, ed. *Black Women Writers at Work.* New York: Continuum, 1983. Pp. 100–16.

Winter, Nina. "On Audre Lorde" and "Audre Lorde." In *Interview with the Muse: Remarkable Women Speak on Creativity and Power.* Berkeley, Calif.: Moon Books, 1978. Pp. 72–81.

—The essay and bibliography have been updated for this edition by Norman W. Jones.

CLARENCE MAJOR
(1936–   )

BRENT HAYES EDWARDS

SINCE THE 1960s, Clarence Major has established himself as one of the most important innovative writers in the United States, through an extraordinarily prolific artistic output that has been as varied as it has been iconoclastic. While Major has produced significant bodies of work as a novelist, poet, painter, anthologist, critic, and lexicographer, he is particularly respected for a series of novels in the 1970s that extended the possibilities of African American fiction beyond the constraints of the naturalistic protest novel. In a 1973 interview, he told John O'Brien that in a novel, "the only thing you really have is words. You begin with words and you end with words. The content exists in our minds. I don't think that it has to be a reflection of anything. It is reality that has been created inside of a book." In Major's view, in other words, the task of literature is not to reflect historical events or social situations in the outside world. Instead, literature is an art that creates a reality "inside of a book," as a systematic and self-conscious construction that the reader experiences in language. Some critics have characterized this position by naming Major's novels "postmodern," "avant-garde," or "metafiction," but Major himself has continually resisted the categorization of his work, reminding interviewers such as Doug Bolling in 1979 that Major's project may be best described as one of "renaming realism"—reconceptual-

izing the creative process to capture in art the complexity, contingency, and fragmentation of life. Major has never considered this endeavor to be limited to literature: thus, in a 1977 interview with the painter Jacob Lawrence, Major told the artist: "Like certain experimental writers, you have, in your own medium, discovered a stronger sense of realism, in the truest sense of that word. You've done this by not trying to create the *illusion* of so-called reality. Instead, the surface, the design creates its own reality."

Early Life

Clarence Major was born on December 31, 1936 in Atlanta, Georgia to Clarence and Inez Huff Major. After his parents divorced in the 1940s, Major moved with his mother and younger sister to Chicago, although he returned often during his childhood for summer visits with his father and grandparents. By the age of 12, he was beginning to write stories and poems and also reading voraciously the works of European authors such as Raymond Radiguet, Arthur Rimbaud, and Joseph Conrad, as well as African American writers such as Richard Wright and Chester Himes. He took private art lessons from Chicago painter Gus Hall and commented in a 1989 autobiographical essay, "Necessary Distance," that "confidence in an ability to express myself *visually* came first," although for Major the impulse to write and the impulse to paint were "always inseparable." In 1994, Major told Larry McCaffery that he considered himself a "visual thinker," making "connections between things more on the basis of visual associations than verbal or logical ones." Even in his juvenile attempts at creative expression, Major evidenced a predilection for artistic form and innovation, finding himself more "fascinated with technique—in painting and in writing—than I was by subject matter. The subject of a novel or a painting seemed irrelevant. . . . What did matter was *how* the painter or storyteller or poet had seduced me into the story, into the picture, into the poem." Major won a Raymond Scholarship to attend sketch and lecture classes at the Art Institute of Chicago when he was seventeen years old, and he continued there until he entered the U.S. Air Force in 1955. Still, he began to concentrate his energies in writing and found time to self-produce a small chapbook of his poems called *The Fires That Burn in Heaven,* which he presented to friends and family in 1954.

In 1957, after his stint in the military, Major returned to Chicago and set out to immerse himself in the city's burgeoning artistic scene. He met the poet Marvin Bell, the painter Archibald Motley and his brother, the novelist Willard Motley, and musicians such as the legendary jazz pianist Lil Hardin Armstrong, who sometimes invited Major and his young friends over to her house to listen to old recordings. He also got married, and fathered two sons, Aaron and Darrell. Major published his first short story in the journal *Olivant* in 1957 and decided to found his own journal, *Coercion,* which ran from 1958 to 1961. As editor, Major published the work of writers including Henry Miller, Lawrence Ferlinghetti, and Kenneth Patchen, and the journal brought him into correspondence with a number of the leading literary lights of the period.

The 1960s

Major moved in 1962 to Omaha, Nebraska, where he worked as a welder and a crane driver to support himself while continuing to write. His first marriage fell apart in 1964, with his sons remaining in Chicago with his former wife; in another ill-fated relationship, he fathered four more children (Serena, Inger, Clarence, and Angela) in the 1960s. In Omaha, Major put out two small poetry collections, while beginning to publish extensively in a number of journals, particularly Walt Shepperd's *Nickel Review.* But his first real prominence in the literary world occurred after he decided to move to New York's Lower East Side in 1966.

In New York, Major found work teaching creative writing at the New Lincoln School in Harlem and at Macomb's Junior High School; he edited anthologies of his students' work in 1967 and 1968. He also worked as a research analyst for the Simulmatics Corporation, studying the reaction of local communities to media coverage of the race riots that tore through the urban United States during that period. While conducting interviews in Detroit and Milwaukee, he produced "Gasoline and Shit," an unpublished sixty-five-page meditation on the riots. Although it would take him three more years to find a publisher, Major had written most of his first important collection of poems, *Swallow the Lake,* by 1967. Many of the poems in the book were culled from periodical publications and two small Coercion Press editions from the mid 1960s. Major became friendly with a number of the artists active in the downtown New York scene in the late 1960s and early 1970s, including the poet Art Berger and the novelists John A. Williams, Quincy Troupe, Steve Cannon, and Ishmael Reed. Toward the end of the decade, he began to teach at universities in the metropolitan area, working at Brooklyn College in 1968–1969 and again in early 1970s and later at Sarah Lawrence College.

In 1969 came two breakthrough publications. First, at the instigation of his friend and mentor Walter Lowenfels, Major assembled *The New Black Poetry,* which came to be one of the most-respected anthologies of poetry published in the renaissance of African American writing in the 1960s. He had published a much-reprinted essay called "Black Criteria" in the *Journal of Black Poetry* in 1967 that was often cited as one of the most eloquent examples of black nationalist criticism, calling for artistic expression to be relevant to the struggles of African Americans for civil rights. In the introduction to *The New Black Poetry*, Major seemed to continue in this vein, writing of the need for a "radical black aesthetic" to take its "impetus in Afro-American nationalism" and proclaiming the "importance of culture—or specifically poetry—in black self-determination." And yet, as Major himself subsequently pointed out, although some poems are militant in tone, the anthology as a whole tends to resist any easy categorization, daringly placing experimental writers such as Russell Atkins, Bob Kaufman, N. H. Pritchard, and Ishmael Reed next to more nationalist writers such as Ed Bullins, Don L. Lee, Larry Neal, and LeRoi Jones (Amiri Baraka). Unlike some of its more strident shelf companions, *The New Black Poetry* also gave significant space to some of the important female poets of the period, including Audre Lorde, Julia Fields, Nikki Giovanni, and Sonia Sanchez. Later, Major would clarify his early resistance to what he considered to be the inadequacy of a nationalist "black aesthetic" that would constrain or prescript an individual artist's expression. He commented in a 1969 interview collected in *The Dark and Feeling*:

I've had to come to realize that the question of a black aesthetic is something that really comes down to an individual question. It seems to me that if there is a premise in an artist's work, be he black or white, that it comes out of his work, and therefore out of himself. Or herself. I think that it's also true with *form*. It has to be just that subjective.

Also in 1969, Major's first novel, *All-Night Visitors*, which he completed during a visit to Mexico in 1967 and referred to as his "epic collage poem," was finally accepted for publication by Maurice Girodias' legendary Olympia Press. Girodias had a long history of publishing experimental and erotically daring works by authors such as Henry Miller, Jean Genet, William S. Burroughs, and Chester Himes. But Major's entry into publication was ambivalent at

best since the press forced him to make substantial cuts in the original manuscript, emphasizing its more explicit sexual passages at the expense of its broader narrative scope. Still, *All-Night Visitors* garnered a good deal of praise and controversy for its vivid descriptions of the ordeals of Eli Bolton, a young black man in Chicago and New York trying to sort through what he calls "the jigsaw puzzle of my heritage" while he drifts through a series of tortured and sometimes abusive relationships.

Eli's quest to understand himself and his place in the world introduces one of the main recurring themes of Major's work. Much of Major's writing echoes with the suggestion in *All-Night Visitors* that any solution to the "huge mystery" of Eli's identity, and to what Eli describes as "the deep, elusive, seeming unjustness and enigma of my immediate familial and lineal history" as an orphan and war veteran, must begin with what is most material: using the blunt force and appetites of his physical existence to begin to make sense of the world around him. Eli rejects any reading of him as a figure in a metaphorical quest, insisting that "this thing that I am, this body—it is me. *I* am it. I am not a concept in your mind, whoever you are! I am *here,* right here, myself, MYSELF . . . I am not *your idea.*" This physical imperative leads to the book's endlessly inventive, self-involved, even baroque fascination with sex. When Eli says that "very early I began furiously to probe anything—method, technique, science, religion—I could come by, searching for clues to the meaning and reality of myself on earth," Major expects the reader to take the word "probe" quite literally. As Eli comments while receiving oral sex from Tammy in the scene that opens the novel:

I realize that I am simply evading so many things by lying around all day like this, letting her play with my dick, sit on my lap, suck it, get down on her knees, upside down, backwards, any way you can think of. I can do nothing else right now. My dick is my life, it has to be. Cathy certainly won't ever come back. I've stopped thinking about the possibility. Eunice has of course gone away to

Harvard, and I'm taking it in stride. My black ramrod *is* me, any man's rod is himself.

Many of the reviewers of *All-Night Visitors* understandably read it simply as a provocation, a phallocentric tour de force—a black man's answer to Henry Miller, as some critics put it. The Olympia Press edition incited a good deal of controversy, with the novel castigated either by feminist critics who found Major's depictions of Eli's long list of female lovers (Tammy, Clara, Hilda, Anita, Linda, Eunice, Cathy) to be troublingly one-dimensional or by black critics who argued that the book reinforced stereotypes of African American men as oversexed primitives. More recently, readers have begun to appreciate the complexity of Major's accomplishment, especially since an unexpurgated edition of the novel (nearly twice as long as the original edition) was published in 1998 by Northeastern University Press. Given that the late 1960s and early 1970s saw a wealth of erotically charged satirical novels by black male writers, some at least as explicit as *All-Night Visitors* (for example, Steve Cannon's 1969 *Groove, Bang, and Jive Around*, Cecil Brown's 1969 *The Life and Loves of Mr. Jiveass Nigger*, and Samuel Delany's 1973 *Tides of Lust*), it has become apparent that the originality of *All-Night Visitors* lies not only in its sexual inventions. In his 1973 interview with John O'Brien, Major explained that he wanted to create the impression that the series of "short broken chapters, little twisted episodes" were a "nightmare in which a whole series of strange things happen." The new edition, restoring virtuosic sections such as "Hilda and Anita" and "Hitting the Apple," foregrounds the inventive rush of Major's prose, which portrays Eli's confused sense of his world through an impressionistic and sometimes surreal crush of images, encounters, dreams, and hallucinations. The disturbing violence in the novel, as in the section "Grunts," where Eli comes across two fellow infantrymen viciously raping and killing a young Vietnamese girl, is a reminder of Major's contention, as he explained in a 1984 essay titled "The Erotic Facts of Life," that "an acceptance of the reality of death and the non-rational vi-olence that permeates eating or love-making is the most profound act giving life a sharp edge of meaning and vitality." In the ending of the restored edition, as in the original, Eli reaches a kind of maturity in deciding to respond to the violence around him when he offers his apartment to a Puerto Rican neighbor with seven children and an abusive husband. Eli feels himself "vibrantly alive" when he realizes that "I could not rationalize my way out of my human responsibility to those ageless sounds of pain that were expropriating this mother from a kind of blemished but necessary social security, the tangible reality of herself simply in the world. *Her* dispossession was my responsibility. . . . I was no victim of complete inner blindness, subjective corruption."

The 1970s

In 1970, Major published the *Dictionary of Afro-American Slang*, a reference compendium of black vernacular speech etymology and usage. Some critics have considered this lexicographical work a departure, since with the exception of *Such Was the Season*, Major's novels are not in the main concerned with a conscious attempt to transcribe the spoken black vernacular (unlike works by other African American writers such as Langston Hughes, Sterling Brown, Zora Neale Hurston, Gloria Naylor, and Gayl Jones). Yet Major himself not only takes great pleasure in his etymological research but also seems to find resonance between it and his creative work, especially in a formal sense. In the preface to the significantly expanded version of the dictionary he published in 1994, retitled *Juba to Jive: A Dictionary of African-American Slang*, Major notes an impulse in slang language that is reminiscent of his own formal experimentation with novelistic form:

I would go so far as to say that *all* alive art is rebellious, and *all* alive speech, slang or otherwise, is rebellious, rebellious in the healthy sense that they challenge the stale and the conventional. . . . African-American slang cuts through logic and arrives at a quick, efficient, interpretative solution to situations and things otherwise difficult to articulate.

The early 1970s brought an astounding succession of poetic output as well. In 1971, a slim volume of poems titled *Private Line* was released in London, and *Symptoms and Madness* was published to a warm reception in New York by Corinth Books, an important imprint that had previously published works by Amiri Baraka, Al Young, Charles Olson, John Ashberry, and Frank O'Hara. *The Cotton Club* was published in 1972 by Dudley Randall's Broadside Press, one of the most-respected black small presses in the country, and *The Syncopated Cakewalk* appeared from a small New York house in 1974 (in 1976, Major would be awarded a Pushcart Prize for the poem "Funeral" in this collection). Major's voice as a poet developed with astonishingly rapidity during this period, from the often willfully obscure and syntactically twisted verses of *Swallow the Lake* to the simple pain of "Funeral," about a boy mourning his father's death, to the jive popular culture signifying of "The Syncopated Cakewalk" to the poems that echo the concerns of his fiction, such as "Words into Words Won't Go" and "Doodle," about a poem that will not behave:

> The girls scream when he suddenly
> takes out his tiny notebook. He reads:
> 'I am a frog with bat wings.
> I want to eat cars on the freeway.
> I want to stroke my mother's butter.'
> Look, go stand in the corner—
> and write a hundred times:
> 'I will understand what it means to be a
>   poem.'

Major continued to write fiction but was attempting to produce high-quality work in both genres and investigating what he had considered from his first attempts at writing as the artificial divisions between them. In a "Self-Interview," collected in *The Dark and Feeling*, Major wrote:

> The distinction I had made all along between poetry and prose I gradually realized

was and had been a serious trap. . . . I came to see that what I had been trying to do in making a novel was the same thing I meant to do in producing a poem: to invest the work with a *secret nature* so powerful that, while it should fascinate, it should always elude the reader—just as the nature of life does.

Major's second novel, *NO*, the majority of which had been written in the summer of 1969, was published in 1973 by a small black publishing house, Emerson Hall, and met a disappointingly small reception. *NO* represents an extension of many of the concerns of *All-Night Visitors* while integrating some of the formal invention of the poetry, with its jagged interwoven sections of text of different type sizes, indented and spaced in complex unconventional arrangements. As in *All-Night Visitors*, the central character is a young black man, Moses Westby, striving to discover his sense of identity. But *NO* leaves that quest much more open, as it shuttles between the story of a young Moses (sometimes called Junebug), growing up in a rural black community, and an adult Moses, who may be the father of the first and who, in the main trauma of the novel, shoots his wife, daughter, son, and himself in a raging determination that, as he puts it, "I ain't going to see you suffer no more."

In *NO*, the quest for identity is represented as a desire to escape from the "prison" of one's background and surroundings. The adult Moses is sometimes called "the guard," while the young protagonist calls himself "the inspector," as he strains to detect a means of exit. "I didn't realize," he says, "that I was really trying to crash out of a sort of penal system in which I was born and grew up. . . . It wasn't really a prison except in an abstract social sense and also in a very personal sense. In truth no one ever really could point out where it began or ended, and it wasn't limited to one country." Moses describes himself as drifting, seeking to come to peace with himself, looking for a place "in which I might feel a certain degree of comfort," but suspecting increasingly that he "somehow was suspended in a kind of pivot between the two, consciousness and unconsciousness. I felt like a creature unable to sleep *and*, at the same time, unable to wake." The novel wanders through strange visions, as when in one erotic encounter, a blue butterfly emerges from a girl's vagina as Moses is entangled in her arms; in another scene, a woman comes out of a toilet bowl and takes the adult Moses into a spaceship. As Major later explained to John O'Brien, he was attempting in the novel "not only to construct a chronological story but one that was psychologically unrestricted by time"; the scenes shift without warning from the rural South to New York, from what seems to be the 1920s to what seems to be the 1970s. The narrator even invites the reader's suspicion, commenting: "Some of you don't trust nor believe in the reality of the 'I.' I know. . . . But I don't really care. Simply trying to get myself together, maybe even one day get *out*side."

Like Eli in *All-Night Visitors*, Moses finally achieves a kind of provisional ethical sense of self—at least a "very necessary . . . vision of how *naked* my presence in the world really is. How absolutely unsafe I'll always be"—when he travels with his wife, Oni, to Latin America. In an unnamed country, one day he jumps over the fence of a bullring in the middle of a bullfight, alarming the spectators, the matadors, and the banderilleros but driven to a risky abandon in his desperation. As he makes his way cautiously toward the bleeding and angry animal, Moses decides:

> [I]f I could touch the bull's head, and survive such a feat, life, from this perhaps unworthy moment, would be invested with essence. In other words I had to give meaning to it and it had to contain courage. And at the same time I argued with the shallowness of it. With myself—with being. . . . He was bleeding and sweating and half dead *but* I touched his head and in a strange and beautiful way that single act became for me a living symbol of my own human freedom.

In the glow of that odd epiphany, Moses leaves Oni and returns to the United States at the end of the novel for what he hopes will be a "new beginning."

After a poetry reading in Connecticut in February 1972 provoked some readers to contend vehemently in the local media that Major's writing was "obscene" and "pornographic," Major responded with an "Open Letter to June Jordan" (an African American writer who had faced similar charges) in the August–September 1973 issue of the *American Poetry Review*, decrying the dangers of censorship. The article was so well received that Major was named a contributing editor to the *American Poetry Review*, composing almost a dozen "Open Letter" columns between 1973 and 1976. These essays covered a wide range of subjects and afforded Major a prominent mainstream venue for his criticism. One letter recounts Major's trip to Yugoslavia for an international poetry conference in 1975, where he met the Senegalese poet Léopold Sédar Senghor; others are meditations on the work of Claude McKay and Willard Motley; still others are reviews of new novels by Jonathan Baumbach, Jerome Charyn, and the just-formed Fiction Collective; and one is an open letter to his creative-writing students on the formal parallels between poetry and painting. The most substantial of the columns focused on "Experimental Fiction by Black American Writers," in which Major claimed a tradition of black literary innovation going back fifty years, which he termed the "black literature of departure." Major argued that there was a line of writers, from Jean Toomer to Zora Neale Hurston, Charles Wright, and Ishmael Reed, whose work spins away from the main body of African American fiction, departing from "subjects involving the racial plight of Black people," as well as from "naturalistic and realistic or deterministic forms" inherited from the mainstream western literary tradition. In 1974, Major collected his criticism in *The Dark and Feeling*, which gathered articles he had written over the past twenty years, mainly for *Essence* magazine and the *Nickel Review*, and also collected a variety of reviews, manifestos (including "Black Criteria" and the "Open Letter" to Jordan), and interviews.

Fiction Collective

In *NO*, Moses wonders at one point: "There's some promise that wasn't fulfilled. But what promise? And why does it necessarily still exist? Can it be moved? Can I stop asking questions? Should questions themselves stop forming?" This kind of interruptive self-questioning becomes the basis of the formal experimentation that drives what most critics consider to be Major's most significant novels, *Reflex and Bone Structure* and *Emergency Exit*. The former marked Major's entry into the Fiction Collective, a group of experimental writers including Ronald Sukenick, Jonathan Baumbach, Peter Spielberg, and Raymond Federman, some of whom Major had met a few years earlier at Brooklyn College. Dissatisfied with the limited opportunities for publishing innovative fiction in the climate of the 1970s, the collective had come together to edit and publish each other's work themselves, in a unique arrangement with a well-known distributor. As Major described it later in an autobiographical essay called "Licking Stamps, Taking Chances," "Painters had formed collectives for years and I was attracted to the idea of writers of fiction doing the same thing."

Reflex and Bone Structure, published in 1975, had been written for the most part over a seven-month period in 1970; in a 1978 interview, Major told Jerome Klinkowitz that up to that point in his career, it was "the most necessary book for me to write" because it "saved me from a great deal of misery and uncertainty and unhappiness and so forth." Discussing the category of experimental American fiction, including early Fiction Collective publications such as Baumbach's *Reruns*, Sukenick's *98.6*, Federman's *Take It or Leave It*, and Major's *Reflex and Bone Structure*, as well as other innovative fiction by authors including Charles Wright and Walter Abish, Major pointed out in a 1979 conversation with Doug Bolling that these authors tend "to minimize *representational effects* in their fictions. They abstract enough of the recognizable in the interest of putting together fictions that, in their various ways, take a unique place in the world as ob-jects through which the reader can have an experience rather than an (ill-conceived) reflection of life." As Major noted, such writing embodies literary experimentation in at least two senses. On the one hand, it insists on the impossibility of capturing life with a system of linguistic representation: "Life *can't* be reflected." The work of fiction, then, "primarily offers a *text* that can be *read* in relation to real experience. It is legitimately a reading experience that allows the reader *to think* and *to imagine* certain possibilities or impossibilities." Thus, *Reflex and Bone Structure* constantly reminds the reader of its inability to capture the world, a message stressed even in the book's epigraph: "This book is an extension of, not a duplication of reality. The characters and events are happening for the first time." At the same time, fiction strives to discover, often *through* fragmentation and digression, new models of representation that will be both self-reflexive about their limitations and also, it is hoped, closer to the complexity of experience. For many of these authors, Major points out, "language itself is often the chief antagonist since many of these writers wish to renew it, reform it, make it work in a new, more effective manner in order to unearth stronger, richer, deeper impressions of and extensions of life itself."

In *Reflex and Bone Structure*, Major, like his contemporaries Ishmael Reed and Samuel Delany, adopts a staple of genre fiction, here the detective novel in particular, as the foundation of his experimentation. He explained to Klinkowitz, "I set out with the notion of doing a mystery novel, not in the traditional sense, but taking the whole idea of mystery." What little plot there is in a conventional sense revolves around Cora Hull, an actress, and her three lovers, who are competing for her attentions: Canada, Dale, and the narrator himself. On the first page, with a single isolated sentence, the novel announces an apparent crime ("The scattered pieces of the bodies were found"), although it is unclear exactly who has been killed and how. Like many of the Fiction Collective novels, *Reflex and Bone Structure* is in the end most concerned with the way a narrator constructs fictional representation, controls and manages a text, while it continually threatens to digress, run on, or hit a dead end. The narrator keeps intruding on scenes in the novel (sometimes to great comic effect), asserting his presence and mastery of the novel's progress: "I'll make up everything from now on. If I want a commercial airline to crash with Cora and Dale on it doing it in the dark, I'll do that. Or have them go down at sea in a steamer caught in a violent typhoon near Iceland, or in an exploration vessel off the West Indies. I'll do anything I like. I'm extending reality, not retelling it."

And yet the narrator is constantly encountering difficulties, obstacles to his construction. Cora herself resists being narrated, just as she sometimes resists the narrator's romantic advances and mercilessly teases him: "You can't keep your mind off me," she cajoles at one point. Later, after having sex with the narrator, she tells him, "This book you're writing isn't nearly as strange as reality. The only way you're going to make any sense is to stick with the impossible. Any resemblance to the past or present should be purely accidental. . . . You'll have to keep making up the most impossible events you can think of to hold my interest." The narrator has similar problems with Canada and Dale, especially the latter, for although he has a certain respect for Canada and his aggressive nature, he has nothing but contempt for Dale: "I have almost no sense of Dale except I know I don't like him." Comically, the narrator worries that he is not able to build up interest in Dale, and at one point he sends Dale to North Dakota because "I needed a break from him." "Too often," the narrator says, "I'm tortured by a sense of dread caused by the fear that I do not really hate Dale, but respond this way to him out of a lack of interest. I mean, I *should* be interested in him since he's one of my creations."

The fragmented narrative returns over and over again to the scene of crime and a description of the police investigating what turns out to have been a bombing that killed Cora and Dale. For the narrator, writing the novel is in a sense a means to remember Cora and to reconstruct the crime through words, through the act of imagination, which are of course the only ways he has to reach his characters:

> I am standing behind Cora. She is wearing a thin black nightgown. The backs of her legs are lovely. I love her. The word standing allows me to watch like this. The word nightgown is what she is wearing. The nightgown itself is in her drawer with her panties. The word Cora is wearing the word nightgown. I watch the sentence: The backs of her legs are lovely.

But *Reflex and Bone Structure* is no traditional detective novel, in which the detective gradually narrows of possibilities of motive and traces the clues back in time to solve a crime. Here the mystery only increases, as "the pieces break into smaller pieces" and the relationship of the characters to one another becomes even more confusing. The narrator laments, "I find everything I touch falling to pieces, and the pieces themselves continue to break into smaller and smaller segments"; this statement describes not just his sense of the plot but also the formal nature of the novel itself, as it breaks down into smaller and less clearly connected passages of text. The novel ends with the narrator himself claiming responsibility for the deaths of Dale and Cora: "They step into a house. It explodes. It is a device. I am responsible. I set the device."

Having taught from 1974 to 1976 at Howard University in Washington, D.C., and then at the University of Washington in Seattle, Major took a tenure-track teaching position in 1977 at the University of Colorado. He gained security in his academic post when he earned a doctorate from Union Graduate School in Ohio at the end of the 1970s, and he was named a full professor at Colorado in 1981. In 1979, the Fiction Collective published what is perhaps his best-known experimental novel, *Emergency Exit*. Its form is even more fragmented than *Reflex and Bone Structure*, often constructed of seemingly abstract, disconnected sentences that are gradually assembled into a narrative, with the main figures introduced slowly into the weave. The novel opens with these sentences: "Stop: The doorway of life. Take this cliché with ancient roots as a central motif." One of the characters, Jim Ingram, later explains to his daughter Julie the book's obsession with doors and thresholds:

> This situation we are involved in stems indirectly from certain Christian assumptions about the function and ritual of the in-and-out motion of things, negative and positive, life and death, rhythm and the static, the doorway and the door, the inlet and the exit, the turnstile, the port and the land, the sea and the earth, the god and the virgin, the male and the female, being and not being. . . . This situation we're in is being rendered in terms of images, and dramatic description. I am using very few things to represent other things. I think the metaphor has its place but the place is historical. Yet I love the metaphor. I love its *visual* tendency. I want you, Julie, to understand that the ultimate *thingness* of our lives operates as a sort of *extended* metaphor.

The slim plot of *Emergency Exit* concerns Allen Morris, a "mentally black" Harlem drug dealer who goes to visit his lover, Julie Ingram, in Inlet, Connecticut, while her parents are away. The town has just passed a new "Threshold Law," continually debated and acted upon throughout the novel, decreeing that all males over twenty-one must carry all females over eighteen over all the thresholds in the town, in a bizarre resurrection of the old tribal custom of carrying new brides across the household boundary. At the same time, Julie's father, Jim, has fallen for his white secretary, Roslyn, who seduced him to win a bet. Jim is considering leaving his wife, Deborah—although the novel sets up such moments of dramatic interest only to pull away from them or to refuse a denouement.

Major has argued that his work lies within what he terms the "digressive" tradition of American innovative fiction, going back most clearly to Melville; and *Emergency Exit* turns away from its own narrative progress at almost every turn. The novel is interrupted by a series of documents so anomalous that the digressions themselves threaten to overwhelm the narrative. It includes a page of names from the Inlet telephone directory, dictionary definitions of words such as "door," a wide variety of epigrams from Will Rogers, Ezra Pound, Harry Truman, Eugene McCarthy, driving manuals, the Bible, and George Herriman's *Krazy Kat,* photographs of Clarence Major in a field of cows, a conference program from "The Annual Door and Threshold Conference" in Inlet, various graphs and charts, and more than two dozen reproductions of Major's own paintings. *Emergency Exit* even offers the reader lists of helpful hints and excuses: "Try to be patient with me," one entry says. "I know I don't always make sense." One page is blank except for nine words in the center: "Well, dear reader, how do you feel about it?" The novel is being proffered as an object for use rather than a reflection to be contemplated; the reader must participate in order to make the narrative work. In the "Open Letter" column in the *American Poetry Review* addressed to his writing students, Major instructs that the "new spirit" of creativity is usually found "at the far side of a deserted junk yard at the edge of the hopeless mind." He adds that when one creates in this state, "feeling one's way in the dark," the work of art "is given to the reader—who has to be taught how to *see* it—who must handle it as another aspect of his own day to day surroundings. It is a functional object, like a plant in the window. Like the door you open."

The 1980s

In 1981–1982, Major was awarded a Fulbright Fellowship to teach in France at the University of Nice. He traveled a great deal during this period, giving readings throughout Europe and visiting Africa as well. It was during these two years that he wrote most of *My Amputations,* which was published by the Fiction Collective in 1986 and which won the Western States Book Award that year. As *Emergency Exit* is dedicated "to the people whose stories do not hold together," *My Amputations* is dedicated "to the people who must find themselves." Mason Ellis is a blocked writer and petty criminal who, while serving a prison sentence in Attica for a crime he claims he did not commit, sees on television a ceremony in which a writer accepts an award Mason comes to believe was meant for him. Mason convinces himself that the writer, whom he calls "the Impostor," has usurped his identity and career, using an assumed name. Out of prison, Mason gathers some shady acquaintances and confronts the Impostor, planning to dispose of him in order to reassume his rightful identity and the fellowship stipend—although the Impostor proclaims his innocence and keeps slipping through Mason's clutches.

My Amputations is written in discrete blocks of prose, in fragmented sections ranging from one-third of a page to eight pages in length. The unidentified narrator, writing in the first person, continually undermines the reader's dwindling confidence in Mason's claims: "The background of such a madman is at least of clinical interest. I strain to find something good to say." From the narrator's hostile perspective, Mason "in the joint had read The Author's works over and over again till he convinced himself he was the writer and no longer the reader." We learn that the assumed name of the Impostor (which Mason in turn begins to use himself in order to take his identity back) is Clarence McKay; a "report" inserted in one of the sections suggests that the Impostor's choice of the name may have "stemmed from a quaint respect" for the Jamaican writer Claude McKay, a writer who "thought of himself as *international.*" Mason realizes that he has "to deal with this shammer in the only way one deals with a conspirator: to out-do him he had to become a supreme impostor himself." Although he doesn't quite understand why critics call the Impostor's work "postmodern," Mason begins to realize that a significant part of what a writer does is impersonate a writer. And so naturally he arranges to go on an international lecture tour:

> Maybe The Impostor *believed* the text represented nothing outside itself. I don't, thought Mason. . . . Text as permanent property—free of outside clut. Okay. Like Cubism: a

peeled conceptual orange oozing Cezanne's blood and sperm: synthetic, analytical, geometric. . . . *Hay,* shouldn't he cut out this shit and call a speakers' bureau? After all, he was a well-known author in need of some immediate action.

My Amputations is thus not only about the search for identity but also about the many ways we strive to confirm our identity by impersonating ourselves—by reproducing what others consider to be recognizable about us. Mason goes from one university to another, across the United States and Europe, telling the story of his search. At the University of Maryland, he stands in front of (rather than behind) the podium and says: "I come here with my life before you: I am a writer whose muse ran off. I'm just beginning to find myself on my own. I want to speak to you about my new effort to recreate myself." At Sarah Lawrence College, he explains, "I'm in the process of inventing myself—in self-defense, of course. Think of me as a character in a book." The audiences tend to ask the same kinds of questions, such as "Did you write *Native Son* and *Invisible Man*?" and "If you're so terrific how come I never heard of you?" After a long stay in Greece, Mason finally decides that perhaps "Africa would offer a way in." In a scene that is reminiscent of Ralph Ellison's *Invisible Man*, Mason is given an envelope to deliver to a Chief Q. Tee in Monrovia, Liberia, who is supposed to reveal the secret of his true identity. But at the novel's end, Mason is sitting, confused, in a village outside Monrovia, wearing a wooden African mask, as though to make the point that identity is never discovered or simply revealed but always performed, always a worn artifact.

Major spent much of 1983 and 1984 in Venice and Paris, where he painted more than fifty watercolors and worked on two books of poems: *Surfaces and Masks,* a book-length poem about Venice, published in 1988, and the 1985 collection *Inside Diameter: The France Poems,* which drew together the poems Major had written during his many visits there. In the spring of 1983, a brief stay as a writer-in-residence at Albany State College in Georgia afforded Major an opportunity to reflect upon his childhood years in the South. The literary result was the 1987 novel *Such Was the Season*.

Critical consensus has been that *Such Was the Season* marked a shift in Major's output, from self-consciously experimental work to a more conventional or straightforward narrative. Major himself has resisted this claim, however, noting that the innovative element in the novel is the careful rendering of the vernacular voice of its narrator, the widow matriarch Annie Eliza Hicks, who describes herself as "just a plain down-to-earth common sense person." "Last week was a killer-diller!" the book opens, and the reader is immediately engaged by one of the most endearing and fully realized narrators in contemporary black fiction. Annie Eliza narrates a busy week when her nephew Dr. Adam North, a pathologist from Yale University who researches the causes of sickle-cell anemia, comes back to Atlanta to give a lecture at Spelman College. Homecomings for Annie Eliza represent "a time of happiness, storytelling, a time when we all come together and membered we was family and tried to love each other, even if we didn't always do it so well," and she attempts to make the return such an occasion. Adam, whom Annie Eliza insists on calling "Juneboy," has his own agenda, however: searching for truth about his father, Scoop (a numbers runner, who was murdered over a gambling dispute), and contemplating his own memories of childhood in the South. "I have been suffering spiritually," he tells her, "longing for something I think I lost a long time ago. . . . I've been running from my early self, and now I want to stop." They make a pilgrimage to Lexington but are unable to find Scoop's grave: the former "colored cemetery" there has been buried under the parking lot at a housing project. Still, Juneboy reconciles himself to his father's death, saying to Annie Eliza:

"... in a way it's a fitting burial for Scoop. It's like he has lent his flesh and spirit to the continuation of the culture. The little kids playing in those parking lots are the ongoing spirits of all those silent souls down beneath the concrete. Scoop's spirit reaches up through the hard surface and spreads like the branches of a summer tree."

Annie Eliza also recounts in garrulous detail the trials and tribulations of her son Jeremiah—who is swept into a tomato-company scandal and then almost killed by his lover—and her daughter-in-law Renee, who has just decided to run for State Senate. But the real subject of the novel is Annie Eliza's voice itself: her way of describing the world around her, even her penchant for digression and rambling—interrupting her tales to offer lists of what she buys at the grocery, extended commentaries on sitcoms and commercials on the television that is always on in her home (providing a kind a constant narrative that to her is as "reliable" as anything else), her memories of her own parents, and remembered folktales from her Cherokee Indian father, Olaudah Equiano Sommer.

In 1983, Major also commenced extensive research among the Zuni, a Native American people in New Mexico, in preparation for two works unique to his canon inspired by Zuni culture: the 1988 novel *Painted Turtle: Woman with Guitar* and the 1989 poetic sequence *Some Observations of a Stranger at Zuni in the Latter Part of the Century*. As the critic Steve Hayward has pointed out, the Zuni books are fundamentally concerned with the question of representation: Who is authorized to speak for a culture, especially a culture that is marginalized, stereotyped, or commodified? Zugowa, the main voice in the poem "In Hollywood with the Zuni God of War" in *Some Observations*, bitingly depicts the exploitation of Native Americans in Hollywood, where "they did not care which tribe we came from":

We all looked alike.
  Being herded and shot
paid better than oranges in S.D.
  County,
or the H.D. in Arizona—that is,
if you could get yourself shot
at least once
per month.

Painted Turtle points out that the Zuni themselves are engaged in the production and protection of identity, cultural authenticity, and ancestry. The novel depicts a young Zuni woman named Painted Turtle who, having left the reservation after being raped, has become a folk singer drawing in part on her Zuni heritage. Her story, which partly concerns her ostracization from her own community, is narrated by another Native American musician, Baldwin Saiyataca (he himself is part Hopi, part Navajo). Since he admits late in the book that he actually "met Painted Turtle in the Blackbird Café in Cuba during her opening night" and is attempting to seduce her, it is not clear how much of his narrative about her life is close to her own perspective and how much of it is his own conjecture. Through these carefully constructed layers of approach, Major is able to frame and reflect on his own "observations" as a "stranger at Zuni" without simply rendering Zuni culture into an static anthropological object of analysis.

The 1990s and Beyond

In the 1960s, while in Nebraska, Major had written an article for the *Nickel Review* on the music scene in Omaha, where a few highly regarded blues and jazz musicians, including the alto saxophonist and singer Eddie "Cleanhead" Vinson, played regularly in Paul Allen's club. Major's 1996 novel, *Dirty Bird Blues*, builds on this experience, telling a leisurely story about African American life in the 1950s in the Midwest, centered around Manfred "Man" Banks, a musician and steelworker in Omaha. Although *All-Night Visitors* already makes recurring references to jazz and scat singing, *Dirty Bird Blues* is Major's first sustained effort at a blues novel, recording Man's development as a musician, particularly through his effort to compose often surreal, often humorous blues lyrics:

> The jailer gave me whiskey,
> The jailer gave me tea.
> I say the jailer gave me whiskey,
> The jailer gave me tea.
> The jailer gave me everything but the key.

Formally, the novel is much more conventional than some of Major's earlier work, but there are still a number of densely wrought impressionistic passages, especially the descriptions of Man's dreams and nightmares:

> He feels the hard new rope resting loosely around his damp neck. A mob of about a hundred jeering dog-faced white men are gathered around the base of a pile of scrap metal on which he stands. He smells fern. He smells apple pie. Dandelions are dangling from his shirt pockets. Closing his eyes, he sees a little birdhouse, and looking through the little hole, inside he sees a little old man sitting in a rocking chair. The old man is himself, a self that will never be. His hands are tied behind his back with a rope made of afterbirth. Overhead high in the dome, birds—golden eagles, red-tailed hawks, snail kites, and white ibises—are flying around in a frantic pattern.

Since the mid-1990s, Major has lived in northern California and taught at the University of California at Davis. He continues to publish extensively and has also turned again to producing anthologies. The 1993 *Calling the Wind* and the 1996 *The Garden Thrives* are collections of twentieth-century African American short fiction and poetry, respectively, projects that for Major represent (as he explained to Steve McCaffery) an attempt "to find the terms on a more personal level to get the best of all the different kinds of cultural influences feeding into my experience, and to come up with a personal aesthetic." He has also collected his own work. In 1990, Major released *Fun and Games*, an entertaining compendium of his short fictions, many of which feature characters from the novels, such as Julie Ingram and Al Morris in "Letters," Juneboy and his father Scoop in "Saving the Children," and Moses Westby in "Ten Pecan Pies." Major also released in 1998 a collection of poems, titled *Configurations*, which contains works from 1958 to 1998 and includes some previously uncollected gems, such as the mature long poems "Un Poco Loco" and "The Slave Trade: View from the

Middle Passage." One fine-tuned lyric inspired by the issues that continue to drive Major's writing is "On the Nature of Perspective," a poem that opens "Sometimes there is a point / without a point of view" and closes with the following lines:

I relax and glean the blossoms, because
I know of time chance makes a fool.
and this is the turning around
in the nick of time that catches
both the soft light and these things
off balance yet just right.

Selected Bibliography

PRIMARY WORKS

NOVELS AND SHORT STORIES

All-Night Visitors. New York: Olympia, 1969. Reprint, with a foreword by Bernard W. Bell. Boston: Northeastern University Press, 1998. (The 1998 publication is an unexpurgated edition of the novel, nearly twice the length of the Olympia Press edition.)
NO. New York: Emerson Hall, 1973.
Reflex and Bone Structure. New York: Fiction Collective, 1975.
Emergency Exit. New York: Fiction Collective, 1979.
My Amputations. New York: Fiction Collective, 1986.
Such Was the Season. San Francisco: Mercury House, 1987.
Painted Turtle: Woman with Guitar. Los Angeles: Sun and Moon, 1988.
Fun and Games: Short Fictions. Duluth: Holy Cow! 1990.
Dirty Bird Blues. New York: Mercury House, 1996.

POETRY

The Fires That Burn in Heaven. Chicago: n.p., 1954.
Love Poems of a Black Man. Omaha, Neb.: Coercion Press, 1965.
Human Juices. Omaha, Neb.: Coercion Press, 1966.
Swallow the Lake. Middletown, Conn.: Wesleyan University Press, 1970.
Private Line. London: Paul Breman, 1971.
Symptoms and Madness. New York: Corinth Books, 1971.
The Cotton Club. Detroit, Mich.: Broadside Press, 1972.
The Syncopated Cakewalk. New York: Barlenmir House, 1974.
Inside Diameter: The France Poems. London and New York: Permanent, 1985.
Surfaces and Masks: A Poem. Minneapolis, Minn.: Coffee House, 1988.

Some Observations of a Stranger at Zuni in the Latter Part of the Century. Los Angeles: Sun and Moon, 1989.
Configurations: New and Selected Poems, 1958–1998. Port Townsend, Wash.: Copper Canyon Press, 1998.

LITERARY CRITICISM AND REFERENCE WORKS

Dictionary of Afro-American Slang. New York: International Publishers, 1970. (Reissued as *Black Slang: A Dictionary of Afro-American Talk.* London: Routledge, 1971.)
The Dark and Feeling: Black American Writers and Their Work. New York: Third Press, 1974.
Juba to Jive: A Dictionary of African-American Slang. New York: Viking Penguin, 1994.

ANTHOLOGIES EDITED BY MAJOR

Writers Workshop Anthology. New York: Harlem Education Project, New Lincoln School, 1967.
Man Is Like a Child: An Anthology of Creative Writing by Students. New York: Macomb's Junior High School, 1968.
The New Black Poetry. New York: International Publishers, 1969.
Calling the Wind: Twentieth-Century African-American Short Stories. New York: HarperCollins, 1993.
The Garden Thrives: Twentieth-Century African-American Poetry. New York: HarperCollins, 1996.

SELECTED ESSAYS

"Ulysses, Who Slept Across from Me." *Olivant* 1:53–56 (1957).
"Weekend Improvisation: Eddie Cleanhead Vinson." *Nickel Review* 4:8 (November 1969).
"Open Letters: A Column." *American Poetry Review* 3:42 (January–February 1974).
"Open Letters: Tradition and Presence." *American Poetry Review* 5:33–34 (May–June 1976).
"Tradition and Presence: Experimental Fiction by Black American Writers." *American Poetry Review* 5:33–35 (May–June 1976).
"Clarence Major Interviews: Jacob Lawrence, the Expressionist." *Black Scholar* 9:14–25 (November 1977).
"Reality, Fiction, and Criticism: An Interview/Essay." With Doug Bolling. *Par Rapport* 2:67–73 (Winter 1979).
"The Erotic Facts of Life: A Personal View." *Revue Française d'Etudes Américaines* 9:261–64 (May 1984).
"Licking Stamps, Taking Chances." In *Contemporary Authors Autobiography Series,* Vol. 6. Edited by Adele Sarkissian. Detroit, Mich.: Gale Research, 1988. Pp. 175–204.
"Necessary Distance: Afterthoughts on Becoming a Writer." *Black American Literature Forum* 23:197–212 (Summer 1989).
"And an Artist with Paris on His Mind." *Washington Post,* February 18, 1996, pp. 39–40.

SECONDARY WORKS

BIOGRAPHICAL AND CRITICAL STUDIES

Bell, Bernard W. *The Afro-American Novel and Its Tradition.* Amherst: University of Massachusetts Press, 1987.

———. "Clarence Major's Homecoming Voice in *Such Was the Season.*" *African American Review* 28:89–94 (Spring 1994).

Bolling, Doug. "A Reading of Clarence Major's Short Fiction." *Black American Literature Forum* 13:51–56 (1979).

Bradfield, Larry D. "Beyond Mimetic Exhaustion: The *Reflex and Bone Structure* Experiment." *Black American Literature Forum* 17:120–23 (Fall 1983).

Byerman, Keith. *Fingering the Jagged Grain: Tradition and Form in Recent Black Fiction.* Athens: University of Georgia Press, 1985.

Coleman, James W. "Clarence Major's *All-Night Visitors*: Calabanic Discourse and Black Male Expression." *African American Review* 28:95–108 (Spring 1994).

Hayward, Steve. "Against Commodification: Zuni Culture in Clarence Major's Native American Texts." *African American Review* 28:109–20 (Spring 1994).

Klawans, Stuart. " 'I Was a Weird Example of Art': *My Amputations* as Cubist Confession." *African American Review* 28:77–86 (Spring 1994).

Klinkowitz, Jerome. "Clarence Major's Innovative Fiction." *African American Review* 28:57–63 (Spring 1994).

———. "The Self-Apparent Word: Clarence Major's Innovative Fiction." In *Studies in Black American Literature.* Vol. 1, *Black American Prose Theory.* Edited by Joe Weixlmann and Chester J. Fontenot. Greenwood, Fla.: Penkevill Publishing, 1984. Pp. 199–214.

Mackey, Nathaniel. "To Define an Ultimate Dimness: The Poetry of Clarence Major." In his *Discrepant Engagement: Dissonance, Cross-Culturality, and Experimental Writing.* New York: Cambridge University Press, 1993. Pp. 49–65.

McCaffery, Larry, and Sinda Gregory. "Major's *Reflex and Bone Structure* and the Anti-Detective Tradition." *Black American Literature Forum* 13:39–45 (Summer 1979).

Quartermain, Peter. "Trusting the Reader." *Chicago Review* 32:65–74 (Autumn 1980).

Roney, C. Lisa. "The Double Vision of Clarence Major, Painter and Writer." *African American Review* 28:65–75 (Spring 1994).

Weixlmann, Joel. "Clarence Major." *Afro-American Fiction Writers after 1955.* Vol. 33 of *Dictionary of Literary Biography.* Edited by Thadious M. Davis and Trudier Harris. Detroit, Mich.: Gale Research, 1984. Pp. 153–61.

INTERVIEWS

Bunge, Nancy. "An Interview with Clarence Major." *San Francisco Review of Books* 7, no. 3:7, 8, 38 (1982).

Klinkowitz, Jerome. "Clarence Major: An Interview with a Post-Contemporary Author," *Black American Literature Forum* 12:32–37 (Spring 1978).

McCaffery, Larry and Jerry Kutnik. " 'I Follow My Eyes': An Interview with Clarence Major." *Black American Literature Forum* 28:121–38 (Spring 1994).

O'Brien, John. "Clarence Major." In his *Interviews with Black Writers.* New York: Liveright, 1973. Pp. 125–39.

Scharper, Alice. "An Interview." *Poets and Writers Magazine* 19:15–19 (January–February 1991).

BIBLIOGRAPHIES

Weixlmann, Joe, and Clarence Major. "Toward a Primary Bibliography of Clarence Major." *Black American Literature Forum* 13:70–72 (Summer 1979).

———. "A Checklist of Books by Clarence Major." *African American Review* 28:139–40 (Spring 1994).

PAULE MARSHALL
(1929–   )

BARBARA T. CHRISTIAN

PAULE MARSHALL'S FICTION epitomizes the black diasporic woman's quest for wholeness, for the integration of the various parts of one's self—race, ethnicity, gender, historical process, and the specific individual in the context of community. Marshall is, to cite critic Dorothy Denniston, a womanist writer, a concept that Alice Walker so succinctly defined in her introduction to *In Search of Our Mothers' Gardens* (1984). An African American of Barbadian ancestry, Marshall in her writing carefully sculpts the complex forms of her African cultural heritage as it appears in the black cultures of the Caribbean, South America, and the United States. In keeping with the significance of women of her ancestry, she consistently crafts the contours of that heritage from a black woman's perspective.

As pivotal as Paule Marshall's works have been to the tradition and literature of African American women and the Third World, she has not received the recognition she deserves—perhaps because she has not cultivated the requisite marketable image, or perhaps because the complex politics of her work cannot be reduced to the neat, brief categories patronized by the mainstream and alternate U.S. literary markets. Her personal history is indicative of why she is the writer she is and why she adheres to an intensely private writer's image.

Marshall was born April 9, 1929, in Stuyvesant Heights, New York (now Bedford-Stuyvesant), the daughter of Ada and Samuel Burke, who like so many other immigrants came to the United States for economic opportunity. Thus one central motif in her work is a major theme of American literature: the adjustment of immigrants to a new material environment and culture and their attempt to retain the spirit and integrity of the Old Country. Yet because Marshall's parents were descendants of slaves forcibly brought from Africa to the New World, her work, like other African American literature, simultaneously confronts the issues of American slavery and racism.

Marshall's African-Caribbean ancestry also gave her insight into another important dimension of the diaspora, the traumatic awareness of colonialism. Furthermore, until recently most writers who ventured to approach these historical processes—slavery, immigration, exploitation, racism, colonialism—did so from a male perspective. A decade before the explosion of literature by women of color in the 1970s, Marshall's fiction emphasized the distinctly sexist character of these phenomena even as she demonstrated how women are significant actors in the making of history. Her writing symbolized a position that would become pivotal in the second wave of American feminism.

In an essay published in the *New York Times Book Review,* "From the Poets of the Kitchen," Marshall underlined the influence of women on her own development as a writer. Like the character Silla in her first novel, *Brown Girl, Brownstones,* Marshall's mother, after a day's work cleaning house, would gather with her women friends around the kitchen table. There, in sessions that prefigured the consciousness-raising meetings of the 1970s women's movement, they would dissect the personalities of their employers, recreate their contexts, and discuss in distinctly Caribbean images and gestures the issues of the day as well as their own community's rituals. In effect these ordinary cleaning women "practiced language as an oral art." As a child who witnessed these dramas, Marshall told Alexis De Veaux in a 1980 interview in *Essence,* she "was always intimidated by the awesome power of these women. That might be one reason that I started writing. To see if on paper I couldn't have some of that power."

She also learned from her mother's kitchen ritual that art is an integral part of life, not, as the pervasive Western definition would have it, an isolated process. As she notes in her essay "Shaping the World of My Art" (1973), central to the African tradition and to its extensions in the New World is the traditional view that the artist is to make into art the rituals of daily life. In calling attention to that particular definition of the artist, Marshall clearly aligns herself with the African tradition and the maintenance of its vitality.

Marshall's kitchen poets also communicated to her that women were not relegated only to domestic concerns. In contrast to the stereotype that women, certainly cleaning women, were not politically involved, her mother and her friends discussed everything from the war to President Franklin Roosevelt and donated their "raw-mouth" pennies to the Garvey movement, which advocated the emigration of American blacks to Africa. De Veaux commented on Marshall's description of this aspect of her childhood: "It was this strong image of the women in her mother's kitchen, an image of women concerned not only with household chores but with the politics of world affairs that was later to be the impetus of Paule Marshall's life-work."

A further influence on Marshall's childhood was Barbados itself. Like many African American children who were sent south during the summer, Marshall visited her parents' birthplace. Although white America promoted the view that blacks had no history, no culture, no rituals, Marshall experienced during her trip the continuity of her community's history, which she beautifully distilled in her work, especially in the short piece "To Da-duh, In Memoriam" (1967). One strength of all of her fiction is this deeply felt sense of black culture that distinguished the distinctiveness of the African world from the pervasive view that blacks exist only because of white racism. She knew from a very young age that her ancestors had created their own wise and complex point of view about what it means to live in this universe.

While her development as a writer was unconsciously being directed by her ancestry and her mother's circle of friends, Marshall was formally schooled in the more conventional American modes of education. Perhaps because of the respect for words she had learned at home, she was drawn to books at school and in the library. Of course the traditional school curriculum of the 1930s and 1940s did not include much writing by blacks or women; still, she learned much from some of the writers she encountered. She tells us that during her adolescence and early twenties she went through "a very heavy Thomas Mann and Joseph Conrad period" and describes *Death in Venice* as "a seminal book for her." She also read the works of two African American writers—Paul Laurence Dunbar and Richard Wright.

During the late 1940s and early 1950s, as the Civil Rights movement escalated, Marshall was strongly influenced by two other African American thinkers, Ralph Ellison, whose *Shadow and Act* (1958) she has called her "literary bible," and James Baldwin, whose essays "were crucial to her formation as a writer and a thinker." Like other writers of the 1950s, Marshall discovered the long-neglected works of African American women writers only in the following decade, when she read Zora Neale Hurston, Dorothy West, and Gwendolyn Brooks, whose *Maud Martha* (1953) she would in 1966 call "the finest portrayal of an African-American woman in the novel to date and one which had a decided influence on my work."

Though they represent different cultures and times the writers who influenced Marshall used language symbolically to represent the complex interrelationships between character and culture. Even when they used the form of the essay, they employed narrative as the frame for their embodied ideas. Although Marshall wrote poetry as a young girl, as a mature writer she exclusively devoted herself to the craft of fiction. She has noted that for her the traditional novel is still a vital form because her reader can see her characters in their context even as she "can explore their inner states and the worlds beyond them."

Despite her interest in literature throughout her adolescence, Marshall certainly did not envision herself as a future writer when in 1948 she entered Hunter College in New York. Indeed, perhaps she might not have become one if two years later, in 1950, having just married her first husband, Kenneth E. Marshall, she had not had to leave school because of illness. While she was convalescing, the bored Marshall wrote letters to friends, one of whom suggested that she pursue writing as a career. She then began practicing and wrote what she called "vignettes," one of which became her first published story, "The Valley Between" (*The Contemporary Reader*, August 1954).

Although the story is immature, its subject—the frustrations of a college-trained woman whose only fulfillments are expected to be motherhood and marriage—anticipated by some twenty years a major theme of American women's literature. Even in her first serious attempts at writing Marshall was a forerunner of future trends. Perhaps as a newly married woman, she feared the restrictions that were beginning to be imposed on her. Yet the characters of her story are white, not black, possibly because she lacked African American female literary models and was still tentative about ap-

Paule Marshall

proaching fiction from that point of view, a circumstance that probably affected other potential black women writers at the time.

Even when Marshall completed Brooklyn College in 1953 with a degree in English, she did not consider fiction writing as a career, but rather looked for work on a newspaper or magazine, only to discover that even black journals were not interested in hiring women. The prescribed careers for educated black women were teaching or social work. Unwilling to give up her goal, she finally got a job at a small black magazine called *Our World*, but then only in the fashion and food section. It seemed to her—the only woman on the staff—that "the men were waiting for her to fall." Marshall's experience as a woman trying to break into the professional literary universe was not atypical. It is one important reason why African American women writers would not emerge as major actors in that world until after the convergence of the black and women's movements of the late 1960s.

Brown Girl, Brownstones

Marshall soon realized that writing for a magazine was not satisfying to her. During this period she began to devote her nights, after an exhausting day's work, to writing the novel that would become *Brown Girl, Brownstones;* it was, she said, her "most exhilarating writing experience." Its publication in 1959 established her as a writer who insisted on probing the complexity of African American women in the context of their own culture.

Like *Maud Martha, Brown Girl, Brownstones* is the story of a black girl growing up. And like Brooks's novella, Marshall's first novel is to some extent autobiographical. Both writers used their experiences of growing up within the context of a specific black community as the basis for their work. Yet these two works are primarily novels rather than autobiography in that neither one attempts to reconstruct the facts of the author's life or to validate her existence. Brooks's novella is dominated almost exclusively by the internal meditations of Maud Martha, so as to emphasize that black girls, too, have a subjective imagination through which they interpret the world around them. While the subjective view of Selina is certainly evident in *Brown Girl, Brownstones,* Marshall expands her narrative world to include other complex and diverse characters who are both distinctly themselves yet representative of the cultural characteristics of the Barbadian-American community.

When *Brown Girl, Brownstones* was published in 1959, it had been preceded in African American letters by a small but significant body of texts that featured to one degree or another the growing-up process of a black girl. Today, students of African American literature know about nineteenth-century texts such as Harriet Jacobs' *Incidents in the Life of a Slave Girl* (1861) and Harriet E. Wilson's autobiographical novel, *Our Nig* (1859), the former about a southern slave girl, the latter about a northern indentured black girl. *Plum Bun* (1929), by the Harlem Renaissance writer Jessie Fauset, provides some outline of the experiences of Angela Murray. Similarly, Zora Neale Hurston's *Their Eyes Were Watching God* (1937), Dorothy West's *The Living Is Easy* (1948), and Gwendolyn Brooks's *Maud Martha* all focus on the protagonist's childhood development for some portion of the text. But with the possible exception of *Maud Martha*—which she may not even have seen before writing her first novel, since Brooks's novella went out of print immediately after publication—Marshall had access to none of these works.

To give primary significance to a "brown girl" as the protagonist of a novel was practically unheard of in 1959; to focus on her adolescent years for an entire novel had not been attempted even by Brooks. True, the growing up of black boys had been recently treated in Wright's autobiography, *Black Boy* (1945), and in James Baldwin's *Go Tell It on the Mountain* (1953). As the Civil Rights movement escalated in the 1950s, more attention was paid to the theme of black manhood and therefore to the precarious journey of black boys as they became men. By contrast, little emphasis was placed on black womanhood (except as it related to men) and therefore on how black girls became women. To some extent, it appeared from contemporary American literature that like Topsy of *Uncle Tom's Cabin,* black women "jes grew." With its intense focus on Selina's journey from budding adolescence to questioning womanhood, *Brown Girl, Brownstones* was unique.

Not only was Marshall's protagonist startling; the novel was also remarkable for its insistence on the reality of black culture as the birthright of a people who supposedly had lost their history as a result of their enslavement by a dominant white culture. By her rich delineation of the rituals, mores, and values of the African-Barbadian community in its attempt to situate itself in the United States, Marshall enunciates the lasting power of black culture in the diaspora. The language her characters speak is itself a reflection of that history—the interplay of African, British, and Caribbean elements. And the rituals the Boyces and the Challenors enact, such as the wedding at the center of the novel, are themselves reflections of the journey from Africa through the colonized Caribbean to racist America. Marshall's story grows out of the possibilities as well as the conflicts presented by these elements.

In creating the shape of Selina's journey into womanhood, Marshall takes into account the forces that affect any young girl—her parents, her environment, her biological development—and shows how they relate to the culture of Selina's people as well as to the racism (against blacks) and discrimination (against foreigners) with which she must contend. By emphasizing "brown" and "girl" in the novel's name, Marshall signals her primary focus: that this work is about both the race/culture and the gender of her protagonist. And by placing "brownstones" directly next to "brown girl," she reiterates the importance of context, of environment. Brownstones are associated with urban New York and the waves of immigrants who not only lived in them but used this new environment as a means to economic advancement. These brownstones served as a shelter from the surrounding world of discrimination and racism as well as a place where the values of the old homeland could be preserved. In giving her first novel its title, Marshall reminded us that personal human development is inseparable from history, culture, and environment.

Marshall's sense of the interrelationship of character and context is also evident in the shape of the novel itself, which is divided into four parts. The first book, "A Long Day and a Long Night," introduces the reader to the major characters and their community as well as to the brownstone itself. "Pastorale" lyrically evokes the pleasure and pain of Selina's coming-of-age. The third book, "The War," concerns the conflict between Silla and Deighton Boyce over the purchase of the brownstone and is also set in the context of World War II. In the fourth book, "Selina," the near-adult protagonist challenges her parents and community and comes to terms with her first sexual encounter and with the racism of the white world.

Throughout the novel, the issues of materialism and intrinsic values, of individual relationship to community, of culture and racism, and of the mysteries of men and women are highlighted against the backdrop of Selina's discovery of herself as a person and as part of a community. Central to that understanding is Selina's relationship to her parents, for it is through the parents that a child first learns what it might mean to be a man or a woman.

Gender definitions are critical to the novel as Marshall situates Selina's growing understanding of her parents and of herself in the context of racial politics.

Marshall's emphasis on the mother-daughter relationship in *Brown Girl, Brownstones* was not recognized as a significant theme in literature until the second wave of American feminism questioned conventional assumptions about that bond. Unlike some women writers of the 1970s and 1980s, she did not idealize the mother-daughter bond, a temptation she must have felt, given its trivialization in Western culture and the ways it was assaulted by the racial realities of America. Rather, she celebrated it by probing its complexity and its societal context. The ten-year-old Selina must look to her mother for what it might mean to be a woman; yet she is drawn not to her "wintery," hard mother, but to her springlike, magical father. Why the mother appears formidable but powerful and the father delightful but ineffectual has much to do with the racial and gender stereotypes found in Selina's immediate community as in American society in general.

As a foreign black people trying to make it in America, the Barbadian immigrant community was forced to confront the same racial stereotypes and socioeconomic restrictions that had been imposed for centuries on African American women and men. Since slavery times black women had been portrayed in American popular culture as domineering mammies or as oversexed wenches, while black men were characterized as hedonistic coons or dumb bucks—boys unable to participate in the hard business world of America. These images continued to reverberate in the 1930s and 1940s, as exemplified by the popular radio show *Amos 'n Andy*, which featured Sapphire, who dominates her weak, lazy husband with her lashing tongue.

Such images were not only distortions of blacks but were based on the cultural assumption that men are to be dominant, women subordinate, and that any other gender construct was deviant, wrong. Since the economic realities of life made it impossible for black women to withdraw from the work world and be cuddled and ineffective, and since men were systematically denied access to wealth, these stereotypes were cruel, dangerous, and an excuse for not dealing with the real causes of black poverty. But they were also sexist, since they assumed a specific personality as the appropriate and only one for a man or a woman. Although the Moynihan Report, which emphasized the fact that black families were matriarchal, deviant, and the major reason for poverty and crime in black communities, was not published until 1966, its major tenets were already ingrained in American popular culture. Strong black women who could not be matriarchs given their powerlessness in the society were branded as the reason why black men were supposedly not productive enough and had not formed traditional patriarchal families as whites had. Black girls growing up in this atmosphere, confronted by contradictory societal demands, must have been in conflict about who they could or should become.

In a talk given at the University of California at Berkeley in 1982, Marshall said that she wrote *Brown Girl, Brownstones* not so much for publication as to unravel her own knots. Perhaps as a young Barbadian-American girl she, like Selina, was confused by the contradictory values of her own community. On the one hand, it revered the puritanical values necessary to achieve material success; on the other, it clearly valued sensual pleasure as symbolized in dancing, a motif in this novel. At the same time, Marshall's analysis of Barbadian-American society in *Brown Girl, Brownstones* indicates her profound awareness of the effect of American stereotypes on the Barbadian immigrant's dream to advance economically. Whatever their personalities or attributes, male Barbadian-Americans defined themselves as men by their ability to acquire property and make money, while in accordance with American society's definition of real women, their wives were eventually to be taken care of and live in fine houses. The Challenor family in *Brown Girl, Brownstones* represents that norm. Percy Challenor is a dull, hardworking man who rules his house like a god while his wife subordinates herself to him, to the goal of buying a house, and to marrying their children into other up-

wardly mobile Barbadian-American families. By contrast, other members of the immigrant community such as the sexually free Suggie, the artistic Clive, and the sensual Deighton Boyce instinctively feel that they are giving up too much of themselves to the ideal of acquisition of money and property. They are, however, perceived as a drain by the already beleaguered community.

In particular the Boyce family does not fit the pattern rewarded by their American community. Deighton refuses to be what he considers "a pawn" in the white man's world and will not submit himself to becoming a drudge, which for him is being less than a man. In refusing to submit to the societal definition of manhood, he passes the weight of survival and success to his wife, Silla, who then must become the tough one. She will do anything to secure her own and her children's position in the community, even at the cost of her own femininity.

At least that interpretation of the dynamics in the Boyce household is what the reader first encounters in *Brown Girl, Brownstones*. But that version of their story competes with another. For Marshall not only criticizes the way American materialism undermines the individual; she is also intent on demonstrating how fixed gender roles distort this family and others like it. Her portrayal of Silla as a strong willful woman who makes "her mouth into a gun" precisely because she has so little power departs from conventional ideals. Further, in her dramatization of Silla and her women friends, and especially in her description of Silla's beauty as she and her family prepare to go to the wedding that is at the center of the book, Marshall underlines the fact that this image is related to other cultural definitions of womanhood, which Silla has inherited from her ancestors.

More than any other element in *Brown Girl, Brownstones*, Silla's persistent voice pronounces Marshall's alternate perception of womanhood. Unlike Maud Martha, who only imagines her own point of view, Silla speaks her mind. As woman she will not be silent. She is an actor, and she passes on her willfulness and her womanishness to her daughter Selina. Critic Mary Helen Washington has commented in her afterword to the Feminist Press reissue of *Brown Girl, Brownstones* that Silla "teaches [Selina] almost nothing of the female arts. She tolerates Selina's adventurous spirit with a grudging respect and in subtle ways encourages it." Thus at the end of the novel Selina comes to realize that she is not so much her father's child as she is her mother's daughter. In parting, her mother blesses the daughter's spirit: "G'long! You was always too much woman for me anyway, soul. . . . If I din dead yet, you and your foolishness can't kill much now."

The mother's blessing is not the last scene in the novel, however, for Marshall sees that this bond necessarily exists within the context of the journey Selina will be making in a complex world. At the crux of her growing up is her awareness of herself, not only as a woman but also as a Caribbean and an American. Marshall gives shape to that interrelationship in the formal, final gesture of the book, when Selina throws one of the two traditional silver bangles worn by all West Indian girls into the landscape of urban Brooklyn, while she keeps the other. It is a gesture that has been preceded by similar rituals exemplifying the bicultural tension and energy of this immigrant community. From the women's rituals around Silla's kitchen table, through 'Gatha Steed's hybrid wedding, to the religious revivals of Father Peace and the meetings of the Barbadian-American Association, the novel's rituals reflect the many intersecting and conflicting elements of its characters' heritage—the African, the Caribbean mix of slavery and British colonialism, and the urban and materialistic quality of American culture.

Yet that outline is not necessarily one of progress, as Marshall demonstrates in the rest of her opus. Rather than focusing on urban American life, she moves through time and space to the Caribbean as her literary landscape. This "arc of recovery," as critic Susan Willis puts it, characterizes Marshall's revolutionary journey, her search for wholeness in the diaspora. Whatever material gains West Indians may have made in the United States, the question of what they may have lost and may need to recover looms large in *Brown Girl, Brownstones*. In carefully analyzing the characters of Deighton

and Clive (one an artist without a form, the other a thinker and would-be painter), as well as their virtual ostracism from the community, Marshall asks hard questions about the values adopted by her immigrant community in its quest for material success. And by making the search for the spiritual/intellectual values these men could potentially give their community an intrinsic part of her novel about a brown woman's coming-of-age, Marshall initiates the first lap of her lifelong journey to the recovery of an ancestral wholeness, even as she evokes the dilemmas of the present for peoples of the black diaspora. Perhaps Selina, who is both her father's *and* her mother's daughter, will struggle to that wholeness by unifying these apparent opposites.

Brown Girl, Brownstones was a critical success, with fine reviews appearing in such prestigious publications as the *New Yorker*, the *Saturday Review of Literature*, and the *New York Times*. It was not a commercial success, partly because the theme of a girl's coming-of-age had not yet been recognized as it would be some twenty years later—when Marshall's novel would be praised as a touchstone work in contemporary American women's literature—and partly because of Marshall's refusal to cultivate a marketable image. Nonetheless, the publication of *Brown Girl, Brownstones* had two important immediate effects. The writing of her first novel convinced Marshall that she *had* to be a fiction writer. And the novel suggested to those who did manage to discover it in the 1960s that there was a complexity and richness in black women's lives that had yet to be mined in literature.

Soul Clap Hands and Sing

Two years after the publication of *Brown Girl, Brownstones*, Marshall published another book, a collection of novellas called *Soul Clap Hands and Sing* (1961). Often neglected, this collection is as important as *Brown Girl, Brownstones* not only because of the new literary landscape it charted but also because of the decisions Marshall made in order to write it. Although she called it her "easiest book to write," by now she had become a mother, and, as she noted in her interview with Alexis De Veaux, although her husband was proud that she wrote, he seriously objected to her decision to hire a babysitter for a time every day so that she could write in a friend's apartment.

The role of parenthood has traditionally been an exceedingly difficult one for women artists since societies have tended to define women's creativity exclusively by that role. As Tillie Olsen pointed out in *Silences* (1978), most women who in the past succeeded in becoming writers were childless. Not until the 1970s, in the context of the women's movement, did writers like Olsen, Alice Walker in her essay "*One* Child of One's Own," and Adrienne Rich in *Of Woman Born* encourage and support the mother who was attempting to be a writer. On the contrary, there was a strongly held view in American society that mothers damage their children if they attempt any other serious form of self-fulfillment. That in the 1950s Marshall took the necessary steps, despite strains on her familial relationships, to be a writer indicates her strong determination to be her own woman and to do what *she* needed to do.

Soul Clap Hands and Sing reflects Marshall's expanding awareness of international cultures and politics. As a journalist working on stories for *Our World*, she traveled to the Caribbean and South America, areas she would use as the book's settings. Though the four novellas that make up *Soul Clap Hands and Sing*—"Barbados," "Brooklyn," "British Guiana," and "Brazil"—can be read separately, when read together they resonate as a journey that takes us through the Americas, from Marshall's place of ancestry to the new home of her immigrant community, then back south to British Guiana, then to the interior of a major South American country. In each setting Marshall examines the complexities of race, nationality, and gender relationships, and in so doing traces the complexity of black cultures as they reshape themselves from North to South America.

For many African American readers in the 1960s such a journey must have been a revelation, since so few were aware of the tremendous black presence in the Western Hemisphere that extended beyond the United States. In charting this geography, Marshall chose a new terrain: in effect she claims the entire hemisphere as an appropriate subject for the black writer. Ironically, however, Marshall herself believed that in *Soul Clap Hands and Sing* she had focused her geographical sights more narrowly since she had felt overwhelmed by the United States. She called the emphasis she would now place on West Indian settings "a more manageable landscape" through which she could deal with the same issues as those existing in the United States. Moreover, her focus on the West Indies and South America provided her with an opportunity to contemplate the West Indian ancestry she had tried to deny as a child growing up in Brooklyn. *Soul Clap Hands and Sing*, then, is a turning point in Marshall's work in that it identifies the West Indies as the pivotal landscape she would use in her work.

The title of the book comes from a line in "Sailing to Byzantium," Yeats's famous poem about aging: "An aged man is but a paltry thing, / A tattered coat upon a stick, unless / Soul clap its hands and sing." The most significant theme of the collection is how each of Marshall's four old men, though apparently outwardly successful, comes to see the lack of depth and commitment in his life, that without soul, without deeply felt values, he is empty. Each man's recognition is set against the context of the effects of racism and colonialism in the New World even as the development of his character shows that he must bear the responsibility for his life.

In each novella, the protagonist's revelation occurs through his relationship with a woman who is either his younger assessor or his mirror reflection. In "Barbados," Mr. Watford, who after joyless years of work in the United States has retired to Barbados to lord it over his own people as the colonial whites had over him, comes to gaze "mutely upon the waste and pretense which spanned his years" when he attempts to dominate his young servant girl. Max Berman, the aging Jewish teacher of French in "Brooklyn," discovers the emptiness of his indifferent life through his attempted thoughtless seduction of one of his students, a Negro girl. In "British Guiana," the upper-class Creole Gerald Motley faces the ruin he has made of his life in giving up politics to take on a meaningless if prestigious job, when his ex-girlfriend, the Negro-Chinese Sybil, returns to the country. And Caliban, the tiny black nightclub entertainer in "Brazil," comes to see the false self he has constructed in the grotesque reflection of his Germanesque partner, the huge, whitish Miranda. Marshall's singular characterization of Miranda reminds us that the voices of women of color are often left out in the attacks Third World men have made against colonial power. In critiquing Shakespeare's *Tempest*, even a critic as eloquent as the West Indian writer George Lamming emphasized the ironies of Caliban's use of the master's language without taking into account Miranda's existence. But Miranda's screams at the end of "Brazil" represent a visceral rendering of the pain of the other figure in this colonial drama.

Like *Brown Girl, Brownstones*, each novella within *Soul Clap Hands and Sing* is constructed so that we see the relationship of character and context, for its intense moment of revelation takes place in a setting that represents the specific geography of each story. Mr. Watford's glimpse of the erotic dance between the servant girl and her lover (a glimpse that precipitates his collapse) occurs in his stunted coconut grove, a typically Caribbean landscape, for example, while the moment of revelation for Gerald Motley takes place in the bush, that impenetrable interior associated with British Guiana. Though they are joined in their inability to risk life, each of the four old men in *Soul Clap Hands and Sing* acts out his fate in images organic to his individual context, that of a New World that offers either new possibilities or stagnation, depending on the choices he has made.

The Chosen Place, the Timeless People

During the 1960s, while struggling to write a new novel, Marshall was divorced. She also be-

gan to receive financial support for her writing from foundations: a Rosenthal Foundation Award in 1962, a Ford Foundation Grant in 1964–1965, and a National Endowment for the Arts Fellowship in 1967–1968. In the same decade she published three short stories: "Reena" (1962), "Some Get Wasted" (1964), and "To Daduh, In Memoriam" (1967). In telling ways, these stories chart her process in transition from the United States/New World setting of her first novel, *Brown Girl, Brownstones*, to the Caribbean/New World geography of her second novel, *The Chosen Place, the Timeless People* (1969).

"Reena," perhaps Marshall's most anthologized piece of writing, was "the first and only commissioned study [she] ever wrote." Asked to do an article on the black woman by *Harper's Magazine* for its special October 1962 supplement, "The American Female," Marshall responded with fiction rather than an essay. Although, as she put it, " 'Reena' is a technically mixed bag," it is a significant story because it was one of the first pieces of contemporary American fiction to employ as its protagonist a college-educated, politically active black woman.

"Reena" has much in common with *Brown Girl, Brownstones*. In keeping with Marshall's portrayal of the distinctiveness of specific communities, Reena narrates her story to a childhood girlfriend at a ritual, a wake for her Aunt Vi. And by focusing on the development of a black woman in the context of a West Indian immigrant community, "Reena" recalls Marshall's portrayal of Selina. Yet this story differs from *Brown Girl, Brownstones* in that its emphasis is on adulthood rather than adolescence. Reena articulates the new options available to black women of her generation in contrast to older women like Aunt Vi; yet she also comes to understand the limits of these options. She *must* search for her African ancestry and its meaning because she feels the discomfort of displacement in this New World. With her unquenchable spirit, sharp intelligence, consistent honesty, and political intensity, Reena serves as a precursor to Merle Kinbona, Marshall's monumental character in *The Chosen Place, the Timeless People*.

While the setting of "Reena" is the United States, "To Da-duh, In Memoriam" takes place in the Caribbean. Marshall calls this piece her "most autobiographical" piece of writing. Based on Marshall's memory of a visit she made at the age of nine to her grandmother in Barbados, the story is a sharp portrayal of the contrast between two worldviews. While the child trumpets the superiority of Western civilization, with its Empire State Building and bright lights, Da-duh holds to the values of much of the underdeveloped Third World—the beauty and pain of the land, the sustenance of tradition.

As Marshall tells us in her headnote to the Feminist Press reissue of this story, Da-duh is an ancestor figure who appears in various forms throughout her work—from the African American Mrs. Thompson in *Brown Girl, Brownstones* to Great-Aunt Cuney in her third novel, *Praisesong for the Widow* (1983). Marshall, like Alice Walker and Toni Morrison, believes in the significance of the ancestors and celebrates them in her fiction, for they are the ground on which she stands. Although the child in "To Da-duh" appears to win the contest of values—for Da-duh dies and she lives—years later she comes to realize the wisdom of her ancestors as she paints scenes of natural environments in the midst of her machine-plagued world. By situating the story in Barbados and by portraying her grandmother, Marshall not only recalls the ancestral land of *Brown Girl, Brownstones* but also carves out the crevices of a character who would be a forerunner of Leesy Walkes, who in *The Chosen Place, the Timeless People* represents the tenacity of history in the Third World.

Unlike the two other short stories of the 1960s, "Some Get Wasted" is about boys—in this case, rival gangs in Brooklyn. At first reading the story seems very different from Marshall's other works, yet its characters recall those of *Soul Clap Hands and Sing* and Deighton in *Brown Girl, Brownstones*, in Marshall's depiction of men who invest their sense of self-worth in the definition of manhood as glory. In addition, "Some Get Wasted" centers on a contemporary phenomenon, the feeling of displacement experienced by African Americans in the United States. The gang serves as a vehicle by which these alienated second-generation West Indian-Americans achieve a sense of belonging while participating in feats of masculine conquest. Ironically, Hezzy, the protagonist of the story, "gets wasted" by the members of his own gang who mistake him for a rival, for the two groups are in fact virtually indistinguishable. In his intense commitment to the gang's definition of manhood, Hezzy also foreshadows Vere (*The Chosen Place, the Timeless People*), who is similarly destroyed by his belief in the definition of manhood as conquest and glory.

The beginning of Marshall's monumental second novel, *The Chosen Place, the Timeless People*, brings together many of the themes and characters featured in her short stories of the 1960s. Merle Kinbona, having just returned from England to Bourne Island (a small Caribbean island), is driving to the airport so that Leesy Walkes can meet her grandson Vere, who is returning from the States, when the road washes away because of unseasonably heavy rains. The plane will bring other major characters to the island: Vere, who is returning to reclaim his manly "inheritance" in his own land; Allen Fuso, an intelligent American researcher of Irish and Italian descent who feels more at home in this razed land than he does in his own; and Harriet and Saul Amron, two newcomers to the island. A blue-blood Philadelphian, Harriet is a direct descendant of the folk who drew their wealth from the triangular slave trade, while her husband, Saul, a Jewish anthropologist, hopes that his research will benefit the people of Bournehills, the rural section of the island.

These first scenes introduce the major actors populating much of the underdeveloped world today—those like Leesy Walkes who have never left their land and see it as their own, natives like Merle and Vere who left their home to seek money or learning in the metropoles of the West, and those like Allen Fuso and the Amrons, who believe they can rescue underdeveloped societies from their economic and social plight.

In her interview with Alexis De Veaux, Marshall notes that *The Chosen Place, the Timeless People* (originally called "Ceremonies in the Guest House") is about a people who "refuse the many stop-gap measures offered to them because, in their minds, the change necessary is a revolutionary change." The novel's epigraph quotes the Tiv of West Africa: "Once a great wrong has been done, it never dies. People speak the words of peace, but their hearts do not forgive. Generations perform ceremonies of reconciliation but there is no end." The inhabitants of Bournehills are descendants of a people whose history in this New World is one of slavery and colonial subjection. Thus *The Chosen Place, the Timeless People* is a novel about one of the most pervasive problems of the contemporary world, neocolonialism, and about the reverberation of past actions in the present. Yet the novel is not a political tract; rather, it carefully explores the ways in which people's relationships are critical to historical process. It investigates the ongoing interaction between the apparently faceless forces of society and the choices human beings make.

The parts of the novel reflect that interaction. Like the title of *Brown Girl, Brownstones*, the title of Marshall's second novel emphasizes the connection between character and context, while extending that connection beyond gender or racial indicators to that of an entire people and their land. The novel is divided into four books, each individual title representing one aspect of that connection. The first book, "Heirs and Descendants," introduces the societal strata of Bourne Island, so determined by its colonial past, and introduces as well the newcomers who believe they have come to change that past. The second book, "Bournehills," focuses on the land itself, which appears to Saul to be "like everyplace that had been wantonly used, its substance stripped away and then abandoned." Despite the world's apparent abuse and then abandonment of them, the people of Bournehills hold to the rhythms of their traditions as a means of sustenance and as a mark of their existence. The third and fourth books, "Carnival" and "Whitsun," are named after ritual times of the year and hence point to both continuity and change. Within this broad structural pattern, Marshall creates intimacy in her novel by her careful delineation of the major

characters, who represent various aspects of Bournehills society even as they most decidedly represent themselves, and by the juxtaposition of pairs of characters who are similar yet oppose each other on issues critical to the novel's themes. Perhaps the most intensely opposed characters in *The Chosen Place, the Timeless People* are Harriet Amron, the supremely sane and wealthy white Philadelphian, and Merle Kinbona, the apparently neurotic black West Indian. In her interview with De Veaux, Marshall points out that she "wanted the women in *The Chosen Place, the Timeless People* to embody the whole power struggle of the world." Not only does Harriet (who Marshall sees as symbolic of the West) exercise power and control over others because she is white and wealthy; she *needs* to do so, because as a woman in Western society her only route to power is her influence on the men in her life. That constraint results in her manipulative schemes. On the other hand, Merle, who Marshall sees as "the history of the hemisphere," is so many things that she lacks wholeness. Although she is a vibrant and complex character, Merle is split, as symbolized by the catatonic spells to which she periodically succumbs. And she cannot achieve harmony as an individual, for her fragmentation is the fragmentation of the society itself. She must therefore attempt to change the entire society if she is to become a person at peace with herself.

Merle Kinbona is an extraordinary prefiguration of other contemporary African American women characters who, wounded by their emotional knowledge of Western society's evils, must seek wholeness not only in their personal lives but in their political context. This revolutionary initiative is central to the quest of Meridian in Alice Walker's *Meridian* (1976) and of Velma Henry in Toni Cade Bambara's *The Salt Eaters* (1980).

As impressive a character as Merle is, so equally memorable are Marshall's portrayals of the ordinary people of Bournehills—Gwen, Stinger, Ferguson, Leesy. It is they finally who enact Ned Cuffee's slave rebellion every Carnival, a scene that employs the past for the needs of the present, and it is they who insist on real rather than apparent change. It is they, Marshall suggests, who will finally give birth to the new society in this New World. Ironically, Marshall began writing *The Chosen Place, the Timeless People* in Grenada, a Caribbean island that suffered an aborted social revolution during the 1980s because of its own internal disharmonies as well as the intense pressures imposed upon it by its giant neighbor, the United States.

Like *Brown Girl, Brownstones, The Chosen Place, the Timeless People* received excellent reviews in prestigious journals and newspapers; yet it did not become well-known despite the emphasis then current in the media on black issues. Perhaps because the novel was published in 1969, when so much African American literature focused on the theme of the urban ghettos, when the popular genres of the black movement were poetry and drama, and when so many of the major literary works focused on male conquest and exclusively black characters, Marshall's complex and convoluted novel did not suit the tenor of the times.

Given the rise of the American women's movement and Marshall's emphasis in her novel on Merle Kinbona as a female political actor, one might have expected the book to have received more support. But Marshall's portrayal of white women in *The Chosen Place, the Timeless People* did not lend her work to the predominant themes of this first phase of the second wave of American feminism. In characterizing the West in the figure of Harriet, Marshall may have upset many white women in the movement. And the novel's portrayal of Merle's lesbian relationship with her London patroness as symbolic of exploitation may have registered as an example of homophobia in literature, as Hortense Spillers has suggested in her essay on the book.

Although *The Chosen Place, the Timeless People* did not become a well-known novel in the United States, the noted Caribbean poet Edward Braithwaite wrote two essays on it in the 1970s. Although the novel is first and foremost a Third World novel, Barbara Christian's 1980 survey *Black Women Novelists* described the work as integral to the development of a black female novel tradition in the United States; and in 1987, Susan Willis' *Specifying*, a work subtitled "Black Women Writing the American Experience," characterized *The Chosen Place, the Timeless People* as Marshall's novel of revolutionary struggle.

As well as being a graphic sign of Marshall's immersion in Caribbean societies, *The Chosen Place, the Timeless People* also marked important changes in her life in the decade following its publication. In 1970, she remarried. Her second husband, Nourry Menard, was a Haitian businessman with whom she lived in what she has called "an open and innovative marriage." But although she spent much time in the Caribbean, she also continued to live in the United States. Affected by the paucity of grants awarded to writers during this decade, Marshall taught at prestigious universities such as Columbia and Yale, an activity that no doubt cut into the intense periods of concentration she devoted to writing.

Although Marshall did not publish a novel during the 1970s, during that decade her work began to receive much more attention from critics than it had the previous decade. With the emergence of a group of critics who emphasized the literature of African American women, Marshall's fiction began to be taught in classes in the fields of literature, African American studies, and women's studies, and to be explored and analyzed in serious essays and critical books. In the 1980s the need to have her work accessible to students, readers, and critics resulted in the Feminist Press reissue of *Brown Girl, Brownstones* (1981), a paperback issue of *The Chosen Place, the Timeless People* (1982), and the publication of the anthology *Reena and Other Stories* (1983).

Praisesong for the Widow

While teaching and living in both the Caribbean and the United States, Marshall worked on a novel, no doubt influenced by her movement between the two worlds. In her 1980 interview with De Veaux, Marshall noted that her work in progress (*Praisesong for the Widow,* which was published three years later) was about a theme that had always concerned her, "namely the materialism of this country and how it often spells the death of love and feeling, and how do we, as black people, fend it off." The same theme is certainly central to *Brown Girl, Brownstones*. In the earlier novel, however, the issue of materialism is explored through a community of immigrants who have yet to achieve that success. In contrast, in her third novel, Marshall explores that theme through her focus on Avey Johnson, a middle-class, middle-aged black woman who has achieved the American dream.

In focusing on such an unlikely heroine, Marshall once again charted new territory in the area of African American women's literature. Certainly, older women such as Eva in Morrison's *Sula* (1974) or Miss Hazel in Toni Cade Bambara's story "My Man Bovanne" (1978) had been featured in fiction. And increasingly in the 1980s African American women writers—for example, Morrison in *Tar Baby* (1981) and Gloria Naylor in *Linden Hills* (1985)—had approached the question of class schisms in contemporary African American society. But no writer had constructed a "praise-song" for a character such as Avey Johnson, whose life journey explores issues of age and class in relation to the racial, cultural, and political issues of that society.

Praisesong for the Widow is also wide-ranging in its geography, for it is a journey through the Brooklyn of *Brown Girl, Brownstones* and the Caribbean society of *The Chosen Place, the Timeless People* as well as the rural black South of Tatem, South Carolina, and black middle-class North White Plains, New York. In referring to the novel as a "praise-song" (an African form still very much alive), Marshall recalls an ancestral worldview that might act as an antidote, as a source of healing for the disease of materialism so rampant in this modern world. The protagonist Avatara (Avey for short) is a symbol of diasporic healing, as the term "avatar" denotes one who is regarded as a complete or exemplary manifestation of a quality or concept.

Praisesong for the Widow is indeed a novel of healing, as its structure emphasizes. Dedi-

cating the work to her ancestral figure, Da-duh (Alberta Jane Clement), Marshall divides the book into four parts that delineate the journey from disease to health for those affected by the contradiction of being "old" in this New World. In Marshall's first section, "Runagate," named after African American poet Robert Hayden's poem about the flight of a runaway slave, Avey Johnson feels the disease of being a slave to materialism when on her annual perfunctory cruise to the Caribbean, she dreams of her long-dead Great-Aunt Cuney. In this first section of the novel, as throughout the work, Marshall uses ritual as an opening to a hidden worldview that is antithetical to the values acclaimed by the elite of the Americas. "Runagate" is followed by "Sleeper's Wake," in which "wake" represents both a ritual of death and awakening; "Lavé Tête," which is both a ritual of cleansing and, symbolically, that of being clothed in the raiments of a different worldview; and "The Beg Pardon," which refers both to a ritual of the letting go of the old and to the reclaiming of an older collective legacy.

In that journey, Avey—whose name echoes that of a title character from one of the vignettes in Jean Toomer's *Cane* (1923)—fulfills the promise that Toomer so poetically prophesied for black women of this century. Pointedly, Marshall emphasizes in *Praisesong for the Widow* that the fulfillment of that promise cannot be achieved without a visceral understanding of the past. So Avey is guided by two elders, one female, one male: her Great-Aunt Cuney, who knew that "her body she always usta say might be in Tatem but, her mind was long gone with the Ibos," and Liebert Joseph, "whose dirt floor under Avey Johnson's feet felt as hard and smooth as terrazo, and as cool." From these two survivors in the diaspora, one from the rural U.S. South, the other from the rural Caribbean, Avey Johnson learns that to *feel* that artificiality and materialism is a disease is the first step toward health, and that to feel "the nurturing ground from which [we] have sprung and to which [we] can always turn for sustenance" is necessary to fulfillment.

Precisely because she responds to the call of these elders, and because she undergoes her journey in her body as well as in her mind, Avey Johnson comes to deserve her praisesong. Only then can she recognize her true name and become an elder on whom others can stand. Marshall ends the novel with Avey's practical application of that truth, as she suggests that the journey through the black diaspora must be rooted in a visceral understanding of the past, which must be continually sung, continually reiterated in the present:

> And at least twice a week in the late afternoon, when the juniper trees amid Tatem began sending out their cool and stately shadows, she would lead them, grandchildren and visitors alike, in a troop over to the Landing.
> "It was here that they brought them," she would begin—as had been ordained. "They took them out of the boats right here where we're standing."

Daughters

Marshall's novel *Daughters* (1991) is an African diasporic text, one that connects issues affecting blacks in the United States to those affecting blacks in the Caribbean. Like *The Chosen Place, the Timeless People, Daughters* revisits and weaves together a number of issues that are central in Marshall's earlier work: black peoples' struggle against neocolonial and imperial forms of subjection in the Caribbean islands and in urban U.S. communities; the importance of ancestral connections and rituals in sustaining diasporic communities; the complexity of black men's and women's relationships with each other given the experiences of enslavement and colonialism as well as constraining race, gender, and class imperatives; and, most significantly, black women's attempts to form meaningful relationships with each other—either as mothers and daughters or as sisterfriends.

At the center of *Daughters* are a number of crisscrossed relationships involving what Marshall presents as a "constellation" or a cluster of women, some located on the island of Triunion, others located in the United States but connected nonetheless across space and time as daughters of the African diaspora. The novel's plot traces several events: the spiritual and emotional development of the protagonist Ursa MacKenzie away from the overshadowing authority of her father; the struggle of Triunion's other daughters, including Ursa's mother Estelle, to break their dependence on men, especially on Primus MacKenzie, Ursa's father; and Primus' own inner struggle to maintain integrity in the face of trenchant neocolonial advancements on Triunion.

Just as the constellations Ursa Major and Ursa Minor are populated by seven spectacular stars known respectively as the Big Dipper (Big Bear) and the Little Dipper (Little Bear), so too Marshall peoples *Daughters* with seven striking women characters (Ursa MacKenzie, Estelle MacKenzie, Celestine Bellgarde, Astral Forde, Malvern, Vincereta [Viney] Daniels, and Mae Ryland) around whom several of the novel's chapters are structured. Marshall's symbolic and allegorical use of astronomical configurations such as the constellation, the polestar, and celestial names as major structuring devices for the novel provides some insight into the individual significance of her characters as well as their relationships with each other. Four of her female characters' names—Ursa, Estelle, Astral, and Celestine—resonate with symbolic star imagery, foregrounding their relationship with the male protagonist Primus MacKenzie, whose character as son and as premier of Triunion plays on the symbolic imagery of the sun as a central celestial figure around which other, supposedly "smaller," stars orbit. The title Marshall uses for book one, "Little Girl of All the Daughters," signifies the symbolic importance of the protagonist Ursa as a "Little Dipper" in relation to a line of epic female ancestors, most importantly, in relation to Congo Jane, the premier female ancestor and symbol of women's resistance in Triunion. Both Ursa MacKenzie's grandmother, Ms. Mack, and the repeatedly emergent figure Congo Jane constitute indispensable female ancestral presences in the text, presences which, though they do not speak forthrightly to Marshall's female characters, shadow these characters throughout the text and embody historical experiences critical to these women characters' spiritual development and to their use of memory as a catalyst for political action.

Inasmuch as *Daughters* points toward a female line of ancestry, it also suggests, first through the pairing of Congo Jane and Will Cudjoe and then through a series of male/female dyads, that black political action against neocolonialism and racism must be a united effort carried out by both men and women. Marshall implies a strong correlation between men's and women's "togetherness" and the consequent successes of their political struggles. She emphasizes this point by ritually invoking the memorialized couple Congo Jane and Will Cudjoe, who orchestrated a liberation struggle against their slavemasters, and by juxtaposing this ancestral couple's history next to the modern day experiences of her characters. Such juxtapositions imply that the characters in *Daughters*, particularly the male/female dyads (Primus and Estelle, Ursa and Lowell, Beufils and his wife, Mae Ryland and Sandy Lawson), are Congo Jane and Will Cudjoe's progeny, similarly engaged in a struggle of political resistance against the ravages of colonialism and the residual effects of enslavement. Marshall's point, as her narrator puts it, is that: "slavery, for all its horrors, was a time when black men and women had it together, were together, stood together. . . . there were Congo Janes and Will Cudjoes—both here [in the United States] and in the islands."

But if slavery "was a time when black men and women had it together," *Daughters* begs the question of what happened to that togetherness following that time; in fact, the novel seems to mourn, nostalgically, the passing of black men and women's collective cooperation even as it critiques the subordinated positions women occupy in male/female relationships that are both politically focused and sexual in nature. Estelle's relationship with Primus, Mae Ryland's relationship with Sandy Lawson, Ursa's relationships with her father and Lowell Curruthers, and Viney's relationships with her mates and her son all indicate what appears on Marshall's part to be a deliberate effort at interrogating black male patriarchy, constraining gender imperatives affecting black women's social and political development, and the unsatisfactory results such constraints yield in black liberation movements. As Marshall explains in an interview with Sylvia Baer, *Daughters* examines "the subtle deferring to men that was so much a part of my childhood and the childhood of many women." Ultimately, Marshall seems to both engage and disavow the feasibility or even the desirability of male-female pairings; what is left nebulous in the constellation of dyads she constructs is the position women are to have in relation to men both socially and politically. Readers are left to ponder what configuration of partnership is to be developed between black men and women—that is to say, whether or not black women should critique and resist black male patriarchy and sexism as the first step in inaugurating mature interventions against colonialism or whether they should refrain from substantive critiques of male leaders such as Primus MacKenzie and Sandy Lawson lest they be judged unsupportive and divisive.

In this regard, the novel remains somewhat ambivalent about several of the resolutions presented through its daughters. Ms. Mae Ryland, for example, makes a plea for pardoning Sandy Lawson, whose lack of judgement and opportunistic manipulation of his community has led to its partial destruction in favor of a new highway. Similarly, despite Estelle's clandestine betrayal of Primus during the election—an intervention we might interpret as covert correction and critique—she has muffled her voice and faithfully tolerated Primus' sexual and political indiscretions over a number of years. Her daughter Ursa has had to fight hard not to emulate Estelle's example. Viney, on the other hand, speaks out against men's oppression. Ironically, the text implies that Viney is an unwhole character, one who, in Ursa's imagination, stands with a gaping hole at her side akin to the hollow cardboard cutout dolls of Ursa's childhood. True to the spirit of her name Vincereta, which means conqueror, Viney artificially inseminates herself and raises her son Robeson alone only to realize that though she may be able to provide Robeson with the best of material acquisitions, her ability to communicate to him the experiential realities of what it means to be black and male in America is inescapably limited. This situation calls to mind the old African proverb: "it takes a whole village to raise a child."

Depending on which perspective the reader chooses, one may draw freely on the associative play implicit in the notion of a hole in order to interpret this hole Ursa imagines as a sign of lack *or* as a sign of wholeness, a sign of unity in the self. In either case, the implication remains strong in *Daughters* that there are inseparable connections between the prerogative (not the ability) to bear children and women's autonomy, power, and responsibility as arbiters over the ancestors' reentry into the world and over the political destiny of black communities/nations. Ursa and Astral's decisions to abort their children, Estelle's string of abortive pregnancies and her determined resolve to bear a child, and Viney's decision to artificially inseminate herself all conjure up the observations of the inspiriting sage Nana Peazant in Julie Dash's film *Daughters of the Dust*, who concludes that "the ancestors and womb they one and the same."

Since the publication of *Daughters* in 1991, Marshall's work has received much critical attention. Several scholarly book-length studies consider *Daughters* in relation to Marshall's earlier work. Heather Hathaway's *Caribbean Waves: Relocating Claude McKay and Paule Marshall* (1999) both compares Marshall's and McKay's Caribbean-American experiences and features chapters that discuss issues of location, migration, and immigration in *Brown Girl, Brownstones* and *Daughters*; Eugenia DeLamotte's *Places of Silence, Journeys of Freedom* (1998) examines the "double visions" of Marshall's art through close readings of *The Chosen Place*, *Praisesong*, and *Daughters*, while Dorothy Denniston's comprehensive study *The Fiction of Paule Marshall: Reconstructions of History, Culture, and Gender* (1995) undertakes Marshall's oeuvre, including a reading of "Transformation and Recreation of Female Identity in *Daughters*." Both Lean'tin Bracks's *Writings on Black*

Women of the Diaspora: History, Language, and Identity (1998) and Joyce Pettis' *Toward Wholeness in Paule Marshall's Fiction* (1995) foreground the diasporic dimensions of Marshall's work and emphasize the importance of black women's spirituality in Marshall's writing. Bernhard Melchior's *Re/Visioning the Self Away From Home* (1998) outlines the relationship between Marshall's Caribbean heritage, her life experiences, and her writings. With increasing interest in African Diaspora studies, Marshall's work continues to be the subject of numerous dissertations and journal articles and will enjoy significant attention in years to come.

Marshall now divides her time between Richmond, Virginia, and New York City. She is a professor of English and Creative Writing at New York University, where she teaches a fiction workshop and sponsors the "Paule Marshall and the New Generation Symposium." In keeping with Marshall's commitment to encouraging young black writers, this yearly symposium features emerging novelists reading from their first published books. It has featured such promising writers as Shay Youngblood, A. J. Verdelle, Edwidge Danticat, Colson Whitehead, and Danny Senna. In 1990 Marshall received the John Dos Passos Prize for writing, and in 1992 she received the prestigious MacArthur Fellowship. Her latest novel, *The Fisher King*, was chosen as the fall 2000 Book of the Month Club selection.

Selected Bibliography

PRIMARY WORKS

NOVELS

Brown Girl, Brownstones. New York: Random House, 1959.
Soul Clap Hands and Sing. New York: Atheneum, 1961.
The Chosen Place, the Timeless People. New York: Harcourt Brace & World, 1969.
Praisesong for the Widow. New York: Putnam's, 1983.
Daughters. New York: Atheneum, 1991.
The Fisher King. New York: Scribners, 2000.

SHORT STORIES AND ESSAYS

"Reena." *Harper's Magazine* 225:154–63 (October 1962).

"Some Get Wasted." In *Harlem U.S.A.* Edited by John Henrik Clarke. East Berlin: Seven Seas, 1964.

"The Negro Woman in American Literature." *Freedomways* 6:20–25 (Winter 1966).

"To Da-duh, In Memoriam." *New World Quarterly* 3:97–101 (1966–1967).

"Shaping the World of My Art." *New Letters* 40:97–112 (October 1973).

"From the Poets of the Kitchen." *New York Times Book Review*, January 9, 1983.

SECONDARY WORKS

BIOGRAPHICAL AND CRITICAL STUDIES

Bracks, Lean'tin. *Writings on Black Women of the Diaspora: History, Language, and Identity.* New York: Garland Publishers, 1998.

Braithwaite, Edward. "West Indian History and Society in the Art of Paule Marshall's Novel." *Journal of Black Studies* 1:225–38 (December 1970).

———. "Rehabilitations." *Critical Quarterly* 13:175–83 (Summer 1971).

Christian, Barbara. "Sculpture and Space: The Interdependency of Character and Culture in the Novels of Paule Marshall." In *Black Women Novelists.* Westport, Conn.: Greenwood, 1980. Pp. 80–136.

———. "Ritualistic Process and the Structure of *Praisesong for the Widow.*" *Callaloo* 18:74–84 (Spring–Summer 1983).

———. "Paule Marshall: A Literary Biography." In *Dictionary of Literary Biography.* Vol. 33, *Afro-American Fiction Writers After 1955.* Edited by Thadious M. Davis and Trudier Harris. Detroit: Gale Research, 1984. Pp. 161–70.

DeLamotte, Eugenia. *Places of Silence, Journeys of Freedom.* Philadelphia: University of Pennsylvania Press, 1998.

Denniston, Dorothy. "Early Short Fiction by Paule Marshall." *Callaloo* 18:31–45 (Spring–Summer 1983).

———. *The Fiction of Paule Marshall: Reconstructions of History, Culture, and Gender.* Knoxville: University of Tennessee Press, 1995.

De Veaux, Alexis. "Paule Marshall—In Celebration of Our Triumphs." *Essence* 11:96–98, 123–34 (May 1980).

Ferguson, Moira. "Of Bears and Bearings: Marshall's Diverse Daughters." *Melus* 24:177–95 (Spring 1999).

Hathaway, Heather. *Caribbean Waves: Relocating Claude McKay and Paule Marshall.* Bloomington: Indiana University Press, 1999.

Marshall, Paule. "Holding on to the Vision: Sylvia Baer Interviews Paule Marshall." *Women's Review of Books* 3, no. 10:24–25 (1991).

Melchior, Bernhard. *Re/Visioning the Self Away From Home: Autobiographical and Cross-Cultural Dimensions in the Works of Paule Marshall.* Frankfurt am Main: Peter Lang Publishers, 1998.

Pettis, Joyce. *Toward Wholeness in Paule Marshall's Fiction.* Charlottesville: University Press of Virginia, 1995.

Spillers, Hortense. "*The Chosen Place, the Timeless People:* Some Figurations on the New World." In *Conjuring: Black Women, Fiction, and Literary Tradition.* Edited by Marjorie Pryse and Hortense Spillers. Bloomington: Indiana University Press, 1985. Pp. 151–75.

Washington, Mary Helen. Afterword to *Brown Girl, Brownstones,* by Paule Marshall. Old Westbury, N.Y.: Feminist Press, 1981. Pp. 311–24.

Willis, Susan. "Describing Arcs of Recovery: Paule Marshall's Relationship to Afro-American Culture." In *Specifying: Black Women Writing the American Experience.* Madison: University of Wisconsin Press, 1987. Pp. 53–82.

—The essay and bibliography have been revised for this edition by Suzette A. Spencer.

CLAUDE MCKAY
(1890–1948)

WAYNE F. COOPER

FROM THE PERSPECTIVE of literary history, Claude McKay's reputation as a pioneer in the development of twentieth-century African American literature seems secure. His literary influence was felt far and wide, in the West Indies and in Jamaica, his native island, as well as in the United States and Africa. Poets as diverse as J. J. Rabearivelo from Madagascar, Aimé Césaire from Martinique, Léopold Sedar Senghor from Senegal, and Langston Hughes in the United States all at one time or another expressed their debt to McKay. In the post-World War I United States his verses inspired a whole generation of "New Negro" writers associated with the Harlem Renaissance of the 1920s. His poetry broke the constraints of Victorian respectability and drew without reserve from his deepest feelings as an African American man.

In his fiction McKay affirms the self-sufficiency of black folk cultures. African American basic values, he believed, derived from their own experiences, cultural traditions, and racial heritage more than from a Western tradition that had historically tried to exclude black experiences. Western progress, McKay argued, continued to endanger black life and black culture. To him, industrialization, urbanization, and bureaucratization, whether managed by the Left or the Right, was killing the souls of Western men and women by cutting them off from their ancient relationship to the natural world. African American culture, McKay believed, deeply rooted as it was in rural folkways, many of which derived from Africa, not only had resisted the oppressive exploitation of slavery and racial segregation but still stood in opposition to the soul-destroying tendencies of modern life. Like all pastoralists, McKay believed that those who led an agricultural life and followed the rhythms of the seasons, as most African Americans did prior to World War I, were more closely attuned to nature's ways than urban dwellers in the industrial West. In his novels and short stories, McKay affirmed black culture at its most elemental level by celebrating the lives of its most marginal members in the urban ghettos of the northern United States and in the small, isolated mountain villages of his native Jamaica. In the 1930s, his novels inspired the founders of the French West African and West Indian Negritude movements. Those in the United States, such as the critics George Kent and Addison Gayle, as well as others, who defend the idea of black cultural autonomy acknowledge McKay's importance as a forerunner to their own ideas.

McKay made his odyssey from Jamaica through the United States, the Soviet Union, Western Europe, and North Africa decades before other West Indian expatriate intellectuals and literary artists more familiar to modern readers, among them C. L. R. James, Frantz Fanon, Derek Walcott, and V. S. Naipaul. McKay was, in a sense, doubly an expatriate. After leaving Jamaica, he made the United States his second home, and then he joined the American expatriate caravan in France during the 1920s, thereby preceding, once again, better-known African Americans, such as Richard Wright and James Baldwin. Even before Paul Robeson was lionized in the Soviet Union, McKay had received similar treatment there in 1922 and 1923. Because he had experienced his radical political phase a full decade or more before most African American writers and intellectuals who came of age in the 1920s or 1930s, McKay's anti-Communist stance as a member of the Federal Writers' Project in New York in the 1930s placed him sharply at odds politically with many of his fellow writers and with critics.

Among all the writers associated with the Harlem Renaissance, McKay remains the most controversial. During his lifetime, he was a man whose personality and works provoked strong, conflicting reactions. To some he seemed an opportunist who, blown by shifting ideological winds, merely wrote whatever was acceptable to the reading public, largely white in his day. In 1937, the then Marxist critic and poet Melvin Tolson called McKay a black Ulysses who never found his way home; in the same year Alain Locke dismissed him as "the playboy of the Negro Renaissance" and its aging enfant terrible who had by 1937 "repudiated all possible loyalties." Although he had his detractors, he also had steadfast defenders, among them such varied figures as James Weldon Johnson, Max Eastman, and John Dewey.

Since his death, critics have been as divided about McKay's achievements as his contemporaries were during his lifetime. A few have insisted that McKay's poetry and prose were pioneering works of genius. A French Catholic, Jean Wagner, and a black nationalist critic, George Kent, have both given high praise to McKay, though for diametrically opposed reasons. To Wagner, McKay's poetry exhibits a universality of appeal that elevated his work above "folklorists" like Langston Hughes and Sterling Brown. Kent, by contrast, finds McKay's work important because it prepared the way for a self-consciously independent black literature. For Kent, McKay displayed "a positive *niggerhood*, . . . a naturalness of being to be maintained in the face of the most complex patterns of western culture."

Others, however, have dismissed his poetry, his fiction, or both as dated, uneven in quality, and generally lacking in artistic merit. To such critics, he was at best a transitional figure of passing historical importance. At worst, they have endorsed his enemies' contentions that his career was fatally flawed by ideological contradictions, opportunism, and a general failure of vision. Harold Cruse claims McKay peddled Communist nostrums, S. P. Fullenwider accuses him of pandering to white tastes, and Nathan Huggins argues that he generally lacked artistic merit. Still others, such as Robert Bone, Stephen Bronz, and James R. Giles, have sought more balanced assessments of McKay, concluding that although he had a significant impact as a literary figure, his own artistic achievements in poetry, the novel, and the short story were limited.

Anyone whose work has been so variously judged over so many years deserves careful attention. McKay's life mirrored in complex ways important aspects of the African American experience in the first half of the twentieth century. The anger, alienation, and rebellion he expressed in his poetry and the search for community he attempted in his fiction reflected not only his own life stages from youth to maturity but also the efforts of African Americans to triumph over the adversities that beset them. He was also deeply involved with the larger society, its social and political movements, and its literary trends. As an editor of the *Liberator* in New York City and the *Workers' Dreadnought* in London after World War I, and as a committed but critical international socialist and opponent of Western imperialism during the interwar years, McKay consistently presented a black viewpoint where one was otherwise seldom heard. Clearly, his importance as a pioneering African American writer lay not only in his specific artistic accomplishments, but

Claude McKay

which my fellow-expatriates could sympathize but which they could not altogether understand. For they were not black like me. Not being black and unable to see deep into the profundity of blackness, some even thought that I might have preferred to be white like them. They couldn't imagine that I had no desire merely to exchange my black problem for their white problem. For all their knowledge and sophistication, they couldn't understand the instinctive and animal and purely physical pride of a black person resolute in being himself and yet living a simple civilized life like themselves. Because their education in their white world had trained them to see a person of color either as an inferior or as an exotic.   (p. 245)

The key words in this passage—"a black person resolute in being himself and yet living a simple civilized life like themselves"—indicate the dilemma that, as W. E. B. Du Bois had pointed out long before, lay at the heart of the black man's struggle in America. To resolve this problem, McKay insisted throughout all his work that blacks, as one identifiable race and many distinct ethnic groups, must insist upon their right to be themselves, fully and without reservation, and also to be participants in the world's larger community, both as individuals and as a group. But first, McKay insisted, African Americans had to recognize and embrace their own communal life as the foundation of their existence—as McKay himself did in his own life and art.

McKay was born on 15 September 1890 on the family farm, Sunny Ville, located in the mountainous center of upper Clarendon Parish in Jamaica. His parents, part of the independent black peasantry that had emerged there after emancipation in the 1830s, successfully educated all their children. The eldest, U'Theo, became a planter, businessman, and civic leader well known throughout Jamaica. In McKay's childhood, U'Theo was just beginning his career as a schoolteacher. In fact, between the ages of seven and fourteen, Claude lived with and received almost all his primary education from U'Theo in various schools around Mon-

also and more broadly in his ability to project African American concerns through his art and career upon the broadest possible stage and to claim for African Americans a voice and a role in the unfolding drama of world history and literature.

At the same time, McKay's work itself, so closely related to his life at every stage, deserves closer scrutiny. Underneath its apparent failures and contradictions, one can discern in his poetry, fiction, and essays a consistency of vision that in the end defines the man and artist as a writer of genuine achievement. McKay defined the problem he so forthrightly faced in his life and art when he wrote in *A Long Way from Home* (1937) of the differences that separated him from white American expatriates in Paris during the 1920s:

Color consciousness was the fundamental of my restlessness. And it was something with tego Bay and in Clarendon Parish. A graduate of Mico Teachers College in Kingston, U'Theo was a free thinking agnostic and rationalist who communicated his intellectual independence to his youngest brother.

At the time, Jamaica was a poor but proud backwater colony of Great Britain. Its heyday as a producer of great wealth in the sugar trade had long passed, but Britain had remained to cast upon her impoverished black subjects the reflected glories of great empire. For the youthful McKay, to be a part of the British Empire seemed adventurous and romantic. As he observed ruefully in his late memoir, *My Green Hills of Jamaica* (1979), "the direction of our schooling was of course English, and it was so successful we really believed we were little black Britons."

As a descendant of black African slaves, however, McKay also had a different heritage to which he early laid claim. In a poem, first published in the Kingston *Daily Gleaner* in 1912, "Gordon to the Oppressed Natives," he identified with Jamaica's history of slave rebellions and more specifically with the postslavery Morant Bay Rebellion of 1865, which had led to substantial governmental reforms in Jamaica. The complex heritage of McKay's Jamaica—British and African, free peasant and imperial colony—was reflected in his Jamaican dialect poetry. Out of this heritage emerged his lifelong literary themes. These themes are largely pastoral—the innocence and joys of childhood, the superiority of black rural community values over the degradations of the alien, white-dominated city. These pastoral themes clashed in the dialect poetry with a striking realism in his treatment of the economic limitations of black peasantry and their social frustrations under British colonial rule. His dialect poetry expresses the spirit of protest and the complete identification with the sufferings of his race that figure prominently in his later American verse.

The poems collected in *Songs of Jamaica* and *Constab Ballads* (both published in 1912) were written between 1910 and 1912. During at least six months of that period, McKay served on the island constabulary and heard many complaints from the island's black peasants about the difficulties of earning a living in and around Kingston. Their complaints were also directed against black policemen, such as himself, whom the black Jamaican peasantry, as they moved between country and city, identified as tools of the ruling British. Thus, in "A Midnight Woman to the Bobby" (in *Songs of Jamaica*), a Jamaican woman taunts a "constab" who has questioned her motive for being on the street so late at night, by reminding him that until he donned the uniform of the constabulary, he, like many he now accosts, had been a half-starved, ill-clad country fellow: "You lef' you district, big an' coarse, / An' come join buccra Police Force."

The best poems in McKay's *Songs of Jamaica* and *Constab Ballads* are dramatic monologues like "A Midnight Woman" and "The Apple-Woman's Complaint" or vivid descriptions of the poor in town or country such as "Two-an'-Six," "Pay-Day," "Knutsford Park Races," and "Papine Corner." In these early volumes, though sentimentally drawn to England and compelled by a naive allegiance to anti-Christian, pro-evolutionary rationalism, McKay emphatically states his basic loyalty to the Jamaican peasantry, "My people, my people, me owna black skin" (in *Constab Ballads*). He pledges to them a return to the countryside of his happy childhood and renounces the temptations of the city. Although, in fact, he soon left Jamaica and never went home again, he carried with him a deep loyalty to rural black folk and a mythic memory of childhood innocence in a self-sufficient black peasant community. This pastoral vision nurtured his creative energies for the rest of his life.

After the publication of his dialect poems in 1912, McKay was persuaded by Walter Jekyll that he could not earn his living as a poet. He consequently decided that he would return to the countryside only as a trained agronomist, and left Jamaica to study at Booker T. Washington's Tuskegee Institute in Alabama. McKay's education in the United States was largely financed by Walter Jekyll, an English "gentleman" resident in Jamaica, who had befriended McKay and tutored him in European literatures and languages. An admirer of the Jamaican peasantry, Jekyll had encouraged the young poet to write Jamaican dialect poems and had found a publisher for them. He also guided the inexperienced young author through the publishing process, supplied both volumes with a glossary and footnotes, and wrote a preface to *Songs of Jamaica*. An ex-minister who had left the Church of England to become an exponent of free thought and social Darwinism, Jekyll himself wrote several books on a variety of topics, such as *The Art of Singing* (1884), *The Bible Untrustworthy* (1904), *The Wisdom of Schopenhauer* (1911), and *Jamaica Song and Story* (1907), a classic collection of Jamaican songs and folklore.

McKay arrived at Tuskegee in the early fall of 1912 but stayed only a few weeks before transferring to Kansas State University in Manhattan, Kansas. Tuskegee had disappointed him. He hated its discipline and rules, and its student body and curriculum fell below his academic expectations. He remained at Kansas State for two years before deciding he had had enough of agronomy and college. His next move was in 1914, to New York City. There he married his Jamaican sweetheart, Eulalie Emelda Lewars. With money from Jekyll, McKay opened a small West Indian restaurant. Neither his business nor his marriage lasted long. The dynamism and variety of the city, both day and night, combined with the variety and vitality of its growing black community, distracted McKay from both business and marriage. His restaurant went bankrupt, and Eulalie, pregnant and dissatisfied with her husband's inattentiveness, returned to her family in Jamaica to have their baby. Although not divorced, the McKays never lived together again. A daughter was born of their brief union; McKay never met her, but she eventually maintained a long correspondence with him. A portion of his irregular and often meager earnings went to her support in Jamaica.

McKay's sexual preferences proved highly unorthodox and clashed at every point with conventional notions of marriage. He believed in free love, he was bisexual, and he had affairs with whomever attracted him, man or woman. In New York, perhaps for the first time, he was able to give free reign to his homosexual inclinations, which he had previously implied in his dialect poetry (see "Bennie's Departure," in *Constab Ballads*).

Freed of marriage and the responsibility of business, McKay took a series of menial jobs and resumed his writing career. From 1914 until 1919, he worked and wrote poetry in his spare moments. In his new verses he moved away from dialect poetry and wrote short, rhymed lyrics, many of them sonnets, about his Jamaican childhood, love, and aspects of the racial conflict in America. Stylistically, they were modeled upon the Elizabethan and Romantic models most admired by Jamaicans, but in them McKay infused his own passions and concerns for racial justice.

McKay's renewed literary efforts began at a fertile time and in a fertile place. In the United States, the assault against Victorian gentility was already well under way, and New York would soon be its center. McKay avidly read the city's newspapers and literary magazines. He also familiarized himself with the radical political movements and journals of the day. His first New York publication was in *Seven Arts*, which published the poems "The Harlem Dancer" and "Invocation" in October 1917. *Pearson's Magazine* included four of his poems—"The Conqueror," "Harlem Shadows," "Is it Worthwhile," and "To the White Fiends"—in its September 1918 issue. And in its July 1919 issue Max Eastman's *Liberator* published two pages featuring his sonnets and other lyrics that included "If We Must Die," McKay's defiant call for blacks to fight back against white mobs that were attacking blacks that summer. The post-war period in the United States saw violent white reactions against blacks eager to share the fruits of democracy. "If We Must Die" brought McKay immediate fame among African Americans, and he became a regular contributor to the *Liberator*, then America's foremost journal of radical art and literature.

Late in 1919 McKay accepted an offer of free passage to England from an admirer; from the late fall of 1919 through 1920, he lived in London and wrote articles and poems for Sylvia Pankhurst's Communist weekly, the *Workers'*

Dreadnought. Under his own name and the pseudonyms Eli Edwards and Hugh Hope (the pseudonyms used to keep his employer from knowing he was a writer), McKay wrote revolutionary poetry and political articles in which he clearly defined his belief that those involved in international communism and colonial movements for national independence were natural allies against European and American imperial domination. British and American Communists, he said, must accept the colored peoples of the world as equals and assist in the demise of European imperialism abroad if they desired revolution at home. He stated that he was supporting Marcus Garvey's international black nationalist movement because "for subject peoples, at least, nationalism is the open door to communism."

McKay's sojourn in London coincided with the efforts of Pankhurst's group and other radical socialists in England to form the British Communist Party. As a participant in Pankhurst's faction, McKay gained valuable experience as a radical journalist and observed closely the strengths and shortcomings of Communists in Great Britain. Although he trusted Pankhurst because she championed blacks and supported the Irish and other colonial independence movements, from the start, McKay adopted a generally critical stance toward most Communists. For them to succeed, he believed they had to accept blacks as absolute equals, just as the Industrial Workers of the World (IWW) had done earlier in the United States.

Although deeply involved politically with Pankhurst's *Workers' Dreadnought,* McKay went elsewhere to publish his poetry. For it, he sought out C. K. Ogden, the editor of the prestigious *Cambridge Magazine.* In the summer 1920 issue Ogden published twenty-three of McKay's nonpolitical lyrics. Ogden ranked McKay with Siegfried Sassoon and Rupert Brooke as the young poets of the World War I generation he most admired. He persuaded the London publisher Grant Richards to print McKay's verse in a slender volume entitled *Spring in New Hampshire and Other Poems* (1920). Ogden even called upon his friend and fellow critic I. A. Richards to write a short introduction to the volume.

Shortly after *Spring In New Hampshire* appeared in the fall of 1920, Pankhurst and some of her associates were jailed for printing articles that violated Great Britain's wartime Defence of the Realm Act. The articles dealt with disaffection in the Royal Navy. They had been written by a young British sailor whom McKay had befriended and encouraged. McKay destroyed the original articles and letters by the sailor and made sure that when agents from Scotland Yard visited his room, they found only poems. With Pankhurst's arrest, however, her associates split into quarreling factions and McKay decided to return to the United States. Early in 1921 he was back in New York, where he spent 1921 and most of 1922 as an associate editor of the *Liberator.* For a while in 1922, after its chief editor, Max Eastman, had left the *Liberator,* McKay co-edited the magazine with Michael Gold, the author of the semiautobiographical novel *Jews Without Money* (1930).

In his earlier sojourn in New York, between 1914 and 1919, McKay had been politically closest to Hubert Harrison, Harlem's foremost pre-war socialist and IWW organizer. He had also met or corresponded with A. Phillip Randolph and Chandler Owen, editors of the *Messenger,* a black socialist monthly based in Harlem. In addition, there were a few other West Indian socialists in Harlem at this time whose ideas concerning the connections between the Bolshevik Revolution, European imperialism, and colonial independence movements influenced McKay's political thought. Besides Harrison, a Virgin Islands native, these included W. A. Domingo and Cyril Briggs both fellow Jamaicans. When Marcus Garvey's Universal Negro Improvement Association and African Communities League (UNIA) emerged as a mass movement after World War I, all these men, including McKay, tried to assist it in various ways, but Garvey proved unamenable to their socialist thought. By the time of McKay's return in 1921, Harrison had become an independent lecturer, while Briggs was directing his own semisecret African Blood Brotherhood (founded in 1919), which would shortly merge with the Communist party. McKay himself wrote an article critical of Garvey's unrealistic attitudes and goals, "Garvey as a Negro Moses," for the *Liberator* (5:8–9 [April 1922]).

Aside from Max Eastman, McKay's most valuable literary benefactor was Joel Spingarn, a distinguished professor of literature at Columbia University. Spingarn was also an important official of the National Association for the Advancement of Colored People, already the nation's leading black civil rights organization, with headquarters in New York City. Through Spingarn's influence, McKay had published his first verses in the United States in 1917. After his return from London, McKay resumed his contact with Springarn, who was also instrumental in getting Harcourt, Brace to accept his next volume of poetry, *Harlem Shadows*, an enlarged version of *Spring in New Hampshire*, in 1922.

McKay's heart lay, however, with *Liberator* and its predecessor, *Masses*, which had been suppressed during World War I. The artists and writers of *Masses* and *Liberator* were free-spirited, innovative, and yet politically committed to remaking society along socialist lines. He could join them without giving up any of his concerns as a black man. When offered the chance by Max Eastman to help edit the publication in 1921, he had accepted the challenge without any hesitation. He loved the camaraderie of its editors and contributors, the bohemian life of Greenwich Village, and the sense of achievement he felt with the appearance of each issue. He developed a lasting friendship with Max Eastman, the magazine's guiding spirit, whose attachment to conventionally romantic verse forms he shared. He also became friends with significant American artists who contributed to the magazine and many other notable writers and personalities of the period. He had a good time, a stimulating and rewarding time. But through it all, he remained committed to revolutionary change. He joined Briggs's African Blood Brotherhood and no doubt influenced its wholesale commitment to the recently emerged American Communist party. At the same time, he continued his criticism of white Communists and urged upon

them the importance of international socialism of blacks and colonials.

While engaged in all these activities, he continued to write sonnets and remained committed to his literary career, a career that he in no way regarded as subservient or secondary to his career as a political journalist. On the Left in post-World War I America, political ideologies had not yet hardened to the point where artistic freedom and left-wing politics had become incompatible. In fact, McKay and others like him believed their allegiance to radical politics was simply an extension of their artistic concerns. In 1922, *Harlem Shadows*, McKay's fourth book of poetry, appeared. It was an enlarged version of *Spring in New Hampshire*, from which McKay's most militant racial protest poems and political verse had been omitted. He had grown ashamed of these omissions, and *Harlem Shadows*, with its inclusion of "If We Must Die" and other protest poems, pleased him immensely. Critics, especially black critics such as James Weldon Johnson and Walter White, received *Harlem Shadows* enthusiastically, and McKay found himself praised as a leading voice among the newer black poets.

Although he patterned his poetry upon the Elizabethan and Romantic models that had become the cliché of Victorian England, McKay, after 1914, slowly elaborated his own vision of the past and present condition of himself and his race. The persona who emerges from these World War I verses is a Romantic, pastoral poet who worships beauty and truth but is mired, like his race generally, in a society that has attempted to deny him not only fundamental social and political rights, but the basic fullness of life itself. In McKay's American poetry he depicts blacks still struggling upward from slavery, which in Orlando Patterson's illuminating definition was a kind of social, if not literal, death (*Slavery as Social Death*, 1982). McKay's protest sonnets written between 1914 and 1922 are in fact impassioned descriptions of the liminal state blacks found themselves in for generations after Emancipation, caught between the old social death that was slavery and the new suppressed status of freedmen still powerfully linked to their slave forebears. In the poem "In Bondage" (in *Spring in New Hampshire*), McKay writes:

> Somewhere I would be singing, far away.
> . . . .
> But I am bound with you in your mean
>   graves,
> O black men, simple slaves of ruthless
>   slaves.

And again in "Outcast" (in *Harlem Shadows*), echoing John Keats's "Ode on a Grecian Urn" (1819), McKay laments the loss of his ancestral African culture and his assumption of Western ideals, for in the process,

> Some vital thing has gone out of my heart,
> And I must walk the way of life a ghost
> Among the sons of earth, a thing apart;
> For I was born, far from my native clime,
> Under the white man's menace, out of
>   time.

In "Mulatto" (first published in *Bookman* [September 1925], later included in Wagner's *Les poètes nègres*), another key sonnet for understanding the roots of McKay's alienation, anger, and rebellion in its American context, the poet literalizes his dilemma of double heritage by assuming the persona of a mulatto. The "mulatto" of the poem should also be interpreted as a symbol of the cultural and social condition of all American blacks for whom slavery in the New World meant the acquisition of and participation in a culture that continued to reject them as equals. In creating black slavery, the white culture of America also fathered the black American's striving for social equality and full recognition of his rights as a part of the "American family." Without such recognition there can be no resolution of racial conflict in America, because without it American blacks can never cease to hate those who, in effect, deny them the fullness of life, which in human terms includes the certainty of belonging to a body politic that recognizes your kinship and includes you in its legitimate social life. In "Mulatto," McKay concludes:

> Because I am my cruel father's child,
> My love of justice stirs me up to hate,
> A warring Ishmaelite, unreconciled,
> When falls the hour I shall not hesitate
> Into my father's heart to plunge the knife
> To gain the utmost freedom that is life.

The late Jean Wagner was the first critic to analyze the unusually penetrating and courageous frankness of McKay's discussion of black hatred of white injustices. In a late untitled sonnet found in his unpublished "Cycle Manuscript" at Yale, McKay exclaimed that "I stripped down harshly to the naked core / of hatred based on the essential wrong!" In "The White House" (in the *Liberator* [May 1922], later included in *Selected Poems*), he makes clear that it is "the potent poison" of white hate, the harsh exclusiveness of white society, that has aroused his own anger, which is at times almost uncontrollable—so white hot, so incandescent that "The pavement slabs burn loose beneath my feet, / A chafing savage, down the decent street." To balance such rage he must at "every hour" find "wisdom . . . To hold me to the letter of your law!" To those who protested that McKay expressed too much bitterness in his work, he replied:

The spirituals and the blues were not created out of sweet deceit. There is as much sublimated bitterness in them as there is humility, pathos and bewilderment. And if the Negro is a little bitter, the white man should be the last person in the world to accuse him of bitterness. For the feeling of bitterness is a natural part of the black man's birthright as the feeling of superiority is of the white man's. It matters not so much that one has had an experience of bitterness, but rather how one has developed out of it. To ask the Negro to render up his bitterness is asking him to part with his soul. For out of his bitterness he has bloomed and created his spirituals and blues and conserved his racial attributes—his humor and ripe laughter and particular rhythm of life.

(*Passion of Claude McKay*, pp. 134–135)

In reviewing *Harlem Shadows*, Robert Littel of the *New Republic* pointed out that McKay's "hospitality to echoes of poetry he has read" too often "obscured a direct sense of life and made rarer those lines of singular intensity" that revealed his "naked force of character" (12 July 1922, p. 196). Such criticism perhaps obscures another truth. McKay often used such echoes in fresh and often ironical ways to illuminate directly and intensely aspects of the psychology of the oppressed vis-à-vis his oppressors. By articulating so forcefully and directly not only naked hatred but also much subtler psychological effects that slavery had upon black slaves and white slave owners alike, McKay communicated in his sonnets aspects of American race relations that succeeding generations of scholars and writers still have trouble grasping or confronting. The objective of McKay's quest as a poet was wholeness, as a man and as a member of a racial group long denied the opportunity to be truly free to develop their full potential. Only as a child in Jamaica had he known the psychological freedom and unity with his community that he sought as an adult, and some of the best-realized verses in *Harlem Shadows* are those in which he evokes his pastoral vision of Jamaica: in "Flame-Heart," "My Mother," "Adolescence," and "The Tropics in New York."

Harlem Shadows received generally good reviews, but once again, he moved on shortly after the book appeared. In June 1922, McKay resigned from the *Liberator*. For the rest of the summer, he planned a trip to Moscow to attend the Fourth Congress of the Third International in November. Although nominally a Communist party member, he was not active enough in party affairs to be chosen an official delegate. Unable to raise enough funds through the special sale of *Harlem Shadows*—friends and admirers were asked to buy signed copies at a premium price—McKay in the late summer of 1922 sailed as a stoker on a merchant ship as far as England. From there he journeyed to Berlin and obtained a visa to the Soviet Union.

He arrived there in time to participate in the Fourth Congress as a special delegate-observer, despite the objections of the American party delegates, who wished to see him expelled. He ended up criticizing them severely because, he alleged, they still harbored common prejudices against blacks and did not understand the critical position of black laborers in America. His color, good looks, and happy smile won over the Moscow crowds, and the Moscow leadership subsequently sent him on a six-month tour of Moscow, Leningrad, and their environs. Through it all, however, he insisted he was primarily a poet, not a politician, and though he thoroughly enjoyed the wooing, he left the Soviet Union determined to resume an independent literary career. He had grown disillusioned with his British and American comrades, and he had begun to suspect that the dominance of the Soviet national party in the Third International meant the subservience of other national revolutionary movements to the Soviet Union's national interest. While there, McKay had written for Soviet newspapers and journals a series of articles and short stories on the racial situation in the United States, which were collected into two pamphlet-sized books. One was an analysis of the black situation in the United States, *Negry v. Amerike (The Negroes in America*, 1923); the other was a slim volume of short stories entitled *Sudom lincha (Trial by Lynching*, 1925).

After leaving the Soviet Union in the spring of 1923, McKay lived and worked in Western Europe and North Africa until 1934. While abroad McKay turned to fiction. From 1923 until 1927, he struggled in France and Spain to produce a marketable novel. With the financial and artistic assistance of many friends, he managed to survive several illnesses—including syphilis, grippe, and high blood pressure—and to persevere in his apprenticeship in fiction. Louise Bryant, the widow of John Reed, persuaded him to engage William Aspenwall Bradley, the leading American literary agent in Paris, as his representative. Bradley secured him a contract with Harper & Brothers that called for three novels and a collection of short stories. McKay responded by producing his first published novel, *Home to Harlem*, in 1928. It appeared in New York at the height of white publishing interest in blacks, received good publicity, and for a while made the local best-seller lists. It presented a story of marginal, working-class black migrants and their stark scrabble for love and a living in Harlem. Black readers were divided in their opinion of *Home to Harlem*. Some thought McKay was merely pandering in it to white enjoyment of black stereotypes. Others defended McKay's story of the hedonistic, instinctually positive hero, Jake Brown, as simply a healthy assertion of the black man's basic strength and vitality. Since his departure in 1922, a new generation of African American writers had emerged to give substance in literature to Alain Locke's assertion in "The New Negro" that a "New Negro" had come forth whose "mind" had "slipped from under the tyranny of social intimidation and [was] shaking off the psychology of imitation and implied inferiority." In the process, many had begun to assert empathically the positive aspects of black folk life in country and city. Langston Hughes was one such writer, and he in particular welcomed Claude McKay's contribution from afar. Hughes insisted in a letter to McKay that *Home to Harlem* was "undoubtedly . . . the finest thing 'we've' done yet." Not everyone in the black intellectual community agreed with him. McKay's characters were rough, hard-drinking, and hard-living. In their everyday pursuits, many skated a thin line between legality and illegality. To W. E. B. Du Bois and many other reviewers, a novel in praise of such characters was simply reprehensible.

McKay wrote *Home to Harlem* in the tradition of the picaresque. Jake Brown is an idealized folk type, a black man who during World War I deserts his army labor unit in Brest, goes to London, and exists there as a stevedore for a few months. Well after the war, he ships as a stoker on a merchant ship back to New York and Harlem, where he has a series of loves and adventures while working as a cook on the Pennsylvania Railroad. Through Jake's movement from episode to episode, McKay reveals aspects of black working-class existence as he himself experienced it as a solitary male in New York City between 1914 and 1919.

There are no children in *Home to Harlem*, no married couples, no ministers, and few professionals of any sort, with the exception of Ray, the Haitian intellectual who, as Jake's fellow worker on the railroad, forms a friendship with him. Ray acts as McKay's thinly disguised alter ego who comments periodically upon Jake and the conditions in which he lives. To Ray, Jake is a natural man who lives for the moment, happily meeting the daily challenges of an unfair world with natural wit, humor, courage, and intelligence. He cannot be beaten down but rolls like an unsinkable ship across America's stormy ocean of racial strife and oppression. Jake is McKay's triumphant primitive. He is only the best of a good lot in *Home to Harlem*. Those with whom he mingles share his essential virtues in lesser degrees. The gambler and loan shark, Billy Biasse; Jake's inept rival in love, Zeddy; and the pathetic but self-reliant Gin-head Suzy—all are lovingly portrayed by McKay. In sharp contrast, only Ray—literate, lonely, and confused—suffers from self-doubt and self-consciousness. *Home to Harlem* was a deliberate insult to respectability, black and white, and a glorification of the staying power of the poor, the ignorant, and the dispossessed.

McKay continued his assault on black respectability in his second novel, *Banjo: A Story Without a Plot* (1929), in which he shifts and expands his locale to include a new, international set of black characters, a group of beached seamen, adrift in that fleshpot of international commerce, Marseilles's *vieux port* (or the Ditch, as McKay's characters call it). Once again, his hero is an archetypal black primitive, Lincoln Agrippa Daily, or "Banjo," as he is called because of his mastery of that stereotypically black instrument. Around Banjo there gather several West Indian and black American seamen, who like him are temporarily without a ship and living by their wits in the Ditch. They form a band and play for handouts and meals. In Marseilles are Africans from various French colonies, as well as a few black students from the French West Indies. Even more than Jake, Banjo is adrift upon the alien sea of Western civilization and enjoying it. As McKay remarks, he and those like him refuse to "disappear under the serried crush of trampling white feet." They are a puzzle and a mystery, a challenge, like a "red rag to the mighty-bellowing, all-trampling civilized bull." In Marseilles, Banjo meets Ray, the Haitian intellectual from *Home to Harlem*, who, like McKay, has fled the United States to become an expatriate writer in France. Together Ray and Banjo encounter Jake, who has become a seaman in order to support a wife and child.

This international mélange of uprooted black men drinks, sings, dances, fights, and philanders its way through the Ditch, all the while discussing every possible aspect of the problems faced by blacks in Africa, the Caribbean, and the United States. McKay's fundamental position is expressed through his archetypal "natural" man, Banjo, and his own fictional alter ego, Ray. Banjo lives the role, while Ray explains how blacks survive in a hostile white society that seeks to hold them literally in a ditch. McKay argues in both *Home to Harlem* and *Banjo* that blacks are a people in closer proximity to the soil, and hence to nature, than industrialized, urbanized, white Europeans. They are more natural, more spontaneous, less driven by greed, less hampered by sexual inhibitions and other neurotic complexes. And they possess, too, rich racial attributes of humor, rhythm, courage, and physical and psychological resiliency, out of which they fashioned for themselves New World cultures strong enough to see them through slavery. Whether consciously or unconsciously (and one suspects a bit of both), McKay was seizing upon traditional stereotypes and using them as positive images of black racial differentiation. Blacks emerged from slavery with rich legacies of music, stories, humor, and history. These attributes and legacies, McKay insisted, were not embodied in racial leaders and black social climbers, but in the common people and especially in the best of the common folk who, like Jake or Banjo, could fashion satisfying lives for themselves because they knew their own strengths, related to each other and their neighbors as fellow humans, and preserved a self respect nothing could destroy.

McKay believed black leaders everywhere had to build upon this already existing folk community. Only with nurturing roots deep sunk in their own experiences, values, and culture could blacks expand and develop economically, politically, and socially. In this regard, blacks, he believed, and especially African Americans, were no different from other ethnic groups. Like the Jews, the Italians, the Poles, and many others, they must become conscious of their inalienable rights as a group to act together for their own self-advancement. Thus, in *Banjo* Ray angrily advises a French West Indian student not to try to become a black Frenchman but to build from his island culture an identity he already has but refuses to acknowledge as legitimate and self-sufficient in its own right. Ray goes on to explain that if the student wishes to emulate whites, he should turn to the promoters of "the Irish cultural and social movement," to the Russian writers who espoused the cause of the peasants before the Russian Revolution, and to Gandhi's movement in India. He should also learn some of the languages of Africa and its cultures instead of feeling embarrassed and ashamed of them and the poor African laborers of the Marseilles dock.

Banjo was McKay's last picaresque novel. *Gingertown* (1932), a collection of short stories, represented an effort to break new ground stylistically and thematically. Some of the Harlem stories in *Gingertown* told of characters very like those found in his novels, but in his Jamaican stories his whole tone changed to a lush pastoral mode that he sustained in his last novel, *Banana Bottom*, which appeared the next year. This novel, McKay's most mature and artistically successful prose effort, was his attempt to find his way back home, to reintegrate himself imaginatively with the black community of his youth. McKay became eager to write about the Jamaica of his childhood after he settled in Tangier, Morocco, in 1930. For seven years he had lived the precarious life of the expatriate writer in Paris, Nice, Marseilles, and various other cities in France and Spain. He was forty in 1930 and felt the need to settle somewhere and establish a more stable existence. He needed a retreat, and he found it in Tangier. Morocco's French colonial existence during the interwar years, with its blend of ethnic groups and strong West African influences, reminded him of Jamaica. Now middle-aged and shaken, physically and emotionally, from all his experiences, he retreated imaginatively to Jamaica to record the community of his dreams, a black community strong upon its own foundations.

In *Banana Bottom*, the artistic soul who returns to Jamaica after years of education in England is a woman, Bita Plant. She is raped as a young girl by an insane mulatto fiddler of genius called Crazy-Bow; afterward she is sent to England by sympathetic but misguided missionaries for a "proper" education. When she returns, they envision for her a marriage to a native minister. Together, the young couple might carry on the civilizing mission they themselves had dedicated their lives to achieving. None of this happens. Bita finds the ministerial student stuffy and boring. She is happy to rediscover for herself the quiet pleasures of her parents' rural life, the excitement of country dances, and the temporarily beguiling enticements of a seductive but feckless local Romeo called Hopping Dick. The ministerial student is caught in flagrante delicto with a nanny goat. The white missionary and Bita's father, a deacon in the church, drown while attempting to ford a flood-swollen stream as they return from a distant church meeting. For consolation Bita turns to Jubba, a black orphan boy of the hill country, raised by her parents in her absence, who has grown into a quiet, self-assured peasant farmer. He assumes control of the family farm after the death of Bita's father.

As Bita's story unfolds, McKay re-creates in rich, loving, and humorous detail the distant Jamaican hill country and the stable peasant culture of his youth. In *Banjo*, he writes that Ray's efforts as an expatriate "to be educated black and his instinctive self was something of a big job to put over." In *Banana Bottom*, he accomplishes this task for himself by returning to the pastoral innocence of youth and by choosing as his main character a woman who could do what the character Ray in *Home to Harlem* and *Banjo* could never do: reconcile through marriage her educated self with her peasant origins in a black community that had created for itself a way of life free from white

missionary efforts to mold it wholly in Western patterns of morality and behavior.

In reality, of course, matters were more complicated, both for himself and for Jamaica. Though *Banana Bottom* received fair reviews, it appeared in 1933 at the height of the Depression and sales were dismal. *Gingertown* had also sold poorly. McKay found himself suddenly isolated, penniless, and without any prospects in Tangier. With assistance from friends, he managed to return to New York City early in 1934. For the remainder of the decade he struggled hard to continue his literary career and to regain the limited financial success that had briefly been his after *Home to Harlem* and *Banjo*. Despite periods of utter poverty, between 1934 and 1940, he managed to produce a memoir, *A Long Way from Home* (1937) and a study, *Harlem, Negro Metropolis* (1940). Both volumes had only modest sales and received mixed reviews. To support himself, McKay appealed to foundations and wrote numerous articles on Harlem's labor scene and grass-roots social movements for a variety of newspapers and magazines. He also worked for the New York Federal Writers Project (FWP). The FWP both saved him financially and enabled him to collect the large body of information about Harlem folk life and movements that he used in his articles and in *Harlem, Negro Metropolis*.

The FWP also involved him deeply in the political disputes in which it had been mired from its inception. McKay had returned from Europe disillusioned with the course of the Bolshevik Revolution and disinclined to join its Trotskyist opposition or any other political movement. As early as 1925, he had predicted the course of Stalinist tyranny and had written Eastman of his disgust with revolutionary parties in the other countries that were willing to follow obediently Moscow's ideological line. He had turned to fiction and ceased political agitation. Once back in Harlem, however, he began to argue that African Americans should not join the American Communist party, nor should they ally themselves with it. He considered the party a tool of Soviet foreign policy. Blacks had enough trouble, he pointed out, without identifying themselves with alien national interests and goals. He also opposed the underhanded tactics used by the Communist party in the FWP to silence its critics, and he warned American writers that Stalinist policies in literature had led to the death of all free expression in the Soviet Union.

At the same time, McKay remained basically a socialist and a black populist, a free spirit who severely criticized the established black leadership in America. Group improvement, and not integration and the acquisition of legal rights alone, should be the immediate goal of African American leadership, he insisted. Black communities such as Harlem, he believed, remained essentially leaderless because African Americans, alone among all ethnic groups, hated and rejected their communities because they identified them with white-imposed segregation. Segregation was a policy, McKay believed, that should be abolished.

But in the meantime, he emphasized, African Americans had to embrace their communities, recognize the legitimate aspirations of their grass-roots labor and religious movements, and build upon the yearnings of their own people for a better life and a real community with labor, business, and social institutions capable of cleansing "the Augean stables" in which they lived. After all, McKay reasoned with admirable prescience, the acquisition of equal civil rights and the abolition of all legal segregation would not mean the disappearance of "the Negro" as an ethnic group in America. African Americans must not wait but must act decisively to build for themselves within their own communities the infrastructure of civic, business, labor, and social institutions common to every community in America. Otherwise, unable to integrate as a whole into American life, they would remain a permanently backward, crime-ridden, and unhealthy sore upon the American body politic. African American leaders, McKay passionately declared, must cease to evade their community responsibilities by using white racism as a permanent excuse for all black ills. The black masses were eager for improvement but lacked the leadership they needed.

McKay's harsh critique won him few friends. A. Phillip Randolph encouraged him; Zora Neale Hurston admired his frankness; and James Weldon Johnson never deserted him. But McKay was viewed by most black leaders as a harping outsider. Nevertheless, his criticism poured forth in the pages of the *New Leader*, the *Nation*, the New York *Amsterdam News*, the *Jewish Frontier*, and other journals.

Finally, however, illness, poverty, and isolation led McKay to enter the Roman Catholic church. In 1944 he moved to Chicago, joined the church, and worked, between bouts of illness, for Bishop Bernard J. Sheil's Catholic Youth Organization until his death in 1948. McKay's conversion surprised most of his friends because he had been an agnostic all his life. However, he was ill, he had found no place within international socialism he could accept, and he likewise had found no security within the African American community or in the United States generally. He needed solace and a cessation of spiritual strife. He sought them in the church and in memory. McKay had envisioned for the black community, as he envisioned for himself, psychological and spiritual freedom to be themselves. Only then could they be proud black citizens of their country and the world. He had found such freedom only in the Jamaican hill country of his youth, and in the last months of his life, it was there he returned by composing a final memoir of his youth, *My Green Hills of Jamaica*.

Selected Bibliography

PRIMARY WORKS

NOVELS

Home to Harlem. New York: Harper & Brothers, 1928.
Banjo: A Story Without a Plot. New York: Harper & Brothers, 1929.
Banana Bottom. New York: Harper & Brother, 1933.
Harlem Glory: A Fragment of Aframerican Life. Chicago: Kerr, 1990.

POETRY

Constab Ballads. London: Watts & Co., 1912.
Songs from Jamaica. London: Augener, 1912. (Six dialect poems set to music by Walter Jekyll.)

Songs of Jamaica. Kingstown, Jamaica: Aston W. Gardner, 1912.

Spring in New Hampshire and Other Poems. London: Grant Richards, 1920.

Harlem Shadows. New York: Harcourt, Brace, 1922.

SHORT STORIES

Sudom lincha. Moscow: Ogonek, 1925. Translated as *Trial by Lynching: Stories About Negro Life in North America* by Robert J. Winter. Edited by Alan L. McLeod. Mysore, India, 1979.

Gingertown. New York: Harper & Brothers, 1932.

MEMOIRS

A Long Way from Home. New York: Lee Furnam, 1937.

My Green Hills of Jamaica and Five Jamaican Short Stories. Edited by Mervyn Morris. Kingstown and Port of Spain, Jamaica: Heinemann Educational Books, 1979.

OTHER WORKS

Negry v Amerike. Translated into Russian by P. Okhrimenko. Moscow: Gosudarstvennoe, 1923. Translated as *The Negroes in America* by Robert J. Winter. Edited by Alan L. McLeod. Port Washington, N.Y.: Kennikat Press, 1979.

Harlem: Negro Metropolis. New York: E. P. Dutton, 1940.

COLLECTED WORKS

Selected Poems of Claude McKay. New York: Bookman Associates, 1953.

The Dialect Poems of Claude McKay. Vol. 1, *Songs of Jamaica.* Vol. 2, *Constab Ballads.* Freeport, N.Y.: Books for Libraries, 1972.

The Passion of Claude McKay: Selected Poetry and Prose, 1912–1948. Edited by Wayne F. Cooper. New York: Schocken Books, 1973.

MANUSCRIPTS AND PAPERS

The Claude McKay Papers are in the James Weldon Johnson Collection of Negro Literature and Art, American Literature Collection, Beinecke Rare Book and Manuscript Library, Yale University.

SECONDARY WORKS

BIOGRAPHICAL AND CRITICAL STUDIES

Binder, Wolfgang. "A Black Icon in the Flesh: The Afro-American Writer in Europe, the Case of Claude McKay." In *L'Amerique et l'Europe: Realites et representations.* Edited by Neil Larry Shumsky. Aix-en-Provence: University of Provence, 1985. Pp 137–51.

Blary, Liliane, et al. "Claude McKay and Black Nationalist Ideologies (1934–1948)." In *Myth and Ideology in American Culture.* Edited by Regis Durand. Lille: Centre d'Etudes et de Recherches Nord-Américaines et Canadiennes, Université de Lille, 1976.

Breitinger, Eckhard. "In Search of an Audience: In Search of the Self: Exile as a Condition for the Works of Claude McKay." In *The Commonwealth Writer Overseas: Themes of Exile and Expatriation.* Edited by Alastair Niven. Bruxelles: M. Didier, 1976.

Chauhan, P. S. "Rereading Claude McKay." *CLA Journal* 34, no. 1:68–80 (September 1990).

Chin, Timothy S. " 'Bullers' and 'Battymen': Contesting Homophobia in Black Popular Culture and Contemporary Caribbean Literature." *Callaloo* 20, no. 1: 127–41 (Winter 1997).

Condit, John Hillyer. "An Urge toward Wholeness: Claude McKay and His Sonnets." *CLA Journal* 22: 350–64 (1979).

Dorris, Ronald. "Claude McKay's Home to Harlem: A Social Commentary." *The McNeese Review* 29:53–62 (1982–1983).

———. "Rhythm in Claude McKay's 'Harlem Dancer.' " In *'This Is How We Flow': Rhythm in Black Cultures.* Edited by Angela M. S. Nelson. Columbia: University of South Carolina Press, 1999.

Fabre, Michel. "Aesthetics and Ideology in Banjo." In *Myth and Ideology in American Culture.* Edited by Regis Durand. Lille: Centre d'Etudes et de Recherches Nord-Américaines et Canadiennes, Université de Lille, 1976.

Greenberg, Robert M. "Idealism and Realism in the Fiction of Claude McKay." *CLA Journal* 24, no. 3:237–61 (March 1981).

Griffin, Barbara J. "Claude McKay: The Evolution of a Conservative." *CLA Journal* 36, no. 2:157–70 (December 1992).

———. "The Last Word: Claude McKay's Unpublished 'Cycle Manuscript.' " *Melus* 21:41–49 (March 1, 1996).

Hamalian, Leo. "D. H. Lawrence and Black Writers." *Journal of Modern Literature* 16, no. 4:579–96 (Spring 1990).

Keller, James R. " 'A Chafing Savage, Down the Decent Street': The Politics of Compromise in Claude McKay's Protest Sonnets." *African-American Review* 28, no. 3:447–56 (Fall 1994).

LeSeur, Geta. "Claude McKay's Romanticism." *CLA Journal* 32, no. 3:296–308 (March 1989).

———. "Claude McKay's Marxism." In *The Harlem Renaissance: Revaluations.* Edited by Amritjit Singh et al. New York: Garland, 1989.

Lively, Adam. "Continuity and Radicalism in American Black Nationalist Thought, 1914–1929." *Journal of American Studies* 18, no. 2:207–35 (August 1984).

Lueth, Elmer. "The Scope of Black Life in Claude McKay's Home to Harlem." *Obsidian II: Black Literature in Review* 5, no. 3:43–52 (Winter 1990).

McLeod, A. L. "Memory and the Edenic Myth: Claude McKay's Green Hills of Jamaica." In *Individual and Community in Commonwealth Literature.* Edited by Daniel Massa. Msida: University of Malta Press, 1979.

———, ed. "Claude McKay as Historical Witness." In *Subjects Worthy of Fame: Essays on Common-*

wealth Literature in Honour of H. H. Anniah Gowda. Edited by A. L. McLeod. New Delhi: Sterling, 1989.

———. Claude McKay: Centennial Studies. New Delhi: Sterling, 1992.

McLeod, Marian B. "Claude McKay's Russian Interpretation: The Negroes in America." CLA Journal 23: 336–51 (1980).

Miller, James A. "African-American Writing of the 1930s: A Prologue." In Radical Revisions: Rereading 1930s Culture. Edited by Bill Mullen and Sherry Lee Linkon. Urbana: University of Illinois Press, 1996.

Ojo-Ade, Femi. "McKay's Tragic Confusion: An African's Comments on Tyrone Tillery's Claude McKay." Literary Griot: International Journal of Black Expressive Cultural Studies 6, no. 2:54–59. (Fall 1994).

———. "Claude McKay: The Tragic Solitude of an Exiled Son of Africa." In Of Dreams Deferred, Dead or Alive: African Perspectives on African-American Writers. Edited by Femi Ojo-Ade. Westport, Conn.: Greenwood, 1996.

Pedersen, Carl. "Review of Claude McKay: Rebel Sojourner in the Harlem Renaissance." Research in African Literatures, June 22, 1997. Pp 198–99.

Roberts, Kimberly. "The Clothes Make the Woman: The Symbolics of Prostitution in Nella Larsen's Quicksand and Claude McKay's Home to Harlem." Tulsa Studies in Women's Literature 16, no. 1:107–30 (Spring 1997).

Russ, Robert A. " 'There's No Place Like Home': The Carnival of Black Life in Claude McKay's Home to Harlem." In Harlem Renaissance Re-examined: A Revised and Expanded Edition. Edited by Victor A. Kramer and Robert A. Russ. Troy, N.Y.: The Whitston Publishing Co., 1997.

Smith, Robert P., Jr. "Rereading Banjo: Claude McKay and the French Connection." CLA Journal 30, no. 1:46–58 (September 1986).

Spencer, Suzette A. "Swerving at a Different Angle and Flying in the Face of Tradition: Excavating the Homoerotic Subtext in Home to Harlem." CLA Journal 42, no. 2:164–93 (December 1998).

Thomas, H. Nigel. "Claude McKay's Banana Bottom: A Black Response to Late Nineteenth and Early Twentieth Century White Discourse on the Meaning of Black Reality." In Nationalism vs. Internationalism: (Inter)National Dimensions of Literatures in English. Edited by Wolfgang Zach and Ken L. Goodwin. Tubingen, Germany: Stauffenburg, 1996.

TONI MORRISON
(1931 –   )

WAHNEEMA LUBIANO

ALTHOUGH LITERARY HISTORY has been so much produced and owned by the canonical gatekeepers of particular social formations that one cannot always count on it to "tell the truth" about the cultural production of a marginalized group, such has not been the case with the work of Toni Morrison. She is, and will continue to be, part of the "truth" about African American literature, partly because her work as novelist, editor, and critic has been "caretaken" by critics of African American literature; partly because she has been instrumental in facilitating the work of other contemporary African American writers; and partly because she has actively engaged in the debates of the critical discourse of her time. Her novels have created space for black and feminist texts, changing the overwhelmingly male makeup of the African American literary canon. Most important, however, she produced some of the most artistically, historically, and politically important work of the twentieth century as well as some of the most formally scintillating and thematically surgical prose in the overlapping bodies of American and African American literature.

Political and cultural analyst Frantz Fanon's delineation of the work of the native intellectual as a project of reclamation, committed to awakening his or her people, is a fitting description of Morrison's work. She herself was nurtured by her parents' insistence on narrating their own experiences, by her education, and by her own recognition of her connections to her ancestors. When Morrison says that she wants her work to come out of a specific African American structure and to keep a reader on edge the way a jazz chord does, she is enlisting in the project that Fanon describes as resistance to the cultural silencing of the marginalized by the dominant group. She makes visible what was invisible both within African American culture and, across the boundaries of race, outside African American culture. Her texts are worldly, emerging from and cutting across the political, social, economic, historical constraints of her particular culture. Her work and her discussion of it have helped us pinpoint her sense of that group in the world, while our reading of it has reminded us of the complexities of its worldliness and of our own. Believing that the best art is political—and that it can be made political and beautiful together—Morrison consistently presents the political, despite her occasional fear that within the terms of the kind of world we inhabit, her work does very little. Nonetheless, because her work remaps the terrain of African American cultural and social history and allows for a community of the imagination, it interrupts the ideology that produces the kind of world we inhabit.

In the wake of her increasing presence in the international context—as attested to by the multiplicity of languages in which her novels have been translated and the attention to her work from scholars, critics, and readers from all over the world—and especially in the wake of her winning the Nobel Prize for Literature in 1993, Morrison has become a figure that challenges preexisting notions of an American writer, a black writer, a woman writer, and a black intellectual. Her writing has taken her around the globe but her movement has taken place in more spaces than bookstores alone. As part of a transnational group of intellectuals and cultural producers, Morrison moves in circles such as the International Parliament of Writers, the Africa and Helsinki Watch Committees, earlier presence in the worlds of publishing and the academy allow us to further complicate our understandings of those places as much as it challenges the various categories of writer and producer I allude to above.

One way to think about "what" Morrison has produced is to think about "how" Morrison has produced herself. On October 7, 1988, Toni Morrison entered the world of literary criticism with the Tanner Lecture on Human Values at the University of Michigan, a presentation entitled "Unspeakable Things Unspoken: The Afro-American Presence in American Literature." With this lecture she made apparent the most recent manifestation of her remarkable ability to recognize, seize, and intervene in the important moments of her time. In deciding to write and talk about literary criticism, Morrison joins Amiri Baraka, Ralph Ellison, Richard Wright, and Sterling Brown as critic and theorist of her own work and as a theorist about the presence of African Americans and their writing in the domain of American literature. In a gesture as timely as it was brilliant, she joined a community of scholars in order to revise and remake critical history.

The road to that lecture was long and marked by Morrison's narrative and editorial projects. The University of Michigan lecture was presented five years before she became the first African American to win the Nobel Prize and on the heels of the 1988 Pulitzer Prize for fiction for her fifth novel, *Beloved*, ten years after the 1978 National Book Critics' Circle Award for *Song of Solomon* (the first African American novel since Richard Wright's *Native Son* to be chosen as a main selection of the Book-of-the-Month Club), and thirteen years after the 1975 National Book Award nomination for *Sula* (an alternate selection of the Book-of-the-Month Club that also was condensed in *Redbook* magazine). Morrison's debut as a critic was both an indication to the world that acts of creative imagination can be formally tied to acts of analysis and a reminder that the writer has been as much a part of a formal intellectual tradition as she is a descendant of storytelling forebears. In its enlarged and enriched published form, *Playing in the Dark* (1992), that lecture has circulated throughout the world of literary studies and has enormous presence in the collective literary historical and critical project of revising our construction of American literature, adding to that project Morrison's interpretive prowess and critical acumen as she refigures some of American literature's most canonical texts.

Life

Although Morrison's early life is full of the signposts to her later creativity, the Western myth (or cliché) of the artist as a singular, completely private, autonomous, and isolated individual does not accurately characterize Morrison's development. With one exception, Morrison has consistently eschewed the tendency to think of herself in terms of narratives of originative and genius imagination. She grew up in a family of storytellers and musicians; both parents told ghost stories, and her grandmother played the numbers by decoding dream symbols. Although narratives of "other" kinds of reality were pastimes throughout her childhood, Morrison admitted, in an interview with Gloria Naylor, to having once thought of herself—when writing *The Bluest Eye*—as unique, under the erroneous impression that nobody else was writing the way that she was or was going to do so. She explained that she had fallen prey to that kind of thinking because she had been ill-taught and did not know about people like Zora Neale Hurston and Wallace Thurman. Her discovery that she herself participates in a community that at one time she had not known existed—that there is a powerful narrative dynamic within African American culture that informs a tradition—affirmed her sense that the world the way black women perceive it really exists.

Morrison insists on a political reading of her biography and asserts her recognition of having lived within a community with class solidarity and class critique. That class recognition and critique informs all of her texts, as does the generative power and specificity of the culture out of which she writes. She said in "Memory, Creation, and Writing": "I simply wanted to write literature that was irrevocably, indisputably Black, not because its characters were, or because I was, but because it took as its creative task and sought as its credentials those recognized and verifiable principles of Black art."

It was in the family and as part of a coherent community that Morrison the novelist, editor, and teacher was made and made herself. She was born on February 18, 1931, in Lorain, Ohio, as Chloe Anthony Wofford, the second of four children of George Wofford, a car washer, steel mill welder, and road construction and shipyard worker, and Ramah Willis Wofford, who worked at home and sang in church. Her mother's parents had come north from Alabama via Kentucky, where her grandfather had worked in the coal mines, to get away, as so many others before and after them, from poverty and racism. Her father, who came from Georgia, bore the imprint of the racial violence of that state. Her mother once responded to an eviction notice by tearing it up, and she wrote to President Franklin Roosevelt to complain of bugs in the corn meal. Although neither parent was especially optimistic about the ability of whites to transcend their racism, they believed, nonetheless, in neighborhood community. Lorain was and is a steel town, multiracial and consistently poor, but Morrison learned early on what it meant to live in an economically cooperative neighborhood.

Toni Morrison

From Lorain High School, Morrison went on to earn her B.A. degree from Howard University, where she worked with the Howard University Players and traveled through the South with a faculty-and-student repertory troupe. Audiences were for the most part black; she reports that she had virtually no contact with white people. After receiving her degree in 1953, she went to Cornell University for graduate work in English, completed a thesis on William Faulkner and Virginia Woolf, and received her M.A. degree in 1955.

Morrison taught at Texas Southern University for two years (1955–1957), and then until 1964 at Howard University, where the Black Power activist Stokely Carmichael was one of her students. She described herself then (during the early stages of the Civil Rights movement) as not really interested in the integration movement. Although she knew of the terror and abuses of segregation, she was afraid that assimilation would have a diminishing effect on African American culture, and she was unpersuaded by the assumption that black children would learn better with white children. This thinking was an echo of arguments that Zora Neale Hurston had made in the 1930s and 1940s. Morrison insisted that what African Americans needed was economic investment in materials for schools, in faculty, in buildings; she argued, as Hurston had before her, that with money black neighborhoods could be the sites of schools, and that mixing people of different races and classes would not solve the problems of racism and poverty.

While teaching at Howard she met and married Harold Morrison, a Jamaican architect, and gave birth to two sons, Harold Ford and Slade Kevin. Morrison describes these years as a period of almost complete powerlessness, a time when she wrote quietly and participated in a writers' workshop, putting together a short story that would eventually become *The Bluest Eye*.

Morrison left Howard in 1964, divorced her husband, and a year and a half later moved to Syracuse, New York, where she began her career as an editor for the textbook subsidiary of Random House. In that time she would publish her book, *College Reading Skills*. She moved to a senior editorship at Random House's New York City headquarters in 1967. She continued to teach—at Yale, at Bard College, at the State University of New York campuses at Purchase and at Albany, and at Rutgers University. In 1989 she became a member of Princeton University's faculty as Robert F. Goheen Professor of the Humanities; she also held the International Condorcet Chair at the École Normale Supérieure and College de France (1994) and spent one year (1998) as the A. D. White Professor-at-Large at Cornell University. As might be expected, Morrison's writing and teaching careers are studded with awards—national and international—and honorary degrees.

What might be less expected, and certainly less well-known, is the importance to black American intellectual history of Morrison's career in publishing. In her position as senior editor at Random House, Morrison facilitated the careers of an array of black American intellectuals, making it possible for important fiction and nonfiction—including critical analysis, history, poetry, and biography—by numerous black writers to be published. Her work at Random House, which by the end of the twentieth century included a distinguished list of more than twenty authors and thirty-five texts, made possible the emergence of some of the most important work by black American authors of the last third of the twentieth century. She edited, among other projects, Leon Forrest's *There Is a Tree More Ancient than Eden* (1973), *The Bloodworth Orphans* (1977), and *Two Wings to Veil My Face* (1983), George Jackson's *Blood in My Eye* (1972), Ivan van Sertima's *They Came before Columbus* (1976), the fiction and essays of Toni Cade Bambara—including Bambara's posthumous novel, *Those Bones Are Not My Child* (1999)—Gayl Jones's first three novels, June Jordan's *Things That I Do in the Dark* (1977), Chinweizu's *The West and the Rest of Us* (1975), and Angela Davis' *An Autobiography* (1974) and *Women, Race, and Class* (1981).

Morrison also helped bring into being *The Black Book* (1974), a collection of materials from black history—representations of black lives as well as black cultural expression. It contains newspaper clippings, photographs, songs, advertisements, slave bills of sale, Patent Office records, receipts, rent-party jingles, and other memorabilia—in short, African American history as revealed in elements of material culture. Morrison produced this book at a time when many feared that the Black Power movement would be reduced to rhetoric and empty images, that its fading salience would silence past reminders of African American history, reminders that would not fit into the rhetoric of the moment or into black collective consciousness. While Morrison's name appears nowhere on it, the collection was, according to Marilyn Mobley, Morrison's idea, her project. Morrison saw it as the history made by unknown black folks, a record that framed the parameters of black existence in terms of the quotidian, giving their due to the noncelebrated and demystifying the relationship of blacks to their history in order to write new histories. *The Black Book* was Morrison's intervention into historical discourse, a gesture that echoes Zora Neale Hurston's commentaries on her anthropological gatherings in the 1920s and 1930s, and her argument in the essay "Characteristics of Negro Expression." Morrison's intervention into historical discourse has also produced, so far, two collections of essays on topical issues: *Race-ing Justice, En-gendering Power* (1992) and *Birth of a Nation'hood* (1997). These essay collections, addressing the Clarence Thomas and Anita Hill controversy and the response to the O.J. Simpson trial respectively, are the result of her ability to make space for progressive politically-engaged academic contributions to the concerns of the nation as those concerns cohere around extraordinary events.

Equally important as the details of Morrison's biography and her writing and academic careers are the contexts for the production of her books, the larger history of African Americans and women. *The Bluest Eye* (1970) was written during a period of an emerging black aesthetic, the cultural arm of the black militancy movement. The book's opening lines imply the keeping of a secret—and it is a dirty little secret, not just of personal aesthetics but of race (there at the end of the Civil Rights movement) and of class.

Sula (1973) was produced in the midst of the reinvigorated feminist movement and debate. Morrison maintains that throughout their history in America, black women have been protofeminists—aggressive, the objects of a labor history as oppressive as men's, and required to do physical labor in competition with them. The relation between black men and black women turned out to be more of a comradeship than the conventional patriarchal pattern of male dominance/female subordination because of the demands of the labor: the requirements of the work were the same. Black women did not have the luxury of middle-class white women, were unable to "choose" to work or to be at home. Morrison's thinking about feminism also bears the influence of her family experience—she has said that within her family, her parents confronted crises as they arose without adhering to a system of gender-divided responsibilities. She views the cooperative and ad hoc nature of their relationship, like the marriages of older generations of blacks, as having been a comradely partnership—a dynamic that she views as having died out as blacks came to participate more and more in the gender illness of the general culture.

Song of Solomon (1977), *Tar Baby* (1981), and *Beloved* (1987) are extended engagements with larger issues of group history. *Song of Solomon* sets that group history within the parameters of the family romance; *Tar Baby* focuses on the relationship of colonialism and its attendant history to the family dynamics and antithetical cultures within a multiracial household; and *Beloved* negotiates history as a narrative of the ownership of the most concrete fact of human existence—the body—as well as the most abstract of human relationships—love.

Jazz (1992) and *Paradise* (1998) extend the narrative and historical projects of Morrison's first five novels and focus in even more intense fashion on the problems of narrative itself and its relation to the complexities, difficulties, and impossibilities of history. *Jazz* makes of the telling of individual stories a conversation about the parallel, intersectional, and contradictory dynamics of large and small history; of romance as adventure as well as sexual interplay; of the making of a city as well as the fractures and fissures of neighborhoods; and of the weaving of multiple relationships. This work of multiple story structures is further complicated by the novel's playful engagement with reading and rereading as a representation of the textual presence itself. A reader reading *Jazz* serves as a cat's-paw to the novel as the novel reads and rewrites itself. "Jazz" as a metaphor in the title might most productively be read as a matter of attuning the mind's eye and ears to the intertwined play of reading and storytelling, where the same narrative can be repeated with infinite variation. The climax of the novel asks us to rethink what we know about erotic desire in terms of reading pleasure. *Paradise* continues the parallel, intersectional, and contradictory attention to history that *Jazz* offers and is, at the same time, a further adventure into the constituting of community by the means of the mechanism of storytelling via the vehicle of control over the bodies of black women by describing the limitations and imperatives of those bodies.

Toni Morrison accepting the Nobel Prize in 1993.

The Bluest Eye

One could say that Morrison's first novel is a story of a barely pubescent girl, Pecola, told through the voice of another barely pubescent girl, Claudia. The story is a simple chronicle of Claudia's journey to social maturation that also describes the psychological destruction of Pecola. Pecola is convinced by her family, classmates, and community that she is ugly. That knowledge, coupled with her rape by her father, destroys her. As with many descriptions that distort the reality of a narrative by reducing it to a summary without necessarily stating outright falsehoods, there would be some truth in that description. The text, however, quickly reveals itself as much more.

"Quiet as it's kept, there were no marigolds in the fall of 1941" we are told as the novel commences. Why quiet? We are being let in on a secret—not just the secret of the detritus of ideas of physical aesthetics but also the secret of the relationship of such ideas to racism and class oppression. The secret kept quiet in the fall of 1941 is that the community, having in-

ternalized the racism of the dominant group, is itself largely the reason for the failure of one of its flowers, Pecola Breedlove, to thrive. That that failure has its roots in the ground of a particular African American community forces readers to rethink the norms of our social formation, especially when the aberrations of those norms (black people's physical appearance) play themselves out in juxtaposition to their most conventional representations (blond, blue-eyed dolls, movie actresses, models in advertisements, and pictures on Shirley Temple cups).

The novel states its agenda early when Claudia admits that narrating Pecola's story is so painful and difficult that "one must take refuge in how" that story came to be rather than "why" it came to be. *The Bluest Eye* is a history of abstractions—racism and physical aesthetics—and their manifestation in a concrete world: in the distorting of one young black girl's life. Pecola is the means by which her community pledges allegiance to an idea of personal beauty; however, her story is as much about the failure of patriarchal family values when those values are based on restrictions of gender definitions and are at the mercy of the pressures of poverty and racism. The horror of Pecola's existence is even more evident when it is set against the nurtured and nurturing lives of the MacTeer sisters, Claudia and Frieda.

The novel proper is preceded by subversion of the small and imperfect universe of the Dick and Jane story. That story, even in its conventional form, is already endangered: Jane can't find a playmate, Dick can't be found, the kitten won't play. Still, despite these intimations of disorder, Mother laughs and Father smiles. The possible chaotic rendering of the family's unity, however, seems to be held at bay by the very conventionality of the story's textuality: proper punctuation, spelling, grammar, straightforward syntax, and uniform spacing and margins. The passage is repeated twice, and with each repetition the words are pushed closer and closer until the paragraph is meaningless. Squashed into incomprehensibility under textual compression, the deformed paragraph represents the deformation of Pecola's family: under the pressures of economic impoverishment and the stultifying effects of past and present racism, the entire family is without the means and the confidence to hold its shape, to center itself, to make itself whole.

With the first epigraph from the Dick and Jane story (following the introductory chapter),

HEREISTHEHOUSEITISGREENANDWH
ITEITHASAREDDOORITISVERYPRETT
YITISVERYPRETTYPRETTYPRETTYP

the text sets the terms. The last word, the key word "pretty," is repeated completely four times, but the fifth attempt at the word stops with *p*. The word has no real existence because this section of the narrative is about the Breedlove storefront home, about which there is nothing intrinsically "pretty": this house is hideous to the mother, Pauline, contrasted as it is with her white, middle-class standards of beauty. The house is ugly, and even the addition of a new couch can't make it "pretty" because the couch arrives damaged. The limits of Pauline's vision are made manifest in the next sec-

tion of the story, which is introduced by a passage focusing on the key word "happiness," again repeated several times but truncated after the *h* at the end.

The family has no history of happiness. Pauline's life has been economically and intellectually stunted, and Cholly's life has been economically and psychosexually stunted by his racist experience as a teenage boy with white males who observe and interfere as he and a teenage girl have sexual intercourse. The children of the family are miserable and withdrawn. From such beginnings the narrative uses the rest of the Dick and Jane story to preview and parallel the deterioration of the Breedlove family even as it uses the seasons of the year to suggest the optimism of a cyclical universe. A reader is fooled into hoping that if one can get through the decay of "Autumn" and the dormancy of "Winter," then perhaps the fecundity of "Spring" and the harvest of "Summer" will renew the malfunctioning world of the text's beginning. Instead, however, the harvest of summer is monstrous—by its end (also the end of the text), Pecola has been raped by her father, assaulted by the world's degradation of her appearance, and, finally, left only with the comfort of her madness—a dream of possessing the "bluest," and hence the most beautiful and desirable, eyes.

Claudia's narrative of Pecola's story attempts to describe and account for what happens to her friend, but the story is bigger and more horrific than one young female child's narrative can contain. While Claudia's own story allows us to discover her world with her—that impatient and overworked mothers still clean up vomit and don't want their sick children to die, that adults "issue orders without providing information"—and shows us Claudia criticizing herself (in short, "becoming" her own narrative), by the end of the novel even Claudia's story is almost as severely circumscribed as Pecola's: Pecola's downfall has become Claudia's guilt. Claudia is the one person to recognize that the responsibility for Pecola's madness lies within every member of the community who did not fight to root out the possession of the black imagination that internalized racism takes.

This novel is a chronicle of Pecola and her family under attack, an attack issuing from the pressures of racism. Cholly's twisted psyche results from his inability to sustain his family economically in a world that both makes it impossible for him to do so yet demands that he must. The attack is made more vicious by Pauline's infatuation with American movie aesthetics and middle-class standards of taste in place of connections to an older southern culture that might have sustained her in the North. Further, she works as a maid and is consumed by a damaging set of aesthetic identifications with her well-off white employer, identifications that prevent her from exercising her imagination or utilizing the coping mechanisms that enrich the MacTeer family both economically and culturally.

By extension, Pauline is part of what destroys her daughter; Pecola is done in by poverty, not just the poverty of the spirit that comes from living within the circumference of her mother's damaging aesthetic but also the poverty of denied aspirations, the vicious cultural poverty that is the logical outcome of racism and the lack of economic mobility. Pecola is raped and made mad not because she is essentially an unloved and ugly victim, or because her community constructs her as ugly, but because she and her family represent the ugly secret beneath the surface of the Shirley Temple cup. That cup represents the attractiveness forced on the young black girls of the story; such "attractiveness" is further enforced by the parameters of the Dick and Jane happy household story. The cup and the story belong to a world that is aestheticized in a particular way and underwritten by an economically comfortable existence. Pecola is the poor, black underside of that story, which by its presence serves to mark the value of its opposite.

Sula

The relationship between micro and macro history in her first novel also informs Morrison's second. *Sula* pulls together a real history of a community forgotten behind the language of "a joke. A nigger joke." The story parallels the history of a black community (the Bottom) and its origins in the false promise of a white farmer with the family histories of two young black women, Sula Peace and Nel Wright, and the military-induced psychosis of a black veteran.

What holds the Bottom together is a shared history both in that place and in the places in the South from which the residents have come. The history of Nel's mother, Helen, the straitlaced daughter of a whore, becomes the engine driving her retreat into, and her insistence on (for her daughter), a life of arid, gentrified, and conventional deprivation nonetheless tragic for Helen's inability to see its stranglehold on her and her daughter's vitality.

The story is a multilevel narrative that pivots on the story of Shadrack the veteran, a schizophrenic who can conquer his fear of death only by externalizing it into a once-a-year ritual, "National Suicide Day," and on the story of a man-loving female dynasty headed by Eva Peace, Sula's grandmother. Shadrack's psychosis draws in the entire community, just as Eva's dynasty does. The complexities of this dynasty are manifested by the inability of Eva's daughter, Hannah, to withhold herself from any man who wants her—she cannot understand why any woman would build her life around just one man—and by the ability of Eva to kill by setting fire to the one male most consistently responsible for her sense of herself as a mother.

It is these complexities that make possible the central richness of the text: its insistence that it is the multiple complications of interwoven identities that allow a community to be both a collection of individuals and an incubator of a common will. The Bottom both produces and contains the friendship of Nel and Sula, just as it valorizes the gender restrictions that make Nel a shadow of conventionality while providing the crucible that constructs the figure of adventure and curiosity that is Sula. Sula is, according to Deborah McDowell, the representation of a character as a process, not an essence. The narrative interweaves this "process" with the text's presentation of Nel as the most historically conservative of constructions—the powerless, careful, and virginal "nice girl"—and thus highlights the interplay between Sula's assumption of the male privilege not to be held down and Nel's insistence on making the expected, stable, held-in-place "good life" for herself. The friendship between the two women is a powerful one, its potency made believable by the text's excavation of how identity is both socially constructed and abrogated.

Toward the end of *Sula*, the same community that had allowed Nel and Sula to forge the terms of their togetherness by making their differences a subject of discussion, and not a reason for exile, constructs Sula as the demon witch "other" who, at least temporarily, causes the matrons of the Bottom to "become" better mothers by allowing them to define their "virtue" against her "evil," just as earlier they had made moral alliances against her mother's promiscuity.

While one grieves for such false consciousness and its deadly manifestions in this community of poor black people, for the series of tragedies throughout the novel—the deaths of a small child, of a sibling and parent, of a marriage, or even of an entire community (when the tunnel caves in on "National Suicide Day")—the broken friendship between the two women evokes the deepest response. Their connection made the other relationships more coherent and salient, and made possible the exploration of what one was not, of what one might otherwise not have done:

"We was girls together," she said as though explaining something. "O Lord, Sula," she cried, "girl, girl, girlgirlgirl."

It was a fine cry—loud and long—but it had no bottom and it had no top, just circles and circles of sorrow.

In mapping the terrain of possibility within the constantly negotiated spaces of race and gender, *Sula* ends with the severed connection between Nel and Sula, a sundering that is clearly more than the death of a friendship, that in fact represents the cessation of fluidity and its being forced into final fixity.

Song of Solomon

Morrison herself has made clear her interest in what is at stake in a critique of fixity, of stability, and it is on the ground of undermining the false comfort of an unquestioned economic, emotional, and familial stability that *Song of Solomon* rests. This third novel is the battleground for undermining the powerful but fallacious hold that fixity, unity, and closure have had on representations of African American culture. While most commonly regarded by critics as the working out of a mythic search for group and self, the politically and psychologically complex *Song of Solomon* is a novel of explicit and implicit critique. It is a critique of ownership psychology, patriarchal culture, and obsessive searches for narratives of authentic and stable "truth." It is a text that takes seriously the tensions of the relationship between individual history and group politics.

At the same time, the text is a multilayered narrative whose protagonist learns to "read" through the layers of history that surround and intersect his life. The narrative explores the ways individuals and communities construct reality and political formations, and, within the dynamic play of African American vernacular language, it refuses to allow the reader to ferret out a single "truth," the "real story," the solution(s) to the mystery(ies).

The text sets up racial and economic oppositions without foregrounding whites and racist oppression; while it does not leave out external racism, it constructs that oppression from the black side. It begins with a community that is defined in negative reaction to a larger community: it is *not* on the "right" side of the tracks, its main thoroughfare is "Not Doctor Street," and the hospital where the narrative threads are laid is "No Mercy Hospital."

The characters must find their ways through the morass of that which defines them, just as the African American community outside of, as well as inside of, this text must think its way through the various possible political strategies. These two parallels meet in the fate of the protagonist, Milkman. Born on the grounds of No Mercy Hospital on Not Doctor Street, Milkman is the human nexus of the forces engaged from the beginning of the narrative.

This is a narrative that complicates place. Home, for example, is where Milkman and his family live and rest, but it is also a place of obsession with money and death. Macon, Milkman's father, has an office that is described not in terms of address or geographical relationship but in terms of its relation to its previous history, "Sonny's Shop," which is how the community sees it. Only Macon thought of it as his office and painted the word "office" on its door. Macon's determination to "fix" meaning also is represented by a business concern (a summer community) named "Honor" on the lake—not a place as much as an exchange marker for the middle-class African Americans who can afford summer homes there.

Place is not simply location; it is what happened at that site, what was felt about that happening, and what people said about it. In response to the question of where her father was murdered, Macon's sister Pilate answers, "off a fence," "on our farm," or "Montour County," and all the answers say something while none of them leaves the questioner satisfied. Pilate herself conveys a meaning of which she is unaware, as Valerie Smith puts it. She sings a partial version of the biblical Song of Solomon wherever she goes, which means the family history is carried to various places by one who knows the text but not its relationship to its history or its meaning.

Pilate also embodies the mediating ground between the polarities of the political selves represented by Milkman and his more explicitly political friend, Guitar. She is, throughout the text, the locus for delineating history, personal connection, and alternatives to time and concrete reality. She maintains a political life—a critique of power relations—without explicitly discussing politics and represents the funky coming together of the modern and the folk. Pilate also represents, in her knowledge of all of the aspects of her world, the ability to manipulate that world, to alter, to make fluid what is "real," but she retains the sense of responsibility that comes through in her history: "You can't just fly on off and leave a body."

It is finally that insistence on responsibility which stays with the reader and which undermines the assumption that Milkman's flight at the end, over her dead body, is an untroubled and transcendent answer to his quest for his history. Even when successful as escape, flight leaves people behind, mourning. When unsuccessful, it leaves people behind, dead. Flight even facilitates the final and lethal showdown between bare-handed but no less inimical friends, the outcome of which is left open to conjecture.

Tar Baby

The indeterminacy of *Song of Solomon* is even more evident in *Tar Baby*, a far less read and written-about text. The difficulty with this novel may stem from the lack of distance from its content on the part of critics, who, like the central character, Jadine, are likely to have had elite educations, and on the part of readers, who, again like Jadine, are likely to be middle- or upper-class. It is more difficult to respond hopefully to a text that so ruthlessly demystifies both education and sentimentality in a way which suggests that neither education nor emotional engagement offers an easy resolution to problems of race and class. The text is also unsettling in its contemporary immediacy: readers cannot escape through it into another world—brand and corporate names so permeate the text that one's nose is rubbed in the "this world-ness" of the story. And the dichotomies that are apparent are too "real," too pointed, for the story's lovers (or readers) to easily transcend the differences which are so interwoven a part of the text.

Set on a Caribbean island representing a microcosm of benevolence and benign intentions on the part of its white owners, the novel probes the more sordid underside and history of that benevolence. Valerian Street, the powerful white male figure, wears Margaret, his "Principal Beauty" wife, as an ornament. This human ornament is as cold and functionless as any of the inanimate sort: she cannot nurture her child—in fact, she is a secret child abuser.

The conflicted household also contains Ondine and Sydney—the black domestic workers—whose niece Jadine is the surrogate child for Valerian and Margaret. Ondine nurtures Valerian and Margaret's son and also knows Margaret's secret. Gideon and Thérèse are the black "outside" workers, who do not exist for the "inside"—they are an undifferentiated part of the natural world that the inside world of artifice covers over. Thérèse's name is not even part of the "owners" story—Margaret calls her Mary. And finally, there is Son—whose very name suggests a familial connection to the three couples that cannot be sustained and who is the catalyst for the action of the story.

The various dyads represent the conflicted grounds in the relationships between nature and nurture and between identity and responsibility. Jadine represents the embodiment of a possible bridge between the worlds, though ultimately she cannot reach and connect all the different sides.

The island on which the characters live and on which Son's presence intrudes is a place that, according to legend, struck slaves blind. Amid the lushness of the "natural" foliage of the island lives the "unnaturalness" of maternal abuse with its counterpoint in the natural, primal, yet dangerous ants and trees. Stuck on the island for different reasons—she visits out of love for the inhabitants and he, out of fear for his life—Jadine and Son are both "tar babies," both equally cultural icons, representations of cultural myths, and both equally unreal. To the reader and to each other they represent caricatures of the arguments that seek to account for racial difference. Jadine has been nurtured much as a white middle- or upper-class young woman would have been; Son has been allowed, by the circumstances of his impoverished childhood in the South, to grow up essentially unsocialized, at least according to bourgeois norms and mores. The text puts the two together spatially with sexual attraction as the glue that causes them to "stick" to each other—they are tar babies with a certain fatal attraction for each other.

The subtext of the novel forces a reader to consider not only the dynamics of "nurture" (or lack thereof) and "nature," but also the difficulty of defining a love affair that is caught on the horns of the dilemmas of gender and class. If Jadine is a particular kind of black woman and Son is a particular kind of black man, is the possibility of their joining arbitrary? Or does the text make their differences so thoroughgoing that the inevitability of "love" or sexual attraction is made a problem by recourse to representations of its difficulties when run through a matrix of polar differences? The text makes fun of the easy and romantic assumption that "love will find a way," insisting instead that love lives in the world, and that the world is political.

At one end of the spectrum is the entirely comfortable world of Jadine's surroundings. Yet that world is comfortable only because Valerian is blind to Margaret's inability to care for their son, because Margaret has been content all of her life to be the "Principal Beauty," and because the power of that household (represented by Valerian) remakes everyone in it to Valerian's specifications, his need. Jadine is comfortable insofar as she represents someone who is constructed according to the desire of others. She is not "naturally" the child of Ondine or Sydney, although she is part of a kin relationship; she is only artificially Valerian and Margaret's child; and she is attractive to Son only because he cannot see past the glitter of her surface to the emptiness below it. But Jadine is as much the product of her world as Son is the product of his. And this is not a text that will allow us to romanticize the "old South," Eloe, from whence he comes. Against his own nostalgia for that place is the clarity of Jadine's gaze on its incredible poverty, oppressive social mores, and restrictions based on gender.

The most fascinating aspect of this text is the interplay between Jadine's gaze on Eloe and Son's gaze on Valerian's world—the two are incredibly critical of each other's world at the same time they are both incredibly blind to the fact that each embodies his or her own world. Both Jadine and Son make the person to whom each is attracted "the other"; both find that "otherness" sexy, but both are finally defeated by the implications of that otherness. Jadine considers Son the physical side of herself, Son desires the carefully nurtured artifice of Jadine, and in their commentary on their relationship the two take on the difficult definition of "blackness."

In a colonialist world, the Isle des Chevaliers, who is really free to be "black"? Everyone is owned, including the owners, who are trapped by the responsibilities that go with owning the land and the humans who work on it and in the house. The "Philadelphia Negroes" (a play on W. E. B. Du Bois's stunning sociological study of the black bourgeoisie in Philadelphia) is a title proudly claimed by Ondine and Sydney, who are domestic servants empowered by their proximity to the real owners and whose niece, Jadine, educated by the owners, represents the new native elite.

Within the constraints of this story, answers to the questions posed by the existence of these people, in that time and in that topsy-turvy landscape of anthropomorphic rivers and trees, are made impossible by the complexities present at the onset. What does it mean to be a black man or woman within the terms of colonialism? What is love when desire continually attaches itself to false exoticism? Whose vision can we trust when all people have power inequities from which they speak or financial interests to negotiate? *Tar Baby* is not a love story as much as it is the ground for first world and third world collision.

Beloved

Beloved, like *Tar Baby*, is a history and a representation of the complexities of love and sexual attraction. It is a more hopeful story because while it suggests that racism and memory never die, it also suggests that it is the negotiation of history, both one's own and that of the group, which makes love possible. This novel is, finally, a text about the community as a site of complications that empowers, as much as its social history within the larger formation debilitates, its members. What is most hopeful about the way in which the characters work their way through the complexities of that community and their relationship to history

and memory is their realization that desire and autonomy are necessarily intertwined.

Beloved foregrounds the alienation of the slave's body; it focuses not only on the use of that body for labor but also on the uses of that body's surplus production—affection from any slave (male or female), the children, and the milk of the slave woman. It delineates the incredible "othering" of the slave system, an othering that allows "owning" humans to put "bits" in the mouths of "owned" humans in the name of socialization and efficiency. The text defines the sexuality of male slaves by virtue of depictions of the inaccessibility of their desires.

More than a recounting of slave history, however, *Beloved* forces on our minds the implications of slavery's existence in the emancipated present. Sethe escapes with her children from the actual scene of her enslavement, but because the tentacles of slavery follow her, she attempts to kill her children and succeeds with one of them. Long after the end of slavery, after the end of her societal punishment, the legacy of slavery—the obsessive presence of the dead baby's spirit—manifests itself in the unhappy and traumatic atmosphere of the house, 124 Bluestone Road. The other part of Sethe's slave past, Paul, comes into that house and provides the catalyst for the physical intrusion of the jealous part of Sethe's slave past. The battleground among Sethe; her living daughter, Denver; her lover, Paul; and the spirit of the dead baby, Beloved, is also the place where rewritten history and memory construct the possibility for at least a negotiated autonomy. The characters learn to love because as survivors of a time when even love was so circumscribed that it had to take as its objects abstractions that could not be taken away by the owners, they realize that freedom finally allows a satisfaction that results from reconsidering everyone's connections to everyone else and to memory. Slavery exists as a hold on the imagination; the relearning of human attachment is the way in which that hold is loosened.

Slavery is a narrative that draws on monologic memory—the horror of the material relation overwhelms every other kind of relation;

against that monologism, *Beloved* foregrounds the dialogic tendencies of memory and its imaginative capacity to construct and reconstruct the significance of the past. The narrative of slavery is chronologically linear; *Beloved*, on the other hand, meanders, circles back, and moves spirally. It takes into account different versions of the past, not to construct a complete, whole, and monolithic account but to complicate any attempt at a monolithic account.

Morrison has repeatedly articulated her sense of awe of the incredible psychic power that ordinary black men and women had to exercise to resist the devastation of slavery. In *Beloved* she pays tribute to that power by not having recourse to a singular and heroic style of narrative, by not simply imposing one personal style. She allows the fractures and ruptures of individuals' retellings of their stories to add layers of the narrative. The text avoids the trap of becoming a parade of mythic suffering woven into a cathartic maternal melodrama by insisting on historicizing everyone's emotional responses, by delineating the individual strategies of resistance, and by including the clinical details of horrific instances like the severing of Beloved's head so that readers are not lost in a maze of Sethe's anguish. This is not a text that allows one to draw back and simply feel; instead, one is forced to look, to think, and to listen to characters account for themselves and for the forces acting on them. If the most damaging aspect of slavery was its insistence that black humans were animal-like in their lack of a psyche, this text reinscribes the complexities of those psyches with a vengeance.

Jazz

The complexities of psyches and their engagement with and through history moves through *Jazz* and are moved by an urban cacophony of mobility: *Jazz* captures the wildness of the rural South moving North, trailing the possibilities and detritus of mysterious and mystified family romances; the momentum of social challenges to the racial house—the United

States—against the attempts of that house to stabilize and control boundaries among people; the impulse to carry and hold fast the embodiment of a dream. Joe's murder of Dorcas is a palimpsest of male attempts to exert control over desire and the object of desire. It is the means by which he secures an unchanging vision of himself, a momento—a totem, even—of his self-idealization. And that murder looms larger or dwindles depending on the movement of the refracturing eye or "I" of history's perception, the text's perception, and the reader's perception. A nonlinear set of tensions and negotiations—entanglements that are sometimes competing, sometimes intersecting, and sometimes knotted and webbed— make up the mess that is a city.

The migration into and transformation of the city is one of the means by which we understand modernity. In *Jazz*, we read of the city's changing animation as the wildness of the South enlivens it, the novel also leads us to understand technology as the means by which personification is established in this new environment—as in the photography of Dorcas. But photography is also the mode of expression that makes Dorcas's personification contingent, ephemeral. Dorcas is alive one moment, as her representation speaks to Violet, and dead the next, as an objet d'art and a finished story on a shelf.

The city rolls over, around, under, and through the circulation of stories and affairs—love, family, friendship—and provides a concrete staging ground for the parade of politics. Harlem stages itself, and the text provides a voice-over. But along with big and small spectacles, big and small machines—on the street, in the home, and in the beauty parlor, come the ghosts of old and new stories. *Jazz* and the "something" driving this text ask us repeatedly: Who are these people?

Morrison addressed the possibilities of the city for black writers in her 1981 essay "City Limits, Village Values," wherein she positions the city as a space of negotiation. The city for black writers is not the scene of loss that it has often figured as for white writers—the loss of unbounded freedom, autonomy, and power.

Nor is it the scene of alienation. Instead, the city serves as the ground of knowledge; it offers the concentration of the village ancestors and the complexity of life lived in dense layers of sound, sight, smell, touch, and taste.

The city is a text, which means it is a mystery as conventional as the son's discovery of his father and as innovative as the making of female friendships and relationships out of the old shackles of a burned-out heterosexual romance. The friendships that Violet makes and the relationships that she sustains in the wake of Dorcas's death and the burial of her own "old" marriage makes possible a different Violet and a more complicated new love affair. Nonetheless, nothing in *Jazz* is ever completely resolved, made, or thoroughly known. The possibilities are just reconfigured, the players repositioned, and another perspective voiced or revoiced.

Paradise

That complexity of positioning and telling so central to *Jazz* also drives *Paradise*. The town Ruby, Oklahoma, created out of a promise, a covenant, that comes out of U.S. racial history, is the concrete embodiment of a foundational myth of purity, authenticity, and power as heavy and opaque as the oven that holds the town in place. Like all foundational myths, the circulation of Ruby's history is deadening. It is meant to keep memory alive, but like the ghost of a corpse weighing on the living, it silences the young for whom it is supposed to promise a different future.

By contrast, the various women who make their ways to Ruby, by chance and by choice, retreating from male-centered difficulty, make a space—the convent—that allows people to return from the dead. They move, in other words, from the places of traditional male control to a place of self-control. The convent is a place for healing, for coexistence that does not demand personal erasure as its price for making community. The stories are not told in strict chronological or linear fashion. They are interrupted, they spiral, and even turn in on themselves. The convent is a challenge to the older ways and the older battles that produced Ruby. We could think of the convent as the embodiment of Morrison's call (in her essay "Home") for a "third, if you will pardon the expression, world"—a space where "one can imagine safety without walls, can iterate difference that is prized but unprivileged." A space where one learns community as something embedded, not imposed.

As is the case with all of Morrison's novels, history is represented, is told, as an interplay of larger forces and structures of power, as a force resisted and opposed, and as the intertwining of family narrative within a tapestry made up of larger stories. The history of the present is more fully apparent in *Paradise* than in any of her other novels with the exception, perhaps, of *Tar Baby*. But where *Tar Baby* takes up the history of colonialism as imbricated in the relationship between Jadine and Son, *Paradise* gives us a sharply critical take on black cultural commonsense as predicated on attempted male colonialization of female bodies and psyches.

That most of the women who become the objects of the black male executioners are themselves also black fractures the myth of racial solidarity. That one of the women is white but not identified specifically in the narrative allows us to question (without the certainty of a completely satisfying answer) what the representation of race does: where it tells us something, where it does not. That all who die are women is the final plank in the narrative's building of a critical representation of masculinist black nationalist fantasies of control. Finally, however, the presence of death and life, or life in death, at the novel's end allows us a sense of possibility: there are limits to the ability of "reality" to tell us all we need to know, there are limits of knowing itself. What kind of resurrection might be possible is the work of imagination.

Morrison's texts have in common the project that she herself has articulated for black literature in general: if it is not concerned with the village or the community (however critically, one might add), then it has no reason for being.

Selected Bibliography

PRIMARY WORKS

NOVELS

The Bluest Eye. New York: Holt, Rinehart & Winston, 1970.

Sula. New York: Knopf, 1973.

Song of Solomon. New York: Knopf, 1977.

Tar Baby. New York: Knopf, 1981.

Beloved. New York: Knopf, 1987.

Jazz. New York: Knopf, 1992.

Paradise. New York: Knopf, 1998.

NONFICTION

College Reading Skills. New York: Knopf, 1965.

Playing in the Dark: Whiteness and the Literary Imagination. Cambridge: Harvard University Press, 1992. (Essays.)

The Nobel Acceptance Speech. New York: Knopf, 1994. (Delivered in Stockholm on December 7, 1993.)

The Dancing Mind. New York: Knopf, 1996. (Morrison's speech in acceptance of the National Book Foundation Medal for Distinguished Contribution to American Letters, November 6, 1996.)

WORKS EDITED OR COAUTHORED BY MORRISON

Race-ing Justice, En-gendering Power: Essays on Anita Hill, Clarence Thomas, and the Construction of Social Reality. New York: Pantheon, 1992.

Deep Sightings and Rescue Missions: Fiction, Essays, and Conversations. New York: Pantheon, 1996. (A collection of writings by Toni Cade Bambara.)

Birth of a Nation'hood: Gaze, Script, and Spectacle in the O. J. Simpson Case. Coedited with Claudia Brodsky Lacour. New York: Pantheon, 1997.

The Big Box. Coauthored with Slade Morrison. New York: Hyperion, 1999. (For children.)

ESSAYS, REVIEWS, AND STORIES

"What the Black Woman Thinks about Woman's Lib." *New York Times Magazine,* August 22, 1971, pp. 14–15, 63–64, 66.

"Cooking Out." *New York Times Book Review,* June 10, 1973, pp. 4, 16.

"Behind the Making of *The Black Book.*" *Black World* 23:86–90 (February 1974).

"Rediscovering Black History." *New York Times Magazine,* August 11, 1974, pp. 14ff.

"Reading." *Mademoiselle* 81:14 (May 1975).

"Slow Walk of Trees (as Grandmother Would Say) Hopeless (as Grandfather Would Say)." *New York Times Magazine,* July 4, 1976, pp. 104ff.

"City Limits, Village Values: Concepts of Neighborhood in Black Fiction." In *Literature and the Urban Experience: Essays on the City and Literature.* Edited by Michael Jaye and Ann Chalmers Watts. New Brunswick, N.J.: Rutgers University Press, 1981. Pp. 35–43.

"Recitatif." In *Confirmations: Stories by Black Women.* Edited by Amiri Baraka and Amina Baraka. New York: William Morrow, 1983. Pp. 243–61.

"Memory, Creation, and Writing." *Thought* 59:385–90 (December 1984).

"Rootedness: The Ancestor as Foundation." In *Black Women Writers (1950–1980): A Critical Examination.* Edited by Mari Evans. Garden City, N.Y.: Anchor/Doubleday, 1984. Pp. 339–45.

"The Site of Memory." In *Inventing the Truth: The Art and Craft of Memoir.* Edited by William K. Zinsser. Boston: Houghton Mifflin, 1987.

"Unspeakable Things Unspoken: The Afro-American Presence in American Literature." *Michigan Quarterly Review* 28:1–34 (Winter 1989).

"The Marketing of Power: Racism and Fascism." *Nation* 260, no. 21:760 (May 29, 1995).

Preface to *Deep Sightings and Rescue Missions.* Edited by Toni Morrison. New York: Pantheon, 1996.

"Home." In *The House That Race Built: Black Americans, U.S. Terrain.* Edited by Wahneema Lubiano. New York: Pantheon, 1997. Pp. 3–12.

"Strangers." *New Yorker,* October 12, 1998, p. 68.

SECONDARY WORKS

BIOGRAPHICAL AND CRITICAL STUDIES

Awkward, Michael. "Roadblocks and Relatives: Critical Revision in Toni Morrison's *The Bluest Eye.*" In *Critical Essays on Toni Morrison.* Edited by Nellie Y. McKay. Boston: G. K. Hall, 1988. Pp. 56–68.

———. *Inspiriting Influences: Tradition, Revision, and Afro-American Women's Novels.* New York: Columbia University Press, 1989.

Backus, Margot Gayle. " 'Looking for That Dead Girl': Incest, Pornography, and the Capitalist Family Romance in *Nightwood, The Years,* and *Tar Baby.*" *American Imago* 51, no. 4:421 (Winter 1994).

Badt, Karin Luisa. "The Roots of the Body in Toni Morrison: A Matter of 'Ancient Properties.' " *African American Review* 29, no. 4:567 (Winter 1995).

Bischoff, Joan. "The Novels of Toni Morrison: Studies in Thwarted Sensitivity." *Studies in Black Literature* 6, no. 3:21–23 (1975).

Bjork, Patrick Bryce. *The Novels of Toni Morrison: The Search for Self and Place within the Community.* New York: Peter Lang, 1992.

Blake, Susan L. "Folklore and Community in *Song of Solomon.*" *MELUS* 7:77–82 (Fall 1980).

Bloom, Harold, ed. *Toni Morrison.* Broomall, Pa.: Chelsea House, 2000.

Butler-Evans, Elliott. *Race, Gender, and Desire: Narrative Strategies in the Fiction of Toni Cade Bambara, Toni Morrison, and Alice Walker.* Philadelphia: Temple University Press, 1989.

Christian, Barbara. *Black Women Novelists: The Development of a Tradition, 1892–1976.* Westport, Conn.: Greenwood Press, 1980.

Coleman, James. "The Quest for Wholeness in Toni Morrison's *Tar Baby.*" *Black American Literature Forum* 20:63–73 (Spring–Summer 1986).

Duvall, John. "Descent in the 'House of Chloe': Race, Rape, and Identity in Toni Morrison's *Tar Baby.*" *Contemporary Literature* 38, no. 2:325 (Summer 1997).

Erickson, Peter B. "Images of Nurturance in Toni Morrison's *Tar Baby.*" *CLA Journal* 28:11–32 (September 1984).

Gates, Henry Louis, Jr., and K. Anthony Appiah, eds. *Toni Morrison: Critical Perspectives Past and Present.* New York: Amistad, 1993.

Handley, William R. "The House a Ghost Built: Allegory, Nommo, and the Ethics of Reading in Toni Morrison's *Beloved.*" *Contemporary Literature* 36, no. 4:676 (Winter 1995).

Harding, Wendy, and Jacky Martin. *A World of Difference: An Intercultural Study of Toni Morrison's Novels.* Westport, Conn.: Greenwood Press, 1994.

Holloway, Karla. "*Beloved:* A Spiritual." *Callaloo* 13, no. 3:516 (1990).

Holloway, Karla, and Stephanie Demetrakopoulos. *New Dimensions of Spirituality: A Biracial and Bicultural Reading of the Novels of Toni Morrison.* New York: Greenwood Press, 1987.

Holton, Robert. "Bearing Witness: Toni Morrison's *Song of Solomon* and *Beloved.*" *English Studies in Canada* 20, no. 1:79–90 (1994).

Horvitz, Deborah. "Nameless Ghosts: Possession and Dispossession in *Beloved.*" *Studies in American Fiction* 17, no. 2:157 (Fall 1989).

Hovet, Grace Ann, and Barbara Lounsberry. "Flying as Symbol and Legend in Toni Morrison's *The Bluest Eye, Sula,* and *Song of Solomon.*" *CLA Journal* 27:119–40 (December 1983).

Kolmerten, Carol A., Stephen M. Ross, and Judith Bryant Wittenberg, eds. *Unflinching Gaze: Morrison and Faulkner Re-envisioned.* Jackson: University of Mississippi Press, 1997.

Lee, Dorothy H. "The Quest for Self: Triumph and Failure in the Works of Toni Morrison." In *Black Women Writers (1950–1980): A Critical Evaluation.* Edited by Mari Evans. Garden City, N.Y.: Anchor/Doubleday, 1984. Pp. 346–60.

Lester, Rosemarie K. "An Interview with Toni Morrison, Hessian Radio Network, Frankfurt, West Germany." In *Critical Essays on Toni Morrison.* Edited by Nellie Y. McKay. Boston: G. K. Hall, 1988. Pp. 47–54.

Lubiano, Wahneema. "The Postmodernist Rage: Political Identity and the Vernacular." In *New Essays on "Song of Solomon."* Edited by Valerie Smith. Cambridge, U.K.: Cambridge University Press, 1995.

McDowell, Deborah E. " 'The Self and the Other': Reading Toni Morrison's *Sula* and the Black Female Text." In *Critical Essays on Toni Morrison.* Edited by Nellie Y. McKay. Boston: G. K. Hall, 1988. Pp. 77–90.

McKay, Nellie Y. "An Interview with Toni Morrison." *Contemporary Literature* 22:413–29 (Winter 1983).

———, ed. *Critical Essays on Toni Morrison.* Boston: G. K. Hall, 1988.

Middleton, David, ed. *Toni Morrison's Fiction: Contemporary Criticism.* New York: Garland, 1997.

Miner, Madonne M. "Lady No Longer Sings the Blues: Rape, Madness, and Silence in *The Bluest Eye.*" In *Conjuring: Black Women, Fiction, and Literary Tradition.* Edited by Majorie Pryse and Hortense Spillers. Bloomington: Indiana University Press, 1985. Pp. 176–91.

Mobley, Marilyn E. *Folk Roots and Mythic Wings in Sarah Orne Jewett and Toni Morrison.* Baton Rouge: Louisiana State University Press, 1991.

———. "Narrative Dilemma: Jadine as Cultural Orphan in Toni Morrison's *Tar Baby.*" *Southern Review* 23, no. 4:761–70 (Autumn 1987).

Moglen, Helene. "Redeeming History: Toni Morrison's *Beloved.*" In *Female Subjects in Black and White: Race, Psychoanalysis, Feminism.* Edited by Elizabeth Abel, Barbara Christian, and Helene Moglen. Berkeley: University of California Press, 1997. Pp. 201–20.

Moraru, Christian. "Reading the Onomastic Text: 'The Politics of the Proper Name' in Toni Morrison's *Song of Solomon.*" *Names* 44, no. 3:189 (September 1996).

Naylor, Gloria, and Toni Morrison. "A Conversation." *Southern Review* 21:567–93 (July 1985).

O'Meally, Robert. " 'Tar Baby, She Don' Say Nothin.' " *Callaloo* 4:1–3 (February 1981).

Otten, Terry. *The Crime of Innocence in the Fiction of Toni Morrison.* Columbia: University of Missouri Press, 1989.

Page, Phillip. "Traces of Derrida in Toni Morrison's *Jazz.*" *African American Review* 29, no. 1:55 (Spring 1995).

Peterson, Nancy J., ed. *Toni Morrison: Critical and Theoretical Approaches.* Baltimore: Johns Hopkins University Press, 1997.

Reyes, Angelita Dianne. "Ancient Properties in the New World: The Paradox of the 'Other' in Toni Morrison's *Tar Baby.*" *Black Scholar* 17:19–25 (March–April 1986).

Rodrigues, Eusebio L. "Experiencing *Jazz.*" *Modern Fiction Studies* 39, nos. 3–4:733 (Fall 1993*).

Samuels, Wilfred D. *Toni Morrison.* Boston: Twayne, 1990.

Smith, Valerie. *New Essays on Song of Solomon.* Cambridge, U.K.: Cambridge University Press, 1995.

———. "The Quest for and Discovery of Identity in Toni Morrison's *Song of Solomon.*" *Southern Review* 21:721–32 (Summer 1985).

———. *Self-Discovery and Authority in Afro-American Narrative.* Cambridge, Mass.: Harvard University Press, 1987.

Stepto, Robert B. " 'Intimate Things in Place': A Conversation with Toni Morrison." *Massachusetts Review* 18:473–89 (Autumn 1977).

Weever, Jacqueline de. "The Inverted World of Toni Morrison's *The Bluest Eye* and *Sula*." *CLA Journal* 22:402–14 (1979).

Willis, Susan. *Specifying: Black Women Writing the American Experience*. Madison: University of Wisconsin Press, 1987.

BIBLIOGRAPHIES

Fikes, Robert, Jr. "Echoes from Small Town Ohio: A Toni Morrison Bibliography." *Obsidian* 5:142–48 (Spring–Summer 1979).

Martin, Curtis. "A Bibliography of Writings by Toni Morrison." In *Contemporary Women Writers: Narrative Strategies*. Edited by Catherine Rainwater and William J. Scheick. Lexington: University Press of Kentucky, 1985. Pp. 205–07.

Middleton, David L. *Toni Morrison: An Annotated Bibliography*. New York: Garland, 1987.

VIDEO RECORDINGS

Four Girls and Toni Morrison. Landmark Media, 1994.

Identifiable Qualities: Toni Morrison. Corentyne Productions, 1989.

In Black and White. Part 3, *Toni Morrison*. Six Profiles of African American Authors series. RTSI Swiss TV/ California Newsreel, 1992.

Toni Morrison with A. S. Byatt. Writers Talk: Ideas of Our Time series. ICA Video, 1989.

A Writer's Work with Toni Morrison. World of Ideas with Bill Moyers series. PBS Video, 1990. (Interview by Bill Moyers.)

GLORIA NAYLOR
(1950–   )

ERIC L. HARALSON

A SHARP EYE for moral and emotional dilemmas, a keen sympathy for the trials and triumphs of her characters, a vibrant response to the challenge of her own self-authorization, and a compelling prose style that is gritty and sensuous, incantatory and apocalyptic—these have been the hallmarks of Gloria Naylor's career. In discussing her calling, especially those moments in which the writing takes wing, she has been known to employ a religious vocabulary: "It's as if I've arrived in a place where it's all spirit and no body—an overwhelming sense of calm. . . . I actually begin to feel blessed." At the same time, she disdains proselytizing and didacticism, claiming that her only obligations are "a certain honesty to the world that I'm creating on that page and a measure of integrity to myself."

Though her work primarily celebrates the unique experience of African American women, Naylor has suggested that the practice of her craft itself—by its very intensity—transcends our usual definitions and divisions: "99 44/ 100% of the process is . . . not only genderless and raceless, it's even humanless. . . . It's about dredging up things that are down there . . . in the gut." Her five novels to date—*The Women of Brewster Place* (1982), *Linden Hills* (1985), *Mama Day* (1988), *Bailey's Café* (1992), and *The Men of Brewster Place* (1998)—bear ample witness to the profundity of her own "dredging."

Gloria Naylor was born on January 25, 1950, in New York City, the first of three daughters of Roosevelt and Alberta McAlpin Naylor, who had recently moved from small-town Mississippi and subsequently worked as a subway motorman and a telephone operator, respectively. "From grade school," Naylor has said, "I had been told that I had potential, while I only knew that I felt most complete when expressing myself through the written word." After high school, she decided against entering City College and instead became a Jehovah's Witness missionary, serving in New York, North Carolina, and Florida for the next seven years (1968–1975). Having become disenchanted with the organization, Naylor returned to New York, where she briefly studied nursing at Medgar Evers College before enrolling in Brooklyn College, from which she received a B.A. in English in 1981. In 1983 she received a master's degree in Afro-American studies from Yale.

It was during her sophomore year at Brooklyn College, at age twenty-seven, that Naylor read Toni Morrison's *The Bluest Eye* (1970), a crucial event in her emergence as an author. Whereas "the writers [she] had been taught to love were either white or male," Morrison's example gave Naylor "the *authority* . . . to enter this forbidden terrain":

599

It said to a young poet, struggling to break into prose, that the barriers were flexible. . . . And it said to a young black woman, struggling to find a mirror of her worth . . . not only is your story worth telling but it can be told in words so painstakingly eloquent that it becomes a song.

(Ironically, Naylor was on the National Book Award panel that passed over Morrison's *Beloved* [1988], a top contender for that prestigious award and later a Pulitzer Prize-winning novel; while it is not known how Naylor voted, the episode caused considerable stir in the literary community.)

Although she admires women—such as Zora Neale Hurston—who have "turned their backs on the world . . . been selfish to some degree . . . gone against the grain," Naylor recognizes the dangers of a creative life in which "you are rewarded for staying inside, for becoming a recluse." Accordingly, she has sought to complement her writing with activities that require engagement with the world-above all, teaching. Since 1983, she has been a visiting writer in residence, professor, fellow, and lecturer at George Washington University, Princeton, the University of Pennsylvania, New York University, Boston University, Brandeis, Cornell, and the University of Kent, Canterbury, England. Naylor's honors include an American Book Award for first fiction (1983, for *The Women of Brewster Place*), a National Endowment for the Arts Fellowship (1985), the Candace Award of the National Coalition of One Hundred Black Women (1986), a Guggenheim Fellowship (1988), and the Lillian Smith Award (1989).

Naylor has written essays and screenplays as well, most notably adapting her first novel *The Women of Brewster Place* into a popular miniseries both starring and produced by Oprah Winfrey in 1989. The miniseries was nominated for two Emmys. After this gratifying experience working in television, Naylor began her own independent, multimedia company called One Way Production in 1990, with the express aim of "being able to control the production of images to a larger audience." Since then, she has received a New York Foundation for the Arts Fellowship for screenwriting and participated in Robert Redford's Sundance Institute as a Sundance Fellow to workshop *Mama Day*, the feature-length script based upon her third novel. In addition, she has adapted *Bailey's Café* for a reading at Lincoln Center and performance at the Hartford Stage Company. She has also edited an anthology of black short stories entitled *Children of the Night: The Best Short Stories by Black Writers, 1967 to the Present* (1997).

In spite of her success in many creative realms, she remains best known for her novels. The critical reception has been positive, applauding her brave sensitivity to the struggles of her characters. Most reviewers also cite her virtuosity in a mixed genre—an often poetic prose that strives for universal meanings while grounding the narrative in realistically portrayed incidents and figures. Her writing has even been compared with the magical realism of Latin American writers such as Gabriel García Márquez.

Some commentators argue that Naylor occasionally asks the mundane lives of her characters to take on more mythic or symbolic freight than they can bear. A *New York Times* reviewer, for instance, though generally praising *Mama Day*, observes that Naylor is "less proficient in making the familiar wondrous than in making the wondrous familiar." Others suggest that the passions that so patently inspire her stories (and in a sense dictate her choice of genre) sometimes bring her perilously near the brink of sentimentality and melodrama. For all of this, critics are almost unanimous in praising her willingness to take these risks, which inhere in the ambitious emotional range of her projects. The best way into Naylor's fictional world, of course, is through attentive perusal of the works.

The Women of Brewster Place

The Women of Brewster Place is a study of life in the street that time forgot—a dead-end street in every sense, literally walled off from its home city (which is unnamed, but inferably in the industrial Northeast, near New York). Conceived after World War II as a "bastard child" of pork barrel politics, Brewster has grown up with the twentieth century, watching its own children—first Irish, then Italian immigrants—move away in quest of the American dream, only to be replaced (in the novel's present) by the "multi-colored 'Afric' children of its old age." Brewster particularly loves its "colored daughters," who battle the disintegrative effects of poverty and racism, and who embody vitality, sensuality, domestic artistry, but also paradox, for they are at once "hard-edged, soft-centered, brutally demanding, and easily pleased." Naylor traces the intertwining lives of several of these women, beginning with the book's dominant presence, Mattie Michael.

Mattie first appears in her early fifties, moving into Brewster amid images of grayness, cold, and decay. A stray odor of cooking reminds her of fresh-cut sugarcane (associated throughout with the sweetness and terror of sex), which triggers an extended flashback of the sad chain of events that has brought her there from her backwoods Tennessee childhood. Her father, Samuel, is recalled as a somber, religious man who both overprizes his daughter and stifles her growth as a woman. When Butch Fuller leads young Mattie into the cane fields one day, she yields to long-repressed urges and becomes pregnant, prompting a rupture with her father. Especially provoking is her refusal to name Butch as her partner ("this baby didn't really belong to him" in any case, Mattie decides), which Samuel finds an intolerable breach of the "unquestioning obedience" he has come to expect. Following a savage beating by her father, Mattie departs—alone and four months pregnant—for Asheville, North Carolina. There Mattie and her newborn son, Basil, have the good fortune to be taken into the home of "Miss Eva" Turner, a wise and resilient survivor of five husbands, who provides both sustenance and solidarity: "The young black woman and the old yellow woman sat in the kitchen for hours, blending their lives so that what lay behind one and ahead of the other became indistinguishable." But even in Asheville the warping impress of the past continues to make itself

Gloria Naylor

felt. Mattie compensates for her losses by investing heart and soul in Basil, thus inviting him to practice a kind of tyranny over her. Though she soon comes to think of Miss Eva as a second mother, Mattie becomes defensively angry whenever the old woman chides her for coddling her son and neglecting her own needs.

The elder woman dies, leaving Mattie the house, which is imaged as a sort of ark meant to convey her progeny into a secure future. But by now, Basil has had thirty years to suffer and to profit by his mother's overindulgence, and his "stomach condition" (in its figurative aspect) has gone from bad to worse. Jobless, aimless, and resentful, he drifts into a netherworld, and one night kills a man in a barroom brawl.

Propelled by habit and a guilt that Basil knows how to manipulate, Mattie puts up her precious house as collateral for his bond. Even before he bolts, she sees her terrible mistake: "There was a void in [Basil's] being that had

601

been padded and cushioned over the years, and now that covering had grown impregnable. . . . God had given her what she had prayed for—a little boy who would always need her." The reward for her self-sacrifice—which Naylor presents as equal parts of maternal love, courage, folly, and practical necessity—is a cramped walk-up apartment in Brewster Place, where houseplants that once enjoyed limitless space and sun must now "fight for light on a crowded windowsill." A sign of Mattie's enduring strength is that she pities her plants instead of pitying herself.

Naylor devotes the rest of the work to women whose lives are somehow touched by Mattie, who (like Miss Eva) puts her dearly bought wisdom at their service, becoming mentor, mother, nurse, and confidante. First comes Etta Mae Johnson, a childhood friend who has chased the mirage of lasting love and good times around the country, and who returns to Brewster in calculatedly high style, sporting a pretty dress "only ten minutes old," oversized sunglasses to hide fatigue, and a strutting "body that had finished a close second in its race with time."

The other women of Brewster are Kiswana Browne, a would-be revolutionary who turns her back on college and a bourgeois family to organize poor tenants; Lucielia "Ciel" Turner (Miss Eva's granddaughter, abandoned by her parents), who undergoes an abortion to keep her feckless lover, Eugene, and then loses her young daughter Serena ("the only thing I have ever loved without pain") when the child sticks a fork into an electrical socket; Cora Lee, a beleaguered welfare mother whose love of babies makes her easy prey for male "shadows" and leaves her with a boisterous brood to clothe, feed, and school; and Theresa and Lorraine, a lesbian couple whose arrival leads to unrest and pernicious rumor.

Each of these stories centers on a particular conflict, and each gives off a glimmer of potential hope. Kiswana and her mother, despite differing notions of racial pride, find common ground in certain fundamental facts of kinship and sexuality. Cora Lee (with Kiswana's sisterly aid) takes her children to an African American

production of Shakespeare and is inspired to revitalize herself and her family. Lorraine forges a surrogate child-father relationship with Ben, Brewster's old handyman who drinks to drown all memory of his own awful losses.

Perhaps the most moving scene in the book is Mattie's rescue of Ciel Turner from catatonic despair after the death of Serena. In Naylor's superb handling, the older woman symbolically gives (re)birth to the younger, in a passage that rehearses the history of crimes against maternity and childhood:

Mattie rocked [Ciel] out of that bed . . . into a blue vastness just underneath the sun and above time. . . . over Aegean seas so clean they shone like crystal, so clear the fresh blood of sacrificed babies torn from their mother's arms and given to Neptune could be seen like pink froth on the water. . . . past Dachau, where soul-gutted Jewish mothers swept their children's entrails off laboratory floors. . . . past the spilled brains of Senegalese infants whose mothers had dashed them on the wooden sides of slave ships. . . .

She rocked her into her childhood and let her see murdered dreams. . . . back into the womb, to the nadir of her hurt, and they found it—a slight silver splinter, embedded just below the surface of the skin. And Mattie rocked and pulled—and the splinter gave way, but its roots were deep, gigantic, ragged, and they tore up flesh with bits of fat and muscle tissue clinging to them. They left a huge hole, . . . but Mattie was satisfied. It would heal.

The action of Brewster Place culminates in graphically rendered violence. A band of delinquents headed by C. C. Baker comes to feel sexually threatened by the lesbian couple, eventually translating their brute fury into the gang rape of Lorraine. As she crawls away from the scene, half dead and deranged, Lorraine encounters old Ben; and blindly striving to quiet "the motions that were running and shouting from every direction in the universe," she pummels him to death with a brick. In the aftermath, during a week of steady rain, the bloodied ghost of Lorraine haunts the dreams of every female resident of Brewster.

In Mattie's dream, a long-planned block party reunites the women, and as a cold, purifying shower beats down, they join hands to dismantle the emblem of their isolation and subjugation: "Women flung themselves against the wall, chipping away at it with knives, plastic forks, spiked shoe heels, and even bare hands." Mattie wakes to find her friends preparing for the actual party, while the morning sun shines on Brewster Place and storm clouds gather in the distance.

It would not do justice to Naylor's first novel to understate the broader social critique informing her treatment of these separate lives (an intention announced in the epigraph, Langston Hughes's "A Dream Deferred"). The reader is persistently reminded that the failures of caring, eruptions of hatred, and patterns of sexism being dramatized are rooted in a long legacy of racism, poverty, and dislocation. When the embattled parishioners of Mattie's church sing the spirituals of slavery days, it is "with the frantic determination of a people who realized that the world was swiftly changing but for some mystic, complex reason their burden had not." And as the preacher sets about exorcising this burden, at least for the duration of a sermon, Naylor imagines the congregation's response as:

Yes, Lord—grind out the unheated tenements! Merciful Jesus—shove aside the low-paying boss man. Perfect Father—fill me . . . till there's no room . . . [for] that great big world out there that exacts such a strange penalty for my being born black.

It was hard work. There was so much in them that had to be replaced.

Even though Naylor obviously criticizes the men who harm her heroines, she still takes the larger view, a perspective she fleshes out in further detail in *The Men of Brewster Place*. Naylor never seeks to exonerate her characters, male or female, but asks us to see most of them (Baker's gang is the clear exception) as more sinned against than sinning, and to place an equal—if not a greater—blame for their acts

and omissions on the broken promises of American society.

An elegiac epilogue, entitled "Dusk," indicates that any hope for the future must be qualified at best. But even though the offspring of moribund Brewster Place will move on only "to inherit another aging street and the privilege of clinging to its decay," still, its "colored daughters . . . get up and pin [their] dreams to wet laundry . . . they're mixed with a pinch of salt and thrown into pots of soup, they're diapered around babies. They ebb and flow, ebb and flow, but never disappear."

Linden Hills

In *Linden Hills* (1985) Naylor offers a tour of the heaven to which the denizens of Brewster pray to ascend, and shows it to be a hell on earth presided over by the devil (re)incarnate. The devil's name stays the same, Luther Nedeed ("de-Eden" backward), whether he appears as the original Luther of the 1820s, a freedman who buys the steep, barren face of a plateau, sets up a mortician's shop at the very foot of it, and rents out shacks to his people on the slopes above; or as his son, the second Luther, who expands the family estate and business, meanwhile granting virtually eternal leases to his neighbors; or as the still later Luther who shepherds the increasingly affluent community through the Great Depression; or, finally, as the Luther of the 1980s, ruling the now thriving African American enclave of Linden Hills.

From the start, the Luther Nedeeds are possessed by a vision of what their little world should be. Like his father, Luther number two foresees that "the future of America . . . was going to be white: white money backing wars for white power because the very earth was white . . . white gold, white silver, white coal running white railroads and steamships, white oil fueling white automotives. . . . Yes, the very sky would be white." Knowing he can never hold real power in such a future, this postbellum Luther aspires to make his burgeoning township "a beautiful, black wad of spit right in the white eye of America." Although the Luther of the

1930s images the same aspiration more elegantly, projecting the Hills as "an ebony jewel . . . so bright that it would spawn dreams of dark kings with dark counselors leading dark armies against the white god," he, too, understands that the gem's scintillations will always be illusive—"nothing but light from a hill of carbon paper dolls." The current Luther, whose story forms the core of the novel, has lived to see the dream of his progenitors

> finally crystallized into that jewel, but he wore it like a weighted stone around his neck. . . . These people were to reflect the Nedeeds in a hundred facets and then the Nedeeds could take those splintered mirrors and form a mirage of power to torment a world that dared think them stupid . . . [and] impotent. But there was no torment . . . for the white god . . . because there was no white god. . . . When men begin to claw men for the rights to a vacuum . . . [the] Almighty Divine is simply the will to possess.

The Nedeeds, then, have failed at their game owing to a flawed premise, but what is it that makes Luther (especially in his latest incarnation) the "equivalent of Satan," as Naylor has called him? First, the Luther Nedeeds stand guilty of crimes against their own people. In trying to trick the white "fools" outside, they have deliberately stocked their microcosm with persons who are all too willing to renounce the African American heritage in favor of materialism and cultural neutrality. Because "empty goblets let through the most light," the Depression-era Luther eliminates any residents whose "hopes of building on, not over, their past" might lead them to "produce children who would dream of a true black power. . . . He'd cultivate no madmen like Nat Turner or Marcus Garvey."

This strategy, partly a concern for community prosperity and partly a symptom of egotistic monomania, works so well that by the 1980s "Linden Hills wasn't black; it was successful. The shining surface of their careers, brass railings, and cars . . . only reflected the bright nothing that was inside of them." Confronted with such a perverse quirk of fate, the modern Luther sinks to new depths of cynicism. "He would just let the fools keep coming. . . . His dark face at the bottom of the hill served as a beacon to draw the blacks needed as fuel for that continually dying dream." When this Luther decides to make his wife the main scapegoat for the dying dream, he is simply embellishing another constant of his demonic inheritance—the oppression of women.

Women have historically served only one purpose in the Nedeed household, and that is to reproduce Luther. Tolerated because their bodies are needed to reissue that same squat figure, with his "dark, immobile face" and his "huge, bottomless globes" for eyes, the sequent Mrs. Nedeeds have each been stripped of identity and then (their reproductive chore at an end) relegated to oblivion. But in choosing a mate the modern Luther has deviated from the policy of his forefathers. Whereas all earlier wives had been young octoroons selected "for the color of their spirits," he has married a somewhat older woman who seemed "better than pale—a dull, brown shadow," but who has given him "a white son . . . a ghostly presence that mocked everything his fathers had built." The story proper of *Linden Hills* begins in the Christmas season as the last Luther Nedeed, suspecting adultery, confines his wife and mortally ill child in the basement (the original morgue) of the house, vowing that "it would be a cold day in hell before he saw some woman tear . . . down" the fruits of his patrimony.

But before turning to the special ordeal of Willa Prescott Nedeed, Naylor begins to elaborate a surface narrative about the community itself, dispatching a pair of twenty year olds named Lester Tilson and Willie Mason as her tour guides. Seeking odd jobs for extra holiday cash, the young men slowly descend the "eight curved roads" threading the "abyss" that terminates at the frozen lake surrounding the Nedeed manor. (The system of Naylor's hell is conspicuously Dantean, as Catherine Ward has shown in detail.) Being the grandson of the late Grandma Tilson, a strenuous opponent of Nedeedism in her time, Lester watches scornfully as his neighbors strain their way toward the more opulent lower reaches, unaware that this odd mode of "upward" mobility ("up means down in the Hills") is also *morally* inverted. His friend Willie, a sensitive, lower-class youth from outside the Hills, sympathizes with Lester's hostility but knows that being poor is a poor alternative. Together they set out to enlarge each other's (and the reader's) understanding of the soul-killing milieu of Linden Hills.

The damaged lives they witness include those of Winston Alcott, a gay attorney forced into a career-furthering marriage; of Maxwell Smyth and Xavier Donnell, who climb the corporate ladder at the expense of natural feeling and racial identification; of the Reverend Michael Hollis, whose rise in the clerical hierarchy has cost him all faith in his calling; and of Laurel Dumont, who acquires power in the business world and makes a prominent marriage, only to find that her life is fatally vacant.

The starkest tale of demise (apart from what transpires in Nedeed's own home) is that of Laurel Dumont. Raised in rural Georgia by her grandmother, Roberta, Laurel comes to love music and water as the only elements capable of "keeping her afloat, keeping her moving, keeping her free." Synchronized swimming leads to Berkeley and a business degree, which leads to a top spot at IBM, which leads to marriage into an old-line Hills family. When she pauses in her headlong rush, however, she sees her past as nothing but an endless transience toward an ever-elusive feeling of "home." Marriage and career collapse as she becomes a self-absorbed recluse. With her grandmother's help, Laurel makes a last-ditch effort to return to the shining life, but even as she busily prepares for Christmas, she knows that "Roberta's presence, the decorated rooms, the endless chatter . . . weren't filling the void, but feeding it . . . [There was] nothing inside her to connect up to them." When Luther Nedeed demands that Laurel vacate the house, he effectively gives the shove that sends her plummeting to her death from a high diving platform into an empty pool.

The problem with Linden Hills is that, unbeknownst to its "inmates," there is no "there" there. The novel is saturated with the language and imagery of hollowness, self-alienation, and false brilliance. Willie Mason is quick to see that "something was missing from the jeweled sparkle." The something missing, Naylor underscores, is spirit, spontaneity, and passion. By uncritically accepting the white power structure's value system, and slavishly imitating its behavioral imperatives, Linden Hills has suffered its soul to be replaced by a "bright nothing."

Beneath this surface narrative runs a chilling account of the events unfolding (and being unfolded) in Nedeed's subterranean morgue, where Willa Nedeed discovers that the wives of the previous Luthers have left records of their misery. Wrapped in the first wife's bridal veil is a Bible filled with jottings that document her descent into schizophrenia, self-mutilation, and the final conviction that "there can be no God." The recipe books of a later Mrs. Nedeed chronicle a desperate bid to gain her husband's love by cooking with magical ingredients, followed by a period of bulimic self-abuse that ends with a suicidal Christmas treat of ice cream and prussic acid. The fate of Willa's immediate predecessor is captured in a series of photographs in which the woman's body is gradually eclipsed by the shadow of her son ("The only thing growing in these pictures was her absence"); the last photo shows her as a dim, faceless image, and "scrawled across the empty hole . . . was the word *me*."

These dire stories help the present Mrs. Nedeed to see how she has participated in her own erasure. Naylor's touch is nowhere more deft than in her handling of Willa's arduous process of self-recuperation—a process that requires rejecting Luther's authority, proving to herself that she exists, reclaiming her birth name and taking charge of her own history, and realizing that if she had made her own bondage by relinquishing identity and will, she could make her own freedom by forging a new (or renewed) self. This last insight forms a "singular germ of truth," the embryo of her parthenogenetic rebirth.

On Christmas Eve, Willa finally mounts the basement stairs, symbolically reversing the downward "steps" of her self-negation, while the unsuspecting Luther trims his tree with tiny houses, boats, and birds that replicate the "cardboard paradise" of Linden Hills. In an ending that blends biblical apocalypse with gothic horror, Willa and Luther become locked in a death struggle (their son's corpse wedged between them) that turns the Nedeed home into an inferno. Having concurred with the first Mrs. Nedeed that "this house couldn't still be standing if there were a God," Willa serves as an agent of divine retribution, vindicating the line of wives and mothers and obliterating all traces of a diabolical patriarchy.

Is annihilation the only answer for Linden Hills? The novel contains hints (albeit muted ones) of a more positive alternative. Although she pays with her life, Willa epitomizes the kind of self-recovery that others may undergo in order to regain "that silver mirror God propped up in your soul"—Grandma Tilson's figure for the source of peace and integrity (which enjoys special privilege as the book's epigraph). Beyond that, Willa is survived by a kindred spirit in young Willie Mason, whose sensitivity to the sins against race, sexuality, womanhood, and self inherent in the Nedeed model of progress—as well as in the greater American model it subserves—represents a slender ray of hope for a more valid and egalitarian future. The work closes with Willie and Lester escaping over a storm fence as Luther Nedeed's home blazes behind them: "Hand anchored to hand, one helped the other to scale the open links." Perhaps the redemptory ascent out of hell has begun.

Mama Day

Mama Day (1988) marks Naylor's departure for new geographic and thematic terrain. Mainly set on an extraordinary island that lies off the Georgia-South Carolina coast (yet belongs to neither state), the novel is a modern love story, replete with all the complications of modern love.

The origins of Willow Springs are obscure, but local legend holds that in 1823 Sapphira Wade, a "slave woman who brought a whole new meaning to both them words," wrought a revolution in her insular world. The actual circumstances—just how she compelled her white master to deed the land to his slaves, in what manner he met his death (allegedly by her hand), and how she made her way back to Africa—remain the source of lively speculation in Willow Springs. According to the narrative "voice" of the island, even Sapphira's skin tone varies from one account to the next, becoming "satin black, biscuit cream, red as Georgia clay: depending upon which of us takes a mind to her." The voice explains that Sapphira defies simple specification because she "don't live in the part of our memory we can use to form words" but resides instead in the communal consciousness as an awesome mythic embodiment of African American freedom.

Willow Springs is both quaintly real and strangely unreal, with supernatural happenings and a pervading quality of timelessness—of the eternal return of the same: "It ain't really what you'd call change. It's all happened before and it'll happen again with a different set of faces." The different faces that figure most significantly in the present chapter of the island's history are two of Sapphira Wade's descendants, Miranda Day (the "Mama Day" of the title) and her grandniece Ophelia.

Mama Day is the aged matriarch of the place, both revered and feared as a healer, midwife, portent reader, and conjure woman. Naylor suggests that much—though by no means all—of Miranda's "magic" amounts simply to freeing up the human mind for positive belief and helping natural rhythms to run their course. Mama Day emerges as Naylor's walking compendium of earthly, commonsensical wisdom in matters of love and hate, life and death. But lest her portrait become too charmingly folksy, the author emphasizes that Miranda's role as "Mama" was forced upon her all too early in life, and at great personal cost. As she looks back on her mother's suicidal madness after the loss of another daughter, named Peace, Miranda realizes that she had never had "time to be young":

Little Mama. The cooking, the cleaning, the mending, the gardening for the woman who sat in the porch rocker, twisting, twisting on pieces of thread. Peace was gone. *But I was your child, too.* The cry won't die after all these years. . . . Being there to catch so many babies that dropped into her hands. Gifted hands, folks said. You have a gift, Little Mama. . . . Gave to everybody but myself. Caught babies till it was too late to have my own. Saw so much heartbreak, maybe I never wanted my own. . . . I've had—Lord, can't count 'em—into the hundreds. Everybody's mama now.

Miranda's relationship with the feisty Ophelia is one of sharp friction but also of deep love born of their common ancestry. Although the old woman thinks of her grandniece as having been "a little raw demon from the start," she also proudly acknowledges that "it's only an ancient mother of pure black [Sapphira Wade] that one day spits out this kinda gold." Ophelia's course has taken her to the great and dubious world beyond the bridge, ultimately to New York City, where she has fallen in love (ever so warily) with George Andrews, a self-made man in the Horatio Alger mode. After tracing their fitful progress through the familiar ambivalences and vulnerabilities of contemporary romance, Naylor brings the now married couple to Willow Springs for a visit, setting the stage for Mama Day's biggest test ever.

"A stone city boy" by island standards, George nonetheless takes to the place and its people instantly. Having been raised in a cheerless boys' shelter, the son of a prostitute and an unknown john, he finds in the lush habitat and familial mood of Willow Springs an unbounded paradise. Mama Day and her sister Abigail (Ophelia's grandmother) lavish attention on the young man but gingerly avoid initiating him into the mysteries of life in their community. This is just as well, for George—an engineer by training and a pragmatist by necessity—has founded his life on the empirically provable and has no use for either religion or superstition. "I've always made my own luck," he tells Miranda, while she—half admiring, half pitying him—observes that "he believes in himself . . . 'cause he ain't never had a choice."

The action reaches its pitch when Ophelia—through the agency of a jealous neighbor woman, another worker in folkloric magic—falls dangerously ill in body and mind. Because a hurricane ("what could only be the workings of Woman") has destroyed the sole bridge to the mainland, George frantically seeks an alternative means of escaping the island to find medical care for Ophelia, recklessly ignoring his own coronary condition. Exhausted and desperate, he finally turns to Mama Day, who persuades him to place his belief not in modern medicine but in the incalculable healing power of love—not in the mechanical but in the spiritual power of his own hands. Those hands, working in concert with Mama Day's, succeed in snatching Ophelia back from the verge of death, but in the process George dies of a heart attack, lapsing into "total peace" beside his sleeping wife.

In guiding George toward his leap of faith, Mama Day achieves a breakthrough of her own, which Naylor typically renders as a mother-child reunion effected in a dream. Opening "door upon door upon doors" Miranda at last arrives at a place of reconciliation with the many deprivations of her life:

Daughter. The word comes to cradle what has gone past weariness. She can't really hear it cause she's got no ears, or call out 'cause she's got no mouth. There's only the sense of being. Daughter. Flooding through like fine streams of hot, liquid sugar to fill the spaces where there was never no arms to hold her up, no shoulders for her to lay her head down and cry on, no body to ever turn to for answers. . . . Melting, melting away under the sweet flood waters pouring down to lay bare a place she ain't known existed: Daughter. And she opens the mouth that ain't there to suckle at the full breasts, deep greedy swallows of a thickness like cream. . . . Full and warm to rest between the mounds of softness, to feel the beating of a calm and steady heart. . . . which tells her look past the pain.

As the novel nears its end, Mama Day gazes out over the bay in which George's ashes have been scattered and forecasts a time when Ophelia will reach back to "learn about the beginning of the Days" and acquire the potent atavistic knowledge of her line. The book concludes with Miranda watching as Ophelia (now eleven years older, remarried, and the mother of two sons) embarks on this very project. While the younger woman sits beside the bay, communing with the spirit of her late husband, Mama Day sees "a face that's been given the meaning of peace. A face ready to go in search of answers."

Bailey's Café

Bailey's Café (1992) is Naylor's fourth effort, rounding out her self-described quartet of novels begun in the eighties. As she describes them: "*Women of Brewster Place* was the emotive novel, *Linden Hills* was the cerebral novel, *Mama Day* was the spiritual novel, and I consider *Bailey's Café* to be the sexual novel. . . . I had a four-book plan that would take me through an apprenticeship with my craft." (In view of her novel *The Men of Brewster Place*, published in 1998, her oeuvre now resembles a quintet of interconnected tales.) A novel equally as experimental as *Linden Hills*, *Bailey's Café* situates its characters within the nebulous contours of a folksy eatery "right on the margin between the edge of the world and infinite possibility." Though at first glance we encounter a straightforward greasy spoon located in Brooklyn in 1948, we soon discover that the quotidian aspects of the restaurant are counterbalanced by its mystical origins and effects. The central narrator and guide to this alternative temporal and spatial realm is the café owner, a man who goes by the name of Bailey because that was the name of the café when he arrived.

In Bailey's humble estimation, all of his customers "boil down to one type, or they wouldn't be here in the first place." The book's characters find themselves there, either as proprietors or customers, after they have reached a crossroads in their life characterized by utter despair. For those who can no longer bear life's

injustices, the café's "back door opens out to a void," a zone of oblivion reserved for suicide. Conversely, the front door of the café opens up to the edge of the world, offering a place of potential salvation and reentry for those who feel ready. In this way, the café resembles a way station for the living where real time is frozen, a liminal haven that materializes when people most require it—as the narrator remarks, "we're only here when they need us." Consequently, "you can find Bailey's Café in any town." The only other features of this surreal landscape are Eve's boarding house-brothel and Gabe's pawnshop, which is seldom open to the public.

Like Naylor's other novels, *Bailey's Café* is a book comprised of a series of portraits focused primarily on the complex circumstances that bring a handful of women to a critical point of despair in their lives. What separates the book from Naylor's previous efforts is the central presence of her male narrator. (Bailey's role alongside two of the novel's most compelling stories, his own and that of the male Miss Maple's, anticipates *The Men of Brewster Place*, a work that retraces the perspectives of the male characters who populate her first novel.) The stories are told sometimes by Bailey, sometimes by the players themselves, and sometimes in the third person. All of the tales are introduced in an overtly musical manner. In this way, Naylor overlays the novel's extended metaphor of the café as way station with the motif of jazz and blues improvisation: the first chapter is entitled "Maestro, If You Please . . ." and it is followed by chapters with names such as "The Jam," "Mood: Indigo," "Eve's Song," and "Miss Maple's Blues." Invoking a confluence of lyrical stories, a virtual chorus of voices, Naylor achieves the emotional magnitude of traditional African American musical forms, conveying extremes of pain and pleasure, sadness and joy. Grounded in communal storytelling conventions, the novel adopts the immediacy of a performance staged for a gathering of acquaintances. It foregrounds narrative invention as a means of survival and the imperative roles of telling and listening within this process. As Bailey warns us from the outset, "Every one-liner's got a life underneath it. . . .

Every point's got a counterpoint. . . . Anything really worth hearing in this greasy spoon happens under the surface. . . . You need to know that if you plan to stick around here and listen while we play it out."

And limn the depths Naylor does, with humor, pathos, and insight, addressing the vexed and often violent terrain of female sexuality within a racist, sexist, and capitalist landscape. The black women in her novel grapple with a continuum of sexual exploitation and violence, from child prostitution and sadomasochistic pedophilia to female genital mutilation. As a result, one especially beautiful woman engages in self-scarring while another becomes a heroine addict to dull her pain. Each of these women eats at Bailey's Café and resides at Eve's boarding house down the street. In a simple and direct prose style, Bailey tells us the tragic story of Sadie, an aging alcoholic with class, whose mother referred to her as "The One the Coat Hanger Missed" and put her on the streets to earn an income as a hooker at the age of thirteen. After a deeply unsatisfactory marriage to a man twice her age, she loses the meager house she has painstakingly kept up, and she becomes a wino, turning tricks to maintain her supply of alcohol. At the café, she finally meets a man who offers her love and a home. Satisfied but ultimately unable to change the sad trajectory of her life story and accept his offer, Sadie walks into the void, leaving him behind.

The next chapter is narrated by Eve, Bailey's first customer. Fittingly, Eve's tale is a retelling of the biblical story of the fall from grace from her perspective, a story of a young girl who discovers sexual pleasure and an individuated sense of self through masturbation. For this transgression, her own godfather, the minister of the Delta community, casts her out with no clothes or food to wander the countryside. She arrives at the café after making a considerable fortune in New Orleans with the realization that "It seemed there was nowhere on earth for a woman like me." Eve becomes the all-powerful proprietress of the brothel, the particularly female realm of Bailey's netherworld. Humorless and unmoved by charity, she decides whom shall stay and whom shall go. On the grounds of her brownstone, she grows a wondrous garden of wildflowers that includes a specific variety of flower for each woman who boards there. In order to be attended to, the gentleman callers must buy the correct flower as an initial offering.

Sadie's and Eve's stories are followed by tales of Esther's sadomasochism, Mary's self-mutilation, Jesse's heroine addiction, and Mariam's immaculate conception. The longest and perhaps most gripping story of the collection belongs to the heterosexual, cross-dressing bouncer at Eve's boarding house—Stanley Beckwourth Booker T. Washington Carver (a.k.a. Miss Maple)—and his journey toward his own acceptance of his masculinity. All of these players stay with Eve in order to come to terms with their suffering: there, they learn how to take charge of their own sexual experiences by dictating the terms of exchange with the men they choose to see intimately. Only by navigating these relationships and narrating their own stories can they hope to emerge even partially whole. For, as Jesse remarks rhetorically, "it's all about who's in charge of keeping the records, ain't it?" These portraits are striking in the degree to which Naylor maintains a particularity of oppression, a uniqueness of each story and teller. At the same time, she provides her readers with a trenchant critique of the interrelated workings of racism, sexism, and capitalism. Bailey describes this perspective when he accounts for his conversations about racism and anti-Semitism with Gabe, who is Jewish: "neither of us is considered a national treasure in our countries, and that's where the similarity ends. . . . We don't get to comparing notes on who did what to whom the most. . . . The way I see it, there is no comparison." While the book presents us with few comparisons, there are common denominators that gird each story. It is no accident that prostitution repeatedly surfaces as the final option for women once they have lost their familial and communal sources of support. As a mode of employment, it literalizes women's bodies as objects of exchange in a patriarchal economy. In Sadie's case, the fact that her mother would sacrifice her to this livelihood demonstrates the insidious and intertwined reach of capitalism and misogyny.

Ultimately, *Bailey's Café* asks us to consider the redemptive possibility of narrative itself. As we come to understand the extended metaphor of the café, more a psychic space than a geographical location, Naylor asks us to view ourselves as fellow customers. In these stories, we are able to enter figuratively into "the margin between the edge of the world and infinite possibility" and experience the vital role that imagination plays in our own processes of meaning-making and self-invention. Naylor equips her characters with the means of telling their stories and in so doing, she asks us to think about the ways we narrate ourselves "midway in [our] own stories."

The Men of Brewster Place

Perhaps it is this ethic that prompted Naylor to return to Brewster Place once more and pick up the masculine threads of that world in her novel *The Men of Brewster Place* (1998). Naylor has indicated in interviews that this novel was in part a response to the Million Man March on Washington and the death of her father. Once again, we encounter Ben, the deceased wino; Basil, Mattie Michael's spoiled son; Eugene, Ciel's sexually ambivalent husband; C. C. Baker, the thug who instigates Lorraine's gang rape; Reverend Moreland T. Woods, the preacher who seduces Etta Mae Johnson; and a few other players as well. As this list demonstrates, Naylor effectively reverses a standard patriarchal lineage, for we recognize these men initially because of their relationships to the women of her first novel. Ben, the narrator, amplifies this point: "with each of 'em—no matter who he was—there was always a Her in his story." While Naylor never attempts to explain away the shortcomings of her male characters, she asks her readers to grasp their singular lives not only in connection with her women characters but within a broader matrix of racism, poverty, and heterosexism as well.

Echoing the narrative structure of *The Women of Brewster Place*, the masculine street life of Brewster Place becomes palpable through the intertwined stories of seven men. Naylor takes the liberty of resurrecting Ben, the drunken janitor who Lorraine beats to death after she has been raped in the first novel. Leaving behind his sharecropping existence in Tennessee to join the great migration north in the thirties, Ben moved into the neighborhood as it changed from Italian to Irish to African American. In the prologue, "Dusk" (the title of the epilogue in Naylor's first novel), Ben declares, "This street gave birth to more than its girl children, ya know." Interestingly, as he attempts to account for Brewster Place's overlooked male inhabitants, he personifies the street as female, thereby establishing a foundational link between masculine persona and a generative, feminine place. He interjects, "Let me tell you about men: If you put him on the likes of Park Avenue and he feels he has no worth, then it's not Park Avenue. If you put him on the likes of a Chicago south side and he feels he has worth, then it's not the South Side. We all live *inside*." Here, Ben asserts a fundamental tenet found in each of Naylor's novels: as Naylor adopts a stance formulated by literary precursors such as Ann Petry and Richard Wright—that unjust socioeconomic factors consign poor people of color to inadequate, segregated living conditions—she suggests that the most devastating effects of this environment for its residents are psychological. In a cyclical pattern, her character's internal, psychic terrain determines their experience of the world around them, yet this interior geography is constructed by their formative encounters with the inequalities of the outside world. In this way, Naylor uses place as an implicit character in her stories, but she complicates the conventional function of environment within a naturalist narrative by asking her readers to consider place as the sum total of those who live within it.

Ben's own chapter provides us with the story of his humble beginnings in the South. Raised by his grandparents, both former slaves, Ben recalls the one story his grandfather "had to tell [that] was never told to [him] or even Grandma Jones," a story about the sexual violation and murder of his grandfather's sister by the overseer on the plantation where they worked as children. At the funeral, no one denounces the brutal circumstances of her death; this interminable silence forms the foundation of his grandfather's bitter existence. When Ben tells the story, he speaks the unspeakable, simultaneously rectifying this grievous omission in the record and establishing his authority as an interpreter and intuitor of stories, told and untold. With this story in place, Ben tells his own tale, about his greedy, "evil" wife Elvira who essentially prostitutes their own daughter to the wealthy white landowner for whom they sharecrop. Though their daughter informs them of the farmer's unwanted advances, Elvira dismisses her complaints and Ben allows the situation to continue, in spite of his impulse to fight the man and shoot his wife. We witness family history repeat itself. Constrained by his subservient position to the landowner and Elvira's constant accusations that he is a poor provider, Ben is culpable in his silence. A man ruined by the violent misogyny directed toward his daughter and his own inability to conceive of an effective, nonviolent masculinity, Ben concludes, "Nobody knows my true story . . . it is my turn to be the silent old man as I inherit more than my share of the pain riding on the question, What does it mean to be a man?"

For Basil, this question eventually leads him back to the father he never knew, Butch Fuller, and his own venture into fatherhood. After Basil is jailed for killing a man, his mother, Mattie Michael, puts up her house as collateral for his bond. She ends up losing the house and moving in to Brewster Place. As we learn in *The Men of Brewster Place*, Basil ducks out of his sentence and earns all of the money he owes her, only to arrive too late—she has already died. At a crossroads in his life, he promises "to be the father he never had," but first he must locate his own father. Once he does, he realizes that his maternal grandfather kept Butch from marrying Mattie or even contacting her; his father tells him that it was for the best because he "ain't the marrying type." Basil then overcompensates for the loss of his family, searching for an appropriate wife and kids (he is impotent, so cannot have children himself). He

eventually finds Keisha, a negligent and abusive young mother of two sons without fathers. They marry with the agreement that she can date as much as she wants to as long as he is allowed to parent the children. After two years, they quarrel bitterly and Keisha calls the police, who come and arrest Basil for involuntary manslaughter, the sentence he evaded five years before. Six years later, when he comes back to father the boys again, they are already lost to him, one remote and the other a delinquent. In this tale, then, like Ben's, we see a family pattern emerge: Basil repeats the mistakes of his mother and father but with a difference. Duplicating his mother's blind devotion to him, his commitment to the idea of becoming a "family man" transforms into a fierce love for Keisha's sons. Yet he enters into an untenable situation with Keisha. Moreover, he has failed to take responsibility for murdering a man. As the narrative outcome seems to suggest, because of this failure (and in spite of his good intentions), he is in no position to take responsibility for the boys. In this way, paradoxically, Basil repeats his mother's mistake only to find himself fulfilling the stereotypical script of the absent father he sets out to erase. In this way, we see the toll male violence takes upon a man who seemingly means to challenge a system of racist, patriarchal power that perpetuates such behavior. Once again, we are left with Ben's refrain, "What does it mean to be a man?"

Like the block party in Mattie's dream in the conclusion of *The Women of Brewster Place*, in the last section of this novel we are introduced to the barbershop, the last stand in the face of the street's imminent demolition, where men come together and talk. As Ben says, "These chairs done seen many a good man as well as the bad, and the ugly. . . . They done seen rejoicing and they done seen grief. . . . Although a man grieves different from a woman, a whole lot more is kept inside to bite him a little here, a little there, until the blood begins to flow." In a literal manifestation of this assessment, Greasy, the homeless customer who regularly comes in for a free haircut, slits his own throat while sitting in a barber chair. His suicide leaves the rest of the men shocked and ashamed of their previous need to castigate Greasy to make themselves feel better. Even this safe, communal space of emotional exchange cannot stave off the psychic price of socioeconomic exclusion for black men—Greasy is one more casualty, another man "bleeding inside."

In "Abshu," Naylor provides us with a glimmer of hope. Kiswana's activist counterpoint, Abshu is a young man who grew up on Brewster Place and has dedicated his life to helping young men at the community center. After Reverend Moreland T. Woods is elected to public office and promotes the demolition of the neighborhood for middle-income housing, Abshu figures out an ingenious method of deposing him, gathering together a sizable group of women who claim that Moreland has fathered their unborn children. Tellingly, only by working together with the women of the community is he able to wreak justifiable and nonviolent revenge. In spite of this victory, Brewster Place is slated for demolition. In the novel's epilogue, "Dawn," Abshu walks through the abandoned street, gathering his resolve to keep fighting for the dispossessed of Brewster Place. In this way, the street lives on in Abshu, informing and sustaining his activism: "this one tired warrior is the best that Brewster Place has to offer the world. . . . But one man standing is all that's needed—one manchild for the millennium—as the music plays on . . . and on." At once a eulogy and a redemption song, the epilogue signals the stakes of this epic battle for dignity and the necessity of black men like Abshu (and black women like Kiswana) to carry on the good fight in other neighborhoods and other cities.

No summary retelling—with its inevitable elision of lesser figures, themes, and subplots—can hope to capture the richness of Gloria Naylor's impressive novels. Nor can any such summary convey the fluent pleasure of reading these books, a good part of which lies in the sense that Naylor has freed her characters to live and grow as they will, regardless of the fashionable pieties (or impieties) of the times, and occasionally regardless of the author's own wishes. (She reports having been angry for a week at Willa Nedeed for spoiling the intended ending of *Linden Hills* by unexpectedly validating herself as a conventional wife and mother.)

What we sense, in other words, is an organic correlation between the values of tolerance, mutuality, and self-empowerment celebrated in Naylor's work and the values of restraint and respect that inform her practice as an artist. This generosity extends as well to her readers, whom she urges toward larger sympathies and a more critical intelligence, all the while leaving them room to make their own readings. Perhaps the island's "voice" in *Mama Day* says it best: "Think about it: ain't nobody really talking to you. We're sitting here in Willow Springs, and you're God-knows-where. . . . ain't but a slim chance it's the same season where you are. Uh, huh, listen. Really listen this time: the only voice is your own."

Selected Bibliography

PRIMARY WORKS

NOVELS

The Women of Brewster Place. New York: Viking, 1982.
Linden Hills. New York: Ticknor & Fields, 1985.
Mama Day. New York: Ticknor & Fields, 1988.
Bailey's Café. New York: Vintage, 1992.
The Men of Brewster Place. New York: Hyperion, 1998.

OTHER WORKS

"A Message to Winston." *Essence,* November 1982, pp. 78–81.
Naylor, Gloria, ed. *Children of the Night: The Best Short Stories by Black Writers, 1967 to the Present.* New York: Little and Brown, 1997.

SECONDARY WORKS

BIOGRAPHICAL AND CRITICAL STUDIES

Andrews, Larry R. "Black Sisterhood in Gloria Naylor's Novels." *CLA Journal* 33:1–25 (September 1989).
Awkward, Michael. *Inspiriting Influences: Tradition, Revision, and Afro-American Women's Novels.* New York: Columbia University Press, 1989.
Collins, Grace E. "Narrative Structure in *Linden Hills.*" *CLA Journal* 34, no. 3:290–301 (March 1991).
Cox, Karen Castellucci. "Magic and Memory in the Contemporary Story Cycle: Gloria Naylor and Louise Erdrich." *College English* 60, no. 2:150–73 (February 1998).
Donlon, Jocelyn Hazelwood. "Hearing is Believing: Southern Racial Communities and Strategies of Story-listening in Gloria Naylor and Lee Smith."

Twentieth Century Literature 41, no. 1:16–36 (Spring 1995).

Eckard, Paula Gallant. "The Prismatic Past in *Oral History* and *Mama Day*."*MELUS* 20, no. 3:121–36 (Fall 1995).

Eko, Ebele. "Beyond the Myth of Confrontation: A Comparative Study of African and African-American Female Protagonists." *Ariel: A Review of International English Literature* 17:139–52 (1986).

Felton, Sharon, and Michelle Loris, eds. *Naylor: The Critical Response to Gloria Naylor*. Westport, Conn.: Greenwood Press, 1997.

Fowler, Virginia. *Gloria Naylor: In Search of Sanctuary*. New York: Twayne, 1996.

Gates, Henry Louis, Jr. "Significant Others." *Contemporary Literature* 29:606–23 (Winter 1988).

Gates, Henry Louis, Jr., and K. A. Appiah, eds. *Gloria Naylor: Critical Perspectives Past and Present*. New York: Amistad Press Inc, 1993.

Harris, Trudier. *The Power of the Porch: The Storyteller's Craft in Zora Neale Hurston, Gloria Naylor, and Randall Kenan*. Athens: University of Georgia Press, 1996.

Homans, Margaret, "The Woman in the Cave: Recent Feminist Fictions and the Classical Underworld." *Contemporary Literature* 29:369–402 (Fall 1988).

Kelley, Margot Anne, ed. *Gloria Naylor's Early Novels*. Gainesville: University of Florida Press, 1999.

Kubitschek, Missy Dehn. "Toward a New Order: Shakespeare, Morrison, and Gloria Naylor's *Mama Day*." *MELUS* 19, no. 3:75–91 (Fall 1994).

Lattin, Patricia Hopkins. "Naylor's Engaged and Empowered Narratee." *CLA Journal* 41, no. 4:452–70 (June 1998).

Matus, Jill L. "Dream, Deferral, and Closure in *The Women of Brewster Place*."*Black American Literature Forum* 24, no. 1:49–65 (Spring 1990).

Meisenhelder, Susan. " 'The whole picture' in Gloria Naylor's *Mama Day*." (Women's Culture Issue) *African American Review* 27, no. 3:405–20 (Fall 1993).

Metting, Fred. "The Possibilities of Flight: the Celebration of Our Wings in *Song of Solomon, Praisesong for the Widow*, and *Mama Day*." *Southern Folklore* 55, no. 2:145–67 (Fall 1998).

Montgomery, Maxine Lavon. "The Fathomless Dream: Gloria Naylor's Use of the Descent Motif in *The Women of Brewster Place*." *CLA Journal* 36, no. 1:1–12 (September 1992).

———. "Authority, Multivocality, and the New World Order in Gloria Naylor's *Bailey's Café*." *African American Review* 29, no. 1:27–34 (Spring 1995).

Page, Philip. "Living with the Abyss in Gloria Naylor's *Bailey's Café*." *CLA Journal* 40, no. 1:21–46 (Sep-

tember 1996).

Puhr, Kathleen M. "Healers in Gloria Naylor's Fiction." *Twentieth Century Literature* 40, no. 4:518–28 (Winter 1994).

Ranveer, Kashinath. *Black Feminist Consciousness*. Jaipur, India: Printwell, 1995.

Restuccia, Frances L. "Literary Representations of Battered Women: Spectacular Domestic Punishment." (Bodies of Writing, Bodies in Performance) *Genders* no. 23:42–72 (Spring 1996).

Stanford, Ann Folwell. "Mechanisms of Disease: African-American Women Writers, Social Pathologies, and the Limits of Medicine." *NWSA Journal* 6, no. 1:28–48 (Spring 1994).

Stave, Shirley A., ed. *Gloria Naylor: Strategy and Technique, Magic and Myth*. Newark: University of Delaware Press, 2000.

Storhoff, Gary. "The Only Voice is Your Own: Gloria Naylor's Revision of 'The Tempest.'" *African American Review* 29, no. 1:35–45 (Spring 1995).

Tanner, Laura E. "Reading Rape: *Sanctuary* and *The Women of Brewster Place*." *American Literature* 62, no. 4:559–83 (December 1990).

Toombs, Charles P. "The Confluence of Food and Identity in Gloria Naylor's *Linden Hills*: 'What we eat is who we is'." *CLA Journal* 37, no. 1:1–19 (September 1993).

Tucker, Lindsey. "Recovering the Conjure Woman: Texts and Contexts in Gloria Naylor's *Mama Day*." *African American Review* 28, no. 2:173–88 (1994).

Ward, Catherine C. "Gloria Naylor's *Linden Hills*: A Modern Inferno." *Contemporary Literature* 28:67–81 (Spring 1987).

Wardi, Anissa J. "The Scent of Sugarcane: Recalling *Cane* in *The Women of Brewster Place*." *CLA Journal* 42, no. 4:483–85 (June 1999).

Whitt, Margaret Earley. *Understanding Gloria Naylor*. Columbia: University of South Carolina Press, 1999.

INTERVIEWS

Carabi, Angels. "Belles Lettres Interview: Gloria Naylor." *Belles Lettres: A Review of Books by Women* 7, no. 3:36–43 (Spring 1992).

"Do You Think of Yourself as a Woman Writer?" *Furman Studies* 34:2–13 (December 1988).

Naylor, Gloria, and Toni Morrison. "A Conversation." *Southern Review* 21:567–93 (Summer 1985).

Rowell, Charles H. "An Interview with Gloria Naylor." *Callaloo* 20, no. 1:179–93 (Winter 1997).

—The essay and bibliography have been revised for this edition by Sonnet Retman.

ANN PETRY
(1908–1997)

MARILYN MOBLEY MCKENZIE

ANN PETRY BROUGHT a unique double perspective to the craft of writing when she began her literary career in the 1940s: the perspective of her own black middle-class upbringing in a small, predominantly white New England community and the perspective of her years of living and working among the black poor of New York City. The weight of her observations from the second perspective prompted her to write *The Street* (1946), her best-selling novel about a black woman's struggle to survive in a hostile Harlem neighborhood. It is in *The Narrows* (1953), the most finely crafted of her three novels, however, that she most skillfully merges both cultural perspectives into a fully developed aesthetic vision and establishes her unique place in the African American literary tradition.

Yet prior to reconciling these two distinct viewpoints, Petry shifted her literary angle of vision from urban scenes in New York to rural villages in New England, and thus began to draw on her personal memories of Connecticut in her writing. This shift is most apparent in her second novel, *Country Place* (1947), which portrays the stark contradictions between the outer image and inner life of small New England towns. *Country Place* not only illustrates Petry's technical versatility but also demonstrates that she was equally adept at depicting black inner-city life and white small-town life.

Although her critical reputation is based on her novels, her fifteen short stories, thirteen of which are published in *Miss Muriel and Other Stories* (1971), demonstrate this ability to shift the angle of vision between urban and rural settings, black and white life. Petry began with and continually returned to the genre of the short story to develop and refine the aesthetic vision that typifies her novels, poetry, historical biographies for young adults, and books for children. Indeed, her entire body of work bears witness to the influence of the two worlds she knew best from her own life. Though her writing has obviously been influenced by various factors, in her opinion, the most important influences have been the circumstances of her birth, her childhood, and her family.

Ann Petry was born Ann Lane in Old Saybrook, Connecticut, on 12 October 1908, upstairs above her father's drugstore. The second daughter of Peter C. Lane and Bertha James Lane (a sister, Helen, preceded her by two years), she was born into a black middle-class family and therefore enjoyed a life of relative privilege and comfort. Although Petry's family was one of only two black families in the small town of Old Saybrook, her parents' professional status made it easier to adjust to a somewhat hostile environment. Her father was a pharmacist who owned his own drugstore, and her mother, a licensed chiropodist, was also a hairdresser, barber, manufacturer, and entrepreneur. Her mother's sister, Anna Louise James, graduated from the Brooklyn College of Pharmacy in 1908, where she was the only woman in her graduating class. After becoming the first woman to be licensed as a pharmacist in the state of Connecticut, Anna Louise opened her own drugstore in Hartford. She moved in with the Lane family in Old Saybrook and acquired Peter Lane's drugstore when he took a job in Hartford working for a wholesale druggist. Petry's mother's brother, Fritz, and his wife were also pharmacists. They owned a drugstore in the neighboring town of Old Lyme, Connecticut. In light of this family tradition in pharmacy, it is not surprising that she drew on her family memories and personal experiences to create the settings of the "drugstore" stories in *Miss Muriel and Other Stories* or to develop the character of Doc, the druggist, in *Country Place.*

Yet many of the memories that shaped Petry's sensibility as a writer have less to do with the family business than with the cultural and historical circumstances of growing up as a black female in a white community. Her family's professional status did not shield her from the racism that periodically disrupted life in Old Saybrook, a picturesque town whose reality was quite different from its relatively serene appearance. Even when racism did not disrupt her life directly, as it did in childhood incidents of harassment by her white male schoolmates, it was nevertheless a felt presence, as in the case of a gravestone erected in the extreme rear of the town cemetery and facing the wrong direction simply because it was in memory of "a colored woman," as its inscription stated. Petry's discovery that racial segregation could profane even death was an early lesson that racism in America had no boundaries. Her personal encounter with segregation also came early. In a 1946 article, "My Most Humiliating Jim Crow Experience," she describes how a Congregational church Sunday school beach outing when she was seven years old became a lesson in race relations: her teacher offered no resistance to the guard's demand that her class leave the beach because "no niggers [were] allowed" there. These and other manifestations of racial oppression that she experienced and observed evoked a sense of outrage that remained with her for years. Later, Petry transformed into fiction the outrage that grew from the painful memory of being harassed as a child; in "Doby's Gone" (1944), a young black girl defends herself against the physical attack and verbal abuse of her white classmates.

Juxtaposed to these memories of racial prejudice from the outside white world are Petry's memories of the warm, protective environment her parents created to ensure her survival against the effects of bigotry and isolation. At the same time that she describes herself as an "outsider" whose tie to New England is a tenuous one, she nevertheless boasts that her roots include four generations of African American New Englanders who were born in Connecticut. Her own sense of self-confidence and self-worth can be attributed not only to the numerous professional female and male role models in her immediate and extended family, but also to their rich oral tradition of storytelling. As a child she looked forward to frequent visits of relatives, for family gatherings inevitably led to lively storytelling sessions. From family stories she learned of aunts who were conjurers and root-workers, of a grandfather who was a runaway slave, and of her father, who successfully resisted a racially motivated attempt to drive him out of town for opening his own drugstore. These stories and numerous others not only gave her a sense of family history and racial heritage but, in her words, "transmitted knowledge, knowledge of how to survive in a hostile environment. They were part of my education." The historical fiction she later wrote for young people—such as *Harriet Tubman, Conductor on the Underground Railroad* (1955)—reflected her desire to pass this knowledge on to succeeding generations of black children.

But her family's storytelling tradition also introduced Petry to the power of the word to transport the listener beyond the confines of time and place. Through her uncle's tales she vicariously escaped the often prosaic monotony of life in Old Saybrook. Moreover, hearing stories from relatives, combined with listening to her mother read stories such as Grimms' fairy tales, inspired an early love for narrative and made her an avid reader. By her own account, her early reading included everything from poems of Paul Laurence Dunbar and narratives of Frederick Douglass and Booker T. Washington to Wilkie Collins's *Moonstone* and Louisa May Alcott's *Little Women*. According to Diane Isaacs, Petry's parents created an environment where reading was encouraged, and her mother wrote "jingles" to provide literary inspiration for her young daughter. In this sense, her mother was the early model that Alice Walker has claimed is so important to the development of any artist, but especially of the writer. Indeed, this early exposure to and appreciation of the power of the spoken and written word engendered in the young Petry the authority to choose writing as an accessible form of creative expression.

Petry first began writing while she was in high school, where she earned five dollars for creating a slogan for a perfume company. Motivated by this monetary incentive and bolstered by the encouragement of her English teachers, she began writing stories and one-act plays. When she graduated from Old Saybrook High School in 1929, however, she had not yet chosen writing as a career. Instead, she decided to follow family tradition by pursuing a career in pharmacy. She graduated from the Connecticut College of Pharmacy with a Ph.G. degree in 1931 and returned to Old Saybrook to work in the family drugstore. After five years she went to Old Lyme to manage the other family drugstore, where she worked for two years until she married and moved to New York. During the seven years that she worked as a pharmacist, Petry was observing and listening to the townspeople who later inspired her fictional representations of small-town New Englanders. Bored with pharmacy, she was nevertheless afforded the unique perspective she later ascribed to Doc in *Country Place,* who knows his fellow townspeople "so well . . . [he] can tell you what they loved and what they hated, what they hoped for and what they feared." As Marjorie Greene asserts, Petry "had to get away from bottles and medicinal mixtures on to paper, words, images,

Ann Petry

and plots." Pharmacy, therefore, was simply one of several phases in her evolution as an artist.

In 1938 Ann Lane married George D. Petry, a New York mystery-story writer, whom she had met in 1936. Although few accounts of her marriage and subsequent move to New York elaborate on it, the decision to leave Connecticut was a significant turning point in her life. Moreover, the move itself represented a break with family tradition. Unlike most of her family, who had chosen to remain in the small towns of Connecticut, she was attracted to big-city life in New York. While many in her family had chosen careers in pharmacy, she made the conscious, difficult decision to abandon pharmacy and pursue writing, her true vocation. She simultaneously declared her female vocational independence from the family custom of pursuing careers in more conventional, financially secure professions in science, business, and education.

Even before she left Old Saybrook, however, Petry discovered that the process of becoming a writer meant learning to deal with rejection slips and returned manuscripts. Arriving in Harlem in 1938, she decided that the best way to facilitate her development as an author was to find work related to writing, and she went to work for the *Amsterdam News*, the Harlem weekly newspaper. From 1938 to 1941 she sold ad space and wrote copy for the advertising department, while continuing to write short stories in her free time. On 19 August 1939, she succeeded in getting her first story published in the *Afro-American*, a Baltimore weekly newspaper. "Marie of the Cabin Club," which she published under the pseudonym Arnold Petri, is a romantic melodrama set in a Harlem nightclub reminiscent of the famous Cotton Club. For this story the newspaper paid her a mere five dollars. Although she had used a pseudonym, in the tradition of other pulp writers, she was nevertheless pleased to be published at last. The strategy of using a male name for her excursion into popular fiction not only concealed her identity but also signaled her desire to have authorial control over what Louis Renza calls the "arena of public literary evaluation." She would reserve the use of her own name for when she wrote "serious" fiction and was ready to be evaluated by more formal literary criteria.

In 1941 Petry went to work as a reporter for the *People's Voice*, Harlem's rival weekly newspaper. Even though she credits her experience at the *Amsterdam News* with teaching her how to meet deadlines, it was her five years at the *People's Voice* that had the most significant influence on her writing. She became a full-fledged journalist, working in nearly every aspect of the newspaper business, from editing the women's page to covering general news. She observed her Harlem neighbors at close range and acquired an intimate knowledge of the oppressive conditions that circumscribed their lives. She gained insight into the ways in which racial oppression, poverty, hunger, and poor education ruined lives and devastated families. As women's editor, she wrote about such topics as the exploitation of black women, the treatment of black soldiers, and the high crime rate. Her own experiences of growing up in Old Saybrook, fused with her sensitivity to these issues, provided her with an empathic perspective and a social consciousness that were apparent in her news articles and that later became the hallmark of her best fiction. Whether in news articles or in fiction, she sought not to present black people as types but, as she told *Crisis* reporter James Ivy, "to show them as people with the same capacity for love and hate, for tears and laughter, and the same instincts for survival possessed by all men."

Journalism was not the only path Petry took to develop her expertise as a writer. She read widely in such disciplines as psychology, psychiatry, and sociology. In addition, she read the autobiographies of other writers to gain greater insight into the writing process. She cites her reading of Arthur Train's autobiography, *My Day in Court*, as the impetus for her decision to enroll in Mabel Louise Robinson's workshop at Columbia University. Train apparently recommended this course as worthwhile for any young, unpublished writer. Petry credits Robinson with teaching her to critique her own writing, to read other writers with a "critical eye," and, most important, to believe in herself. Petry later paid tribute to Robinson by dedicating her third novel, *The Narrows*, to her.

But Petry's literary apprenticeship did not end with simply reading in order to understand the social conditions and psychological makeup of poor black people in Harlem; nor did it end with reading other writers or taking a creative writing course. Instead, her evolution as an artist extended beyond these endeavors and relied on what Mabel Robinson had already prophetically identified as Petry's literary assets: experience, wisdom about people, and sound judgment in using the English language, a combination Robinson said amounted to a "gift" and the potential for success in fiction. Indeed, before Petry committed herself totally to her craft, she undertook a number of projects that sharpened her insights and deepened the perspective she had already acquired as a journalist. In essence, she shifted from objective observation to direct interaction with the people of Harlem. For example, she founded Negro

Women, Inc., a political group organized to provide consumer information, to protest racial discrimination, and to advocate economic empowerment of women. In 1944 she became a recreation specialist at P.S. 10, a Harlem elementary school at 116th Street and St. Nicholas Avenue, where she designed programs for so-called problem children. This job brought her in contact with the kind of folk who later peopled *The Street*. She also studied painting, acted in *Striver's Row*, an American Negro Theater production, took piano lessons, and taught a business letter-writing course at the Harlem branch of the NAACP.

All the while that Petry led this very active civic and social life, she continued to pursue a literary career as a short-story writer. Throughout the 1940s her stories appeared in *The Crisis*, *Opportunity*, *Phylon*, and other literary magazines. The turning point in her career came in 1943, when the *Crisis* (the official organ of the NAACP) published "On Saturday the Siren Sounds at Noon." Houghton Mifflin expressed an interest in her work after seeing this story. The publishing company not only encouraged her to consider writing a novel but invited her to apply for one of its literary fellowships. Although she had not previously entertained the idea of writing a novel, she eventually gave it much thought: "I decided . . . that I would work for nobody, and at nothing else—that I would spend every single minute of my day just writing." The implications of her decision recall Virginia Woolf's assertion that a "woman must have money and a room of her own if she is to write fiction." Petry laments: "It wasn't an easy decision exactly. It meant that I had to live on my husband's allotment check—the only income I had. He was with the armed forces. In New York, that check meant a pittance. After all expenses for the apartment were paid, I had a bare five dollars a week for food." (Greene, p. 79).

Nevertheless, her decision had its own reward. On the strength of the first five chapters and a synopsis of *The Street*, Petry won a Houghton Mifflin literary fellowship of twenty-four hundred dollars in 1945. In 1946 *The Street* was published, and Petry became an instant ce-

lebrity. Alain Locke, an eminent scholar of African American literature, declared in *Phylon* that it was the "artistic success of the year." The story "Like a Winding Sheet" also won national acclaim and was selected for Martha Foley's *Best American Short Stories of 1946*. Petry's second novel, *Country Place*, was published in 1947. By the time she and her husband returned to Old Saybrook in 1948, Petry had established herself as an independent writer. Yet she wrote only one novel, *The Narrows* (1953), after leaving New York. Her energies were dispersed instead among raising her only child, Elisabeth Ann, writing books for young people, writing short stories and collecting them into a single volume, and trying to balance her public career with her desire for a more private life.

Ann Petry's place in the African American literary tradition can best be appreciated on the basis of a close reading of her three novels, the genre upon which much of her critical reputation rests. Yet historically, until the emergence of feminist scholarship, most critical attention was directed toward her first novel, *The Street*, and its similarities to the black male narrative tradition of social protest and naturalistic writing best exemplified in Richard Wright's 1940 novel, *Native Son*. Unfortunately, because Wright's reputation overshadowed hers, critics such as Robert Bone underestimated the significance of Petry's work and relegated her to marginalized status in the African American literary canon. Such comparisons overlooked the ways in which her unique vantage point on black experience, especially black female experience, empowered her not only to challenge the cultural and ideological limitations that the protest and naturalistic modes of writing placed on her literary imagination, but to revise them as well. As Nellie McKay argues in her introduction to *The Narrows*, Petry "borrowed heavily from elements in the naturalistic tradition, but her view of the world was significantly less one-dimensional than that of a more lauded peer like Wright." Petry's statements of authorial self-definition that identify Harriet Wilson as her literary ancestor suggest that she sought to be read in a broader context than naturalism: "Having been born black and female,

I regard myself as a survivor and a gambler, writing in a tradition that dates back to 1859 when *Our Nig*, the first novel written by a black woman in this country, was published in Boston, Massachusetts." Petry's statement confirms Henry Louis Gates Jr.'s well-argued contention that the black tradition emerged "because writers read other writers" and engaged in the conscious process of "literary revision." *The Street* can be read as a text that continues the tradition by consciously evoking it in order to revise it. Indeed, the nexus of race, gender, and class so profoundly informs Petry's fictional representation of black life and culture in *The Street* that the novel must be examined in the context of the black female literary tradition of which it is a part. Thus examined, the novel is both a cultural critique and a cultural response to the conditions Petry had observed during her years in Harlem.

The Street is the story of Lutie Johnson, an ambitious, working-class black woman who supports her son and unemployed husband by working as a maid for the Chandlers, a white family in Lyme, Connecticut. After a year of working for them, she begins to absorb their middle-class values and to long for their material trappings of success. She assumes that if she is good enough and works hard enough she can obtain a similar life for herself and her family. Under the influence of the Chandlers' economic security and her personal adoption of Benjamin Franklin as a model of success, she works longer and longer hours to advance her plan of upward mobility. Lutie is forced to abandon her own suburban home in Queens, New York, when she discovers that her husband, Jim, frustrated with his inability to find work and angry about her absence, is having an affair. The novel begins with her search for an apartment and her decision to rent one on the top floor of a Harlem tenement on 116th Street. From the time Lutie moves into the apartment until the end of the novel, the reader bears witness to her valiant struggle against the poverty, racism, and sexism that undermine her aspirations to leave the ghetto. The forces against her are embodied in three men: Jones, the superintendent of her building, who tries to rape her

and who eventually tricks her son into stealing mail; Boots, the bandleader at the club where she sings, who first befriends but later exploits her; and Junto, the white casino-owner, who tries to exploit her by offering gifts and sex rather than the salary he owes her.

In the process of working and going to school, she is regularly forced to leave her son home alone. The super, determined to get revenge for Lutie's rejection of his sexual advances, takes advantage of her circumstances and tricks her son into stealing mail from tenant mailboxes. When Bub is taken to a shelter for delinquent children, a lawyer deceives her by charging two hundred dollars for services that should have been free. In desperation, she asks Boots for the money. He tries to convince her that Junto will give her the money if she is "nice" to him. Correctly interpreting "nice" to mean she must sleep with Junto to get the money, Lutie is repulsed both by the thought of sleeping with a white man and by Boot's suggestion that she even consider such an offer. She attempts to leave, but Boots is so annoyed with what he considers her uppity scruples and so driven by his own hatred of Junto that he tries to force Lutie to sleep with him first. No longer able to contain herself in the face of yet another sexual assault, Lutie lets her accumulated rage and suppressed anger erupt in the violent murder of Boots in self-defense. She flees the scene and buys a one-way ticket to Chicago. The novel ends with her on the train, wondering what will become of her son and tracing the tragic pattern of her life.

On the surface, the plot supports Petry's expressed narrative intention "to show how easily the environment can change the course of a person's life." Having lived and worked in Harlem for nine years, Petry was well aware of how racism and environmental determinism affected the lives of black people. In fact, the novel is based on an actual news story of a superintendent teaching a young boy to steal mail. The inspiration for many of Petry's stories came from real-life incidents. Through detailed documentation, the language of the text represents the kind of neighborhood Lutie confronts. She thinks at one point that "streets like the one she lives on were . . . the lynch mob" of the North—"the method the big cities used to keep Negroes in their place." She thinks of her life in terms of entrapment in a "small cage" or "ever-narrowing space."

Yet in a 1950 essay, "The Novel as Social Criticism," Petry explains her reluctance to describe *The Street* as a naturalistic novel. While she does not subscribe to the notion of art for art's sake, she nevertheless questions the validity of the naturalistic depiction of characters as mere "pawns in the hands of a deaf, blind, stupid social system." For Petry, this depiction is problematic because it gives society the role of fate, and the "burden of responsibility for their actions is shifted away from the characters." While her portrayal of Lutie is no less problematic, it nevertheless exposes for the reader much of the complexity that naturalistic interpretations ignore. At the same time that she portrays Lutie as a victim of racism and economic oppression, forces she relentlessly critiques throughout the novel, she also portrays her as a character who must do battle with herself, who must make choices, even though the environment has diminished her choices. More importantly, Lutie's desire for the American dream and her unexamined acceptance of white middle-class values cause her to work against her own best interests and to undermine her own efforts to succeed.

Petry's reluctance to accept the label of naturalism might also be attributed to the black feminist concerns that inform her writing. She could not critique the issues of race and class and ignore the politics of gender that account for Lutie's plight. Lutie is just as much a victim of male sexual desire as she is a victim of racism and economic oppression. Moreover, Petry could not portray Lutie as a mother and ignore the ways in which her environment compromised conventional expectations of motherhood. Petry clearly understood that the plight of an urban black mother is complicated by forces that black male writers had not acknowledged or written into their fiction. Thus she sought to write into her text the untold story of what it means to be black and female. The result, as Barbara Christian has noted, was that she be-

came the first woman novelist to depict a black mother's struggle to survive in the inner city.

The rhetorical strategies Petry uses to mediate the disparity between what Lutie does and what the environment does to her account not only for the narrative tension that moves the novel forward, but for the power of the novel as a whole. For example, at the very beginning of the novel, Petry introduces Lutie in the process of reading ads for vacant apartments—literally sign-reading. Because she has "to blink in order to read the words on the sign swaying back and forth" in the wind, she can barely focus on the words "Three rooms, steam heat, parquet floors, respectable tenants. Reasonable." Although she knows there is a disparity between what the sign says and what is really available (" 'steam heat' meant . . . rattling radiators . . . 'parquet floors' . . . meant the wood was . . . old and discolored . . . 'respectable tenants' . . . where colored people were allowed to live included anyone who could pay the rent," and so on), she takes the apartment anyway. Petry illustrates with painstaking detail scene after scene where Lutie must assess negative alternatives and choose the lesser evil. She reveals the complexity of inner-city life and revises the naturalistic rendering of black people, especially black women, as helpless, passive victims that dominates Wright's fiction and that of other black male writers. Robert Stepto suggests that Petry's task was not only one "of redeeming Bessie," the girlfriend Bigger Thomas silences in *Native Son*, "but of revising Bigger as well." In this regard, Petry's perspective not only connected her to black women writers who predated her, but anticipated the next generation of black women writers such as Gwendolyn Brooks, Paule Marshall, Toni Cade Bambara, Alice Walker, Toni Morrison, and Gloria Naylor.

Petry's second novel, *Country Place*, represents a sharp departure from *The Street* and from much of the African American literary tradition. Often regarded as her "raceless" novel because it focuses almost exclusively on white characters in a small town in Connecticut, it nevertheless draws on a geographic location and a set of values and cultural attitudes with which

Petry was very familiar. In describing her knowledge of small-town life, Arthur Davis asserts it is a subject that "in all probability she knew better than the life she wrote about in *The Street*." Her narrative intentions in *Country Place* seem clear: to call into question and even deflate the romanticized "picture-postcard" image of small-town New England by exposing the ugly conflation of bigotry, petty vindictiveness, and greed that lay beneath this image. In a sense, Petry returns in *Country Place* to a community much like that of the Chandlers in *The Street*. This time, however, it is not briefly introduced as an objectified symbol of the American dream. Instead, it becomes a closely scrutinized subject, the narrative center of the entire novel. By focusing on the inner life of this community, Petry exposes the reality behind the myth of small-town perfection and thereby challenges the idealized image that Lutie had accepted without question.

The first observation any reader is likely to make about *Country Place* is that the narrator begins his account with an elaborate, almost self-conscious justification of his right to tell the story. As the town's only druggist, Doc Fraser establishes his narrative authority by assuring us that he is "in a better position to write the record of what took place . . . than anyone else" because "all the people concerned were customers" of his and he had "acquired an intimate, detailed knowledge of all of them." Through his first-person retrospective narrative, he informs us that the town of Lennox, Connecticut, is a "quiet place, a country place" like many other New England towns. He acknowledges, however, that despite appearances to the contrary, "Lennox could hardly have been called a quiet, sleepy village." As the seer/sayer, narrator/philosopher, he expresses the theme around which the narrative revolves: "There is always a vein of violence running under the surface quiet." *Country Place*, then, focuses on the various manifestations of violence that belie the town's picturesque serenity. Having established his authority, however, Doc undercuts it by reminding the reader that despite his belief in the truth of his account, "truth has many sides." Petry occasionally abandons Doc's

perspective to allow other characters to share in the telling, thereby fleshing out the collective personality of the town and portraying its townspeople in all their complex humanity.

The basic plot of *Country Place* is fairly simple. Johnnie Roane, the protagonist, returns home from World War II with an idealized expectation of a loving reunion with his wife, Glory. From the moment he enters the taxicab of Weasel, the town gossip, on the day of his return, until he sadly boards a train a week later and departs for New York, he gradually realizes his wife was merely "the soapbubble, the dream, the illusion" he had held on to for too long. On the day of his return, it is Weasel's sinister innuendo of his wife's affair with Ed Barrell, the town leech, that first raises his apprehensions. When he discovers the truth of this innuendo, his violent confrontation with Ed and Glory convinces him to relinquish the relationship altogether. Realizing "nothing was ever the same . . . either on the surface or underneath," he ultimately admits he has outgrown the town and should pursue a new life in New York.

If Johnnie represents entrapment by dreams and the inevitability of change, then Mrs. Gramby, the wealthiest woman in town, represents entrapment by outmoded traditions and resistance to change. The plot gets complicated as much by the violent storm that sets the characters to "reluctant examination of their lives" as by Weasel, whose malicious gossip both creates and propels the conflict virtually along class lines. There are the ordinary working people—Glory, her mother, Lillian, and Ed—trapped by movie-image fantasies, selfish materialism, and wanton lust, respectively. By contrast, there are Mrs. Gramby and her son Mearns, whose indifference to wealth and status frustrates his mother's dreams and plans for his life. Weasel's sadistic meddling in the affairs of these separate groups, as well as their violent responses to the truths he uncovers, creates at once the narrative cohesion and tension of the novel. He is responsible not only for Johnnie's discovery of Ed and Glory's adulterous rendezvous, but for Mrs. Gramby's discovery that Mearns's wife, Lillian, has also had an affair with Ed Barrell. Motivated by greed for her portion of the Gramby inheritance, Lillian attempts to kill the diabetic Mrs. Gramby by withholding her insulin. In response to this failed attempt and her discovery that Lillian has cheated on her son, Mrs. Gramby disinherits her and adds insult to injury by selecting a Jewish lawyer to assist with the will and by including the black maid and the Portuguese janitor in the will instead of Lillian. By so doing, Mrs. Gramby transcends the narrow-mindedness of her neighbors and reaches out to the very minorities Lillian had treated with scornful condescension. At the end of the novel, Mrs. Gramby pushes Ed to his death as she falls to her own on the courthouse stairs, thus symbolizing the ultimate triumph of justice over wrongdoing.

Although the plot of *Country Place* occasionally borders on melodrama, as some reviewers and critics have noted, the novel nevertheless reveals Petry's skill at characterization and the manipulation of point of view. In selecting Doc as narrator, she not only pays tribute to her pharmacist father but also creates a surrogate for herself as storyteller. At the same time, however, she revises the convention of a single narrator by dispersing the narrative among several tellers to expose collective histories and multiple viewpoints and to dispel the notion that anyone can have a monopoly on the truth of any human experience. Moreover, her conscious decision to shift from her perspective in *The Street* to portray the lives of white characters both demonstrated her insightful versatility as an artist and asserted her freedom to write about subjects other than race.

In her third novel, *The Narrows*, Petry displays her artistic versatility and sharpens the insights that distinguish her first two novels. Having focused on a black community in Harlem in *The Street* and a white community in Connecticut in *Country Place*, Petry seeks in *The Narrows* to write about the relationship between black and white people. To exploit the possibilities of bringing both groups together in one geographic location, she uses a tragic interracial affair and a New England town's response to it as the narrative center of the novel. This strategy also provides an opportunity for her to examine black life in a small New England town not simply to evoke the subject of racial oppression, but to depict dimensions of black culture that had been neglected in literature. Arthur Davis notes that Petry introduces "virtually an untried field for the black writer." Ostensibly an examination of the dynamics of race, gender, and class in American culture, *The Narrows* is at once the most ambitious and most complex of Petry's three novels.

The central plot of *The Narrows* focuses on the interracial affair between Lincoln (Link) Williams, a handsome, black Phi Beta Kappa graduate of Dartmouth, and Camilla (Camilo) Treadway Sheffield, the beautiful white heiress to the Treadway Munitions Company fortune and the wife of a well-known businessman. The couple meet by chance in an area of Monmouth, Connecticut, "known variously as The Narrows, Eye of the Needle, The Bottom, Little Harlem, Dark Town, Niggertown—because Negroes had replaced those other earlier immigrants, the Irish, the Italians and the Poles." Embedded within these name changes are the very historical and cultural conflicts of race and class that gradually complicate and destroy this couple's relationship. In a sense, however, the relationship seems doomed from the start because of the question of identity. Neither is aware of the other's racial identity at first, and Camilo fails to disclose her wealth or marital status. Link's accidental discovery of her deception enrages him, but it also forces him to see their affair in the historical context of white exploitation of black people. He feels she has bought him as though he were a commodity, "a stud." When he tries to end their affair against her wishes, she gets retribution by falsely accusing him of rape. Her accusation exploits the stereotype of black men as violently desirous of white women, a stereotype that is perpetuated by the newspaper her family controls. Moreover, Camilo takes advantage of two interconnected historical realities: that relationships between black men and white women are taboo, and that a charge of rape from a white woman against a black man is a virtual death sentence. At the end of the novel, Camilo's husband and father carry out this death sentence by murdering Link for breaking this taboo and for making their family the focus of town scandal. Their corrupt domination of the town is brought to an end when they are arrested for Link's murder.

In and of itself, the plot of *The Narrows* borders on the sensational. What saves it, however, is the artistic maturity that Petry demonstrates through the novel's intricate thematic development, complex narrative structure, and remarkable stylistic diversity. The theme of the novel—the inescapable influence of the past—is expressed in the thoughts of Link's adoptive mother, Abbie Crunch: "On how peculiar, and accidental a foundation rests all of one's attitudes toward a people. . . . Accident? Coincidence? It all depended on what happened in the past. We carry it around with us." The truth of this statement is best understood by Link, who reassesses everything—from his failure to become a historian to his employment at the Last Chance Bar, from his chance meeting with Camilo to the disillusioning end of their affair—as "all part of the education of one Link Williams." Yet because of her interest in educating her reader, Petry stops short of yielding to an easy fatalistic vision. In response to those who blame Link's death on Camilo, a woman who "starts an evil action, just by her mere presence," Abbie thinks: "We all had a hand in it, we all reacted violently to those two people, to Link and that girl, because he was colored and she was white." For Petry human experience is always an admixture of circumstance and choice, never one without the other.

Petry develops the plot with a complex narrative structure of numerous subplots and minor characters whom she fleshes out with immense detail and psychological depth. As a consequence, *The Narrows* is the first novel where Petry shifts her perspective from outside the black community to look within it, examining the cultural dynamics of its inner life—such as the oral tradition, language play, the vernacular, the blues, black pride, intraracial prejudices, male/female relationships, attitudes toward white people, and responses to racism. Petry also looks within the white community to examine how the dynamics of racial preju-dice, unearned privilege, and exploitative power operate and wreak havoc not just on the lives of black people but on the lives of white people as well. It is probably this ability to move into the interior life of both black and white communities that prompted Arna Bontemps, in his review of *The Narrows*, to refer to Petry as "a neighborhood novelist."

The most distinguishing feature of *The Narrows* is its stylistic diversity. To illustrate the significance of the past, the plot does not move in a linear fashion, but meanders back and forth between past and present. More specifically, Petry uses dramatic shifts in time, multiple points of view, interior monologues, flashbacks, and foreshadowing to emphasize the interconnectedness of experience and the psychological consequences of human choice. While early critics such as Robert Bone and Addison Gayle neglected *The Narrows* in preference for *The Street*, contemporary critics, such as Mary Helen Washington and Nellie McKay, have viewed this novel as the best of Petry's literary canon.

To appreciate this canon, however, one must examine Petry's use of the short story, the genre in which she began her literary career. It is possible to trace in *Miss Muriel and Other Stories* the development of her craft and to discover how her stories often operated as literary workshops for her experimentation with theme, structure, and style. For example, in "In Darkness and Confusion," written in 1943, she examines the racial violence that can erupt from the kind of circumstances Lutie faces in *The Street*; "Like a Winding Sheet," published in 1945, illustrates the relationship between racism and domestic violence; and both stories reveal Petry's early attempt to use Harlem as a setting for fiction. Likewise, "The Bones of Louella Brown" (1947) is an ironic portrayal of the New England narrow-mindedness and bigotry that appear in *Country Place* and *The Narrows*. In her later stories, such as "The News Mirror" (1965) and "Miss Muriel" (1969), she focuses on black female consciousness and writes her most autobiographical fiction. Her changes in perspective from story to story not only reveal her artistic growth, but bear witness to her ability to tell a good story at the same time she scrutinizes the two cultures that shaped her aesthetic vision and social consciousness.

From the publication of *The Narrows* in 1953 to the publication of *Miss Muriel and Other Stories* in 1971, Petry devoted most of her time to writing for children. Prior to 1953, she had written only one book for children, *The Drugstore Cat* (1949), a fable about the value of exercising wisdom with self-assertiveness. Two historical biographies, *Harriet Tubman, Conductor of the Underground Railroad* (1955) and *Tituba of Salem Village* (1964), were written for adolescent readers, and *Legends of the Saints* (1970) was her second book for young children. All four books reflect her belief in using African American history and folklore to teach and inspire black youth to learn from black women and men who struggled to survive against various forms of oppression. While the tone of her adult fiction is predominantly tragic, that of her children's literature is more didactic and inspirational. Not content with using literature to critique American society, she was also committed to using it to bring about social change.

Petry began her literary career with the modest ambition of becoming a short-story writer. Yet her commitment to the craft of writing meant she was destined to excel in other genres as well. Indeed, her achievement in fiction is marked by fully realized characters, complex narrative structures, and detailed delineations of black and white life. Whether written from the vantage point of an outsider looking at Harlem or that of an insider looking at New England, her novels offer a rigorous critique of American culture. They not only reveal her knowledge of how the interconnections of race, gender, and class can shape tragic experiences for both black and white people, but also illustrate her desire to represent black people in all their humanity and complexity. Her depiction of black female characters in particular not only connects her to the black feminist literary tradition of her precursors, but establishes her as a precursor to black writers of today. Although critics may have once habitually attempted to enclose her in the narrow space of

the naturalistic tradition, her greatest contribution to the African American literary tradition has been fiction that exposes the limits of naturalistic readings by creating a narrative space to accommodate her unique perspective and that of others who also seek to tell not just one story of black oppression, but many stories of black survival. Ann Petry died in 1997 in a convalescent center near her Old Saybrook home. Just a decade earlier in the 1980s, the reissue of *The Street* brought her critical acclaim from a new generation of readers. Thus, by the time of her death, she had not only enjoyed a literary life beyond her early ambitions, but she had also had the good fortune of bearing witness to renewed attention to her work from a diverse community of readers and scholars.

Selected Bibliography

PRIMARY WORKS

FICTION

"On Saturday the Siren Sounds at Noon." *Crisis* 50:368–69 (December 1943).

The Street. Boston: Houghton Mifflin, 1946. Reprint, New York: Pyramid, 1946, 1961. Reprint, London: Michael Joseph, 1947. Reprint, New York: Signet, 1947. Reprint, Boston: Beacon, 1985. Reissue, Boston: Houghton Mifflin, 1992.

Country Place. Boston: Houghton Mifflin, 1947. Reprint, London: Michael Joseph Ltd., 1948. Reprint, Chatham, N.J.: The Chatham Bookseller, 1971.

The Drugstore Cat. Illustrated by Susanne Suba. New York: Crowell, 1949. Reprint, Boston: Beacon, 1988.

Miss Muriel and Other Stories. Boston: Houghton Mifflin, 1971. Reprint, Boston: Beacon Press, 1989.

"The Moses Project." *Harbor Review* 5–6:52–61 (1986).

NONFICTION

"New England's John Henry." *Negro Digest* 3, no. 5:71–73 (March 1945).

"My Most Humiliating Jim Crow Experience." *Negro Digest*, June 1946, pp. 63–64.

"What's Wrong with Negro Men?" *Negro Digest*, March 1947, pp. 4–7.

"The Great Secret." *Writer* 61, no. 7:215–17 (July 1948).

"Harlem." *Holiday*, no. 4:110–16 (April 1949).

"The Novel as Social Criticism." In *The Writer's Book.* Edited by Helen Hull. New York: Barnes and Noble, 1950.

Harriet Tubman: Conductor on the Underground Railroad. New York: Crowell, 1955. Reprint, New York:

Archway Paperbacks, 1971. Published in England as *A Girl Called Moses: The Story of Harriet Tubman*. London: Methuen, 1960.

Tituba of Salem Village. New York: Crowell, 1964. Reprint, New York: Harper, 1988.

"The Common Ground." In *Horn Book Reflections*. Edited by Elinor Whitney Field. Boston: Horn Book, 1969.

Legends of the Saints. Illustrated by Anne Rockwell. New York: Crowell, 1970.

MANUSCRIPTS AND PAPERS

Unpublished materials and manuscripts are held in the Special Collections of Mugar Memorial Library at Boston University, Boston, Massachusetts; the James Weldon Johnson Collection at the Beinecke Rare Book and Manuscript Library, Yale University, New Haven, Connecticut; and the Moorland-Spingarn Research Center, Founders Library, Howard University, Washington, D.C.

SECONDARY WORKS

BIOGRAPHICAL AND CRITICAL STUDIES

Adams, George R. "Riot as Ritual: Ann Petry's 'In Darkness and Confusion.' " *Negro American Literature Forum* 6:54–57, 60 (1972).

Bell, Bernard W. *The Afro-American Novel and Its Tradition*. Amherst: University of Massachusetts Press, 1987.

———. "Ann Petry's Demythologizing of American Culture and Afro-American Character." In *Conjuring: Black Women, Fiction, and Literary Tradition*. Edited by Marjorie Pryse and Hortense J. Spillers. Bloomington: Indiana University Press, 1985. Pp. 105–15.

Bell, Roseanne P., Bettye J. Parker, and Beverly Guy-Sheftall, eds. *Sturdy Black Bridges: Visions of Black Women in Literature*. New York: Anchor Press, 1979.

Bone, Robert H. *The Negro Novel in America*. New Haven, Conn.: Yale University Press, 1958.

Christian, Barbara. *Black Women Novelists: The Development of a Tradition 1892–1976*. Westport, Conn.: Greenwood Press, 1980.

Clark, Keith. "Distaff Dream Deferred? Ann Petry and the Art of Subversion." *African American Review* 26, no. 3:495–505 (1992).

Condon, Garrett. "Street Wise: The Rediscovery of Ann Petry and Her Timeless Stories of the Cruel City." In *Northeast*. Sunday supplement of the *Hartford Courant*, November 8, 1992, pp. 8, 13, 18–20.

Davis, Arthur P. *From the Dark Tower: Afro-American Writers (1900–1960)*. Washington, D.C.: Howard University Press, 1974.

Dempsey, David. "Uncle Tom's Ghost and the Literary Abolitionists." *Antioch Review* 6:442–48 (September 1946).

Gates, Henry Louis, Jr. "In Her Own Write." Foreword to *The Schomburg Library of Nineteenth-Century Black Women Writers*. New York: Oxford University Press, 1988.

Ervin, Hazel Arnett. *Ann Petry: A Bio-Bibliography*. New York: G. K. Hall, 1993.

Fein, Esther. "Author's Look at Harlem of the '40s to Be Reissued." *New York Times*, January 8, 1992, pp. B1–2.

Gayle, Addison. *The Way of the New World: The Black Novel in America*. New York: Anchor, 1975.

Greene, Marjorie. "Ann Petry Planned to Write." *Opportunity* 24:78–79 (April–June 1946).

Harper, Michael S., and Robert B. Stepto. *Chant of Saints: A Gathering of Afro-American Literature, Art, and Scholarship*. Urbana: University of Illinois Press, 1979.

Harris, Trudier. *From Mammies to Militants: Domestics in Black American Literature*. Philadelphia: Temple University Press, 1982.

Hernton, Calvin C. *The Sexual Mountain and Black Women Writers: Adventures in Sex, Literature, and Real Life*. New York: Anchor, 1987. Reprint, 1990.

Holladay, Hilary. "Creative Prejudice in Ann Petry's 'Miss Muriel.' " *Studies in Short Fiction* 31:667–74 (1994).

———. *Ann Petry*. New York: Twayne, 1996.

Hughes, Carl Milton. *The Negro Novelist 1940–1950*. New York: Citadel Press, 1970.

Hull, Gloria T., Patricia Bell Scott, and Barbara Smith, eds. *All the Women Are White, All the Blacks are Men, But Some of Us Are Brave: Black Women's Studies*. Old Westbury, N.Y.: Feminist Press, 1982.

Isaacs, Diane Scharfeld. *Ann Petry's Life and Art: Piercing Stereotypes*. Ph.D. diss., Columbia University Teachers College, 1982; Ann Arbor, Mich.: University Microfilms International, 1982.

Ivy, James W. "Ann Petry Talks about First Novel." *Crisis* 53:48–49 (January 1946). Reprinted in *Sturdy Black Bridges: Visions of Black Women in Literature*. Edited by Roseann P. Bell, Bettye J. Parker, and Beverly Guy-Sheftall. New York: Anchor Press, 1979.

Jones, Gayl. "Jazz/Blues Structure in Ann Petry's 'Solo on the Drums.' " In *Liberating Voices: Oral Tradition in African American Literature*. Cambridge: Harvard University Press, 1991. Pp. 90–98.

Lattin, Vernon E. "Ann Petry and the American Dream," *Black American Literature Forum* 12, no. 2:69–72 (Summer 1978).

Lee, Robert A., ed. *Black Fiction: New Studies in the Afro-American Novel Since 1945*. New York: Barnes and Noble, 1980.

Littlejohn, David. *Black on White: A Critical Survey of Writing by American Negroes*. New York: Grossman, 1966.

Madden, David. "Ann Petry: 'The Witness.' " *Studies in Black American Literature* 6:24–26 (1975).

Maund, Alfred, "The Negro Novelist and the Contemporary Scene." *Chicago Jewish Forum* 12:28–34 (1954).

McDowell, Margaret. "The Narrows: A Fuller View of Ann Petry." *Black American Literature Forum* 14:135–41 (1980).

McKay, Nellie Y. "Ann Petry's *The Street* and *The Narrows*: A Study of the Influence of Class, Race and

Gender on Afro-American Women's Lives." In *Women and War: The Changing Status of American Women from the 1930s to the 1950s*. Edited by Maria Diedrich and Dorothea Fischer-Hornung. New York: Berg, 1990. Pp. 127–40.

———. Introduction to *The Narrows*. Boston: Beacon, 1990.

Naylor, Gloria, and Toni Morrison. "A Conversation." *Southern Review* 21:567–93 (July 1985).

O'Brien, John, ed. "Ann Petry." In *Interviews with Black Writers*. New York: Liveright, 1973. Pp. 153–63.

Pryse, Marjorie. " 'Pattern Against the Sky': Deism and Motherhood in Ann Petry's *The Street*." In *Conjuring: Black Women, Fiction, and Literary Tradition*. Edited by Marjorie Pryse and Hortense Spillers. Bloomington: Indiana University Press, 1985. Pp. 116–131.

Renza, Louis A. " 'A White Heron' and the Question of Minor Literature." Madison: University of Wisconsin Press, 1984.

Riis, Roger William. "A Story of 'Hemmed in' Lives." *Opportunity* 24, no. 3:157 (1946).

Rosenblatt, Roger. "White Outside." *Black Fiction*. Cambridge: Harvard University Press, 1974.

Sarkissian, Adele, ed. "Ann Petry." In *Contemporary Authors: Autobiography Series*. Vol. 6. Detroit: Gale Research, 1988. Pp. 253–69.

Shinn, Thelma J. "Women in the Novels of Ann Petry." *Critique: Studies in Modern Fiction* 16, no. 1:110–20 (1974).

Streitfield, David. "Retraced Steps on a Grim Street." *Washington Post*, February 25, 1992, pp. E1–E2.

Thomson, Rosemarie Garland. "Ann Petry's Mrs. Hedges and the Evil, One-Eyed Girl: A Feminist Exploration of the Physically Disabled Subject." *Women's Studies* 24, no. 6:599–614 (September 1995).

Washington, Gladys J. "A World Made Cunningly: A Closer Look at Ann Petry's Short Fiction." *CLA Journal* 30, no.1:14–29 (September 1986).

Washington, Mary Helen. *Invented Lives: Narratives of Black Women, 1860–1960*. Garden City, N.Y.: Doubleday, 1987. Pp. 297–306.

Weir, Sybil. "*The Narrows*: A Black New England Novel." *Studies in American Fiction* 15, no. 1:81–93 (Spring 1987).

Wilson, Mark. "A *MELUS* Interview: Ann Petry—The New England Connection." *MELUS* 15, no.2:71–84 (Summer 1988).

ISHMAEL REED
(1938–   )

HENRY LOUIS GATES JR.

ISHMAEL REED, OFTEN cast as the enfant terrible of black letters, has been and continues to be among the most misunderstood of African American writers, indeed of American writers in his time. Whether marked as the preeminent black postmodernist, as the quintessential curmudgeon whose satires respect no one and no idea, or as a misanthrope falling into bouts of misogyny and homophobia, Reed's capacity to generate controversy has only been outpaced by his amazing ability to remain prolific over the decades since the 1960s on which his writing has commented. His attitude toward literary and cultural protocols of the particular day in which he writes remains always irreverent, always playful. But the spirit of play that infuses almost all of Reed's work emerges from his deep love not only of the cultural traditions that he lambastes (yet remains tied to) but also his love for those to whom he feels most beholden, the everyday people whose agency and integrity are lost in what he views as the consistent media blackout of communities of color in the United States.

Two metaphors from Reed's work reflect his writerly stance, a stance that can consistently be described as at once earthy and cosmic, even (and especially) when one feels that each new work—whether novel, poem, essay, or play—seems to contradict his previous piece. First, as he puts it in his oft-anthologized poem "I Am a Cowboy in the Boat of Ra," he is a "vampire outlaw of the milky way," who feeds on the detritus and glories of Western culture (and its misappropriations of non-Western traditions). Although Reed appears to be reveling in the ruins of "civilization," in fact, he is suggesting that exposing its underpinnings, its most impure origins, is the method by which civilization may be saved. For it is in the tainted elements of what Reed calls "multi-America" that we begin to uncover the profoundly syncretic and uneven truths that constitute the unique culture of the United States.

The second metaphor is that of a boxer; Reed has assumed a role as the Muhammad Ali of literature and culture, where "writin' is fightin'." His critical jabs may hit various aspects of conventional U.S. life, but his animus, his knockout punch, is almost always saved for the "establishment media," those especially in print journalism who consistently seem to misconstrue his work.

Reed is often characterized as the true satirist of his time, a mantle he accepts with relish. As more than one critic has discovered, you can dress him up in theory, but you can't take him anywhere: Reed's satiric impulse is no respecter of persons, pieties, or proprieties. How, then, does one reconcile his profile as a corrosive satirist with his highly nurturing presence as an editor and publisher, in which capacity he has supported a wide range of artistic endeavors slighted by mainstream publishing? What does one make of this vampire outlaw whose work tries to create havoc of the most cherished myths of Western culture, but who in other moments writes poignantly of the tragedies and mortalities of his neighbors? How should one read this career of writerly boxing, at constant war with the establishment, the media, the academy, when this very career enabled Reed to win a coveted MacArthur Foundation "genius grant" in 1998? Indeed, Reed is a writer with not a few contradictions. But it is in these contradictions, where no resolution can—or should—take place, that one can see Reed's capacity to remain responsive to the world around him, and in turn demand responses of us to that world.

Early Life

Ishmael Scott Reed was born in Chattanooga, Tennessee, on February 22, 1938, to Henry Lenoir, a fund-raiser for the YMCA, and Thelma Coleman, a homemaker and saleswoman. Later in the 1930s Reed's mother married Bennie Stephen Reed, an autoworker. In 1942 Reed moved with his mother to Buffalo, New York, where she worked in various war industries and he attended public schools. He was an erratic student, first at Buffalo Technical High School (1952–1954) and then at East High School, from which he graduated in 1956.

Reed began his college education at the University of Buffalo's night school division, Millard Fillmore College, supporting himself as a clerk in the Buffalo public library system during the day. Writing proved an agent of mobility for Reed. His satirical short story "Something Pure" (which depicts the Jesus of the Second Coming as an advertising agent whose unorthodox sales strategy earns him ridicule, scorn, and certain exile) alerted an English professor to his extraordinary gifts of storytelling and parody, and secured for him perhaps his first positively reinforcing experience in academia. Such positive reactions from academic critics would be elusive in the next two decades.

While a student at the University of Buffalo (1956–1960), Reed was influenced by many professors: several members, especially Lyle Glazer, of the department of American studies; Terrence Hawkes, in the English department; and George Trager and Henry Lee Smith, two linguists who helped him to understand the potential of the African American vernacular as a literary resource. Both influences—a "canonical" training in the Western tradition and a nuanced appreciation of the resonance of the several dictions and "dialects" of contemporary "hyphenated-Americans"—formed a distinctive blend even in Reed's earliest poems and stories. In September 1960, Reed married Priscilla Rose and, faced with a dire shortage of funds, withdrew from the university and moved into the Talbert Mall housing project. There he learned to shed the social and class distinctions that he associated with American higher education. Reed described life in the lower-class black housing project as "a horrible experience" compounded by his increasing awareness of cycles of poverty that seemed to resist individual control. The result was a period of political activism during the latter stages of the Civil Rights movement and the opening stage of the Black Power movement. But his period of activism, Reed recounts, "was followed by one of cynicism."

Reed's professional career began with a Buffalo newspaper, the *Empire Star Weekly*, for which he was a staff correspondent. With the *Star*'s editor, Reed served as cohost of a radio program, "Buffalo Community Roundtable," on station WVFO. The program was controversial from the start because of its innovative format and presentation of political opinions and personalities even farther to the left than those of civil rights advocates. The radio station finally canceled the program after Reed interviewed Malcolm X, then the most visible leader of the black nationalist organization the Nation of Islam. Reed's interest in puncturing the confines of conventional opinion and his delight in outraging orthodox sensibilities were amply in evidence in his earliest journalistic endeavors and have remained a central aspect of his career.

In 1962 the Reeds' daughter, Timothy Brett, was born. The following year, Reed and his wife separated; they were divorced in 1970. Reed also entered the world of local theater, performing in Edward Albee's *The Death of Bessie Smith*, Tennessee Williams' *Camino Real*, Lorraine Hansberry's *A Raisin in the Sun*, and Jean Anouilh's *Antigone*. Although he is known mostly as a novelist, poet, and essayist, Reed's passion for theater (both on stage and in writing) has continued throughout his career. Reed moved from Buffalo to New York City in 1962. He was active in a number of cultural organizations during his residence there, a period that witnessed the culmination of the Civil Rights movement, the assassinations of John F. Kennedy and Malcolm X, and the birth of the Black Arts and Black Power movements and various radical "underground" integrated political-cultural organizations. During this seminal period in American letters, Reed served as editor in chief of *Advance*, a Newark, New Jersey, weekly. His friend the painter Walter Browart collaborated with Reed on the initial number of *Advance*, and Reed in turn gave his assistance when Bowart founded the *East Village Other*. Reed also was a major participant in the Umbra Workshop, a black writers' group that, he believes, "began the inflorescence of 'Black Poetry' as well as many other recent Afro-American styles of writing." Reed's New York period was crucial in his evolution as an artist, marked as it was by his emerging identity among black and white writers, his organization of the 1965 American Festival of Negro Art, and the writing of his first novel, *The Free-Lance Pallbearers*, published in 1967.

In 1967 Reed moved to Berkeley, California. Since then he has taught at the University of California, Berkeley; the University of Washington, Seattle (1969, 1989); the State University of New York, Buffalo (1975, 1979); Yale (1979); Dartmouth (1980); Harvard (1987); and the University of California, Santa Barbara (1989). For the most part Reed has been a resident of the San Francisco area, where he lives with his second wife, Carla Blank, a modern dancer he married in 1970; they have a daughter, Tennessee, born in 1977. In 1971, with

Ishmael Reed

Steve Cannon and Al Young, Reed founded the Yardbird Publishing Company; in 1973, he started the Reed, Cannon, and Johnson Communications Company (later called Ishmael Reed Books); and in 1976, with Victor H. Cruz, he established the Before Columbus Foundation. Each of these organizations is intended to expand our ideas of exactly what "American" literature might be. To Reed, the United States is "unique in the world: the world is here." His vision of a national literature is one that is Chicano and Chinese, Yiddish and Native American, Anglo-Saxon and African American, multicolored, multivocal, and multicultural.

As the author of an ever-growing number of novels, books of poems, and collections of essays, writer and producer of numerous plays and television programs, and editor and publisher of several anthologies, Reed stands as one of the cardinal figures in the African American literary tradition. And yet his place in the tradition is, as has been suggested, more than a little ironic. For Reed has chosen to establish his presence as an artist not by repeating and revising the great black texts in that tradition, but by challenging the formal conventions that these texts share through the always fragile arts of satire and parody.

Whatever their settings—the Harlem Renaissance in *Mumbo Jumbo* (1972), the antebellum plantation in *Flight to Canada* (1976), the mythical Western never-never land in *Yellow Back Radio Broke-Down* (1969), or the fantastic futuristic kingdom of "HARRY SAM" in *The Free-lance Pallbearers* (1967), and, in a more contemporary setting, the parallel universes of *The Terrible Twos* (1982), its sequel, *The Terrible Threes* (1989), *Reckless Eyeballing* (1986), and *Japanese by Spring* (1993)—Reed's novels share some basic assumptions. He sees the historical present as an extension of the past, yesterday's evils now in full bloom as today's nightmares. Even his futuristic antithetical universes are reflections of the present, logically extended. Reed's allegorical narratives convey their moral point with an ironic wit, a cold, keen eye for economic exploitation—one that does not spare the victims of that process, both the exploited and the exploiter—and a slender but persistent optimism for the determined souls who transcend their immediate environment and penetrate illusions by daring acts of will.

Still, it would be a mistake to imagine Reed primarily as a social reformer. Although his work is immediately concerned with racism, sexism, and economic exploitation, a closer reading suggests that his parody targets, in the first instance, literary conventions themselves. Reed's use of "subcultural" or "subliterary" forms—such as the Western, modes of film narration, and the detective novel—are not merely devices for telling a story. Rather, they engage other, inherited strategies of narration that become as much a part of a people's "experience," narrated in literature, as does the ostensible "content" of that experience.

Reed's subversive but not unaffectionate relation to inherited literary convention leads to a sustained engagement with the fictions of

Ralph Ellison, Richard Wright, and James Baldwin, among other canonical writers of African American literature. He has said of his writing, "I try to do what has never been done before." And while Reed's satire has affinities with the works of Rudolph Fisher, George Schuyler, and Wallace Thurman, he has no true precursor in the African American tradition. Along with Amiri Baraka, Reed may be one of the two most controversial artists in that tradition. But whereas Baraka's controversy arises from the successive political ideologies he has adopted and abandoned over two decades, Reed's source of controversy is his penchant to parody even our most sacred and shared beliefs.

Ishmael Reed's novels consistently manage to consolidate disparate, seemingly unrelated characteristics of black written and unwritten formal expression, and thereby to redefine the very possibilities of the novel as a literary form. His novels are almost essays on the art of black fiction making. His use of satire is no accident. Thematically, as in *Mumbo Jumbo*, he seems determined to force readers to rediscover the still largely untold role of blacks as creators of American culture or as word sorcerers who maintain a secret culture that, from time to time, pervades all of American life. Formally, as in *Flight to Canada*, by taking imaginative liberties not only with plot, structure, and point of view, but also with classical notions of time and space, he effectively draws attention to the artifice of writing. His is an art based on the tension of dissonance—on the power of art to "say" more than it states—as opposed to an art where normative judgment turns on a "likeness" to the world we experience every day.

A close reading of Reed's works strongly suggests his concerns with the received form of the novel, with the precise rhetorical shape of the African American literary tradition, and with the relation of the African American tradition to the Western tradition. His concerns, as exemplified in his narrative forms, seem to be twofold: first, he is aware of the relation his own art bears to his black literary precursors; and second, he undertakes the process of willing-into-being a rhetorical structure, a literary language, complete with its own figures and tropes, that allows the black writer simultaneously to criticize both the metaphysical presuppositions inherent in Western ideas and forms of writing and the metaphysical system in which the "blackness" of the writer and his experience have been depicted as a "natural" absence. In a series of demanding novels, Reed has criticized, through parody, what he perceives to be the conventional structures of feeling that he has received from the African American tradition. He has proceeded almost as if the process of analysis can clear a narrative space for the next generation of writers as decidedly as Ellison's narrative response to Wright and naturalism cleared a space for Leon Forrest, Toni Morrison, Alice Walker, James Alan McPherson, and, of course, Reed himself.

Through the perilous art of pastiche, Reed takes to task the African American idealism of narrating a universal, singular black subject, in whose experiences with obstinate, social obstacles might be found easy and adequate literary representation in received Western forms and figures. Reed's fictions argue that the so-called black experience cannot be thought of as static, but as a dynamic, even conflictual, process of identity-and-change. His narratives do not even opt for a dialectical vision of black identity, but rather he foregrounds the particularity and contingency of individual experience that can bear different fruit, even on the same soil.

The Free-Lance Pallbearers

Reed's first novel creates a set of general expectations for reading the rest of his works. *The Free-Lance Pallbearers* (1967) is, above all else, a parody of the confessional mode that is the fundamental, undergirding convention of African American narrative, received, elaborated upon, and transmitted in a chartable heritage from Briton Hammon's captivity narrative of 1760, through the antebellum slave narrative, to black autobiography (most notably Booker T. Washington's 1901 *Up from Slavery*), and into black fiction, especially the fictions of Zora Neale Hurston, Wright, Baldwin, and Ellison.

The narrative of Reed's Bukka Doopeyduk is a pastiche of the classic black narrative of the questing protagonist's "journey into the heart of whiteness"; but it parodies that narrative form by turning it inside out, exposing the character of the originals and thereby defining their formulaic closures and disclosures.

Doopeyduk's tale ends with his crucifixion. As the narrator of his own story, therefore, Doopeyduk articulates, literally from among the dead, an irony implicit in all confessional and autobiographical modes, in which any author is forced by definition to imagine himself or herself to be dead. Yet while the conventional confessional narrative may anticipate the author's death by detailing a life worth writing about— the wisdom gained from experience and struggle, or what Bukka in the novel refers to as "Inchin' Along"—Reed in this novel lambastes this vision of cultural and social mastery. Bukka narrates from the dead after he is impaled on a meat hook and is left hanging publicly for three days: dissatisfied with his life story of Alger-esque diligence, he tries to concoct a new story for himself, only to exclaim as he finally gives up "his ghost," "What's the use?" Clearly serving as a parody of Christ's "accomplishment" in the archetypical crucifixion scene, Bukka's execution signals a rejection of both the black Horatio Alger ethic of casting down one's bucket, and the myth of the necessary black martyr—the martyr white society is glad to worship in place of the live person with whom they would have to contend. No proclamation of a completed, fulfilling task, no commending of the spirit to a higher ideal—Reed's first novel is a world so degenerate, so far beyond the possibility of repentance that the despotic rule of HARRY SAM is made ludicrously complete by Reed's description at the end of the story. Bukka's death is memorialized only by the blinking neon sign of Harry Sam's motel flashing the same message over and over: "EATS-SAVE GREEN STAMPS-BINGO WED-EATS . . ." only changed by the fact that it is "WRITTEN IN CHINESE NO LESS." This last piece of information, of a society increasingly catering to, populated by, and perhaps even ruled by Asians would return, with all its cultural implications, in Reed's 1993 novel *Japanese by Spring*.

At the end of *The Free-Lance Pallbearers* Reed tell us that the novel was finished in Hell's Kitchen, New York, in the summer of 1966, a detail that should prompt us to think about the social upheavals taking place during the time the novel was written. The second "long-hot summer" in the wake of the Pyrrhic victory of an earlier form of the Civil Rights movement, the seeming optimism that culminated in the passage of the Voting Rights Act of 1965, gave way to a new political radicalism largely from urban communities ignored by the same people who had been well-wishers of the Freedom Riders in the U.S. South. Moreover, Reed wrote this novel as President Lyndon Johnson simultaneously launched a "war on poverty" and escalated the war in Southeast Asia. *The Free-Lance Pallbearers* highlights the extent to which such contradictions made a kind of insane sense when one dispenses with the idea that social policy, like the mimetic thrust of neosocial realism that Reed vilifies here and elsewhere, must maintain a rational logic in order for policy to work in practice. The story's society is called "HARRY SAM," named after its leader, the dictatorial and cannibalistic Harry Sam, whose throne of white power, Bukka discovers, is a giant toilet. Reed's penchant for scatology (treatment of obscene matters) at the same time that he makes reference to political figures such as John F. Kennedy, Lyndon Johnson, Richard Nixon (and his dog Checkers), Franklin Roosevelt, and Neville Chamberlain is meant at first to outrage urbane sensibilities and create havoc out of the historical stuff from which he derives his material for the novel. But even as his thematic and formal excess defies simple allegorical reference, Reed's first novel reminds us of the potency of Swiftian anger: *The Free-Lance Pallbearers* distills satiric rage toward a culture that he regards with the most baneful of laughter.

But laughter towards his contemporary culture only amounts to part of the project significant in *The Free-Lance Pallbearers*, equally important in this novel are Reed's subversions of the black literary and cultural tradition into which he self-consciously writes. Reed pays ironic homage to (through use of parody and ironic repetition) Wright's *Black Boy* and Baldwin's *Go Tell It on the Mountain* in a critique that can be read as an epigraph to the novel: "read growing up in soulsville first of three installments—or what it means to be a backstage darky." Reed foregrounds the "scat-singing voice" that introduces the novel against the "other" voice of Bukka, whose "second" voice narrates the novel's plot. Here, Reed parodies both Hurston's use of free indirect discourse in *Their Eyes Were Watching God* and Ellison's use in *Invisible Man* of the foregrounded voices in the prologue and epilogue that frame his nameless protagonist's picaresque account. In a classic inversion of narratorial authority, Bukka speaks with the affectations of formal, stiff English in sharp contrast to the opening narrative voice, which employs slang, profanity, the aspects of English considered nonformal, nonstandard. And significantly, this "scat" voice is echoed by those in power, such as Harry Sam, who proposes as his political project, "When they act up and give you some lip, bomb the fuken daylights out of um. . . . That goes for spicks and gooks and all the rest what ain't like us." If Bukka is enslaved initially by his unreconstructed allegiance to and mimicry of formal English, the second voice offers no respite for liberation: language unfettered by the king's rules, Reed suggests, can still be used in the service of political tyranny. Such inversion is one of the techniques Reed uses most often to exemplify his deconstruction of both the pretense of a "pure" (and therefore powerful) English and the myth of the inherent revolutionary possibilities of speaking the seemingly unauthorized tongue of the marginalized.

The Free-Lance Pallbearers was the only novel that Reed wrote in New York. While the novel placed him immediately on the literary map, Reed felt that the artistic world of New York, clustered around the Soho and East Village sections of Manhattan, provided a too limited vision of what was considered acceptable writing. Reviews seemed to confirm Reed's fears. In a review for *Harper's Magazine*, Irving Howe complained that the novel never reached its satirical objectives and instead deflated into "*Mad Magazine* silliness." Reed, in Howe's view, could not accurately reflect the conditions and dilemma facing black communities in this turbulent era.

Yellow Back Radio Broke-Down

The focus on Reed's "inaccuracy" is telling. In his second novel, *Yellow Back Radio Broke-Down* (1969), the first of many written from the Bay Area in California, Reed continues to critique the specious divide between realism and modernism. And not surprisingly, a figure emerges in the novel mouthing the aesthetic protocols of neosocial realism and sounding strangely enough like Howe. Consider the following exchange between Bo Shmo and the Loop Garoo Kid:

It was Bo Shmo and the neo-social realist gang. They rode to this spot from their hideout in the hills. Bo Shmo leaned in his saddle and scowled at Loop, whom he considered a deliberate attempt to be obscure. A buffoon an outsider and frequenter of sideshows. . . .

The trouble with you Loop is that you're too abstract, the part time autocrat monarchist and guru finally said. Crazy dada nigger that's what you are. You are given to fantasy and are off in matters of detail. Far out esoteric bullshit is where you're at. Why in those suffering books that I write about my old neighborhood and how hard it was every gumdrop machine is in place while your work is a blur and a doodle. I'll bet you can't create the difference between a German and a redskin.

What's your beef with me Bo Shmo, what if I write circuses? No one says a novel has to be one thing. It can be anything it wants to be, a vaudeville show, the six o'clock news, the mumblings of wild men saddled by demons.

All art must be for the end of liberating the masses. A landscape is only good when it shows the oppressor hanging from a tree.

Right on! Right, on, Bo, the henchmen chorused.

Did you receive that in a vision or was it revealed to you?

Of course, Howe has not been the only person to voice the idea that art should be in the service of a particular political ideology or program. This is a debate central to the conversation between African American writers. A key figure in this debate was Richard Wright, whose shadow loomed over black writers during the 1950s and 1960s, and whose descendants a generation later called for an artistic enterprise that would directly "serve the people." This passage, therefore, comprises only one of many in which Reed deliberately reflects upon the history of the black tradition's debate over the nature and purpose of art.

Reed should not be mistaken here. It is not that he does not believe that art, and in particular his writing, should not work to chart new terrains of possibility and change. Nor does he privilege "esoteric bullshit," or in more conventional terms "avant-garde" writing, that eschews any attention toward his readers. In fact, Reed would be the first to claim that his work is not esoteric or inaccessible at all, and that his writing clearly falls within what he calls a deeper, richer, and more historical "popular Afro-American tradition." Rather, what Reed deplores is the idea that the narrative of black freedom and liberation travels only one road. The assumption of just one narrative road necessarily leaves the writer locked in an aesthetic of neorealism that actually hinders, Reed implies, rather than facilitates the social liberation to which its practitioners and critics seem so committed. In a 1972 interview, collected in *Conversations with Ishmael Reed* by Dick and Singh, Reed framed the confrontation between Loop Garoo Kid and Bo Shmo this way: "Loop Garoo Kid . . . sees 'reality' on many levels. Bo Shmo is a guy who has two minds. Garoo has an infinite number of minds." Embedded in this statement are both a critique of a dualism that stultifies black writers by defining determinism (something that Reed actually does believe in) into a kind of fatalism and an indication of Reed's reconstructive efforts to explore the possibilities latent in the "infinite number of minds" that Loop Garoo Kid exemplifies in *Yellow Back Radio Broke-Down.*

From his criticism of Westernized Christianity to his castigation of simplistic nationalism during the 1960s and 1970s to his skepticism of rigid, orthodox Marxist writers and critics, a struggle against dualistic thinking pervades all of Reed's work. This theme is illustrated wittily in one of Reed's earliest poems, aptly entitled "Dualism: Ralph Ellison's Invisible Man," published in 1972 in *Conjure.* In this short poem, Reed has Ellison's unnamed protagonist visiting "history," a caged figure:

I am outside of
history. i wish
i had some peanuts, it
looks hungry there in
its cage

i am inside of
history. its
hungrier than i
thot

The poem suggests the impossibility of writing beyond one's present while at the same time it warns of the danger of falling prey to a kind of fatalistic determinism. More important, Reed's critique of dualism points to his own alternative vision of writing within the spaces of history without being eaten by it. History's "hunger" can also be the read as a kind of artistic desire, from which one might generate new forms of aesthetics and narrative charting that enables more choices than the paltry two afforded to Ellison's protagonist.

Mumbo Jumbo

Reed extends his fight against literary dualism and at least some provisional solutions to the problem that plagues Ellison's main character in subsequent work. Reed's third novel, *Mumbo Jumbo* (1972), is a novel about writing itself— it is both a book about texts and a book of texts, a composite narrative composed of subtexts, pretexts, posttexts, and narratives within narratives. It is both a definition of African American culture and its deflation. Exemplifying Reed's verbal art at its most complex, the book repays close attention.

"The Big Lie concerning Afro-American culture," the dust jacket states, "is that it lacks a tradition." The "Big Truth" of this novel, on the other hand, is that this very tradition is as rife with ossified conventions as is the rest of the Western tradition. Reed's parody of tradition begins with his book's title. "Mumbo jumbo" is the received and ethnocentric Western designation for the rituals of black religions as well as for all black languages. A vulgarized Western "translation" of a Swahili phrase, *mambo, jambo,* "mumbo jumbo," according to *Webster's Third New International Dictionary,* connotes "language that is unnecessarily involved and difficult to understand: gibberish." The *Oxford English Dictionary* cites its etymology as "of unknown origin," illustrating the significance of Reed's title and the book's central presence, the phenomenon of Jes Grew, which recalls the myth of Topsy in *Uncle Tom's Cabin,* who, with no antecedents, "jes' grew"—a phrase with which James Weldon Johnson characterizes the creative process of black sacred music. *Mumbo Jumbo,* then, reveals Western etymology for what it is: abusive Western practices of deflation through misnaming. The title also expresses Johnson's specious, albeit persistent, designation of black creativity as anonymous.

But there is even more parody in this title. Where Ellison ironizes the myth of presence in Wright's titles *Native Son* and *Black Boy* through his title *Invisible Man,* Reed parodies all three titles by employing as his title the English-language parody of black language itself. Swahili speakers know that the phrase "mumbo jumbo" derives from the common greeting *jambo* and its plural *mambo,* which, loosely translated, mean "What's happening?" Reed is also echoing and parodying Vachel Lindsay's ironic poem "The Congo," which exerted such a baneful influence on the Harlem Renaissance poets. From its title on, *Mumbo Jumbo* serves as a critique of black and Western literary forms and conventions and of the complex relations between the two. Thus, again, we see Reed taking to task a culture that privileges itself over another and the desperate need to maintain one's cultural purity: in other words, the novel attempts to debunk the myth of cultural dualism.

This critique of dualism is implicit in *Mumbo Jumbo*'s central speaking character, PaPa LaBas. "Speaking" has emphasis here because the novel's central character, Jes Grew, never speaks and is never seen in its "abstract essence," only in discrete manifestations or "outbreaks." Jes Grew is the supraforce that sets the text of *Mumbo Jumbo* in motion, as Jes Grew and Reed seek their texts, as all characters and events define themselves against this omnipresent, compelling force. Jes Grew emerges as a clever parody of similar forces invoked in the black novel of naturalism, most notably in Wright's *Native Son*.

Unlike Jes Grew, PaPa LaBas does indeed speak. He is the chief detective in hard-and-fast pursuit of both Jes Grew and its Text. PaPa LaBas's name is a conflation of two of the several names of Esu, the Pan-African trickster. Called "Papa Legba" as his Haitian honorific and invoked through the phrase *eh là-bas* in New Orleans jazz recordings of the 1920s and 1930s, PaPa LaBas is the African American trickster figure from black sacred tradition. His surname is French for "over there," and his presence unites "over there" (Africa) with "right here." He is indeed the messenger of the gods, the divine Pan-African interpreter, pursuing, in the language of the text, "The Work," which is not only *vaudou* but also the work (and play) of art itself. PaPa LaBas is the figure of the critic in search of the text, decoding its telltale signs in the process. Even the four syllables of his name recall *Mumbo Jumbo*'s play of doubles. Chief sign reader, LaBas also, in a sense, is a sign himself.

The prose of *Mumbo Jumbo* can be explained as a textbook, complete with illustrations, footnotes, and a bibliography. A prologue, an epilogue, and an appended "Partial Bibliography" frame the text, again in a parody of Ellison's framing devices in *Invisible Man*. (Reed supple-ments Ellison's epilogue with the bibliography, parodying the device both by its repeated presence and by the subsequent asymmetry of *Mumbo Jumbo*.) This documentary scheme of notes, illustrations, and bibliography parodies the documentary conventions of black realism and naturalism, as does Reed's recurrent use of lists and catalogs. Reed fails to separate these "separate" items with any sort of punctuation, thereby directing attention to their presence as literary conventions rather than as sources of information, particularly about the "black experience." Reed's text also includes dictionary definitions, epigraphs, epigrams, anagrams, photoduplicated type from other texts, newspaper clips and headlines, signs (such as those that hang on doors), invitations to parties, telegrams, "Situation Reports" that come "from the 8-tubed Radio," yin-yang symbols, quotations from other texts, poems, cartoons, drawings of mythic beasts, handbills, photographs, book-jacket copy, charts and graphs, playing cards, a representation of part of a Greek vase, and a four-page handwritten letter. Just as our word "satire" derives from *satura* (medley), so Reed's form of satire is a version of "gumbo," a parody of form itself.

Here Reed parodies and underscores our notions of intertextuality, present in all texts. The "Partial Bibliography" is Reed's most brilliant stroke, since its unconcealed presence (along with the text's other undigested texts) parodies both the scholar's appeal to authority and all studied attempts to conceal literary antecedents and influence. All texts, claims *Mumbo Jumbo*, are intertexts, full of intratexts. Our notions of originality, Reed's critique suggests, are more related to convention and material relationships than to some supposedly transcendent truth. Reed lays bare that mode of concealment and that illusion of unity which characterize modernist texts. Coming as it does after the epilogue, the "Partial Bibliography" is an implicit parody of Ellison's ideas of craft and technique in the novel and suggests an image of Ellison's nameless protagonist, buried in his well-lighted hole, eating vanilla ice cream smothered in sloe gin, making annotations for his sequel to *Invisible Man*. The device, moreover, mimics the fictions of documentation and history that claim to order the ways societies live. The presence of the bibliography also recalls Ellison's remarks about the complex relationship between the "writer's experience" and the writer's experiences with books.

Reed's parodic use of intertextuality shows *Mumbo Jumbo* as a postmodern text par excellence. But—to pose a seemingly naive question—what is its parody of the Jazz Age and the Harlem Renaissance about, and for whom do the characters stand? Reed's novel is situated in the 1920s because, as the text explains, the Harlem Renaissance was the first full-scale, well-patronized attempt to capture the essence of Jes Grew in discrete literary work. Jes Grew had made its first appearance in the 1890s, when "the Dance" swept the country. Indeed, James Weldon Johnson appropriated the phrase "jes' grew" to refer to the composition of the musical texts of ragtime, which depended upon signifying riffs to transform black secular, and often vulgar, songs into formal, repeatable compositions. The power of Jes Grew was allowed to disappear in the 1890s, Reed argues, because it found no literary texts to contain, define, interpret, and thereby will it to subsequent black cultures.

Although the Harlem Renaissance did succeed in the creation of seminal works of art and criticism, most critics agree that it failed to find its voice, which lay muffled beneath the dead weight of Romantic convention, which most black writers seemed not to question but to adopt eagerly. This is essentially the same critique rendered by Wallace Thurman in his *Infants of the Spring* (1932), a satirical novel about the Harlem Renaissance by one of its most thoughtful literary critics. Few of Reed's characters stand for historical personages; most are figures for types. Hinckle Von Vampton suggests the writer and critic Carl Van Vechten; but his first name, from the German *hinken* (to limp), could suggest the German engraver Hermann Knackfuss, whose name can roughly translate to "a person with a clubfoot." Abdul Sufi Hamid recalls a host of black Muslims, most notably Duse Mohammed Ali, editor of the *African Times and Orient Review*, as well

as Elijah Muhammad's shadowy mentor, W. D. Fard. The key figures in the action of the plot, however, are the Atonist Path and its military wing, the Wallflower Order, on the one hand, and the NeoHooDoo detectives, headed by PaPa LaBas, and its "military" wing, the Mu'tafikah, on the other. "Wallflower Order" is a pun on "Ivy League," while Mu'tafikah puns on a twelve- (or "dozen"-) letter word ("motherfucker") that signifies chaos. Also, "mu" is the twelfth letter of the Greek alphabet, suggesting "the dozens," which forms a subdivision of the black ritual of signifying; in Reed's novel, the Mu'tafikah plays the dozens on Western art museums. Knackfuss created a heliogravure from Wilhelm II's allegorical drawing of the European authority to go to war against the Chinese. This heliogravure, *Volker Europas, wahrt eure heiligsten Guter* (People of Europe, Protect What Is Most Holy to You), was completed in 1895. It appears in *Mumbo Jumbo* as part of a chapter in which members of the Wallflower Order plot against the Mu'tafikah. The pun on "Knackfuss" and *hinken* is wonderfully consistent with Reed's multiple puns on the "Wallflower Order" and "Atonist."

The meanings of "Atonist" multiply here. "One who atones" is an atonist; a follower of Aton (Pharaoh), Akhnaton's Supreme Being who "reappears" as Jehovah, is an Atonist; and one who lacks physiological tone, especially of a contractile organ, is an atonist. The Atonists and the Jes Grew Carriers (J.G.C.s) allegorically reenact a primal, recurring battle between the forces of light and the forces of darkness, between forces of the Left Hand and forces of the Right Hand, between the descendants of Set and the descendants of Osiris, all symbolized in Knackfuss's heliogravure.

We learn of this war in *Mumbo Jumbo*'s marvelous parody of the scene of recognition so fundamental to the structure of detective fiction, which occurs in the library of a black-owned villa at Irvington-on-Hudson, called Villa Lewaro, "an anagram," the text tells us, "upon the Hostess' name, by famed tenor Enrico Caruso." "Lewaro" is an anagram for "we oral," but it is also the actual name of the villa of the famed black entrepreneur Mme C. J.

Walker. This recognition scene, in which PaPa LaBas and his sidekick, Black Herman, arrest Hinckle Von Vampton and his sidekick, Hubert "Safecracker" Gould, parodies its counterpart in the detective novel by its exaggerated frame. When forced to explain the charges against Von Vampton and Gould, LaBas replies, "Well if you must know, it all began 1000s of years ago in Egypt, according to a high up member in the Haitian aristocracy." He then proceeds to narrate, before an assembled company of hundreds, the myth of Set and Osiris and its key subtext, the myth of the introduction of writing into Egypt by the god Thoth. The parody involved here is the length of the recapitulation of facts—of the decoded signs—which LaBas narrates in a thirty-one-page chapter, the longest in the book.

The myth, of course, recapitulates the action of the novel up to this point of the narrative, but by an allegorical representation through mythic discourse. By fits and starts, we realize that Von Vampton and the Wallflower Order are the descendants of Set, by way of the story of Moses and Jethro and the birth of the Knights Templar in 1118. Von Vampton, we learn, was the Templar librarian; he found the sacred Book of Thoth ("the 1st anthology written by the 1st choreographer"), which is Jes Grew's sacred Text. In the twentieth century, Von Vampton subdivided the Book of Thoth into fourteen sections, just as Set had dismembered his brother Osiris's body into fourteen segments. He anonymously mailed the fourteen sections of the anthology to fourteen black people, who are manipulated into mailing its parts to one another in a repeating circle, in the manner of a "chain book." Abdul Sufi Hamid, one of the fourteen who are unwitting Jes Grew Carriers, calls in the other thirteen chapters of the anthology, reassembles the Text, and translates the Book of Thoth from the hieroglyphics.

Sensing its restored Text, Jes Grew surfaces in New Orleans, as it had in the 1890s with the birth of ragtime, and heads toward New York. Ignorant of the existence or nature of Jes Grew and of the true nature of the sacred Text, Abdul destroys the Book, and then, when he refuses to reveal its location, is murdered by the Wall-

flower Order. LaBas, Von Vampton's archenemy, master of HooDoo, devout follower of Jes Grew ("PaPa LaBas carries Jes Grew in him like most other folk carry genes"), chief decoder of signs, recapitulates this complex story in elaborate detail to the assembled guests at Villa Lewaro, thereby repeating through the recited myth the figures of Mumbo Jumbo's own plot, functioning as what Reed calls "the shimmering Etheric Double of the 1920s. The thing that gives it its summary."

Despite numerous murders, the arrests of Von Vampton and Gould, and their repatriation to Haiti for trial by the *loas* of *vaudou*, neither the mystery of the nature of Jes Grew nor the identity of its Text is ever resolved. The epilogue presents PaPa LaBas in the 1960s, delivering his annual lecture to a college audience on the Harlem Renaissance and its unconsummated Jes Grew passion.

But just as we can define orders of multiple substitution and signification for Reed's types and caricatures, as is true of allegory generally (for instance, Von Vampton/Van Vechten, *hinken*/Knackfuss), so we can find many levels of meaning that could provide a closure to the text. The first decade of readers of *Mumbo Jumbo* attempted, with great energy, to find one-to-one correlations, decoding its allegorical structure by looking to counterparts in, for example, the Harlem Renaissance and the Black Arts movement. As is true with his earlier and subsequent novels, Reed's inspiration for *Mumbo Jumbo* arose from his immediate cultural contexts: in this case, the social upheavals of the late 1960s and early 1970s, made most manifest in the meteoric rise and decline of Black Power, the student uprisings (especially in the Bay Area) whose calls for ethnic studies shook the foundations of Western-centered education, and in the Watergate scandal that was rocking the country as a whole.

Surely, however, *Mumbo Jumbo* resists a purely historical reduction, opting instead to *redact* key historical figures into typologies that enable the narrative to set into motion crucial contestations of culture and power. To this degree, *Mumbo Jumbo* accomplishes both vertical (historical) and horizontal (contemporaneous) reverberance. But the relation of Reed's mode of narration to a critique of traditional notions of closure in interpretation is equally germane. Reed's most subtle achievement in *Mumbo Jumbo* is to parody the notions of closure implicit in the key texts of the African American canon. *Mumbo Jumbo*, in contrast with that canon, is a novel that figures and glorifies indeterminacy. In this sense, *Mumbo Jumbo* stands as a critique and an elaboration upon the convention of closure, and its metaphysical implications, in the black novel.

Flight to Canada

Reed's criticisms of major black writers such as Ellison are most vociferous over the question of what he considers Ellison's narrow prescriptions that demand a certain "craft" in order to tell a story. Even beyond a laying bare of fallacious dualistic tendencies, Reed's work has always sought to tell people's stories without remaining bound to conventional narrative paths, not even normative understandings of temporality. Such is the case with his fourth novel, *Flight to Canada* (1976), a narrative that like *Mumbo Jumbo* employs pastiche; only this time Reed plays with our notions of time and space, lacing with anachronism a story about antebellum American society. Ostensibly, *Flight to Canada* is Uncle Robin's slave narrative, written by Raven Quickskill—"the first one of [Arthur] Swille's slaves to read, the first to write, and the first to run away." The novel turns on the relationship between the demonic and decadent slaveholder Arthur Swille and three or four absolute "types" of slaves that sociologists have invented for the sake of convenience.

The title of the novel invites a double reading. There is the historical flight to Canada undertaken by U.S. slaves, those emblematized in the character of Quickskill. But the way in which he escapes to Canada is one that no other slave has done before: Raven literally takes a flight to Canada, seated first-class in a jumbo jet. According to his note to Swille, written in free-verse, Quickskill "Had / Champagne / Compliments of the Cap'n," on the plane, and stole money from Swille's safe as "Down payment on my back / wages." We are far from a vision of slave identity that Harriet Beecher Stowe would have written (a figure who is consistently lambasted in the novel). And read alongside another popular novel (and later television miniseries) published around the same time as Reed's, namely Alex Haley's *Roots* (1976), *Flight to Canada*'s rendition of slave society, in which slaves watch television after working the fields, Coffee-Mate is replaced by (and mistaken for) a slave mother's milk, and Robin, a slave-turned-plantation-owner rides up to his new home in a limousine. Reed's novel not only forces us to look anew at the nineteenth century (something that Haley's novel did not do, its narrative and story all too familiar for its audience) but also compels us to question the extent to which the latter-half of the twentieth century has performed better in its treatment of people of color. As Reed puts it so well, almost a meta-statement of the underlying warrant of his novel, "Strange, history. Complicated, too. It will be a mystery, history. New disclosures are as bizarre as the most bizarre fantasy."

In addition to Raven Quickskill, the popular slave poet, there is Cato the Graffado ("So faithful that he volunteered for slavery . . . the slaves voted him all-Slavery"); Stray Leechfield, who exploits his exotic blackness to satisfy the fantasies of a repressed Calvinistic culture; Mammy Baracuda, a parody of Henry Bibb's unfaithful wife; and, most of all, Uncle Robin, who, unlike Raven, never left Swille's plantation. The following exchange between Robin and Swille succinctly demonstrates Reed's trademark satirical wit, one which underscores the fact that those with power often have it without correlative knowledge: "Robin, what you heard about this place up North," Arthur Swille asks his loyal servant. "I think they call it Canada?" "Canada," Uncle Robin replies, "I do admit I have heard about the place from time to time, Mr. Swille, but I loves it here so much that . . . I would never think of leaving here. . . . Most assuredly, Mr. Swille, this is my Canada. You'd better believe it." Robin's knowledge about Canada, a place about which he supposedly knows little, as the mythic space of black freedom is almost betrayed by his overzealous oath of loyalty to Swille. Swille, however, remains obtuse to Robin's momentary slip; we, Reed's readers, know better and await the fruits of Robin's trickery.

Curiously, it is the relationship between slaveholder and loyal slave that is drawn most compellingly in Reed's novel. Though we are meant to laugh at Arthur Swille, there lurks in his character a masterful depiction not of mere evil but of the hubris demanded to defy the natural order. For Swille is a man deranged by his own netherside:

Nigger fever. Niggers do something to you. I've seen white people act strange under their influence. First you dream about niggers, little niggers mostly; little niggers, sitting eating watermelons, grinning at you. Then you start dreaming about big niggers. Big, big niggers. Big, big niggers walking all on top of you; then you got niggers all over you, then they got you. . . . As long as they're in this country, this country is under their spell.

Not only is Swille pursued by his own demonic nature, he seeks to merge with it, to consummate his reverence for it. As death approaches him in the form of the ghost of his dead sister, with whose corpse he has been engaged in a deeply satisfying necrophilic liaison, the nature of Swille's true evil becomes vividly clear: his is the transgression of human limits and the construction of a nightmare world to justify that transgression.

And what of Uncle Robin after the sudden and tragic demise of his beloved master Swille? Uncle Robin rewrites Swille's will and inherits the great Virginia mansion of his master. Moreover, he rejects Harriet Beecher Stowe's subsequent attempts to buy his story and then sends to Canada for Raven Quickskill.

As much as about any good-versus-evil dichotomy, Reed is writing about what Robert Stepto calls "authorial control"—the possession of one's own story, be that our collective history or one's own autobiography. He wants to wrestle the text away from those who would control it—whether the well-intentioned abolitionists who "authenticated" the slave narratives, or even Clio, the muse of history. "Why isn't Edgar Allan Poe recognized as the principal biographer of that strange war?" asks the narrator. "Fiction you say? Where does fact begin and fiction leave off? Why does the perfectly rational, in its own time, often sound like mumbo-jumbo?"

One senses in *Flight to Canada* a sort of ending for this aspect of Reed's earlier fiction: The search for the Word, which Reed began in *Mumbo Jumbo*, has finally realized itself in the successful search for the Text, or more mundanely but equally importantly, the Story—the text that at all points comments upon itself. Arthur Swille says in a disarmingly perceptive aside on the uses of black literacy:

And the worst betrayal of all was Raven Quickskill, my trusted bookkeeper. Fooled around with my books, so that every time I'd buy a new slave he'd destroy the invoices and I'd have no record of purchase; he was also writing passes and forging freedom papers. We gave him Literacy, the most powerful thing in the pre-technological pre-post-rational age— and what does he do with it? Uses it like that old Voodoo . . .

If a plane ride, the demonstrable symbol of mobility in our age, is Quickskill's path to freedom, then writing one's story or the story of another remains equally if not more important in the struggle for liberation. It is, Reed suggests, the most powerful of technologies for latter-day conjurers.

Shrovetide in Old New Orleans

The relation between literacy and "Voodoo," as Swille puts it, frames much of Reed's nonfiction. *Shrovetide in Old New Orleans* (1978) is a motley collection of articles and essays, published between 1972 and 1977, in which Reed discusses what he calls "the multi-cultural" influences on his own fiction, pays homage to the black artists to whom he feels indebted, and shares in detail the often bitter controversies that he seems too adept at generating. Even more important, he reveals at length the nature of *vaudou* (voodoo or hoodoo, as it is known popularly) and traces the patterns it assumes in his own work. It is this attention to *vaudou*, the key metaphorical system that threads its way through all of Reed's work, that gives this collection its unity.

Throughout, in disarmingly revealing asides, Reed seems concerned to put to rest his image of the artist as an embattled man. "Writing has made me a better man. It has put me in contact with those fleeting moments which prove the existence of soul." Even more, he seems intent on using various methods of exposition in the essays to "show that I know the difference between an essay and a work of fiction." If the matter were an open question, it remains so no longer, for in these pieces Reed uses H. L. Mencken's techniques of wry irony and a biting wit to draw a self-portrait that is alternately humorous and polemical, but at all times perceptive, honest, and human.

Reed's concerns are those of a self-conscious artist. In a long interview with the satirist and essayist George S. Schuyler, as well as in two insightful critical essays on the novels of Chester Himes and on Wright's *Native Son*, Reed takes his stand against what he calls "social realism" as defined by those who "feel that life has to be a heavy Russian Doestoevskian din of intense pain, as some critics . . . require black writers to believe." His art and his critical judgments are committed, he emphasizes, "toward overcoming the consciousness barrier erected by an alliance of Eastern-based black pseudo-nationalists and white mundanists who in the 1960s sought to dominate Afro-American intellectual thought with their social realist position papers." What he values most in all forms of human cultural expression is an art that manages to contain the triumph of even the absurdly human over the demonic forces of despair. Even more adamantly, Reed opposes those who would reduce the complexity of the human experience to mere cant or to gross generalization.

In his three long essays on *vaudou* in *Shrovetide*, finally, Reed not only describes in vivid detail the form and function of this metaphysical system that syncretized various African and European religions but also demonstrates just how this system of thought has become his metaphor for the black man and the essential philosophical framework for his fiction. By deriving his symbols, physical laws, and ethical values from this still largely misunderstood system of signs, Reed implicitly reveals the arbitrary biases that undergird our traditional notions of order, ethics, and aesthetics. He contends that his is "an art form with its own laws," one that demands "the necessary scholarship" for its decoding, which more than any other reason explains the often bitter and generally confused critical reviews he receives. But Reed has taught us more about the penetration of appearances and about the remarkably persistent strength of black culture than anyone has since Ellison. Reed's essays, like his fiction, are "songs turning back onto themselves," at all points urging a more encompassing concept of reality than a merely Western one. Toward what goal? Reed answers, "The goal of racial understanding" that will come "through cultural revolution, the way most profound revolutions occur: A man enters the city on the back of an ass; his autobiography becomes the empire's best seller." With these essays, Reed reinforces his importance to modern writing by making explicit the assumptions implicit in his fictions.

In his subsequent novels of the 1980s and 1990s, Reed engages with more directness the contemporary period, and, as he did in *The Free-Lance Pallbearers*, parodies what he regards as the misdirection of those in charge of resources and representation in the United States. But unlike his first novel, Reed displays in his later fiction a willingness to provide a corrective voice in his satire, one most likely gestating in his novels during the 1970s. *The Terrible Twos* (1982) was the first of this prolific novelist's works since *The Free-Lance Pallbearers* in which he engages in an analysis—a critique through satire—of the nature and functioning of American political and economic systems, this time the system of the Reagan-Bush era.

The Terrible Twos and *The Terrible Threes*

In *The Terrible Twos*, along with its sequel, *The Terrible Threes* (1989), Reed makes his readers laugh, all the while rendering exact judgments. The book's title derives from the common phrase that describes the psychic state of two-year-old toddlers and that Reed employs as a metaphor for an America two centuries old. As the novel's fake Santa Claus says:

> Two years old, that's what we are, emotionally—America, always wanting someone to hand us some ice cream, always complaining, Santa didn't bring me this and why didn't Santa bring me that? . . . Nobody can reason with us. Nobody can tell us anything. Millions of people are staggering about and passing out in the snow and we say that's tough. We say too bad to the children who don't have milk. I weep as I read these letters poor children sent to me at my temporary home in Alaska.

Central to Reed's critique, that the wealthy and elite are really conspiratorial children, is the coalescence of political, economic, and cultural power in the upper echelons of U.S. society. The government, the media (print and broadcast), corporations, and right-wing Christian groups are in cahoots with one another to control and expand repressive measures masking as commercial desire. To develop this idea, Reed has created a fictional America in the decade between 1980 and 1990, in which a small, newly rich California elite, inextricably tied to oil money, runs the White House.

If all of this sounds perilously familiar, it is supposed to. Creatively fusing several ingredients, like a good chicken gumbo, including the Macy's Thanksgiving Parade, the hagiography of the traditional model for Santa Claus, Saint Nicholas, Charles Dickens's *A Christmas Carol*, Dante's *Inferno*, the novels of social realism, and Rastafarian-*vaudou* symbolism, Reed has written a novel about tiny groups of people who seek to turn a profit at the expense of blacks, Indians, and the vast poor. Christmas comes under the monopoly of Oswald Zumwalt's North Pole Development Corporation in Alaska, which controls all rights to the one true Santa Claus, a failed actor from the soaps.

Reed's characters include President Dean Clift, a former model-become-president because he is manipulable by Big Oil; Nance Saturday, black and sexy sleuth on the trail of the real Santa; and Jamaica Queens, a sensual reporter who penetrates the inner sanctum of the Nicolaites (those who would restore Saint Nicholas to the church) only to discover Black Peter, everyone's favorite hoodoo man and wizard. The shades of Dwight Eisenhower, Harry Truman, and Nelson Rockefeller that President Clift encounters in his Dickensian descent into the American hell are all tortured eternally for their political crimes: Truman for Hiroshima ("Japanese faces, burnt, twisted, and peeling, with no eyeballs"), Rockefeller for the slaughter at Attica.

The story thus far sounds a little morbid, but in *The Terrible Threes*, Reed actually allows some of his characters room for redemption. Diverging significantly away from his Reagan-esque reference, the now-ousted President Clift undergoes a tectonic change in his political views. Once the figurehead, if not architect, of the "Terrible Twos"—the secret plan to eradicate the "surplus" (read: colored) populations around the world and in the United States—Clift now seems to embrace the country's multicultural reality and beauty:

> He had read avidly of the world's literature: from Africa, Asia, India, Afro-America, and he had also talked to many of the contemporary authors and intellectuals from around the world. His speech would quote from the world's literature as well as from the Bible, which, in his view, had been exploited by televangelists and fundamentalists over the years. He could imagine Christ, armed as he

was when he chased the moneylenders from the temple, flogging the TV evangelists until they fled their pulpits. . . . Clift had decided that he would quote sections about the poor and about peace.

What accounts for Clift's repentance? It is in part because he has become victim of the very repressive mechanisms that he used on others—the most radicalizing of situations. More important, Reed seems to suggest his own fantasy of an insurgent coalition of the disenfranchised, one which joins secular and sacred, material and mystical, forces together to foment the kind of social change necessary to produce the semblance of a "revolution." In *The Terrible Threes*, the "true" Black Peter struggles for market dominance against his nemesis, Saint Nicholas, but we realize by the end of the novel that "Bro Peter" and "Bro Nick" derive from the same Yoruban myth. And while the novel ends with the prospect of a year-round Christmas shopping season—aptly called "Xmas forever"—Reed at least opines that the insurgents, now in hiding, may someday reemerge to disrupt the circles of power bent on commodifying and repressing everything.

Writin' Is Fightin'

Reed continues to employ a wide range of genres in conducting his literary and political polemics. It is from *Writin' Is Fightin'* (1988) that he argues that a "black boxer's career is the perfect metaphor for the career of a black male." In that collection of essays he shows that he takes the metaphor very much to heart: "Regardless of the criticisms I receive from the left, the right, and the middle," he vows, "I think it's important to maintain a prolific writing jab, as long as my literary legs hold up." But what's really striking about the metaphor—the image of a one-on-one match—is that it suggests far better odds than most cultural critics give themselves. At least in the twentieth century, the most influential of those writers who have engaged in a sustained, contestatory way with American literary politics—Dwight Macdon-

ald, Edmund Wilson, Lionel Trilling—usually have seen themselves as members of a tiny and embattled mandarinate, surrounded on all sides by the unwashed masses (the title of one of Trilling's essays, "Reflections on a Lost Cause," pretty much captures the tone). Reed speaks for the vernacular against the Latinists, and while he is equally aggrieved, his agon is far more personal.

Writin' Is Fightin' provides an opportunity to assess Reed's evolving role as a cultural critic. It's clear, for example, that Reed differs from most oppositional critics in that, for all his contumely, he genuinely likes his country, likes the particolored cast of contemporary culture. And at the heart of his polemical agenda is an exalted vision of the United States "as a planet-nation—a nation that is generated by diversity and cultural exchange between people of different backgrounds"; in several essays, he explores the diverse traditions bequeathed by the African diaspora in particular. The United States can, he feels, "become a place where the cultures of the world crisscross . . . This is possible because the United States is unique in the world: The world is here." These are the passions of nationalism in the service of internationalism; or possibly vice versa.

Reed's major disputes, accordingly, are with the "educational and cultural Elect"; with the "monoculturalist" who "attempts to impose his small-screen view of political and cultural reality upon a complex world." In the venerable name of "Western civilization," he fears, they want to purge American culture of its rich, multiethnic character, and turn a "thick bouillabaisse" into a thin gruel. As a consequence of such cultural puritanism, Reed observes pungently, "We learn about one another's cultures the same way we learn about sex: in the streets." What concerns him about "the current literary-industrial complex of publishers, critics, writers, and slowpoke academia is that it can see cultural repression when it happens in other states but can't recognize it when it's practiced by its own states." Reed thus displays the one defining feature of the true intellectual: his primary animus is directed against other intellectuals. And here he is implacable. "Many black intellectuals," he charges, "yearn for the kind of one-party police states, operating in the rest of the world, where debate is stifled." As a naturalized Californian, he flaunts the skepticism of his state about the so-called New York intellectual establishment: "One of the reasons the United States seems always to be on the verge of an apocalypse," he informs us soberly, is that "the media are based in New York." In the same oppositional mood, he eloquently champions authors, such as Chester Himes, who were luminaries abroad but suffered critical neglect at home.

Yet Reed may appear to better advantage in his less pugilistic moments. *Writin' Is Fightin'* begins with two autobiographical pieces, "My Oakland: There Is a There There," and more of this self-situating runs through the rest of the book: we learn piecemeal about wife and daughter, about the houses and neighborhoods in which he has lived, and the objects he collects. Mike Davis and other cultural critics have taken Reed to task for what they perceive to be his capitulation to the Reagan-Bush "war on drugs" ideology in the second part of "My Oakland," in which Reed casts black drug dealers as "Black terrorists" and "crack fascists" and even seems to flirt with the idea of imposing a curfew on young *adult* men between the ages of eighteen to twenty-four in Oakland. But it is important to note that Reed also denounces state terrorism in the form of police abuse. The conundrum facing black working-class communities in the Bay Area, and across the country, makes "My Oakland" one of the most complex—and for him, most depressing—essays Reed has ever written. In this essay, Reed wears his pain on his literary sleeve, as he yearns for but cannot see any real solutions for his neighborhood, except to fight a war on its own terms.

Thus although he is cast primarily in the role of being the preeminent black, even American, satirist, Reed's work defies this simplistic category. Even as he takes aim at the myths and lies that keep the United States from becoming the multicultural civilization that he envisions as being its greatest potential, Reed consistently demonstrates in his writing his deep love and advocacy of the working, poor folk who dare to

challenge the skepticism of contemporary intellectuals, who, like their Frankfurt School predecessors, believe in the pervasive alienation of modern life. These are his neighbors on Fifty-third Street in Oakland, a neighborhood where "people look out for one another" even in the most despairing of times. Reed's poetry of the late 1980s highlights this other side of his creative energy, one that is short on the invective and anger for which he is most known, and long on the ironic, tragic, and ultimately human struggles of everyday people living in the midst of palpable mortality. This decidedly unsatirical writing is best seen in one of his most poignant poems, "Oakland Blues" (1988). The piece opens as follows:

> Well it's six o'clock in Oakland
> and the sun is full of wine
> I say, it's six o'clock in Oakland
> and the sun is red with wine
> We buried you this morning, baby
> in the shadow of a vine

Reed's use of the blues is even more deliberate than the form's history of voicing personal and collective pain and injustice. His image of Oakland's evening sun "full" and "red" with wine echoes the famous opening line to W. C. Handy's early twelve-bar "St. Louis Blues": "I hate to see de evenin' sun go down." But while Handy's song tells the story of a woman forlorn for her lover having left town with another (white) woman, Reed's lyric speaks of a deeper loss, that of one left behind after a lover has died. And like the phenomenon of "Jes Grew" in *Mumbo Jumbo*, this feeling belongs to no one in particular and therefore is one shared by everybody.

Even more significant are clues of what the speaker is lamenting, the collective sorrow signaling a larger communal crisis: "they told you of the sickness / almost eighteen months ago / You went down fighting, daddy. Yes / You fought Death toe to toe." Oakland in the 1980s, like other urban communities across the country, was struggling in the throes of the AIDS epidemic. And while the "sickness" of this lost lover could be the result of any number of diseases—natural or human-made—it is hard not to read these lines as an elegy to the disproportionate number of black people who have died from AIDS, those whose suffering would otherwise remain out of sight. Elsewhere in the collection *Points of View*, of which "Oakland Blues" is a part, Reed writes of love as both "full of wine" and "political"—noting that love kills "if you're gay." There is certainly a satirical, even racial, barb in the poem in Reed's juxtaposition of blindingly white egrets flying over Lake Merrit while "blackbirds roost in trees," perhaps an allegory of the uneven development taking place between the more affluent Oakland–Berkeley Hills area and the rest of the deindustrialized city. But the larger arc of "Oakland Blues" takes on the time-worn subjects of love and death, and turns even the clichéd last line of the poem, "footsteps in the dark," into a poignant, blues-inflected moment of mystical *and* urban pathos.

Reckless Eyeballing

There is rarely any distinction between the polemical and the personal with Reed, who disdains the Olympian perch most cultural critics have favored. And like many celebrated heavyweights, who spend half their careers announcing their impending retirement, Reed cannot stay out of the ring for long. Sometimes, of course, critics wish he would. Reed has never been accused of judiciousness, and in the 1980s and 1990s the subject of black feminism has exerted a fascination that has led him occasionally to make bizarre overstatements. And, as we should expect, his animus has taken the form of a novel, *Reckless Eyeballing* (1986), which conjures with a conspiracy theory in which black feminists are pawns of white feminists in their war against black males. When, in *Writin' Is Fightin'*, he calls the male allies of "feminists and womanists" "bimps and wimps," he sounds uncomfortably like the character in *Reckless Eyeballing*, who ties up black feminists and chops off their hair, explaining that this is what the French did to Nazi collaborators.

Japanese by Spring

Likewise, in his 1993 novel *Japanese by Spring*, Reed writes of a milquetoast African American college teacher, Professor Benjamin "Chappie" Puttbutt, whose diatribes against affirmative action, black people (men in particular), and multiculturalism in order to receive tenure at Jack London College seem a redacted typology of the rise of black conservative voices in U.S. cultural debates. This conceit of the novel is significant: Puttbutt has been learning Japanese from a Mr. Yamato, and he later realizes that his lessons with Yamato are propitious for other reasons. Despite the many overtures he makes in an attempt to placate his white colleagues, Puttbutt and his accommodationist antics do not prevent his being denied tenure as a result of a conspiracy between black feminist and white male colleagues. But it is at this point when Puttbutt's Japanese becomes serendipitous: Puttbutt joins forces with Yamato as the elder Japanese man takes over Jack London College and turns it into the seeding ground for a Shogunite revival. The new administration appoints Puttbutt as second in command, and the now-powerful Puttbutt helps Yamato eradicate all Western influences in the curriculum. Soon, however, Puttbutt becomes disillusioned with Yamato (who imprisons and tortures his dissenters) and works with his father, a black air force general, to thwart the Japanese regime and reinstall the old order.

Throughout the novel, Reed's satire cuts across a whole range of figures and scenes, not the least of which is the story's conceit: that of an impending Asian takeover. Reed clearly is pressing on an issue pervasive during the late 1980s and early 1990s, namely, the fear of an "Asian invasion," whether of actual people (a fear made most obvious when one regards the surge in anti-Asian hate crimes) or of Asian-based products (which help spur on such violence). But in floating the idea of what the United States or the world might look like if a non-Western culture assumed hegemony, Reed suggests that ethnocentrism would still prevail. One chauvinism is replaced by another, and eventually is displaced once again. Yet within this shuttling of power lies Ishmael Reed, himself a character in the novel, who works as the narrative's trickster figure, disrupting Western and non-Western attempts at domination and calling to others to form a multicultural band of rebels bent on ridiculing the power-brokers, whether in higher education or elsewhere.

Yet even here, Reed displays a bizarre attitude with regard to gender. We learn of Puttbutt's ignominious past, of his affair with a Japanese wife of a former teacher. Upon the discovery, the teacher beheads his wife and kills himself; Puttbutt is expelled. Although Reed has rightly pointed out that many of those who have criticized him for advocating misogyny have not read his work, scenes such as these lend credence to a certain problematic that continues to keep Reed embroiled in controversy over his attitude toward feminism and women in general. And while he approvingly cites a black feminist to the effect that the rift between black men and women is "media inspired," Reed fails to see how his own divisive polemics against "feminist ideologues" plays into this factitious media event. This is not to deny that legitimate criticisms can be made about those feminists who perpetuate ideologies of racial or sexual essentialism. But it must be said that feminism has not been waiting for Ishmael Reed to set it straight: black feminists such as Angela Davis and Bell Hooks have already delivered the critique, loud and clear.

Airing Dirty Laundry

Reed has continued to cast barbs against a "media-industrial complex" that he believes has it in for black people, and especially black men. In his 1993 collection of essays, *Airing Dirty Laundry*, Reed again plays advocate for black men given infamous spotlight—Clarence Thomas, Mike Tyson, rap artists such as Big Daddy Kane and Ice-T—and rails against the "McIntellectuals" and other pundits who glibly throw around terms like "underclass" without full exposition of either its concept or its cultural implications. Reed names names here, never pulling a punch to call out specific re-

porters whom he feels have made careers on the (misrepresented) backs of black people. Yet equally significant in *Airing Dirty Laundry* are Reed's attempts to understand and find solidarity with other oppressed groups: "An Outsider in Koreatown" displays Reed's struggles to make connections between black poverty (which he does not believe is a result of an "underclass" pathology), the underpaid, superexploited travails of Latinos who have become the dominant group in Southern California's plurality, and the ordeals of Korean Americans who suffered the destruction of their mom-and-pop stores during the 1992 uprisings in Los Angeles that followed the Rodney King trial. And while much of the critical response to *Airing Dirty Laundry* has centered around his castigation of certain groups—mainly white gays and feminists, for buying into the stereotypes of black men—most of the collection focuses on Reed's advocacy of underreported, unnoticed writers, artists, and activists such as Elaine Brown, John Edgar Wideman, and Paul Robeson. Most significantly and above all, Reed champions—as is evident in his essay "American Poetry: Is There a Center?"—younger and less-publicized writers whose work quietly pushes the edges and indeed shifts the center of the core of U.S. poetry. True culture, Reed suggests, does not lie in the hands of those broadcasting fallacious visions of black and brown people on CNN or preparing yet another series of articles on the "underclass" in the *New York Times*. Instead, American culture is located most preciously in its younger poets, those whom he regards are most open to the migrancy of sensibility: "A lot of American poets can't sit in one position that long because they're itching from spirits and can't keep still. Demons pour out of their mouths and issue from their fingertips. Others may have their Fourth Estate but poets have their Estate of the Second Sight Seers." It is on behalf of these culture movers, most of all, that Reed feels that he must continue to be the metaphorical boxer in the literary world.

Reed is widely viewed as the best satirist in the African American tradition today, and satire, especially one filled with diatribe against the United States' most cherished institutions, has never been a very nice sport. Yet for Reed, investing himself so much in the "culture wars" is the only way to achieve what he calls "cultural peace," one in which the United States can finally welcome rather than grudgingly tolerate its capacity to become what he calls "multi-America." It is this vision that he wants us to take seriously, and perhaps nothing else. Everything else, he acknowledges, whether the myths he continues to debunk, or the controversies around his own work that he often enflames, demands yet another send-up and roasting.

A critic would be foolhardy indeed to try to predict the future course of Reed's work; but posterity will, most likely, take little interest in his hobbyhorses and pet peeves. His best work resists being reduced to any political or social message. What is so easy to forget—and so important to remember—is that Reed, complex artist that he is, tells a good story. One tends to be surprised by just how funny, and erotic, he can be simply by naming for us the deeper structures, myths, and presuppositions by which we, and contemporary American society, order our lives. But of course, there's nothing "simple" about telling a tale that is both humorous and riveting and simultaneously teaches its audience a lesson, with the magical indirection of the best parables and allegories. For all the ire that he generates, it is therefore no surprise that Reed received the MacArthur Fellowship in 1998, one of only twenty-nine recipients that year. Yet even this accolade will probably not deter him for raising eyebrows or tempers again.

Whatever direction his work takes, Ishmael Reed, like his biblical namesake, will be recalled at least in part for his self-willed expulsion from the literary tradition that he parodies, for his fierce political and literary individuality, and for his skill as a satirist. But it may be that, in the end, we read him because he names things for us, as any great orator or preacher does: He fingers for us "the jagged grain" of our character, the ways in which our very identities can be used to manipulate us; he lays bare the invisible network within which we are bound and regulated, and which few will admit exists.

Ishmael Reed, like the greatest black comics (and the phrase is intended in both senses) tells us not only who we are and where we as a society are, but why.

Selected Bibliography

PRIMARY WORKS

NOVELS

The Free-lance Pallbearers. Garden City, N.Y.: Doubleday, 1967.
Yellow Back Radio Broke-Down. Garden City, N.Y.: Doubleday, 1969.
Mumbo Jumbo. Garden City, N.Y.: Doubleday, 1972.
The Last Days of Louisiana Red. New York: Random House, 1974.
Flight to Canada. New York: Random House, 1976.
The Terrible Twos. New York: St. Martin's Press/Marek, 1982.
Reckless Eyeballing. New York: St. Martin's Press, 1986.
The Terrible Threes. New York: Atheneum, 1989.
Japanese by Spring. New York: Atheneum, 1993.

POETRY

Catechism of d neoamerican hoodoo church. London: P. Breman, 1971.
Conjure: Selected Poems, 1963–1970. Amherst: University of Massachusetts Press, 1972.
Chattanooga: Poems. New York: Random House, 1973.
A Secretary to the Spirits. New York: NOK, 1978.
Cab Calloway Stands in for the Moon. Flint, Mich.: Bamberger, 1986.
New and Collected Poems. New York: Atheneum, 1988. (Includes the collection *Points of View.*)

ESSAYS

Shrovetide in Old New Orleans. Garden City, N.Y.: Doubleday, 1978.
God Made Alaska for the Indians: Selected Essays. New York: Garland, 1982.
Writin' Is Fightin': Thirty-seven Years of Boxing on Paper. New York: Atheneum, 1988.
Airing Dirty Laundry. Reading, Mass.: Addison-Wesley, 1993.

PLAYS

The Ace Boons. 1980.
Hell Hath No Fury. 1982. (Later titled *Mother Hubbard.*)

ANTHOLOGIES EDITED BY REED

Nineteen Necromancers from Now. Garden City, N.Y.: Doubleday, 1970.
Yardbird Lives! Edited with Al Young. New York: Grove Press, 1978.

Calafia: The California Poetry. Berkeley, Calif.: Yardbird, 1979.

The Before Columbus Foundation Fiction Anthology. Edited with Kathryn Trueblood and Shawn Wong. New York: Norton, 1992.

Multi-America: Essays on Cultural War and Peace. New York: Viking, 1997.

SECONDARY WORKS

BIOGRAPHICAL AND CRITICAL STUDIES

Carter, Steven R. "Ishmael Reed's Neo Hoo Doo Detection." In *Dimensions of Detective Fiction.* Edited by Larry Landrum, Pat Browne, and Roy B. Browne. Bowling Green, Ohio: Popular Press, 1976. Pp. 265–90.

Cowley, Julian. "What If I Write Circuses?: The Space of Ishmael Reed's Fiction." *Callaloo* 17, no. 4:1236–44 (Fall 1994).

Davis, Charles T. *Black Is the Color of the Cosmos: Essays on Afro-American Literature and Culture, 1942–1981.* Edited by Henry Louis Gates Jr. New York: Garland, 1982. Reprint, Washington, D.C.: Howard University Press, 1989.

Davis, Matthew R. " 'Strange, History. Complicated, Too': Ishmael Reed's Use of African-American History in *Flight to Canada.*" *Mississippi Quarterly* 49, no. 4:743–44 (Fall 1996).

Davis, Robert Murray. "Scatting the Myths: Ishmael Reed." *Arizona Quarterly* 39, no. 4:406–20 (Winter 1983).

De Arman, Charles. "The Black Image in the Black Mind: Or, *Flight to Canada.*" *CLA Journal* 33, no. 2:157–77 (December 1989).

Dick, Bruce, and Amritjit Singh, eds. *Conversations with Ishmael Reed.* Jackson: University of Mississippi Press, 1995.

Ford, Nick Aaron. "A Note on Ishmael Reed: Revolutionary Novelist." *Studies in the Novel* 3:216–18 (Summer 1971).

Fox, Robert Elliot. "Blacking the Zero: Toward a Semiotics of Neo-Hoodoo." *Black American Literature Forum* 18, no. 3:95–99 (Fall 1984).

———. *Conscientious Sorcerers: The Black Postmodernist Fiction of LeRoi Jones/Amiri Baraka, Ishmael Reed, and Samuel R. Delany.* Westport, Conn.: Greenwood, 1987.

Gates, Henry Louis Jr. " 'The Blackness of Blackness': A Critique of the Sign and the Signifying Monkey." *Critical Inquiry* 9, no. 4:685–723 (June 1983). Reprinted in *Figures in Black: Words, Signs, and the "Racial" Self.* New York: Oxford University Press, 1987. Pp. 235–76.

Harris, Norman. "The Gods Must Be Angry: *Flight to Canada* as Political History." *Modern Fiction Studies* 34, no. 1:111–23 (Spring 1988).

Henry, Joseph. "A *MELUS* Interview: Ishmael Reed." *MELUS* 11, no. 1:81–93 (Spring 1984).

Hoffman, Donald L. "A Darker Shade of Grail: Questing at the Crossroads in Ishmael Reed's *Mumbo Jumbo.*" *Callaloo* 17, no. 4:1245–56 (Fall 1994).

Howe, Irving. Review of *The Free-Lance Pallbearers. Harper's Magazine* December 1969, pp. 130–41.

Hume, Kathryn. "Ishmael Reed and the Problematics of Control." *PMLA* 108, no. 3:506–18 (May 1993).

Jessee, Sharon A. "Laughter and Identity in Ishmael Reed's *Mumbo Jumbo.*" *MELUS* 21, no. 4:127–39 (Winter 1996).

Johnson, Carol S. "The Limbs of Osiris: Reed's *Mumbo Jumbo* and Hollywood's *The Mummy.*" *MELUS* 17, no. 4:105–15 (Winter 1991).

Johnson, Lemuel A. " 'Ain'ts,' 'Us 'ens,' and 'Mother Dear': Issues in the Language of Madhubuti, Jones, and Reed." *Journal of Black Studies* 10:139–66 (December 1979).

Joye, Barbara. "Literature of Race and Culture: Satire and Alienation in Soulville." *Phylon* 29, no. 4:410–12 (1968).

Klinkowitz, Jerome. "Ishmael Reed." In *The Life of Fiction.* Urbana: University of Illinois Press, 1977. Pp. 117–27.

Lindroth, James. "Images of Subversion: Ishmael Reed and the Hoodoo Trickster." *African American Review* 30, no. 2:185–96 (Summer 1996).

Lowe, John. "Monkey Kings and Mojo: Postmodern Ethnic Humor in Kingston, Reed, and Vizenor." *MELUS* 21, no. 4:103–26 (Winter 1996).

Ludwig, Sami. "Ishmael Reed's Inductive Narratology of Detection." *African American Review* 32, no. 3:435–44 (Fall 1998).

Mackey, Nathaniel. "Ishmael Reed and the Black Aesthetic." *CLA Journal* 21:355–66 (March 1978).

Martin, Reginald. *Ishmael Reed and the New Black Aesthetic Critics.* London: Macmillan, 1986.

———. "The Freelance Pallbearer Confronts the Terrible Threes: Ishmael Reed and the New Black Aesthetic Critics." *MELUS* 14, no. 2:35–49 (Summer 1987).

Mason, Theodore O., Jr. "Performance, History, and Myth: The Problem of Ishmael Reed's *Mumbo-Jumbo.*" *Modern Fiction Studies* 34, no. 1:97–109 (Spring 1988).

McGee, Patrick. *Ishmael Reed and the Ends of Race.* New York: St. Martin's, 1997.

McKenzie, James. "Pole Vaulting in Top Hats: A Public Conversation with John Barth, William Gass, and Ishmael Reed." *Modern Fiction Studies* 22:131–51 (Summer 1976).

Medwick, Lucille. "The Afro-American Poet in New York." *New York Quarterly*, no. 6:102–18 (1971).

Northouse, Cameron. "Ishmael Reed." In *Conversations with Writers.* Vol. 2. Detroit: Gale Research, 1977. Pp. 212–54.

O'Brien, John, ed. "Ishmael Reed." In *Interviews with Black Writers.* New York: Liveright, 1973. Pp. 165–83.

Punday, Daniel. "Ishmael Reed's Rhetorical Turn: Uses of 'Signifying' in *Reckless Eyeballing.*" *College English* 54, no. 4:446–61 (April 1992).

Review of Contemporary Fiction 4, no. 2 (Summer 1984). Special issue devoted to Ishmael Reed.

Schmitz, Neil. "Neo-HooDoo: The Experimental Fiction of Ishmael Reed." *Twentieth Century Literature* 20:126–40 (April 1974).

———. "The Gumbo That Jes Grew." *Partisan Review* 42, no. 2:311–16 (1975).

Stepto, Robert. *From Behind the Veil: A Study of Afro-American Narrative*. Urbana: University of Illinois Press, 1979. 2d ed., 1991.

Stepto, Robert, and Michael S. Harper, eds. *Chant of Saints: A Gathering of Afro-American Literature, Art, and Scholarship*. Urbana: University of Illinois Press, 1979.

Turner, Darwin. "A Spectrum of Blackness." *Parnassus* 4, no. 2:202–19 (Spring/Summer 1976).

Walsh, Richard. " 'A Man's Story Is His Gris-Gris': Cultural Slavery, Literary Emancipation, and Ishmael Reed's *Flight to Canada*." *Journal of American Studies* 27, no. 1:57–71 (April 1993).

Watkins, Mel. "An Interview with Ishmael Reed." *Southern Review* 21, no. 3:603–14 (Summer 1985).

Weixlman, Joe. "Politics, Piracy, and Other Games: Slavery and Liberation in *Flight to Canada*." *MELUS* 6, no. 3:41–50 (1979).

———. "African American Deconstruction of the Novel in the Work of Ishmael Reed and Clarence Major." *MELUS* 17, no. 4:57–79 (Winter 1991).

Zamir, Shamoon. "The Artist as Prophet, Priest, and Gunslinger: Ishmael Reed's 'Cowboy in the Boat of Ra.' " *Callaloo* 17, no. 4:1205–35 (Fall 1994).

BIBLIOGRAPHY

Settle, Elizabeth A., and Thomas Settle. *Ishmael Reed: A Primary and Secondary Bibliography*. Boston: G. K. Hall, 1982.

—The essay and bibliography have been revised for this edition by James K. Lee.

NTOZAKE SHANGE
(1948–)

SANDRA L. RICHARDS

BLACK WOMAN, POET, playwright, dancer, and mother, Ntozake Shange explores life's "nappy edges," the metaphoric terrain just beyond neatly fixed social definitions. There, the sweat of pursuing an intimate, humane connection with the world as well as with one's innermost selves is manifested as a dynamic, affirmative rawness. Hers is a holistic vision within which language, music, movement, icon, and time and space are manipulated so that poetry becomes drama and dance; the political is simultaneously the aesthetic and the personal; and spirituality offers insights which ultimately empower one to grapple with a problematic social world.

With the 1976 production of *for colored girls who have considered suicide/ when the rainbow is enuf*, Ntozake Shange exploded upon the American national consciousness, claiming for black women a beauty and artistic validity previously denied them. Though her subsequent theater texts have failed to garner the controversial public attention accorded that first play, Shange has nonetheless remained a significant voice in American theater. Among the hallmarks of her distinctive style are a disregard for conventional, linear dramatic structure; a crafting of arresting, poetic imagery; shrewd manipulation of nonrational modes of insight; and daring commitment to what are perceived as personal and public truths. In the context of American theater, Shange's dramaturgy is most closely related to that of Adrienne Kennedy and Amiri Baraka; within a larger Western tradition, her most immediate references are the French playwright Antonin Artaud and the German Bertolt Brecht. Though these four writers may appear quite different, particularly in relation to their interest in sociopolitical issues, they are similar in their pursuit of dramatic forms that do not reside wholly within a Euro-American framework. For Artaud and Brecht, inspiration was to be found in the nonillusionist theaters of Asia; for Kennedy, Baraka, and Shange herself, the creative source is African culture as lived in the diaspora.

Born Paulette Williams on 18 October 1948, to surgeon Paul T. Williams and psychiatric social worker Eloise Owens Williams, Shange was raised initially in Trenton, New Jersey. The oldest of four children, she seems to have enjoyed a childhood blessed with material security and loving parents who traveled widely, maintained an international set of friends, and transmitted a pride in African and African American cultures. They exposed the precocious girl to a variety of influences ranging from musicians Dizzy Gillespie and Chuck Berry to writers like Paul Laurence Dunbar, Countee Cullen, and T. S. Eliot. Sunday-afternoon family variety shows might consist of her mother offering selections from Shakespeare, her father performing magic tricks or improvising on the congas, and the children doing a soft-shoe or playing such instruments as the violin, cello, flute, and saxophone. As she was later to reveal in a self-interview entitled "i talk to myself," included in her 1978 poetry collection *Nappy Edges*, family members voraciously pursued whichever arts struck their fancy, so that "any explorations of personal visions waz the focus of my world."

When Shange was eight, the family moved to St. Louis, Missouri, where they lived for five years. There she was among the first black children to integrate the public school system. As later fictionalized in the novel *Betsey Brown* (1985), that experience seemingly left a sense of anger and betrayal at being thrust out of the security of the black community into the known violence of the white world. But apparently it also strengthened Shange's fighting spirit and pride in her own abilities, for in the poem "nappy edges (a cross country sojourn)" she answers actual and would-be oppressors:

> my dreams run to meet aunt marie
> my dreams draw blood from ol sores
> these stains & scars are mine
> this is my space
> i am not movin
> (*Nappy Edges*, p. 88)

Though her parents took a keen interest in events throughout the African diaspora, that progressive perspective was nonetheless counterbalanced by a black, middle-class conservatism. As a means of advancing in America, its adherents preached individual initiative and a noblesse oblige understood through W. E. B. Du Bois's "talented tenth" model of relating to the impoverished masses; repression of sexual impulses and other potentially nonconformist instincts; and disavowal of unrefined aspects of African American culture, as often defined by the white mainstream. As Shange admitted in a 1976 *Village Voice* interview with Michelle Wallace, the vacuousness of that class perspective initially led her to rebel by adopting the idioms of the live-in maids who had cared for

her as a child. Indeed, only some nine years later with the lush rite-of-passage novel *Betsey Brown* would she be able to represent aspects of her middle-class background.

When Paulette Williams was thirteen, the family moved back to New Jersey, settling this time in Lawrenceville. She had written short stories in elementary school but had been deterred by racial insults. Similarly, at Morristown High School she wrote poetry, some of which was published in the school magazine, but derogatory comments concerning her choice of black subject matter caused her to again abandon this mode of self-expression. During these years she became progressively more frustrated that young black girls had virtually no appropriate models of success. As she confided in the Wallace interview, "There was nothing to aspire to, no one to honor. Sojourner Truth wasn't a big enough role model for me. I couldn't go around abolishing slavery."

In 1966, Williams entered Barnard College; a year later, at the age of nineteen, she attempted suicide, despondent over a recent separation from her law-school husband and enraged at a society that penalized intelligent, purposeful women. Although she made three other suicide attempts during these college years, she also managed to graduate from Barnard with honors in American Studies in 1970. Relocating to Los Angeles, Williams pursued formal education by enrolling in a master's program in American Studies at the University of Southern California and furthered an informal apprenticeship by living with other writers, dancers, and musicians. In 1971 two South African friends baptized her in the Pacific Ocean with a name selected to express the personality she was already manifesting. Thus, she became Ntozake, meaning "she who brings her own things," and Shange, "one who walks with lions."

After earning a master's degree in 1973, Shange moved north to the San Francisco Bay Area, where she taught humanities and women's studies courses at Mills College in Oakland, the University of California Extension, San Francisco, and Sonoma State College, Sonoma. She reports in an essay documenting the history of *for colored girls . . .* that working with such po-

Ntozake Shange

ets and teachers as J. J. Wilson, Wopo Holup, and Joanna Griffin allowed her to delve further into women's history and to theorize via poetry on the quality of women's experiences such that seemingly disparate figures like Isis, Calamity Jane, Zora Neale Hurston, and Anna May Wong could be linked.

San Francisco, which had nurtured an earlier generation of Beat poets, at that time offered a fertile environment in which the talents of Third World and white women artists could particularly flourish. Janice Mirikitani, Jessica Hagedorn, Avotcja, Carol Lee Sanchez, Kitty Tsui, Thulani, and others were exploring through poetry the implications of liberation movements as they affected the lives of women of color, while white women like Susan Griffin, Barbara Gravelle, and Judy Grahn, whose book of poems *The Common Woman* (1973) would serve as a model for *for colored girls* . . . , were

similarly rejecting the claims of patriarchy. Bars like Specs, Malvina's, Minnie's Can-Do Club, the Coffee Gallery, and Ribeltad Vorden sponsored poetry readings, and small presses like Shameless Hussy and the Oakland Women's Press Collective published women's writings.

Incorporating the writing of men as well as women, Janice Mirikitani coproduced during this period a sassy, first-of-its-kind anthology of American-born Third World writers, *Time to Greez! Incantations from the Third World* (1975). Included in this volume was Shange's "Steada Slingin Hash/Waltzin Proper & Wanderin Demure," a poem that unlike many others has not reappeared in any of her collected poetry, plays, or novels.

At this time Shange was reciting poetry with the Third World Collective and was also dancing with Raymond Sawyer and Ed Mock, whose class routines and formal choreography linked specific folk traditions of West Africa and the Caribbean to the vaudeville and street dance traditions of Afro-America. By discovering in movement some of the intricacies and strengths of her identity as a black woman, Shange found that she was also discovering her voice as a poet. Thus, as she was to write in describing the creative context of her San Francisco years, "The freedom to move in space, to demand of my own sweat a perfection that could continually be approached, though never known, waz poem to me, my body & mind ellipsing, probably for the first time in my life."

The theme of the body and dance as sites of a knowledge whose rhythms constitute poetry is one to which Shange would return again and again. Its importance is related to her likely exposure at this time to such New World African religions as Vodun, found in Haiti, and Santéia, practiced in Cuba. The famed choreographer Katherine Dunham had established a basic vocabulary for black dance instruction based upon her field research in the Caribbean. Teachers like Sawyer could be expected to have followed Dunham's practice of educating students concerning the social and religious contexts out of which the various body isolations or movements grew. Choreographer Halifu Osumare remembers that during this time Shange was collaborating with musicians and dancers who practiced Sant"ia, and that it was partially because of Shange's familiarity with African religious practices that she cast Shange as a priestess in her 1973 dance-drama "The Evolution of Black Dance." Representing the syncretism of West African belief systems of the Fon and Yoruba with Roman Catholicism, these diasporic religions would contribute significantly to the aesthetic structure and vocabulary of Shange's works.

Osumare's troupe The Spirit of Dance offered Shange her first experience of women's theater, for the ensemble of four women performed in the Oakland and Berkeley public schools as part of Ethnic Studies offerings. Not only did Shange learn strategies for producing pieces with few financial resources, but—as she reports in the preface to her first theater piece—she also became imbued with Osumare's confidence in the legitimacy of their own women-centered/African-centered visions. After seventy-three performances, Shange left the company in the summer of 1974 to collaborate with Paula Moss, a horn trio called The Sound Clinic, and Jean Desarmes & His Raggae Blues Band. The various poems, dance, and music on which they worked would be called *for colored girls who have considered suicide/ when the rainbow is enuf.*

The initial locations for these performances were the same ones she had frequented earlier. Starting with Joanna Griffin's Bacchanal Bar near Berkeley, the group played other bars, caf", Women's Studies departments, and poetry centers. The response was positive, as poets, dancers, and feminists showed up to support this new vision of theater, and *The Bay Guardian* dubbed the ensemble a "must see" event. Buoyed by their success, Paula Moss and Shange drove across country to present "the show," as it was simply called then, at the Studio Rivbea in New York. The production continued to change and assume a more crystalline shape, as Oz Scott was brought in first to advise and then to direct, and dancers like Aku Kadogo and Laurie Carlos joined the group. Enthusiastic word of mouth grew with every change in venue, so that the piece catapulted out of the intimacy of

the bars first when Woodie King first produced it as a showcase at the Henry Street Settlement House, and then when Joseph Papp optioned it for the Public Theater. Papp subsequently took the show to the Booth Theater on Broadway, where it opened in September 1976 before going on to tour nationally and internationally.

The production of *for colored girls . . .* was like nothing America had previously experienced. Jettisoning the national preference for linearly structured, realistic plays, the text manipulated poetry and dance so as to create a swirl of imagery, emotions, colors, and movement proclaiming a woman's experience a fit subject for dramatic representation. For many women and men, the performance became akin to a consciousness-raising event. At the outset, seven women, distinguishable from each other primarily by the color of their simple dresses, set forth the image of a black girl

[who's] been dead so long
closed in silence so long
she doesn't know the sound
of her own voice
her infinite beauty
                                            (p. 4)

They announce that what is to follow is a gift or a song calculated to restore her to life. The subsequent collage of danced poems—or "choreopoem," as Shange labeled the text—traces a black girl's eager transition from adolescence (high school graduation and loss of virginity) into an adulthood of stormy relationships with men and eventual self-recognition of a personhood whose legitimacy is divinely natural. Yet, because the women play multiple unnamed characters, what emerges is not an individual protagonist but an essential Every-woman.

Moments of transcendence intersect with what Shange was later to call a labored breathing necessitated by the attempt to withstand racist and sexist social definitions. To the exuberant 1960 sounds of the Motown rhythm-and-blues songs about love, the women initially do the pony, the swim, and other popular dance steps. Sliding effortlessly into the Afro-Latin beat of Willie Colon, they also execute the merengue and the bomba, all in celebration of the wondrous vitality of their bodies and graduation from "mama to what ever waz out there." But a sudden lighting change pierces their joy, plunging them into a misogynist, material realm.

One early poem is particularly remarkable, for it conjoins definitions of woman and of theater treated separately throughout much of the play. Most simply expressed, "sechita" concerns a down-on-her-luck tent dancer who performs for the country yokels in Natchez, Tennessee, while dreaming of the bygone, elegant quadroon balls in St. Louis, Missouri. The splendor of a Creole society insulated from the hostility of poor whites is fleetingly suggested as a counterpoint to the dancer's tawdry, patchwork circumstances in which female sexuality, constructed so as to titillate male desire, is the currency for insuring economic survival. Accustomed to gin-stained, itchy black stockings and a mirror which "made her forehead tilt backwards/ her cheeks appear sunken/," Sechita cannot dispel the feeling that here in Natchez humiliation is not merely societal but natural, for "god seemed to be wipin his feet in her face/." Thus, dissociating her soul from her person, she dances to reassert her primal connections, seemingly ever more vigorously the more the drunken men aim gold coins between her thighs.

Because Sechita is not simply an object of male fantasy, the actress must do more than narrate a story of degradation. She must also exhort a powerful subject or agent to make her presence known. For that reason, the actress utters the character's praise names: "the full moon/ sechita/ goddess/ of love/ egypt/ the 2nd millennium." Through sound, rhythm, and repetition, through what the Yorubas of West Africa term *ase,* or the power to make things happen (which resides in language), she strives to call into being that primordial spirit who presides over the perpetuation of life. Similarly, the performer who dances Sechita's narrative both retraces the ancestral history of female agony and partakes of divine potency. Her experience potentially approximates that of a Vodun devotee who, in dancing and opening her body

to trance, serves as a medium of the gods and thereby reconnects herself and the community to all history, past, present, and yet unlived. Through the dynamic of conjuring, as manipulated by speaker, dancer, and musician, Sechita is presented victorious, kicking past the coins thrown onto the makeshift stage to commune with the stars. The poem has thus operated within an African conception of theater, being simultaneously representational and presentational, functioning both to construct a fictive event as though it were real and to constitute a moment of transcendence when, dependent on the performers' skills and the audience's beliefs, the human and the divine merge in the body of the dancer.

From this moment of union follows a series of vignettes, most of which are firmly anchored within recognizable social realities and structured to operate within a representational mode. A young girl finds an adolescent hero who might match the Toussaint L'Ouverture of her dreams; a West Coast transplant to Harlem learns that the slightest hint of openness in this urban jungle invites psychological and physical aggression; and three friends find through male betrayal a sisterhood that both binds them together and isolates each one in grief. But the yearning for intimacy is now coupled with an insistence upon the part of this collective protagonist that she be accepted for what she is: a colored girl (read nonwhite), big-hipped, scarred by a rage and strength inflicted by racism, consigned to scavenging through jazz and rhythm and blues for a way out of pain. Locating herself in a matrix that precedes gender designations, this heroine improvises an affirmation that serves to clear the air for the choreopoem's funniest and most devastating moments.

"Somebody almost walked off wid alla my stuff" introduces the kind of blues humor that arises when an individual has gained sufficient perspective on catastrophe to joke and transmute private despair into a public declaration of survival. The degree to which that articulation is made with wit, telling imagery, and a sense of mastery—in effect, a grace under pressure—determines the blues piece's overall artistry. Against urban rhythms that play with the multiple, contradictory connotations of black street language, the speaking voice in "somebody . . ." constructs from such mundane items as old skirts, fried plantains, Sun-Ra records, dance steps, and poems a series of images that collectively constitute her "stuff," or self. In much the same way as her lover fails to recognize her as a sentient, vulnerable being, she humorously portrays herself as an object of little worth in order to emphasize her eventual recognition that value is foremost self-determined, and relationships must be built upon mutual respect for and sharing of each person's "stuff." The other women ratify this position by further extending blues humor. Adopting familiar, male gestures and intellectualizations, they rehearse a variety of "i'm sorry" poses used to rationalize callous behavior. Furthermore, boldly claiming responsibility for their own actions, they challenge men to do likewise, while relishing the reversal of roles and enjoying being undependable and insensitive.

Seemingly, their self-confident wit has had a cathartic effect that enables one woman to voice a history, to which all other male-female encounters significantly pale in comparison. "A nite with beau willie brown" recounts the gradual collapse of a family unit plagued by poverty, poor education, domestic violence, and post-combat trauma. After years of suffering at the hands of her childhood sweetheart Beau Willie Brown, twenty-two-year-old Crystal has obtained a restraining order denying him access to their children, Naomi and Kwame. But Beau Willie claims that he wants to function as a father and husband. Nightmares about atrocities committed in Vietnam, memories of failed attempts to economically support the family, and confused equations between family unity and increased veterans' benefits mix with alcohol and other drugs to propel this deeply troubled man into attempting a scenario of familial reunification and personal justification. Suddenly he projects kindness, so that first his daughter and next Crystal relax their vigilance. Then with the two young children dangling from his arms out the opened window, and the neighbors screaming at him in horror, Beau Willie demands that Crystal promise to marry

him. When seemingly she can respond neither quickly or loudly enough, he drops Naomi and Kwame five flights to their death.

The power of this poem, which in performance is usually met with total silence, stems not only from the sustained image of social dysfunction but also from the treatment of voice or enunciatory stance of the speaker. That is, to signal her distance from the material, the actress deploys a third-person narrative throughout most of the poem. Occasionally she switches into direct quotation in order to represent Crystal's scathing responses to Beau Willie's repeated, desperate marriage proposals. Only at the last horrific moment does she utilize the first person. The effect is as though actress and character have merged into one undifferentiated identity, as though through the process of retelling the speaker has finally obliterated all distance to name her pain and fully embrace the misogyny to which women are vulnerable. As in the "sechita" poem, representational and presentational modes coincide, but in contrast to that earlier piece, here the trajectory is not upward toward a transcendent triumph.

From a shared low the women must endeavor to rise. Echoing and extending each other's thoughts, they admit to missing a spiritual sensibility. But because these women are ignorant of their own holiness, the transfer of an energy external to the supplicant, usually accomplished by a laying on of hands, will not suffice. Rather, each one must undertake an individual quest. Thus, events in the closing poem are structured according to the experiences of trance and testifying. The lady in red, who had related "a nite with beau willie brown," now speaks of a crisis situation in which she had wished for death or some release from feelings. From too much emotion she next succumbs to a numbness in which it seems as though she merges with the natural world. Successively baptized by cold, heat, dawn, and tears, she is released into the intuition, "i found god in myself/ & i loved her/." Having offered this verbal testimonial, she repeats her insight, this time seeking to register its abstract force in the rhythms of an improvised song. Tentatively at first, the other women join this chant, creating out of it a gospel song, which as it gathers in volume and emotional intensity, captures the emerging confidence of "colored girls" who have moved beyond racial and gender distortions to discover the ends of their own self-determined rainbows.

The initial production and subsequent national tour of *for colored girls . . .* garnered praise throughout the media, vaulting Ntozake Shange overnight into a celebrity status from which, as she would later acknowledge, it would take years to recover a sense of privacy and focus. It provoked an avalanche of responses that seemingly became a barometer of audience members' identification with larger, feminist issues. As suggested earlier, for many women and men the text was refreshingly honest in naming some of the tensions experienced in heterosexual relationships. Feminism, heretofore represented primarily as the preserve of middle-class, white women, was seen to have tangible relevance to the lives of black women and women of color.

But for some in the black community in particular, the text constituted a virulent attack that left untouched the real power source, namely, white men. No positive male-female interactions were presented, and the "beau willie" poem, coming at the end of a long catalog of male insensitivities, functioned so as to accuse all black men of pathological behavior. For that reason, argued proponents of this view, white male critics, whose positions with New York newspapers gave them national influence, could celebrate a newly discovered humanity with black women; they could publicly rejoice in feeling not the least bit threatened, as they presumably had been by the earlier Black Arts plays of Amiri Baraka and others.

In this black community debate, two somewhat separable issues were conflated, namely the audience's interpretation or production of meaning and the media's hegemonic function in shaping individual responses to reinforce values espoused by the dominant power structure. While there is a certain validity to the textual objections concerning Shange's portrayal of black men, the animus behind some of the negative responses seems more related to the latter

issue of the media's function. That is, *for colored girls . . .* violated the unspoken code of the 1960s by rejecting the equation of black liberation with male privilege. In bringing certain "family" or intraracial problems out of the proverbial closet, the text appeared to validate existing negative stereotypes used to rationalize the oppression of black men. Moreover, it did so in an arena that has historically denied black men and women significant opportunities for projecting their own counternarratives.

But ironically, were it not for a mass media controlled by white men, the text never would have involved large numbers of black people in a much-needed reexamination of male-female relationships. There is yet another irony about which virtually no critic has commented. That is, most of the representations of Shange and the actresses in photographs, posters, or interviews projected images of anger or extreme distress. Underneath all the notoriety and praise was a subtext of aberrant behavior, an insinuation that the play's feminist message could be attributed to suicidal impulses. From either standpoint, white patriarchy was clearly the beneficiary. But as the foregoing discussion has demonstrated, it is nonetheless possible to produce readings that resist these hegemonic designs and refigure the black woman as a self-empowered subject.

The New York years 1976—1982 were quite productive for Shange. The Public Theater produced such plays as *A Photograph: A Still Life with Shadows / A Photograph: A Study in Cruelty* and *Where the Mississippi Meets the Amazon* (1977), *Spell #7* (1979), and *Mother Courage & Her Children* (1980), an adaptation of Bertolt Brecht's play, and Dianne McIntyre's dance company produced *Black & White Two-Dimensional Planes* (1979) and *It Has Not Always Been This Way* (1981). *Boogie Woogie Landscapes* (1979) was first produced by the Frank Silvera Writers' Workshop; *Mouths* (1981), which was subsequently revised as *From Okra to Greens* and produced by the Mark Taper Forum Lab in Los Angeles as *Three For a Full Moon and Bocas*, was initially produced at The Kitchen, New York City, and the Women's Interart Center in New York sponsored *Dream*

Laurie Carlos and Ntozake Shange in a scene from *for colored girls*.

Dwellings (1981), an installation and performance piece for which Shange collaborated with Wopo Holup.

Shange's *for colored girls* . . . won the 1977 Obie, Outer Critics Circle, Audelco, and *Mademoiselle* awards and received Tony, Grammy, and Emmy nominations. Her Brecht adaptation brought her a 1981 Obie; the collection of plays *Three Pieces* garnered the *Los Angeles Times Book Review Award* for poetry in 1981; and that same year Shange was granted a Guggenheim Fellowship and Medal of Excellence by Columbia University as well as being appointed a member of the New York State Council of the Arts and an artist-in-residence at Houston's Equinox Theatre. During this creative period Shange also published a collection of poetry and prose entitled *Natural Disasters and Other Festive Occasions* (1977), the book of poetry *Nappy Edges* (1978), and the novella *Sassafrass* (1976), which was later expanded, published as *Sassafrass, Cypress & Indigo* (1982), and theatrically produced as *The Dancin Novel: Sas-*

safrass, Cypress & Indigo (1982). In 1977 she married again, this time to musician David Murray, and in 1981 a daughter, Savannah Thulani Eloisa, was born.

Of Shange's long list of accomplishments, several merit special consideration here. Given the stylistic and thematic innovations of *for colored girls* . . . , *A Photograph*, which was produced a year after Shange's 1976 Public Theater success, seems disappointing. Using a more traditional dramatic structure of realism building toward the individual male protagonist's enlightenment, the text centers on the character Sean David, a photographer who fantasizes himself both Alexandre Dumas, literary giant, notorious womanizer, and black outsider in French society, and Dumas *fils*, the bastard son angrily seeking his father's acceptance. As his projection of self-hatred suggests, Sean can see black culture only in terms of pathology; he dreams of a material success which will confirm that he is visible to whites. Through his life pass several former, present, and would-be lovers, all the walking-wounded perverted by racism and sexism. Only the dancer Michael retains an affinity to nature; she envisions a seemingly mythic world where male and female are united, made whole. Through her help Sean arrives at a threshold where his sense of self and hence his artistic vision become clarified.

Unfortunately, the sociohistorical context shaping these characters is not clearly delineated; the bizarre, sordid, and painful seem simply gratuitous; and women are relegated to the typical role of servicing men's needs, while leaving their own largely unattended. Glimmering in the work may be the theme of the artist who virtually destroys himself in the process of creating, but because the writing allows the public no easy access, it fails to suggest how the characters' pain is on some level our own.

The contrast with *Spell #7*, offered the following year, is instructive. Here, a blackface minstrel mask, which dominates the set and thus establishes a confrontational presence before the actors have even appeared, locates the text both within a specific historical context and a temporally undifferentiated psychic terrain. Underneath this hideous representation of blacks in the American popular imagination, Lou, the magician who acts as master of ceremonies, promises to cure the desire for whiteness by executing a novel kind of magic which will guarantee, "you gonna love it/bein colored/ all yr life/ colored & love it." But before the cure can begin, it becomes necessary to fully confront the pain the antidote is designed to counter. Thus, Lou's fellow performers skillfully reenact some of the song and dance idioms associated with black entertainment in America, i.e., washboard rhythms, acrobatics, tap dance routines, du-wop tunes, and exotic showgirl chorus numbers. Displaying their considerable craft for the audience's delighted consumption, for a finale the cast strikes the famous extended-arm, kneeling-mammy pose used by Al Jolson in the movie *The Jazz Singer*. In effect they manipulate the unsuspecting viewer into applauding the ideology of subservience.

But Lou cuts these ironic pleasures short. Challenging viewers instead to imagine the violence attendant upon integrating a public school in 1955, he stimulates a performer to rip off the minstrel mask in order to articulate more truthfully his narrative of terror. As the others dare to follow suit, viewers are given the codes of behavior (which governs their acceptance) on an excursion behind the mask to a land where blacks are free to create identities unfettered by white assumptions.

you are welcome
to my kingdom my city my self
but yr presence must not disturb these
    inhabitants
leave nothing out of place / push no dust
    under my rugs
. . . .
there are no maids here no days off
for healing no insurance policies
for dislocation of the psyche
aliens/foreigners/are granted resident status
we give them a little green card
as they prove themselves non-injurious
to the joy of my nation

(pp. 12–13)

In this exorcised space, the actors explore a complexity seldom accorded black characters. They enact the narratives of Fay from Brooklyn, who is looking for a good time but is not a whore; of Lily, who dreams of brushing a head of hair from which such wonders as pomegranates, ambrosia, and Ishmael Reed essays all flow forth; and of Alec, who wants a moment of national apology when the dehumanization wrought upon black lives is acknowledged. However, two confessions (one placed at the end of each act) threaten to rupture the whimsical or contained quality of most of these narratives: the story of Sue-Jean, who kills her child named Myself, and that of Maxine, who buys South African gold as atonement for blacks' seemingly willful abandonment of ethical sensibilities that had survived slavery. Both tales exemplify what Barbara Christian in an essay on Alice Walker terms "contrariness" or what W. E. Abrahams in his book on African culture describes as "control over deformity." Both characters arrest a process of self-discovery, opting instead for a liminal state where they remain on the verge of creative action.

The pregnant Sue Jean, a young woman of no consequence to anyone in her community, becomes "gay & gracious: she waz someone she had never known/she waz herself with child & she waz a wonderful bulbous thing." She is determined to protect her baby from the poverty and racism she has always known, but when the male child Myself grows old enough to crawl and explore, she kills the boy. Drinking his blood, she prefers to believe herself "full all her life/ with "myself" . . . who'll be out/any day now." Similarly, as a child Maxine was convinced that black people were blessed with divine protection from such epidemics as polio because they never appeared on any of the posters soliciting donations; as an adult, however, she learns that they are susceptible to the same diseases of body and spirit as whites. Hence as the distortions mount, she buys more and more gold jewelry because, as she admits,

> i wear all these things at once/ to remind the black people that it cost a lot for us to be here/ . . . i weep as i fix the chains around my neck/ my wrists/ my ankles. . . . no one understands that surviving the impossible is sposed to accentuate the positive aspects of a people. (p. 51)

Because Sue Jean's and Maxine's stories are marked by a pain almost beyond resolution, Lou interrupts to reassure audiences that they will indeed love his black magic. The cast joins him in repeating the refrain "bein colored & love it," aiming to create between themselves and viewers an emotion that approximates the joyous celebration of church. With Lou's final, defiant affirmation of blacks' right to exist however they choose to define themselves, the minstrel mask returns, and the audience is free to depart.

While Christian's term "contrariness" refers more to the social realm, and Abrahams' "control over deformity" to the metaphysical, both describe situations that, in departing from be-

havioral norms, insinuate the presence of some vaguely familiar and therefore tantalizing, but ill-defined and therefore disruptive energy beyond a collective epistemology. By carefully manipulating her medium to suggest that which presently eludes specification, to simultaneously beckon and repel, Shange fashions a testament that invites its audience to redefine and revitalize those values holding it together as a community.

The closing tension between the ritualized validation of potentiality, encoded in the gospel chant, and the social sign of fixed ontological designations, present in the mask, marks the text's affinities to what may be for Western readers the more familiar dramatic traditions of Artaud and Brecht. That is, in its onslaught on the senses, the script recalls Artaud's formulation of theater as a cleansing plague, while its episodic structure and challenge to imagine alternative social formations are related to Brecht. Of equal significance is the text's location within an African cultural matrix. A prominent index of that matrix is the interlock of competing energies, as accomplished through the development of mask, dance, ritualized repetition, densely textured testimonial, and multiple narratives. The resultant total theater experience not only appeals equally to the intellect and the senses, but it also demands that audiences attempt to impose some interpretive resolution upon the conflicts, both as they are dramatized onstage and as they resonate in the world outside the theater.

This attempt to articulate a resolution is an enormous struggle, as Shange acknowledges in such articles as the prefatory essay to *Three Pieces* (1981), entitled "unrecovered losses/ black theater traditions." Eavesdropping on audiences, she notes that some white viewers were surprised to find themselves identifying with the fantasies expressed in *Spell #7*, while some blacks confessed that these dreams express emotional experiences for which they had hitherto found no words. Both reactions, Shange contends, attest to the manner in which language functions as a racist prison outlawing certain modes of thought. Hence her frontal attack on English, as represented most overtly by unorthodox capitalization, punctuation, and spelling, and more indirectly by the reproduction of black verbal rhythms and a deep cultural imbed-dedness. The consequences for many Shange readers are that a once familiar language now conveys less than familiar representations and demands different modes of critical apprehension. Continually juxtaposing, in her pursuit of a more holistic approach, elements that are conventionally conceptualized as unrelated or that coexist in a dialectical tension, she is locating herself within an African cultural matrix. Radical or cultural feminists might also argue that such a perspective locates the playwright within a woman's culture that has historically been suppressed by patriarchy.

The preference for a provocative complexity in which tensions are often left unresolved is, of course, also characteristic of Shange's non-theatrical work. To date, she has written one novella, *Sassafrass*, and two full-length novels, *Sassfrass, Cypress & Indigo* and *Betsey Brown*. The evolution from novella to novel is indicative of the manner in which Shange often reworks her materials, putting them into new contexts that substantially complicate the production of meaning. For example, poems projecting a unitary female voice, when transferred to the stage, sometimes become dialogue dispersed among both female and male performers and thereby challenge audiences' perceptions of gender differences. Or, as in the development from novella to novel, a single narrative acquires additional, ambivalent resonance through its juxtaposition to other stories.

Opening with the lines "nothin but tenor sax solos ever came outta that house/ sometimes you cd hear a man & a woman arguin/ almost always some kinda music/ . . . ," the novella *Sassafrass* details the protagonist's attempts to construct for herself out of such tasks as cooking, dancing, writing, or loving a life that approximates the vibrant colors, yet interwoven threads of the wall hangings she fashions. One of the primary obstacles to the realization of that desire is her lover Mitch, a horn player and painter, drug addict, and male chauvinist. For a time the couple separates, until Mitch concedes his need and demands that Sassafrass re-

turn home. Just as the text starts with a reference to Mitch and to arguments that music as a primal energy force cannot totally dispel, so, too, does it end. Sassafrass's deep enjoyment of the blues, within which she senses is encoded a spirit of survival, is shattered by Mitch, who needs money to pay off drug debts. Momentarily thrown off balance, she then decides to give him her stash of drugs to sell because "she didnt care/ abt her dreams if her truth/ her real life/ waz hurtin & mitch waz real life/ & needin from her/ somethin she cd give/ & did/." Though the novella ends with an ambiguous blues lyric promising sexual pleasure, a reader may be more likely to suspect that Sassafrass has opted for further self-degradation.

Coming after the self-conscious, affirmative stance of *for colored girls . . . ,* the novella's conclusion may appear retrogressive. In an interview with Claudia Tate, however, Shange reiterates Adrienne Rich and Susan Griffin's contention that women writers must endeavor not only to discover the sources of women's pain but also to accord it respect; they must strive to craft their work so that women's lives— whatever their choices, triumphs, or defeats— are experienced as both valid and valiant. Expanding upon the idea of the affective challenge novels should pose, Shange asserts that she wrote *Sassafrass* with virtually no punctuation or paragraph breaks so that the reader would be unable to impose any distance by putting the book down before finishing it. For Shange, characters are like people: an encounter with them on the printed page or stage should be full to the point where emotions are allowed their explosive climax. Thus, it may be that the novella's conclusion is also calculated to be provocative, to stimulate the reader to quarrel and, perhaps, to come to terms with the protagonist's choice.

With the novella's expansion into *Sassafrass, Cypress & Indigo* and its publication by a major press, the author's characteristic attack on English has been standardized through the use of periods, capitals, and conventional spellings and paragraph and chapter breaks. While the intensity of a single, uninterrupted focus is lost, the novel is richly textured. The sisters' narratives, along with letters from their mother, are like bold, primary-color threads spun out against a more muted background of recipes and journal entries.

The opening sentence, "Where there is a woman there is music," telegraphs the novel's concerns, for all three women—the weaver Sassafrass, the dancer Cypress, and the midwife Indigo—venture off from their Charleston roots seeking to realize themselves as creative, purposeful persons. Their mother, Hilda Effania, serves alternately as a comically well-intentioned but maddeningly conservative chorus commenting upon the array of options her daughters enjoy. By novel's end, having met with varying degrees of success, the sisters find themselves home again. Though the constancy of their mother's love (which has in a certain sense made possible their pursuits) is affirmed, this gesture toward closure must necessarily appear suspect upon further reflection by the reader. As the voice of prevailing community standards regarding acceptable female behavior, Hilda can be expected to eventually force her children to flee into a stress-filled world of greater freedoms and less predictable networks of support.

Cypress's narrative is particularly noteworthy, given the silence that has for the most part determined representations of black lesbians and the problematic manner in which they are depicted here. Disgusted by the misogyny of the predominantly homosexual Kushites Returned dance troupe, Cypress rooms with two dancers of the Azure Bosom. In the latter's dance and living quarters, lines have been superseded by curves; everything celebrates womanhood, so that no matter where Cypress looks she sees herself reflected and affirmed. A concert becomes for performers and women in attendance akin to a communal ritual: "then there was celebration. Celebration of menses; of why she can be daughter, why she can be mother. How girl from woman. . . . The woman of Azure Bosom became the female body exalted." Having freed themselves from patriarchy's one-dimensional definition of female physiology as destiny, the dancers can explore their relationships to the female principle represented by the Haitian goddess Erzulie, and they can fashion and luxuriate in their own eroticism.

Ultimately, Cypress rejects the Azure Bosom collective. At the outset she had noticed that though these women exulted in their femaleness, they also spent a good deal of energy venting their anger at men. Meeting her lover Idrina again after the breakup of their affair, Cypress has a dream in which that hatred of men has metamorphosed into a post-holocaust women's colony located off the coast of Britain. There, heterosexuality and motherhood are severely punished, and species survival is guaranteed by Third World "bearers" of the sperm of imprisoned men. Fleeing from a world that would reenslave her parents, she resolves to make her presence a weapon against all those who would maim or destroy her lineage, as it extends both backward and forward in time. Out of that intuitive insight comes one of the final actions in Cypress's narrative, namely her decision to join a dance troupe pursuing a radical politics.

Important to note is the conflation of issues that allows Cypress's nightmare to function as a validation of the choice of heterosexuality. Initially, lesbianism is presented on a par with heterosexuality, because both in her relationship with Idrina and in that with the musician Leroy, Cypress finds that which nurtures her. Yet the closing image in this sequence, Idrina sleeping peacefully in Cypress's arms, is not rendered strongly enough to counteract the vividness of Cypress's dream. Through a metonymic gesture, the Third World women's active dislike of men comes to stand for an Orwellian fascism that replicates international, North-South geopolitical relations.

This validation of heterosexuality is further ratified when, at the conclusion of Cypress's story, Leroy decides to abort his successful European tour, return home, and marry her. But though the text clearly applauds the affirmation of commitment signaled by marriage, it embeds within that proposed union the seeds of potential disintegration, for both Cypress and Leroy must compromise aspects of their artistic visions in order to wed.

The positive value assigned heterosexuality is additionally subverted when one places an analysis of the Sassafrass narrative next to that of Cypress. As in the novella, Sassafrass is involved with Mitch. His continuing drug addiction guarantees that both parties will remain trapped in a pathological dependency upon each other, despite all Sassafrass's prayers and sacrifices to the Santéa gods of the self-proclaimed African diasporic community to which they have moved. Though Sassafrass finally discovers the strength to leave Mitch and return home to her mother and sisters, the consequences of her move, like those of Cypress's move, are not unequivocal, for she is pregnant with Mitch's baby, who may prove to be irrevocably scarred by the father's cocaine habit.

Through a series of layered contradictions, lesbianism and heterosexuality are again rendered equivalent, their moral value dependent upon the nurturing effects either choice has upon individuals and the larger society. But it is important to note that because the text offers a series of nuanced assertions and subversions, where the reader chooses to place interpretive emphasis may ultimately be a function of his or her own sexual orientation. That is, just as the placement and detail of the "nite with beau willie brown" poem contribute to the interpretation of *for colored girls* . . . as an anti-black male text by many readers, so too the graphic quality of Cypress's nightmare may overshadow the more subtle critique of heterosexual relations. In such an instance, the representation of lesbians may appear to some readers as negative or homophobic.

The holistic approach of the dramas and novels is also found in Shange's poetry. Readers interested in Shange's aesthetics would do well to consult *Nappy Edges*, where such poems as "takin a solo/ . . . ," "wow . . . yr just like a man!" "inquiry," "de poems gotta come outta my crotch"" or "between a dancer & a poet" specifically address such issues as craft and vision, as the latter is shaped by gender. Similarly, *Ridin' the Moon in Texas: Word Paintings* (1987) represents an attempt to converse with the visual arts through the medium of poetic language. Whereas dance is for Shange a means of existing in a realm of pure possibility totally divorced from societal constrictions, poetry, in

that it communicates by channeling the abstract quality of rhythm into the specificity of language, becomes an analog to dance, a means by which the author seeks to transform a transcendent vision into a physical reality. Shange's free verse captures the rhythms of vernacular urban black speech patterns, and in collections such as *Nappy Edges* or *A Daughter's Geography* (1983) often purposefully transgresses the boundary between prose and poetry. The structure of her imagery suggests a creative process akin to that of the visual artist Romare Bearden. In such lines as the following (from *Spell #7*), not only are sensations of pleasurable fullness simulated, almost tangible to the fingers or tongue, but a giddy world is conjured up in which the familiar and the startling jostle each other, expanding the perimeters of consciousness.

> . . . my hair'll grow pomegranates & soil/rich as round the aswan/ i wake in my bed to bananas/ avocados/ collard greens/ the tramps' latest disco hit/ fresh croissant/ pouilly fuiss" ishmael reed's essays/ charlotte carter's stories / all stream from my hair
>
> (*three pieces*, p. 27)

In the early 1980s Shange left New York for Houston, where she was appointed Mellon Distinguished Professor of literature at Rice University and an associate professor of drama in the Creative Writing Program at the University of Houston from 1983 to 1986. Her publications during the 1980s include *See No Evil: Prefaces, Essays & Accounts 1976–1983* (1984); the autobiographical novel *Betsey Brown* (1985) that was subsequently transferred to the New York Shakespeare Festival in 1983; the volume of poems *Ridin' the Moon in Texas* (1987); and the play *Daddy Says* (1989).

In 1994 Shange published her third novel, *Liliane: Resurrection of the Daughter*. Interspersing psychoanalytic sessions between Liliane and her white male therapist with reminiscences from her friends and lovers, this novel challenges the reader to assemble Liliane's history from narratives that weave back and forth over the period from the waning days of legal segregation in the United States to the present. The cast of characters constitutes a virtual African diaspora, with solidly middle-class relatives and boyfriends from Mississippi, East St. Louis, Creole New Orleans, and Queens; a working-class New Jersey school chum; and an Afro-Latino photographer and lover all offering stories that productively complicate the reader's sense of Liliane.

Starting from a point where she can barely breathe whenever her environment is quiet, Liliane uses psychoanalysis to process the loss of her artist-friend Roxie and of her mother, who is suggestively named S. (Sunday) Bliss. Roxie had, despite her friends' pleading to leave, chosen to remain with an abusive boyfriend who ultimately murders her, while Liliane's imaginative, idiosyncratic mother decided to pursue her own dreams, abandoning staid, Southern domesticity for interracial, extramarital love. Both losses pose for Liliane questions as to how she will balance responsibility to her individual vision with the need for close connections to family and friends.

Two of the most distinctive voices in this novel belong to Bernadette and Victor-Jésus María. Bernadette is a working-class Jersey girl who is alternately fascinated by and contemptuous of Liliane and her middle-class friends; her narrative argues that in seeking to authenticate their racial identity by befriending Bernadette and her brother, these teens are oblivious to how their self-assured assumption of personal freedom signifies class privilege separating them from the so-called "real" black folk. Yet Bernadette's contentions of middle-class vacuousness are partially contradicted by the story of Liliane's friend Hyacinthe, a "sixth generation Malveaux," a high yellow or light-skinned African American, driven crazy by the racism that corrodes black lives in general and that has specifically resulted in Hyacinthe's brother Sawyer's death at the hands of darker-skinned, lower-class black males.

Nuyorican Victor-Jésus tells a tale of sexual desire, possession, and female autonomy; his lush language and emphatically machismo rhythms convey a relationship that is seductive and disturbing. While he idealizes Liliane, he also seems intent upon subduing her artistry to his own creativity. The novel ends much the same way as does George C. Wolfe's drama *The Colored Museum*, itself a parody of segments of Shange's *for colored girls . . .* and *Spell #7*. That is, the novel concludes on a celebratory note with a wedding whose "rituals are opportunities for the continuation of clans, dreams, fields of fancy, and realms of the spirits." Indeed, caught in Victor-Jésus' camera lens are the auras of the departed Roxie, Sawyer Malveaux, and S. Bliss herself, mingling with this diverse, diasporic crowd. Challenging Victor to quit the sidelines by putting down his camera and joining the dance, Liliane promises to paint the movement they presently enjoy. Seemingly like Shange, having tasted both the pain and pleasure of life's intricate, fluid rhythms, Liliane will embrace the daunting task of representing them within a fixed form of paint on canvas.

As with many other Shange pieces, portions of this novel have been "recycled" into other formats. In 1994 Sydné Mahone published some of the psychoanalytic sessions in her anthology of contemporary black women playwrights, producing a seemingly static drama in marked contrast to Shange's other plays. Similarly, Shange combined a portion of these sessions with Victor-Jésus' narrative to form a section of *I Live in Music (A Work in Progress)*; it was subsequently published (1997) by Miguel Algarín and Lois Griffith in an anthology of plays from the Nuyorican Poets Café. In this version, Shange includes as many as four musicians and six dancers in the cast, so that, surrounded by music, the analyst seems less emotionally neutral than he appears in either the novel or the excerpt in the Mahone anthology. In winter 2000 actress-playwright Regina Taylor included the novel's playful parody of male constructions of the Muse, entitled "Every Time My Lil World Seems Blue, I Just Haveta Look at You and Learn Eye-Hand Coordination," in her one-woman show, *Millennium Mambo*, produced by the Goodman Theatre in Chicago.

In fact, *I Live in Music* exists in at least two published forms. As a poem that exists on the printed page, it is coupled with Romare Bearden paintings to suggest a black culture composed of such disparate, musical elements as traditional African idioms used for communal festivals or translated for the concert stage, solo guitars, Louis "Satchmo" Armstrong's jazz artistry and near-minstrel smile, and big bands with people jitterbugging in a wash of red color. Bearden's paintings and Shange's poem convey what Ralph Ellison describes as the "sharp breaks, leaps of consciousness, distortions, paradoxes, . . . telescoping of time, and surreal blending of styles" characteristic of the African American experience. For the Nuyorican Poets Café, the text includes the powerful "Crack Annie" poem, whose representation of familial dysfunction rivals the famous "Beau Willie Brown" poem of *for colored girls. . . .* Shange creates a chilling portrait of a mother so addicted to crack cocaine that she offers her eight-year-old daughter to her drug supplier. Surprised when he violently abuses her virginal gift, Annie recognizes too late that she has confined herself to a living hell; she sees in her daughter's pained, uncomprehending eyes and little-girl voice the accusation "mommy what kinda mother / are you / mommy . . ." and hears ". . . the blues in her eyes / an unknown / virulent blues / a stalkin' takin' no answer but yes to me blues / a song of etta james." This poem had been published earlier in 1991 as part of the "I Heard Eric Dolphy in His Eyes" segment of *The Love Space Demands, A Continuing Saga.* Dedicated to "her beaux [political theorist] C. L. R. James and Romare Bearden," *The Love Space Demands* explores analogies between music and love in the context of distrust and conservatism borne of the epidemic of AIDS and sexually transmitted diseases. This collection of poems has been performed by Shange and her band Syllable, which has included John Purcell on reeds, Jean-Paul Borelly and Kelvin Bell on guitar, Rasul Siddik on trumpet, Tyler Mitchell and Don Pate on bass, and Ronnie Bourrage on percussion. Billy Bang and Billy "Spaceman" Patterson Jr. composed the music for various poems in this performance piece, while Mickey Davidson has served as choreographer and dancer.

In *If I Can Cook / You Know God Can* Ntozake Shange returns to her valuation of cuisine as a mode of knowledge seen in her earliest novel, *Sassafrass* (1976). Categorized as nonfiction in a listing of Shange's publications, this work imagines answers to such questions as ". . . what did L'Ouverture, Pétion, and Dessalines share for their victory dinner, realizing that they were the first African nation, slave-free, in the New World?" and, "what if at some point during our sojourns in the New World we decided we did not want to eat to live: that we did not want to live at all?" Shange offers recipes and personal anecdotes about cooking as a means of exploring the migratory histories of black people in the Americas and of raising questions about the extent to which people of African descent continue to honor that history. Unlike most cookbooks whose directions imply only one way to prepare a dish authentically, Shange's recipes continually invite the readers' creativity, thereby insinuating that African diasporic societies though sharing commonalities also expect improvisational flair.

Ntozake Shange has once again moved from the East coast to Texas. She continues to teach, write, and enjoy production opportunities nationally at such venues as Brown University's Rites and Reason Theatre and the Freedom Theatre in Philadelphia.

Selected Bibliography

PRIMARY WORKS

PLAYS

for colored girls who have considered suicide / when the rainbow is enuf. New York: Macmillan, 1977.
Negress. 1977.
Black and White Two-Dimensional Planes. 1979.
Mother Courage & Her Children. 1980.
carrie. (Operetta.) 1981.
mouths. 1981.
A Photograph: Lovers-in-Motion. New York: Samuel French, 1981.
three pieces: spell #7, a photograph: lovers in motion, boogie woogie landscapes. New York: St. Martin's Press, 1981.
Three for a Full Moon and Bocas. 1982.
Educating Rita. 1983.
From Okra to Greens / A Different Kinda Love Story. New York: Samuel French, 1983.
Spell #7. London: Methuen, 1985.
Three Views of Mt. Fuji / A Poem with Music. 1987.

Daddy Says. In *New Plays for the Black Theatre.* Edited by Woodie King Jr. Chicago: Third World Press, 1989.

Liliane: The Resurrection of the Daughter. In *Moon Marked & Touched by the Sun.* Edited by Sydné Mahone. New York: Theatre Communications Group, 1994.

Nomathemba. 1996.

I Live in Music (A Work in Progress). In *Action: The Nuyorican Poets Café .* Edited by Miguel Algarín and Lois Griffith. New York: Simon & Schuster, 1997.

POETRY

Melissa & Smith. St. Paul, Minn.: Bookslinger, 1976.

Natural Disasters and Other Festive Occasions. San Francisco: Heirs, 1977.

Nappy Edges. New York: St. Martin's Press, 1978.

A Daughter's Geography. New York: St. Martin's Press, 1983.

From Okra to Greens. St. Paul, Minn.: Coffee House Press, 1984.

Ridin' the Moon in Texas: Word Paintings. New York: St. Martin's Press, 1987.

The Love Space Demands, a Continuing Saga. New York: St. Martin's Press, 1991.

I Live in Music: Poem by Ntozake Shange, Paintings by Romare Bearden. New York: Welcome Enterprises, 1994.

PROSE

Sassafrass. San Lorenzo, Calif.: Shameless Hussy Press, 1977.

Sassafrass, Cypress & Indigo: A Novel. New York: St. Martin's Press, 1982.

See No Evil: Prefaces, Essays & Accounts, 1976–1983. San Francisco: Momo's Press, 1984.

Betsey Brown: A Novel. New York: St. Martin's Press, 1985.

Liliane: Resurrection of the Daughter. New York: St. Martin's Press, 1994.

NONFICTION

If I Can Cook / You Know God Can. Boston: Beacon Press, 1998.

AUDIOTAPES/VIDEOTAPES

Beneath the Necessity of Talking, Ntozake Shange Live with Syllable. American Audio Prose Library, 1989.

Ntozake Shange with Syllable: Live at the Victoria Theater, San Francisco. San Francisco Poetry Center, 1989.

Serial Monogamy. New York: WNYC, 1989. (Video performance of Ntozake Shange and Billy "Spacemen" Patterson.)

SECONDARY WORKS

BIOGRAPHICAL AND CRITICAL STUDIES

Bond, Jean Carey. "For Colored Girls Who Have Considered Suicide." *Freedomways* 16:187–91 (Third Quarter 1976).

Brown, Elizabeth. "Ntozake Shange." In *Dictionary of Literary Biography.* Vol. 38, *Afro-American Writers After 1955: Dramatists and Prose Writers.* Edited by Thadious M. Davis and Trudier Harris. Detroit: Gale Research, 1985.

Brown-Gillory, Elizabeth. *Their Place on the Stage: Black Women Playwrights in America.* New York: Greenwood Press, 1988.

Christian, Barbara. "No More Buried Lives: The Theme of Lesbianism in Audre Lorde's *Zami,* Gloria Naylor's *The Women of Brewster Place,* Ntozake Shange's *Sassafrass, Cypress and Indigo,* and Alice Walker's *The Color Purple.*" In *Black Feminist Criticism: Perspectives on Black Women Writers.* Edited by Barbara T. Christian. New York: Pergamon Press, 1985. Pp. 187–204.

DeShazer, Mary K. "Rejecting Necrophilia: Ntozake Shange and the Warrior Re-Visioned." In *Making a Spectacle: Feminist Essays on Contemporary Women's Theatre.* Edited by Lynda Hart. Ann Arbor: University of Michigan Press, 1989. Pp. 86–100.

Elder, Arlene. "*Sassafrass, Cypress and Indigo:* Ntozake Shange's Neo-Slave/Blues Narrative." *African American Review* 26, no. 1:99–107 (Spring 1992).

Geis, Deborah R. "Distraught Laughter: Monologue in Ntozake Shange's Theater Pieces." In *Feminine Focus: The New Women Playwrights.* Edited by Enoch Brater. New York: Oxford University Press, 1989. Pp. 210–25.

Flowers, Sandra Hollin. "*Colored Girls:* Textbook for the Eighties." *Black American Literature Forum* 15: 51–54 (Summer 1981).

Keyssar, Helene. "Rites and Responsibilities: The Drama of Black American Women." In *Feminine Focus: The New Women Playwrights.* Edited by Enoch Brater. New York: Oxford University Press, 1989. Pp. 226–40.

Lester, Neal A. "Shange's Men: *for colored girls* Revisited, and Movement Beyond." *African American Review* 26, no. 2:319–28 (Summer 1992).

———. *Ntozake Shange, a Critical Study of the Plays.* New York: Garland Publishing, 1994.

Mitchell, Carolyn. " 'A Laying on of Hands': Transcending the City in Ntozake Shange's *for colored girls who have considered suicide / when the rainbow is enuf.*" In *Women Writers and the City: Essays in Feminist Literary Criticism.* Edited by Susan Merrill Squier. Knoxville: University of Tennessee Press, 1984. Pp. 230–48.

Olaniyan, Tejumola. "Ntozake Shange: The Vengeance of Difference, or the Gender of Black Cultural Identity." In *Scars of Conquest/Masks of Resistance: The Invention of Cultural Identities in African, African-American, and Caribbean Drama.* New York: Oxford University Press, 1995. Pp. 116–38.

Peters, Erskine. "Some Tragic Propensities of Ourselves: The Occasion of Ntozake Shange's *for colored girls who have considered suicide / when the rainbow is enuf.*" *Journal of Ethnic Studies* 6:79–85 (1978).

Peterson, Bernard L. Jr. "Ntozake Shange." In *Contemporary Black American Playwrights and Their Plays: A Biographical Directory and Dramatic Index*. New York: Greenwood Press, 1988. Pp. 417–21.

Richards, Sandra L. "Conflicting Impulses in the Plays of Ntozake Shange." *Black American Literature Forum* 17:73–78 (Summer 1983).

———. "Under the 'Trickster's' Sign: Toward a Reading of Ntozake Shange and Femi Osofisan." In *Critical Theory and Performance*. Edited by Janelle Reinelt and Joseph Roach. Ann Arbor: University of Michigan Press, 1992. Pp. 65–78.

Splawn, P. Jane. " 'Change the Joke[r] and Slip the Yoke': Boal's 'Joker' System in Ntozake Shange's *for colored girls . . .* and *Spell #7*." *Modern Drama* 41, no. 3:386–398.

Staples, Robert. "The Myth of Black Macho: A Response to Angry Black Feminists." *The Black Scholar* 10:24–33 (1979).

Talbert, Linda Lee. "Ntozake Shange: Scarlet Woman and Witch/Poet." *Umoja* n.s. 4:5–10 (Spring 1980).

Wallace, Michelle. "For Colored Girls, the Rainbow Is Not Enough." *Village Voice* August 16, 1976, pp. 108–9.

Watson, Kenneth. "Ntozake Shange." In *American Playwrights Since 1945: A Guide to Scholarship, Criticism, and Performance*. Edited by Philip C. Kolin. New York: Greenwood Press, 1989. Pp. 379–86.

Waxman, Barbara Frey. "Dancing Out of Form, Dancing Into Self: Genre and Metaphor in Marshall, Shange, and Walker." *MELUS* 19, no. 3:91–107 (Fall 1994).

INTERVIEWS

Betsko, Kathleen, and Rachel Koenig, eds. *Interviews with Contemporary Women Playwrights*. New York: Beech Tree Books, 1987. Pp. 365–76.

Blackwell, Henry. "An Interview with Ntozake Shange." *Black American Literature Forum* 13:134–38 (Winter 1979).

Bowles, Juliette, ed. "Interview with Ntozake Shange." (With James Early.) In *Memory and Spirit of Frances, Zora, and Lorraine: Essays and Interviews on Black Women and Writing*. Washington, D.C.: Institute for the Arts and Humanities, Howard University, 1979.

Lester, Neal A. "At the Heart of Shange's Feminism: An Interview." *Black American Literature Forum* 24, no. 4:717–30 (Winter 1990).

Splawn, P. Jane. "An Intimate Talk with Ntozake Shange: An Interview." In *Black Women Film and Video Artists*. Edited by Jacqueline Bobo. New York: Routledge, 1998.

Tate, Claudia, ed. *Black Women Writers at Work*. New York: Continuum, 1983. Pp. 149–74.

THE SLAVE NARRATIVE IN AMERICAN LITERATURE

MASON LOWANCE JR.

THE SLAVE NARRATIVE occupies a special place in American literature because it represents the continuation of an autobiographical form of writing always prominent in American culture. It also offers a view of the "promised land" that contrasts markedly with the millennial and Edenic visions of the New World proposed by explorers and early white settlers. Among the Puritans of New England recording the experience of eminent figures was the most obvious means of articulating the place of the New World in providential history and of proving that New England and her people stood in a covenanted relationship to God. Borrowing their biographical methodology from the Bible, they argued that God's providential design for his "new English Israel" could best be realized in the life stories of leading figures, just as the history of ancient Israel is told through accounts of the lives of, among others, Abraham, Moses, Joseph, Deborah, and David.

Most slave narratives, the dominant mode of early African American writing, also carry the providential metaphor as an informing structural principle. The guidance and salvation of many escaped slaves was credited to God's providence. Moreover, the slave narrative as a literary genre combined elements of the Puritan spiritual accounts to give the reader another parallel to the biblical Israelites. Both groups were persecuted wayfarers who could look for-

ward to a better life in the next world. Negro spirituals, the folk songs of the slave culture, were imbued with these biblical parallels. The Israelites' deliverance from suffering in Egypt was perceived to be a foreshadowing of God's deliverance of the southern slaves from a more contemporary but equally merciless ordeal. "Crossing Over Jordan" and other spirituals reinforce the conviction that somehow God would provide deliverance and that the everlasting life would await the faithful believer. Moreover, the abolitionist editors of many of the slave narratives were consciously exploiting biblical parallels in order to appeal to a predominantly white audience that would be very familiar with the sufferings of the ancient Israelites from their study of scripture.

But the slave narratives as a genre are very different from the early Puritan autobiographies because they focus more on the individual self and its emergence through human experience than on divinely guided personal accounts. Slave narratives flourished in the first half of the nineteenth century, specifically 1830–1865, when the abolitionist movement—supported by William Lloyd Garrison's *Liberator* and other abolitionist papers—gathered momentum for a final confrontation with the institution they held to be inconsistent with the values and ideals of the newly founded democratic society. Eighteenth-century slave narratives shared the design of New England spiritual autobiography in recording the life of a member of a tribal group that was guided by divine providence. The life was usually expressed as the journey of a Christian wayfarer from the earthly city of Babylon to the eternal and holy "city upon a hill," Jerusalem. Literary precedents for these early slave narratives include Plutarch's *Lives* and the Bible, and parallels may also be drawn with John Bunyan's *Pilgrim's Progress* (1678) and *Grace Abounding* (1666), in which Bunyan spiritualized his own life story. When Ralph Waldo Emerson remarked in *Representative Men* (1850) that "there is properly no history, only biography," and Thomas Carlyle, whose English Calvinist background resembled Emerson's, asserted that "history is the essence of innumerable biographies," they had specific reference to the lives of eminent men.

The slave narratives, by contrast, are the life accounts of victims, tales of unendurable suffering and torment that alert the reader to a counterculture present in America even as Emerson penned *Representative Men*. The early narratives are also spiritual autobiographies; their authors' perceptions of the colonial experience provide an excellent counterpoint to the assurances of divine guidance that pervade Puritan biographical and historical narratives. Like the Indian captivity narratives they closely resemble, the slave accounts tell the story of individuals in hostile environments against which they are forced to struggle continuously for survival. The slave narratives, however, reverse the judgments of such representative captivity narratives as Mary Rowlandson's *The Captivity and Restoration of Mary Rowlandson* (1682) and John Williams' *The Redeemed Captive, Returning Unto Zion* (1708). For example, if the white settlers were portrayed as martyred saints in the Indian captivity narratives, they are represented as bestial villains in the slave accounts. Both types were structured as individual journeys, which provide the metaphorical framework for all slave accounts—the movement from enslavement to freedom or deliverance. This may be paralleled by an escape from the southern states to the North, and this geographic paradigm resembles the movement of ancient Israel from Egypt to Canaan, the promised land.

The slave narrative also shares the "before" and "after" structure of the spiritual autobiography. Each account is focused on the experience of a protagonist who speaks in the first person, and the protagonist's point of view is that of a freed person looking back on the experience of chattel slavery. This movement from slavery to freedom in the context afforded by hindsight gives each narrative a curiously ironic tone: the writer searches into the harsh reality of his or her personal past in order to establish the condition of slavery from which the later portions of the narrative will illustrate a blessed deliverance.

The essential elements of spiritual autobiography include: the first-person account of a deliverance from earthly peril by divine providence; the journey motif, suggesting a circular migration governed by God, who moves the action forward toward a predetermined end, known only to him; and the essential, innate depravity of mankind, excepting those saintly few who are especially designated to carry forward the course of divine history.

The slave narratives of the nineteenth century were part of a larger antislavery literature written by abolitionists as responses to the presence of the institution of slavery in a democracy consecrated to the enlightenment ideal that "all men are created equal." These responses were as varied as they were numerous, crossing genre lines from slave narratives to sermons to poetry and other more conventional literary forms. Novels were the most prominent form of literature circulating in antebellum America, and they were a popular vehicle for representing sentiment for or against slavery. Proslavery idealized plantation portraits, such as John Pendleton Kennedy's *Swallow Barn* (1832) or Mary Eastman's *Aunt Phillis's Cabin* (1852), a direct response to Harriett Beecher Stowe's *Uncle Tom's Cabin*, the powerful antislavery novel of that same year, sought to discredit the gothic horrors of slavery represented in the slave narratives and the antislavery writings of the abolitionists. Tract writing by the abolitionists between 1830 and 1865, and the heroic work of William Lloyd Garrison in editing the *Liberator* from 1831 until 1865, provided an antislavery literature that paralleled the work of the slave narrators.

There are literally hundreds of slave narratives, especially from the period 1830–1865, the "Abolitionist Crusade" during which antislavery societies were extremely active both in Britain and the United States. Prominent authors of these accounts include William and Ellen Craft; the famous Sojourner Truth; Henry "Box" Brown, who was sent to freedom in a shipping crate; and the abolitionist William Wells Brown. This essay focuses on the most representative eighteenth- and nineteenth-century examples for analysis, including *The Interesting Narrative of the Life of Olaudah Equiano, or Gustavus Vassa, the African, Written by Himself* (1789); an eighteenth-century slave narrative that includes a graphic and gothic description of the infamous "middle Passage" across the Atlantic on a slave ship, a description that Stephen Spielberg appropriated in his filming of the Amistad mutiny.

Josiah Henson, The Life of Josiah Henson (1842), ostensibly the prototype for the character of Uncle Tom in Stowe's 1852 antislavery novel, *Uncle Tom's Cabin*. In response to severe criticism from Southerners that she lacked any experience of the plantation system in the South, Stowe issued, in 1853, a compilation entitled A Key to Uncle Tom's Cabin, in which she listed and analyzed her sources for the novel, in an attempt to gain authenticity and credibility for her fictional work. In this Key, she cited the Henson narrative as her source for the character of Uncle Tom. *A Narrative of the Life of Frederick Douglass, an American Slave* (1845); Frederick Douglass' *My Bondage and My Freedom* (1855); which extends the author's experience by a decade and revises the entire dramatic narrative, and the encyclopedic 1881 *The Life and Times of Frederick Douglass* (1881); which includes some of his public life [Douglass eventually became an advisor to four United States Presidents and was himself named Consul General to Haiti. He was also very active in the women's rights movement that paralleled the antislavery movement, and deliv-

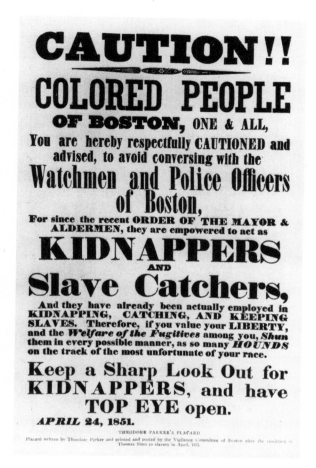

An antislavery poster.

ered an address at the Seneca Falls Convention in 1848 and had spoken at a women's voting rights meeting on the day of his death in 1896].

Harriett Jacobs' *Linda: Incidents in the Life of a Slave Girl* (1861); and Harriet Beecher Stowe's *Uncle Tom's Cabin* (1852). This text, written several years before 1861 but not published until just prior to the outbreak of the Civil War, is technically a sentimental novel, with fictional names thinly disguising the real persons they represent. However, its powerful narrative voices clearly show the author's consistent dedication to the ending of chattel slavery, especially the brutal treatment of female slaves, through the rhetorical strategy of combining the sermonic voice with the narrative structure of a sentimental novel.

These are, of course, only six of over one hundred such titles, all of which were serious literary responses to the peculiar institution of slavery, and they follow conventional patterns of spiritual, autobiographical narration, including: (1) a journey motif in which the narrator's personal experience is metaphorically paralleled by a spiritual awakening to freedom; (2) a sense of the narrator's isolation in a hostile environment that imposes barriers that must be crossed in the journey to freedom; (3) several prominent episodes along the way where transformations occur, such as the gaining of an awareness of the importance of literacy to freedom; (4) the presence of multiple voices, as the adult narrator recapitulates earlier experiences in slavery and then provides commentary both moral and interpretative; (5) a litany of gothic representations of the horrors of slavery, including flogging and auction scenes; (6) the narrative movement of a stressful pursuit, in which the predator and prey are always closely allied in an intense chase, whether of an escaped slave or, in the case of Harriet Jacobs, a sexual predator chasing after the object of his desire; and (7) an emphasis on the slave's family, including attempts to establish an authentic genealogy where possible. Often, for the slave, this effort was fruitless, as most slaves were not aware of their exact paternal parentage. Frederick Douglass, a mulatto product of a slave mother and a white father, never discovered his true father's identity, and yet the opening pages of his 1845 *Narrative* contain the record of his efforts to establish his genealogy.

These fundamental characteristics of slave narratives, some of which are shared with the antecedent models of Puritan spiritual autobiography, constitute a typology for the American antebellum slave narrative. However, it would be incorrect to argue that these qualities prove that the abolitionist editors like William Lloyd Garrison or Lydia Maria Child edited or even wrote these documents simply because they appear to follow a common formula. Rather, all slave narratives shared the common objective of bringing an end to the institution of chattel slavery, and whatever emphases seemed to work with the reading public they utilized in realizing this objective.

The slave narrative has gained much prominence since the 1960s, with the introduction of African American history courses, programs and departments, and the "canonization" of once marginalized texts by slaves and women into the mainstream of American literature. Similarly, postwar scholarship has focused on the experience of the slave in America. Benjamin Quarles and John Hope Franklin were pioneers who, as African Americans, were often denied access to university libraries where important resources were held. In spite of these restrictions, Franklin produced the magisterial *From Slavery to Freedom* in 1947, which has been revised many times and has sold well over a million copies. Scholarly and critical studies include: William Andrews, *To Tell a Free Story: the First Century of Afro-American Autobiography, 1760–1865* (1986); Charles Davis and Henry Louis Gates Jr., *The Slave's Narrative* (1985); and John Sekora and Darwin Turner, *The Art of the Slave Narrative* (1982). The Davis and Gates volume contains a useful full bibliography of American antebellum slave narratives.

It is important to distinguish this group of antebellum slave narratives, which followed conventional literary models and were all designed to bring an end to the institution of chattel slavery, from the reminiscences by former slaves written during Reconstruction and particularly those orally delivered by elderly former slaves to Works Progress Administration (WPA) workers during the 1930s (see George Rawick in the bibliography to this essay). These reminiscences are generally unstructured accounts in which some episodes are highly romanticized; few could be characterized as having the determined agenda of illuminating the horrors of slavery in an effort to bring about its demise. It is the antebellum slave narrative (1745–1865) that has so significantly influenced twentieth-century African American writing, including such prominent figures as Nobel Prize winner Toni Morrison, whose *Beloved* follows closely the typology of antebellum slave narration while violating its chronology;

Ralph Ellison, whose narrative voice in *Invisible Man* closely resembles that of antebellum slave narrators; Octavia Butler *(Kindred)*; James Baldwin *(Nobody Knows My Name)*, Sherley Anne Williams *(Dessa Rose)*, Charles Johnson *(Oxherding Tales)*, and Ishmael Reed *(Flight to Canada)*. These modern writers have recuperated the slave narratives either through plot, characterization, voice, or some combination of these narrative elements. As Hazel Carby has argued, "the idea that the ex slaves wrote themselves into being through an account of the condition of being a slave is woven into the very fabric of the Afro-American literary imagination and its critical reconstruction."(see Hazel Carby, "Ideologies of Black Folk: the Historical Novel of Slavery," in McDowell and Rampersad, Slavery and the Literary Imagination, 1987, pp. 125–41)

The Morrison and Butler texts recapitulate the horrors of chattel slavery, and particularly *Beloved* recuperates the common phenomenon of antebellum slavery, infanticide, represented in the nineteenth century by the historically real Margaret Garner episode. Morrison's novel does not follow the strictly chronological order of the antebellum slave narrative, but uses the narrative techniques of James Joyce or William Faulkner to suggest that historical time is less important than the ethical and moral issues raised by a society where the taking of the life of one's own child is preferable to allowing it to live a life of slavery. Mark Twain has his heroine, Roxy, wrestle with the same question in Puddn'head Wilson(1895). Not only is the nineteenth-century historical moment challenged morally and spiritually; the modern reader is also forced to confront the ethical dilemma faced by Sethe in *Beloved*. Stowe's examination of the issue of infanticide is found in "The Quadroon's Story," Cassy's slave narrative, that is inserted into *Uncle Tom's Cabin*. As Paul D., in *Beloved*, remarks, "there could have been a way. Some other way."

Butler and Morrison abandon the strictly chronological structure for a more disjunctive, episodic narrative technique. As Lisa Siegmann observes, "this modern manipulation of voices both gives the author freedom and range not enjoyed by the antebellum slave narrators, and gives the modern reader an opportunity to respond to the text with his own moral perspective, just as the more historically focused antebellum texts sought to develop moral outrage in the reader. Both the antebellum narratives and the slavery fiction of the twentieth century are cumulative expressions of a culture, a race, and not the voices of individual writers working in isolation." It is important to recognize that black men wrote the majority of the published slave narratives, while black women wrote fewer than 12 percent of the antebellum documents, as Deborah McDowell has observed. She also notes the correlative that the modern authors using slave narrative structures are predominately female and suggests that these authors write not about what was done to slave women but rather what the slave women themselves did in response to the institution of slavery. This is of course the perspective adopted by Toni Morrison in *Beloved* for her main character, Sethe.

The antebellum slave narratives are expressions of personal heroism and achievement as central to the American experience as Benjamin Franklin's Autobiography. If Franklin were the "new man, this American," in response to Hector St. Jean de Crevecoeur's rhetorical question, then Frederick Douglass is an equally powerful voice in determining the identity of the new inhabitants of North America. The flogging scenes of the slave narratives, and pathetic attempts at discovering one's "roots" or genealogy, the separation of families through the auction system, all serve the slave narrator's purpose in showing the obstacles that had to be overcome in the movement from personal slavery to personal freedom. But this movement was always paralleled by the the story of the race, by history of a people, struggling not only for the most basic forms of personal emancipation, but struggling, along with America herself, for a new identity, a new value system, and a new beginning in this new land. As such, the slave narrative is as much the "great American novel" as Moby-Dick or The Great Gatsby. Its long history of neglect by American professors of literature and history is the result of a cultural arrogance and a failure to recognize the value of a minority culture that has in the past one hundred years not only survived the racial hostility of Jim-Crow segregation and Reconstruction, but has in one century managed, as William Faulkner observed about the spirit of man in his Nobel Prize acceptance speech, not only to "endure, but to prevail." African-Americans have made enormous contributions to American society in many areas, and the jazz music that evolved from the spirituals of the nineteenth century(mentioned in the Douglass narratives,) is possibly the single most important cultural contribution of the United States to world culture. The slave narratives show the beginnings of this expression among the most oppressed of America's future citizens, and the place of the slave narrative in the American literary landscape is now permanently assured. What follows is an analysis of the most prominent of these narratives, and the essay concludes with a bibliography of primary and secondary sources that will make further study accessible to the scholar and the general reader.

Eighteenth-Century Slave Narratives: Olaudah Equiano (1745–1797)

The best-known and most powerful of the eighteenth-century slave narratives are Briton Hammon's *A Narrative of the Uncommon Sufferings, and Surprizing Deliverance of Briton Hammon, a Negro Man. . . .* (1760), John Marrant's *A Narrative of the Lord's Wonderful Dealings with John Marrant, a Black, Now Going to Preach the Gospel in Nova Scotia, Born in New York, in North America* (1785), Venture Smith's *A Narrative of the Life and Adventures of Venture, A Native of Africa* (1798), and the masterpiece among the early accounts, Olaudah Equiano's *The Interesting Narrative of the Life of Olaudah Equiano, or Gustavus Vassa, the African, Written by Himself* (1789). This essay will examine the Equiano narrative as a representative eighteenth-century text.

The most representative examples of the greatest period of slave narrative composition,

between 1820 and 1865, include Frederick Douglass's Narrative of the Life of Frederick Douglass, an American Slave (1845), a central document of the abolitionist movement that formed the basis of Douglass's two subsequent autobiographies (1855, 1881), and Harriet Jacobs's Incidents in the Life of a Slave Girl, Written by Herself (1861). Harriet Jacobs and Frederick Douglass have provided extraordinary visions of the hardships suffered by slaves of both sexes, and together, these three documents—Equiano, Douglass, and Jacobs—illustrate the characteristic rhetorical strategies of this genre. The pervasive metaphor for all life-writing of this type is the teleological journey, that purposeful trek from birth to death that is punctuated by episodes and digressions but united by the metamorphosis of the central character, through whose voice the story is narrated. The individual's life may be redeemed spiritually and artistically by the guidance of providence and the earthly agents of God (often kind or helpful whites, usually women, sometimes called "angels"), but each narrative also depends heavily on the self-reliance and determination of the protagonist.

Because nineteenth-century slave narratives were often published by abolitionist or anti-slavery societies, and because they were frequently edited by prominent abolitionists, the issue of credibility and veracity was raised in objection to their firsthand accounts of slavery. For example, William Lloyd Garrison and Wendell Phillips both authored introductory essays for Frederick Douglass' *Narrative of the Life of Frederick Douglass, an American Slave* and Lydia Maria Child edited and introduced *Linda: Incidents in the Life of a Slave Girl.* These prominent Boston abolitionists provided verification for the narratives that followed their introductory statements; however, there was much speculation that the documents themselves were not genuine or authentic.

The case of Equiano's *The Interesting Narrative of the Life of Olaudah Equiano, or Gustavus Vassa, the African, Written by Himself* deserves special attention because it represents a much earlier account than those sponsored by the abolitionists and because it has recently come under attack for credibility by scholars of slave narration, notably the critic Vince Carretta. In most slave narratives of both centuries, the phrase "written by himself (or herself)" was used to suggest authenticity; however, the very presence of lengthy introductions by prominent Bostonians cast doubt on these assertions and, in some cases, led to further speculation that Garrison, Phillips, or Child might have composed the entire document. The problem for Equiano was that his elegant, eighteenth-century Johnsonian style gave rise to speculation that he also might have been assisted in the composition, given the limitations of his education and background. As the Carretta critique suggests, these issues of credibility and veracity have not even been resolved in our own time, and ultimately, it is left to the reader to accept or reject the account of each slave narrative. If this sounds dangerously like "reader response theory"—by which each reader of a text brings to the reading his or her own perspective and values and shades of interpretation—it is the way most slave narratives have been received. Many nineteenth-century readers who were proslavery advocates chose to deny the accounts of the antebellum slave narratives and the fictional slave narration of Stowe's *Uncle Tom's Cabin.* However, modern studies of slavery, such as John Blassingame's *The Slave Community* or William Andrews' *To Tell a Free Story: The First Century of African American Autobiography* clearly show that most of the incidents in slave narration were genuine and not fabricated.

Equiano clearly established the model for the slave narrative genre. His first-person, retrospective recapitulation of the past leads the reader along a purposeful journey. The language of this account is erudite and polished, obviously the work of an educated, even learned writer. Like many of the eighteenth-century narratives it commences with an apology, which contains many of the conventional apostrophes to God, but which in this instance reveals much about the personality of the author. Very self-conscious about thrusting his life story before a predominantly white readership, Equiano argues that "it is not a little hazardous in a pri-

vate and obscure individual, and a stranger, too, thus to solicit the indulgent attention of the public, especially when I offer here the history of neither a saint, a hero, nor a tyrant." This modesty, more a contemporary style of address than a confession, pervades the narrative, and Equiano, like Phillis Wheatley in her poetry, ascribes the good things of his life to the operations of divine providence: "I might say that my sufferings were great; but when I compare my lot with that of most of my countrymen, I regard myself, as a particular favorite of heaven, and acknowledge the mercies of Providence in every occurrence of my life." What follows these prefatory remarks is a detailed description of tribal life in Africa, from which Equiano was abducted into slavery and then transported to America. The Equiano account is important not only because it is an early example of the slave narrative but also because it exhibits many characteristics that were to be associated with later development of the genre. Survival, for example, is the protagonist's primary goal, but the Equiano account also establishes the narrative voices later writers would employ, including the sermonizing and direct address to the reader, and a harsh critique of the hypocrisy of white, Christian antebellum society, north and south.

The reader of these accounts sometimes assumes that they were composed by former slaves who wished to retell the gothic horrors of their previous experiences, in much the same way that contemporary Holocaust survivors intend to bear witness to the truth and to reveal the extreme cruelty of the German death camps. These accounts were not only intended to recall the cruelties of the past, however; they were clearly designed to reform the institution, if not to end it altogether, and many were financially supported by the abolitionist movement. Therefore, they are also political documents, and they differ from the Holocaust survival narratives in that they were not composed in secret during an episode of history that was hidden from much of the world at the time it took place. Rather, the slave narratives reveal the feelings, isolation, history, and experience of human beings whose conditions were not always well known to the nation that tolerated and supported the institution.

Personal Identity and the Autobiography

As in all autobiographies the primary characteristic or theme of the slave narrative is that of self-definition. But in the slave account, the definition of the persona is intrinsically linked to the narrator's impulse toward personal freedom. This conflation of the desire for freedom and the identity of the subject of the autobiography pervades all slave narratives; indeed, the power of this central theme governs one of the most complex paradoxes in all slave autobiography. The slave narrator is compelled to recall his former state, even a former self, just as he has reached the "promised land" of freedom and has achieved that purpose toward which the entire objective of his experience has been directed. As Annette Niemtzow has summarized, "The slave, happily ceasing to be a slave, describes his or her slave self to preserve it just as it is about to cease to be a condition under which the self lives." Thus the persona developed is very different from other contemporary autobiographical figures. For example, where Benjamin Franklin was able to inscribe the first part of his *Autobiography* (written in 1771, published in 1818) to a familial audience by commencing, "Dear Son," and then to broaden his appeal to a much larger public audience by creating a sequence of personae who reveal a directed, self-created image of ascendancy and the American dream, the author of the slave narrative seeks identity in two opposing ways: first, he attempts to establish the usual genealogical account of his past just as Franklin did in art 1 of the *Autobiography,* and second, he seeks a new identity in the new world that will replace his African Heritage. But the slave's attempt to establish genealogical identity is frustrated by a frequent absence of information about this past; for example, Frederick Douglass offers a stark contrast to Franklin's genealogy by writing, on the first page of his narrative:

I have no accurate knowledge of my age, never having seen any authentic record containing it. By far the larger part of the slaves know as little of their age as horses know of theirs, and it is the wish of most masters within my knowledge to keep their slaves thus ignorant. I do not remember to have ever met a slave who could tell of his birthday. . . . A want of information concerning my own was a source of unhappiness to me even during childhood.

Moreover, the slave may be the illegitimate offspring of an owner and a slave, whose identity may be traceable only to the mother. Douglass continues: "My father was a white man. He was admitted to be by all I ever heard speak of my parentage. The opinion was also whispered that my master was my father; but of the correctness of this opinion, I know nothing; the means of knowing was withheld from me." That "means of knowing" was of course the mother, who might have provided the child with sufficient information about his parentage. But Douglass never really knew his mother:

My mother and I were separated when I was but an infant—before I knew her as my mother. . . . I never saw my mother, to know her as such, more than four or five times in my life; and each of these times was very short in duration, and at night. She was hired by a Mr. Stewart, who lived about twelve miles from my home. She made her journeys to see me in the night, travelling the whole distance on foot, after the performance of her day's work. She was a field hand, and a whipping is the penalty for not being in the field at sunrise. . . . I do not recollect of ever seeing my mother by the light of day. . . . She would lie down with me, and get me to sleep, but long before I waked she was gone. Very little communication ever took place between us. Death soon ended what little we could have while she lived, and with it her hardships and suffering. She died when I was about seven years old.

By contrast, Olaudah Equiano knew a lot about his background, as he was abducted in

Africa and came from a tribal past with a family structure that he describes quite fully. Chapter 2 of his narrative gives a geographic, cultural, and genealogical account of this heritage: "My father, besides many slaves, had a numerous family, of which seven lived to grow up, including myself and a sister, who was the only daughter." But the identity of the self in any autobiography is not confined to genealogy, and Equiano soon loses one vital element in the process of self-discovery: his ability to retain his own name. In chapter 3 Equiano treats this subject sensitively and intelligently, long after he has survived the voyage by sea in a slave ship, discussing the way in which he was successively renamed on his emergence as an African slave in America (both his African and imposed names are used on the title page of the autobiography, indicating this acceptance or merging of identities):

> In this place I was called Jacob; but on board the African Snow [the slave ship], I was called Michael. . . . Some of the people of the ship used to tell me they were going to carry me back to my own country, and this made me very happy. I was quite rejoiced at the idea of going back; and thought if I could get home what wonders I should have to tell. But I was reserved for another fate, and was soon undeceived when we came within sight of the English coast. While I was on board this ship, my captain and master named me *Gustavus Vassa* [after a Scandinavian chief]. I at that time began to understand him a little, and refused to be called so, and told him as well as I could that I would be called Jacob; but he said I should not, and still called me Gustavus: and when I refused to answer to my new name, which I at first did, it gained me many a cuff; so at length I submitted, and by which I have been known ever since.

Thus the masters assert their authority over the slave subject by dictating the very names by which they will be known, eradicating their previous identities even though in some instances they might have been regal and powerful in the African societies from which they were abducted. In the later narratives of the nineteenth century, this process is less central to the story because identity has already been established in the slave culture; however, naming and the process of self-realization takes another form, the achievement of literacy.

Slave Literacy

In all slave narratives, the acquisition of literacy in English parallels the gaining of freedom. The impulse toward freedom remains the central theme of all slave narratives; however, freedom without literacy in an alien, hostile culture is inconceivable. The literary power with which Equiano, Douglass, and Jacobs narrate their stories results in each case from a determination to learn the language of their oppressors in the New World. Equiano articulates the frustration he felt on realizing that the most formidable barrier between himself and his captors was not just race but literacy:

> I had often seen my master and Dick employed in reading; and I had a great curiosity to talk to the books as I thought they did, and so to learn how all things had a beginning. For that purpose I have often taken up a book, and have talked to it, and then put my ears to it, when alone, in hopes that it would answer me; and I have been very much concerned when I found it remained silent.

Both Harriet Jacobs, represented by her created persona-narrator Linda Brent in *Incidents*, and Frederick Douglass are taught to read initially by sympathetic owners' wives. Douglass informs the reader:

> Very soon after I went to live with Mr. and Mrs. Auld, she very kindly commenced to teach me the A, B, C. After I had learned this, she assisted me in learning to spell words of three or four letters. Just at this point of my progress, Mr. Auld found out what was going on, and at once forbade Mrs. Auld to instruct me further, telling her, among other things, that it was unlawful, as well as unsafe, to teach a slave to read. To use his own words,

further, he said, "If you give a nigger an inch, he will take an ell. . . . If you teach that nigger (speaking of myself) how to read, there would be no keeping him. It would forever unfit him to be a slave. He would at once become unmanageable, and of no value to his master. As to himself, it could do him no good, but a great deal of harm. It would make him discontented and unhappy." . . . I now understood what had been to me a most perplexing difficulty—to wit, the white man's power to enslave the black man. [Literacy] was a grand achievement, and I prized it highly. From that moment, I understood the pathway from slavery to freedom.

Toward the end of his narrative, Douglass recalls that it was this epiphany that led to his understanding of the complex relationships between the realization of the self, the achievement of freedom, and the gaining of literacy. Because his tutorials with Mrs. Auld were terminated, he had to resort to his own cunning and later tricked or bribed white boys with whom he was associated to continue his literacy lessons. For Douglass, the value and importance of literacy in gaining his full freedom was never in question.

In a real sense, the gaining of literacy and freedom belong together because all of these narratives carry the burden of bearing witness to the truth, of recounting the past through speech and language that are often inadequate to the task. The apologies that preface each of the narratives are more than quaint, antiquated statements that serve conventional roles in the writing of the period; rather, they are frequently heartfelt statements about the powerlessness felt by the narrators in the face of their task of communicating the truth about their experiences to predominately white audiences, whom they wish to convince of the illegality and injustice of the institution of chattel slavery. The critic William Andrews examines two narratives' open confession of this sense of inadequacy:

As early as 1790, the black preacher John Marrant lamented in his *Journal* the failure of his "stammering tongue" and of language

itself to signify his experience of divine love: "O where shall we find language sufficient to celebrate his praises." In his *Narrative* of 1849, the fugitive Henry Bibb echoed Marrant on the inadequacy of language, although by this time the unspeakable hellishness of slavery, not the ineffable bliss of salvation, had become the text of most black autobiography. "Reader," Bibb wrote, "believe me when I say, that no tongue, nor pen ever has or can express the horrors of American slavery. Consequently, I despair in finding language to express adequately the deep feelings of my soul, as I contemplate the past history of my life."

This frustration of expression, coupled with the anger of the freed slave as he recalls the past "self" from which he has been delivered, compels the writer to powerful declarations of the new self that contrast with the patterns of oppression and suffering that characterize the past. As the literary historian Andrews put it, using the vocabulary of modern rhetorical discourse:

In a number of black autobiographies of this era, a quest more psycholiterary than spiritual can be discerned. It is spurred by many motives, perhaps the most important of which is the need of an other to declare himself through various linguistic acts, thereby rectifying his abstract unreality, his invisibility in the eyes of his readers, so that he can be recognized as someone to be reckoned with. Such declarative acts . . . include the reconstructing of one's past in a meaningful and instructive form, the appropriating of empowering myths and models of the self from any available resource, and the redefining of one's place in the scheme of things by redefining the language used to locate one in that scheme.

Abuse of Slaves

Unlike Benjamin Franklin or Henry Adams, the slave autobiographer is attempting to escape the past and to recapture it simultaneously, a process of writing history that is further complicated by the problems of writing in English, which is an acquired language, especially for the early slave narrators who had suffered the "middle passage" from Africa. For this reason, the earlier narratives often appear more formal and less angry than nineteenth-century accounts. However, in the Equiano narrative, the formal structure quickly drops away and a more direct appeal to the reader's conscience is addressed in several episodes where the narrator witnesses or suffers torture and abuse by owners, masters, or seamen on the slave ship. These episodes provide another characteristic moment in the slave narratives: the white culture's attempt to dominate and repress the slave through physical abuse. These compelling narratives are successfully governed by rhetorical strategies that give the reader varying exposure to the horrors of chattel slavery. Equiano, for example, does not attempt to sanitize his photographic memory for detail. In one objectively related passage, he describes "the bit," a device used by William Byrd at Westover Plantation in Virginia and cited no fewer than nine times in Byrd's *Secret Diary* (written between 1709 and 1712, published in 1941), and recalled by Toni Morrison in her novel *Beloved* (1987). Equiano remembers:

> When I came into the room . . . I was very much affrighted at some things I saw, and the more so as I had seen a black woman slave as I came through the house, who was cooking the dinner, and the poor creature was cruelly loaded with various kinds of iron machines; she had one particularly on her head, which locked her mouth so fast that she could scarcely speak; and could not eat nor drink. I was much astonished and shocked at this contrivance, which I afterwards learned was called the iron muzzle.

The slave, forced to wear the bit even while working in the house or field, was unable to eat or drink. Most important, the device prevented speech and limited communication among the slaves, another form of identification—dominance over the oppressed by the oppressor. The bit came to symbolize in slave literature the owners' objectives to prevent their "property" from gaining identity as persons and to complicate the process of self-realization.

Identification as oppressed people and acceptance of this condition was clearly the opposite of the impulse to escape into freedom. And yet, the conditions were so intolerable, particularly on the slave ships, that narrators often recount how some "cargo" would prefer the escape of death to continued suffering. Equiano provides such an account, which merits being quoted in full:

> The stench of the hold while we were on the coast was so intolerably loathsome, that it was dangerous to remain there for any time, and some of us had been permitted to stay on the deck for the fresh air; but now that the whole ship's cargo were confined together, it became absolutely pestilential. The closeness of the place, and the heat of the climate, added to the number in the ship, which was so crowded that each had scarcely room to turn himself, almost suffocated us. This produced copious perspirations, so that the air soon became unfit for respiration, from a variety of loathsome smells, and brought on a sickness among the slaves, of which many died—thus falling victims to the improvident avarice, as I may call it, of their purchasers. This wretched situation was again aggravated by the galling of the chains, now become insupportable; and the filth of the necessary tubs, into which the children often fell, and were almost suffocated. The shrieks of the women, and the groans of the dying, rendered the whole a scene of horror almost inconceivable. . . . Often did I think many of the inhabitants of the deep much more happy than myself. I envied them the freedom they enjoyed, and as often wished I could change my condition for theirs. Every circumstance I met with, served only to render my state more painful, and heightened my apprehensions, and my opinion of the cruelty of the whites. . . .
> One day, . . . two of my wearied countrymen who were chained together, . . . preferring death to such a life of misery, somehow

made through the nettings and jumped into the sea: immediately, another quite dejected fellow, who, on account of his illness, was suffered to be out of irons, also followed their example; and I believe many more would very soon have done the same, if they had not been prevented by the ship's crew. . . . Two of the wretches were drowned, but they got the other, and afterwards flogged him unmercifully, for thus attempting to prefer death to slavery.

Equiano's graphic and gothic description of the infamous "Middle Passage" was appropriated by Steven Spielberg in his filming of the Amistad mutiny.

The Equiano narrative, like the later Douglass and Jacobs narratives, also places great importance on familial relations. Equiano is abducted in Africa with his only sister, from whom he is eventually separated but whom he comforts briefly in their initial incarcerations. Later, in the nineteenth century when many slave narratives were edited by the abolitionists who promoted them, domesticity and family relations were often exploited as a rhetorical strategy by which a predominantly female, white audience would be able to identify with the wrenching horror of family disruption among the black slaves. Equiano, writing well before the organized abolitionist movement, anticipates this rhetorical device. The account carries numerous digressions and intrusions by the narrator, who denounces the institution of slavery and its abominations, but perhaps none so ringing as the one at the conclusion of chapter 2, where Equiano attacks the hypocrisy of those who profess Christianity even as they cruelly separate the slave family:

O, ye nominal Christians! might not an African ask you—Learned you this from your God, who says unto you, "Do unto all men as you would men should do unto you?" Is it not enough that we are torn from our country and friends, to toil for your luxury and lust of gain? Must every tender feeling be likewise sacrificed to your avarice? Are the dearest friends and relations, now rendered more dear by their separation from their kindred, still to be parted from each other, and thus prevented from cheering the gloom of slavery, with the small comfort of being together, and mingling their sufferings and sorrows? Why are parents to lose their children, brothers their sisters, or husbands their wives? Surely, this is a new refinement in cruelty, which, while it has no advantage to atone for it, thus aggravates distress, and adds fresh horrors even to the wretchedness of slavery.

This connection of oppression, cruelty, and the destruction of the nuclear family unit is a persistent theme in slave narratives and abolitionist literature of the nineteenth century, including the most powerful abolitionist tract of them all, Harriet Beecher Stowe's *Uncle Tom's Cabin* (1852). Curiously, only in recent years has the now obvious connection between oppression of women and cruelty to black slaves become a prominent subject for critical discourse, though both Stowe and Harriet Jacobs articulated this connection as early as the 1850s. The work of Ann Douglas, Jane Tompkins, Elaine Showalter, Deborah White, Nell Irvin Painter, and Hazel Carby has done much to issue corrective notions about this critical indifference; moreover, one succinct expression of this association and its representation in slave narrative literature of the nineteenth century was well stated by Carolyn Porter:

As a result of the nexus between race and gender in antebellum discourse, the South in Northern eyes was not only black but to a remarkable extent female as well. As the work of the social historians has made clear, nineteenth-century Americans came to embrace a domestic ideology of separate spheres for men and women. Women were enshrined in the private sphere of the home so as to neutralize the threat to masculine control presented by a social scene in which women were increasingly visible—as part of a volatile labor force, as outspoken abolitionists, or as the popular novelists whom Hawthorne disparaged as "scribbling women." Ascribing to women the innate traits of a natural Christian—moral purity, passive obedience, and a habit of maternal self-sacrifice—domestic ideology in effect feminized them . . . By the 1840s, the identification of Afro-Americans and women on the grounds of their shared feminine traits was a common theme among anti-slavery clergymen . . . [and] such appropriations of domestic ideology proved problematic for militant abolitionists like Theodore Parker. As early as 1841, Parker delivered a sermon in which a note of contempt can be heard for the slave's alleged docility. "If the African can be so low that the condition of slavery is tolerable in his eyes, and he can dance in his chains, then it is all the more a sin in the cultivated and strong, in the Christian, to tyrranize over the feeble and defenseless."

What Ann Douglas has called "the feminization of American culture" is represented here; the identification of the slave culture with docility, domesticity, and above all, with Christian meekness and acceptance provided the proslavery advocates with a version of American society that did not correspond to the impulses toward freedom articulated by democratic principles and the rhetoric of abolitionist literature.

Nineteenth-Century Slave Narratives: Frederick Douglass (1818–1895) and Harriet Jacobs (1813–1897)

The most representative examples of the greatest period of slave narrative composition, between 1820 and 1865, include Frederick Douglass' *Narrative of the Life of Frederick Douglass, an American Slave* (1845), a central document of the abolitionist movement that formed the basis of Douglass' two subsequent autobiographies (1855, 1881), and Harriet Jacobs' *Linda: Incidents in the Life of a Slave Girl, Written by Herself* (1861). Jacobs and Douglass have provided extraordinary visions of the hardships suffered by slaves of both sexes.

The Douglass narrative employs the family structure to reveal problems inherent in the social relations of slave families with the owner's family. While a prominently accepted false impression of the "happy slaves" was circulated by such proslavery opponents of abolition as George Fitzhugh, whose *Sociology for the South; or, The Failure of Free Society* (1854) and *Cannibals All!* (1857) depicted the slaves happily living in the shadow of the master's "big house," a much more accurate and articulate picture of the realities of slave experience may be found in the pages of Douglass' and Jacobs' narratives. For example, many slaves had to endure the double relationship of servant and child to their master and father. Douglass himself was such a mulatto product of a white father and a slave mother, and he observes that

such slaves invariably suffer greater hardships, and have more to contend with, than others. They are, in the first place, a constant offence to their mistress. She is ever disposed to find fault with them; they can seldom do any thing to please her; she is never better pleased than when she sees them under the lash, especially when she suspects her husband of showing to his mulatto children favors which he withholds from his black slaves. The master is frequently compelled to sell this class of his slaves, out of deference to the feelings of his white wife; and, cruel as the deed may strike any one to be, for a man to sell his own children to human flesh-mongers, it is often the dictate of humanity for him to do so; for, unless he does this, he must not only whip them himself, but must stand by and see one white son tie up his brother, of but a few shades darker complexion than himself, and ply the gory lash to his naked back; and if he lisp one word of disapproval, it is set down to his paternal partiality, and only makes a bad matter worse, both for himself and the slave whom he would protect and defend.

Recent critics like Ann Douglas and Jane Tompkins have described the relationship between the tradition of sentimental fiction in

England, such as Samuel Richardson's *Pamela; or, Virtue Rewarded* (1740) and *Clarissa; or, The History of a Young Lady* (1747–1748), and slave narrative literature, including Stowe's *Uncle Tom's Cabin*. The feminizing of southern culture suggested earlier is also represented in slave narratives by the few kindnesses shown young slaves by mistresses who wish to teach their daily companions to read, such as Mrs. Auld in the Douglass account. However, these unusual people are contrasted with more predictable characters who represent the masculine harshness of the dominant and oppressive system of chattel slavery. In Harriet Jacobs' *Incidents*, for example, the Flints are portrayed as a cruel master and mistress who are antagonistic to Jacobs' persona-narrator, Linda Brent, throughout the account:

> Mrs. Flint, like many southern women, was totally deficient in energy. She had not strength to superintend her household affairs; but her nerves were so strong, that she could sit in her easy chair and see a woman whipped, till the blood trickled from every stroke of the lash. She was a member of the church; but partaking of the Lord's Supper did not seem to put her in a Christian frame of mind. If dinner was not served at the exact time on that particular Sunday, she would station herself in the kitchen, and wait till it was dished, and then spit in all the kettles and pans that had been used for cooking. She did this to prevent the cook and her children from eking out the meagre fare with the remains of the gravy and other scrapings. The slaves could get nothing to eat except what she chose to give them.

Similarly, Dr. Flint is described as cruel and inhuman in his relations to the slaves, regardless of his compassion as a physician to whites in the narrative:

> Dr. Flint was an epicure. The cook never sent a dinner to his table without fear and trembling; for if there happened to be a dish not to his liking, he would either order her to be whipped, or compel her to eat every mouthful in his presence. . . . They had a pet dog, that was a nuisance in the house. The cook was ordered to make some Indian mush for him. He refused to eat, and when his head was held over it, the froth flowed from his mouth into the basin. He died a few minutes after. When Dr. Flint came in, he said the mush had not been well cooked, and that was the reason the animal would not eat it. He sent for the cook, and compelled her to eat it. He thought that the woman's stomach was stronger than the dog's; but her sufferings afterwards proved that he was mistaken. This poor woman endured many cruelties from her master and mistress; sometimes she was locked up, away from her nursing baby, for a whole day and night.

Southern women like Mrs. Auld appear as models of Christian charity; others, like Mrs. Flint, would represent the cruel and inconsistent side of the Christian faith, which throughout the abolitionist and proslavery debate was cited for support by both sides.

The style and structure of the Jacobs narrative have been compared to those of the traditional sentimental novel, like Richardson's *Pamela* and *Clarissa*. It is important to distinguish Jacobs' experiential account, however, from novels such as Stowe's *Uncle Tom's Cabin*, which also makes use of sentimental conventions. Stowe's account is fictional, a product of the imagination. Jacobs' account is a record of her remembered experience. Jacobs writes in her preface:

> Reader, be assured this narrative is no fiction. I am aware that some of my adventures may seem incredible; but they are, nevertheless, strictly true. I have not exaggerated the wrongs inflicted by Slavery; on the contrary, my descriptions fall far short of the facts. I have concealed the names of places, and given persons fictitious names. I have no motive for secrecy on my own account, but I deemed it kind and considerate towards others to pursue this course.

The Jacobs narrative dramatically interweaves the personal account of Linda's efforts to evade the sexual predator, Dr. Flint, with glimpses of the horrors of slavery. However, unlike the Equiano narrative with its graphic description of the Middle Passage, or the Douglass narrative with its dramatic accounts of the flogging of Aunt Hester and Hetty, the Jacobs narrative does not attempt to shock its readers into a recognition of the horrors of slavery. That task is left to the sermonic voice of the narrator, who intrudes into the work more than Douglass' narrative voice to interpret and sermonize about the peculiar institution. For example, Jacobs does give a few specific examples of the brutal horrors of slavery, but only in glimpses or, literally, sound bites. In chapter 9, "Sketches of Neighboring Slaveholders," Jacobs describes an event where a male slave was tied to the ground underneath a roasting pork, so that, as the meat cooked, "scalding drops of fat continually fell on the bare flesh." She also describes an incident in which a runaway slave was captured and punished by his placement between the screws of a cotton gin—a prison that he does not escape alive. But the purpose of her narrative was not to provide the reader with alarming accounts of physical abuse, and she avoids the graphic details often presented in other slave narratives. One of the most important statements of her own experience makes this intention clear:

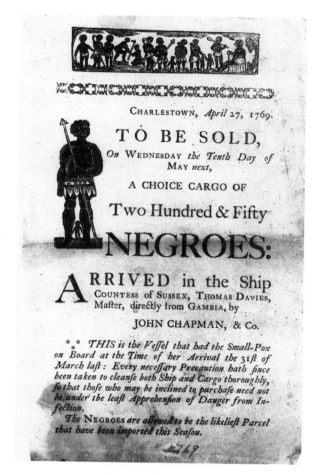

A notice from 1769.

I was never cruelly overworked; I was never lacerated with the whip from head to foot; I was never so beaten and bruised that I could not turn from one side to the other; I never had my heel-strings cut to prevent my running away; I was never chained to a log and forced to drag it about while I toiled in the fields from morning till night; I was never branded with a hot iron, or torn by bloodhounds. . . .But, though my life was comparatively devoid of hardships, God pity the woman who is compelled to lead such a life!

Of course the litany of torture described in the previous passage may have never been Harriet Jacobs' plight; however, the implication of this passage is that these torments were routinely applied to her fellow slaves, her brothers and sisters in bondage. The dramatic effect thus created is one of the most effective rhetorical strategies of her entire narrative.

The slave narrator retrospectively examines his own past, intensely personal experience. But the objective of the narrative is to represent a linear development between that experience and the achievement of freedom. Thus the perspective of the narrator is that of a storyteller, narrating events as they happened but providing the context of purpose and narrative structure. Unlike Holocaust narratives, which were often firsthand accounts of episodes smuggled out of the concentration camps at a time roughly contemporary with those events, the slave narrative's unique retrospective account follows a purposeful teleology.

Douglass' Persona

Of the nineteenth-century slave narrators, Frederick Douglass was the most prolific. He produced three autobiographical accounts: *Narrative of the Life of Frederick Douglass, an American Slave* (1845); *My Bondage and My Freedom* (1855); and *The Life and Times of Frederick Douglass* (1881). The first and last accounts contained the phrase "written by himself" in the title, suggesting the need to verify the narratives at the beginning and the end of his career. But the three accounts are very different from each other, in more ways than simply that the later accounts add material that was not available in the earlier narratives. Each of these narratives—as in all autobiographical writing—contains a "persona" of the author, a representative figure whom the author wishes to project to his reading audience. Benjamin Franklin's four-part *Autobiography* moves quickly from a personal history to Franklin the civic and public figure. Similarly, the three Douglass accounts all begin with his life as a slave and the importance of personal freedom as well as the parallel concern, freedom for all enslaved persons. While Douglass never lost sight of these parallel concerns, his later narratives, especially the *Life and Times*, seem to add factual data to bring the reader up to date on his public success. (Douglass went from slavery to advising four presidents during Reconstruction.) In the several editions of the *Life and Times*, Douglass abandons the consistency and unity of the first two narratives and seems only to add information about his life.

Self-representation is a tricky business, and Douglass provides the reader with two extremely disciplined and controlled narratives. As William Pannapacker put it, "Douglass's 1845 *Narrative* details how the former slave managed to overcome systematic exclusion from the advantages of middle-class domestic life: a birthday, a mother, siblings, marriage, and literacy. Douglass's determination to struggle with Covey, the 'nigger-breaker,' racially charged as it is, elides the issue of race by transforming Douglass from a 'slave' into a generalized 'man.' Douglass's struggle thereby becomes universalized as one of dominance and submission. Ultimately, *Douglass*, with a name taken from the history of Scottish resistance—is aligned with the rhetoric of the American Revolution." This early incarnation of the self, the "man who was made a slave" and the "slave who became a man" in the confrontation with Covey, is not entirely abandoned by Douglass in his next autobiographical incarnation, *My Bondage and My Freedom*. Here, the reader is not only provided with an additional decade of Douglass' life; he or she also views an altered Douglass, one more conscious of his public role as an abolitionist and one whose confidence and determination seem more secure, now that his freedom has been purchased by British admirers.

As Douglass himself stated it, seeming to critique his own persona of the early years, "You must not judge me now by what I then was—a change of circumstances, has made a surprising change in me. Frederick Douglass, the *freeman*, is a very different person from Frederick Bailey, the *slave*." This kind of attempt to distance the self-as-author from earlier personae of the self, represented in earlier writings or public appearances, is not unusual for autobiographers who compose more than one version of their narratives (for example, Douglass, Walt Whitman, or P. T. Barnum). As Pannapacker argued, "Most generally stated, autobiographical revision reveals the alienation of an author from earlier textual constructions of his or her identity. Revisers, perhaps more than other autobiographers, express dissatisfaction with the self-text relationship. Even as the pen moves across the page, the 'I' of the previous sentence becomes increasingly discontinuous from the self in the present; the 'I' becomes an historical construct, an impersonation, a fiction that should be in the third person usually remains in the first. This essential flaw in the genre is particularly problematic when the subject engages in autobiography at a relatively young age, as Douglass, Barnum, and Whitman all did. To avoid complication, an autobiography should be written just before death, when the self has less potential to change and alienation from the textual self becomes less likely."

The three Douglass narratives thus present an evolutionary view of the man, from the abject misery of chattel slavery to one of America's most "representative men," as Ralph Waldo Emerson would call this pantheon of heroes. And with each revision of the original 1845 *Narrative,* not only are readers given new information; they are also presented with an altered figure of the autobiographical self.

Two types of scenes inevitably occupy prominent places in all slave narratives: the flogging or whipping and the slave auction. These scenes, intended to incite readers to agitate for abolition, are brutal, but they are not generally embellished nor are they as numerous in the slave narratives as they no doubt were in the everyday experience of chattel slaves. In the Douglass narrative, for example, the transformation from dependent and uncertain adolescence to full and assertive manhood is represented through a violent confrontation in which Douglass threatens the slave breaker Covey. The confrontation with Covey is clearly designed to illustrate Douglass' emergence into adulthood through courage. "You have seen how a man was made a slave; you shall see how a slave was made a man," he writes by way of introduction. He then recalls how in 1833, on a hot day in August, exactly six months into his year of "slave training," Covey required arduously heavy work that strained Douglass physically:

When I could stand no longer, I fell, and felt as if held down by an immense weight. . . . He came to the spot, and, after looking at me awhile, asked me what was the matter. I told him as well as I could, for I scarce had strength to speak. He then gave me a savage kick in the side, and told me to get up. I tried to do so, but fell back in the attempt. He gave me another kick, and again told me to rise. . . . While down in this situation, Mr. Covey took up the hickory slat . . . and with it gave me a heavy blow upon the head, making a large wound, and the blood ran freely;

and with this again told me to get up. . . . I made no effort to comply, having now made up my mind to let him do his worst. . . . Mr. Covey had now left me to my fate.

Douglass escapes for the night to his master, Thomas Auld, who had sent him to Covey for breaking. But he was forced to return and received no sympathy from Auld, despite his brutalized appearance. Thus Douglass was forced to confront Covey physically, and it became the making of him as a man:

Mr. Covey seemed now to think he had me, and could do what he pleased; but at this moment—from whence came the spirit I don't know—I resolved to fight; and, suiting my action to the resolution, I seized Covey hard by the throat . . . My resistance was so entirely unexpected, that Covey seemed taken all aback. He trembled like a leaf. . . . He asked me if I meant to persist in my resistance. I told him I did, come what might; that he had used me like a brute for six months, and that I was determined to be used so no longer. . . . We were at it for nearly two hours. Covey at length let me go . . . saying that if I had not resisted, he would not have whipped me half so much. The truth was, that he had not whipped me at all. . . .

This battle with Mr. Covey was the turning-point in my career as a slave. It rekindled the few expiring embers of freedom, and revived within me a sense of my own manhood. It recalled the departed self-confidence, and inspired me again with a determination to be free.

The Covey confrontation becomes, in the retrospective narrative structure, a rite of passage by which Douglass achieves manhood within the context of slavery. But this scene appears relatively late in the narrative, and it is paralleled by one very early in chapter 1, where the seven-year-old Douglass learns what it means to be a slave by witnessing the flogging of his aunt:

The overseer's name was Plummer. Mr. Plummer was a miserable drunkard, a profane swearer, and a savage monster. He always went armed with a cowskin [whip] and a heavy cudgel. I have known him to cut and slash the women's heads so horribly, that even master would be enraged at his cruelty, and would threaten to whip him if he did not mind himself. Master, however, was not a humane slaveholder. It required extraordinary barbarity on the part of an overseer to affect him.

This passage also suggests the evil effects of slavery as an institution on the owners and overseers; the demonic other in the slave narrative is the institution itself, and it is incarnated in its most visible representatives, the slave owner, the slave trader, the slave breaker, and the overseer. No one involved in the institution escapes its barbaric influence; slaves are not the only human beings victimized by the institution. In some respects, heroic figures like Douglass and Jacobs rise above their origins through the course of their narratives to triumph over the institution in ways that their masters and overseers are unable to do. Being "hardened by a long life of slaveholding," a phrase Douglass applies to owners and masters, suggests an opposing perspective the narrator has gained that will never be available to the master. The episode that follows confirms this observation:

> He would at times seem to take great pleasure in whipping a slave. I have often been awakened at the dawn of day by the most heartrending shrieks of an own aunt of mine, whom he used to tie up to a joist, and whip upon her naked back till she was literally covered with blood. No words, no tears, no prayers, from his gory victim, seemed to move his iron heart from its bloody purpose. The louder she screamed, the harder he whipped; and where the blood ran fastest, there he whipped longest. He would whip her to make her scream, and whip her to make her hush; and not until overcome by fatigue, would he cease to swing the blood-clotted cowskin.

Here, Douglass recalls a scene in which he probably witnessed the physical rape of his Aunt Hester, who would have been approximately twenty-five years old when he was seven. The language of this passage clearly shows a rhythmic crescendo of sexual orgasm, after which the exhausted male rapist retires from the bloody scene. He was, after all, a man who had been "hardened" by a "lifetime of slaveholding." To the modern reader, this message is not altogether subtle; however, in the context of Douglass' 1845 account, this was an encoding of the physical violence against women that slaves were often required to witness.

Multiple Narrative Voices

The Douglass narrative operates on two levels simultaneously, as do most of the slave accounts. These "levels of narration" are, in turn, related to the "voices" used by the author to represent the events of the past. Multiple voices or personae appear in all autobiographical writing, but the use of at least two voices is essential to slave narration especially. First, there is the voice of the person recounting a specific experience of the past, which is immediately followed by a commentary by the adult author, who retrospectively recalls the event and moralizes or sermonizes on it. This "contextualizing" of experience characterizes the narrative method of almost all antebellum slave narratives. Few are simply literal accounts without commentary or evaluation by the narrator. The interior narrative here tells the story of a bildungsroman, the narrator's movement from youth to adulthood through coming to terms with the environment external to his developing self. But it also addresses a larger, external audience, with graphic scenes like the brutal whipping of his aunt, which are designed to alert the reading audience to the evils of slavery as an institution as much as to recall an event as it was perceived by the youthful protagonist. This didactic function was sometimes exploited by the abolitionist supporters who edited the slave narratives, but the tension in each document relies on a balance between the interior and exterior narratives. Jacobs' *Incidents* offers the intimate details of Linda Brent's feelings and reactions as she develops into adulthood, chronicling some of the most horrifying institutional abuses found in the slave literature, most particularly the sexual abuse of the slave women by the slave masters. Similarly, the Douglass Aunt Hester whipping episode serves a dual purpose for its author, who provides a retrospective commentary on it by way of conclusion:

> I remember the first time I ever witnessed this horrible exhibition. I was quite a child, but I well remember it. I never shall forget it whilst I remember any thing. It was the first of a long series of such outrages, of which I was doomed to be a witness and a participant. It struck me with awful force. It was the blood-stained gate, the entrance to the hell of slavery, through which I was about to pass. It was a most terrible spectacle. I wish I could commit to paper the feelings with which I beheld it. . . .
>
> I was so terrified and horror-stricken at the sight, that I hid myself in a closet, and dared not venture out till long after the bloody transaction was over. I expected it would be my turn next. It was all new to me. I had never seen any thing like it before.

Here, the narrator conflates the point of view of a preadolescent youth witnessing the sadistic beating of a seminude woman whose offense was that she had been "unfaithful" to the master through her romantic attentions to a fellow slave, Ned Roberts. The motif of the master's jealous rage belongs to the interior narrative of the experience of young Douglass; the scene itself and the injustice perpetrated on the powerless victim of this sexual and physical abuse belongs to the narrative's intended purpose of revealing to a primarily white audience the evils inflicted on black slaves by their perverted masters and overseers. The birthing metaphor suggests the beginning of his awareness that he was a slave.

A similar scene appears near the beginning of Jacobs' narrative, and again, the spectacle both illustrates the growth of the protagonist and alerts the readers to the evils of slavery. The effect is in some ways heightened by the way in which the brutality is witnessed; Linda Brent hears rather than sees the beating: "When I had been in the family a few weeks, one of the plantation slaves was brought to town, by order of his master. It was near night when he arrived, and Dr. Flint ordered him to be taken to the work house, and tied up to the joist, so that his feet would just escape the ground. In that situation he was to wait till the doctor had taken his tea."

This deliberate juxtaposition of brutality and gentility in the single figure of Dr. Flint reinforces the identity grouping that the slave narrative imposes upon its characters. At once, Dr. Flint elevates himself above the slave victim by ordering the punishment about to be inflicted; the slave repeatedly learns his identity in the evil system by reminders of his powerlessness in the hands of brutes who are, to the external world, ladies and gentlemen. Only the slave victim as inside narrator can tell the true story of the master's character:

> I shall never forget that night. Never before, in my life had I *heard* hundreds of blows fall, in succession, on a human being. His piteous *groans,* and his "O, pray don't, massa," *rang in my ear* for months afterwards. . . . I went into the work house the next morning, and saw the cowhide still wet with blood, and the boards all covered with gore. The poor man lived.   (emphasis added)

Note that Jacobs witnesses the flogging audially; Douglass actually *sees* the flogging of his Aunt Hester.

This episode is accompanied by a third motif, which in some narratives provides the most revealing indictment of slave abuse: the victimized man was accused of saying that his master was the father of his wife's child. "There were many conjectures as to the cause of this terrible punishment. Some said master accused him of stealing corn; others said the slave had quarreled with his wife, in the presence of the overseer, and had accused his master of being the father of her child. They were both black, and the child was very fair." Just as Douglass had alerted his readers to the sociology of slave owners and their slave mistresses, Jacobs intro-

687

duces the jealous wife as a villainous character who extends the brutality of her husband's infidelity to the object of his lust: "I once saw a young slave girl dying soon after the birth of a child nearly white. In her agony she cried out, 'O Lord, come and take me!' Her mistress stood by, and mocked at her like an incarnate fiend. 'You suffer, do you?' she exclaimed. 'I am glad of it. You deserve it all, and more too.' "

Slave Treatment

An important theme in the Douglass account of the brutal whipping of his aunt is that of sexual abuse of female slaves. The Jacobs narrative extends and develops this aspect of the slave experience by examining the tensions in human experience when virtue must be compromised and then is rewarded. This feature of the sentimental novel, from *Pamela* and *Clarissa* to *Jane Eyre*, becomes an organizing principle in the Jacobs narrative; however, it is also based on the actual life experience of the author, so that the "virtue rewarded" convention is just that, a literary and narrative convention that is appropriated for organizational purposes. Jacobs repeatedly appeals to her predominately white, female audience that she not be held to the same moral standards of virtue that they hold each other and themselves to. She clearly distinguishes between the plight of the female slave and the white woman in antebellum society.

Jacobs' narrative indicts both the men and the women in white slave society for abusing the victimized black woman slave. Her long, episodic narrative, ingeniously related through the persona Linda Brent, adheres to a teleology of purpose as she moves from incarceration toward personal freedom, which is thwarted by the sexual assaults she suffers from Dr. Flint. This pattern is established very early in the story; when Brent is quite young, she is given an identity in relation to Flint that initially terrorizes her, but that creates a revulsion toward her persecutor and motivates her escape from his lustful grasp:

For my master, whose restless, craving, vicious nature moved about day and night, seeking whom to devour, had just left me, with stinging, scorching words; words that scathed ear and brain like fire. O, how I despised him! I thought how glad I should be, if some day when we walked the earth, it would open and swallow him up, and disencumber the world of a plague. . . . When he told me that I was made for his use, made to obey his command in *every* thing, that I was nothing but a slave, whose will must and should surrender to his, never before had my puny arm felt half so strong.

The imagery here is biblical, and the creature who "walked to and fro upon the earth" in the Old Testament's Book of Job was Satan.

The analogies to disease and to beasts are also commonplace in slave narratives. Using a technique of inversion, the narratives depict the hypocritical Christian slave owners as pigs, dogs, worms, and creatures below man in the hierarchy of creation, thus ironically reversing the literally subhuman treatment inflicted on the slaves by their white masters.

The social perspective of the Jacobs account is exceptionally rich because the protagonist moves from the South to the North and then travels to England as the companion of a deceased friend's child, where she makes comparisons between American slavery and the conditions of the rural poor of nineteenth-century England:

I heard much about the oppression of the poor in Europe. The people I saw around me were, many of them, among the poorest poor. But when I visited their little thatched cottages, I felt that the condition of even the meanest and most ignorant among them was vastly superior to the condition of the most favored slaves in America. They labored hard; but they were not ordered out to toil while the stars were in the sky, and driven and slashed by the overseer, through heat and cold, till the stars shone out again. Their homes were very humble; but they were protected by law. No insolent patrols could come, in the dead of night, and flog them at their pleasure. The father, when he closed his cottage door, felt safe with his family around him. No master or overseer could come and take from him his wife, or his daughter. They must separate to earn their living; but the parents knew where their children were going, and could communicate with them by letters. The relations of husband and wife, parent and child, were too sacred for the richest noble in the land to violate with impunity. Much was being done to enlighten these poor people. Schools were established among them, and benevolent societies were active in efforts to ameliorate their condition. There was no law forbidding them to learn to read and write; and if they helped each other in spelling out the Bible, they were in no danger of thirty-nine lashes, as was the case with myself and poor, pious, old uncle Fred. I repeat that the most ignorant and the most destitute of these peasants was a thousand fold better off than the most pampered American slave.

Family Ties

The emphasis in the Jacobs narrative on family unity and the sacred ties of family bonds is characteristic of slave narrative literature. However, Linda Brent's experience as a mother and wife is most poignant because she was separated from her children when they were very young and only after their father, Mr. Sands, purchased them from Dr. Flint was Linda able to observe their growth and development from her hiding place in a small shed adjacent to her grandmother's living quarters. This episode was based on Jacobs' actual seven years of confinement. Her small children were unaware of her presence in the closet. She observed them through peepholes in the wall, maintaining steadfast silence not only because she feared discovery by Dr. Flint but also because her own children might inadvertently reveal her secret whereabouts. The story of those seven dreadful years, when the heroine was unable to stand or to sit or even to see in order to read, are some of the most dramatic in the narrative and they are based on the actual life experience of Har-

riet Jacobs. They are paralleled and reinforced by the hideous scenes of the slave auctions, where families are divided by the auctioneer's hammer. In one brief chapter, "The Slaves' New Year's Day," Jacobs recaptures the anguish of this moment:

> Hiring-day at the south takes place on the 1st of January. On the 2d, the slaves are expected to go to their new masters. On a farm, they work until the corn and cotton are laid. They then have two holidays. Some masters give them a good dinner under the trees. This over, they work until Christmas eve. If no heavy charges are meantime brought against them, they are given four or five holidays, whichever the master or overseer may think proper. Then comes New Year's eve; and they gather together their little alls, or more properly speaking, their little nothings, and wait anxiously for the dawning of day. At the appointed hour the grounds are thronged with men, women, and children, waiting, like criminals, to hear their doom pronounced. The slave is sure to know who is the most humane, or cruel master, within forty miles of him. . . . If a slave is unwilling to go with his new master, he is whipped. . . . The whip is used till the blood flows at his feet; and his stiffened limbs are put in chains, to be dragged in the field for days and days!

There are literally hundreds of vivid accounts of slave auctions, including narratives and journal entries written by whites who sympathized with the abolitionist cause or who simply recorded events as they were witness to them. One such account of a slave auction in Richmond, Virginia, was written by the landscape architect Frederick Law Olmsted, designer of the Boston Common and New York's Central Park and an acquaintance of William Lloyd Garrison.

The Jacobs narrative intensifies the family disruption cited objectively in the Olmsted account; however, the effect of disunion in each is tragically recalled:

> But to the slave mother, New Year's Day comes laden with peculiar sorrows. She sits

on her cold cabin floor, watching the children who may all be torn from her the next morning; and often does she wish that they might die before the day dawns. She may be an ignorant creature, degraded by the system that has brutalized her from childhood; but she has a mother's instincts, and is capable of feeling a mother's agonies.

On one of these sale days, I saw a mother lead seven children to the auction-block. She knew that *some* of them would be taken from her; but they took *all*. The children were sold to a slave-trader, and their mother was bought by a man in her own town. Before night her children were all far away. She begged the trader to tell her where he intended to take them; this he refused to do. How *could* he, when he knew he would sell them, one by one, wherever he could command the highest price? I met that mother in the street, and her wild, haggard face lives today in my mind. She wrung her hands in anguish, and exclaimed, "Gone! All gone! Why *don't* God kill me?" I had no words wherewith to comfort her. Instances of this kind are of daily, yea, of hourly occurrence.

Nor are children and mothers the only poignant victims of the institution's indifference to human feeling. Elderly slaves were regarded as property with diminishing value, and they were often cast off as they became weaker and less able to work.

The Narrator's Voice

The inhumanity of the auction scenes and the arbitrary nature of the sales, the commodification of humans as "lots" and "labor," provide the slave narrative with dramatic force. In the Jacobs narrative, as in many contemporary accounts, the protagonist is striving to escape from the clutches of many antagonists, slave owners, slave breakers, slave overseers, and slave catchers. But looming very large in the background of each of the narratives is the overarching evil, the pervasive depravity, of the institution of slavery itself. Each narrative relates particular instances and experiences within the institutional and historical moment; however, the evil victimizes everyone associated with slavery, and all the narratives strive for abolition not only to free the black slaves but also to free society from a blight that will forever tarnish character, humanity, and the democratic, free society the United States was supposed to be. Thus the credibility of each narrative must be assessed in relation to this larger purpose of abolishing slavery as well as the peculiar relation of a personal history.

As in all writing, the voice of the narrator is an important factor in determining the veracity of the story. This becomes especially important in a narrative that addresses a specific reader— as the slave narratives were usually addressed to a predominately white female audience— whom the writers wished to convince of the evils of chattel slavery. These accounts resemble each other so closely that the reader of many will be inclined to think that they were composed according to a formula that was circulated among literate former slaves who had agreed on a convention of narration that would best persuade northern (and some southern) readers that slavery should be abolished. The narratives have many common, formulaic elements: for example, the transition from slavery to freedom as a structural and organizational principle, graphic descriptions of beatings and floggings, indictments of the sexual abuse of female slaves, reports of the hostility of the narrator's environment to his or her development as a person, the focus on family (both slave's and master's), and a first-person delivery that is frequently punctuated by direct addresses to the reader. It is well known that many slave narratives originated in an oral tradition that depended on formulaic patterns to facilitate the speaker's memory. Few slaves could read, so the narratives depend heavily on repeated episodes that are transmitted accurately because they are expressed in oral formulas. And it is also true that the politically active abolitionist movement sponsored the publication of slave narratives as a way of dramatizing their social and moral objectives, so that in some cases editing of the narratives was done to maximize their effectiveness as political documents. The

Douglass narrative, for example, was edited and introduced by William Lloyd Garrison, publisher of the *Liberator*, an abolitionist newspaper.

Nevertheless, the slave narratives also arose from personal experience, so that the credibility of each account should be assessed on its individual merits. No two narratives are so similar that modern readers should regard them as false historical documents; indeed, one of the ways in which the credibility of a narrative was guaranteed was by the inclusion of textual proof, a bill of sale or reward notice, which anchored the narrative in a specific historical moment. The broadside printed to offer a reward for the recapture of Harriet Jacobs is such a document, and the inclusion of it in the narrative has a chilling effect on the reader:

$100 REWARD WILL be given for the apprehension and delivery of my Servant Girl HARRIET. She is a light mulatto, 21 years of age, about 5 feet 4 inches high, of a thick and corpulent habit, having on her head a thick covering of black hair that curls naturally, but which can be easily combed straight. She speaks easily and fluently, and has an agreeable carriage and address. Being a good seamstress, she has been accustomed to dress well, has a variety of very fine clothes, made in the prevailing fashion, and will probably appear, if abroad, tricked out in gay and fashionable finery. As this girl absconded from the plantation of my son without any known cause or provocation, it is probable she designs to transport herself to the North.

The above reward, with all reasonable charges, will be given for apprehending her, or securing her in any prison or jail within the U. States.

All persons are hereby forewarned against harboring or entertaining her, or being in any way instrumental in her escape, under the most rigorous penalties of the law.

JAMES NORCOM
Edenton, N.C. June 30

The presence of this documentary notice does more than verify the Jacobs account; it also gives the narrative voice historical immediacy.

Rhetorically, it is a valuable and essential component of the narrative's force.

Another rhetorical strategy employed by the slave narratives was to call on well-known abolitionist leaders to provide prefatory testimonials to the historical veracity of the narratives that followed. Douglass' narrative includes both a preface by William Lloyd Garrison and a letter from Wendell Phillips. Jacobs' own thorough prefatory explanation of the facts of her narrative, signed by "Linda Brent," is followed by the testimonial of her careful editor, Lydia Maria Child, who writes:

The author of the following autobiography is personally known to me, and her conversation and manners inspire me with confidence. . . . I believe those who know her will not be disposed to doubt her veracity, though some incidents in her story are more romantic than fiction. At her request, I have revised her manuscript; but such changes as I have made have been mainly for the purposes of condensation and orderly arrangement. I have not added anything to the incidents, or changed the import of her very pertinent remarks. With trifling exceptions, both the ideas and language are her own.

This kind of rhetoric attempted to disarm the cynic and the proslavery opponent who might otherwise have used the document to discredit the narrator by focusing on biased authorial intention and inaccuracy of relation, though some reviewers remained skeptical. As William Andrews puts it,

Ultimately, the mode of black autobiographical discourse itself undertakes the task of validating its own claims to reality and its author's claims to an identity. Early black autobiographers seem preoccupied with authenticating their stories and themselves by documenting both according to their fidelity to the facts of human nature and experience that white Americans assumed to be true. . . . Black autobiography is designed to establish the grounds on which one may decide what will count as fact in a narrative and what mode of interpretation is best suited to a full comprehension of that fact. As a rhetorical mode, black autobiography then employs various methods of persuading (or manipulating) the reader to make decisions about truth and significance in a narrative consonant with the aim of the autobiographer. Thus Afro-American autobiography mediates between historical, rhetorical, and tropological truth within the discursive framework of narrative patterns of the recovered life, and dramatic patterns of the evolving act of recovery.

The slave narratives are directed toward a reading audience, the contemporary white oppressor, and any interaction between reader and author perceived in the narrative dynamic must keep in focus the two historical personae each narrative employs, the narrator's real voice and the voice that answers to the reader's assumed response. Considered in this historical context, the slave narratives of the American eighteenth and nineteenth centuries offer some of the most troubling insights into the American past. As literature, they are valuable precisely because they intelligently employ rhetorical strategies and a mode of discourse that had to be learned outside formal educational traditions. If they are occasionally romantic and sentimental, they are also graphically realistic and horrifying, perhaps even gothic. They are, in short, comprehensive human literature, and they powerfully represent one of the most difficult stages in the growth of the United States from youth to maturity.

Uncle Tom's Cabin

Finally, it is important to recognize the influence of the slave narrative as literature on the emerging canon of American writing, not only in the recapitulation of slave narrative techniques in the novels of Toni Morrison and Octavia Butler in the twentieth century but also in the more direct importance to the most influential work of the nineteenth century, Harriet Beecher Stowe's *Uncle Tom's Cabin.*

Both Stowe and Jacobs appropriated the format and structure of the sentimental novel, a popular form that had entertained readers for over a century and one that provided opportunities for melodramatic death scenes and searing accounts of families separated at slave auctions.

There are other, more subtle parallels between the Jacobs hand account of slavery and the Stowe fiction modeled on the slave experience. For example, both Stowe and Jacobs ask the reader to identify with the plight of a heroine in distress. After hearing that someone had bought her children at auction, but before learning that the purchaser was their father, Mr. Sands, Jacobs "bit her lips till the blood came to keep from crying." In Stowe's account, after learning that Harry was about to be sold away from her, Eliza's heart "has no tears to give,—it drops only blood, bleeding itself away in silence." Jacobs loosely follows a chronological structure in her narrative, but the primary formal organizing principle is the seduction novel. The incidents that are organized around the persona of Linda Brent form the plot of the narrative, and these pearls on a strand are gathered by the author, and the reader, to form an organized whole. While there is a continuous theme of retrospective commentary through the secondary narrative voice, there is also the sympathetic central figure of the heroine, who is relentlessly pursued by Dr. Flint as both an object of sexual obsession and a retrieval of lost property. Similarly, Stowe provides the reader with a loosely organized plot structure, one that Charles Dickens harshly critiqued as "artless" and "disorganized." There are, of course, many parallels between the Douglass 1845 *Narrative,* Stowe's 1852 *Uncle Tom's Cabin,* and Jacobs' 1861 *Incidents.* These almost exactly contemporary antislavery writings employed a variety of rhetorical strategies to persuade the readership of the evils of slavery, including the popular trickster tales so common in William Augustus Longstreet's *Georgia Scenes.* As Lewis Hyde observes in *Trickster Makes This World,* "it may seem odd to seek out a vein of trickster consciousness in a person as serious and moralizing as Frederick Douglass," but Douglass and George Harris in *Uncle Tom's Cabin* both employ trickster devices in their escapes from bondage and it is clear that the authors of these texts were exploiting well-known devices of the genre in composing their own narratives. In twentieth-century accounts, such works as Ishmael Reed's *Flight to Canada* recuperate the nineteenth-century antebellum slave narrative, where Quickskill even calls his escape a "Liza Leap" recalling the escape of Eliza and Harry from Kentucky to Ohio over the ice floes of the river. However, more than any other nineteenth- or twentieth-century writer, Harriet Beecher Stowe explored the potential for fictionalizing the slave narrative into a document of moral and persuasive power, what the abolitionist movement called "moral suasion." Lacking political power and having essentially no voice in public affairs, women like Stowe and Lydia Maria Child used their talents as writers, attempting to reach a wide audience through narrative rhetoric rather than the political speech or sermon delivered from pulpits commanded by men. It worked; the influence of Stowe's book was greater than any speech or sermon of the three decades preceding the Civil War, and Abraham Lincoln was not far off the mark when he welcomed Stowe to the White House in 1863 by observing, "So this is the little lady who started this great big war."

As Stowe makes clear in her 1853 *A Key to Uncle Tom's Cabin*, the antecedent slave narratives were her most prominent literary resource. Both Douglass and Stowe castigate the hypocrisy of the Christian Church, and Stowe, who was the sister of six ministers, daughter of the evangelical president of Lane Seminary in Cincinnati, Lyman Beecher, and wife of Calvin Stowe, minister and professor of religion at Bowdoin College in Maine, unleashes her most powerful criticism in the novel against the Christian Church. Douglass admonishes: "I therefore hate the corrupt, slaveholding, women-whipping, cradle-plundering, partial and hypocritical Chrtistianity of this land," where Stowe concludes her novel with a dramatic challenge to the church: "O Church of Christ, read the signs of the times!" going on to show how the church has failed because it has allowed chattel slavery to continue and has in fact justified it through proslavery sermons. Larry Tise, in *The Proslavery Argument*, shows that of the fifty-five proslavery sermons published in the decade from 1830 to 1840, thirty seven of them were written by northern ministers! Stowe clearly indicts the church, both North and South, in her critique of the hypocrisy of a society that allowed chattel slavery to coexist with democracy committed to the notion that "all men are created equal." She has little patience with the proslavery view that the institution could be justified by Biblical precedent, nor did she accept the "technicality" that the Jeffersonian equality phrase so often used to contrast with the practice of allowing slavery in the United States, "all men are created equal" is in the Declaration of Independence and not included in the document of law, the Constitution. Such facile legal distinctions meant little to Stowe, whose concern was with the moral argument against slavery rather than with the Biblical or legal disputation that had permitted slavery to continue in American society for over two hundred years.

Stowe's appropriation of the slave narrative had much to do with the success of her novel, Living in Cincinnati, Harriet Beecher was provided with a firsthand look at American slavery; Lane Seminary often hosted escaped slaves who came across the river from Kentucky, and she interviewed these slaves. Not only is her work corroborated by the slave narratives examined in this essay; her account is also supported by one of her most prominent sources, Theodore Dwight Weld's *American Slavery As It Is: the Testimony of a Thousand Witnesses* (1839). This book is a journalistic account of slavery and dramatizes the horrors of the institution by gathering newspaper accounts and advertisements for runaway slaves. It stands opposed to such proslavery narratives as Mary Eastman's *Aunt Phillis's Cabin* (1852), which views southern slavery as a paternalistic institution that made salvation available to pagans and demonstrates preference for family life in the monogamous, Western mode made available to the polygamous tribal Africans fortunate enough to be sold into American slavery. The proslavery advocates met a formidable adversary in Harriet Beecher Stowe.

Stowe's appropriation of the slave narrative had much to do with the success of her novel. In the first week of April 1852, *Uncle Tom's Cabin* sold ten thousand copies. By the end of six months it had sold three hundred thousand copies. The printers were unable to keep up with the demand, and in 1861, on the eve of the Civil War it had helped to instigate, the novel was being read in sixteen languages and had sold over four and one half million copies. This is a remarkable statistic even today; in 1861, however, the population of the United States was only thirty-two million and some five million of that number were semiliterate slaves living in the South, where the book was effectively banned. Moreover, the population remaining among whom the book circulated was only twenty-two million, of whom only sixteen million were sufficiently literate or old enough to read the book through. There was therefore one copy of *Uncle Tom's Cabin* for every four of five readers in America in 1862.

The importance of these figures is that ultimately, *Uncle Tom's Cabin* is the most influential slave narrative of them all. As it appropriated not only the content but also the rhetorical strategies and the methodology of the slave narratives, it stands as a powerful reflection of the structure, style, and message of these uniquely American documents. The slave narratives of antebellum America were, like jazz, an original art form contributed to the canon of American literature by the most victimized members of the population in the antebellum United States, for they were not yet US itizens, a political move that would come in 1867, following the Emancipation Proclamation of 1863 and the Thirteenth Amendment to the Constitution in 1865. The slave narratives have gained a permanent place in the canon of American literature, one that is long overdue given the immense influence they have always had on both American literature and the movement of American history before the Civil War.

Selected Bibliography

PRIMARY SOURCES

Allison, Robert J., ed. *The Interesting Narrative of the Life of Olaudah Equiano, Written by Himself*. Boston: Bedford Books of St. Martin's Press, 1995.

Andrews, William L., ed. *The Frederick Douglass Reader*. New York: Oxford University Press, 1996.

Baym, Nina, et al., eds. *The Norton Anthology of American Literature*. Vol. 1, 5th ed. New York: Norton, 1998.

Blight, David, ed. *Narrative of the Life of Frederick Douglass, an American Slave, Written by Himself*. Boston: Bedford Books of St. Martin's Press, 1993.

Brown, William Wells. *The Travels of William Wells Brown, including the Narrative of William Wells Brown, a Fugitive Slave, and The American Fugitive in Europe*. Edited by Paul Jefferson. New York: M. Weiner, 1991.

Cain, William E., ed. *William Lloyd Garrison and the Fight Against Slavery: Selections from the "Liberator."* Boston: Bedford Books of St. Martin's Press, 1995.

Child, Lydia Maria. *An Appeal in Favor of that Class of Americans Called Africans*. Edited with introduction by Carolyn Karcher. Amherst: University of Massachusetts Press, 1996.

———. *A Lydia Maria Child Reader*. Edited by Carolyn Karcher. Durham, N.C.: Duke University Press, 1997.

———. *The Frederick Douglass Papers*. Edited by John Blassingame. New Haven, Conn.: Yale University Press, 1979.

———. *My Bondage and My Freedom*. Edited with an introduction by William Andrews. Urbana: University of Illinois Press, 1987.

———. *Narrative of the Life of Frederick Douglass, an American Slave*. In *The Norton Anthology of American Literature*. Vol. 1, 3d ed. Edited by William Pritchard. New York: Norton, 1989.

Equiano, Olaudah. *The Interesting Narrative of the Life of Olaudah Equiano, or Gustavus Vassa, the African, Written by Himself*. Edited by Francis Murphy. In *The Norton Anthology of American Literature*. Vol. 1, 5th ed. New York: Norton, 1998.

Greenberg, Kenneth S. *The Confessions of Nat Turner and Related Documents*. Boston: Bedford Books of St. Martin's Press, 1996.

Hammon, Briton. *A Narrative of the Uncommon Sufferings, and Surprizing Deliverance of Briton Hammon, a Negro Man. . . .* Boston: Green & Russell, 1760.

Kemble, Fanny. *Journal of a Residence on a Georgian Plantation in 1838–1839*. Edited with an introduction by John A. Scott. New York: Knopf, 1970.

Marrant, John. *A Narrative of the Lord's Wonderful Dealings with John Marrant, a Black. . . .* London, 1785.

McKitrick, Eric. *Slavery Defended: The Views of the Old South.* Englewood Cliffs, N.J.: Prentice-Hall, 1963.

Reed, Ishmael. *Flight to Canada.* New York: Random House, 1976.

Smith, Venture. *A Narrative of the Life and Adventures of Venture, A Native of Africa.* Boston, 1798.

Stowe, Harriet Beecher. *Uncle Tom's Cabin.* Edited by Elizabeth Ammons. New York: Norton, 1994.

Thomas, John. *Slavery Attacked: The Abolitionist Crusade.* Englewood Cliffs, N.J.: Prentice-Hall, 1963.

SECONDARY SOURCES

BIOGRAPHICAL AND CRITICAL STUDIES

Abzug, Robert. *Cosmos Crumbling: American Reform and the Religious Imagination.* New York: Oxford University Press, 1994.

Andrews, William. *To Tell a Free Story: The First Century of Afro-American Autobiography, 1760–1865.* Urbana: University of Illinois Press, 1986.

———, ed. *Critical Essays on Frederick Douglass.* Boston: G. K. Hall, 1991.

Baker, Houston. *Long Black Song: Essays in Black American Literature and Culture.* Charlottesville: University Press of Virginia, 1972.

———. *The Journey Back: Issues in Black Literature and Criticism.* Chicago: University of Chicago Press, 1980.

Bell, Bernard W. "Afro-American Writers." In *American Literature 1764–1789: The Revolutionary Years.* Edited by Everett Emerson. Madison: University of Wisconsin Press, 1977.

———. *The Afro-American Novel and Its Tradition.* Amherst: University of Massachusetts Press, 1987.

Berlin, Ira. *Many Thousands Gone: The First Two Centuries of Slavery in North America.* Cambridge, Mass.: Belknap Press of Harvard University, 1998.

Blassingame, John W. *The Slave Community: Plantation Life in the Antebellum South.* New York: Oxford University Press, 1972; rev. enl. ed., 1979.

Blight, David W. *Frederick Douglass's Civil War: Keeping Faith in Jubilee.* Baton Rouge: Louisiana State University Press, 1989.

Bloom, Harold, ed. *Modern Critical Interpretations: Frederick Douglass's Narrative of the Life of Frederick Douglass, an American Slave.* New York: Chelsea House, 1988.

Broadhead, Richard. "Sparing the Rod: Discipline and Fiction in Antebellum America." *Representations* 21:67–95 (Winter 1988).

Butterfield, Stephen T. *Black Autobiography in America.* Amherst: University of Massachusetts Press, 1974.

Carby, Hazel. "Ideologies of Black Folk: The Historical Novel of Slavery." In *Slavery and the Literary Imagination: Selected Papers from English Institute.* Edited by Deborah McDowell and Arthur Rampersad. Baltimore, Md.: Johns Hopkins University Press, 1989. Pp. 125–41.

Cott, Nancy F. *The Bonds of Womanhood: Woman's Sphere in New England, 1780–1835.* New Haven, Conn.: Yale University Press, 1977.

Davis, Charles T., and Henry Louis Gates Jr. *The Slave's Narrative.* New York: Oxford University Press, 1985.

Davis, David Brion. *The Problem of Slavery in Western Culture.* New York: Oxford University Press, 1966.

Douglas, Ann. *The Feminization of American Culture.* New York: Knopf, 1977.

Dubois, Ellen. "Women's Rights and Abolition: The Nature of the Connection." In *Feminism and Suffrage: the Emergence of an Independent Women's Movement in America, 1848–1869.* Ithaca, N.Y.: Cornell University Press, 1978.

Dumond, Dwight Lowell. *Antislavery: The Crusade for Freedom in America.* Ann Arbor: University of Michigan Press, 1961.

Elkins, Stanley. *Slavery: A Problem in American Institutional and Intellectual Life.* Chicago: University of Chicago Press, c.1959.

Filler, Louis. *The Crusade Against Slavery, 1830–1860.* New York: Harper and Row, 1960.

Finkleman, Paul, ed. *Articles on American Slavery: An Eighteen-Volume Set Collecting Nearly Four Hundred of the Most Important Articles on Slavery in the United States.* New York: Garland Publishing, 1989.

Fisher, Dexter, and Robert Stepto, eds. *Afro-American Literature: The Reconstruction of Instruction.* New York: Modern Language Association, 1979.

Fitzhugh, George. *Cannibals All!, or, Slaves Without Masters.* Edited by C. Vann Woodward. Cambridge, Mass.: Harvard University Press, 1964.

Foster, Frances Smith. *Witnessing Slavery: The Development of Ante-Bellum Slave Narratives.* Westport, Conn.: Greenwood Press, 1979.

Fredrickson, George M. *The Black Image in the White Mind: The Debate on Afro-American Character and Destiny, 1817–1914.* New York: Harper and Row, 1971.

———. *The Arrogance of Race: Historical Perspectives on Slavery, Racism, and Social Inequality.* Middletown, Conn.: Wesleyan University Press, 1988.

Gates, Henry Louis, Jr. "Binary Opposition in Chapter One of *Narrative of the Life of Frederick Douglass, An American Slave Written by Himself.*" In *Afro-American Literature: The Reconstruction of Instruction.* Edited by Dexter Fisher and Robert Stepto. New York: Modern Language Association, 1979. Pp. 212–32.

Genovese, Eugene. *Roll, Jordan, Roll: The World the Slaves Made.* New York: Pantheon, 1974.

Gougeon, Len. *Emerson's Antislavery Writings.* Athens: University of Georgia Press, 1988.

———. *Virtue's Hero: Emerson, Antislavery, and Reform.* Athens: University of Georgia Press, 1990.

Helper, Hinton Rowan. *The Impending Crisis of the South: How to Meet It.* Edited by George Fredrickson. Cambridge, Mass.: Harvard University Press, 1968.

Jordan, Winthrop. *White Over Black: American Attitudes Toward the Negro, 1550–1812.* New York: Norton, 1968.

Kolchin, Peter. *American Slavery, 1619–1877.* New York: Hill and Wang, 1995.

Kraditor, Aileen S. *Means and Ends in American Abolitionism: Garrison and His Critics on Strategy and Tactics, 1834–1850.* New York: Pantheon, 1960.

Lane, Ann J., ed. *The Debate Over Slavery: Stanley Elkins and His Critics.* Urbana: University of Illinois Press, 1971.

Lowance, Mason. "Biography and Autobiography in Early America." In *The Columbia Literary History of the United States.* Edited by Emory Elliott. New York: Columbia University Press, 1988.

———. "Frederick Douglass." In *African American Writers.* Edited by Lea Bacheler and A. Walton Litz. New York: Scribners, 1991.

———. "Negro Spirituals of the Nineteenth Century." In *The Encyclopedia of American Poetry.* Edited by Eric Harelson. Chicago: Fitzroy-Dearborn, 1998.

———, ed. *The Stowe Debate: Rhetorical Strategies in "Uncle Tom's Cabin."* Amherst: University of Massachusetts Press, 1994.

Martin, Waldo E. *The Mind of Frederick Douglass.* Chapel Hill: University of North Carolina Press, 1984.

Matlack, James. "The Autobiography of Frederick Douglass." *Phylon* 40:15–28 (March 1979).

McDowell, Deborah. "Negotiating between Tenses: Witnessing Slavery After Freedom—Della Rose." In *Slavery and the Literary Imagination: Selected Papers from English Institute.* Edited by Deborah McDowell and Arthur Rampersad. Baltimore, Md.: Johns Hopkins University Press, 1989. Pp. 144–63.

McPherson, James M. *The Struggle for Equality: Abolitionists and the Negro in the Civil War and Reconstruction.* Princeton, N.J.: Princeton University Press, 1964.

Minter, David. "Conceptions of the Self in Black Slave Narratives." *American Transcendental Quarterly* 24:62–68 (1974).

Pannapacker, William. "Revised Lives: Studies in the Changing Constructions of Authorial Identity in Nineteenth-Century Anglo-American Culture." Ph.D. diss., Harvard University, 1999.

Pease, Jane, and William Pease. *The Antislavery Argument.* Indianapolis: Bobbs-Merrill, 1965.

———. *Bound with Them in Chains: A Biographical History of the Antislavery Movement.* Westport, Conn: Greenwood Press, 1972.

Porter, Carolyn. "Social Discourse and Nonfictional Prose." In *The Columbia Literary History of the United States.* Edited by Emory Elliott. New York: Columbia University Press, 1988.

Quarles, Benjamin. "Frederick Douglass: Black Imperishable." *Quarterly Journal of the Library of Congress* 29:159–61 (July 1972).

———. *The Black Abolitionists.* New York: Oxford University Press, 1979.

Rawick, George P., ed. *The American Slave: A Composite Autobiography.* 18 volumes, Westport Conn.: Greenwood Press, 1972; 12 volume *Supplement,* 1977.

Rose, Willie Lee Nichols. *Slavery and Freedom.* Edited by William Freehling. New York: Oxford University Press, 1982.

Sekora, John, and Darwin Turner. *The Art of the Slave Narrative: Original Essays in Criticism and Theory.* Urbana: University of Illinois Press, 1982.

Siegmann, Lisa. "The Slave Narrative and Twentieth-Century African-American Literature." Amherst, Mass: University of Massachusetts, Department of English, Fall 1999.

Stampp, Kenneth M. *The Peculiar Institution: Slavery in the Antebellum South.* New York: Knopf, 1961.

Stone, Albert E. "Identity and Art in Frederick Douglass's *Narrative.*" *CLA Journal* 17:192–213 (December 1973).

Sundquist, Eric. *To Wake the Nations: Race in Nineteenth-Century American Literature.* Cambridge, Mass.: Harvard University Press, 1986.

———, ed. *Frederick Douglass: New Literary and Historical Essays.* New York: Cambridge University Press, 1990.

Takaki, Ronald. *Iron Cages: Race and Culture in Nineteenth-Century America.* New York: Knopf, 1979.

Tise, Larry E. *Proslavery: A History of the Defense of Slavery in America, 1700–1740.* Athens: University of Georgia Press, 1987.

Tompkins, Jane. *Sensational Designs: The Cultural Work of American Fiction, 1790–1860.* New York: Oxford University Press, 1985.

Tragle, Henry. *The Southampton Slave Revolt of 1831: A Compilation of Source Material.* Amherst: University of Massachusetts Press, 1995.

White, Deborah. *Ain't I a Woman: Female Slaves in the Plantation South.* New York: Norton, 1985.

Wish, Harvey, ed. *Antebellum Writings of George Fitzhugh and Hinton Rowan Helper on Slavery.* New York: Capricorn Books, 1960.

Yellin, Jean Fagan. *The Intricate Knot: Black Figures in American Literature, 1776–1863.* New York: New York University Press, 1972.

Yetman, Norman R., ed. *Voices from Slavery: Selections from the Slave Narratives Collection of the Library of Congress.* New York: Holt, Rinehart, and Winston, 1970.

SPIRITUAL AUTOBIOGRAPHY

KATHERINE CLAY BASSARD

AFRICAN AMERICAN SPIRITUAL autobiography emerges as a distinct literary genre out of larger concerns for African American self-expression or, as William Andrews puts it, out of the desire "to tell a free story." African American autobiographical writing began in the second half of the eighteenth century, the period of the heaviest traffic along the transatlantic slave trading route. Against a backdrop of bondage and ownership, individual African American writers gave expression to the cry of an entire people for freedom and self-determination. While the slave narrative is prototypical of this quest for personal and literary freedom, African American spiritual autobiography casts the issues of personal and communal liberty in the light of a Christian framework of salvation and redemption.

To some extent, almost all African American autobiographies of this period make some reference to salvation, Christian conversion, and deliverance. Thus, important early texts like Briton Hammon's *Narrative of the Uncommon Sufferings and Surprizing Deliverance of Briton Hammon, a Negro Man* (1760) and Olaudah Equiano's *Interesting Narrative of the Life of Olaudah Equiano, or Gustavus Vassa, the African, Written by Himself* (1789), while not classified as spiritual narratives per se, have strong religious motifs and language in common with spiritual autobiography, as well as the use of language from the King James version of the Christian Bible. In chapter 10 of his *Interesting Narrative* for example, Equiano recounts his sojourn through Roman Catholicism and a variety of Protestant denominations before converting to Methodism, a kind of spiritual autobiography within a slave narrative.

Thus the paradigm of Christian conversion—from sinner to saint and from sin to salvation—made popular in Puritan and Anglo-American spiritual autobiography, afforded many African American autobiographers the language with which to represent a variety of psychological, social, and political themes. Moreover, while the terms "spiritual autobiography," "spiritual narrative," and "spiritual journal" are often used as synonyms, there are distinctions among them. The keeping of a spiritual journal or diary in colonial and nineteenth-century America was encouraged for all literate Christians by many Protestant churches as an essential spiritual exercise to foster individual introspection. Yet journals are often little more than listings of events and dates, offering little in the way of storyline or development. Spiritual narratives, a more general category of writings, include hybrid texts like those of Daniel Coker, Maria W. Stewart, Nancy Prince, or Sojourner Truth, in which a brief conversion narrative appears amid a variety of other writings by the same author. Spiritual autobiographies proper, although they often build on a writer's keeping of a journal or log, and many times contain other types of writing, can be distinguished by their narrative structure, which relies on the stages of Protestant Christian conversion for their basic storyline.

Many of the narratives contain, as part of their title, the phrase "religious experience." This reliance on the experiential places the conversion event centermost in the telling of the life story. Thus, African American spiritual autobiographies derive their narrative frameworks from Protestant understandings of salvation, which divide the conversion experience into two stages. First, the narrator experiences *conviction* of sin as the narrator becomes aware of his or her guiltiness before God and need for redemption. At this point in the narrative, the protagonist may be in great anguish of soul, even entertaining thoughts of suicide. The second stage, *justification* from sin through belief in Jesus Christ, follows the narrator's coming before God for salvation and creates a release from the inner turmoil of conviction. Although justification produces a state of equilibrium, the narrator often enters a period of doubt that the salvation experience is genuine. Many times this period of doubt may place the protagonist in a state similar to that of conviction. In many spiritual autobiographies, especially the more introspective narratives of the Puritans and Quakers, this tension of release and struggle continues throughout the autobiography with a state of peaceful equilibrium projected onto an afterlife in heaven.

Other narratives, particularly those written by women who had embraced early doctrines of holiness, include a third stage, *sanctification* from sin, the state of one's will being entirely conformed to the will of God. Sanctification allows the state of equilibrium—release from tension and doubt—to be resolved once and for all as the narrator gains confidence in the efficacy of the salvation experience. Importantly, sanctification appears most often in narratives in which the autobiographer seeks to refute some challenge to the authenticity of the conversion or the call to the ministry.

Many African American spiritual autobiographers were ministers. Because some Protestant denominations require evidence that clergy have received a personal call from God, the protagonist often relates events that may include hearing a voice or voices, supernatural dreams and visions, miraculous or fortuitous circumstances, and illumination of special passages of scripture. In addition, the call may be confirmed by the community, as other characters give voice to the validity of the autobiographer's ministry, usually through affirming the gift of preaching.

The development of African American spiritual autobiography can be broken down into three main historical periods: 1770–1830, 1830–1865, the late nineteenth and the twentieth centuries. The first period begins about two decades after the First Great Awakening in America (c. 1739–1750) with the first flowering of African American poetry and prose. It encompasses as well the transatlantic slave trade (abolished in 1808) and gradual emancipation. Moreover, this era saw the establishment of independent African American churches and denominations, culminating in the incorporation of the African Methodist Episcopal Church, the first African American denomination, in 1816. The second period begins during the decade of the 1830s at the zenith of the Second Great Awakening and the inception of the abolitionist movement and the early women's rights movement. It encompasses the signing of the Emancipation Proclamation into law (1862) and lasts roughly to the end of the Civil War. It is during this period of high achievement in the genre that African American women's spiritual autobiography emerges. Spiritual autobiographies of the final period became popularized into forms of travel writing and ministerial autobiography. Often sponsored by church organizations, these autobiographies reflect the increasing institutionalization of postbellum African American churches.

Beginnings: 1770–1830

Representative texts of the earliest phase of spiritual autobiography (1770–1830) include James Albert Ukawsaw Gronniosaw, *A Narra-*

698

tive of the Most Remarkable Particulars in the Life of James Albert Ukawsaw Gronniosaw, an African Prince* (1770); John Marrant, *A Narrative of the Lord's Wonderful Dealings with John Marrant* (1785); George White, *A Brief Account of the Life, Experiences, Travels, and Gospel Labours of George White, an African, Written by Himself and Revised by a Friend* (1810); John Jea, *The Life, History, and Unparalleled Sufferings of John Jea, the African Preacher* (c. 1811); and Daniel Coker, *Journal of Daniel Coker, a Descendant of Africa* (1820). In its early development, the spiritual narrative often combined several literary genres, as the story of the writer's spiritual journey was embedded within travel writing (for example, James Albert Ukawsaw Gronniosaw and Daniel Coker), captivity narrative (for example, John Marrant), or slave narrative (for example, John Jea). In addition, issues of literacy and authorship (the use of amanuenses and editors to accommodate illiteracy or marginal literacy) that shaped the development of the slave narrative are important in spiritual autobiography as well. Because of the presumption that all African Americans were illiterate, the title of George White's autobiography, for example, includes information on its production: "Written by Himself and Revised by a Friend." Unlike the classic slave narrative, however, African American spiritual autobiography, while often incorporating a narrative of the writer's journey from slavery to freedom (for instance, see the section on Richard Allen below), maintains the primary emphasis on the journey from sin to salvation, from spiritual bondage to inner freedom. Moreover, they differ from Anglo-American spiritual autobiographies because the writers had to address larger social concerns of oppression and racism—as the phrases "an African Prince," "An African," and "the African Preacher" in three of the above titles suggest. Thus the writer's individual spirituality was given shape by his or her social condition as a part of an oppressed community.

Several sociohistorical factors contributed to the growth of African American spiritual autobiography before 1830. First, gradual emancipation laws in the North following the American Revolution produced a large, increasingly literate, free black population. Second, this new emphasis on education and literacy (though the vast majority of free African Americans lived in extreme poverty and illiteracy) coincided with the evangelization of African Americans by Methodists and Baptists, resulting in a new religious community consciousness. This community—when challenged with racism and injustice within the Anglo-Christian churches and denominations—would soon spawn separate and distinct African American congregations and churches, culminating in the formation of the African Methodist Episcopal Church in 1816.

Within this literary and social context, the classic form of spiritual autobiography emerges in the work of George White. In his *Brief Account of the Life, Experiences, Travels, and Gospel Labours of George White, an African* (1810), White chronicles not only an inward spiritual journey, but his journey through the institution of the Methodist church, whose leadership at this time was made up of an all-white (as well as all-male) hierarchy. White's quest for the right to preach from the Christian Bible sets the tone for the development of African American spiritual autobiography as simultaneously a recording of the individual soul's search for God and the communal challenge of a people to institutions of oppressive power and authority that threatened to limit all African Americans' claims to humanity and freedom.

Maturity: 1830–1865

This dual purpose (the recording of an inner journey and an outward struggle) is more clearly delineated in texts that form the second period in the development of African American spiritual autobiography. It is significant that the genre reaches its highest creative expression in the era spanning roughly two decades (1830s and 1840s) that encompass the evangelistic fervor of the Second Great Awakening in America. African Americans made up a significant segment of the congregations at revivals and camp meetings as religious revival swept through America. The informal, often emotional, style of worship at revival camp meetings increased the appeal of Christianity to African Americans, and this period saw the largest number of African American converts to Protestant denominations of Christianity. In addition, the Second Great Awakening had important social consequences as religious revival spilled over into the social and political arenas, giving rise to the U.S. abolition movement, which in turned spawned the early women's movement. It is no surprise, then, that many of the finest African American spiritual autobiographies were published during these decades.

This blending of the spiritual and political is reflected in an important spiritual narrative by Maria W. Stewart. Published in Boston in 1835, *Productions of Mrs. Maria W. Stewart* is a hybrid text that compiles essays Stewart wrote for William Lloyd Garrison's abolitionist paper the *Liberator* as well as speeches and addresses, prayers and meditations. Born in 1803, Stewart was orphaned at age five and bound out as an indentured servant to a clergyman's family. In 1826 she married James W. Steward (Stewart) and was widowed three years later. Stewart was converted in 1830 and made her public profession of Christian faith in 1831, becoming a member of the politically active First African Baptist Church in Boston. In the conversion-story section of her narrative, Stewart articulates the dual focus that is the hallmark of African American spiritual autobiography of the antebellum period:

> From the moment I experienced the change, I felt a strong desire, with the help and assistance of God, to devote the remainder of my days to piety and virtue, and now possess that spirit of independence, that, were I called upon, I would willingly sacrifice my life for the cause of God and my brethren.

For Stewart, the quest for individual "piety and virtue" and the collective struggle for the liberation of her African American "brethren" are two parts of the same call from God. This duality runs throughout the spiritual autobiographies of this period. However, the two most outstanding examples are Richard Allen's *Life, Experience, and Gospel Labors of the Rt. Rev. Richard Allen* (1833) and Jarena Lee's *Life and Religious Experience of Jarena Lee, a Coloured Lady, Giving an Account of Her Call to Preach the Gospel* (1836).

Nineteenth-Century Spiritual Autobiography: Richard Allen (1760–1831)

Richard Allen was born a slave to the Quaker lawyer Benjamin Chew, who served as chief justice of Pennsylvania from 1774–1777. Allen was sold to a Mr. Stokeley near Dover, Delaware, and at the age of seventeen he converted to Christianity. Allen's first contact with Methodism was through his attendance at a religious gathering called a "class meeting" in a forest. He was called to preach and licensed in 1782, and began an itinerant ministry in the Mid-Atlantic states the following year. In 1799 Allen was ordained a deacon, and later an elder, by the Methodist bishop Francis Asbury. Allen died on March 26, 1831.

Published in Philadelphia two years after Allen's death, *The Life, Experience, and Gospel Labors of the Rt. Rev. Richard Allen . . . Written by Himself, and Published by His Request* serves as a prototype of nineteenth-century African American spiritual autobiography. Building on George White's earlier account of his challenge to Methodism, Allen's narrative is both an individual testimony—the journey of the individual soul from sinner to saint, and the individual person from slave to free—and a story of collective struggle. Allen not only tells his own story, but recounts the bold breaking away of African American worshipers from St. George's Methodist Episcopal Church in Philadelphia because of the racism they encountered there. Allen and others went on to form the Free African Society, a religious and political organization, in 1789, and later they founded the Bethel African Methodist Episcopal Church, an independent denomination with an all-black congregation. Difficulties with the Methodist Episcopal denomination, again on ra-

Richard Allen

Through the juxtaposition of physical and spiritual slavery and freedom, the language of Allen's text begins to take on double meaning. Following his conversion, Allen describes a period of spiritual anguish—including doubting his conversion and feeling burdened with his sins—worthy of the early Puritan narratives. Allen goes on to relate his first contact with Methodism through attendance at a class meeting. It is here, however, that a defining difference emerges. As a slave, Allen must ask permission of his unconverted master to attend religious services.

This tension allows Allen to portray himself as both physically bound and spiritually free, in contrast to his master who, while enjoying physical liberty and privilege, remains in spiritual bondage. Thus Allen is able to represent himself as the "insider" whose duty it is to enlighten and convert the oppressor. When Allen and his brother, also a Christian convert, overhear a neighboring slaveholder remark that "the privilege of attending meeting" would make them unfit for slavery, they resolve to work even harder "so that it would not be said that religion made us worse servants." When the brothers are observed to have missed a meeting, the following exchange takes place between the two slaves and their master:

cial and cultural grounds (disputes over style of worship, music, liturgy, and so forth) led to the organization and incorporation of the African Methodist Episcopal (AME) denomination in 1816, with Allen as its first bishop.

Allen's autobiography begins like a typical slave narrative: "I was born in the year of our Lord 1760, on February 14th, a slave to Benjamin Chew, of Philadelphia." Yet having established the details of his physical birth, Allen immediately moves to recount his spiritual (re)birth through conviction and justification:

My mother and father and four children of us were sold into Delaware state, near Dover; and I was a child and lived with him [Stokeley] until I was upwards of twenty years of age, during which time I was awakened and brought to myself, poor, wretched and undone, and without the mercy of God must be lost. Shortly after, I obtained mercy through the blood of Christ, and was constrained to exhort my old companions to seek the Lord.

When our master found we were making no provision to go to meeting, he would frequently ask us if it was not our meeting day, and if we were not going. We would frequently tell him; "No, sir, we would rather stay at home and get our work done." He would tell us: "Boys, I would rather you would go to your meeting; if I am not good myself, I like to see you striving yourselves to be good."

By portraying the two religious slaves as the moral superiors to the master, Allen is specifically refuting racist stereotypes of African Americans as lazy and morally deficient. Moreover, he accomplishes this by having the white master proclaim the hard-working, industrious slaves "good." This reversal in terms results in the conversion of Allen's master, who then "could not be satisfied to hold slaves, believing it to be wrong." The master agrees to let Allen and his brother buy their freedom for 609 pounds gold or silver or $2,000 Continental money. Thus spiritual freedom leads Allen and his brother to physical freedom as these two narratives merge into one.

After agreeing with his master on the price of his freedom, Allen has difficulty finding enough work to raise the money. Allen kneels in prayer and asks God to "open some way for me to get my living." Here Allen's autobiography moves to the relating of his "gospel labors," a term that echoes with the labor of slavery and physical work. As Allen writes, "I was employed in cutting wood . . . although I preached the Gospel at nights and on Sundays. My dear Lord was with me and blessed my labors—Glory to God—and gave me souls for my hire." Thus Allen uses the language of labor in two senses—labor to make ends meet and provide his material needs, and preaching as labor to save souls.

The reliance on narrative doubling and linguistic duality reflects the social context of Allen's spiritual autobiography—an America deeply divided through racism. Thus Allen's narrative begins to become racially coded as he mentions, at first almost incidentally in one place, "most of my congregation was white." With the first mention of race, the tone of the narrative begins to shift. Allen relates a meeting with the great Methodist clergyman the Reverend Bishop Francis Asbury, who invites Allen to travel and preach with him. Yet what looks like a momentous opportunity for Allen becomes his entry into the institutionalized racism within the Methodist denomination:

He told me that in the slave countries, Carolina and other places, I must not intermix with the slaves, and I would frequently have to sleep in his carriage, and he would allow me my victuals and clothes. I told him I would not travel with him on these conditions. He asked me my reason. I told him if I was taken sick, who was to support me? and that I thought people ought to lay up something while they were able, to support themselves in time of sickness or old age. He said that was as much as he got, his victuals and clothes. I told him he would be taken care of, let his afflictkions be as they were, or let him be taken sick where he would, he would be taken care of, but I doubted whether it would be the case with myself. He smiled, and told me he would give me from then until he returned from the eastward to make up my mind. . . . But I made up my mind that I would not accept of his proposals.

This fundamental misunderstanding of the material conditions of African Americans—here portrayed as a miscommunication between two individuals—foreshadows the racial split within Methodism that led to the formation of the AME denomination.

At this point, the narrative builds toward the climactic scene as the narratives of conversion and gospel "labors" give way to the recounting of the formation of the AME Church. Allen describes his preaching assignment at St. George's Methodist Episcopal Church, the scene of the schism: "Preaching was given out for me at five o'clock in the morning at St. George's church. I strove to preach as well as I could, but it was a great cross to me; but the Lord was with me." However, the early preaching hour—five o'clock in the morning—and the fact that Allen was only allowed to preach to black worshipers dampened Allen's enthusiasm for the assignment. Not long after this Allen writes that he "saw the necessity of erecting a place of worship for the coloured people." The proximity of these two statements sets the stage for the emotional peak of the autobiography, the encounter of racism within the very sanctuary of St. George's Church:

A number of us [African Americans] usually attended St. George's Church in Fourth street; and when the colored people began to get numerous in attending the church, they moved us from the seats we usually sat on, and placed us around the wall, and on Sabbath morning we went to church and the sexton stood at the door, and told us to go in the gallery. He told us to go, and we would see where to sit. We expected to take the seats over the ones we formerly occupied below, not knowing any better. . . . Meeting had begun, and they were nearly done singing, and just as we got to the seats, the elder said, "Let us pray." We had not been long upon our knees before I heard considerable scuffling and low talking. I raised my head up and saw one of the trustees . . . having hold of the Rev. Absalom Jones, pulling him up off of his knees, and saying . . . "You must not kneel here. . . . Get up now, or I will call for aid and force you away." . . . we all went out of the church in a body, and they were no more plagued with us in the church.

From this emotional climax, the autobiography focuses less and less on the individual self and increasingly relates the details of building physical structures and creating institutional documents. Having agreed with other African American clergy formally to separate from the Methodist denomination, Allen recounts the actual building of Bethel AME Church in Philadelphia:

The day was appointed to go and dig the cellar. I arose early in the morning and addressed the throne of grace, praying that the Lord would bless our endeavors. Having by this time two or three teams of my own—as I was the first proposer of the African church, I put the first spade in the ground to dig a cellar for the same. This was the first African church or meeting-house that was erected in the United States of America.

With the building of the church edifice, the narrative gives way to a variety of documents, including articles and amendments for the AME Church, as well addresses and sermons from Richard Allen that demonstrate Allen's desire to influence and shape the African American community. Thus Allen's spiritual autobiography has, in a sense, come full circle, from the recounting of his individual physical and spiritual birth to the birth of an African American denomination and newly empowered community.

African American Women's Spiritual Autobiography: Jarena Lee (1783–?)

Jarena Lee was born in Cape May, New Jersey, probably free, in 1783. Like Maria W. Stewart, from the age of seven she was separated from her family and "bound out" to serve in a white family as a domestic—the first in a series of domestic labor situations. Lee converted to Methodism at the age of twenty-one and received a call to preach in 1807. At first ignoring the call, Lee married Joseph Lee, pastor of a Methodist society, and they moved to Snow Hill, about six miles outside Philadelphia. The isolation of the location caused Lee to experience depression and chronic illness. About six years later, Lee was widowed and left with two young children. At this point, she reconsidered her call to preach and in 1822 began her itinerant ministry. In the course of her ministry, she traveled thousands of miles, as far north as Canada, as far west as Ohio, and south into the slave territories of Maryland.

In 1836 Jarena Lee published *The Life and Religious Experience of Jarena Lee, a Colored Lady . . . Written by Herself.* Though she had financed the printing of the 1836 autobiography on her own and even distributed copies at camp meetings and on the street, in 1844 she found herself appealing to the AME book committee for permission to publish an expanded version of her autobiography based on more than a decade of journal keeping. The all-male members of the AME Book Concern rejected the manuscript on the grounds that it was "written in such a manner that it is impossible to decipher much of the meaning contained in it." Undaunted by this rejection, Lee financed the printing of her *Religious Experience and Journal of Mrs. Jarena Lee, Giving an Account of Her Call to Preach the Gospel* in 1849.

Lee's spiritual autobiographies were, indeed, "written by herself," as well as published and distributed by herself, a fact that stands in contrast with her self-portrait as a "poor colored female instrument." In the 1836 *Life and Religious Experience*, Lee presents a twist on the narrative duality that is evident in spiritual autobiographies written by men. On the one hand, her texts speak to the structures of social domination of nominally free African Americans in the urban North; on the other hand, she gives voice to the politics of gender exclusion within an African American community still in the process of institution building and community formation. Thus for Lee, the climactic scene of her autobiography is not a confrontation with white authority but an interruption of black male leadership, which threatened to silence her voice.

In its opening pages, Lee's spiritual autobiography follows the classic paradigm of conversion narratives: conviction, justification, and sanctification: "the spirit of the Lord never entirely forsook me, but continued mercifully striving within me, until his gracious power converted my soul." Significantly, her first communication with God takes place through revelation and outside of any formal religious structure. Her parents were "wholly ignorant of the knowledge of God," thus, when "the spirit of God moved in power through my conscience, and told me I was a wretched sinner," it is a moment of pure revelation between God's spirit and Lee's soul.

Lee's first experience with organized religious structures comes in 1804, when she attends the services of a Presbyterian missionary. She recalls the first verse of a psalm that was read at this service:

Lord, I am vile, conceived in sin,
Born unholy and unclean.
Sprung from man, whose guilty fall
Corrupts the race, and taints us all.

Compare Psalms 51: 1–5 (from the King James Version):

Have mercy upon me, O God, according to thy loving kindness: according unto the multitude of thy tender mercies blot out my transgressions.

Wash me thoroughly from mine iniquity, and cleanse me from my sin.

For I acknowledge my transgressions: and my sin is ever before me.

Against thee, thee only, have I sinned, and done this evil in thy sight: that thou mightest be justified when thou speakest, and be clear when thou judgest.

Behold, I was shapen in iniquity; and in sin did my mother conceive me.

Lee's response to this versified scripture is immediate and intense. "At the reading of the Psalms," she writes, "a ray of renewed conviction darted into my soul." Yet while this early religious experience produces conviction, it does not relieve the tension brought on by guilt over her sin. Following this incident, Lee at one point considers suicide, and she suffers physical illness. Finally, she leaves her employer for Philadelphia.

Here, Lee's narrative moves beyond the story of her individual conversion as she begins to relate her search for a "church home" in terms of a search for racial and cultural community. While in Philadelphia, Lee visits the congregation of a minister named Pilmore at St. Paul's Episcopal for three months: "While sitting under the ministrations of this man ... it appeared that there was a wall between me and a communion with that people ... and seemed to make this impression upon my mind, *this is not the people for you.*" The search for religious instruction and for a church "home" now becomes a search for community, for a "people." One day she asks a black cook working for her mistress about the Methodists. It is then that Lee goes to the African American church, Bethel AME, and hears Richard Allen preach for the first time (1808): "During the labors of this man that afternoon, I had come to the conclusion, that *this is the people to which my heart unites,* and it so happened, that as soon as the service closed he invited such as felt a desire to flee the wrath to come, to unite on trial with them—I embraced the opportunity" (emphasis added). This time the religious service ends with Lee embracing the community of African American worshipers at Bethel Church.

It is within this context that Lee describes her experience of justification, focusing again on her individual spirituality: "That instant, it appeared to me, as if a garment, which had entirely enveloped my whole person, even to my fingers' ends, split at the crown of my head, and was stripped away from me, passing like a shadow from my sight—when the glory of God seemed to cover me in its stead."

Despite this high moment, Lee continues to search her heart for hidden sin. At the mention of Allen's text, "Thy heart is not right in the sight of God" (Acts 8:21), Lee recalls that "there appeared to *my* view . . . *one* sin; and this was *malice* against one particular individual, who had strove deeply to injure me, which I resented." The mention of *"one* sin" recalls the opening page of the narrative where Lee recounts her first "sin" at the age of seven, an act of resistance against her first mistress, Mrs. Sharp:

Not long after the commencement of my attendance on this lady, she had bid me do something respecting my work, which in a little while after, she asked me if I had done, when I replied, Yes—but this was not true.

At this awful point, in my early history, the spirit of God moved in power through my conscience, and told me I was a wretched sinner.

Having told Mrs. Sharp a sinful lie Lee immediately feels guilty: "so great was the impression [of conviction], and so strong were the feelings of guilt, that I promised in my heart that I would not tell another lie. But notwithstanding this promise my heart grew harder."

This spiritual guiltiness continues in a later scene, in which Lee recounts her sin of malice. After a verbal forgiveness of the transgression of others, however, Lee experiences complete forgiveness of her own transgressions: "I felt not only the sin of *malice* was pardoned, but all other sins were swept away together." As if to leave no doubt of the genuineness of her salvation, Lee goes on to relate the experience of sanctification: "I have now passed through the account of my conviction and also of my conversion to God; and shall next speak of the blessing of sanctification."

Yet as the accounts of Lee's personal conversion and sanctification and her quest for religious community are resolved, her call story centers on a new conflict. The move that formed the highlight of Richard Allen's autobiography, from St. George's Methodist Episcopal Church to Bethel AME, transferred power from all-white to all-black, but still all-male, clergy. In the AME Church, rights and powers—to be ordained as ministers, vote in trustees, and sit on important committees—were restricted to "the male colored members" by the formal articles of association that guided the AME Church. Women were allowed to exhort (provide reflections on sermons delivered by male preachers), hold prayer meetings, and speak at revivals and camp meetings, but they were prohibited from preaching from a pulpit and from "taking a text" from the Bible.

Because of the precariousness of her position as an African American woman preacher, Lee's text relies more heavily than does Allen's on authenticating her call to the ministry. In Allen's narrative, little attention was paid to his call to preach the gospel. In fact, his preaching is mentioned almost incidentally, in the context of manual labor. Lee, however, spends a major portion of her narrative (in two chapters, "My Call to Preach the Gospel" and "The Subject of My Call to Preach Renewed") describing the supernatural incidents like visions, dreams, and divine revelation that authenticate her call to preach. Immediately after "a voice" urges her to "Preach the Gospel!" Lee envisions herself standing behind a pulpit: "there appeared to my view the form and figure of a pulpit, with a Bible lying thereon, the back of which was presented to me as plainly as if it had been a literal fact." Just as Allen's narrative focuses on the exterior structure of the church building as a sign of autonomy, Lee uses the interior space of the pulpit to symbolize her quest for authority. Though denied (at this point) the authority to preach from a pulpit, Lee claims that authority in her narrative: "I took a text, and preached in my sleep."

Significantly, Bethel Church, where Lee discovered the people to which her heart united, is the scene of the climactic moment in Lee's text:

But to return to the subject of my call to preach. Soon after this, as above related, the Rev. Brother Williams was to preach at Bethel Church, where I with others were assembled. He entered the pulpit, gave out the hymn, which was sung, and then addressed the throne of grace; took his text, passed through the exordium, and commenced to expound it. The text he took is Jonah, 2d. chap. 9th verse—"Salvation is of the Lord." But as he proceeded to explain, he seemed to have lost the spirit; when in the same instant, I sprang, as by an altogether supernatural impulse, to my feet, when I was aided from above to give an exhortation on the very text which my brother Williams had taken.

Though Lee calls this an exhortation, her interruption of the male speaker serves as a critique of his preaching ability ("he seemed to have lost the spirit") and a challenge to the prohibition against women preachers. Rather than ending in her censure, however, Lee's bold action results in Richard Allen himself acknowledging her call to preach and verbally licensing her. Given the emphasis in Lee's spiritual autobiography on community and religious fellowship, it is significant that she represents this dramatic scene not as divisive, but as the basis for community reformation.

Although there is no recorded death date for Jarena Lee, her 1849 *Religious Experience and Journal of Mrs. Jarena Lee, Giving an Account of Her Call to Preach the Gospel* continues her life story up to 1842. While Richard Allen's spiritual narrative ends with the building of an institution and becomes more "fixed," Jarena Lee's narrative becomes more focused on her itinerant ministry. Moreover, it is in this longer version of her autobiography that Lee reports greater opposition to her ministry as the AME Church became even more institutionalized. Literacy requirements for clergy, for example, made it more difficult for women to qualify for ministry. As late as 1852, a motion to ordain women preachers was defeated by a large majority. Thus Lee recalls, among other incidents, being accused by one hostile person of being "a man dressed in female clothes."

Lee's *Religious Experience and Journal* goes on to chronicle an exhausting schedule of preaching and speaking in travels that take her north, west, and even south, as Lee's vision of religious community grows even more expansive. This expanded vision characterizes spiritual autobiography of the later nineteenth century. In many ways, Lee's 1849 text looks simultaneously backward to the eighteenth-century travel narratives and forward to the end-of-the-century itinerant narratives of women like Amanda Berry Smith (see her 1893 *Autobiography: The Story of the Lord's Dealings with Mrs. Amanda Smith, the Colored Evangelist*). Indeed, the Bible's Great Commission spoken by Jesus in Matthew 28:19 (King James Version), "Go ye therefore, and teach all nations, baptizing them in the name of the Father, and of the Son, and of the Holy Ghost," gave occasion for African American women spiritual autobiographers to take on an expansive focus that reshaped their sense of self and community.

Perhaps the earliest example of the global focus of African American women's spiritual autobiography is Zilpha Elaw's *Memoirs of the Life, Religious Experience, Ministerial Travels, and Labours of Mrs. Zilpha Elaw, an American Female of Color . . . Written by Herself* (1846). Elaw, a contemporary of Lee, also experienced private and public opposition to her ministry. Yet her narrative is distinguished by a broader focus: her travels to England to preach for her denomination, the white Methodist Episcopalians, involve her in issues of nationality as well as gender, race, and class differences.

Elaw's text reminds us that not all African American spiritual autobiographers belonged to black congregations and denominations. Another writer whose texts point to the variety of African American religious experience is Rebecca Cox Jackson. Jackson's spiritual journals were written between 1830 and 1864 and collected and edited in 1981 by Jean Humez as *Gifts of Power: The Writing of Rebecca Jackson.* Jackson also provides us with one of the last historical references to Jarena Lee as she relates a meeting with the then seventy-three-year-old Lee on New Year's Day in 1857:

Sister Jarena Lee called to see me, under the influence of a very kind and friendly spirit. She spoke very lovingly, and I found that she was sincere. I was constrained to give God the glory, for when I looked back to the time and times that she was one of my most bitter persecutors, I said in my mind, "Is not this the Lord's doing?"

Though Jackson calls Lee "sister," she also reveals that Lee had been "one of [her] most bitter persecutors." Like Jarena Lee, Jackson's quest for authentic spiritual experience led her to try several churches and denominations, including African Methodism, before joining the Shaker sect in 1844. Jackson had been raised in the AME faith, but when she started her itinerant preaching in 1833 she found the churches of her denomination closed to her. Even other believers in holiness and sanctification found Jackson's teachings—including her belief in celibacy as the only way to true holiness—too radical. Jackson did return to Philadelphia in 1851 after living for seven years in the Shaker communal lifestyle. She returned, however, neither to African Methodism nor to the Holiness Movement. Rather she returned more firmly committed to the doctrine of celibacy (a central tenet of Shaker theology) and established a Shaker "out-family"—a small congregation of believers living together communally— and became the first African American woman Shaker eldress. Given the fierce opposition to her ministry, it is perhaps no surprise that Jackson's writings rely even more heavily than Lee's on supernatural events as authenticating devices; recollections of long, densely symbolic dream-visions, spontaneously composed spiritual songs, and even visitations from departed loved ones characterize her narratives.

During the quarter century from 1850 to 1875, the genre continued to be dominated by African American women. Two texts published in 1850 are noteworthy. The first is Nancy Prince's *Narrative of the Life and Travels of Mrs. Nancy Prince*, which recounts Prince's travels to Russia in service to the Russian court. The second is Sojourner Truth's *Narrative of Sojourner Truth*, which chronicles the life of one of the nation's leading abolitionists and women's rights activists. In contrast to Truth's fame, an almost anonymous writer known only as "Elizabeth" published a short narrative entitled *Memoir of Old Elizabeth, a Colored Woman* in 1863 at the age of about ninety-seven. Published in 1854, Daniel Peterson's *The Looking Glass: Being a True Report and Narrative of the Life, Travels, and Labors of the Rev. Daniel H. Peterson, a Colored Clergyman* recalls the style of George White and Richard Allen and looks ahead to the postbellum rise of African American ministerial autobiography.

Decline: The Late Nineteenth and the Twentieth Centuries

The popularity of African American spiritual autobiography declined in the half-century after Reconstruction (1875–1925). In this period, African American churches became even more institutionalized and hierarchical, losing many of the distinctive features of New World African worship that they had enjoyed during the antebellum period. Thus, many of the spiritual narratives began to be published under the auspices of the churches, with fewer narrators operating with the "free agency" of a Richard Allen or a Jarena Lee. As more or less "official" documents of religious institutions, these autobiographies are often more didactic than the earlier texts.

A refreshing exception is Julia A. J. Foote's *A Brand Plucked from the Fire: An Autobiographical Sketch* (1879), which continues African American women writers' involvement in the holiness movement, using spiritual experience to challenge increasing institutionalization of the churches. Published in the same year, Maria W. Stewart's *Meditations from the Pen of Mrs. Maria W. Stewart* is an expanded version of her 1835 *Productions*. Toward the end of the century, Amanda Berry Smith's lengthy *Autobiography: The Story of the Lord's Dealings with Mrs. Amanda Smith, the Colored Evangelist* (1893) continued the tradition

Daniel Payne

of depicting the spiritual journey in concert with travel narrative.

The most important development after Reconstruction was the rise of ministerial autobiography, as African American churches and denominations became more patriarchal in structure. Daniel A. Payne's *Recollections of Seventy Years* (1888) is representative as it relates the parallel development of both man and institution. Continuing the tradition of Richard Allen. Payne, a prominent AME bishop and the denomination's historiographer, used a compiler to arrange material from lengthy journals "extending over half a century." Adopting more of a "story of great men" tone, Payne's *Recollections* seems more akin to Booker T. Washington's 1901 autobiography *Up from Slavery*, as spiritual experience is almost a backdrop for the achievements of a self-made individual.

At the beginning of the twenty-first century, the genre of African American spiritual autobiography was primarily relegated to popular forms, for example, Pauli Murray's *Proud Shoes*

(1956), which tells of her struggle to become the first African American woman Episcopal priest, or Rosa Parks's *Quiet Strength: The Faith, the Hope, and the Heart of a Woman Who Changed a Nation* (1994). Certainly the form has lost its structural distinctiveness, and examples such as these writings by Murray and Parks are classified more readily as popular celebrity autobiographies. While religion and spirituality remain important topics in African American literature, the genre of spiritual autobiography clearly had its heyday in the nineteenth century. The issues of freedom, human dignity, and the quest for the spiritual empowerment, however, remain timeless themes in the literary tradition.

Selected Bibliography

PRIMARY SOURCES

Allen, Richard. *The Life, Experience, and Gospel Labors of the Rt. Rev. Richard Allen to Which Is Annexed the Rise and Progress of the African Methodist Church in the United States of America.* Philadelphia: Martin and Boden, 1833.

Coker, Daniel. *Journal of Daniel Coker, a Descendant of Africa . . .* Baltimore: Edward J. Coale, 1820.

Elaw, Zilpha. *Memoirs of the Life, Religious Experience, Ministerial Travels, and Labours of Mrs. Zilpha Elaw, an American Female of Colour . . . Written by Herself.* London: Self-published, 1846. Reprinted in *Sisters of the Spirit: Three Black Women's Autobiographies of the Nineteenth Century.* Edited by William L. Andrews. Bloomington: Indiana University Press, 1986.

Elizabeth. *Memoir of Old Elizabeth, a Coloured Woman.* Philadelphia: Collins, 1863. Reprinted in *Six Women's Slave Narratives.* Edited by William L. Andrews. New York: Oxford University Press, 1988.

Equiano, Olaudah. *The Interesting Narrative of Olaudah Equiano, or Gustavus Vassa, the African, Written by Himself.* London: Self-published, 1789. Reprinted in *The Classic Slave Narratives.* Edited by Henry Louis Gates Jr. New York: New American Library, 1987.

Foote, Julia A. J. *A Brand Plucked from the Fire: An Autobiographical Sketch by Mrs. Julia A. J. Foote.* Cleveland, Ohio: Self-published, 1879. Reprinted in *Sisters of the Spirit: Three Black Women's Autobiographies of the Nineteenth Century.* Edited by William L. Andrews. Bloomington: Indiana University Press, 1987. A later edition (from 1886) is reprinted in *Spiritual Narratives.* Edited by Susan Houchins. New York: Oxford University Press, 1988.

Gronniosaw, James Albert Ukawsaw. *A Narrative of the Most Remarkable Particulars in the Life of James Albert Ukawsaw Gronniosaw, an African Prince.* Edited by W. Shirley. Bath, U.K.: S. Hazzard, 1770.

Hammon, Briton. *A Narrative of the Uncommon Sufferings and Surprizing Deliverance of Briton Hammon, a Negro Man.* Boston: Green and Russell, 1760. Reprinted in *Early Negro Writing, 1760–1837.* Edited by Dorothy B. Porter. Boston: Beacon Press, 1971.

Jackson, Rebecca Cox. *Gifts of Power: The Writings of Rebecca Jackson, Black Visionary, Shaker Eldress.* Edited by Jean McMahon Humez. Amherst: University of Massachusetts Press, 1981.

Jea, John. *The Life, History, and Unparalleled Sufferings of John Jea, the African Preacher.* Portsea, U.K.: Self-published, c. 1811. Reprinted in *Black Itinerants of the Gospel: The Narratives of John Jea and George White.* Madison, Wis.: Madison House, 1993.

Lee, Jarena. *The Life and Religious Experience of Jarena Lee, a Coloured Lady. Giving An Account of Her Call to Preach the Gospel.* Philadelphia: Self-published, 1836. Reprinted in *Sisters of the Spirit: Three Black Women's Autobiographies of the Nineteenth Century.* Edited by William L. Andrews. Bloomington: Indiana University Press, 1986.

———. *Religious Experience and Journal of Mrs. Jarena Lee, Giving an Account of Her Call to Preach the Gospel, Revised and Corrected from the Original Manuscript, Written by Herself.* Philadelphia: Self-published, 1849. Reprinted in *Spiritual Narratives.* Edited by Susan Houchins. New York: Oxford University Press, 1988.

Marrant, John. *A Narrative of the Lord's Wonderful Dealings with John Marrant, a Black.* Edited by the Reverend W. Aldridge. London: Self-published, 1785. Reprinted in *Early Negro Writing, 1760–1837.* Edited by Dorothy B. Porter. Boston: Beacon Press, 1971.

Payne, Daniel A. *Recollections of Seventy Years.* 1888. Reprint, New York: Arno Press, 1968.

Peterson, Daniel H. *The Looking Glass: Being a True Report and Narrative of the Life, Travels, and Labors of the Rev. Daniel H. Peterson, a Colored Clergyman.* New York: Self-published, 1854.

Prince, Nancy Gardener. *A Narrative of the Life and Travels of Mrs. Nancy Prince.* Boston: Self-published, 1850.

Smith, Amanda Berry. *Autobiography: The Story of the Lord's Dealings with Mrs. Amanda Smith, the Colored Evangelist.* Chicago: Meyer, 1893.

Stewart, Maria W. *Maria W. Stewart, America's First Black Woman Political Writer: Essays and Speeches.* Edited by Marilyn Richardson. Bloomington: Indiana University Press, 1987. (Includes full text of both the 1835 *Productions* of Mrs. Maria W. Stewart and the 1879 *Meditations from the Pen of Mrs. Maria W. Stewart.* Another reprint of the 1835 *Productions* is in *Spiritual Narratives,* edited by Susan Houchins, New York: Oxford University Press, 1988.)

Truth, Sojourner. *The Narrative of Sojourner Truth, a Northern Slave.* Boston: Self-published, 1850.

White, George. *A Brief Account of the Life, Experiences, Travels, and Gospel Labours of George White, an African, Written by Himself and Revised by a Friend.* New York: John C. Totten, 1810.

SECONDARY SOURCES

Andrews, William L. *To Tell a Free Story: The First Century of Afro-American Autobiography, 1760–1865.* Urbana: Illinois University Press, 1986.

———, ed. *Sisters of the Spirit: Three Black Women's Autobiographies of the Nineteenth Century.* Bloomington: Indiana University Press, 1986.

Bassard, Katherine Clay. "Gender and Genre: Black Women's Autobiography and the Ideology of Literacy." *African American Review* 26, no. 1:119–29 (Spring 1992).

———. *Spiritual Interrogations: Culture, Gender, and Community in Early African American Women's Writing.* Princeton, N.J.: Princeton University Press, 1999.

Braxton, Joanne. *Black Women Writing Autobiography: A Tradition within a Tradition.* Philadelphia: Temple University Press, 1989.

Carby, Hazel V. *Reconstructing Womanhood: The Emergence of the Afro-American Woman Novelist.* New York: Oxford University Press, 1987.

Connor, Kimberly Rae. *Conversions and Visions in the Writings of African American Women.* Knoxville: University of Tennessee Press, 1994.

Eakin, Paul John. *Fictions in Autobiography: Studies in the Art of Self-Invention.* Princeton, N.J.: Princeton University Press, 1985.

Evans, James H., Jr. *Spiritual Empowerment in Afro-American Literature: Frederick Douglass, Rebecca Jackson, Booker T. Washington, Richard Wright, Toni Morrison.* Lewiston, N.Y.: Edwin Mellen Press, 1987.

Foster, Frances Smith. *Written by Herself: Literary Production by African American Women, 1746–1892.* Bloomington: Indiana University Press, 1993.

Frazier, E. Franklin. *The Negro Church in America.* New York: Schocken Books, 1974.

George, Carol V. R. *Segregated Sabbaths: Richard Allen and the Emergence of Independent Black Churches, 1760–1840.* New York: Oxford University Press, 1973.

Houchins, Susan, ed. *Spiritual Narratives.* Schomburg Library of Nineteenth-Century Black Women Writers. New York: Oxford University Press, 1988.

Humez, Jean McMahon. " 'My Spirit Eye': Some Functions of Spiritual and Visionary Experience in the Lives of Five Black Women Preachers, 1810–1880." In *Women and the Structure of Society: Selected Research from the Fifth Berkshire Conference on the History of Women.* Edited by Barbara Harris and JoAnn McNamara. Durham, N.C.: Duke University Press, 1984. Pp. 129–43.

Kagle, Steven E. *American Diary Literature, 1620–1799.* Boston: Twayne, 1979.

Lejeune, Philippe. *On Autobiography.* Translated by Katherine Leary. Edited by Paul John Eakin. Minneapolis: University of Minnesota Press, 1989.

709

Litwack, Leon F. *North of Slavery: The Negro in the Free States, 1790–1860.* Chicago: University of Chicago Press, 1961.

Loewenberg, Bert James, and Ruth Bogin, eds. *Black Women in Nineteenth-Century American Life: Their Words, Their Thoughts, Their Feelings.* University Park: Pennsylvania State University Press, 1976.

Mays, Benjamin E. *The Negro's God, as Reflected in His Literature.* New York: Negro Universities Press, 1969.

Morgan, Edmund S. *Visible Saints: The History of a Puritan Idea.* New York: New York University Press, 1963.

Payne, Daniel A. *History of the African Methodist Episcopal Church.* Edited by the Reverend C. S. Smith. Nashville, Tenn.: Publishing House of the AME Sunday School Union, 1891.

Peterson, Carla. *"Doers of the Word": African American Women Speakers and Writers in the North, 1830–1880.* New Brunswick, N.J.: Rutgers University Press, 1998.

Porter, Dorothy B., ed. *Early Negro Writing, 1760–1837.* Boston: Beacon Press, 1971.

Raboteau, Albert J. *Slave Religion: The "Invisible Institution" in the Antebellum South.* New York: Oxford University Press, 1978.

Richardson, Harry V. *Dark Salvation: The Story of Methodism as It Developed among Blacks in America.* Garden City, N.Y.: Anchor Press, 1976.

Ruether, Rosemary Radford, and Rosemary Skinner Keller, eds. *Women and Religion in America.* Vol. 1, *The Nineteenth Century.* San Francisco: Harper and Row, 1981.

Ruether, Rosemary Radford, and Eleanor McLaughlin, eds. *Women of Spirit: Female Leadership in the Jewish and Christian Traditions.* New York: Simon and Schuster: 1979.

Shockley, Ann Allen. *Afro-American Women Writers, 1746–1933: An Anthology and Critical Guide.* New York: New American Library, 1988.

Smith, Sidonie. *Where I'm Bound: Patterns of Slavery and Freedom in Black American Autobiography.* Westport, Conn.: Greenwood Press, 1974.

Smith, Theophus H. *Conjuring Culture: Biblical Formations of Black America.* New York: Oxford University Press, 1994.

Sobel, Mechal. *Trabelin' On: The Slave Journey to an Afro-Baptist Faith.* Westport, Conn.: Greenwood Press, 1979.

Sterling, Dorothy, ed. *We Are Your Sisters: Black Women in the Nineteenth Century.* New York: Norton, 1984.

Weems, Renita J. "Reading Her Way through the Struggle: African American Women and the Bible." In *Stony the Road We Trod: African American Biblical Interpretation.* Edited by Cain Hope Felder. Minneapolis: Fortress Press, 1991.

Whitson, Robley Edward, ed. *The Shakers: Two Centuries of Spiritual Reflection.* New York: Paulist Press, 1983.

Williams, Richard E. *Called and Chosen: The Story of Mother Rebecca Jackson and the Philadelphia Shakers.* Edited by Cheryl Dorschner. Metuchen, N.J.: Scarecrow Press, 1981.

MELVIN TOLSON
(1898–1966)

WILBURN WILLIAMS

OF ALL THE black writers of his generation—with the exception of Richard Wright—Melvin Beaunorus Tolson was born into circumstances least likely to nurture a major poet. Langston Hughes, four years Tolson's junior, could, and did, see his own greatness prefigured in forebears who played significant roles in the struggle to end slavery, and Countee Cullen, adopted into one of the most prominent black families in New York, could dream of a writing career from a vantage point of real privilege. By contrast, Tolson's father, the son of a former slave and her white master, had only eight years of formal schooling; biographers do not indicate that Tolson's mother received any formal schooling at all. The father's dogged efforts to rise in the Methodist Episcopal Church (he took correspondence courses and taught himself Latin, Hebrew, and Greek) met little success, and during most of Melvin's youth the family moved from one small parish to another in Missouri and Iowa, pursuing a higher status that, like the horizon, steadily receded before them. According to a family friend writing in support of Melvin's bid for financial aid to attend Lincoln University, the father simply was unable to do anything for the boy."

Tolson's development as a poet was every bit as slow as his father's advance as a preacher. The first works of Hughes and Cullen were published when they were in their twenties.

Tolson turned forty-six the year his first book appeared, and he was past fifty before he found his mature voice. As a college professor at Wiley College in Texas and then at Langston University in Oklahoma, Tolson was cut off from the Harlem Renaissance so vital to the early careers of Hughes and Cullen, and, unlike them, he never became identified with any particular movement in African American literature. He did, however, achieve some notoriety as a spokesman for radical political causes. One former student, James Farmer, director of the Congress of Racial Equality and leader of the Freedom Riders of the 1960s, cites Tolson's teaching as a major inspiration, but Tolson's place in history ultimately must rest on his poetry.

There certainly were few readers of that poetry during Tolson's lifetime. Far more people read the "Caviar and Cabbage" column Tolson wrote for the *Washington Tribune* between 1937 and 1944 than ever heard of his poetry, and to this day Tolson remains, even to specialists in black literature, something of an embarrassment: a poet they know they should, but don't, know. When Allen Tate, then at the height of his critical authority, tried to introduce Tolson to a wider readership, the preface he wrote for *Libretto for the Republic of Liberia* (1953) quickly became more famous than the poem itself. One year before Tolson's death in 1966, his

711

longtime friend and supporter Karl Shapiro wrote in the introduction to Tolson's *Harlem Gallery* (1965):

> A great poet has been living in our midst for decades and is almost totally unknown, even by the literati, even by poets. Can this be possible in the age of criticism and of publication unlimited? It is not only possible but highly probable. Poetry today is an established institution which has many of the characteristics of a closed corporation. (One of the rules of the poetic establishment is that Negroes are not admitted to the polite company of the anthology.) Poetry as we know it remains the most lily-white of the arts. A novelist and pamphleteer like Baldwin is world famous; Tolson, easily the literary equal of any number of Baldwins, is less honored in his own country than the most obscure poetaster.   (p. 11)

Three book-length studies and numerous articles have since assuaged the neglect Shapiro decried, but no critical consensus on Tolson's reputation has emerged, even among literati, even among poets. Tolson is the most controversial figure of his generation in African American poetry, and he is not easily assimilated into a critical history of black literature. His work is notable for evoking extreme responses. Admirers place him with Hughes, Gwendolyn Brooks, and Robert Hayden, among the very best in the tradition of black poetry. His more severe detractors would banish him from that tradition altogether, claiming that he writes, in his celebrated late work *Harlem Gallery*, in an esoteric idiom wholly alien to anything that might be authentically black. Sarah Webster Fabio, for example, writes that Tolson's "vast, bizarre, pseudo-literary diction is to be placed back in the American mainstream where it rightfully and wrongmindedly belongs." For such as she, Tolson is at best a mere imitator of the high modernist mode established by T. S. Eliot and Ezra Pound, bowing and scraping in the knee pants of servility to establish his credentials for a place in the white literary establishment.

Tolson, naturally, saw the matter quite differently, and he thoroughly anticipated the chorus of catcalls emanating from his detractors. He once proudly called himself the first modern black poet, and the only Marxist poet, in America. Both claims fall short of the truth, but they reveal Tolson's deep-seated awareness of his complex relationship to Marxism, the rise of modernism, and the maturation of a distinctly black poetry in the twentieth century. Like no other black poet of his time, Tolson purposely invited comparisons between himself and modern masters like Eliot and Pound. He studied their technique assiduously, was indeed deeply, and guiltily, indebted to them; but his poetry violently rejects the reactionary social and philosophical values he saw embedded in their work.

That Tolson's mature work superficially resembles that of Eliot and Pound has caused much confusion about the nature and meaning of his poetry. What, it is often asked, could such learned, allusive poetry have to do with the raw earthiness of black folktales, sermons, and the blues? What does the blunt grittiness of the black vernacular have to do with the Byzantine intricacy of Tolson's language?

The answer to both questions is, a very great deal. Long before the term acquired its current popularity, Tolson called himself an "African-American" poet. For him there was no contradiction in seeing himself as heir to both a poetry rooted in the oral traditions of black folk and a modern poetry rooted in the written traditions of Europe and white America. The hyphen that separates the two halves of his inheritance paradoxically joins them, and Tolson shared with William Blake, one of his favorite poets, the ironic realization that opposition is true friendship. Like the Curator of *Harlem Gallery*, whose biological ancestors include the Irish, the African, and the Jew, Tolson as a poet stands at the confluence of diverse streams of influence. By sheer force of style he blends them into an unmistakable idiom that is at once down-home and cultured, plainspoken and recondite, black and white.

Race, class, and identity are the major themes of Tolson's poetry. In a broad sense, all three concepts represent vain attempts to impose fixity on the flux of life, vain attempts to substitute a soothing reductionist simplicity for the exhilarating and baffling complexity of existence. It is absurd, Tolson says, to judge an individual on the basis of race or class, and it is futile to think that any person's identity can ever be established firmly. Notions of race, class, and identity are *historical* facts, but they are *scientific* fictions; and again and again Tolson finds his freedom in the realization that the world and all who are in it are ultimately unknowable: "Who knows, *without no*, / the archimedean pit and pith of a man?" asks the Curator in *Harlem Gallery*.

All knowledge is provisional, subject to change without notice, but it is in this very uncertainty that Tolson finds liberation from the tyranny of the "realities" of race, class, and identity. It is no accident that in *Harlem Gallery*, where Tolson's thoughts about this subject are most explicit, all three main characters defy reductive categorization: the Curator is blonde, blue-eyed, and black; Obi Nkomo, born, he says, a Zulu savage, has a Ph.D.; and Hideho Heights publishes lucid racial ballads for the public domain while writing esoteric private poems in the modern vein.

It is difficult to resist finding the origins of these themes in Tolson's complex attitudes toward the ambiguities of his own racial inheritance and class status. Born on 6 February 1898, in Moberly, Missouri, Melvin was the first child of Alonzo Tolson and Lera Ann Hurt to survive infancy (two elder siblings died before his birth). In "The Odyssey of a Manuscript" (1981) Tolson remembered his mother as a "little walnut-hued woman [who] was fiercely proud of being an American Negro, although in her veins flowed Irish, French, Native American, and African blood." His sister Helen, however, remembered Lera's parentage differently; both, according to her, were Cherokee Indians. Since ideas about racial identity in the Missouri of Lera's day were relatively plastic compared with those operative in the Deep South, it is quite possible that both Melvin's and Helen's recollections of their mother's background are true. In any event, it was Lera who encouraged

Melvin Tolson

Melvin's early ambition to write, and he later looked back upon his career as the vicarious fulfillment of Lera's own thwarted desire to write. Bedridden with the cancer that would take her life on 1 April 1934, Lera said, "Son, I always wanted to write. I had many things to tell people. But now that I am going to die, you'll have to do it for me."

Alonzo Tolson's origins seem to have been part of a dark family secret, shrouded in guilt and shame, and it is to him especially that one must look for clues to Melvin's attitudes toward race and class in American culture. According to Tolson's best biographer, Robert Farnsworth, the name of Alonzo's father was never mentioned, at Alonzo's insistence, in family discussions. The best evidence indicates that he was a white slave owner, a descendant of settlers of pre-Revolutionary Virginia, a member of a family known for its intelligence, industry, and conservatism. He fathered six, possibly seven, children with Suzie Tolson, Alonzo's mother. The relationship appears to have begun when Suzie was his chattel, and it continued after the Civil War and emancipation. "I've got Caucasian blood in my veins," Melvin told his *Washington Tribune* readers in 1941, "but I'm ashamed to tell you how it got there." Tolson family legend holds that one of the offspring of this relationship, Alonzo's sister Susie, passed for white. It was no doubt Susie whom Melvin had in mind when he sadly observed, "I had an aunt who was a good woman. But she believed that black persons are evil."

So far as we know, Tolson never directly and publicly revealed either the white slave-master identity of his paternal grandfather or his aunt's desertion of her black kin. It is impossible to tell with any certainty, therefore, precisely how they affected his outlook. But the burden of having to bear in secret this awful knowledge about them must have been a heavy one for a sensitive, inquisitive boy like Melvin. To ask Alonzo about *his* father—the natural thing for any child to do—would mean running the risk of Alonzo's anger. Seeking out the grandfather he had never seen might mean losing the affection of the father he did know. To discuss, among strangers, Susie's defection—a defection that Melvin likely understood to be a rejection of his own self—meant betraying a family confidence.

There must have been moments when Melvin asked what any normal child would have asked under such circumstances: What is so wrong with me that my grandfather and my father's sister have abandoned me? And Tolson the adult, living in a country where a black boy like Emmet Till could be lynched with impunity for merely whistling at a white woman, surely must have repeatedly asked: Why did my grandmother continue to sleep with that white man, who once *owned* her, *after* Emancipation? In *Harlem Gallery* the Curator reflects, in one of the most touching passages in that great poem:

> For dark hymens on the auction block,
> the lord of the mansion knew the macabre
> score:
> not a dog moved his tongue,
> not a lamb lost a drop of blood to protect a
> door.

> O
> Xenos of Xanthos,
> What midnight-to-dawn lecheries,
> in cabin and big house,
> produced these brown hybrids and yellow
> motleys?

In all likelihood the shame and guilt associated with the secret burden of the grandfather's identity and the defection of Aunt Susie go far in accounting for the intensity of Tolson's obsession with race, his fascination with the idea of occult identity, and his antipathy to snobbery and class distinctions. As a college professor in a day when most blacks were lucky to finish high school, Tolson more than qualified for induction into the black bourgeoisie, but in prose and in poetry he scorned identification with his proper social class and delighted in exposing the shallowness of their pretensions. It is no accident that the John Laugart painting that outrages the monied patrons of *Harlem Gallery* takes its title from E. Franklin Frazier's savage dissection of black middle-class life, *Black Bourgeoisie* (1957).

In the same "Caviar and Cabbage" column in which he furtively alluded to his white grandfather and his aunt's passing for white, Tolson viciously attacked the black bourgeoisie for pretending to a pride of race that they so obviously lacked. Victims of racism themselves, they ironically perpetuated racism in their treatment of their dark-skinned brothers and sisters:

> From the pictures of Negro women in Negro newspapers [note well here that the *Washington Tribune* was one], I'm sure there are no black women in America. Society leaders are near-white. There are no black women in Negro colleges, for "Miss Chittling Switch College" and "Miss Freedom College" are queens who're near-white. No good-looking Negro women have kinky hair. Negro doctors, businessmen, and professors marry (accidentally) high-yellow women. Chorus girls are (accidentally) high yellows.
> Even black women speak of improving Sambo's Race by marrying yellow men. Ain't

it the truth? Brownskins are flattered when you tell them they look Spanish, Hindu, Italian, Japanese—anything but African. Society matrons invite me to "A Night in Africa"?

Yet the blacks and yellows and browns assure me that they're proud to be Negroes! They urge me in this column to speak for the Race. They tell me to butt my wooly head against the white man's barriers of racial prejudice. Yet, on every hand, I'm confronted with the Color Lines within the Color Line! Because my hair is wooly and kinky, as God made it, they tell me my hair is "bad." Who in the hell says straight hair is "good"? The white man, of course! And his Uncle Tom Negroes! I've got Caucasian blood in my veins, but I'm ashamed to tell you how it got there! (*Caviar and Cabbage*, p. 95)

Tolson attacks color prejudice among the black bourgeoisie with such relish because he is at the same time trying to exorcise the terrible knowledge that his grandmother slept with her master and an aunt passed for white. Although he has done nothing to feel guilty about, he senses that he is somehow sullied by his grandmother's and aunt's betrayal of race pride. Immediately after noting that Aunt Susie "believed that black persons are evil," he writes: "Dirty Negroes are always worse than dirty white folk! And they always have worse odor. I've heard Negro aristocrats say that. They are duped and doped!" And Tolson is dirtied, too, by a sense of shame and guilt, in need of a cleansing confession that family loyalty denies him. And consider for a moment the near-identity of the grandmother's and aunt's names. The thought could not have escaped a poet, so renowed for his sensitivity to sound, that the grandmother's betrayal might defy absolution, passing, like her name, to the next generation and perhaps beyond. The sins of the grandmother are visited upon her daughter, and the grandson's teeth are set on edge.

In this light, the few examples of writing from Tolson's teens and twenties discovered by Farnsworth assume a new significance. Taken together with the literary training Tolson received in high school and at Lincoln, they offer

a clue to the puzzling belatedness of his poetic development. The high school writings suggest that Tolson veered away from personal experience and racial themes. To deal with such would have brought him too close to secrets the family forbade him to reveal. The stories in the high school yearbooks of 1917 and 1918 are particularly illuminating in this regard. They are exercises in the baroque, featuring vaguely conceived characters traipsing through ill-defined exotic landscapes. The language is lush and dreamy, and the stories might have succeeded as parodies of Poe if Tolson had in fact intended them to be parodies.

In college Tolson's writing did not fare any better. After a year at Fisk University in Nashville, Tennessee, Tolson transferred to Lincoln University in Pennsylvania, where his father's connections in the Methodist Episcopal Church helped him to attain financial assistance. Tolson majored in journalism and theology, and he won prizes in English, oratory, and debate. He caught the eye of the faculty and was invited to teach a freshman English class during his junior year. Apparently none of the poetry he wrote in college survives (and Lincoln, at any rate, was hardly the kind of place to nurture genuine creativity in literature). Lincoln was a prestigious but conservative sectarian institution, and Tolson got no encouragement from its all-white faculty to respond to the new developments then taking place in American poetry. Tastes there were soberly Victorian, and the black student body was a remarkably passive lot. Langston Hughes, who entered Lincoln in 1926, discovered in his senior year that fully two-thirds of the students opposed having blacks as permanent faculty for fear that they would not be objective evaluators of students. Lincoln could hardly be considered the center of a black consciousness movement.

When Tolson graduated with honors in 1923, already with the responsibilities of a husband and father—he had married Ruth Southall on 29 January 1922, and their son Melvin, Jr., was born on 19 June 1923—he seemed to have no inkling of the renaissance in black literature already under way in Harlem. Tolson lagged far behind his precocious black contemporaries.

715

Jean Toomer, four years older than Tolson, had just completed *Cane* (1923), perhaps the single best book to come out of the Harlem Renaissance. Langston Hughes had written one of his best poems, "The Negro Speaks of Rivers" (1921), and Countee Cullen was by then well known to readers of the NAACP's *The Crisis* magazine. Moreover, the great modernists who were to prove essential to Tolson's development were utterly unknown to him at this time. Farnsworth observes that a 1926 Tolson story, "The Tragedy of the Yarr Karr," published at Wiley College in Marshall, Texas, where Tolson taught from 1923 to 1947, "suggests that his youthful romantic fantasies were as yet far more compelling than the later sterner disciplines of his imagination." Like the juvenilia of the high school yearbooks, "Yarr Karr" seems an embarrassingly unself-conscious parody of the very worst melodrama.

Tolson wrote nothing of literary value until he began *A Gallery of Harlem Portraits* while studying for an M.A. in comparative literature at Columbia in the academic year 1931–1932, and it is important to note that he began it during the same year he started writing his thesis on the Harlem Renaissance writers. *Harlem Portraits* went unpublished during Tolson's lifetime, and the M.A. thesis borrows too heavily from Alain Locke to lay claim to originality, but both were part of a decisive break with Tolson's past reluctance to deal with race. With them he broke through the inhibitions blocking his imagination. Another fifteen years would pass before Tolson found his proper style, but 1932 at least gave him his theme.

Looking back on that year in 1938, Tolson wrote:

> In 1932 I was a Negro poet writing Anglo-Saxon sonnets as a graduate student in an Eastern university. I moved in a world of twilight haunted by the ghosts of a dead classicism. My best friend there was a German-American who'd sold stories to the magazines. We read each other's manuscripts and discussed art, science, and literature instead of cramming for the examinations. My ignorance of contemporary writers was abysmal.

> One cold wet afternoon the German-American read my sonnet *Harlem*, cleared his throat, and said: "It's good, damned good, but—"

> "The word Abut" suspended me in space. I could hear the clock on the desk; its tick-tock, tick-tock, swelled into the pounding of a sledge-hammer on an iron plate. The brutal words knifed into my consciousness: "You're like the professors. You think the only good poet is a *dead* one. Why don't you read Sandburg, Masters, Frost, Robinson? Harlem is too big, too lusty, for a sonnet. Say, we've never had a Negro epic in America. Damn it, you ought to stop piddling!"

> I placed the sonnet at the beginning of my thesis on the Harlem Renaissance. Under the painstaking supervision of Dr. Arthur Christy I had learned the beauty of the inevitable word.

> At the end of four years and 20,000 miles of traveling and the wasting of 5,000 sheets of paper, I had finished the epic *A Gallery of Harlem Portraits*.

> ("Odyssey of a Manuscript," pp. 8–9)

Whether this anecdote is factually true is altogether beside the point. (Tolson was not above creative dissembling. He once conducted a self-interview without warning his readers of the fact.) Here he acknowledges that his earlier writing constituted an enormous evasion of the truth, not just about Harlem but also about himself and his family's past. The words of the German-American plunge like a knife not just through Tolson's consciousness but through his *conscience*, for his loyalty to Alonzo's attempt to repress awareness of the perfidy of his grandmother and aunt had constituted a betrayal of his own talent: being true to his father meant being false to himself.

It is no accident that the encounter with the German-American is related in the same 1938 essay, "The Odyssey of a Manuscript," where we find the dying Lera Tolson obliging her son to do the writing she would never do. The mother's deathbed wish converts the father's command to be silent into an obligation to speak. The writing of *Harlem Portraits*, therefore, must be seen as part of a complex process in which fidelity to the mother compensates for defiance of the father. The writing of *Harlem Portraits,* for Melvin Tolson, constitutes a psychic drama not unlike the biblical story of Abraham and Isaac: Tolson takes the role of Abraham, his ambitions for poetry that of Isaac, and Alonzo and Lera divide God's role between them—*that* role, of course, being a tad too large for one parent.

Tolson never did free himself entirely from the embarrassment of his grandmother and aunt, but in his thesis and in *Harlem Portraits* he took the first steps of an odyssey that would end with *Harlem Gallery* in 1965. In the thesis, which he did not complete until 1940, Tolson located his own imaginative ground midway between Cullen's poetry in traditional forms and Hughes's heady explorations in the black vernacular. "Countee Cullen and Langston Hughes," he wrote, "represent the antipodes of the Harlem Renaissance. The former is a classicist and conservative; the latter, an experimentalist and radical. However, they are staunch friends and mutual admirers." Like the Curator and Dr. Nkomo of *Harlem Gallery,* Cullen and Hughes shine like Castor and Pollux in the sky of Tolson's art. Their paradoxical pairing leavens the classicism of Lincoln and Columbia with the experimentalist spirit of modernism.

Tolson modeled *Harlem Portraits* on Edgar Lee Masters' *Spoon River Anthology.* Tolson states his ambition to catalog every aspect of 1930s Harlem life in the final stanza of the opening poem:

> Radicals, prizefighters, actors and deacons,
> Beggars, politicians, professors and redcaps,
> Bulldikers, Babbitts, racketeers and jig-
>   chasers,
> Harlots, crapshooters, workers and pink-
>   chasers,
> Artists, dicties, Pullman porters and
>   messiahs . . .
> The Curator has hung the likeness of all
> In *A Gallery of Harlem Portraits.*

Harlem Portraits is a loose, baggy monster— 162 poems strewn over 230 pages. It is a series of static portraits with no consistent point of view and no narrative development. Robert Browning and Walt Whitman are often cited as influences, but Masters, Vachel Lindsay, and Carl Sandburg—lesser lights, to be sure—are more immediately present. Tolson read his Browning and Whitman with a severe selectivity. None of the portraits approach the subtlety of Browning's dramatic monologues, and Tolson's Whitman is the bearded purveyor of barbaric yawp dear to the anti-Romantic heart rather than the brooding tragic genius of "As I Ebb'd with the Ocean of Life." But *Harlem Portraits* is nevertheless fascinating for its energetic frankness (note the bulldikers and jigchasers), and Tolson's artful exploitation of the blues marks him as a worthy successor to Hughes and Sterling Brown.

Two themes in *Harlem Portraits* merit special attention: the failure of the Harlem Renaissance and the imminence of Marxist revolution. The poems "Elbert Hartman," "Miss Felicia Babcock," and "Ray Rosenfeld" collectively echo Sterling Brown's view that Harlem Renaissance artists pandered to their white patrons' obsession with black primitivism. Tolson's satiric genius is on full display in these three poems, and they are his way of saying that missing out on the New Negro movement of the 1920s perhaps was not such a great loss after all. In "The Underdog," which closes the book, Tolson voices his revolutionary fervor:

> Kikes and bohunks and wops,
> Dagos and niggers and crackers . . .
> Starved and lousy,
> Blind and stinking—
> We fought each other,
> Killed each other,
> Because the great white masters
> Played us against each other.
>
> Then a kike said: *Workers of the world,*
>   *unite!*
> And a dago said: *Let us live!*
> And a cracker said: *Ours for us!*
> And a nigger said: *Walk together, children!*
>
> WE ARE THE UNDERDOGS
> ON A HOT TRAIL!

Such crude sloganeering was common enough in the 1930s, and with it Tolson announced his intention to join Richard Wright, Frank Marshall Davis, and others in correcting the mistakes of the Harlem Renaissance by producing a realistic, earthy, and overtly political literature.

But the decline in the market for poetry during the Great Depression made publication of *Harlem Portraits* impossible, despite Tolson's vigorous efforts at self-promotion. Tolson told Joy Flasch, his first biographer, that the rejection of his manuscript led him to abandon writing for several years, but Farnsworth shows that the late 1930s and early 1940s were productive years in which Tolson experimented in drama and the novel, and found outlets for his poetry in *Modern Monthly, Common Ground,* and other magazines.

In 1940 a panel of judges that included Langston Hughes, Arna Bontemps, and Frank Marshall Davis awarded Tolson's "Dark Symphony" first prize in a poetry contest sponsored by the American Negro Exposition in Chicago. Reprinted in the *Atlantic Monthly* in September 1941, the poem led to publication of *Rendezvous with America* in 1944. Tolson's first book sold well and was widely and favorably reviewed. Margaret Walker, winner of the prestigious Yale University Younger Poet's Award in 1942, wrote: "These poems are full of arresting images . . . and [Tolson] handles difficult forms and metres with comparative ease. No one can say here is another naive Negro poet. He is a poet to be reckoned with by all poets." To this praise Richard Wright added: "Tolson's poetic lines and images sing, affirm, reject, predict, and judge experience in America, and his poetry is direct and humanistic. . . . The strong men keep coming and Tolson is one of them."

Rendezvous with America is surely all that, but it is ironic that "Dark Symphony," which is so unlike Tolson's best work, is perhaps his most widely read poem. Written at a time when the early victories of the Axis powers made America the last, best hope of democracy, it struck just the right balance between protest against racial bigotry at home and solidarity with the cause of freedom abroad. The funda-mental rhetorical strategy of "Dark Symphony" projects the history of African American experience as a prophecy of the fate of the world; to understand the African American past is to foresee the world's future. At the outset, however, the poem acknowledges a tension between the untold heroism of blacks and the whitewashed history enshrined in textbooks. Crispus Attucks, not Patrick Henry, is the proper ideal of revolutionary self-sacrifice:

> Black Crispus Attucks taught
> Us how to die
> Before white Patrick Henry's bugle breath
> Uttered the vertical
> Transmitting cry:
> "Yea, give me liberty or give me death."

Tolson's New Negro, "Hard-muscled, Fascist-hating, Democracy-ensouled," takes his inspiration from Nat Turner, Frederick Douglass, and Sojourner Truth, rather than the familiar periwigged faces of Enlightenment America. Marching "Along the Highway of Today / Toward the Promised Land of Tomorrow," he "thunders the Brotherhood of Labor." The poem concludes on a predictably upbeat note with black men chanting:

> Out of abysses of Illiteracy,
> Through labyrinths of Lies,
> Across waste lands of Disease . . .
> We advance!
>
> Out of dead-ends of Poverty,
> Through wildernesses of Superstition,
> Across barricades of Jim Crowism . . .
> We advance!
>
> With the Peoples of the World . . .
> We advance!

This is the kind of uplifting bombast high school teachers love to inflict on their captive students, but it is not great poetry. "Dark Symphony" is full of archaic inversions ("Men black and strong"), bloodless abstractions ("Democracy," "Justice," "Poverty," "Jim Crowism"), and dull figures ("juggernauts of despotism," "freedom's gates").

What is missing in "Dark Symphony" and in *Rendezvous* generally is a language capable of dramatizing the particularities of the black experience. In *Rendezvous* Tolson ignores the expressive possibilities of the black vernacular; he abandons the folk forms, like the blues and the spirituals, that he began to exploit in *Harlem Portraits*. He tells us what black experience is *about*, but he fails to embody that experience in a language adequate to his subject. In *Harlem Portraits* he had accepted the challenge laid down by James Weldon Johnson in 1922, when Johnson said that the black poet

> needs a form that is freer and larger than dialect, but which will still hold the racial flavor; a form expressing the imagery, the idioms, the peculiar turns of thought, and the distinctive humor and pathos, too, of the Negro, but which will also be capable of voicing the deepest and highest emotions and aspirations, and allow of the widest range of subjects and the widest scope of treatment.
>
> (p. xli)

In *Rendezvous*, Tolson declined this challenge and produced a poetry that, despite the importance of its theme, falls curiously flat.

The shortcomings of "Dark Symphony" could go so generally unremarked because criticism of black literature had for decades displayed little concern for the formal properties of literary works. In a 1950 essay on the history of black criticism, Ulysses Lee observed that criticism

> has generally been a handmaiden of progress, illuminating not the works themselves but the wonder that they exist, analyzing not the problems and methods of the authors but their effect, actual and probable, upon their audiences. . . .
>
> [Black literature's] critics . . . have had to judge the works with which they are concerned less as literature than as new evidence of advance and achievement, to be shared and gloried in by all members of the race.
>
> (pp. 328, 329)

This tradition of criticism had a profound effect upon twentieth-century black poetry, be-

cause its anti-formalist impulse was inherently inimical to the concern for language and form essential to understanding the great moderns—Eliot, Pound, William Butler Yeats, and William Carlos Williams, just to mention a few. With the exception of Jean Toomer, the color line excluded the writers of Tolson's generation from the social orbit in which the latest news of the modernist revolt circulated, and their idea of what constituted modern poetry lagged far behind current developments. Their situation was not at all helped by the fact that Pound, Eliot, and Yeats were notorious for their conservative, even fascist, politics.

Sometime between the publication of *Rendezvous* and the publication of the first version of *Libretto for the Republic of Liberia* in 1950, Tolson immersed himself in an intensive study of modern poetry and emerged utterly changed. The claim that Allen Tate inspired the transformation has proven false, and, since there is no evidence to the contrary, what Pound said of Eliot probably holds true for Tolson: he simply modernized himself. The full extent of the change is startlingly clear in the opening lines of *Libretto*:

> *Liberia?*
> No micro-footnote in a bunioned book
> Homed by a pendant
> With a gelded look:
> You are
> The ladder of survival dawn men saw
> In the quicksilver sparrow that slips
> The eagle's claw!
>
> *Liberia?*
> No side-show barkers bio-accident
> No corpse of a soul's errand
> To the Dark Continent:
> You are
> The lightning rod of Europe, Canaan's key,
> The rope across the abyss,
> *Mehr licht* for the Africa-To-Be!

The language here is alive, fanciful yet deeply serious, and artfully compressed. The interplay between *bunioned* and *footnote* is rather obvious, perhaps grotesquely so, but *bunioned* must also be read as *Bunyaned*, for in line 116 the Liberian emigrants are called "Black Pilgrim Fathers." Their exodus thus becomes a quest for spiritual perfection, "a soul's errand," as well as a physical flight from the slavery symbolized in the claw of the American eagle. Rich suggestions lurk in "ladder of survival" as well. The religious context of the Liberian experiment evokes the ladder seen by Jacob (Genesis 28:12–15) in a dream in which God promises to bless him with land for himself and his descendants. The carnival barker in line 10 inevitably recalls the ladder of Yeats's "The Circus Animal's Desertion" ("I must lie down where all the ladders start, / In the foul rag-and-bone shop of the heart"), so the ladder promises a renewal of poetic creativity as well. The images of Liberia as ladder, lightning rod, and rope, which symbolically connect disparate realms of experience, collectively constitute Tolson's version of "The Bridge" of Hart Crane, whose earlier attempt to undo the pessimism of Eliot's *The Waste Land* inspired the *Libretto's* attempt, in Tolson's words, to answer "the mysticism of the *Four Quartets*."

The wealth of reference here is daunting, and critics like Fabio are quick to dismiss it as so much showing off. But Tolson does not always write in such a difficult style. His evocation of the fall of West African empires to Europe is extraordinary, at once broodingly tragic and frighteningly sinister:

And now the hyenas whine among the
    barren bones
Of the seventeen sun sultans of Songhai,
And hooded cobras, hoodless mambas, hiss
In the gold caverns of Falémé and Bambuk,
And puff adders, hook scorpions, whisper
In the weedy corridors of Sankoré *Lia! Lia!*

The ease with which Tolson incorporates diverse historical, mythological, biblical, and literary data into a poetry all his own is what Allen Tate had in mind when he said, in the introduction to *Libretto,* "For the first time, it seems to me, a Negro poet has assimilated completely the full poetic language of his time and, by implication, the language of the Anglo-

American poetic tradition." One might object that Tolson was not the first black poet to do so, or one might say, like Fabio, that the game is not worth the candle to begin with; but Tate is surely right when he says, "For there is a great gift for language, a profound historical sense, and a first-rate intelligence at work in this poem from first to last."

Libretto deserves far more attention than it can be given here, but a few pertinent remarks are in order. Tolson was commissioned to write the poem for the Liberian centennial in 1947. Tolson's alma mater, Farnsworth notes, was originally the Ashmun Institute, founded by the American Colonization Society to train blacks for service in Africa and named after Jehudi Ashmun, one of the founders of the Liberian colony. Horace Mann Bond, a friend of Tolson's and president of Lincoln University, probably had a hand in the commission. Tolson completed the first version of the poem within a year, and sent the fourteen-page manuscript to Tate in February 1949, asking him to write a preface as a gesture of interracial cooperation. Tate's introduction and what is now section seven of *Libretto* appeared in *Poetry* in July 1950. Throughout this time, and even after, Tolson revised and added to the poem. The final version, twenty-nine pages of text and sixteen pages of Tolson's notes, was published in 1953.

A libretto is the text of an opera; the remark quoted in the note to line 495—"Dictatorship is always an aria, never an opera"—implies that the poem opposes an abiding vision of freedom to the transient reality of tyranny. The eight sections of the poem are named for the notes of the diatonic scale, which is one of Tolson's symbols for the ambiguous nature of historical change. Insofar as the diatonic scale arranges the notes in ascending order, it is emblematic of the view of historical change as a linear progression toward an ultimate state of perfection. But since the notes begin and end with *do,* change can also circle back on itself, yielding the figure of history as a tautological nightmare, an endless treading of the same dreary ground. Neither view, in Tolson's opinion, is privileged—Tolson abhors determinist theories—for the course of history can be bent to the human will, but, as the optimistic conclusion of *Libretto* makes clear, his sympathies lie in the progressivist camp.

Tolson devotes the first six sections of the poem to observing the official necessities of his commission. They are a compressed rendering of the history of West Africa and the settling of Liberia, but they comprise less than a third of the poem. The final two sections are given over to dark reflections on the horrors of the twentieth century and have almost nothing to do with the actual Liberia—a happy, deliberate omission for celebrants of the centennial, because Tolson was severely critical of the exploitation of the Liberian masses by the unsavory collusion of the American-Liberian elite with the Firestone Rubber Corporation.

These two sections are notoriously difficult going, even with Tolson's notes. They can be seen as a duet sung—or, more precisely, a duel fought—by the "old she-fox today" (line 489) and an unnamed protagonist representing Tolson. Her "eyes dead letters mouth a hole in a privy" (line 490), the she-fox personifies cowardly capitulation to the enemies of race and class, the White Sphinx and Red Enigma of line 376. Her song catalogs the ruinations of these stubborn ideas, and Tolson numbers among them Stalin's perversion of the Marxism so dear to his heart. The she-fox is an acute observer, but she mistakenly concludes that race warfare and class warfare are inevitable products of a corrupt human nature that can never change. As Tolson puts it in the long note to line 619, she "confuses the feral with the societal"; instead of opposing the enemies of race and class, she shortsightedly concedes that some race or class will always oppress some other.

The protagonist has great difficulty answering the she-fox because he must agree that her pessimistic vision finds support in history. Indeed, his own sense of contemporary disarray is every bit as deep as hers, and at times the voices of the two are virtually indistinguishable. His first attempt to foresee a world in which all men are brothers—see his invocations of Goethe's *Höhere* of Gaea's children in lines 403ff.—is undone by the song of the she-fox. Only after in effect acknowledging her partial truth can he

sustain the vision of the Futurafrique that closes the poem; and even here, Tolson admonishes in the note to line 619, some vestiges of the disasters of the past will remain.

Libretto, despite Tate's approbation, did not win Tolson the recognition he expected. As Farnsworth and others have noted, reviewers in the main were cautious in their praise even though they had to admit Tolson's power. Tate's obiter dictum that the African American poet's attempts to exploit black forms and idioms have largely "limited the Negro poet to a provincial mediocrity in which one's feelings about one's difficulties [in being black] become more important than poetry itself" struck a raw nerve in black readers, many of whom well knew that Tate was hardly in the forefront of the struggle for black civil rights. Tolson, disappointed but not disheartened, returned to Harlem, the subject that inspired his first, still unpublished book.

Harlem Gallery: Book I, The Curator (1965) is the full title of Tolson's masterpiece. Tolson originally planned a five-volume epic of African American history, but only the first got beyond the planning stage. *Harlem Gallery* is 154 pages long, so we can only begin to suggest its riches here. It is a quest romance narrated by the Curator—he has no name—who seeks answers to three questions: What is art? What does it mean to be a black artist? What is the proper role of the critic who mediates the artist's relationship to the public? Companions on this quest include Obi Nkomo, an expatriate African and the Curator's alter ego; Hideho Heights, a poet who resembles, but in crucial respects differs radically from, Langston Hughes; and John Laugart, a great but neglected painter. Mister Starks (Mister is his given name, not a title), a pianist and avant-garde composer, observes the interaction of the questers from a distance, but the manuscript he bequeaths to the Curator upon his death provides the key to understanding the Curator. There are a host of memorable minor characters, and their brief portraits are drawn with Dickensian skill. Most of the action takes place in the Harlem Gallery and the Zulu Club, a popular nightspot where lowbrows and highbrows, pimps and preachers, meet. As an intellectual quest romance, most of *Harlem Gallery* is talk—glorious, bawdy, witty, endless talk—and takes place over a period of roughly forty years, from the Harlem Renaissance of the 1920s to the early 1960s.

The poem is divided into twenty-four cantos, named after the letters of the Greek alphabet. Ten are monologues spoken by the Curator, giving us his thoughts about art and life in Harlem; the other fourteen contain the narrative heart of *Harlem Gallery*, the spirited debates about art and the politics of race that give Tolson the freedom to deploy the full range of his encyclopedic knowledge. The wealth of allusions is even greater than that in *Libretto*, but passages in foreign languages are mercifully few. There are no notes.

We can approach an appreciation of Tolson's immense achievement by examining the first three stanzas of the poem, which illuminate the crisis confronting Harlem and the Curator's response to it:

> The Harlem Gallery, an Afric pepper bird,
>   awakes me at a people's dusk of dawn.
> The age altars its image, a dog's hind leg,
> and hazards the moment of truth in pawn.
>   The Lord of the House of Flies,
>   jaundice-eyed, synapses purled,
>   wries before the tumultuous canvas,
>   *The Second of May*—
>   by Goya:
>   the dagger of Madrid
>   vs.
>   the scimitar of Murat.
> In Africa, in Asia, on the Day
> of Barricades, alarm birds bedevil the Great
>   White World,
> a Buridan's ass—not Balaam's—between
>   no oats and hay.
>
> Sometimes a Roscius as tragedian,
>   sometimes a Kean as clown,
> without Sir Henry's flap to shield my neck,
> I travel, from oasis to oasis, man's Saharic
>   up-and-down.
>
> As a Hambletonian gathers his legs for a
>   leap,

> dead wool and fleece wool
> I have mustered up from hands
>   now warm or cold: a full
>   rich Indies' cargo;
> but often I hear a dry husk-of-locust blues
> descend the tone ladder of a laughing
>   goose,
>   syncopating between
>   the faggot and the noose:
>   "Black Boy, O Black Boy,
>   is the port worth the cruise?"

The Harlem Gallery is both the Curator's place of work and the black masses of New York, who are forced to sit in the galleries of its segregated theaters. The pepper bird, noted for its morning song, is sometimes called the alarm clock of West Africa. The Curator is irritated by its demand that he wake up and get about his work because he does not know what the day portends. We must recall here that "dusk of dawn" was coined by W. E. B. Du Bois to express his wonder whether the stirrings in the Black South at the turn of the century presaged a sinking into a deeper bondage or a casting off of the chains of enthrallment, "the twilight of nightfall or the flush of some faint-dawning day." The Curator tellingly refers to the Harlem Gallery as *a*, not *my*, people, and by this we take the measure of his alienation from them. He had once chosen, like Tolson's Aunt Susie, to pass for white; having revealed his identity at "an Olympian powwow of curators," he is forced to work at a gallery whose patrons are black Babbitts—and miserly ones at that.

The pepper bird metamorphoses into the alarm birds of Asia and Africa, for the crisis of Harlem, poised at the outset of the tumultuous 1960s, is part of a global crisis that threatens the hegemony of the white world. Beelzebub's writhing before the engagé art of Goya indicates the sanative power of authentic art; if his jaundiced eyes were cleansed, "every thing would appear to [him] as it is, infinite." But, like the she-fox, he comprehends only a partial reality. A question mark, the shape of the dog's hind leg raised in urinating, is the appropriate figure for an age beset by doubt, an age that delegates to underlings the hard task of confronting its crisis. Unlike the biblical ass that saved Baalam by being able to see the vengeful angel Baalam could not see—blindness is a major symbol in this poem—the ruling class is even worse than that of Jean Buridan's sophism. (Buridan's ass, it was argued, would starve to death out of indecision if placed between equally attractive piles of fodder. The Great White World lacks these alternatives, being "between no oats and hay.")

The Curator wanders through this wasteland in disguise—Quintus Roscius was a comic actor, Edmund Kean played tragic roles—but still vulnerable (he lacks the flap devised by Sir Henry Havelock to shield the necks of Britain's imperial armies from the desert sun).

As a collector of art, he has salvaged works by living and dead artists. *Wool gathering* refers at once to the idle imaginings of this absent-minded former professor and the pastoral obligations to Harlem he would gladly relinquish. The rich collection of paintings hanging in the Harlem Gallery is proof that he knows his art, but like Prufrock he does not know whether it has been worth it after all. The accumulation of rhymes leading up to the blues song of the laughing goose (a real bird, here symbolically the pepper bird's antagonist) recalls the virtuoso rhyming so prominent in black folk poems like "The Signifying Monkey," and they prepare our entry into lines of poetry that are black in their form as well as in their subject. The faggot and the noose allude to Walter White's 1929 study of lynching, *Rope and Faggot*, and it is well to remember that White, the NAACP secretary, was able to witness actual lynchings of blacks because, like the Curator, he could pass for white. This blues-singing goose is not trapped by his own indecision; he is trapped between *real* alternatives, both destructive. Yet, like the blacks whose condition his plight symbolizes, he makes music—cool, husky, jazzy music—while dancing between them. He challenges the Curator's resolve even as he enacts the resolution of hateful contraries that the Curator must learn to imitate. Tolson's goose is the lineal descendant of the animal tricksters of black folk tales, and like the many other speaking animals in *Harlem Gallery*, every bit as canny as Br'er Rabbit.

The Curator is too caught up in his ambivalent relationship to Harlem to recognize it for what it is, much less identify its source and resolve it. The moment of recognition comes when he reads an account of a conversation he himself had with Dr. Nkomo in the dead Mister Starks's *Harlem Vignettes:* "I used to say," Mister Starks's account begins, "if I knew the differences between / the Curator and Doctor Nkomo, / I'd know the ebb and flow of tides of color." As the Curator sips a glass of cream, Nkomo, "guileless . . . [as] a whore in a virgin's wedding gown," asks, "Why cream, O Nestor, instead of milk?" The Curator replies that he is "fascinated by / the opacity of cream," that is, the blackness of its whiteness, its superiority to the milk it rises above. Dr. Nkomo angrily replies that the Curator's belief in the natural superiority of cream is analogous to the racist's belief in the natural superiority of whites: "Garbed in the purple of metaphors, / the Nordic's theory of the cream separator / is still a stinking skeleton!" The Curator answers: "Since cream rises to the top . . . / blame Omniscience—/ not me." He states that white supremacy, like cream's superiority to milk, is divinely ordained. This being the case, he gloomily advises Nkomo to "*taste* the milk of the skimmed / and *sip* the cream of the skimmers."

For Nkomo—and for Tolson—this appeal to Nature and to God privileges the art of the elite—the cream of the skimmers—at the expense of the masses. By implication the Curator's appeal to God and the natural order rationalizes the existence of racial hierarchies. Like the she-fox of *Libretto*, the Curator *knows* that hierarchies of race and class are immoral, but he is unwilling to challenge them. Dr. Nkomo gets the final word when he says that a mind conscious of the right thing

"is not a hollow man who dares not peddle
the homogenized milk of multiculture,
in dead ends and on boulevards,
in green pastures and across valleys of dry
bones."

723

The Curator, having finished reading Starks's poem, confesses:

> [Starks] had seen in me
> the failure of nerve
> Harlem would never see—
> the charact in the African
> that made
> him the better man.

The essential message—moral, if you will—of *Harlem Gallery* is not very different from that of *Libretto*. What troubles humankind is not a defect of knowledge but a failure of will. But the language of *Harlem Gallery* is very different from that of *Libretto*. It is in this last poem that Tolson demonstrates his mastery of Anglo-American tradition, which we understand, unlike Tate, to *include* the idioms and forms of the black oral tradition. Tolson shows, by the ease with which he slips from arch, Mandarin sonorities into the audacious, funky tones of the black vernacular, that the full range of the English language is available to him; and he demonstrates that black speech is indeed capable of giving voice to the highest thoughts, to speaking with authority on every subject.

Harlem Gallery won Tolson the kind of recognition *Libretto* deserved to win. The American Academy of Arts and Letters gave him its annual award for poetry and playwrighting and $2,500 to go with it. Tuskegee Institute gave him an endowed professorship in 1965, but Tolson did not have it for long. He died of cancer on 29 August 1966.

It is still too early to adequately measure the extent of Tolson's influence on subsequent American poetry. Although poems such as *Harlem Gallery* might be considered too demanding for a general readership, poets and critics continue to reflect upon Tolson's work, particularly in discussions about the relation of art to its audience. Regardless of Tolson's critical reception, two things are certain: *Harlem Gallery* remains one of the most ambitious, imaginative works in African American poetry to date, and one of the great long poems of the twentieth century.

Selected Bibliography

PRIMARY WORKS

POETRY

Rendezvous with America. New York: Dodd, Mead, 1944.
"E. & O. E." *Poetry* 78:330–42, 369–72 (September 1951).
"The Man From Halicarnassus." *Poetry* 81:75–77 (October 1952).
Libretto for the Republic of Liberia. New York: Twayne, 1953.
Harlem Gallery. Book I, The Curator. New York: Twayne, 1965.
A Gallery of Harlem Portraits. Edited by Robert Farnsworth. Columbia: University of Missouri Press, 1979.

NONFICTION

"Richard Wright: *Native Son.*" *Modern Quarterly* 11:19–24 (Winter 1939).
"Claude McKay's Art." *Poetry* 83:287–90 (February 1954).
"A Poet's Odyssey." In *Anger and Beyond.* Edited by Herbert Hill. New York: Harper & Row, 1966.
"The Odyssey of a Manuscript." *New Letters* 48:5–17 (Fall 1981).
Caviar and Cabbage. Edited and with an introduction by Robert Farnsworth. Columbia: University of Missouri Press, 1982.

THESIS

"The Harlem Group of Negro Writers." Columbia University, 1940.

SECONDARY WORKS

BIOGRAPHICAL AND CRITICAL STUDIES

Basler, Ray P. "The Heart of Blackness—M. B. Tolson's Poetry." *New Letters* 39:63–76 (Spring 1973).
Benet, William Rose. "Two Powerful Negro Poets." *Saturday Review* 28:34–36 (24 March 1945).
Bérubé, Michael. "Avant-Gardes and De-Author-izations: *Harlem Gallery* and the Cultural Contradictions of Modernism." *Callaloo* 12:192–215 (Winter 1989).
———. "Masks, Margins, and African American Modernism: Melvin Tolson's *Harlem Gallery.*" *PMLA* 105:57–69 (January 1990).
———. *Marginal Forces/Cultural Centers: Tolson, Pynchon, and the Politics of the Canon.* New York: Cornell University Press, 1992.
Bone, Robert. "A Poet With a Fame Deferred." *Change* 11:65–67 (October 1979).
Brooks, Gwendolyn. "Books Noted." *Negro Digest* 14:51–52 (September 1965).
Dove, Rita. "Telling it Like it I-S: Narrative Techniques in Melvin Tolson's *Harlem Gallery.*" *New England*

Review and Bread Loaf Quarterly 8:109–17 (Autumn 1985).

Fabio, Sarah Webster. "Who Speaks Negro?" *Negro Digest* 16:54–58 (December 1966).

Farnsworth, Robert M. "What Can a Poet Do? Langston Hughes and M. B. Tolson." *New Letters* 48:19–29 (Fall 1981).

———. *Melvin B. Tolson, 1898–1966: Plain Talk and Poetic Prophecy*. Columbia: University of Missouri Press, 1984.

Flasch, Joy. *Melvin B. Tolson*. New York: Twayne, 1972.

Johnson, James Weldon, ed. *The Book of American Negro Poetry*. New York: Harcourt, Brace, 1922.

Lee, Ulysses. "Criticism at Mid-Century." *Phylon* 11:328–37 (1950).

Miller, R. Baxter, ed. *Black American Poets Between Worlds, 1940–1960*. Knoxville: University of Tennessee Press, 1986.

Mootry, Maria K. " 'The Step of Iron Feet': Creative Practice in the War Sonnets of Melvin B. Tolson and Gwendolyn Brooks." *Obsidian II* 2:69–87 (Winter 1987).

Nielsen, Aldon L. "Melvin B. Tolson and the Deterritorialization of Modernism." *African American Review* 26:241–55 (Summer 1992).

Randall, Dudley. "Portrait of a Poet as Raconteur." *Negro Digest* 15:54–57 (January 1966).

Redmond, Eugene B. *Drumvoices*. Garden City, N.Y.: Doubleday, 1976.

Russell, Mariann. *Melvin B. Tolson's "Harlem Gallery": A Literary Analysis*. Columbia: University of Missouri Press, 1980.

Shapiro, Karl. "The Decolonization of American Literature." *Wilson Library Bulletin* 39:843–53 (June 1965).

———. "The Critic Outside." *American Scholar* 50:197–210 (Spring 1981).

Smith, Gary. "A Hamlet Rives Us: The Sonnets of Melvin B. Tolson." *CLA Journal* 29:261–75 (March 1986).

Thompson, Gordon E. "Ambiguity in Tolson's Harlem Gallery." *Callaloo* 9:159–70 (Winter 1986).

Tolson, Melvin B., Jr. "The Poetry of Melvin B. Tolson (1898–1966)." *World Literature Today* 64:395–400 (Summer 1990).

Werner, Craig. "Blues for T. S. Eliot and Langston Hughes: the Afro-Modernist Aesthetic of *Harlem Gallery*." *Black American Literature Forum* 24:453–72 (Fall 1990).

Woodson, Jon. "Melvin Tolson and the Art of Being Difficult." In *Black American Poets between Worlds, 1940–1960*. Edited by R. Baxter Miller. Knoxville: University of Tennessee Press, 1986.

—The bibliography has been updated for this edition by Keidra Morris.

JEAN TOOMER
(1894–1967)

NELLIE Y. MCKAY

HIS PARENTS NAMED him Nathan Pinchback Toomer—giving him his father's and his mother's names. At the insistence of his grandfather, for several years of his childhood he was called Eugene Pinchback—forced to disinherit his Toomer connections and assume as surname that of the grandparents with whom he and his mother lived after his father deserted them. As a child he responded to several nicknames: he was Pinchy to his friends, Booty to his mother, Whippersnapper to his grandfather, and Kid and Snoots to different uncles. In his mid twenties, when he began to write, he adopted the name Jean because he thought that it suggested the poet, or the man of letters, and Eugene did not. Much later, he called himself Nathan Jean to indicate his gender clearly to those who did not know him. Jean Toomer is the name that literary posterity inherits, but the name changes serve well as a metaphor for the search for identity that seems to have governed Toomer's life.

Jean Toomer was born in Washington, D.C., on 26 December 1894, the son of Nathan Toomer, a Georgian and self-described gentleman planter, and Nina Pinchback, daughter of Pinckney Benton Stewart Pinchback, a prominent Louisiana politician during the Reconstruction. Toomer's father and grandfather were men whose appearances, despite their mixed blood, did not necessarily indicate black Afri-

can ancestry. P. B. S. Pinchback nevertheless made his reputation by claiming his racial heritage. Nathan Toomer never went out of his way to do likewise. Jean Toomer, also fair-skinned, viewed the issue of race from a different perspective entirely. He had an innate distaste for categories such as race that created stereotypes of individuals. In his early teens he independently developed a concept of his identity that enabled him to acknowledge the various races and nationalities of his forebears without isolating and privileging or marginalizing any one part of his background. This concept played an essential role in his subsequent life choices.

Toomer's life through young adulthood was marked by familial stormy times. Lacking financial means of support, and deserted by the husband she had married against her father's wishes, in 1896 Toomer's mother returned to her parents' house, also in Washington, with her infant son. Toomer's accounts recall that his mother, a young woman of upper-class refinement, refused to be intimidated into passiveness by Pinchback's strong and dominating personality. Perhaps to escape the conflicts of her parents' home, Nina Pinchback remarried in 1906 and moved first to Brooklyn and then to New Rochelle with her (white) husband and her son.

While Jean Toomer recalled early fondness for the stories read to him by his mother and by her brother Bismarck, who also lived under P. B. S. Pinchback's roof, his conscious love of literature originated in the New York period of his life. During this time, he discovered the library and his love for reading. In New Rochelle his imagination was also stimulated by the outdoors, and he engaged in activities that permitted him the solitude he craved: bicycling, swimming, fishing, and sailing. In his small sailboat, a gift from his stepfather, whose overtures of friendship he otherwise refused, he explored the waters along the harbor of Long Island Sound. Later he recalled those times in stories that he wrote.

In 1909 Nina Pinchback died suddenly from complications following an appendectomy; soon after, Toomer returned to Washington to live with his grandparents. Major changes had occurred in the family's circumstances during his absence. The Pinchbacks, affluent in the 1890s, suffered severe financial reverses in the early twentieth century. His grandparents had moved out of the mansion in the largely white upper-class section of town where Toomer lived when he was a young child. In 1910 fourteen-year-old Jean Toomer found himself in a middle-class interracial community where, for the first time, he lived in close contact with significant numbers of people of color. He took pleasure in the change, enjoying and participating in the infectious exuberance of his new environment.

School life embodied the usual adolescent fluctuations of successes and failures for Jean Toomer. During his first year at the M Street High School (now the Paul Laurence Dunbar High School), one of the most famous black secondary schools in the country, he did well. But in the following year, and intermittently thereafter, he was tormented by sexual anxieties that left him emotionally drained. Struggles with his stern grandfather, usually over money, which, despite Pinchback's depleted resources, Toomer felt the older man owed him, raged between them until Pinchback's death in 1922. Toomer undertook an obsessive program of body building and health promotion activities in an effort to resolve his inner distresses. His excellent physical condition brought him admiration from those around

him, although he continued to experience debilitating emotional turmoil. This ability to project self-control and physical and psychological well-being to the world even as internal chaos devoured him became a permanent characteristic of Jean Toomer's life.

Had Pinchback had the resources, Toomer would probably have attended Harvard College. The old man, whose three sons graduated from prestigious institutions of higher education, wanted the best for his only grandson, who in turn believed that he had a right to the best that life afforded. But financial exigencies made going to Harvard out of the question. Toomer decided instead to go to the University of Wisconsin at Madison, where he intended to study scientific agriculture. Later, in an autobiographical account, he said that he chose Wisconsin largely to put distance between himself and the middle-class goals and aspirations of the people he knew in Washington. He felt a need to eschew conventional expectations, to establish his individuality, and to reject blind conformity.

After graduating from high school at mid-year, Toomer had several months to contemplate the nature of his college career before leaving home. During this time he gave substantial thought to the meaning of racial identity in one's relationship to the world at large. For most of his life he had lived within an almost all-white world; for a shorter period, his world had been an integrated one. His high-school peers were the next generation of the black middle class. Toomer thought they seemed to have accepted the social separation of the races without the same degree of resistance that he felt toward such a dichotomy. On the one hand, he had suffered little on account of race. Although his grandfather insisted on the primacy of his African blood, by dint of their color and their economic and social standing the Pinchbacks enjoyed white middle-class status. On the other hand, Toomer was aware of the degrading conditions that the majority of black people endured. He worried most about the limitations that race imposed on nonwhites, and he passionately resisted any categorization that made him vulnerable to such external restrictions. He wondered what his white counterparts at Wisconsin would think of him when they discovered that he had attended an all-black high school.

Toomer's thinking led him to formulate a concept of an "American race"—a group that would encompass most Americans, since the bloodlines of the majority of people in the United States stretched across nations and continents. The commonality they shared was their Americanness. Throughout his life, Toomer rejected the idea that he should have to choose between defining himself as white or black, and insisted that he belonged to the American race. When others challenged the accuracy of such a category, he claimed that while all Americans belonged to this race, and others would come to this knowledge in time, he was the first conscious member of the group.

Although his Wisconsin stay was brief—a summer and one semester—it was at that university that Toomer gained his first mature introduction to the world of literature. An English professor urged him to write and made him aware of important periodicals like the *New Republic*, the *Nation*, and the *Manchester Guardian*. His college years lasted from 1914 to 1919 and were spent in more institutions of higher education than the aggregate of years in which he attended them. During these years he explored widely diverse areas of study, including scientific agriculture and literature, and he quarreled incessantly with his grandfather over money—or, rather, the lack of it. Amid the turmoil of these years, he read and was influenced by the literary works of Victor Hugo, George Bernard Shaw, and Henrik Ibsen in particular. He was equally influenced by Charles Darwin and the sociological writers Lester Ward and Clarence Darrow. Toomer, in trying to explain his inability to decide on a single course of study during his five years of college, noted that he had been yearning to find "a sort of whole into which everything fits . . . a body of ideas which holds a consistent view of life." He glimpsed possibilities in systems of thought such as socialism, but he was never able to settle on a field of study that wholly satisfied him. Finally, in 1919, without having done sufficient

Jean Toomer

work in any single institution to earn a degree, he gave up on the life of the academy.

From the spring of 1919 through the first half of 1921, Toomer—who during this time thought of himself as a political and economic socialist—began to think of writing as a serious career choice. For part of that time he lived in Greenwich Village in New York City, where he met writers and critics who introduced him to the culture of writers and artists. He also read Walt Whitman, Edwin Arlington Robinson, Witter Bynner, Waldo Frank, Fyodor Dostoyevski, Leo Tolstoy, Gustave Flaubert, Charles-Pierre Baudelaire, Sinclair Lewis, Theodore Dreiser, and Sigmund Freud. Other American writers who made an impression on him were Sherwood Anderson and Robert Frost, and he read in world religions, including Eastern religions and the Christian Bible. By the middle of 1920, however, his financial circumstances forced him back to Washington, where he lived with and received a small allowance from his indigent grandparents for taking care of them. The arrangement was not satisfactory, however, and he suffered the frustrations of the unfulfilled writer. In one of his autobiographical fragments he observed that at the time his efforts yielded a literal trunk of manuscripts, none of which were good enough to publish. Still, the distractions of outside employment would have been worse, so he stayed with his family.

During what he subsequently called the "difficult winter" of 1920–1921, Toomer had one important success: he wrote a long poem, "The First American." In it he set out the theory of race that he had first formulated in 1914 at the beginning of his college career, but now with the keener insights that his wanderings from Washington to Wisconsin, Massachusetts, Chicago, and elsewhere had given him. Although not published then, the poem represented a major breakthrough for him: he was beginning to find a voice of his own, and he felt he truly had something to say. For more than a decade and a half he continued to refine it, until 1936, when it appeared in print as "The Blue Meridian."

The climax to Toomer's literary apprenticeship came in the fall of 1921, when, leaving his grandparents in the care of others, he went south to take a position as a substitute teacher for a friend on a mission north to collect funds to support the school. Living in what he called a "hut" in rural Georgia, not far from Sparta, where his father had lived, from mid September to mid November Toomer heard folk songs and spirituals sung in a manner he had never before experienced. For the first time he understood that despite overt white racism and oppression of blacks, there was a prodigious black folk culture that was not yet diluted by white cultural mores. Ironically, segregation had thus far preserved that folk culture. But Toomer recognized that the way of life he was witnessing would disappear soon. Young black people, as they moved to urban areas in search of lives away from the backbreaking labor of the land, were appropriating more of white America's

cultural values for their own. He was moved by what he heard and saw of the remnants of the folk culture, but more important, he found a voice to express his discovery. From the South he sent a poem, "Georgia Dusk," to the *Liberator*, and on the train back to Washington in November he began to write the vignettes that became the first section of his book, *Cane*.

By the end of December 1921, Toomer had nearly completed the first part of *Cane*. The grandfather with whom Toomer had done battle for most of his life died in that same month. Family feuds notwithstanding, Toomer had loved and respected his grandfather. He took the body to New Orleans, where much of Pinchback's controversial political career had taken place, and buried him in a vault beside his daughter, the young writer's mother. This death marked the end of one important part of Toomer's life and the beginning of another. During that winter he continued to work on his book, and he wrote two plays; *Balo*, a folk drama that was produced by the Howard University Repertory Company during its 1923–1924 season, and *Natalie Mann*, a bold experiment in expressionist theater. This work was never produced, but it appears in Darwin Turner's *The Wayward and the Seeking: A Collection of Writings by Jean Toomer*, published in 1980.

With Waldo Frank (a man of letters who staunchly supported talented new writers, whom Toomer had met in New York in 1920) as his closest friend and adviser, during 1922 Jean Toomer worked furiously and joyously on *Cane*. The Georgia trip had inspired him, giving him new material for writing and filling him with enthusiasm for the task. He saw beauty in the African American folk experience that called forth lyric responses from him. He also became known in literary circles. His reviews, short stories, and poems appeared in publications such as the *Crisis, Double Dealer,* and the *Little Review.* Sherwood Anderson, among others, admired and offered to help him. For a while the two men corresponded, but the relationship between them never became as strong as that between Toomer and Frank, who criticized and offered suggestions to each other on their work. With Hart Crane, too, who was then working on *The Bridge*, Toomer enjoyed a period of similar colleagueship. Acceptance into the literary community as an equal was very important to him, and these men gave him the assurances he needed to reinforce his confidence in his artistic abilities. Although he never lived in Harlem, and over time he knew only a small number of black writers of the period, the Harlem Renaissance literati took an enthusiastic interest in his work. Jessie Fauset, literary editor of the *Crisis,* was especially encouraging in her correspondences with Toomer and predicted that he would become a great writer.

In December 1922 Toomer completed *Cane.* Sherwood Anderson offered to do an introduction for it, but the privilege went to Waldo Frank, who had been one of the first to identify Toomer's talents. On Frank's advice, in January 1923 Boni & Liveright accepted *Cane* for publication, and it appeared in the early fall of that year. It was the first major venture that Toomer had completed in his life: his family, especially his aged grandmother and his beloved uncle, Bismarck Pinchback, were extremely proud of him. Toomer recorded that he was happier than he had ever been before.

Jean Toomer's literary reputation rests on *Cane,* an artistic representation of African America, encompassing the Northern and Southern, the urban and rural experiences. It is divided into three sections depicting South, North, and the unity of South and North, with the first and second parts containing prose vignettes interspersed with poems that provide bridges between the prose pieces. The third part of the book, "Kabnis," is a short drama. Finding a generic name for this combination of forms has been a problem for many critics, especially since Toomer made clear that his text was not a collection of individual pieces but a single entity made up of intrinsically related parts. The wholeness Jean Toomer had unsuccessfully sought in life during his earlier adulthood had been realized with the production of *Cane.* Failure to attain his goals in the past often left him complaining of long periods of inner chaos. The results of the trip to Georgia, at least temporar-

ily, solved that problem. The book, he said, "brought his scattered parts together."

The most immediately striking feature of *Cane* is its language. With great skill, Toomer uses words to create tones and atmospheres. The first section contains stories set in Georgia—of six women, five black and one white, each in a vignette of her own and each with different physical qualities and psychological strengths and weaknesses. The effectiveness of these portrayals is partly achieved through a heavy overlay of nature imagery. Each vignette is a verbal photograph, vivid, mystical, and sensuous, constructed with words that evoke color and sound. For example, in the sketch that opens *Cane*, he describes the young woman Karintha:

> Her skin is like dusk on the eastern
>   horizon
> O cant you see it, O cant you see it,
> Her skin is like dusk on the eastern
>   horizon
> . . . When the sun goes down.

In the first section of *Cane,* black women's beauty is associated with their nurturing qualities as well as their vulnerabilities. Three of the women in particular—Karintha, Carma, and Fern—embody a mystical quality that in each case the narrator finds impossible to penetrate. Karintha is connected to the dusk on the eastern horizon. Yellow-flower-faced Carma, "strong as any man," is associated with the seductive powers of an ancient goddess. An ethereal atmosphere envelops Fern, whose "face flowed into her [irresistible] eyes." As Toomer portrays these beautiful, strong, and vulnerable women, they are symbols of the black community from slavery to the present.

In contrast with the dark beauty of Karintha, colorless Esther, in another vignette, is physically the most unattractive of the women in the book, and Becky, the only white woman in the group, is invisible. Estranged from the rest of the black community by her higher economic status, Esther lives a sensually starved existence of psychological alienation from both black and white communities. Becky, on the other hand, who has transgressed the racial code governing black-white sexuality and given birth to two black babies, has consciously forfeited her white privilege. She is banished from the community and permitted to die for want of help from a devoted group of churchgoers.

The first section of *Cane* closes with a story titled "Blood-Burning Moon," a tragedy of a black woman and two men—one white, one black. Rejecting the imagist portrayals of the earlier narratives, Toomer turns almost completely to realism to carry his message. The black man loves the black woman and anticipates an honorable life with her. The white man wants her for a mistress and cannot tolerate competing against a black man for her. The black man kills the white in self-defense and is lynched by the white community. Louisa, the sexual object of both men's desires, and the final victim, loses her sanity. At the close of the narrative she is sitting outside her door, singing plaintively to the blood-red moon.

"Blood-Burning Moon" addresses one of the most painful aspects of black-white experience in the South. This story is more than a tragedy of ritual murder that reinforces the power of white over black—it points to the inevitable confrontation between black and white men as black men reclaim the birthright of human dignity wrenched from them through slavery, segregation, and other kinds of racial oppression. The irrational violence of "Blood-Burning Moon" lowers the curtain on the first section of the black Southern experience in this book.

Part 2 of *Cane* contains four narratives, five poems, and three prose poems. Immediately striking is the change from the lyrical language of the first section to language that with a paucity of metaphors and nature images embodies approximations of the sounds and vibrations of the city. Set in the urban North, the section's artistic tension arises out of the conflicts between natural human impulses and the covert violence of the man-made environment. Emphasis is on the harshness, mechanization, sterility, and destructiveness of the modern city to the human spirit. Of the prose poems—"Seventh Street," "Rhobert," and "Calling Jesus"—the first (which opens: "Seventh Street is a bastard of Prohibition and the War") is an extended metaphor of urban black life at a particular time

in history; the second and third are allusions to humanity's loss of meaning in the mire of modern city life.

In the narratives in section 2 of *Cane*, realism imposes on the impressionism that marked the earlier part of the book. Toomer uses autobiographical experiences as the bases for the action of at least two of these stories. In "Avey," for instance, the setting is Washington, D.C., with references to the street on which he lived as a young boy and to places where he vacationed with his family, as well as scenes from his days at the University of Wisconsin. Avey, the central figure in the vignette, represents, among other things, the African American folk culture. The unnamed narrator both clings to Avey and tries to fashion her to meet his own selfish needs as he searches for cultural identity. In the end he discovers the futility of attempting to appropriate her strengths only for his self-serving ends.

"Theater," also set in Washington, uses the Howard University theater for its setting. Here Toomer explores class issues among black people, and he presents the dance as an art form that can express the free natures of black people who are not repressed by white Western social conventions. Unfortunately, although the potential for free expression exists, it comes to nothing in "Theater," an environment in which materialism and sterile social conventions take the place of natural, uninhibited behavior between men and women. The same theme appears in "Box Seat," another narrative set in a theater. Its images of disharmony reflect the public discord of a repressed world and the private conflicts of those who live in it. The conflict between those who attempt to hold on to old values and those who reject them weakens the black community and makes it more vulnerable to oppression from the world outside.

The final narrative in the section, "Bona and Paul," like "Blood-Burning Moon" involves direct relations between the races, but without physical violence. The action revolves around a sexual attraction between two college students—one a mulatto young man, the other a young white Southern woman. The setting is Chicago, and the narrative opens in the gymnasium of what might well be the American College of Physical Training, where Toomer was a student in the fall of 1916. In the story, the young man's naive attempt to establish a relationship with the young woman fails because she cannot overcome the hurdle of his race.

The focus on the urban setting in this part of the book explores, first, the restrictions that a segregated society imposes on the human spirit and the failure of African Americans to achieve emotional and psychological wholeness in such a climate and, second, the danger when black Americans reject positive characteristics in black folk life for destructive aspects of white culture. These failures stem from racism in American society, and from restraints sometimes self-imposed by black Americans, which Toomer views as originating in misguided concepts of the significance of certain moral and spiritual values. In looking at sections 1 and 2 of *Cane*, a reader sees that he examined race and sex, city and country, beauty and pain as parts of the double experience of what it meant to be black in America. The folk culture is dying out, but its influence is still a vital force in the lives of many black people and a guidepost for future directions for the race.

Section 3 of this book, "Kabnis," is a sustained folk drama with strong resemblances to *Balo*, the only one of Toomer's plays that was ever produced. This part of the text structurally unifies the Southern and Northern black experiences represented in *Cane*, through the return of a Northern black man to his ancestral South. Kabnis, the protagonist of the piece, is a schoolteacher and poet at a cultural crossroads, searching for meaning in his history. Toomer is not sparing in the extent to which we see the fears, alienation, and ambivalence of Kabnis on this pilgrimage. For one, he is afraid of what might happen to him in the South, of the senseless violence that can erupt around him at any moment. Those fears paralyze him and make it impossible for him to act effectively, no matter what he tries to do. In contrast with his fears, the natural environment, to which he is extremely sensitive, has a double face. On the one hand, it is serene and lovely; on the other, it is full of unknown dangers. Race and religion are also closely allied in this drama: racial inequality and black social and economic subservence rooted in a passive acceptance of religious dogma, versus political action, are fully explored along the way in the young man's psychological journey.

While most of the action points to what seem like unsurmountable problems in the abilities of Kabnis to bring his quest to a successful conclusion, the piece ends on an optimistic note. For one long and tortured night he takes refuge from the fears that he cannot dismiss in the basement of a blacksmith's shop with a group of black Southerners who are representative of black men and women in the South. Also present is an old man, a relic of slavery, who is blind and deaf. Away from a hostile world, Kabnis and the younger women and men give voice to their racial hurts and anxieties. Through an unfruitful attempt to engage the aid of the old man to find answers to his problems, Kabnis comes better to understand his identity. Next morning, the young woman who brings food for the old man assists the emotionally drained Kabnis out of the basement, and he emerges into a brilliant new day. His rise from the cellar coincides with the "birth-song" that the early morning sun sends through the branches of the trees into the streets of the sleeping town. This ending suggests that, taking hold of his fears, Kabnis will sing that song of African American struggle through his art, and because of his experiences his work will capture the complexity of the African American experience. On his arrival in the South, he had believed that he had many things to teach the "backward" black people who lived there, but that he could learn little from them. Instead, he learns the collective history of African Americans from them and discovers his place in that history.

While many poems in *Cane* function as bridges to the prose narratives, a few stand on their own. One such poem is "Song of the Son," the most frequently anthologized work from this book. Included midway through section 1 of the text, it synthesizes many of the themes in the work. "Song" makes it clear that *Cane* is the work of an artist—a poet who, having been separated from his heritage, returns to his paternal homeland to pay homage to the memory, the triumphs, and the sufferings of his fathers. The returning son regrets his long absence from the land of his forebears, but the clear, strong voice of the poem asserts that there is no ambiguity in his position: he is the son of the soil. The culture of the past, especially of slavery, is in danger of loss to history, and it is his responsibility to ensure its preservation and restoration to collective memory. This he will do in art:

> One plum was saved for me, one seed becomes
> An everlasting song, a singing tree,
> Caroling softly souls of slavery,
> What they were, and what they are to me,
> Caroling softly souls of slavery.

His "song" is the emotional outpouring of a poet who recognizes his place in time and in the history of African America. With *Cane*, Toomer fulfills his commitment to save the departing soul of his culture.

A number of critics view *Cane* as an autobiographical work, citing both Toomer's discussions of the book, mostly with Waldo Frank, during the time he was engaged in writing and the many textual parallels with situations in Toomer's life. Toomer writes that before his trip to Georgia his unfulfilled search for inner harmony often left him in deep depression. This changed as soon as he arrived in the South. Not only was he enthusiastic over his discovery of a rich vein of splendid artistic materials, but in his letters to Frank between 1921 and 1923 he acknowledged a strong sense of identity with the elements of his project. Most important, perhaps, was that in writing *Cane* he seemed to have come to an understanding of the dual nature of the African American heritage. On the one hand, he saw its beauty and strength, and he felt a dignity derived from within the folk culture; on the other hand, he understood the depth of the pain and the price of the struggle that American racism exacted from a people it attempted to make less than human beings. "Song of the Son" and "Kabnis" are the segments in the book that best express this duality, and they also reflect Toomer's own relationship to the materials of *Cane*.

When it appeared in 1923, *Cane* was well received by writers and critics alike, praised especially because of Toomer's ability to break with exclusive fidelity to American realism and yet capture the poignancy of the African American experience. The book represented Toomer's ascendancy in the literary world, and many people predicted a brilliant future for him. Unfortunately, however, by the time *Cane* was published Toomer had lost the glow his achievement had brought him immediately after the writing was done. Initially he had felt that he was part of a new generation of writers whose works would retard the onrushing effects of technology and acquisitiveness that were taking hold of Western civilization. But he had begun to feel strong disaffection for the literary world and literature, because of what he saw as the ineffectiveness of literary art in helping to resolve the problems of the modern world, such as alienation and materialism. Furthermore, that in his authorship of *Cane* he was identified as a "Negro writer" made him angry. He wanted to be known as an American writer, whose race was inconsequential to his art, and in that light his hopes for *Cane* were not fulfilled. Late in 1923 he turned his back on the literary world he had worked so hard to enter, and similarly he rejected most of the friends who had supported him in his efforts. His search for a system to foster inner harmony began again. Meanwhile, despite his attitude toward it, *Cane* went on to have a life of its own. Sales were small, but black and white critics and writers were voluminous in their praises of the merits of the book and of its author's talents. *Cane* remains a classic in the tradition of African American literature, and it continues to generate new and interesting criticism.

Soon after the publication of *Cane*, Toomer became involved with the teachings of George Ivanovich Gurdjieff, an Eastern mystic whose disciples attempted to achieve a higher consciousness that would enable them to participate in a more ultimate goal of universal consciousness. Gurdjieff's philosophical and psychological program was intended to engage the physical, mental, and emotional centers of human activity. It included strenuous physical exercises (from long hours of kitchen work to felling trees); a combination of mental and physical exercises accompanied by music; and lectures, discussions, and created "situations" that forced disciples to address interpersonal problems. In the 1920s Gurdjieff's Institute for the Harmonious Development of Man, in the community of Fontainebleau near Paris, attracted many well-known Europeans and Americans. Toomer became a follower in 1924, and between 1925 and 1933 he taught the Gurdjieff method in the United States. Although he broke formally with Gurdjieff in the mid 1930s, tenets of Gurdjieff's philosophy continued to inform Toomer's actions, thinking, and writing for nearly another decade.

While *Cane* is Toomer's only book, his disappointment with art and the literary world did not put an end to his writing. He subsequently published a number of stories, including "Easter," in the *Little Review*, in 1925; "Mr. Costyve Duditch," in the *Dial*, and "York Beach," in *New American Caravan*, in 1929; and "Winter on Earth," also in the *Dial*, in 1933. A poem, "White Arrow," and "Reflections," a small group of aphorisms, appeared in the *Dial* in 1929. Toomer's short stories are heavily laden with the message that modern man (Toomer also meant woman) is rootless and mechanical and in need of redemption from these flaws; human beings have created a world that is contrary to the laws of nature, and thus they have subverted the authentic goal of life, which is human development along the lines of Gurdjieff's teachings.

His scant body of published material bears no relationship to the substantial quantity of Toomer's writings. Some of Toomer's previously unpublished work is now available in Darwin Turner's anthology *The Wayward and the Seeking*. But although Toomer wrote for many years, after *Cane* he could find no publisher to take his work. As early as 1929, he collected a group of ten of his unpublished stories written between 1924 and 1929 and tried

unsuccessfully to publish them. He had no better luck with his novels and his plays. The former include "Transatlantic" (the first draft written in 1929), revised as "Eight-Day World" (in 1933 and 1934); "Caromb" (written during 1932); and "The Gallonwerps," a novel he wrote in 1927 and later revised as a play. His other plays are "A Drama of the Southwest," written in the mid 1930s but never completed, and "The Sacred Factory," which he wrote in 1927. He made several attempts at autobiography, with the same discouraging results. His most successful writing ventures after *Cane* were the essays and articles he wrote for the *Friends Intelligencer* in the 1940s.

Toomer's novels, stories, and plays of the late 1920s through the 1940s are flawed by thinness of plot, weak characters, lack of development or dramatic impulse, moralizing, and his need to act always as a proselytizer for Gurdjieff. His themes were not unlike those of many of the significant writers of the same era, but he could generate no enthusiasm or interest among publishers for his efforts, which lacked the imagination of *Cane* and were hopelessly mired in the dogma of Gurdjieff's philosophy.

Then "Blue Meridian," the poem that began as the unpublished "The First American" in the winter of 1921–1922 and appeared as "Brown River, Smile" in *Pagany* in 1932, was published in the *New Caravan* in 1936. Although the poem did not elicit critical attention at the time of its publication, subsequent critics have considered it a worthy second to *Cane* in the literary achievements of Jean Toomer. In comparison with *Cane*, which looked at the history of America's past to acknowledge and redeem it for its own sake, "Blue Meridian" uses the past to lay out a plan of action for and to predict the future. Toomer spent many years reworking this poem. In final form it is a carefully reasoned, idealistic statement about racial homogeneity in America. Like Toomer's writings of the late 1920s and early 1930s, it articulates much of Gurdjieff's philosophy, but it combines literary elements with social concerns and is a sophisticated work of art.

"Blue Meridian," more than eight hundred lines long, is a poem about America that is usually compared to Walt Whitman's "I Hear America Singing" and Hart Crane's *The Bridge*. It celebrates America for its diversity of races, tribes, and regions; in the poem, all Americans have come to know the meaning of being American. Earlier barriers that separated groups of people have fallen, and all have become one. Meridian—the blue man—is the aggregate human being, without differentiation of sex, class, or color. The new America of this poem is a product of the evolution of a mystical, spiritual process; rather than alienation or fragmentation, it holds only harmony and oneness with universal order. The poem makes its point through a combination of conventional and Gurdjieffian imagery; the "dynamic atom-aggregate" and "Radiant Incorporeal" represent the Gurdjieffian human being in harmony with the universe; the eagle and the airplane are symbols of American strength and power. The poet's aim is to draw our attention to the possibility of transforming his nation into what it originally set out to be—a country in which all people would have dignity and the opportunity to develop to their full human and spiritual potential. Toomer's poem is a public statement in which he offers a philosophical and moral solution to the problems of race, sex, religion, and class in American society.

"Blue Meridian" includes all of North America. The Mississippi, which plays such an important role in North American history, becomes, like its Eastern sister the Ganges, a sacred river that serves as the wash of spirituality which energizes the people of a continent. Many religious symbols find their way into the text. The East and West coasts are the masculinity and femininity of the new land; the middle region of the country is the offspring of these extremes. All of these are brought together in the service of the blue man—the synthesis of all groups of people and the representative ideal toward which all should strive.

For all of its brilliance, "Blue Meridian" did not prove a point of re-entry for Toomer into the world of the arts. In 1936, although he was no longer actively engaged in teaching and recruiting disciples for Gurdjieff, he was following much of what he had learned in the previous decade and was still in search of a system that would offer the personal harmony of which he dreamed. He wanted what he wrote to reach publication, but his focus was on a message that he felt he possessed and needed to convey. He was searching for truth; he believed that, in contrast, most other human beings were dead and did not realize they were. He wanted to awaken them. This tenet dominated everything that he wrote well into the 1940s.

In 1932 his deep commitment to Gurdjieff's work led Toomer to conduct an experiment in living on the model of the Institute for the Harmonious Development of Man. It took place in Portage, Wisconsin, for a period of six months, with six people, in a small house called Witt Cottage. In subsequent writings Toomer named the period spent in Portage the Cottage Experiment. The group at Witt Cottage aimed for physical self-sufficiency by doing all the physical work necessary for their living needs, while at the same time they strove for collective spiritual growth. (Economic security was not involved, for these were upper-middle-class people.) Toomer considered the experiment a success, although later the wife of one participant sued her husband for divorce on grounds of adultery, and newspapers called the communal experiment a love cult. Immediately after the group broke up, Toomer married Margery Latimer, a Wisconsin novelist who had participated in the experiment. The marriage was a happy one for both of them, but a year later she died of complications associated with the birth of their child. In 1934 Jean Toomer married again, a New Yorker named Marjorie Content, whose wealthy father gave the couple a farm outside Doylestown, Pennsylvania. Toomer lived there until his death on 30 March 1967. Although he officially broke with Gurdjieff in 1934, between 1936 and 1940 Toomer attempted to replicate the Witt Cottage Experiment on the Pennsylvania farm, calling it the Mill House Experiment. The participants considered it a worthwhile undertaking, but by 1940 he was suffering from a number of health problems and could no longer direct the program.

In 1939 Toomer took his family on a nine-month pilgrimage to India. Neither that trip nor his various subsequent excursions into the teachings of the mystic Edgar Cayce, Jungian psychoanalysis, and scientology satisfied his yearning to find an approach to life that would yield inner harmony, although his association with the Society of Friends appears to have been valuable to him. He spoke and wrote extensively for the Friends in the 1940s and 1950s.

Although *Cane* has been in print for most of the years since its publication, the whereabouts of Jean Toomer were unknown to most of the literary world between the late 1920s and the early 1960s. His interest in Gurdjieff was of little concern to those who had lionized him as a rising literary star in 1923 and 1924, and he never tried to revive the relationships that had nurtured him as a young artist. During the brief period of his first marriage in 1933, the national media created a controversy over the marriage of a so-called black poet to a white novelist. But Toomer otherwise seems to have gained the racial anonymity he craved as soon as he left the literary world to devote his life to a search for inner harmony. Some critics have accused him of "passing," but Toomer never claimed to be white. He simply refused to be labeled a black man.

Jean Toomer's *Cane* ranks among the greatest achievements in American literature. Nearly three-quarters of a century after its publication it continues to receive critical attention; essays, chapters in books, and dozens of dissertations each year focus on both the writer and his book. Toomer's unique and powerful talent captured the legacy of the African American experience, but he nevertheless insisted throughout his life that the issue of race was, to him, an irrelevant element in comparison with the more important universal human experience. In his long and unsuccessful search for himself, Jean Toomer epitomized the true son of America.

Selected Bibliography

PRIMARY WORKS

BOOKS

Cane. With an introduction by Waldo Frank. New York: Boni & Liveright, 1923; with an introduction by Arna Bontemps. New York: Harper & Row, 1969; with an introduction by Darwin Turner. New York: Liveright, 1975; critical ed., edited by Darwin Turner. New York: Norton, 1987.

Essentials: Definitions and Aphorisms. Chicago: Lakeside Press, 1931. Reprint edited by Rudolph P. Byrd. Athens, Ga.: University of Georgia Press, 1991.

The Wayward and the Seeking: A Collection of Writings by Jean Toomer. Edited and with an introduction by Darwin Turner. Washington, D. C.: Howard University Press, 1982.

The Collected Poems of Jean Toomer and Margery Toomer Latimer. Edited Robert B. Jones and Margery Toomer Latimer, with an introduction and textual notes by Robert B. Jones. Chapel Hill: University of North Carolina Press, 1988.

Jean Toomer's Years with Gurdjieff: Portrait of an Artist, 1923–1936. Edited by Rudolph P. Byrd. Athens, Ga.: University of Georgia Press, 1990.

A Jean Toomer Reader: Selected Unpublished Writings. Edited by Frederik L. Rusch. New York: Oxford University Press, 1993.

Jean Toomer: Selected Essays and Literary Criticism. Edited and with an introduction by Robert B. Jones. Knoxville: University of Tennessee Press, 1996.

UNCOLLECTED SHORT FICTION

"Easter." *Little Review* 11:3–7 (Spring 1925).

"York Beach." In *New American Caravan.* Edited by Alfred Kreymbourg, Lewis Mumford, and Paul Rosenfeld. New York: Macaulay, 1929. Pp. 12–83. (Novella.)

"Of a Certain November." *Dubuque Dial* 4:107–12 (November 1, 1935).

UNCOLLECTED POEMS

"Gum." *Chapbook,* no. 36:2 (April 1923).

"Reflections." *Dial* 86:314 (April 1929).

"As the Eagle Soars." *Crisis* 41:116 (April 1932).

"Brown River, Smile." *Pagany* 3:29–33 (Winter 1932).

"For M. W." *Pembroke Magazine* 6:68 (January 1975).

"Glaciers of Dusk." *Pembroke Magazine* 6:68 (January 1975).

UNCOLLECTED PLAY

Balo. In *Plays of Negro Life.* Edited by Alain Locke and Montgomery Gregory. New York: Harper and Brothers, 1927. Pp. 269–86.

ESSAYS

"Race Problems and Modern Society." In *Problems of Civilization.* Vol. 7, *Man and His World.* Edited by Baker Brownell. New York: D. Van Nostrand, 1929. Pp. 67–111.

"The Hill." In *America and Alfred Stieglitz: A Collective Portrait.* Edited by Waldo Frank et al. New York: Doubleday, Doran, 1934. Pp. 295–303.

"A New Force for Cooperation." *Adelphi* 9:25–31 (October 1934).

LITERARY CRITICISM

"An Open Letter to Gorham Munson." *S4N*, no 25 (March–April 1923).

"Notations on *The Captain's Doll*." *Broom* 5:47–58 (August 1923).

"The South in Literature." *Call* (1923).

"Waldo Frank's *Holiday*." *Dial* 75:383–86 (October 1923).

"Zona Gale's *Faint Perfume*" *Broom* 5:180–81 (October 1923).

"The Critic of Waldo Frank: Criticism, an Art Form." *S4N*, no. 30 (September 1923–January 1924).

"Oxen Cart and Warfare." *Little Review* 10:44–48 (Autumn–Winter 1924–1925).

SECONDARY WORKS

BIOGRAPHICAL AND CRITICAL STUDIES

Abu-Shardoe, Abarry. "Afrocentric Aesthetics in Selected Harlem Renaissance Poetry." In *Language and Literature in the African American Imagination*. Edited by Carol Aisha Blackshire-Belay. Westport, Conn.: Greenwood Press, 1992.

Ackley, Donald G. "Theme and Vision in Jean Toomer's *Cane*." *Studies in Black Literature* 1, no. 1:45–65 (Spring 1970).

Baker, Houston A., Jr. "Journey Toward Black Art: Jean Toomer's *Cane*." In *Singers of Daybreak: Studies in Black American Literature*. Washington, D.C.: Howard University Press, 1975. Pp. 53–80.

Bell, Bernard W. "A Key to the Poems in *Cane*." *CLA Journal* 14:251–58 (March 1971).

———. "Portrait of the Artist as High Priest of Soul: Jean Toomer's *Cane*." *Black World* 23, no. 11:4–19, 92–97 (September 1974).

———. "Jean Toomer's 'Blue Meridian': The Poet as Prophet of a New Order of Man." *Black American Literature Forum* 14:77–80 (Summer 1980).

Benson, Brian Joseph, and Mabel Mayle Dillard. *Jean Toomer*. Boston: Twayne, 1980.

Bontemps, Arna. "The Negro Renaissance: Jean Toomer and the Harlem Writers of the 1920's." In *Anger and Beyond: The Negro Writer in the United States*. Edited and with an introduction by Herbert Hill. New York: Harper and Row, 1966.

Bowen, Barbara. "Untroubled Voice: Call and Response in *Cane*." *Black American Literature Forum* 16, no. 1:12–18 (Spring 1982).

Bradley, David. "Looking Behind *Cane*." *The Southern Review* 21, no. 3:682–94 (Summer 1985).

Brannan, Tim. "Up from the Dusk: Interpretations of Jean Toomer's 'Blood Burning Moon.' " *Pembroke Magazine* 8:167–72.

Brinkmeyer, Robert H. "Wasted Talent, Wasted Art: The Literary Career of Jean Toomer." *The Southern Quarterly* 20, no. 1:75–84 (Fall 1981).

Bus, Heiner. "Jean Toomer and the Black Heritage." In *History and Tradition in Afro-American Culture*. Edited by Gunter Lenz. Frankfurt and New York: Campus, 1984.

Bush, Ann Marie, and Louis D. Mitchell. "Jean Toomer: A Cubist Poet." *Black American Literature Forum* 17, no. 3:106–08 (Autumn 1983).

Byrd, Rudolph P. "Jean Toomer and the Afro-American Literary Tradition." *Callaloo* 8:310–19 (Spring–Summer 1985).

———. "Jean Toomer and the Writers of the Harlem Renaissance: Was He There With Them?" In *The Harlem Renaissance: Revaluations*. Edited by Amritjit Singh, William S. Shiver, and Stanley Brodwin. New York: Garland, 1989.

———, ed. *Jean Toomer's Years with Gurdjieff: Portrait of an Artist, 1923–1936*. Athens, Ga.: University of Georgia Press, 1990.

———. "Shared Orientation and Narrative Acts in *Cane, Their Eyes Were Watching God*, and *Meridian*." *MELUS* 17, no. 4:41–56 (Winter 1991–1992).

Caldeira, Maria Isabel. "Jean Toomer's *Cane*: The Anxiety of the Modern Artist." *Callaloo*, no 25, *Recent Essays from Europe: A Special Issue*. Pp. 544–50 (Autumn 1985).

Cancel, Rafael A. "Male and Female Interrelationship in Toomer's *Cane*." *Negro American Literature Forum* 5, no. 1:25–31 (Spring 1971).

Chase, Patricia. "The Women in *Cane*." *CLA Journal* 14:259–73 (March 1971).

Christ, Jack. "Jean Toomer's 'Bona and Paul': The Innocence and Artifice of Words." *Negro American Literature Forum* 9, no. 2:44–46 (Summer 1975).

Christensen Peter. "Sexuality and Liberation in Jean Toomer's 'Withered Skin of Berries.' " *Callaloo*, no. 36:616–26 (Summer 1988).

CLA Journal 17 (1974). (Special Toomer issue.)

Cooperman, Robert. "Unacknowledged Familiarity: Jean Toomer and Eugene O'Neill." *The Eugene O'Neill Review* 16, no. 1:39–48 (Spring 1992).

Davis, Charles T. "Jean Toomer and the South: Region and Race as Elements Within a Literary Imagination." *Studies in the Literary Imagination* 7:23–37 (Fall 1974).

Dorris, Ronald. "Early Criticism of Jean Toomer's Cane: 1923–1932." *Perspectives of Black Popular Culture*. Edited by Harry Shaw. Bowling Green, Ohio: Popular Press, 1990.

Durham, Frank. "The Poetry Society of South Carolina's Turbulent Year: Self-Interest, Atheism, and Jean Toomer." *Southern Humanities Review* 5:76–80 (Winter 1971).

———, ed. *Studies in "Cane."* Columbus, Ohio: Charles E. Merrill, 1971.

———. "Jean Toomer's Vision of the Southern Negro." *Southern Humanities Review* 6:13–22 (1972).

Farrison, Edward. "Jean Toomer's *Cane* Again." *CLA Journal* 15:295–302 (March 1972).

Faulkner, Howard. "The Buried Life: Jean Toomer's *Cane*." *Studies in Black Literature* 7, no. 1:1–5 (1976).

Flowers, Sandra Hollin. "Solving the Critical Conundrum of Jean Toomer's 'Box Seat.' " *Studies in Short Fiction* 25, no. 3:301–05 (Summer 1988).

Foley, Barbara. "Jean Toomer's Sparta." *Arizona Quarterly* 51, no. 1:103–26 (Summer 1995).

———. "Jean Toomer's Washington and the Politics of Class: From 'Blue Veins' to Seventh-Street Rebels." *Modern Fiction Studies* 42, no. 2:289–321 (Summer 1996).

———. " 'In the Land of Cotton': Economics and Violence in Jean Toomer's Cane." *African-American Review* 32, no. 2:181–98 (Summer 1998).

Fullinwider, S. P. "Jean Toomer: Lost Generation, or Negro Renaissance?" *Phylon* 27:396–403 (1966).

Gibson, Donald B. "Jean Toomer: The Politics of Denial." In his *The Politics of Literary Expression: A Study of Major Black Writers.* Westport, Conn.: Greenwood Press, 1981. Pp. 155–81.

Grant, Mary Kathryn. "Images of Celebration in *Cane.*" *Negro American Literature Forum* 5, no. 1:32–34, 36 (Spring 1971).

Griffiths, Frederick T. "Sorcery Is Dialectical: Plato and Jean Toomer in Charles Johnson's *The Sorcerer's Apprentice.*" *African American Review* 30, no. 4:527–38 (Winter 1996).

Hajek, Friederike. "The Change of Literary Authority in the Harlem Renaissance: Jean Toomer's *Cane.*" In *The Black Columbiad: Defining Moments in African American Literature and Culture.* Edited by Werner Sollors. Cambridge, Mass.: Harvard University Press, 1994.

Hamalian, Leo. "D. H. Lawrence and Black Writers." *Journal of Modern Literature* 16, no. 4:579–96.

Helbling, Mark. "Sherwood Anderson and Jean Toomer." *Negro American Literature Forum* 9, no. 2:35–39 (Summer 1975).

Innes, Catherine L. "The Unity of Jean Toomer's *Cane.*" *CLA Journal* 15:306–22 (March 1972).

Jackson, Blyden. "Jean Toomer's *Cane:* An Issue of Genre." In *The Twenties: Fiction, Poetry, Drama.* Edited by Warren French. Deland, Fla.: Everett/Edwards, 1975.

———. "Jean Toomer as Poet: A Phenomenology of the Spirit." *Black American Literature Forum* 21:253–73 (Fall 1987).

———, ed. *Jean Toomer: Selected Essays and Literary Criticism.* Knoxville: University of Tennessee Press, 1996.

Joyce, Joyce Ann. "Nora Is Calling Jesus: A Nineteenth Century European Dilemma in an Afro-American Garb." *CLA Journal* 21:251–44 (1977).

———. "Gwendolyn Brooks: Jean Toomer's November Cotton Flower." In *On Gwendolyn Brooks: Reliant Contemplation.* Edited by Stephen Caldwell Wright. Ann Arbor, Mich.: University of Michigan Press, 1996.

Kerman, Cynthia. "Jean Toomer? Enigma." *Indian Journal of American Studies* 7, no. 1:67–78 (1977).

Kerman, Cynthia Earl, and Richard Eldridge. *The Lives of Jean Toomer: A Hunger for Wholeness.* Baton Rouge: Louisiana State University Press, 1987.

Kraft, James. "Jean Toomer's *Cane.*" *Markham Review* 2:61–63 (October 1970).

Krasny, Michael J. "Design in Jean Toomer's *Balo.*" *Negro American Literature Forum* 7, no. 3:103–04 (Autumn 1973).

———. "The Aesthetic Structure of Jean Toomer's *Cane.*" *Negro American Literature Forum* 9, no. 2:42–43 (Summer 1975).

———. "Jean Toomer's Life Prior To *Cane:* A Brief Sketch of the Emergence of a Black Writer." *Negro American Literature Forum* 9, no. 2: 40–41 (Summer 1975).

Kulii, Elon. "Literature, Biology and Folk Legan Belief: Jean Toomer's *Kabnis.*" *The Language Quarterly* 25, no. 4:5–7, 49, 54 (Spring–Summer 1987).

Larson, Charles R. *Invisible Darkness: Jean Toomer and Nella Larsen.* Iowa City: University of Iowa Press, 1993.

Lieber, Todd. "Design and Movement in *Cane.*" *CLA Journal* 13:35–50 (September 1969).

Lindberg, Kathryne V. "Raising Cane on the Theoretical Plane: Jean Toomer's Racial Persona." *Cultural Difference and the Literary Text: Pluralism and the Limits of Authenticity in North American Literatures.* Edited by Winfried Siemerling and Katrin Schwenk. Iowa City: University of Iowa Press, 1996.

McKay, Nellie Y. *Jean Toomer, Artist: A Study of His Literary Life and Work.* Chapel Hill: University of North Carolina Press, 1984. (Contains an extensive bibliography.)

McKeever, Benjamin F. "*Cane* as Blues." *Negro American Literature Forum* 4, no. 2:61–63 (July 1970).

Martin, Odette C. "Cane: Method and Myth." *Obsidian* 2, no. 1:5–20 (1976).

Mason, Clifford. "Jean Toomer's Black Authenticity." *Black World* 20, no. 1:70–76 (January 1971).

Miller, Baxter R. "Blacks in His Cellar: The Personal Tragedy of Jean Toomer." *The Langston Hughes Review* 11, no. 1:36–40 (Spring 1992).

Mitchell, Carolyn A. "Henry Dumas and Jean Toomer: One Voice." *Black American Literature Forum* 22, no. 2:297–309 (Summer 1988).

Moore, Lewis. "*Kabnis* and the Reality of Hope: Jean Toomer's *Cane.*" *North Dakota Quarterly* 54, no. 2:30–39 (Spring 1986).

O'Daniel, Therman B., ed. *Jean Toomer: A Critical Evaluation.* Washington, D.C.: Howard University Press, 1988. (Contains an extensive bibliography.)

Quirk, Tom, and Robert E. Fleming. "Jean Toomer's Contributions to the New Mexico Sentinel." *CLA Journal* 19:524–32 (1976).

Rankin, William. "Ineffability in the Fiction of Jean Toomer and Katherine Mansfield." *Renaissance and Modern: Essays in Honor of Edwin M. Moseley.* Edited by Murray J. Levith. Saratoga Springs: Skidmore College Press, 1976.

Reilly, John M. "The Search for Black Redemption: Jean Toomer's *Cane.*" *Studies in the Novel* 2:312–24 (Fall 1970).

———. "Repeated Images in Part One of *Cane.*" *Black American Literature Forum* 17, no. 3:100–05 (Autumn 1983).

———. "Jean Toomer's Early Identification: The Two Black Plays." *MELUS* 13, no. 1–2:115–24 (Spring–Summer 1986).

Saunders, James Robert. "Sonia Sanchez's *Homegirls and Handgrenades:* Recalling Toomer's *Cane*." *MELUS* 15, no. 1:73–82 (Spring 1988).

Schultz, Elizabeth. "Jean Toomer's 'Box Seat': The Possibility for 'Constructive Crisises.' " *Black American Literature Forum* 13, no. 1:7–12 (Spring 1979).

Scruggs, Charles. "Jean Toomer: Fugitive." *American Literature* 47:84–96 (March–January 1959–1960).

———. "The Mark of Cain and the Redemption of Art: A Study in Theme and Structure of Jean Toomer's *Cane*." *American Literature* 44, 276–91 (March–January 1972–1973).

Solard, Alain. "Myth and Narrative Fiction in *Cane:* 'Blood-Burning Moon.' " *Callaloo* no. 25:551–62 (Autumn 1985).

Stein, Marion L. "The Poet-Observer and Fern in Jean Toomer's *Cane*." *Markham Review* 2:64–65 (October 1970).

Taylor, Clyde. "The Second Coming of Jean Toomer." *Obsidian* 1, no. 3:37–57 (1975).

Turner, Darwin T. "A Passing: First Memorial Tribute to Langston Hughes." *Negro American Literature Forum* 1, no. 1:3–4 (Autumn 1967).

———. "Jean Toomer: Exile." In *In a Minor Chord: Three Afro-American Writers and Their Search for Identity.* Carbondale: Southern Illinois University Press, 1971. Pp. 1–59.

———. "The Failure of a Playwright." *CLA Journal* 10, no. 4:308–18 (1967).

———. "Jean Toomer's *Cane*." *Negro Digest* 18:54–64 (January 1969).

Wagner-Martin, Linda. "Toomer's *Cane* as Narrative Sequence." *Modern American Short Story Sequences: Composite Fictions and Fictive Communities.* Cambridge: Cambridge University Press, 1995.

Whyde, Janet M. "Mediating Forms: Narrating the Body in Jean Toomer's *Cane*." *Southern Literary Journal* 26, no. 1:42–53 (Fall 1993).

ALICE WALKER
(1944–   )

MARY MARGARET RICHARDS

IN A 1973 interview, Alice Walker said:

> I am preoccupied with the spiritual survival, the survival *whole* of my people. But beyond that, I am committed to exploring the oppressions, the insanities, the loyalties, and the triumphs of black women.... For me, black women are the most fascinating creations in the world.
>
> Next to them, I place the old people—male and female—who persist in their beauty in spite of everything. How do they do this, knowing what they do? Having lived what they have lived? It is a mystery, and so it lures me into their lives.

This statement is a succinct explanation of what all Walker's work tries to do. In novels, stories, poems, and essays, she explores the issue of the spiritual survival of black people and, indeed, of people of color throughout the world. This search leads her to discuss issues that other writers have avoided and issues that anger many of her critics. Undeterred, Walker continues to find roads to wholeness and to describe those roads in her writing.

She is also committed to causes that go beyond the black community, seeing blacks as a part of a larger world that must be saved from destruction. In her *In Search of Our Mothers' Gardens: Womanist Prose* (1983) she described herself as a "womanist" rather than a "black feminist," defining "womanish" as "referring to outrageous, audacious, courageous or *willful* behavior" and a "womanist" as being "committed to survival and wholeness of entire people, male *and* female." She has spoken out on a variety of women's issues, and has become involved in the civil rights, animal rights, and antinuclear movements, all of which she sees as necessary for the survival of the planet and everyone on it.

Early Life

Walker was born on February 9, 1944, in Eatonton, Georgia, the eighth child of Willie Lee and Minnie Tallulah Grant Walker, who were sharecroppers. Of her childhood Walker remembers being different from the other children, spending more time alone, more time reading. When she was eight, one of her brothers shot her in the right eye with a BB gun; she has been blind in that eye ever since. Decades later, during her research on female genital mutilation, Walker came to see this wound as a "patriarchal wound," convinced that her brother intended to shoot at her, if not specifically at her eye, and drawing a parallel to other injuries, physical and psychological, inflicted on women because of their gender.

Education was a primary concern for the community in which Walker grew up, because parents were convinced that education would provide their children with better futures. Walker remembers the insistence on education in a poem titled "Women" (in *Revolutionary Petunias*), which speaks of the women of her mother's generation as "Headragged Generals," marveling that they "knew what we / *Must* know" and managed to provide education for their children even though they themselves were uneducated. Education was the way out of poverty. When Walker was four, her mother had to go to work, so Walker started first grade then. She began writing poems in a notebook when she was eight, frequently writing in the fields because of the lack of privacy in her family's small, crowded house.

The insistence on education; the community working toward education; the seventy-five dollars the community raised to help Walker get to Atlanta to attend Spelman College—all of these elements shaped her as a writer, and are one reason for her love of the people of her parents' and grandparents' generations. They gave her another gift, however, that was both to validate her own calling as a writer and to furnish her with material for her art: the consciousness—through the stories they told, the gardens they grew, and the quilts they pieced—of the artistic abilities of black women. In the title essay of her collection *In Search of Our Mothers' Gardens*, Walker asks, "How was the creativity of the black woman kept alive, year after year and century after century, when for most of the years black people have been in America, it was a punishable crime for a black person to read or write? And the freedom to paint, to sculpt, to expand the mind with action did not exist." She turns to her mother for the answer:

And so our mothers and grandmothers have, more often than not anonymously, handed on the creative spark, the seed of the flower they themselves never hoped to see. . . . no song or poem will bear my mother's name. Yet so many of the stories that I write, that we all write, are my mother's stories.

In addition to the money raised by the community, Walker received a scholarship for the handicapped that allowed her to attend Spelman College in Atlanta. Walker found Spelman's emphasis on producing "ladies" to be an extreme contrast to the changes occurring because of the Civil Rights movement, in which she was involved. After two years (1961–1963) she transferred to Sarah Lawrence College in Bronxville, New York, an elite, mostly white school, because of her need for a more open, intellectual atmosphere. In her essay "The Unglamorous but Worthwhile Duties of the Black Revolutionary Artist" Walker said of her move to Sarah Lawrence, "I was fleeing from Spelman College in Atlanta, a school that I considered opposed to change, to freedom, and to understanding that by the time most girls enter college they are already women and should be treated as women." It was only after her graduation and move to Mississippi that Walker would see the hole in her education at Sarah Lawrence: no blacks were included in the curriculum, even in courses on the South.

As a result of the Eurocentric curriculum she was taught in college, Walker was influenced in those years primarily by the great works of the European tradition. For example, during her sophomore year she immersed herself in Russian novels, including those of Leo Tolstoy, Fyodor Dostoevsky, Ivan Turgenev, Maxim Gorky, and Nikolai Gogol. Only years later was she bothered by the almost total lack of female Russian writers. The poets she read in college included Emily Dickinson, E. E. Cummings, William Carlos Williams, Robert Graves, Catullus, even Li Po, the great Chinese poet—but no blacks.

The Publication of *Once*

During the summer of her senior year Walker became pregnant while visiting Africa. Returning to school in despair, she felt that unless she could locate an abortionist, she must commit suicide. An abortion was arranged, and, feeling that her life had been given back to her, Walker wrote compulsively, completing almost all of the poems in *Once*, her first volume of poetry, and slipping them under the door of Muriel Rukeyser, one of her teachers, as she wrote them. They were published three years later, in 1968.

The poems in *Once* deal with her experiences in Africa, suicide, the Civil Rights movement, and love. They reveal one result of the loss of her eye: an intense awareness of vision, of the importance both of seeing the beauty in the world and of seeing things accurately. The sharply contrasting images in the Africa poems in *Once* make this double emphasis on beauty and accuracy particularly clear. The poems celebrate the beauty of Africa, yet they refuse to idealize it. For instance, "African Images, Glimpses from a Tiger's Back" celebrates both the beauty and the danger, pairing "Red orchids-glorious!" with the deadly "spinning cobra." Other poems contrast idealizations of Africa with the reality of sickness, ignorance, and ugliness that lies beneath the superficial beauty, as in "Karamojans," which describes "The Noble Savage" —a positive, if obvious, image—with "His pierced ears / Infected." Walker uses short lines and intense images in these poems. In an interview with John O'Brien, she acknowledged the influence of Zen epigrams and Japanese haiku:

> I was delighted to learn that in three or four lines a poet can express mystery, evoke beauty and pleasure, paint a picture—and not dissect or analyze in any way. The insects, the fish, the birds, and the apple blossoms in haiku are still whole. They have not been turned into something else. They are allowed their own majesty, instead of being used to emphasize the majesty of people; usually the majesty of the poets writing.

Becoming a Civil Rights Activist and Teacher

After graduating from Sarah Lawrence in 1965, Walker received a Charles Merrill Writing Fellowship and made plans to move to Senegal. She moved to Mississippi instead, because, as she noted in her essay "Choosing to Stay at Home," "that summer marked the beginning of

Alice Walker

a realization that I could never live happily in Africa—or anywhere else—until I could live freely in Mississippi." In Mississippi she worked with voter registration drives and Head Start programs, and she taught at both Jackson State College and Tougaloo College (1968–1969).

In 1969 one of Walker's assignments as black history consultant for Friends of the Children of Mississippi, a Head Start program, was to teach black history to teachers in the Head Start programs across the state. The women she was teaching, however eager and industrious, had, on average, fifth-grade educations and poor reading skills. She asked the women to write their autobiographies, developing from their experiences a sense of the relationship between their private lives and the wider movements of history, such as World War II or the Great Depression. Walker found that although these women knew little of what the white world refers to as history, they had stories to tell of their lives, of "the faith and grace of a people under continuous pressures," as she noted in her essay " 'But Yet and Still the Cotton Gin Kept on Working. . . .' "

In Mississippi Walker met Melvyn Leventhal, a white civil rights lawyer, whom she married on March 17, 1967. They married, she said in an interview with Gloria Steinem, because "given the history, we couldn't go off into the world and do political work unless we were married. We could challenge the laws against intermarriage at the same time—in addition to which, we really loved each other." The interracial marriage meant that living in Mississippi involved frequent fear of physical attack, or even death. The marriage also caused criticism among blacks. Critics of her writing tended to focus on her marriage as a betrayal of the black community, discussing the marriage rather than her work. Walker responded to this attack by pointing out the interracial marriages among her critics, saying that she had done no differently than they had.

The Third Life of Grange Copeland

Partly in an attempt to keep her husband from being drafted, partly out of curiosity, Walker had a child, Rebecca, who was born in 1969, three days after Walker completed her first novel, *The Third Life of Grange Copeland*. In her essay "*One* Child of One's Own," Walker discussed her misgivings about becoming a mother. "Women's Folly," she writes, told her that she should have multiple children; that she would forget the pain; that her daughter would need a sibling. She was worried that her writing would be adversely affected. Instead, she found that having a child "joined me to a body of experience and a depth of commitment to my own life hard to comprehend otherwise." The ability to see the world as a mother deepened her understanding, and the duties of motherhood did not stop her writing.

In an afterword to *The Third Life of Grange Copeland* (1970), Walker described her purpose in the book:

The black people there [in Eatonton], as in so many parts of the world, are an oppressed colony, and as one of our great African-American writers has said (and I paraphrase), in their frustration and rage they *of course* kill each other. But what, I wondered, would happen if you could show the people in the oppressed colony the futility of this? . . . I believe whole-heartedly in the necessity of keeping inviolate the one interior space that is given to all. I believe in the soul. Furthermore, I believe it is prompt accountability for one's choices, a willing acceptance of responsibility for one's thoughts, behavior and actions, that makes it powerful. The white man's oppression of me will never excuse my oppression of you, whether you are man, woman, child, animal or tree, because the self that I prize refuses to be owned by him. Or by anyone.

The novel tells of three generations of the Copelands—Grange, Brownfield, and Ruth—from 1920 to the arrival of the Civil Rights movement in a small Georgia town. The oldest generation, represented by Grange, finds itself trapped in a sharecropper system in which the bills of the sharecropper are always higher than the pay for his crops—a form of slavery. Feeling frustrated, reduced by the whites to "a mask . . . tight and still," jealous of his wife, impotent to change his conditions, Grange ignores Brownfield, his son, and regularly visits Josie, the prostitute who helps him feel like a man. As his frustration increases, Grange's ability to use language decreases; he only shrugs: "After each shrug he was more silent than before, as if each of these shrugs cut him off from one more topic of conversation."

After Grange goes to the North, his wife, Margaret, poisons herself and her baby, leaving Brownfield to fend for himself. In the North, Grange steals and robs to keep himself alive, eventually developing a doctrine of hate for the white man that he preaches on street corners. He comes home to buy a secluded farm where he can live separate from whites, then realizes that hatred is not productive. Redeemed by his relationship with his granddaughter, Ruth, Grange abandons his hate and seeks to stop the cycle of evil. As a result of his relationship with Ruth, Grange continues to grow and change, as shown by his comment on Martin Luther King, whom he sees on the television news: "The thing about him that stands in my mind is that even with them crackers spitting all over him, he gentle with his wife and childrens."

The second generation is represented primarily by Brownfield, Grange's son. After his mother's suicide, Brownfield wanders into the juke joint run by Josie, unaware that she had been his father's lover. Brownfield marries Josie's niece, Mem, and returns to sharecropping, ignoring his previous conviction that if he once started, he would never escape. In the inevitable frustration and degradation of sharecropping, Brownfield grows to hate his wife for the qualities that had originally attracted him to her— her intelligence, her education, her beauty— and frequently beats her, eventually killing her with a shotgun blast to the face. When he gets out of jail, he tries to regain custody of his daughter, Ruth, from Grange, not because he loves her but to prove his own power.

An occasional glimpse of the person Brownfield could be emphasizes what has been lost. For example, in prison he finds himself reading a newspaper article about his trial, amazed that he can do it. Then he realizes that he had learned to read and write from Mem, a skill forgotten just as he had forgotten the good times they had shared. Such a revelation could be a turning point, but it isn't. He chooses evil, which cannot be explained away or forgiven, especially since Grange had managed to overcome more difficult circumstances.

In a confrontation with Brownfield, Grange explains to Ruth that he accepts his own responsibility for Brownfield's errors and crimes. He goes on, though, to say that Brownfield had "his own opportunity to righten the wrong I done him by being good to his own children, he had a chance to become a real man, a daddy in his own right. . . . But he messed up with his children, his wife and his home, and never yet blamed hisself. And never blaming hisself done made him *weak*. He no longer have to think beyond me and the white folks to get to the root of *all* his problems."

Grange tries to make Brownfield see that both of them are guilty for what they did to their families: "We *guilty*, Brownfield, and neither one of us is going to move a step in the right direction until we admit it." Brownfield responds, "I don't have to admit a damn thing to you . . . and I ain't about to let the crackers off the hook for what they done to my life!" Grange then makes the most direct statement of Walker's theme: "Most of what I'm saying is *you got to hold tight a place in you where they can't come.* You can't take this young girl here and make her wish she was dead just to git back at some white folks that you don't even *know*. We keep killing ourselves for people that don't even mean nothing *to* us!"

The third generation is represented in Ruth, the promise for the future. Circumstances have eased somewhat in the South by the time she is born, and as a teenager she is aware of the Civil Rights movement. In spite of her father's attempt to ruin her life, Ruth manages, with Grange's help, to escape slavery to whites or to her father. Grange's determination that Ruth "survive whole" with her future free from the emotional slavery to which Brownfield wishes to subject her, leads him to murder Brownfield rather than give him custody of Ruth, knowing that he will be killed in turn. To break the cycle of misery, Grange takes ultimate responsibility for his mistakes, paying with his own life.

The novel is told in chronological order, except for what we learn of Grange's time in the North through Grange's later thoughts. This structure has been criticized as being unbalanced, not providing enough discussion of Grange's life in the North. However, Walker is making the point that his life in the North was not really a life at all, but a time when he was depersonalized to the greatest extent. The title is not *The Three Lives*, but *The Third Life*, placing emphasis on Grange's change.

In Love and Trouble, and the Influence of Zora Neale Hurston

In 1970, while working on "The Revenge of Hannah Kemhuff," Walker found in Zora Neale Hurston's anthropological studies the details about southern rootworking and voodoo that she needed for her story. Until this time she had been unaware of Hurston's corpus, which was to become one of the most important influences on her own writing. She went on to read all of Hurston's work; to mark her neglected grave in Fort Pierce, Florida; and to edit *I Love Myself when I Am Laughing,* an anthology of Hurston's writings. In her essay "Zora Neale Hurston" Walker said of Hurston's *Their Eyes Were Watching God* (1937), *"There is no book more important to me than this one."* Walker has described what she thinks characteristic of Hurston's work: "racial health; a sense of black people as complete, complex, *undiminished* human beings. . . ." The sense that a literary ancestor had tried to accomplish what she herself sees as her primary goal—the survival of her people whole—meant that Hurston's life and work validated Walker's. In addition, critics are now comparing Walker's use of black folk language, rootworking, and elements of narration and characterization with that of Hurston.

"The Revenge of Hannah Kemhuff" was included in Walker's first collection of short stories, *In Love and Trouble* (1973), which won the Rosenthal Award of the National Institute of Arts and Letters in 1974. The story, based on an event in Walker's mother's life, uses Hurston's knowledge of authentic voodoo. The narrator, apprentice to the local rootworker, achieves the revenge Hannah wants by skillfully playing on a white woman's fear of voodoo. Hannah, like Walker's mother, has been denied food during the Great Depression because her cast-off clothes, sent by northern relatives, are of better quality than those of the white woman giving out the food. Walker's mother told the story again and again—how she managed to get food from family and friends, and how, years later, she felt satisfaction that the white woman, hunched and shrunken, could walk only with the aid of two canes. Hannah doesn't fare as well as Walker's mother: her husband abandons her; her children die. Shortly before her own death years later, Hannah asks Tante Rosie, the local rootworker, to help her get revenge. The narrator, Tante Rosie's apprentice, goes to the white woman's house and asks for some

hair, nail parings, urine, and feces, explaining that a black woman is seeking revenge and that, if the white woman doesn't believe in voodoo, she won't mind. Terrified, the white woman eats her fingernails and hoards her bodily excretions, driving away her friends and family, who can't stand the smell. She eventually dies in "constant anxiety lest a stray strand of hair be lost . . . the foul odor of the house soon brought to the hands a constant seeking motion, to the eyes a glazed and vacant stare, and to the mouth a tightly puckered frown." Thus Hannah, already dead, has her revenge.

Another tale in the volume, "Everyday Use," has become one of Walker's most widely read stories. "Everyday Use" tells of the return home of a daughter, Dee, who sees her mother and slow-witted sister, Maggie, as quaint, out of step with the present. Dee has changed her name to "Wangero," saying that she is giving up her slave name, despite the fact that she has been named for her aunt and grandmother. Oblivious to the needs of her mother and sister, Dee lays claim to various homemade items faddishly valued as decorations, including quilts made by her grandmother and great-grandmother. Unlike Maggie, she cannot quilt; she has no need for the quilts save to hang them on the wall. She is appalled at the idea that such valuable artifacts could be subjected to everyday use. Yet her mother, seeing Maggie's love for the women who had made those quilts and taught her how to make more, takes the quilts away from Dee, insisting on Maggie's right to them.

The 1970s

Walker received a Radcliffe Institute Fellowship that enabled her to teach at Wellesley and the University of Massachusetts at Boston during the period 1971–1973. At both schools Walker taught a course in black women writers, a course that may well have been the first of its kind. By this time, she had discovered a variety of black writers. Among those she taught were Zora Neale Hurston, Nella Larsen, Frances Watkins Harper, Dorothy West, Ann Petry, and Paule Marshall.

In 1973 Walker published her second volume of poetry, *Revolutionary Petunias and Other Poems*, which won the Lillian Smith Award of the Southern Regional Council. The title poem of this volume concerns Sammy Lou, an "incorrect" woman who has killed her husband's white murderer and, on her way to the electric chair, reminds her children to water her petunias. Of Sammy Lou Walker told O'Brien:

> Sammy Lou, of course, is so "incorrect" she does not even know how ridiculous she is for loving to see flowers blooming around her unbearably ugly gray house. To be "correct" she should consider it her duty to let ugliness reign. Which is what "incorrect" people like Sammy Lou refuse to do.

In other poems in the volume Walker pursues the idea of "incorrectness," of doing whatever is important for the individual rather than what is expected by an anonymous revolution. For example, "While Love Is Unfashionable," dedicated to her husband, celebrates the beauty and importance of love in spite of danger and the fear of death.

In 1974, a particularly difficult year, Walker left the South. Her father, with whom she had an awkward relationship, died, and she was unhappy in Mississippi. Before leaving the South for New York, Walker completed her second novel, *Meridian* (1976), which includes some obvious similarities between Walker's life and that of her title character: growing up in small-town Georgia; going to a women's college in Atlanta; becoming active in the Civil Rights movement. However, as noted by Claudia Tate, Walker has said that the novel is "autobiographical only in the sense of projection"—that is, "what happens often when I write is that I try to make models for myself. I project other ways of seeing."

The "models" Walker creates in *Meridian* are people in the Civil Rights movement, people whom she saw as flawed yet willing to suffer for the cause. The flawed revolutionaries include Anne-Marion, who rejects and vilifies Meridian and becomes a landowning nature poet with a child; Truman Held, who paints huge, big-breasted black women but sleeps with and marries petite white women; Lynne Rabinowitz, who marries Truman and sleeps with other black men out of guilt and despair over her own whiteness. At the center of this group of revolutionaries is Meridian, who is herself flawed and yet seeks for the highest she can reach.

Seemingly locked into a rerun of her mother's life, sacrificed to the exigencies of childbearing, Meridian gives her child away so that she can attend Saxon College, where she continues her involvement with the Civil Rights movement. Struggling against guilt as well as inequality, she develops an illness that causes, among other symptoms, hair loss and catatonia. Badgered by the members of the revolutionary group who demand that she swear to kill for the revolution, Meridian thinks of the black church—a community that would be hurt by killing. Her questions and doubts send her back to the South, where she continues her civil rights work in small communities.

She starts going back to church and finds a community that has suffered the murder of one of its own. A red-eyed man stands before the congregation to reveal the truth of his life: his son has been killed. Meridian discovers that her earlier questioning of her ability to kill resulted from her need to identify not with an abstraction of revolution but with the concrete reality of individuals within a community:

> For she understood, finally, that the respect she owed her life was to continue, against whatever obstacles, to live it, and not to give up any particle of it without a fight to the death, preferably *not* her own. And that this existence extended beyond herself to those around her because, in fact, the years in America had created them One Life. . . . she made a promise to the red-eyed man herself: that yes, indeed she *would* kill, before she allowed anyone to murder his son again.

The issue of destruction as a result of frustration, so important in *The Third Life of Grange Copeland*, is present here as well. As

Brownfield had destroyed his own and others' lives out of a sense of his own powerlessness, so characters in this novel destroy their sources of strength, comfort, and connection with their histories. Meridian's mother, frustrated by her role as mother, has never learned "to be in any other way creative in her home. She could have done so, if she had wanted to. Creativity was in her, but it was refused expression. It was all deliberate. A war against those to whom she could not express her anger or shout, "It's not fair!" In a similar way, when Saxon College students express their frustration at not being allowed to hold the Wild Child's funeral in the college chapel, their actions result in destruction of the Sojourner, the great magnolia tree that had symbolized the voice and nurturing of black people.

Walker has described the structure of the novel as being like a crazy quilt: "You know, there's a lot of difference between a crazy quilt and a patchwork quilt. . . . A crazy quilt . . . only *looks* crazy. It is not "patched"; it is planned. . . . A crazy-quilt story is one that can jump back and forth in time, work on many different levels and one that can include myth." As a character thinks of an earlier event, that event is recounted, with an interesting development of ironic twists because of the juxtaposition. For example, in the chapter telling of Meridian's becoming pregnant by Truman, Truman asks Meridian about her employer, a retired black professor from Saxon. Meridian does not tell Truman of the professor's fondling her, but she thinks about his insistent rubbing against her body in return for tins of tuna and other small gifts that help her eke out her scholarship:

> Every day when she rose to go—having typed letters for him in a veritable swamp fog of bad breath—he clasped her in his arms, dragging her away from the door, the long bones of his thighs forcing her legs apart, attempting to force her to the floor. But she smiled and struggled and struggled and smiled, and pretended she knew nothing of his intentions—a thought which no doubt aroused him all the more.

Immediately after this recollection, Truman complains of his work at the white country club, saying, "God, I hate those bastards. You just don't know how hard a time I have making a little bread." It would never occur to him—and Meridian does not tell him—that black women encounter incredibly demeaning situations, involving not just their pride but their bodies as well, from black men.

This movement back and forth in time results in the impression that throughout the novel one is hearing stories told, that meaning can be made of the present only in the context of the past. The crazy-quilt movement in time can cause confusion; a number of critics have misplaced events in the novel, moving them from state to state. While some of the action of the novel does take place in Mississippi, Alabama, and New York City, most occurs in Georgia: Meridian grows up in a small Georgia town; she goes to college in Atlanta; Truman finds her for the last time in a small town near the Georgia coast.

Walker lived in the borough of Brooklyn in New York from 1974 to 1978. She and Leventhal divorced in 1977, and she subsequently moved to California. A Guggenheim Fellowship (1977–1978) allowed her time to think and write. While beginning work on her next novel, which would be *The Color Purple*, Walker published her second collection of stories and third collection of poetry.

The 1980s and *The Color Purple*

The stories in *You Can't Keep a Good Woman Down* (1981) show some of Walker's experiments with narrative form. For example, in "Coming Apart," written originally as an introduction to a section of *Take Back the Night (1980)*, an anthology of writings about pornography, she intersperses polemical passages on pornography with the fictional material of her story. Another example of her experiments is "Advancing Luna—and Ida B. Wells," a story about interracial rape. Unable to resolve the ending, Walker offers "Afterwords, Afterwards

Whoopi Goldberg and Margaret Avery in Steven Spielberg's 1985
adaptation of *The Color Purple*.

Second Thoughts," "Discarded Notes," "Imaginary Knowledge," and "Postscript," all of which help the reader see the various threads of story and meaning with which the author struggled.

Probably the best story in the collection is "A Sudden Trip Home in the Spring," which concerns a black woman attending a northern college who comes home to Georgia for her father's funeral. She has been unable to paint black men because of the defeat she sees in their faces: "the defeat of black forever defined by white." Looking at her grandfather, though, she sees no defeat, and goes back to school with the determination to learn the skills that will allow her to sculpt her grandfather's face in stone.

The title of Walker's third volume of poetry, *Good Night, Willie Lee, I'll See You in the Morning* (1979), is her mother's farewell to her father at his funeral. Among other topics, the poems in the volume deal with love and the history of slavery. "Early Losses: A Requiem," gripping in its immediacy and simplicity, is the story of a young girl sold into slavery. Her husband had been chosen even before her birth, but she grew up loving a boy her own age. Both are sold into slavery, and she never sees him again. When, later, her own child is torn from her, she calls out the name of her beloved, a word the child does not understand.

Walker's move to California was essential to the writing of *The Color Purple* (1982). She had been working on the novel before the move, but found that the characters would not speak to her in New York City. In "Writing *The Color Purple*" (in *In Search of Our Mothers' Gardens*), Walker explains that New York "was a place the people in *The Color Purple* refused even to visit." She flew to San Francisco, "where all the people in the novel promptly fell silent—I think, in awe" and found a place in the country that the characters liked: "it looked a lot like the town in Georgia most of them were from, only it was more beautiful and the local swimming hole was not segregated. It also bore a slight resemblance to the African village in which one of them, Nettie, was a missionary." The characters visited more frequently as time passed and as Walker enjoyed the country, working on a quilt in a "pattern my mama swore was easy." Walker signed the book "A.W., author and medium" to indicate her sense of transmitting as well as creating the story.

The Color Purple, which won both the Pulitzer Prize and the National Book Award, is the story of Celie, a barely educated black woman, who is raped by her stepfather and then married off to Mr. ———, who needs a good worker to look after his children. Told by her stepfather that she had better tell no one but God about the rape, Celie starts writing letters to God. After her children by her stepfather have been taken away and her sister Nettie has been forced to leave, Celie is wholly alone. However, she slowly develops an extended family that includes Shug—her husband's mistress and only true love—and Sofia, who marries Celie's stepson. The love that Celie and Shug come to share not only awakens Celie's sexuality but also allows her the freedom to say what she thinks and to develop as an independent woman with a sense of self and a creative talent that she eventually expands into a business—making the most comfortable pants available. Eventually, with Shug's help, Celie discovers the letters that Nettie has been writing her for years and that Mr. ——— has been hiding. Reading the letters, Celie finds out the truth about her family, and is so disgusted that God would allow such wrongs that she stops writing to him and starts writing to Nettie. She explains to Shug, "he give me a lynched daddy, a crazy mama, a lowdown dog of a step pa and a sister I probably won't ever see again. Anyhow, I say, the God I been praying and writing to is a man. And act just like all the other mens I know. Trifling, forgitful and lowdown."

Shug shares her conception of God as neither male nor female but present in all creation, and Celie is able by the end of the novel to address a letter of thanksgiving to "Dear God. Dear stars, dear trees, dear sky, dear peoples. Dear Everything. Dear God." She has moved beyond the concept of God as an old white man, to a concept closer to the animism of many indigenous peoples, especially Native Americans and Africans. Celie's celebration of God as "Dear Everything" occurs at the end of the novel, when the characters have grown into rather nice people, free to do whatever their skills and

inclinations allow, and Nettie and the children have come home. Thus, a novel that begins with an isolated, scared black girl of fourteen ends with that same "girl" thirty years later at the center of a loving family and a thriving business, complete with the sister she has missed for all those thirty years.

Critics have pointed out Walker's use of the epistolary form in the tradition of Samuel Richardson and other English eighteenth-century novelists—novelists Walker says she has not read. As these white male writers told women's stories through those women's private, personal letters, so Walker tells the story of a barely educated black woman through hers. Not only does the epistolary form tie the novel to those written by men about women; in addition, as Barbara Christian has pointed out, it recognizes that letters, along with diaries, are one of the few written forms allowed women in Western culture and are an important source of information about women's lives.

One interesting similarity between earlier epistolary novels and *The Color Purple* is Celie's use of blanks—that is, the way she uses Mr. ———, for her husband's name—in spite of the fact that she obviously knows his name. In earlier epistolary novels the blanks would hide the specifics of a supposedly real situation. In Walker's case, however, while the blanks are an ironic reference to the epistolary tradition, they are used primarily to show the distance between Celie and her husband—he is such a stranger to her that she cannot even use his name.

Nettie's letters are a way for Walker to expand the world of the novel beyond what Celie knows. Nettie tells Celie what she discovers about the family as well as about the world. Her letters become more learned as her education improves and as her association with the educated missionaries changes her from a backward Georgia girl to a knowledgeable woman with vastly more experience than Celie. She is, in part, seeking to educate Celie by telling her of all she has seen and learned. Celie, on the other hand, rejects the standard English which Nettie learns to use as not feeling right in her brain. This is Walker's comment on the distance caused by losing one's original dialect in favor of a less colorful, but more widely accepted, standardized way of speaking.

While Walker's first two novels end in the promise of good, *The Color Purple* ends in happiness, reunion, and celebration. Walker has said that she took her great-grandmother's life, which included rape and childbearing at age eleven, and gave it a happy ending. Once again she had begun with one of her ancestors' stories, completing and transmuting it through her art.

As Walker's interracial marriage had caused controversy in the early 1970s, so *The Color Purple* subjected her to extensive, heated criticism in the 1980s. While some critics saw only the abuse by Celie's stepfather and husband early in the novel, others objected to the changes in the men, saying that for Walker's men to be good, they must be feminized. Walker's main point in the novel is her concern in all her works: the survival whole of people, whatever their abilities. Thus Harpo, who prefers cooking to patching a roof, comes to terms with Sofia, who would rather do the roof patching. Mr. ———, who gave up sewing as a child when others laughed at him, learns not only to sew but also to design shirts for men to accompany Celie's pants.

In 1985 the film version of *The Color Purple*, directed by Steven Spielberg, was released to great praise and blame. Walker was excoriated for allowing a white man to direct, and the attacks on her portrayals of black men continued. Walker argued that a film directed by Spielberg would receive wide distribution, even being shown in small towns like Eatonton. She hoped that the film would reach people who could not or would not read the book but could benefit from its message. Spielberg asked Walker herself to write the screenplay for the movie, but after completing a draft, her ill health forced her to relinquish the writing to Menno Meyjes. She remained involved throughout the process of making the movie, though.

More than a decade after *The Color Purple* was made into a movie, Walker published *The Same River Twice: Honoring the Difficult* (1996), a collection of essays, journal entries,

her screenplay for the movie, magazine articles written by others, and correspondence. In this volume Walker tells the story of the making of the movie and, in her own voice and the voices of others, responds to the criticism directed at the book and the movie. She makes it clear that, while the movie did not completely reflect her vision of the book, she was pleased with the result.

In the midst of the attacks on her work, Walker was dealing with upheavals in her personal life. Her mother's health was declining, due to a series of strokes; her partner of many years, Robert Allen, admitted to having an affair; and Walker was suffering from an undiagnosed case of Lyme disease, which would leave her exhausted, weak and weary, for more than three years. Walker and Allen eventually resolved their relationship into one of longstanding friendship and Walker recovered her health, but the sense of vulnerability to hurts had long-term effects: Walker writes in *Same River* that it was "as if my illness had pushed open an inner door that my usual conscience was willing to ignore. I found myself in easy contact with the ancestors"—contact that she would write about in her subsequent essays and novels.

In 1983 Walker published *In Search of Our Mothers' Gardens: Womanist Prose*, a collection of essays and lectures from 1967 to 1983. We have already mentioned the title essay, which may well be Walker's most important. Another important essay in the collection is "Beyond the Peacock: The Reconstruction of Flannery O'Connor," which won the Newswomen's Club of New York's Front Page Award for best magazine criticism in 1976. The article recounts her visit with her mother to the house in which the Walkers had lived in 1952, a sharecropper's cabin on the same road as O'Connor's house, Andalusia. Walker says that she was attracted first by the fact that O'Connor's southerners "are like Southerners that I know." However, more important is that "*essential* O'Connor is not about race at all, which is why it is so refreshing, coming, as it does, out of such a *racial* culture." Part of her conclusion about what she has learned from O'Connor is this: "She destroyed the last vestiges of sentimentality in white Southern writing; she caused white women to look ridiculous on pedestals, and she approached her black characters—as a mature artist—with unusual humility and restraint."

In 1984 Walker both founded a press and published her fourth volume of poetry. Wild Trees Press was designed to publish work by other writers. After publishing six books, it was, according to Walker, "deemed a complete success" and closed in 1988. The volume of poetry, *Horses Make a Landscape Look More Beautiful* (1984), is made up of poems written between 1979 and 1984. The subjects of the poems range from the very personal—her daughter's return, daily exercise—to the political—the assassination of Martin Luther King's mother, Golda Meir's trip to Africa. The political content of these poems reflects Walker's continuing concern with the preservation of people, animals—indeed, of the whole planet.

Her second volume of essays, *Living by the Word* (1988), further reveals her involvement with global issues. One of the essays recounts her participation in antinuclear protests at the Concord Naval Weapons Station at Port Chicago, California, where she was arrested. Another, "Why Did the Balinese Chicken Cross the Road?," discusses her rationale for becoming a vegetarian, which has primarily to do with her conviction that in eating meat we eat the misery we have caused other living creatures.

The Temple of My Familiar

Walker's fourth novel, *The Temple of My Familiar* (1989), continues the expansion of scope in her novels to include all people. In this "romance," as Walker calls it, we find American, Caribbean, South American, and African people, many of whom have ancestors who were white, black, Native American, or Asian. Also, Walker deals here not only with working-class people but also with college professors, the middle class, and artists.

Primarily, the novel tells the story of two marriages. Fanny, the granddaughter of Celie

from *The Color Purple*, divorces her husband, Suwelo, in order, paradoxically, to have a closer relationship with him. He turns to Carlotta, whose musician husband, Arveyda, has become her mother's lover. The process by which these couples save their relationships involves not only an increase in understanding of themselves but also a new understanding of their forebears. Each learns about his or her parents, and Miss Lissie, an elderly black woman whom Suwelo meets because of her long friendship with his uncle Rafe, provides for Suwelo an understanding of the development of the entire species.

Miss Lissie can remember her past lives, during which she has been both black and white, male and female. Through Miss Lissie, Walker develops a creation myth centered on black women in Africa. As Miss Lissie tells Suwelo the stories of her most important lives, he gains understanding of the always difficult relationships between men and women, difficulties dating back 500,000 years, at least.

The novel moves back and forth between narrative lines, with those lines gradually coming together. Miss Lissie's storytelling takes up the most room in the novel, occurring in sections as Suwelo listens to her in person, reads her letters, and hears a tape she makes for him before her death. The other characters also tell stories; in fact, very little actually happens in the present of the novel. For example, Fanny writes to Suwelo from Africa; Arveyda hears the story of Zedé's life, then sings it to Carlotta, who has never heard it from her mother; Fanny's sister talks about her childhood in Africa; Mary Jane Briden reads Eleandra Burnham Peacock's diary. Walker also continues the stories of both Celie's Georgia and Nettie's Africa, telling of Celie and Shug's later years and of the movement from colonialism to black rule in Africa. She tells the story of M'sukta, an African woman who lived in a London museum for fifteen years, always on display, and of Mary Jane Briden, a rich white woman who forsook her immediate family and name only to find the diary of a great-great aunt with a legacy of action on behalf of Africans, including the rescue of M'sukta from her museum prison.

Creativity and art, which appear in so much of Walker's work, are present here as vital, important areas of life, not as forbidden dreams. The artist is sometimes ambivalent about the use to which a product is put, as Zedé is about her feathered garments and Ola is about his plays, but the artist's existence is assumed and the work is paid for. Arveyda is a successful musician. Ola's daughters also write plays, Zedé learns to make feathered capes from her mother, and Carlotta inherits her skill with chimes from her grandmother. Miss Lissie, Mr. Hal, and Mary Jane Briden are all visual artists; indeed, all these characters have extraordinary artistic abilities. Critics have said that the solutions Walker's characters—so extraordinary themselves—find for their problems are remote from those solutions available to most people. However, *The Temple of My Familiar* clearly states Walker's belief in the necessity of seeing the world, and all its people, as a whole.

The 1990s

In 1991 Walker published her collected poems under the title *Her Blue Body Everything We Know*. This collection includes all the poems from her four published volumes and a number of previously uncollected poems. Walker has written a very brief introduction for each of the earlier volumes, locating the poems within her own life experience. As Thadious Davis has pointed out, the poems can be read profitably next to the fiction Walker was writing at the same point in time; the themes are similar, with the poems providing a context for the fiction.

After a decade of declining health, Walker's mother died in 1993, a year after the publication of *Possessing the Secret of Joy*. At this time Walker was deeply involved in publicizing the horrors of female genital mutilation (also known as female circumcision or excision). Walker had known of the practice of female genital mutilation since her first trip to Africa in 1965. It was not until the filming of *The Color Purple*, though, that a photograph showing the blank look of a young girl who had undergone the pro-

cedure led her to two projects: her novel *Possessing the Secret of Joy* (1992) and her documentary film and accompanying book *Warrior Marks* (1993), produced in collaboration with Pratibha Parmar.

The main character in *Possessing the Secret of Joy* is Tashi, the African woman who, as a peripheral character in both *The Color Purple* and *The Temple of My Familiar*, marries Celie's son Adam. As her tribe is being destroyed, losing its identity, Tashi decides to undergo both facial scarification and female genital mutilation as a way of inscribing on her body her tribal identity. She is not aware, because of taboo, of what the mutilation actually entails and is permanently psychically scarred by the ordeal. The novel, using multiple narrators and moving back and forth in time, deals with her psychological difficulties—which include years of analysis and occasional commitments to mental hospitals—as well as her husband's bafflement and family's attempts to help. Eventually Tashi murders the old woman who had mutilated her, stands trial, and is executed. Tashi's psychological problems are partly displayed in her two names: Tashi, her African name, and Evelyn, her American name. Some of the sections she narrates are headed with one name, some with the other; as she moves toward spiritual reintegration and closer to death, her sections are increasingly labeled "Tashi-Evelyn," indicating that the two parts of her personality are coming together.

Walker makes it clear that she is not writing about a practice limited to Africa, but that female genital mutilation is only one of many forms of control exerted over women's sexuality. One example of the way she expands the parameters of her argument lies in Tashi's feelings for her adopted country, America. In her cell in Africa she dreams of America:

In all my dreams there is clear rushing river water and flouncy green trees, and where there are streets they are wide and paved and in the night of my dreams there are lighted windows way above the street; and behind those windows I know people are warm and squeaky clean and eating meat. Safe.

However, Tashi has heard the story of Amy, an elderly white woman from New Orleans whose clitoris was excised—on her mother's orders—when she was three. Unable to comprehend that such actions could occur in her adopted country, Tashi asks, "Is New Orleans America?" Amy replies, "I am telling you that even in America a rich white child could not touch herself sexually, if others could see her, and be safe. It is different today, of course. And even back then not every parent reacted as my mother did. But that I was not the only one this happened to I am sure." Tashi refuses to believe her—"For I saw the healthy green leaves of my America falling seared to the ground. The sparkling rivers muddy with blood." Tashi cannot accept the notion that her place of refuge, of safety, is also a place of cutting the female body—but Walker's point is clearly made: the experience of African women is not entirely alien from that of women in other parts of the world.

The novel presents Tashi's story in a powerful way, but it has met with mixed reviews. Some critics think that the book is too overtly didactic, that its point is hammered home with more force than necessary. Others object to the fact that all the narrators—ranging from Carl Jung, who treats Tashi for a time, to Tashi's mentally retarded son Benny—all sound the same, use the same language. Unlike the letters in *The Color Purple*, which clearly differentiate between Celie's voices and Nettie's, the voices here are practically indistinguishable.

Critics also attacked Walker for her portrayal of female circumcision, saying that as an American she has no right to comment on traditional practices in Africa and that she has ignored the psychological problems inherent in being an outcast from one's tribal group as a result of not undergoing the procedure. They maintain that by labeling female circumcision "torture" Walker is labeling well-meaning mothers "torturers." Walker responds that she is condemning the practice, not the people; that, as a descendant of Africans who may well have undergone circumcision, she has the right to speak; and that this bodily mutilation is just one type of oppression of the many suffered throughout the world.

In the film *Warrior Marks*, Walker interviews many women whose lives have been affected by female genital mutilation—those who have fled Africa to avoid the procedure; those, themselves mutilated, who inflict the procedure on their daughters; the circumcisers themselves; and women who are fighting to stop the practice. Interspersed with these interviews is a dance designed to evoke the emotions of women, both their joy and their pain. The accompanying book is divided into three sections. The first two sections, one each by Walker and Parmar, consist of journals and letters describing the process of conceiving and making the film. The third section contains transcripts of the interviews made for the film. Throughout, photographs document both the making of the film and the harm done by the procedure.

In 1994 Walker was named to receive the California Governor's Arts Award at the same time that two of her stories were removed from a statewide reading test. Walker at first refused the award, sparking much public debate over censorship. Eventually the stories were restored to the list of literature used for the test, and Walker accepted the award. Ironically, the statuette presented to her was that of a woman's torso, headless, armless, and legless—an unintended affront to a writer whose entire career involves seeing people whole.

Walker's third collection of essays, *Anything We Love Can Be Saved: A Writer's Activism* (1997), contains essays on many of Walker's wide-ranging interests: oppression, female genital mutilation, the Million Man March, Winnie Mandela, Fidel Castro, Salman Rushdie, and others. The essays focus on Walker's sense of the importance in every person's attempts to make the world a better place. Her own activism, she writes, comes from her parents' concerns: her mother's love of beauty and order in her house and garden, "her satisfaction in knowing everyone in her environment was sheltered and fed"; and her father's "insistence . . . that black people deserved the vote, black children deserved decent schools."

Two essays in the volume deal with the process of writing two of her novels. In "Turquoise and Coral: The Writing of *The Temple of My Familiar*," Walker discusses the "synchronicity" she felt during the writing process, especially her need to be surrounded with the colors turquoise and coral. The essay on the writing of *Possessing the Secret of Joy* tells of her trip to Carl Jung's house in Bollingen, Switzerland, which is recounted in the novel as the experience of Tashi and Adam. Overall, though, these essays are most concerned with Walker's political causes.

Walker's 1998 novel *By the Light of My Father's Smile* continues many of the themes and narrative techniques of her earlier work. The characters include people of color from all over the world; the central story involves a family of African American missionaries who live for years with a mixed-race tribe in Mexico. The narrative switches from voice to voice, including sections narrated by characters who have died. Walker takes on various causes, including the treatment of Vietnam veterans. The novel also castigates Christianity; explores the effects of the Ice Age on race and power; and explains various myths, nursery rhymes, and old wives' tales in terms of the subjection of women to men and of blacks to whites. Overall, though, the novel's theme is the importance of love, whatever form it takes, and the psychological damage inflicted when a person is punished for loving.

The Robinsons, black anthropologists pretending to be Christian missionaries, spend many years living with the Mundo tribe, whose people are a mix of black and Native American. The father, an agnostic, gradually loses his sense of self in the lie he is living, pretending to be a priest. He beats his older daughter, Magdalena, for making love to Manuelito, a Mundo boy. Susannah, the younger sister, observes the beating through the keyhole. Both daughters are damaged in ways that are never healed in their lifetimes. Magdalena constantly reminds Susannah of the way their father had treated her, forcing Susannah to choose between her love for her father and her love for her sister. Susannah always chooses her sister, denying herself the opportunity to forgive her father and accept his love. Magdalena, seeking constant

revenge for her father's treatment, eats until she is grossly obese. Only after death do they find peace and reconciliation.

While in earlier novels Walker developed creation myths, in this novel she introduces a ritual taught in the initiation ceremony of the Mundo to help the soul achieve peace after death. Manuelito and Magdalena are reunited briefly, with the hope of change in both their lives, but he is hit and killed by a bus. Her dead father, who has been haunting his daughters for years, hovers over the scene and begins to learn from the spirit of Manuelito how to achieve peace with his daughters.

The Mundo believe not in an eternal afterlife, but in a time after death to rectify wrongs committed during life. Manuelito tells the father's spirit, "each of us will have a little bit of time, a window of opportunity, so to speak, to make amends, to say good-bye, to bring love back to a love-forsaken heart. And then we are gone, and no one even thinks of us anymore." The father learns the Mundo initiation song and participates in the ceremony joining Manuelito to the now-dead Magdalena, thus making right the errors he had committed long before.

Walker's vision here moves beyond the happy endings of some of her earlier works to recognize that human hurts are often so deep that they cannot be healed in this life. However, she has been castigated by critics for the physical lovemaking described in the novel and for what critics see as the weirdness of having a father's spirit describing his own daughter's sexual experiences. Echoing the criticism aimed at some of Walker's earlier novels, critics have also complained that the novel is too didactic and that the characters are not adequately developed.

Walker lives in northern California, on forty acres in Mendicino County. Her house, built to her specifications, is called Temple Jook House. In this serene retreat Walker, a very private person, continues her very public struggles to help all the people of the world attain wholeness. No matter what her future course, Walker is likely to attract criticism from those who refuse to recognize her constant attention to issues that allow human beings to be themselves, whole, free and healthy—issues essential to survival.

Selected Bibliography

PRIMARY WORKS

POETRY

Once: Poems. New York: Harcourt Brace and World, 1968.

Revolutionary Petunias and Other Poems. New York: Harcourt Brace Jovanovich, 1973.

Good Night, Willie Lee, I'll See You in the Morning. New York: Dial, 1979.

Horses Make a Landscape Look More Beautiful. San Diego: Harcourt Brace Jovanovich, 1984.

Her Blue Body Everything We Know: Earthling Poems 1965–1990 Complete. San Diego: Harcourt Brace Jovanovich, 1991.

FICTION

The Third Life of Grange Copeland. New York: Harcourt Brace Jovanovich, 1970. Reprint, New York: Pocket Books, 1988, with an afterword by Alice Walker.

In Love and Trouble: Stories of Black Women. New York: Harcourt Brace Jovanovich, 1973.

Meridian. New York: Harcourt Brace Jovanovich, 1976.

You Can't Keep a Good Woman Down: Stories. New York: Harcourt Brace Jovanovich, 1981.

The Color Purple. New York: Harcourt Brace Jovanovich, 1982.

The Temple of My Familiar. San Diego: Harcourt Brace Jovanovich, 1989.

Possessing the Secret of Joy. New York: Harcourt Brace Jovanovich, 1992.

By the Light of My Father's Smile. New York: Random House, 1998.

CHILDREN'S LITERATURE

Langston Hughes, American Poet. New York: Harper & Row, 1974.

To Hell with Dying. Illustrations by Catherine Deeter. San Diego: Harcourt Brace Jovanovich, 1987.

Finding the Green Stone. Illustrations by Catherine Deeter. San Diego: Harcourt Brace, 1991.

EDITED ANTHOLOGY

I Love Myself when I Am Laughing . . . and Then Again when I Am Looking Mean and Impressive: A Zora Neale Hurston Reader. Old Westbury, N.Y.: Feminist Press, 1979.

ESSAYS

In Search of Our Mothers' Gardens: Womanist Prose. San Diego: Harcourt Brace Jovanovich, 1983.

Living by the Word. San Diego: Harcourt Brace Jovanovich, 1988.

Anything We Love Can Be Saved: A Writer's Activism. New York: Random House, 1997.

OTHER WORKS

Warrior Marks: Female Genital Mutilation and the Sexual Blinding of Women. With Pratibha Parmar. San Diego: Harcourt Brace, 1993.

Banned. Introduction by Patricia Holt. San Francisco: Aunt Lute Books, 1996. (Includes "Roselily," "Am I Blue?," an excerpt from *The Color Purple,* and letters and transcripts dealing with the exclusion of these works from California's literature-based reading tests.)

The Same River Twice: Honoring the Difficult. New York: Scribners, 1996.

FILMS

The Color Purple. Screenplay by Menno Meyjes. Directed by Steven Spielberg. Warner, 1985.

Warrior Marks: Female Genital Mutilation and the Sexual Blinding of Women. Produced and directed by Pratibha Parmar. Hauer Rawlence Productions, in association with Our Daughters Have Mothers, 1993.

SECONDARY WORKS

BIOGRAPHICAL AND CRITICAL STUDIES

Abbandonato, Linda. " 'A View from Elsewhere': Subversive Sexuality and the Rewriting of the Heroine's Story in *The Color Purple.*" *PMLA* 106, no. 5:1106–15 (October 1991).

Babb, Valerie. "*The Color Purple:* Writing to Undo What Writing Has Done." *Phylon* 47:107–16 (June 1986).

Bass, Margaret Kent. "Alice's Secret." *CLA Journal* 38, no 1:1–10 (September 1994).

Berlant, Lauren. "Race, Gender, and Nation in *The Color Purple.*" *Critical Inquiry* 14:831–59 (Summer 1988).

Bloom, Harold, ed. *Alice Walker.* New York: Chelsea House, 1989.

Braendlin, Bonnie. "Alice Walker's *The Temple of My Familiar* as Pastiche." *American Literature* 68, no. 1:47–67 (March 1996).

Buckman, Alyson R. "The Body as a Site of Colonization: Alice Walker's *Possessing the Secret of Joy.*" *Journal of American Culture* 18, no. 2:89–94 (Summer 1995).

Buncombe, Marie H. "Androgyny as Metaphor in Alice Walker's Novels." *CLA Journal* 30:419–27 (June 1987).

Butler, Robert James. "Making a Way Out of No Way: The Open Journey in Alice Walker's *The Third Life of Grange Copeland.*" *Black American Literature Forum* 22:65–79 (Spring 1988).

Callahan, John F. "The Hoop of Language: Politics and the Restoration of Voice in *Meridian.*" In his *In the African-American Grain: The Pursuit of Voice in Twentieth-Century Black Fiction.* Urbana: University of Illinois Press, 1988. Pp. 217–55.

Chambers, Kimberly R. "Right on Time: History and Religion in Alice Walker's *The Color Purple.*" *CLA Journal* 31:44–62 (1987).

Christian, Barbara T., ed. *"Everyday Use" [by] Alice Walker.* Edited and with an introduction by Christian, for the series Women Writers: Texts and Contexts. New Brunswick, N.J.: Rutgers University Press, 1994.

Cowart, David. "Heritage and Deracination in Walker's 'Everyday Use.' " *Studies in Short Fiction* 33, no. 2:171–84 (Spring 1996).

Davis, Thadious. "Poetry as Preface to Fiction: Alice Walker's Recurrent Apprenticeship." *Mississippi Quarterly* 44, no. 2:133–42 (Spring 1991).

El Saffar, Ruth. "Alice Walker's *The Color Purple.*" *International Fiction Review* 12:11–17 (Winter 1985).

Estes, David C. "Alice Walker's 'Strong Horse Tea': Folk Cures for the Dispossessed." *Southern Folklore* 50, no. 3:213–29 (1993).

Fifter, Elizabeth. "The Dialect and Letters of *The Color Purple.*" In *Contemporary American Women Writers: Narrative Strategies.* Edited by Catherine Rainwater and William J. Scheick. Lexington: University Press of Kentucky, 1985. Pp. 155–71. Bibliography on pp. 165–71.

Froula, Christine. "The Daughter's Seduction: Sexual Violence and Literary History." *Signs* 11:621–44 (1986). Revised version in *Daughters and Fathers.* Edited by Lynda E. Boose and Betty S. Flowers. Baltimore: Johns Hopkins University Press, 1989. Pp. 111–135.

Gaston, Karen C. "Women in the Lives of Grange Copeland." *CLA Journal* 24:276–86 (March 1981).

Gates, Henry Louis, Jr. "Color Me Zora: Alice Walker's (Re)Writing of the Speakerly Text." In his *The Signifying Monkey: A Theory of Afro-American Literary Criticism.* New York: Oxford University Press, 1988. Pp. 239–58.

Harris, Trudier. "Violence in *The Third Life of Grange Copeland.*" *CLA Journal* 19:238–47 (December 1975).

———. "From Victimization to Free Enterprise: Alice Walker's *The Color Purple.*" *Studies in American Fiction* 14:1–17 (Spring 1986).

Hellenbrand, Harold. "Speech after Silence: Alice Walker's *The Third Life of Grange Copeland.*" *Black American Literature Forum* 20:113–28 (Spring–Summer 1986).

Henderson, Mae G. "*The Color Purple:* Revisions and Redefinitions." *Sage* 2:14–18 (Spring 1985).

Hogue, W. Lawrence. "History, the Feminist Discourse, and Alice Walker's *The Third Life of Grange Copeland.*" *MELUS* 12:45–62 (Summer 1985).

McGowan, Martha J. "Atonement and Release in Alice Walker's *Meridian.*" *Critique* 23, no. 1:25–36 (1981).

Nadel, Alan. "Reading the Body: Alice Walker's *Meridian* and the Archeology of Self." *Modern Fiction Studies* 34:55–68 (1988).

Ross, Daniel W. "Celie in the Looking Glass: The Desire for Selfhood in *The Color Purple.*" *Modern Fiction Studies* 34:69–84 (Spring 1988).

Royster, Philip M. "In Search of Our Fathers' Arms: Alice Walker's Persona of the Alienated Darling." *Black American Literature Forum* 20:347–70 (Winter 1986).

Scholl, Diane Gabrielson. "With Ears to Hear and Eyes to See: Alice Walker's Parable *The Color Purple.*" *Christianity and Literature* 40:255–66 (Spring 1991).

Selzer, Linda. "Race and Domesticity in *The Color Purple.*" *African American Review* 29:67–82 (Spring 1995).

Shelton, Frank W. "Alienation and Integration in Alice Walker's *The Color Purple.*" *CLA Journal* 28:382–92 (June 1985).

Smith, Felipe. "Alice Walker's Redemptive Art." *African American Review* 26:437–51 (Fall 1992).

Souris, Stephen. "Multiperspectival Consensus: Alice Walker's *Possessing the Secret of Joy,* the Multiple Narrator Novel, and the Practice of 'Female Circumcision.' " *CLA Journal* 40, no. 4:405–31 (June 1997).

Stade, George. "Womanist Fiction and Male Characters." *Partisan Review* 52, no. 3:264–70 (1985).

Stein, Karen F. "*Meridian:* Alice Walker's Critique of Revolution." *Black American Literature Forum* 20:129–41 (Spring–Summer 1986).

Tate, Claudia. "Alice Walker." In *Black Women Writers at Work.* Edited by Claudia Tate. New York: Continuum, 1983. Pp. 175–87.

Tavormina, M. Teresa. "Dressing the Spirit: Clothworking and Language in *The Color Purple.*" *Journal of Narrative Technique* 16:220–30 (Fall 1986).

Walker, Robbie Jean. "Implications for Survival: Coping Strategies of the Women in Alice Walker's Novels." *Explorations in Ethnic Studies* 10:9–24 (January 1987).

Wall, Wendy. "Lettered Bodies and Corporeal Texts in *The Color Purple.*" *Studies in American Fiction* 16:83–97 (Spring 1988).

Walsh, Margaret. "The Enchanted World of *The Color Purple.*" *Southern Quarterly* 25:89–101 (Winter 1987).

Washington, J. Charles. "Positive Black Male Images in Alice Walker's Fiction." *Obsidian II* 3:23–48 (Spring 1988).

Weston, Ruth D. "Inversion of Patriarchal Mantle Images in Alice Walker's *Meridian.*" *Southern Quarterly* 25:102–107 (Winter 1987).

BIBLIOGRAPHIES

Banks, Erma Davis, and Keith Byerman. *Alice Walker: An Annotated Bibliography.* New York: Garland, 1989.

Byerman, Keith, and Erma Banks. "Alice Walker: A Selected Bibliography, 1968–1988." *Callaloo* 12, no. 2:343–45 (1989).

Howard, Lillie P. "Alice Walker: An Annotated Bibliography." *MELUS* 15:143–45 (Fall 1988).

Kirschner, Susan. "Alice Walker's Nonfictional Prose: A Checklist, 1966–1984." *Black American Literature Forum* 18:162–63 (Winter 1984).

Pratt, Louis H., and Darnell D. Pratt. *Alice Malsenior Walker: An Annotated Bibliography, 1968–1986.* Westport, Conn.: Meckler, 1988.

Werner, Craig. "Alice Walker." In *Black American Women Novelists: An Annotated Bibliography*. Pasadena, Calif.: Salem Press, 1989. Pp. 238–58.

INTERVIEWS

Dreifus, Claudia. "Alice Walker: 'Writing to Save My Life.' " *Progressive* 53, no. 8:29–31 (August 1989).

O'Brien, John. "Alice Walker." In *Interviews with Black Writers*. Edited by John O'Brien. New York: Liveright, 1973. Pp. 185–212. Reprinted in part as "From an Interview." In Alice Walker, *In Search of Our Mothers' Gardens*. San Diego: Harcourt Brace Jovanovich, 1983. Pp. 244–72.

Sanoff, Alvin P. "The Craft of Survival." *U.S. News and World Report* 110, no. 21:51 (June 3, 1991).

Steinem, Gloria. "Do You Know This Woman? She Knows You: A Profile of Alice Walker." *Ms.* 10, no. 2:35, 37, 89–90, 92–94 (June 1982).

Whitaker, Charles. "Alice Walker: *The Color Purple* Author Confronts Her Critics and Talks about Her Provocative New Book." *Ebony* 47, no. 7:86–90 (May 1992).

White, Evelyn C. "Alice's Wonderland." *Essence* 26, no. 10:84–88 (February 1996).

MARGARET WALKER
(1915–1998)

JANE CAMPBELL

DESCRIBED BY SONIA Sanchez as "a woman celebrating herself and a people," Margaret Abigail Walker was one of the most distinguished and prolific writers of the twentieth century. She produced a novel, several volumes of both poetry and nonfiction, and an extensive number of essays, interviews, and speeches. Walker's vision was a humanistic, spiritual one: although she viewed herself as pitted against a violent, materialistic society dominated by sexism and racism, Walker identified "the feminine principle" of being a daughter, a sister, a mother, and a grandmother as the "inspiring agency" for her work. She viewed womanhood and connections with others as the source of her creativity. Groomed from childhood to appreciate literature and music, Walker, the daughter of a Methodist minister, was also taught to devote herself to a mission. She thus regarded her purpose as a writer as "the healing and annealing hand," celebrating African American history and culture and transforming society.

Walker's view of her art as emerging from her responsibility to others and her healing role is at once ancient and contemporary, and it carries on the African tradition of conjure woman. Historically occupying a high plane in African American culture, representing the power to transcend earthly confinement, conjure women possess superhuman powers of concentration, knowing, magic, and healing. Walker's identi-

fication with womanhood runs throughout her work. Long before "The personal is political" became a feminist commonplace, she spoke of the political integration of her life and her art.

Walker lived through and described eras many people have only read about: post-Reconstruction, the Harlem Renaissance, and the radical thirties. She enjoyed the companionship and friendship of many intellectual giants—W. E. B. Du Bois, Langston Hughes, Zora Neale Hurston, Gwendolyn Brooks, Countee Cullen, and Richard Wright. Walker's commitment to antiracism and social justice began when she was a teenager. She conveyed this commitment through the rhythms and language of her folk heritage, inspiring audiences with all the religious and spiritual fervor she learned from her father. Walker's signature poem, "For My People," expresses her desire to speak directly to and about African Americans everywhere, regardless of education or class.

Walker was brought up to accept and develop her own singularity, and on the surface, gender seemed to have no impact on her introduction to literature and culture. Born in Birmingham, Alabama, on 7 July 1915, a time when most women were discouraged or ridiculed when they sought higher education, Walker knew she must finish college to gain parental approval. The daughter of university-educated, ambitious parents who surrounded her with music and books, Walker grew up linking achievement and identity. Both parents encouraged her to love literature; her mother taught her to read by the time she was four and read her poetry when she was very young. Early in life Walker was exposed to the work of Langston Hughes, James Weldon Johnson, and Zora Neale Hurston; she also read Homer, Shakespeare, and Jane Austen. While Walker lauded her mother for teaching her to read, she credited her father with inspiring her to write, giving her a daybook in which to keep the poems she began writing at the age of twelve. Emerging from this family, Walker, who spoke and read many languages, both embodied the tradition of scholarly African Americans and occupied a unique station among women during the first decades she was publishing. More than once she has enunciated an awareness of her privilege in having been intellectually encouraged and financially supported during her undergraduate education.

Because her parents were instrumental to her perspective, Walker has spoken often and eloquently about them. Her father, Sigismund C. Walker, was born in Jamaica Buff Bay, Jamaica British West Indies, coming to the United States to study for the ministry. Attending Tuskegee Institute for a time, he found its emphasis upon industrial education appallingly limited, and he received his degree from Gammon Theological Seminary in Atlanta. He and Walker's mother, a music teacher named Marion Dozier, fell in love at first sight, marrying and moving to Birmingham, where Walker and her three younger siblings were born. Ten years after Walker's birth, the family relocated to New Orleans. At New Orleans University, where she was a sophomore and her parents were professors, Walker met Langston Hughes. Sixteen-year-old Walker was bold enough to approach Hughes after he read his poetry and to show him some of her own. Impressed with both her confidence and her work, Hughes encouraged her to leave the deep South, and he became a close friend.

Walker's commitment to a creative mission emerged publicly two years later when her first poem appeared in *Crisis* magazine in 1934. At first called "Daydreaming," the poem was later retitled "I Want To Write" and was republished in Walker's *October Journey* (1973). "I Want To Write" conveys her passionate identification with African American culture, her commitment to humanism, and her spirituality. The first three lines bear one of Walker's trademarks, the evocation of her father's rhythmically inspiring sermons:

I want to write
I want to write the songs of my people
I want to hear them singing melodies in the
    dark.

Shortly after this first publication, and before her twentieth birthday, Walker earned a bachelor of arts degree in English from Northwestern University. Presumably this singular achievement garnered accolades from her ambitious parents. At the same time, however, Sigismund Walker expressed his wish that his daughter earn a Ph.D. by the time she was twenty-one. "Luckily," Walker observes wryly, "neither health nor finances would permit it." His stringent expectation dramatizes the pressure laid upon the young Margaret to satisfy him. Clearly, Walker's identity as a daughter—a role she has repeatedly defined as pivotal—hinged on an exaggerated version of success. "My father claimed he was always right," Walker has commented. "Strangely enough, he usually was." With her father serving as the impetus for her writing and with her own desire to please him at all costs, Walker has spent her life reconciling the sometimes conflicting demands of ambitious writer and good woman, with all that those involve.

Walker's desire to be a good daughter, a nurturing woman, and at the same time a productive writer mirrors the role conflicts many women face today. But in 1935, when she joined the Federal Writers' Project in Chicago, woman's role was even more strictly defined. Designed to subsidize promising writers, the project was funded by the Works Project Administration, but it subsidized men more generously than women. The project, according to Walker, taught her "professional tricks of the trade, if not the actual craft of writing"; moreover, it enabled her to work with other significant writers such as Arna Bontemps, Fenton Johnson, Willard Motley, Gwendolyn Brooks, and Richard Wright.

The Writers' Project also allowed Walker to observe and reflect upon discrimination and poverty in the urban North and to compare blacks' experiences in Chicago with those in the South. Thus her years in Chicago were pivotal to Walker's poetic imagination. The project also gave Walker a taste of sexual discrimination. Walker was so thrilled to be accepted on the project it never occurred to her to question her paltry salary of $85 a month despite her degree from Northwestern; later, she discovered that Wright, who had no formal education beyond eighth grade, was making $125. Her relationship with Wright, which she details in the biography *Richard Wright: Daemonic Genius* (1988), was also oppressive. Trusting and giving, Walker edited Wright's work, since he had little knowledge of the conventions of writing; later, when he began *Native Son*, Walker helped him with the prose and did the research for the book. Not only did Wright give her no credit, he later humiliated and rejected her and ended their friendship.

When the government pulled out the funding from under the Writers' Project, Walker decided to pursue a master's degree in creative writing at the University of Iowa. There she completed her first volume of poetry, *For My People* (1942). The book epitomizes Walker's role as critic, healer, and annealer of society, her link with her conjuring heritage. Using elemental symbols of sun, earth, and water, she puts her audience in touch with the pain of their oppression and nurtures their hope of delivery by celebrating the power and magic of African American culture.

The three-part structure of *For My People* begins with a series of poems employing what Walker describes as "a strophic form of free verse." Evocative of the sermons her father inspired her with as she was growing up, these poems introduce the motifs of bitterness, oppression, despair, and deception as well as those of delight, liberation, hope, and love that underlie the volume. The poet then moves to a

series of jubilant folk ballads and concludes with a group of Petrarchan sonnets evoking the despair, the darkness blacks live with daily, and calling for "a union of the two worlds," black and white.

According to Walker, "For My People," the opening poem, was composed "by accident" in fifteen minutes at a typewriter except for the final strophe and stanza. It was originally published in 1937 in *Poetry* magazine. A lucky "accident" indeed, the poem offers a hymn of praise for the dignity, the endurance, and the superhuman strength of African Americans, "singing their slave songs repeatedly," songs of transcendence that seek to make sense out of oppression. Walker piles up image after image, from the "bitter hours when we discovered we / were black and poor and small and different" that mark off the days of school children, to the "blundering and groping and floundering" hours consuming the lives of adults. Fully empathetic to the coping mechanisms that ease the anguish of poverty and abuse, Walker also encourages her audience's awareness of how destructive "losing time being lazy" or "drinking when hopeless" can be. But she places the blame squarely where it belongs: on a racist society that refuses to acknowledge black humanity. Her healing role in this poem lies in her insistence that black folk "rise and take control," reclaim their power and let it "fashion a better way."

Some of the most powerful poems in the first part of *For My People* embrace African American heritage. In many, Walker evokes a female consciousness embodied in the life-giving powers of nature. "Dark Blood" ponders Walker's "bizarre beginnings in old lands," where exquisite beauty and tropical sensuality become a symbolic landscape for ancient wisdom "sucked . . . through my veins with my mother's milk." Romantic images of "sugar sands and islands of fern and pearl" create a lush, primal vision of her father's Jamaican homeland. "Dark Blood" urges Walker's audience to mine the wealth of one's African heritage to heal the wounds imposed by racist America.

"We Have Been Believers" moves "Dark Blood"'s celebration of African heritage in another direction, rejoicing in black America's spirituality, "believing in the conjure of the humble and the faithful and the pure." In this poem, Walker reveals African American woman's centrality in black culture, acting as conjurer and seeress. Simultaneously, Walker expresses bitterness that blacks' humility and trust have been the vehicle for white economic oppression: "With our hands we have fed a people and out of our / strength have they wrung the necessities of a nation." "We Have Been Believers" calls for an end to the false gods of an oppressive country and asks for black Americans to heal themselves by tapping their awareness of imprisonment: "our fists bleed against the bars with a strange insistency."

Just as America has raided the African American spiritual home, so has it robbed blacks of their southern home. The speakers of "Southern Song" and "Sorrow Home" yearn to return to empowering natural beauty, so different from the urban desert of Chicago, but bitterly deride the racist violence that blights the South and has plundered blacks' ownership of their heritage. "Southern Song" and "Sorrow Home" exult in the healing natural powers of the South, where elemental images of "rainsoaked earth" and "spring growth of wild onion" hearken back to the "tropic world" of Jamaica that "sired and weaned" Walker. All the poems in part II revere a connection with the earth that Walker seeks to recapture and communicate so that she can gain strength from a kind of maternal power. "Lineage" enunciates Walker's connection with her matrilineal heritage, a link that these other poems express symbolically. "My grandmothers," Walker writes, "touched earth and grain grew."

Part II of *For My People* contains rousing ballads exalting the power and resourcefulness that form the core of black culture. Walker's folk heroes are larger than life, and they jubilantly proclaim African Americans' belief in magic, trickery, and revenge as tools to surmount poverty and oppression. If Walker champions women's life-giving capacities, their connections with the natural world in part I, she exalts women's connections with the supernatural world in "Molly Means," the poem that opens part II. The ballad depicts an unabashedly evil "chile of the devil, the dark, and sitch," who turns innocent brides into animals and defies ordinary humans to retaliate. Molly suggests Walker's belief in conjure women's unparalleled power, which can not only create but destroy.

Other heroines express earthier but no less impressive abilities to hold their own in a tough, male-dominated world. Kissie Lee learns from painful experience that being good garners only beatings from her lovers. When she listens to her grandmother's advice to pack weapons to defend herself, Kissie evolves into the "meanest mama you ever seen," who "can hold her likker and hold her man" and dies "with her boots on switching blades." Revenge over abusive men emerges in two other ballads. May tricks the ultimate misogynist, Yalluh Hammuh, who killed his own mother, and it is women who spell the doom of Teacher. This womanizer, whose lust "included all / Women ever made," not only the "juicy bait" he lures into his sex trade, suffers well-deserved knifings and shootings from his victims.

Single-minded revenge from women is a cultural imperative in a world peopled by the likes of Yalluh Hammuh and Teacher. But Walker's depiction of men is not entirely negative. In fact, she clearly valorizes Poppa Chicken, the pimp whose charisma commands near adoration from the legions of women "on Poppa's time." Stagolee, whose "bullets made holes no doc could cyo," kills a cop and escapes the lynch mob. In a culture where violence and death are meted out because of skin color, Stagolee becomes the apotheosis of justice. Some of the characters in these ballads exalt superhuman strength as a survival tool. The legendary John Henry, who significantly owes his conjuring skills to women, is "stronger than a team of oxen," and Gus, the Lineman, another mythic figure, handles live wires and survives supposedly fatal illness. Both characters are paradigms of black men forced to work at dangerous jobs in the absence of other options. Ironically, the "juice" that kills Gus is not electrical but alcoholic, and this simple detail speaks volumes about the real danger such "mighty guys" confront in living up to a masculine code enforced by a society that relegates African American men to roles that are strictly physical.

Taken as a whole, Walker's folk heroes affirm the strength and vibrance of African American culture. Enlarging these traits to mythic proportions, Walker celebrates the sensuality, passion, and courage of black folk. Her women and men defy convention, refuse to subscribe to limitations, and consequently transcend oppression. This section of *For My People* foregrounds Walker's role as healer, for she clearly seeks to empower her readers to look within themselves for the qualities they possess to take control of their lives despite poverty, discrimination, and tragedy.

Part III offers a sobering contrast to the riotous rhythms and mythic characters of Walker's ballads. These stark sonnets remind the reader that, despite the humor and energy that Walker celebrates in black life, one must acknowledge the anguish of a people denied human rights in a country supposedly founded on liberty and equality. Images of poverty and despair recur, from the ragged miners, "grumbling undermining all their words," who peopled her childhood, to the sullen-eyed whores she encountered in Chicago. "Memory," the poem at the center of this section, distills these images: "shoulders hunched against a sharp concern," Walker's brooding, lonely tenement dwellers in frigidly hostile Chicago mutter oaths of protest against their oppression but have no power to escape from it.

Closing the volume, "Our Need" and "The Struggle Staggers Us," two of Walker's finest poems, tap the despair described in the rest of *For My People* and call for a redemptive vision, "a wholeness born of inner strength." "Our birth and death are easy hours," Walker remarks here. The only hope is that blacks and whites will come together, embark on "a journey from the me to you . . . from the you to me," which will allow us to understand each other and unify our worlds divided by race. Although "For My People" opens this volume and enunciates Walker's identification with black culture—an identification central to all

her work—"The Struggle Staggers Us," the final piece, underscores her belief that the fates of black and white Americans are intertwined, that the two races must resolve their differences. Throughout her life, Walker has insisted on this position, articulated especially well at a speech she delivered at the National Urban League Conference in New Orleans in 1968:

> Any notions that a wide cleavage in the American people based on race, class, caste, sex, or age—any such notion is unrealistic, naive, negative, and detrimental. . . . Shall we divide and conquer? Who will conquer, and who stands to benefit from such cleavage?

Walker was the first African American to win the Yale Series of Younger Poets Award, and as a result *For My People* was published as part of the Yale Series. Not only is *For My People* Walker's first book; it also serves as an entry into her work and her vision. Walker has stated that she wanted to convey her hope for "another world, another whole earth to come into being." This literary masterpiece fuses the cadence of sermon and folk tale with Western literary tradition. It merges her African heritage and her humanistic and Christian beliefs with a feminist consciousness that sees woman's links with nature and the earth as emblematic of her ability to create new poetic, political, and spiritual worlds.

The year following *For My People's* publication, Walker married Firnist James Alexander, and together they had four children: Marion Elizabeth, Firnist James Jr., Sigismund Walker, and Margaret Elvira. At about the same time, Walker began her career as an English professor, first at West Virginia State College, then at Livingstone College in Salisbury, North Carolina, where she stayed until 1946. From 1949 to 1979 she taught for twenty-six years at Jackson State University, also directing the Institute for the Study of the History, Life, and Culture of Black People. Not surprisingly, the demands of motherhood, marriage, and career interfered with Walker's publishing until *Jubilee* appeared in

1966. What is surprising is that while raising four children and supporting the family because her husband was disabled, she managed the extensive research and composition of the novel's early drafts. During this same period, Walker wrote poems, speeches, and essays, received the Rosenwald Fellowship for Creative Writing in 1944, a Ford Fellowship at Yale University in 1954, and completed her Ph.D. at the University of Iowa in 1965. *How I Wrote Jubilee* (1972) is an eloquent testimony of the obstacles women face while writing. Walker wrote the first three hundred pages of *Jubilee* when she was nineteen, but the arduous shaping into fiction took thirty years because of the pressures and disruptions of Walker's family and career.

Jubilee received the Houghton Mifflin Literary Fellowship in 1966. In writing this novel, Walker transcribed her family's oral history, passed along to her from her grandmother, who often enthralled the child "way past bedtime" with stories of her forebears Vyry and Randall Ware. When Margaret's mother objected to these "tall tales," Walker's grandmother insisted that she was telling her granddaughter the truth. Many of the chapter headings are transcriptions of her grandmother's words. Thus Walker takes on the role of African griot, or oral historian, enlarging her audience by the huge success of *Jubilee:* it has sold millions of copies; has been translated into six languages including French, German, and Swedish; has been made into an opera; and has remained in print since its publication.

Taken as companion volumes, *Jubilee* and *How I Wrote Jubilee* accentuate Walker's identification with womanhood, mothering, and healing, and they demonstrate how her life and art are of a piece. Celebrating her great-grandmother, *Jubilee* is simultaneously a paean to Walker herself, who—despite lifelong discrimination on the basis of race and gender, despite relative critical neglect, despite a negative self-image engendered by cultural animosity to diversity ("there was always something wrong with me—either ragged stockings, or nappy hair")—has steadfastly refused to alter her vision or her image to conform to fashion.

Jubilee presents a panorama of African American history beginning with slavery and ending in Reconstruction. The daughter of her master, Vyry bears striking resemblance to her sister Lillian, the daughter of Big Missy and Marster John. Taken into the house to serve her sister and her father, Vyry suffers hideous abuse from Big Missy, who views Vyry as a symbol of her husband's sexual proclivities for Vyry's mother. Hung by her wrists in a closet for two weeks as punishment for a minor infraction, Vyry survives, typifying the extraordinary strength of African American women historically forced to endure similar treatment. *Jubilee* chronicles Vyry's marriage to Randall Ware, the free black who tries, without success, to liberate Vyry from slavery; Vyry's loyalty to her white family even after Emancipation; her subsequent second marriage to Innis Brown; and the overwhelmingly difficult years during Reconstruction. *Jubilee* ends with Vyry sending her teenage son Jim to live with Randall Ware, so that Jim can study to become a teacher, thus realizing Vyry's dream of triumphing over oppression.

In *How I Wrote Jubilee*, Walker discusses the genesis of her novel, eventually accepted for her Ph.D. dissertation at the University of Iowa. She also defends Vyry's sometimes-criticized lack of bitterness and militance as a faithful rendering of her maternal great-grandmother, who "realized that hatred wasn't necessary and would have corroded her own spiritual well-being." Instead of forcing her heroine into the militant model fashionable at the time *Jubilee* was published, Walker remains true to the spiritual vision passed down through the generations, a nurturing, healing approach to life that mirrors Walker's own attitude.

A Poetic Equation: Conversations Between Nikki Giovanni and Margaret Walker (1974) offers insight into Walker's dislike for antiwhite sentiments, her insistence on a humanitarian, loving solution to racism. "I don't know that that's necessarily great spiritual strength," Walker argues in that book, "to have deep hatred and . . . kill some of these 'honkies.' " Instead, Walker calls for Christian love and spiritual wholeness, the inner peace that sees Vyry through and leads eventually to her transcendence over oppression.

The significance of motherhood underpins *Jubilee*, serving as its core philosophy and linking it with earlier African American writers such as Frances E. W. Harper. The novel begins with Sis Hetta, Vyry's mother, dying in childbirth when Vyry is only two years old. As if losing one mother is not enough, Vyry loses two surrogate mothers, Mama Sukey, who also dies, and Aunt Sally, who is sold to another plantation. Ushering Vyry into her newly orphaned state, Big Missy slaps her, a vicious parody of the life-giving slap a newborn receives to start it breathing.

Rather than harboring bitterness, Vyry responds to her motherless state by nurturing others. She loses the chance to escape slavery because she refuses to leave her children behind, an episode that beautifully symbolizes the double burden that black women carried during slavery. Vyry cares for her sister, Lillian, even after Emancipation because she will not leave Lillian, who has lost her sanity from being attacked by Union soldiers after the war. Only after a relative arrives to take over Lillian's care does Vyry marry Innis Brown and begin the life of a free woman. Lillian serves as a foil for Vyry; she is as weak and incompetent as Vyry is strong and capable.

Vyry's nurturing constitutes a redemptive, humanitarian vision throughout the novel. Certainly her children are the center of her life, a point of view passed on to her by Aunt Sally at the onset of Vyry's menstruation, when Vyry learns that her ability to mother affirms her superiority. At a time of total despair, Vyry miscarries, symbolizing her loss of hope and vitality. Vyry also extends her nurturing beyond her family to the community. When she and Innis move into a house that starving white sharecroppers are vacating, Vyry feeds the white family before they set out on their journey. The meals Vyry prepares are described frequently in *Jubilee*; chosen as a child to become head cook in the Big House, Vyry possesses culinary skills that telegraph her nurturing role throughout the novel. When Vyry offers her services as a midwife and saves a white baby's life without asking for remuneration, her family receives its first safe haven during terrifying, Klan-dominated years of Reconstruction.

This episode signals Vyry's conjuring role, one Walker subtly enshrines throughout *Jubilee*. Vyry's conjuring powers emerge in the latter part of *Jubilee*, as she and Innis move from place to place trying to make a home. Vyry and Innis undergo a series of crises typifying blacks' struggles during the years following the Civil War, when white southerners fought to reinstate slavery and make the lives of black southerners miserable in every way they could. The family is robbed by the landlord for whom it sharecrops, terrorized and torched by the Klan, and intimidated by virulent bigotry. Gifted with non-Western ways of "knowing," Vyry senses danger in Troy, Alabama, long before the Klan burns down her family's new house, and she insists that they wait until she feels the time is ripe before rebuilding. It is significant that her midwifery, the most ancient and creative of women's healing arts, turns around racist sentiment and causes the white inhabitants of Greenville, Alabama, to welcome her family into the community, which offers protection in exchange for Vyry's skill as a "granny."

Rooted in Walker's reverence for women's connections with others—women's proclivities for nurturing, healing, and life-giving—the publication of *Jubilee* was also timely in supplanting the negative connotations of matriarchy that had recently been put forth by Daniel P. Moynihan and popularized by the media. Published one year after Moynihan's destructive, inaccurate study "*The Negro Family: The Case for National Action*" (1965), *Jubilee* counters Moynihan's views of the matriarchal family as fragmented, unstable, and unnatural. Vyry not only holds the family together, she makes all of the decisions, and Innis usually defers to her, though he often argues with her first. As Innis acknowledges, Vyry appears to have miraculous powers of seeing, and her decisions are the right ones. Countering popular views that the matrifocal family leads to violence and delinquency in the African American community, *Jubilee* honors the matriarch.

765

As committed as Walker was to commemorating her great-grandmother and the strength of womanhood, so too was she committed to celebrating the civil rights movement in her next major work, *Prophets for a New Day* (1970), a collection of poetry published just four years after *Jubilee*. Similar to the way Walker sees Vyry's Christian humanism as a solution to societal ills, *Prophets for a New Day* identifies civil rights leaders with biblical prophets, signifying that their vision fuses politics and spirituality.

Prophets for a New Day begins with two poems about young females. "Street Demonstration," the opening piece, is a charming, comic poem based on the urgent statement of an eight-year-old girl, "Hurry up Lucille or we won't get arrested with our group." The speaker of the second poem, "Girl Held Without Bail," espouses passive resistance and alludes to her mother, sister, and girlfriends who share her cell. Walker, by positioning these two poems at the beginning of the volume, enshrines children and young people as symbolic of the hope for a new era. "How Many Silent Centuries Sleep in My Sultry Veins" enunciates a similar view, finding redemption in a proud African heritage that provided us with contemporary heroes: "these modern, sensate sons" who by virtue of their ancestors are "immortal men, and free." Thus, Walker credits women with creating children to take up the banner of freedom. Yet in "Jackson, Mississippi," even motherhood is a lost cause, for grannies have "long since fled."

Prophets for a New Day is a compelling, cohesive volume of memorable poems. Walker's renunciation of cities such as Jackson and Oxford, Mississippi, punctures the gentility masking a racist code. Oxford, "where all the by-gone years of chivalry and poetry and crinoline / are dead," calls up "bright, grim" smiles as survival mechanisms for African Americans. In Jackson, where Walker has lived since 1949, the sun is "raw fire" beating down, suggesting that even nature punishes rather than heals. Juxtaposing white wealth and comfort with black poverty and hopelessness, "wide white avenues / And black alleys of filthy rendezvous," Walker decries the years she has spent developing and passing on liberating visions in a city ruled by demagogues. These trenchant sketches reawaken the anger motivating the civil rights movement. Moreover, they throw into relief Walker's poems about the prophets seeking equal rights.

Typifying the era's hopeful mood, the poems depict exemplary men who carried on the centuries-old tradition of black revolt. "The Ballad of the Free" offers tribute to heroes familiar to African Americans through oral histories, despite their absence from "official" versions taught in schools. Walker sanctifies Nat Turner, Gabriel Prosser, and Denmark Vesey, leaders of American slave revolts; Toussaint L'Ouverture, paradigmatic for freeing slaves in Haiti; and John Brown, hanged for attacking Harper's Ferry. She includes Brown to signal her belief that African Americans and whites can join together in the struggle for racial equality. Her choice of ballad emphasizes the legendary quality of these men, all of whom were martyred for their political actions. "The Ballad of the Free" is written in quatrains followed by a refrain with biblical echoes: "The last shall be first and the first shall be none." Their martyrdom notwithstanding, these five men set the tone of empowerment and risk that earmarks *Prophets for a New Day*.

Modern heroes receive equally inspired treatment. A free-verse sonnet to Malcolm X emphasizes Malcolm's messianic role when Walker queries, "When and where will another come to take your holy place?" Three civil rights workers murdered by Mississippi Klansmen are resurrected in "For Andy Goodman—Michael Schwerner—and James Chaney." In this haunting piece, Walker employs natural imagery to mourn the interrupted youth of these three men, "Black and white together," who relinquished their lives for their political commitment. Delicate images of humming birds, sequoias, trembling blossoms, and wild cardinal calls accentuate the ugliness of death and mutilation hinted at but never graphically mentioned in the poem. The mourning dove, "Mississippi bird of sorrow," recurs throughout the final stanzas, as the writer hopes to discern the meaning of these senseless deaths.

Although Walker attributes prophecy to all of those committed to the civil rights movement, she links biblical prophets with certain exemplary figures. Isaiah, "a man of the court," is perhaps Whitney Young, Roy Wilkins, or Adam Clayton Powell; Joel, who speaks "harsh and bitter words of burning Truth" may be identified with Julian Bond or Eldridge Cleaver. Micah, crying out against racist enemies, is explicitly identified as Medgar Evers. Amos, revered in two poems, doubtless represents Martin Luther King. "Amos—1963" depicts King preaching "a new gospel of love" in "seething" Selma and "bitter Birmingham." In "Amos (Postscript-1968)," Walker transmutes King's death into eternal life.

Prophets for a New Day possesses all Walker's willingness to step aside and let others occupy the front lines. Walker reasserts her conjuring mission, continuing to inspire and support, to heal her audience and her community. By foregrounding African Americans, Walker expresses her belief that the political and spiritual impulse of the sixties originated in black America. As Walker puts it: "We are a people of spirit, we are a people of soul, we are a numinous people."

October Journey, published in 1973, lacks the cohesiveness of the two earlier books of poetry. A collection of autobiographical and occasional pieces, it contains little memorable work aside from Walker's first poem "I Want To Write." Significantly, however, the volume attests to Walker's lifelong desire to celebrate and support people she holds in high regard. It includes, for instance, a long epitaph for her father, sonnets to Paul Laurence Dunbar and Mary McLeod Bethune, and a piece dedicated to Gwendolyn Brooks—whom Walker has known both as a child and a woman. A lively ballad about Harriet Tubman reflects Walker's desire to recreate history and commemorate women as well as men, an impulse she also reveals in short critical pieces about Brooks, Nella Larsen, Georgia Douglas Johnson, and May Miller. Taken as a memento of Walker's commitment to promoting and appreciating others, *October Journey* reveals Walker's adherence to celebrating black voices.

In the 1980s, having retired from Jackson State University to allow herself to devote more time to her writing, Walker produced two major works. *Richard Wright: Daemonic Genius* (1988) and *This Is My Century: New and Collected Poems* (1989).

The biography of Richard Wright reasserts Walker's pattern of celebrating others' works. Walker positions herself as Wright's definitive biographer, in part because of her close friendship with him in the late 1930s. Her approach is psychological, at times almost psychoanalytic, and it reveals some extraordinarily controversial views. Unfortunately the book is quite uneven. Initially compelling, full of provocative notions about the relationship between artist and work, *Daemonic Genius* deteriorates during the last few chapters. The latter part of the narrative reflects poor editing, weakly synthesizing previously composed pieces into the text and repeating sections from earlier chapters.

Walker argues that Wright's art derived from two impulses: the "psychic wound of racism" and his "psychosexual confusion." These she sees as interrelated and reflected in all of his work. As evidence of Wright's confusion, Walker argues that despite his commitment to racial equality and social justice, he harbored internalized racism, hating "his own black self." Connected with Wright's internalized racism, Walker maintains, is his hostility to black women, whom he viewed as unattractive and disloyal to black men: "they only pull you down when you're trying to get up." Wright allegedly castigated black women as exhibiting "animal sexuality," falling easy prey to white men. According to Walker, Wright felt nearly as much hostility for white women as he did for black women, so that his relationships with his white lovers and wives were fraught with trauma. Walker insists that Wright's misogyny emerges clearly in *Native Son*, when Bigger Thomas, with whom she believes Wright identified, murders and maims two women, one white and one black. It is not accidental, Walker continues, that mothers, aunts, and grandmothers appearing in Wright's fiction are negatively portrayed, for Wright used his writing as an outlet for his rage against women.

Walker's biography of Wright nevertheless expresses her reverence for his tortured genius, and she argues that his talent originated in his turbulent psychology. She maintains that Wright's rage and passion reflected his connection with higher planes of awareness, a kind of divine madness. Ambitious and intriguing, *Richard Wright: Daemonic Genius* sparks reconsideration of Wright's work; in that respect it accomplishes one of the aims of biography and complements Walker's "healing, annealing" role. But *Daemonic Genius* communicates almost as much about Walker as it does about Wright. The chapters about Walker's relationship with her subject disclose her resentment at Wright's cavalier treatment of her.

During the last decade, Walker has increasingly lamented the discrimination she has suffered as a result of being an African American woman. Her awareness of critical neglect, unequal pay, and blatant raiding of her work have emerged in interviews and essays such as "On Being Female, Black, and Free." Walker comments there, "The higher you try to climb, the more rarified the air, the more obstacles appear." Walker's description of Wright's cruelty toward her invites the question of whether Walker's book is an act of exorcism. Taken in conjunction with her writing as a whole, it suggests that Walker, in exposing Wright's exploitation and rejection of her, seeks to apply her healing arts to herself.

This Is My Century: New and Collected Poems reveals the full range of Walker's talents and brings her vision full circle. The title announces her reclamation and ownership of the twentieth century, reinforcing her celebratory role and her desire to criticize and shape society. Like *For My People* and *Prophets for a New Day*, the new poems in *This Is My Century* are cohesive, revolving around a central purpose.

In a group of poems titled "Farish Street," a street in Jackson, Mississippi, serves as a microcosm of the African American community. The seven poems affirm various aspects of that community. The African Village represents blacks' efforts to recreate their heritage in America:

In our beginnings our Blackness was not
 thought so
beautiful
but out of bitterness we wrought an ancient
 past
here.

Imagining the homeland's pastoral spirit amid bricks and alleyways, residents seek connections with their ancestry. "Black Magic" humorously warns of the dangers inherent in meddling with that fixture of the community, the root doctor, citing the shibboleth "Lie down with dogs and get up with fleas." The poem "Farish Street" distills the energy and despair of tavern, church, and greengrocer, likening the street to a patchwork quilt "stitched with blood and tears," just as the street is "paved with martyred Black men's flesh and bones." Taken as a group, the poems of "Farish Street" resonate with the anguish, power, and passion of the black community.

In *This Is My Century*, Walker assigns herself the role of teacher, one that allows her to pass on the healing wisdom she has accrued over seventy-five years. She contrasts her youthful and senior visions, commemorates intellectual and creative paragons, affirms Pan-Africanism, recreates significant historic moments, and revitalizes her humanistic perspective. Like all of Walker's work, the book demands—as the end of the century approaches—that her society take a hard look at itself, identify its failures, and take pleasure in its triumphs in order to move to another level of awareness and health.

Walker continues her commitment to commemoration; she lauds such figures as Frederick Douglass, Albert Einstein, W. E. B. Du Bois, and Karl Marx, and she also praises longshoremen, mothers, and "proud park-bench sleepers." She offers a poignant poem to Alex, her late husband, and takes the liberty of applauding herself as the embodiment of African American women in "My Truth and My Flame": "I am the spirit in all living things."

Some of the poems contrasting youth and age in *This Is My Century* complain bitterly that too many years in a racist country have eroded her spirit. In "Old Age" Walker deplores the lifelong stress of dealing with "the clash of race and sex and class." "I Hear a Rumbling" asks "How long must my children cry / to the skies" Walker's gentle irony in "On Youth and Age" notes,

> When I was a little girl
> the little girl on Morton Salt was white;
> She still is.

Walker's frustration at addressing the same issues for seventy-five years emerges especially powerfully in the angry "They Have Put Us on HOLD"; "Fanfare, Coda, and Finale" implores America to "remake the music stifling in my throat."

Walker's belief in spiritual humanism as a healing agency underlies the entire volume. She decries technology, consecrates nature as the repository of spiritual wisdom, expresses faith in a union of black and white, and exalts African heritage. She enunciates her belief that the answer to racial divisions, poverty, gender discrimination, anti-Semitism, and class prejudice is to recognize our shared humanity, "providing a full measure of human dignity for everyone." *This Is My Century* encapsulates Walker's perspective: adhering to her own private, coherent vision regardless of political currents or literary fashions, identifying herself as both a black woman and a writer, Walker survived and prevailed.

She remained remarkably productive into her seventies and eighties. During the last eight years of her life, she published two volumes of essays: *How I Wrote Jubilee and Other Essays on Life and Literature* (1990) and *On Being Black, Female, and Free: Essays by Margaret Walker, 1932–1992* (1997). Edited by Maryemma Graham, these two books contain previously uncollected work. Taken together, the books round out Walker's canon, reminding us that she excelled not only as a poet and novelist, but also as an essayist.

Up until her death, Walker was a vital and committed member of the scholarly community. On October 17, 1998, she made her last public appearance at the Gwendolyn Brooks Writers' Conference held at Chicago State University, where she was inducted into the African American Hall of Fame. Just six weeks later, at the age of 83, she died of breast cancer on November 30 at the Chicago residence of her daughter, Marion Elizabeth Alexander Coleman. Carrying on the African tradition of conjurer, healing and celebrating the black community, Margaret Walker inspired, nurtured, and politicized her audience for nearly an entire century.

Selected Bibliography

PRIMARY WORKS

VOLUMES

For My People. New Haven: Yale University Press, 1942. Poetry.

Jubilee. Boston: Houghton Mifflin, 1966. Novel.

Prophets for a New Day. Detroit: Broadside Press, 1970. Poetry.

How I Wrote Jubilee. Chicago: Third World Press, 1972. Essay.

October Journey. Detroit: Broadside Press, 1973. Poetry.

A Poetic Equation: Conversations Between Nikki Giovanni and Margaret Walker. Washington, D.C.: Howard University Press, 1974.

Richard Wright: Daemonic Genius. New York: Warner Books, 1988. Biography.

This Is My Century: New and Collected Poems. Athens: University of Georgia Press, 1989.

Jubilee and Other Essays on Life and Literature. Edited by Maryemma Graham. New York: Feminist Press, 1990.

On Being Female, Black, and Free: Essays by Margaret Walker, 1932–1992. Edited by Maryemma Graham. Knoxville: University of Tennessee Press, 1997.

ESSAYS

"New Poets." *Phylon* 11, no. 4:345–54 (1950). Reprinted in *Black Expression: Essays By and About Black Americans in the Creative Arts.* Edited by Addison Gayle. New York: Weybright and Talley, 1969.

"Black Writer's Views on Literary Lions and Values." *Negro Digest* 17:23 (January 1968).

"Black Studies: Some Personal Observations." *Afro-American Studies* 1:41–43 (1970).

"The Humanistic Tradition of Afro-American Literature." *American Libraries* 1:849–54 (October 1970).

"Religion, Poetry, and History: Foundations for a New Educational System." In *The Black Seventies.* Edited by Floyd B. Barbour. Boston: Porter Sargent, 1970. Pp. 284–95.

"On Being Female, Black, and Free." In *The Writer on Her Work*. Edited by Janet Sternburg. New York: W. W. Norton & Co., 1980. Pp. 95–106.

"Dr. Nick Aaron Ford: A Man in the Classic Tradition." In *Swords Upon This Hill*. Edited by Burney J. Hollis. Baltimore: Morgan State University Press, 1984. Pp. 116–20.

"Foreword." In *I Wonder As I Wander: An Autobiographical Journey*, by Langston Hughes. New York: Thunder's Mouth Press, 1986.

SECONDARY WORKS

BIOGRAPHICAL AND CRITICAL STUDIES

Barksdale, Richard K. "Margaret Walker: Folk Orature and Historical Prophecy." In *Black American Poets Between Worlds, 1940–1960*. Edited by R. Baxter Miller. *Tennessee Studies in Literature* 30. Knoxville: University of Tennessee Press, 1986. Pp. 104–17.

Bell, Bernard W. *The Afro-American Novel and Its Tradition*. Amherst: University of Massachusetts Press, 1987.

Bonetti, Kay. "An Interview with Margaret Walker Alexander." *Missouri Review* 15:113–31 (Spring 1992).

Campbell, Jane. "Margaret Walker." In *Dictionary of Literary Biography*. Vol. 152, *American Novelists since World War II*. Edited by James R. Giles and Wanda H. Giles. Detroit: Gale Research, 1995. Pp. 273–81.

Carmichael, Jacqueline Miller. *Trumpeting a Fiery Sound: History and Folklore in Margaret Walker's Jubilee*. Athens: University of Georgia Press, 1998.

Caton, Bill. "An Interview with Margaret Walker Alexander." In *Fighting Words: Words on Writing from 21 of the Heart of Dixie's Best Contemporary Authors*. Edited by Bill Caton. Montgomery: Black Belt Press, 1995. Pp. 125–35.

Christian, Barbara. *In Wild Women in the Whirlwind: Afra-American Culture and the Contemporary Renaissance*. Edited by Joanne M. Braxton and Andree Nicola McLaughlin. New Brunswick, N.J.: Rutgers University Press, 1990.

Collier, Eugenia. "Fields Watered with Blood: Myth and Ritual in the Poetry of Margaret Walker." In *Black Women Writers (1950–1980): A Critical Evaluation*. Edited by Mari Evans. New York: Doubleday, 1984. Pp. 499–509.

Egejuru, Phanuel, and Robert Elliot Fox. "An Interview with Margaret Walker." *Callaloo* 2:29–35 (1979).

Freibert, Lucy M. "Southern Song: An Interview with Margaret Walker." *Frontiers* 9:50–56 (1987).

Gabbin, Joanne V. "Conversation: Margaret Walker Alexander and Joanne V. Gabbin." In *The Furious Flowering of African American Poetry*. Edited by Joanne Gabbin. Charlottesville: University Press of Virginia, 1999. Pp. 239–51.

Giddings, Paula. " 'A Shoulder Hunched Against a Sharp Concern': Some Themes in the Poetry of Mar-garet Walker." *Black World* 21:20–25 (December 1971).

Goodman, Charlotte. "From Uncle Tom's Cabin to Vyry's Kitchen: the Black Female Folk Tradition in Margaret Walker's *Jubilee*." In *Tradition and the Talents of Women*. Edited by Florence Howe. Urbana: University of Illinois Press, 1991. Pp. 328–37.

Graham, Maryemma. "The Fusion of Ideas: An Interview with Margaret Walker Alexander." *African American Review* 27:279–86 (Summer 1993).

Gwin, Minrose C. *Black and White Women of the Old South: The Peculiar Sisterhood in American Literature*. Knoxville: University of Tennessee Press, 1985.

Hull, Gloria T. "Black Women Poets from Wheatley to Walker." In *Sturdy Black Bridges: Visions of Black Women in Literature*. Edited by Roseann P. Bell, Bettye J. Parker, and Beverly Guy-Sheftall. Garden City, N.Y.: Anchor Press, 1979. Pp. 69, 86.

Jones, John Griffith. "Margaret Walker Alexander." *Mississippi Writers Talking*. Jackson: University Press of Mississippi, 1983. Pp. 121–46.

Klotman, Phyllis R. " 'Oh Freedom': Women and History in Margaret Walker's *Jubilee*." *Black American Literature Forum* 11:139–45 (Winter 1977).

McDowell, Margaret B. "The Black Woman as Artist and Critic: Four Versions." *Kentucky Review* 7:19–41 (Spring 1987).

Miller, R. Baxter. "The 'Intricate Design' of Margaret Walker: Literary and Biblical Re-Creation in Southern History." In *Black American Poets Between Worlds, 1940–1960*. Edited by R. Baxter Miller. *Tennessee Studies in Literature* 30. Knoxville: University of Tennessee Press, 1986. Pp. 118–35.

Pettis, Joyce. "Margaret Walker: Black Woman Writer of the South." In *Southern Women Writers: The New Generation*. Edited by Tonette Bond Inge. Tuscaloosa: University of Alabama Press, 1990. Pp. 9–19.

Reid, Margaret. "The Defiant Ones: Black Female Voices in Poetic Protest." In *Amid Visions and Revisions: Poetry and Criticism on Literature and the Arts*. Edited by Burney J. Hollis. Baltimore: Morgan State University Press, 1985. Pp. 79–94.

Rowell, Charles H. "Poetry, History and Humanism: An Interview with Margaret Walker." *Black World* 25:4–17 (December 1975).

Russell, Sandi. *Render Me My Song: African American Women Writers from Slavery to the Present*. New York: St. Martin's Press, 1990.

Spears, James E. "Black Folk Elements in Margaret Walker's *Jubilee*." *Mississippi Folklore Register* 14:13–19 (Spring 1980).

Tate, Claudia, ed. *Black Women Writers at Work*. New York: Continuum, 1983. Pp. 188–204.

Traylor, Eleanor W. " 'Bolder Measures Crashing Through': Margaret Walker's Poem of the Century." *Callaloo* 10:570–95 (Fall 1987).

———. "Music as Theme: The Blues Mode in the Works of Margaret Walker." *Black Women Writers (1950–1980): A Critical Evaluation*. Edited by Mari Evans.

Garden City, N.Y.: Anchor Press/Doubleday, 1984. Pp. 513–24.

Williams, Delores S. "Black Women's Literature and the Task of Feminist Theology." In *Immaculate and Powerful: The Female in Sacred Image and Social Reality*. Edited by Clarissa W. Atkinson, Constance H. Buchanan, and Margaret Ruth Miles. Boston: Beacon Press 1985. Pp. 88–110.

BIBLIOGRAPHIES

Chapman, Dorothy Hilton, ed. *Index to Poetry by Black American Women*. New York: Greenwood Press, 1986.

Deodene, Frank, and William P. French. *Black American Poetry Since 1944: A Preliminary Checklist*. Chatham, N.J.: Chatham Bookseller, 1971.

PHILLIS WHEATLEY
(1753–1784)

JOHN C. SHIELDS

THE EXPLOSION OF literary criticism which has occurred in the last ten to fifteen years of the twentieth century has catapulted Phillis Wheatley to the first rank among American authors. The 1970s saw the beginning of efforts to overturn the several myths which, for some two hundred years, had embraced the life and career of the first African American to publish a book, the 1773 *Poems on Various Subjects, Religious and Moral.* Such myths as that Wheatley was merely a derivative writer; that she was so much in awe of her white captors that she failed even to address the issue of slavery; that her piety for her adopted New England Congregationalism was so absolute that she never questioned the contradiction between its professed faith (equality for all believers) and the practice of slaveholding among parishioners; and that her work is entirely the product of the white linguistic and poetic idiom she allegedly imitated, showing no debt whatever to her African heritage—all of these notions made for an unfair and intellectually anemic assessment of this poet's contribution. It is indeed these myths that steadily and implacably promoted for so long a time the idea of a "pseudo-Wheatley" (to adapt a concept elaborated by Paul de Man in *Blindness and Insight*). While the artistry of the true Wheatley is finally being recognized, the pseudo-Wheatley has all too often served the interests of sociopolitical arguments of decidedly racist contours. Now that these myths are being dispelled and the historical Phillis Wheatley is beginning to emerge, critics of her work are discovering that she has produced poetry and prose which is much more complex than was previously assumed. What her deliberate and thoroughly engaged readers are learning is that she composed texts which are richly multilayered and brilliantly constructed. Indeed, the extent of her sophistication has yet to be measured.

The *content* of Wheatley's poems was almost totally ignored until the appearance in 1953 of Arthur P. Davis's groundbreaking "Personal Elements in the Poetry of Phillis Wheatley." Davis argues that examination of the words, phrases, and lines of Wheatley's poetry reveals the presence of a highly personal lyric voice; he is virtually the first to talk not only about this writer's content but about how she wrote. His concern is with Wheatley's works, not with making some sociological or anthropological argument. Only from a close examination of the texts of her poems and prose can one begin to make an honest, fair evaluation of this significant American poet. Such an examination has proved that Wheatley does address the issue of slavery, that her work manifests a keen awareness of her African heritage, and that, rather than composing derivative or imitative verse, she constructs a highly original, even revolutionary poetics that prefigures British and Continental Romanticism. In particular, Wheatley's poem "On Imagination" inspired and influenced such American scholars as the father of anthropology Johann F. Blumemenbck and Thomas Clarkson, as well as the British Romantic figures William Wordsworth and Samuel Taylor Coleridge. Wheatley's work participated in the flow of thought which was becoming Romantic both in the United States and in Britain.

African Origins

According to the memoir of Margaretta Matilda Oddell, Phillis Wheatley was born in or around 1753, probably along the Gambia River in West Africa. Because of her sharp skeletal features and thin lips, evident in the portrait used as a frontispiece for her 1773 *Poems*, she was very likely of the Fulani people. She was approximately seven or eight years old (surmised from the fact that she had just lost her front teeth, though this may have resulted from the meager diet of the horrible middle passage) when John Wheatley, a Boston merchant, bought her "for a trifle" on July 11, 1761 and gave her to his wife, Susana, as a personal maid. It is unlikely, therefore, that Wheatley ever completely forgot her former life in West Africa. It is nevertheless true that all she apparently chose to recall of that former life to her white captors was the memory of her mother pouring out water every day *"before the sun at his rising"* and then "prostrating herself" in the direction of the risen sun.

This ritual suggests that Wheatley's religious training in Africa included some sort of hierophantic solar worship. Since solar imagery constitutes the dominant image pattern in her poetry, this suggestion becomes all the more credible. As this daily ritual entailed her mother's prostrating herself before the object of worship, yet another kind of religious training may have been present to the child. In West Africa, prostration before the dawning sun would have required turning the body toward the east, the direction of Mecca. Since Islam had long before penetrated into the Gambia region, one can conclude that Wheatley's mother may have been performing the first of five daily, obligatory prayers to Allah. The ostensibly simple ritual that Wheatley recalled, then, may actually have represented a more complex, syncretized version of Islam and solar worship.

Margaretta Oddell, who remains Wheatley's principal biographer, observed in her 1834 *Memoir* that "the young girl was frequently seen endeavoring to make letters upon the wall with a piece of chalk or charcoal." Some have speculated that these characters may have been Arabic, thus strengthening Wheatley's ties to Islam which had reached the Gambia region some twenty or thirty years before Wheatley's abduction. Wheatley soon distinguished herself in John Wheatley's household, composed of other slaves and of twin children about six years Phillis's senior, by learning to read and write English when only about nine. She eventually learned Latin as well, as evidenced by her fine translation-adaptation from Ovid, "Niobe in Distress . . . ," published in her 1773 *Poems*. By at least 1765, Phillis was proficient enough in English to correspond with Samson Occom, the Mohegan Native American minister; and on December 21, 1767, at age thirteen or fourteen, she published "On Messrs. Hussey and Coffin." Though she had doubtless experimented by writing several earlier poems, this is her first known poem to have appeared in print. During the next year, 1768, that Wheatley wrote the original version of what was to become her best-known poem, "On Being Brought from Africa to America," which she probably polished for its first publication in the 1773 *Poems*. Wheatley's act of writing was unusual for a slave since the time was simply not available to slaves for this activity. As a "petted slave" Wheatley was most likely put on display much like a circus act—people were very curious about a black woman who could "perform" at so sophisticated a level.

In addition to being her most popular poem, "On Being Brought from Africa" may well be her most controversial piece. Perhaps surprisingly, it shares many qualities with what Jean-Pierre Makouta-Mboukou in *Black African Lit-*

erature: *An Introduction* (1973) characterizes as the moral function of songs sung by African folk poets: "Traditional songs . . . convey a moral—a warning, ridicule, criticism, entreaty, flattery, thanks, abuse, defiance, a demand, repulsion." First written when she was only fourteen or fifteen, this poem is indeed a bold expression for a young slave girl. This decidedly personal lyric (bearing some relation to confession) opens with these apparently innocuous couplets:

'Twas mercy brought me from my *Pagan* land,
Taught my benighted soul to understand
That there's a God, that there's a *Saviour* too:
Once I redemption neither sought nor knew.

> (*Collected Works* 1988, p. 18;
> all quotations from Wheatley's
> works are from this edition.)

Phillis Wheatley

Taken by themselves, these lines attest the enthusiasm of a sincere convert to Christianity. But this young poet is hardly naïve, as the remaining lines reveal. Having given herself as a suitable example of the success of Christian evangelism, or, to place this first half of the poem within the context of Makouta-Mboukou's description, having offered thanks for her conversion, she subsequently moves into a direct indictment of "some" white Christians.

In the first line of the second half of this eight-line lyric, the poet declares: "some view our sable race with scornful eye." It is, then, those numbered among the "some" whom the poet appears to want to address. The inclusive pronoun "our" indicates that Wheatley is under no delusion that she has herself somehow merited exclusion from the gaze of this collective "scornful eye." Then she completes the couplet by quoting, as if to record an aspersion overheard, " 'Their colour is a diabolic die.' " Pointing out the connotations of "nobility and natural dignity" associated with the attributive "sable," on the one hand, and the association of evil and filth inherent in "diabolic," on the other, James A. Levernier has cogently argued

that Wheatley's use of the noun "die" here is an attempt to advance a sophisticated irony: "Like the black slaves brought to America, indigo *dye* and sugar *cane* were products of the triangular trade" (p. 25). Levernier informs us that true Christians among the pre-Revolutionary American colonists—that is, those not included in Wheatley's "some"—boycotted goods produced in the Indies on dye and cane plantations, where the labor was carried out by black slaves.

Wheatley closes this brief but pithy lyric with an undisguised imperative: "Remember, *Christians, Negros,* black as *Cain,* / May be refin'd, and join th'angelic train." What opened with the spirit of confessional closes with an admonition to all whites who, without legitimate grounds, would raise themselves above black people. For according to the Christian message as this young girl has received it, God makes no distinction between white and black; and just as white believers are promised "redemption," conversion has taught Wheatley that, contrary to those whites whose racial bigotry would consign all of her color to hell (implied by the word "diabolic"), all true believers, even *"Negros,"* "May be refin'd" or raised to a higher spiritual state equal to that of any white believer. Wheatley here expresses her earliest written acknowledgment of the rude lesson taught her by the white world, which in a 1774 letter she likens to a "severe schoolmaster." The Janus-like world speaks, even preaches, one message yet clearly practices a contradictory one. But the important point to recognize here is that, unlike her contemporary, black poet Jupiter Hammon, who resigned himself to temporal inequality and set his hope for equality on the spiritual realm, Wheatley blatantly challenges the insidiousness of the white Boston public she knew and then rebukes those same authors of deceit with an unmistakable assertion of equality.

Such courage and forthrightness could only have proved to bigoted whites that this blooming poet was nothing but an "uppity" slave—one who was better silenced than allowed to exercise the freedom of a literate pen. Since "On Being Brought from Africa" was among the titles listed in her first 1772 "Proposals" for a volume that was subsequently rejected by the Boston public, it is possible that some Bostonians knew of Wheatley's uppity notions and therefore refused to support the publication. "On Being Brought" is an extremely important poem to Wheatley's evolving liberation poetics; perhaps the fact that it enjoys a reputation among modern readers as one of her most controversial poems signals its importance. In addition to challenging the injustice of the status quo, Wheatley is here in the act of determining her role as poet. Not at all content with resignation, she steadfastly confronts those who would condemn her and her race and challenges their tyranny over her and hers. Having been in New England for only seven years, perhaps she is recalling traditional African folk songs as she delivers to an unsympathetic audience this highly moral warning, replete with a tone of entreaty, perhaps even of flattery, yet which at the same moment clearly conveys an attitude of defiance, command, and repulsion.

Emergent Poetics and the African Panegyric

Another performance by Wheatley that suggests the recollection of an African musical setting occurs in the companion pieces "An Hymn to the Morning" and "An Hymn to the Evening." Despite the notion that Milton's "L'Allegro" and "Il Penseroso" may have inspired these poems, neither of Wheatley's poems is given to analysis of cheerful or thoughtful man. Rather each constitutes a paean to the sun, recalling the solar worship of Wheatley's mother and also restating the general classical origin of the paean as a genre devoted to celebration of Apollo, Greek god of the sun. Setting aside for the moment the subject of these poems, let us examine their common structure. The first two lines of "An Hymn to the Morning" present an invocation to the Muses; since "An Hymn to the Evening" has no invocation, this pentameter couplet, "Attend my lays, ye ever honour'd nine, / Assist my labours, and my strains refine," serves both poems (note the plural "lays"). Minus this invocation, each piece is eighteen lines in length. Each celebrates the sun's inestimable contribution to the soft, purling streams, gentle gales, and singing birds of spring; then each concludes abruptly. Whereas the morning piece cites the poet's musical intentions in the line "In smoothest numbers pour the notes [not beats or stresses] along," the evening piece absorbs the music within an auditory image, "the birds renew their notes, / And through the air their mingled music floats." This renewal of the birds' song suggests the relationship of statement and response (strophe and antistrophe) that obtains between the two poems. After the sun reaches its noon zenith in the morning hymn, its complementary descending motion is recorded in the evening hymn. Even the use of "hymn" in each of the titles signals the musical structure of an antiphonal anthem.

In his discussion of African vernacular poetry in the *Princeton Encyclopedia of Poetry and Poetics* (1974), Lyndon Harries asserts that lyric, "probably the most common genre of oral poetry in Africa, has a great variety of forms, but basically it is a short poem sung or recited either antiphonally or by an individual." He next describes the subjects of African lyric as "about every conceivable topic in the African experience. Songs about, or attributed to, birds are very common, but the main interest is human life and conduct." Wheatley's two "hymns," among her shortest poems, place great emphasis on the songs of birds, on antiphonal structure, and on the moral lesson to be learned from proper appreciation of the sun as God's gift:

> Fill'd with the praise of him who gives the
>   light,
> And draws the sable curtains of the night,
> Let placid slumbers sooth each weary
>   mind,
> At morn to wake more heav'nly, more
>   refin'd.

In *Oral Literature in Africa* (1970), Ruth Finnegan offers two more details that suggest an affinity between Wheatley's two lyrics and the praxis of lyric in Africa. First she declares that the soloist of antiphonal songs in Africa often "has complete scope to improvise his part of the verse as he chooses (apart perhaps from the very first line, p. 259). Wheatley's repeatedly demonstrated fondness for the invocation to the muse suggests a parallel to the African practice of accepting the first line of a lyric (as part of the soloist's contribution, which frequently opens the entire song) as donnée. Finnegan goes on to detail a second parallel practice: "Sometimes the end is abrupt and the leader simply stops" (p. 260). Wheatley's morning hymn ends: "And scarce begun, concludes th'abortive song." She uses this sort of "abortive" conclusion again in "On Imagination" and in "Niobe in Distress" (if one considers this poem to conclude at line 212 as scholars argue was Wheatley's own intention).

Another manifestation of her African poetic heritage appears in her repeated practice of the panegyric, which Finnegan cites as "one of the most developed and elaborate poetic genres in Africa." She further points out that "cultivation of panegyric poetry . . . [gives] rise to poetry of profound political significance as a means of political propaganda, pressure, or communication." Such poems as "To Samuel Quincy, Esq; a Panegyrick," "To the King's Most Excellent Majesty," "To the Right Honourable William, Earl of Dartmouth," "To His Excellency General Washington," and "Liberty and Peace" all eulogize political events and figures, each of which in itself dramatizes a decisive moment in America's struggle for independence. The political praise poem is a genre of no small significance to Wheatley. Her boldness in composing such commentaries, while functioning under the disadvantages either of being a slave or of being relegated to the status of a black female domestic after having been freed, suggests roots in an African tradition which taught that political praise poems were at the very center of one's responsibility as poet.

Wheatley's panegyrics, however, were not limited to politics. In such poems as "Thoughts on the Works of Providence," "To S. M. a Young *African* Painter, on seeing his Works," and "An Hymn to Humanity," she offers praises to her conceptions of God, individual artistic achievement, and mankind. Each of these poems celebrates some manifestation of freedom. While the verses on "Providence" exalt God in his works of nature and "To S. M." enthusiastically describes the artistic accomplishment of a fellow African, "An Hymn to Humanity" first extols "Divine *Humanity*" and then sounds the ideal of the Age of Reason, tolerance, in these poignant lines spoken by God to his son, " 'my heav'nly fair' ":

> "Descend to earth, there place thy throne;
> "To succour man's afflicted son
>   "Each human heart inspire:
> "To act in bounties unconfin'd
> "Enlarge the close contracted mind,
>   "And fill it with thy fire."

The son of man (or sons of men) is "afflicted" because he is not tolerant, this because of his "close contracted mind." "To act in bounties unconfin'd" is to give the gift of freedom decreed as a gesture of largesse. Written for the 1773 *Poems*, this poem anticipates the more direct plea for racial equality in "On the Death of General Wooster" (1778). "An Hymn to Humanity" does indeed celebrate the human spirit, not for what is has done but for what it promises to do. To be sure, expression of some sort of hope is a donnée among examples of the African genre of the panegyric; it is surely no accident, then, that this same critical but hopeful attitude characterizes much of the literature by black Americans from the time of Wheatley to the present.

Wheatley's Elegies and African Dirges

In addition to the objects of praise already noted in the African panegyric are, in Finnegan's words, "a stress on royal or aristocratic power, and an admiration for military achievement." Certainly such poems as "To the King's Most Excellent Majesty" stress royal power, and others, such as "To His Excellency General Washington," show much approval of military prowess. But Wheatley's debt to the African panegyric is not limited to subject matter alone; it also embraces form. According to Finnegan, typical of the African form is a "loose ordering of stanzas by which a series of pictures of a man's qualities and deeds is conveyed." Since Wheatley best exhibits this structure in certain elegies, a genre of African oral poetry integrally related to the panegyric, an examination of her elegy on George Whitefield, the "voice" of the Great Awakening, provides a vivid illustration. In order to demonstrate how Wheatley's structure differs from the expected English form, a brief comparison of "On the Death of the Rev. Mr. George Whitefield" with two other elegies on the same subject, but by white authors, the colonial poet Benjamin Church and the English hymnodist Charles Wesley, proves instructive.

Wheatley's elegy opens with this arresting image: "Hail, happy saint, on thine immortal throne." In the English elegy of the late eighteenth century, this sort of apotheosis ordinarily occurs, if it occurs at all, in the closing lines. Neither Church's nor Wesley's elegy contains an apotheosis. Church's begins with a complaint against death's "poison," announces

Whitefield's departure, moves to an *ubi sunt* lament (where are the days of a better life?), then progresses into a general treatment of Whitefield's evangelical career interspersed with maudlin expressions of grief: "Forgive the tempest, should our sorrows rave, / while o'er thy moldering dust our heads decline" (p. 213). The poem closes with a stanza asking that some fitting marble monument be erected to Whitefield's glory. The Wesley memorial is, at 536 lines, over five times the length of Church's. It is by far the most reflective and measured of the three elegies. After starting with a lament over Whitefield's passing, the poem moves into a lengthy and detailed rehearsal of the principal spiritual events of his life and ministry, including the author's first meeting with his subject. The last part of the elegy gives a general plea to the unregenerate to be moved by Whitefield's example to seek forgiveness for their sins through conversion.

Wheatley's poem contrasts markedly with these two elegies. Whereas both Church and Wesley have clearly composed laments, Wheatley has constructed an encomium, whose prevailing tone of praise is established in the first line, "Hail, happy saint, on thine immortal throne." Unlike Church and Wesley, Wheatley has written her poem with great economy, for it is a mere forty-seven lines. Church's elegy follows somewhat the typical structure of the so-called Puritan elegy, wherein the subject's biography—broken down into details of vocation or conversion, evidence of good works (sanctification), and the deceased's joyous reception into heavenly reward—is followed by an exhortation to the living to put off mourning and concentrate on earning a similar reward. Church does not detail Whitefield's conversion, probably because such information simply was unknown to him, nor does he include an exhortation to the living. He does, however, speak of Whitefield's work with orphans, of his seven ocean voyages to the colonies on evangelical missions, and of his great success in bringing about converts, as well as of his achievement of heavenly reward.

More surprising is the British poet's faithfulness to the Puritan elegy. Wesley's portraiture is one of the most elaborate I have encountered among elegists writing in English before 1800. It is obvious from the great number of details, including details about his subject's conversion, that Wesley knew Whitefield intimately. (Indeed, at an early point in their careers, John and Charles Wesley and Whitefield together practiced an inchoate form of Methodism.) Wesley assures his readers that Whitefield has earned his heavenly reward, a conclusion that inevitably follows from the overwhelming evidence of the evangel's good deeds; the poet's emphasis on exhortation has already been noted. We observe, then, that Wesley brings out fully the structure of the Puritan elegy.

While Wheatley's celebration of Whitefield assuredly shows familiarity with the Puritan elegy, as do several of her elegies, she does not appear in this elegy, as in many others, to derive her form exclusively from the Puritan genre. With its "series of pictures" and its "laconic and often rather staccato sentences"—descriptions that Finnegan gives of the African panegyric praising a specific individual—this poem establishes a pattern that her possible childhood internalization of African panegyric may well have suggested to her. Confining the motif of lament to such expressions as "we the setting sun deplore" and to drawing a picture of orphans mourning "their more than father [who] will no more return," Wheatley concentrates on Whitefield's power to "inflame the heart, and captivate the mind" (two objectives of her own poetry), on his longing "to see *America* excel," and especially on the universality of Whitefield's message to new converts.

In one extant version of this elegy, apparently printed in London and carelessly entitled by another hand as "An Ode of Verses on the Much-Lamented Death of the Rev. Mr. George Whitefield," Wheatley dramatizes a portion of one of Whitefield's sermons in these affective and noticeably rebellious lines:

Take him, ye *Africans*, he longs for you,
Impartial Saviour is his Title due.
If you will walk in Grace's heavenly Road,
He'll make you free, and Kings, and Priests
　　to God.

In the version contained in the 1773 *Poems*, the last couplet above is muted to read: " 'Wash'd in the fountain of redeeming blood, / You shall be sons, and kings, and priests to God.' " Wheatley's insistence on the equalizing result of conversion echoes her sentiments in "On Being Brought from Africa." The short, staccato effect of the pictures the poet draws here of the deceased, along with her loosely organized but vivid portraiture, contrasts markedly with the more calculated and longer portraits by Church and Wesley. Even her recording of Whitefield's conversion is reduced from Wesley's nearly one hundred lines to a single line subordinated to the subject of his ministry: "That Saviour, which his soul did first receive."

One might argue that such a lack of detail bespeaks merely the poet's unfamiliarity with her subject. However, Whitefield was in Boston only a week before his death in Newburyport, Massachusetts, on September 30, 1770, and he had visited Boston during his sixth trip to America between 1763 and 1765, some two years after Phillis had become a member of the Wheatley household. Given the extant correspondence between Wheatley's mistress, Susanna, and Selina Hastings, Countess of Huntingdon, whose privy chaplain was Whitefield himself, it is probable that Whitefield was offered accommodations when visiting Boston in the Wheatley mansion. Phillis and Whitefield, therefore, may well have met while under the same roof. In any case, it is most probable that Wheatley had heard Whitefield preach on at least two occasions prior to composing her eulogistic elegy. Her elegy preceded Wesley's by several months, which may have contributed to its popularity in England. Having probably come to England aboard the same ship that brought the news of Whitefield's death, Wheatley's poem appeared at a most opportune and timely moment.

The success of Wheatley's elegy was also owing to its brevity, which allowed it to be issued in broadside, making it cheaper to purchase and easier to circulate than Wesley's long poem, which required a more cumbersome and expensive pamphlet for distribution. But particularly attractive to readers must have been Wheatley's economy of form. Whitefield's immense popularity demanded some sort of tribute, and concerned readers must have found Wheatley's brief but pithy testimonial both consoling and appropriate. Her African heritage served her well, for it probably assisted her in constructing a public statement that placed "little stress on personal emotions"—another characteristic of African panegyric described by Finnegan (recall that even Wheatley's plea for equality is not a personal one)—and that conveyed a succinct and recognizable portrait of a well-known figure in "laconic and often rather staccato sentences." I underscore the significance of her success with the Whitefield poem because it definitely assured the patronage of the Countess of Huntingdon, grieved by the loss of her chaplain, and thus led to the appearance of the 1773 *Poems*, a project that otherwise may not have materialized. Wheatley's African heritage may quite simply have been crucial to her success as a poet.

Wheatley's Epyllia and Elegiac Mode in Relation to the African Epic and Elegy

Wheatley's African heritage may also have helped prepare her for the composition of her two experiments with the short epic, "Goliath of Gath" and "Niobe in Distress." Harries, again in the *Princeton Encyclopedia*, asserts that panegyrics are "intermediary between epic and ode, a combination of exclamatory narration and laudatory apostrophizing." Certainly the biblical story of David's confrontation with the giant contributes to praise of the young boy's fitness for kingship, while the Niobe episode warns against too much self-praise. Both of Wheatley's experiments, then, deal with the praise motif, the one emphasizing the positive and the other the negative side of the subject. As these two poems are her longest, running to 222 and 212 lines respectively, Finnegan's observation about long praise poems is relevant: "many of the lengthy praise poems . . . do contain some epic elements and provide the nearest common parallel to this form in Africa." In

altering the traditional tales of young David's heroism and Niobe's pride, Wheatley demonstrates what Makouta-Mboukou has called the African folk poet's art: "The talent of the African folk poet resides only in the practice of the art of his narrative that he embellishes in accord with his own poetic insight. He always works with an accepted traditional tale." The transplanted African then, has, taken two traditional moral tales and embellished each, transforming them through her talent and creating them anew as short epics.

Although Wheatley's handling of the gods in these epyllia, or short epics, may simply be the result of the Old Testament's henotheism ("the worship of one god without denying the existence of other gods," according to Webster's dictionary) and the classical world's religious perspective, it may be indebted as well to the manner in which a much younger Wheatley heard African oral poets represent their (and at that time her) gods. In his discussion of spoken African mythic literature in *The Black Mind: A History of African Literature* (1974), O. R. Dathorne notes that "the gods . . . are frequently humanized or, rather more than that, they are not thought of as being any different from human beings." Perhaps Wheatley's memory of African oral poets at least complemented and made more feasible to her literary imagination the characters of Samuel's Jehovah and Ovid's Apollo. In her epyllia, as in their traditional sources, both "gods" are enraged by challenges to their authority and subsequently take measures to destroy the sources of those challenges; Jehovah sends a messenger who gives Goliath an ultimatum, and Apollo looses his arrows to eliminate the expression of Niobe's pride, all fourteen of her children. In other words, the gods of Wheatley's poems act in predictable, anthropomorphic ways, as they do in the source stories and as deities acted in African tales of the gods.

According to Isidore Okpewho in *The Epic in Africa: Toward a Poetics of the Oral Performance* (1979), the audiences of traditional African epics "sung" by tribal griots believe "the gods are responsible for evil as well as good." Wheatley's own empathy with her heroine, Niobe, would seem to imply that Apollo and his sister, Phoebe (the moon), take their exaction of justice too far. This same empathy suggests another characteristic of African epic that Okpewho isolates: "the tremendous empathy the bard establishes between himself [or herself] and the subjects of his [or her] tale, particularly the hero [or heroine]." Wheatley's feeling for Niobe is amply revealed when she describes her, immediately upon her having lost all seven sons to the swift arrows of Apollo and Phoebe, as "beautiful in woe," a phrase that does not appear in Ovid. While the Classical poets Homer and Virgil do also on occasion display a measure of empathy for their heroes, Ovid in the Niobe episode does not empathize with his mortal queen, who is being punished for blatant pride and blasphemy against the gods (especially against Latona, mother of the twins Apollo and Phoebe). Wheatley's sentiment for Niobe departs remarkably from her original source, but accords well with the African praxis of epic delivery.

A third characteristic of the African oral epic that recurs in Wheatley's work has to do with what Okpewho calls "the overall context of each performance" of the African epic. He cautions that appreciators of the form must consider "the living process by which performance is continually actualized." Okpewho further observes: "In this form of art, the means is more worthy of our attention than the end, for poetry here implies more the moment and process of creation than the finished product itself." Wheatley is herself caught up in the totality of the making of her poems, as her "On Imagination" illustrates. Here she is concerned not only with demonstrating how powerful is the faculty of a poet's imagination but especially with performing a "wond'rous act" of her own—the creation of a poem. For as she asks, with the impact of a declaration, *Imagination!* who can sing thy force?" Her next move is to show how a poet, despite unpleasant realities, can create a pleasant alternative world by means of her power to manipulate words: "Though *Winter* frowns to *Fancy's* raptur'd eyes / The fields may flourish, and gay scenes arise." Wheatley often gave her readers different ver-

sions of the same poem before its appearance in print (this is especially the case with her elegies); so different was each "performance" that Wheatley's verse resembles "the living process" that characterizes the oral African epic.

While the genres of lyric, panegyric, and epyllion demonstrate connections to Wheatley's African heritage, her praxis of the elegy exhibits the most substantial connection to those origins. Her eighteen elegies constitute almost a third of the existing Wheatley canon. Although most of the English and American elegies (as well as all other forms) of her time were written by men, this was not the standard practice among black Africans of the day. Finnegan emphasizes that the saying or singing of elegies (dirges) was usually the province of women. Characterizing elegiac verse as "more private and normally lacking the political relevance of panegyric poetry," she indicates that the elegy "tends to be performed by nonprofessionals (often women) rather than state officials." Since such dirges as sung in Africa "often involve wailing, sobbing, and weeping," they are "particularly suitable for women—for in Africa as elsewhere such activities are considered typically female." Among the Akan peoples, for example, "traditionally all . . . girls were expected to learn how to sing and compose dirges."

Given this heritage it should come as little surprise that Wheatley devoted much of her poetic energies to composing elegies; for very likely engraved upon her childhood memory was the recollection of women and young girls performing dirges. Her heritage may have suggested more to Wheatley than simply the role and responsibility of elegies; indeed, several characteristics of the genre as practiced in Africa recur in her works. For example, according to Finnegan, the dirge singer is expected to make "frequent references to the wisdom of the dead"; these references typically take the form of "the singer lamenting that she no longer has anyone to give her advice." In her elegies on Joseph Sewall (spelled Sewell in the title) and Samuel Cooper, Wheatley carries out these specifications. Of Sewall, who for fifty-six years was pastor of the famous Old South Church of

Boston and whose services the poet attended until his death in 1769, Wheatley wrote: " 'I, too have cause this mighty loss to mourn, / For he my monitor will not return.' " From his youth, according to a variant of the poem, Sewall "sought the Paths of virtue and of Truth." While Sewall apparently served as Wheatley's spiritual adviser during her adolescence, Cooper, who baptized her, served her in another capacity. In her 1784 elegy on this latitudinarian minister of Cambridge's Brattle Street meeting-house, Wheatley, in the year of her own death, identifies Cooper as one "drawn by rhetoric's commanding laws" who "Encourag'd oft, and oft approv'd [my] lays." The poet also celebrates his intellectual gifts in the arresting line "The Sons of Learning on thy lessons hung."

While the elegies on Whitefield by Church and Wesley both extol their subject for his knowledge of Scripture and spiritual matters, neither describes Whitefield as personal counselor. Such personal acknowledgments as appear in Wheatley's elegies on Cooper and Sewall were uncharacteristic of American and English elegies of the time, as was her penchant for the dramatic, which appears in many of her elegies. Whitefield, for example, speaks five verse couplets in Wheatley's elegy; a deceased girl of five utters six lines of advice from her heavenly abode in another poem, while in still other elegies several among the departed describe to the living how they may imitate the behavior of the speaker and thus likewise be received into joyous reward. In his discussion of the African elegy, Dathorne declares that "funeral dirges frequently are directed at the living" and that "frequently the form of the dirge is itself dramatic." Perhaps Wheatley's own flare for the dramatic and her concentration in the elegy on the conduct of the living are still other manifestations of her African heritage.

Given the present dearth of details regarding Wheatley's life in Africa, any investigation of her African origins must remain to some extent speculative. At the same time, however, too many points of positive correlation obtain between her poetry and African oral literature to be ignored. The fact that she saw her role as poet to be largely governed by a responsible moral conviction accords well with African practice, as does her frequent praxis of the lyric. She so enthusiastically embraces the panegyric, Africa's most prevalent genre, that even certain of her elegies spill into panegyric. Her experiments with the epic demonstrate affinities with long African praise poems and with characterizations resembling African gods. And most substantially her praxis of the elegy harmonizes so well with the African that we travel full circle, back to definition of her function as poet; for in Africa, elegies are usually sung by women. Wheatley's biological origin in Africa is incontestable; now we should speak of her literary origin in Africa as well.

Blending Christianity, Humanism, Classicism, and Solar Worship

When Wheatley arrived in colonial Boston in 1761 to be sold on the block, she carried with her a store of African heritage. Almost immediately she was told that her pagan religious practices were grievously erroneous and that she must abandon all allegiance to them in favor of New England Congregational Christianity. Virtually all commentators on the life and work of Wheatley, from her time to the present, have assumed that she converted absolutely to this New England religion. The evidence from her poems, nevertheless, indicates that her religious views shift from those of a naïve convert to those of an enlightened humanist. I do not intend to suggest that she ever became any less sincere in her ideas concerning God, nor that she ever gave up belief in the Deity. She did, however, become more liberal in her religious views, which shows in her poems. A reliable indication of the shift may well be observed in Wheatley's necessary change of religious mentors.

In her elegy commemorating Sewall's death, she calls this wholly orthodox Calvinist "my monitor." Two years before his death, she composed two poems, one against deism and one against atheism, that resemble pious exercises affirming her knowledge of orthodox Calvinism, and that were not included in her 1773 *Poems*. Two years after Sewall's death, however, Wheatley was baptized by Cooper, who penned the line "Imagination! heaven-born maid!" in the 1761 collection *Pietas et Gratulatio*, celebrating the accession of George III. In *Sibley's Biographical Sketches of Those Who Attended Harvard College* (vol. 11; 1960), Clifford Shipton observes of Cooper's ministry: "The church in Brattle Street was known throughout the English-speaking world as one of the most liberal in the Dissenting persuasion." Concerning Cooper's theology, Shipton writes, "The only theological point to which he held firmly was the right of free inquiry. . . . He read the writings of Jonathan Edwards, but they had no effect at all upon him."

After Cooper's baptism of her, Wheatley's poetry begins to show a modification of her former orthodoxy. For instance, what had been a strictly conventional biblical paraphrase of David's confrontation with Goliath in Mather Byles's *Poems on Several Occasions* (1744), after which Wheatley is thought to have designed her 1773 *Poems* (see my "Phillis Wheatley and Mather Byles"), becomes in her creative mind an elaborate epyllion replete with machines, albeit Christian machines, and an eight-line invocation to the muse. The young black poet's interpolation into the biblical narrative of the classical invocation demonstrates a refusal to follow the dictates of convention, and suggests a conscious attempt to syncretize a classical element with Christianity; as a matter of fact, the word "muse" does not occur in either the King James Bible or the Geneva Bible. Another sign of conscious syncretism is the enormous role played by the image of the sun in Wheatley's poetry; solar images far outnumber all others. Especially noteworthy here is that her use of this image greatly exceeds the conventional sun-Son (Jesus as the Christ) motif.

Her mother's solar worship surely is the source of her exaltation of the sun, which she names in her poems nine times as Aurora; as Apollo, seven; as Phoebus, twelve; and as Sol, twice. That she casts this image in terms completely classical provides clear evidence of syncretism of solar worship, Christianity, and classical paganism. George Whitefield, for example, Wheatley laments as "the setting sun." In "Phillis's Reply to the Answer," responding to a poem praising her achievement as a poet, Wheatley describes her native Gambia, in phrases redolent of paradisiacal pastoral, as a realm wherein resides "the tuneful flowing stream, / The soft retreats, the lovers [sic] golden dream"—all conventional enough. What is not quite so conventional is her recollection of Gambia's "soil spontaneous, [which] yields exhaustless stores," and of Phoebus reveling "on her [the river Gambia's] verdant shores." What is not at all the product of European or American convention is her memory of the Gambia region as one "devoted to the God of day!" In her finest poem, "On Imagination," classical paganism, solar worship, and Christianity all merge in the following couplet describing the force of this faculty: "Soaring through air to find the bright abode, / Th' empyreal palace of the thund'ring God." Sun and Zeus with his thunderbolts blend here, constructing one syncretized image of the deity.

Freedom through Imagination: Wheatley's Preromantic Poetics

It is surprising that this intelligent young woman's rebellion against practitioners of the Christian religion—whose tenets emboldened her, at the early age of fifteen, to chide a practically all-white audience in the daring lines of "On Being Brought"—apparently went unnoticed. Several years later, in a 1774 letter to Samson Occom, Wheatley asserts her ardent desire to convince the good Christian citizens of colonial New England of "the strange Absurdity of their Conduct whose Words and Actions are so diametrically opposite. How well the Cry for Liberty, and the reverse Disposition for the Exercise of oppressive Power over others agree,— I humbly think it does not require the Penetration of a Philosopher to determine." This letter appeared in print six times in 1774 and many other times in the following year. Age and experience had not encouraged Wheatley to trust the promises either of her white captors or of their versions of Christianity. She wanted freedom now, in this world, and it is clear she was thoroughly impatient to obtain it. Despite the fact that she was legally manumitted at least by October 18, 1773, shortly after her return from London, where she had seen her *Poems* through the press, the one ground upon which she moved with greatest freedom was the world in her poems. Since the most poignant expression of her personal quest for freedom occurs in "On Imagination," this poem demands close scrutiny.

The poem opens with this arresting four-line apostrophe:

> Thy various works, imperial queen, we see,
> How bright their forms! how deck'd with
>   pomp by thee!
> Thy wond'rous acts in beauteous order
>   stand,
> And all attest how potent is thine hand.

"Thy" of the first line refers to the imagination named in the poem's title. Clearly, for Wheatley imagination exercises a regal presence in full control of her "various works," the poems of the poet. This faculty empowers the poet to build "bright . . . forms" or structures—poetic genres—that she or he ornaments with magnificent or dignified display. Here Wheatley shows herself to be schooled thoroughly in the practice of what William Wordsworth later called poetic diction, and it is worth noting that she revels in this display. Indeed, her entire oeuvre is characterized by a sincere, exhilarated intention to adorn her poetry with elaborate images and by a palpable fascination with her capacity to achieve such adornment. In her own words, "it does not require the Penetration of a Philosopher to determine" that the desire to deck her poetic world in pomp distances that pleasant world from the real world of New England, which she elsewhere describes as "oppress'd with woes, a painful endless train." Wheatley insists that the "wond'rous acts" of imagination, her poems, must stand or arrange themselves "in beauteous order"; in just the same manner, she stubbornly arranges the over-whelming majority of her lines within the restrictions of the neoclassical heroic couplet.

Seldom does she depart from the strict regularity of the couplet or from the rhythmic pattern of the iambic pentameter line. Yet it is her constant desire to ascend to her God, to reach that realm to which she so often appeals in her elegies, as in "To a Clergyman on the Death of His Lady" (1772):

> Where contemplation finds her sacred
>   spring,
> Where heav'nly music makes the arches
>   ring,
> Where virtue reigns unsully'd and divine,
> Where wisdom thron'd, and all the graces
>   shine.

This "vertical" desire to reach her God, to escape to a wholly different world from that of unsympathetic Boston, is juxtaposed to her stubborn adherence to the horizontal order of the iambic pentameter line—hence setting up a tension in her verse between form and content. In other words, the form of most of her poems is firmly grounded in the neoclassicism by means of which she learned to cast her thoughts and desires into English verse; the content, however, pulls away from this horizontal regularity, expressing her intense desire to be free. This contest between the horizontal and vertical, between form and content, achieves resolution in the sense of liberation that the finished product affords its creator and subsequently challenges its readers to experience.

The next line of "On Imagination" clarifies her interest in this faculty: "And all attest how potent is thine hand." The referent of "all" must be "wond'rous acts," which have already been identified as her poems. These poems testify how powerful imagination is by lifting her, however temporarily, out of an unsatisfactory world; her poems liberate her. The fact that she follows this apostrophe with her invocation to the muse rather than opening with this convention, a sequence she never fails to follow in any other occasional piece that calls for an invocation, invites two possible explanations. First, in her ecstatic mood she may simply have forgotten to include it first; this possibility is tenuous at best, because as many have noted she made a practice of tireless revision and could easily have reassembled the poem. To have done so, however, would have done violence to her overall plan. The fact that she places "On Imagination" in the center of *Poems* establishes its significance; the poem and its theory constitute the center of her poetics. Although inspiration is of great importance to her, the subject here is imagination, the one faculty by which this young black female slave can experience liberation, albeit briefly. "*Helicon's* refulgent heights," "Ye sacred choir," and "Ye blooming graces" are all entirely conventional phrases; her intense celebration of imagination as the aesthetic principle of liberation, however, is revolutionary.

What occurs in the succeeding quatrain is at least equally revolutionary:

> Now here, now there, the roving *Fancy*
>   flies,
> Till some lov'd object strikes her wand'ring
>   eyes,
> Whose silken fetters all the senses bind,
> And soft captivity involves the mind.

The activities of the fancy include roving indeterminately, wandering about, gathering an object or objects attractive to the senses, and thence involving the mind or prompting it to action—in this case provoking the imagination into the act of poiesis. Wheatley is making a distinction between imagination as the faculty of control, judgment, order, and even (as we will shortly see) creation, and fancy as a subordinate agent in service to imagination.

In this poem, imagination has become a blend of understanding and wisdom, while fancy, no longer synonymous with imagination, has been relegated to serving imagination. Cooper's "heaven-born maid" may well have played a role in Wheatley's redefinition of these faculties, but more is at work here than simple imitation. Wholly committed to her world of poetry for reasons that should now be obvious, Wheatley requires first a theory of poiesis and second details of that theory—in short, an analysis of mental faculties that will describe, to her own satisfaction, the process of composition. In bringing this redefinition of fruition, she discovers that she requires something like reason as controller but a faculty that, as creator as well, is more flexible or malleable ("plastic") than the cold logic of reason.

The earlier poem "Thoughts on the Works of Providence," written in late 1772 or early 1773, suggests the evolution of Wheatley's thought regarding *poiesis*. This entire poem is devoted to contemplation and celebration of the God of nature, whom the poet calls

> . . . monarch of the earth and skies,
> Whose goodness and beneficence appear
> As round its centre moves the rolling year.

Following this syncretized image of the sun, Wheatley finds that "*Wisdom*, which attends *Jehovah's* ways, / Shines most conspicuous in the solar rays." Toward the poem's conclusion, the poet considers the action, or inaction, of the mind in sleep. Acknowledging that "reason's pow'rs by day our God disclose," she asks,

> Say what is sleep? . . .
> When action ceases, and ideas range
> Licentious and unbounded o'er the plains,
> Where *Fancy's* queen in giddy triumph
>   reigns.

Is fancy's queen here reason? Does sleep represent those moments when reason acts to free the mind, to "range / Licentious and unbounded"? The poet continues: "On pleasure now, and now on vengeance bent, / The lab'ring passions struggle for a vent." With pleasure and anger at cross-purposes, mirrored in the chiasmus of this couplet's first line, whatever faculty is active in sleep is much in need of a controller.

The controller Wheatley identifies in this rhetorical question: "What secret hand returns the mental train, / And gives improv'd thine active pow'rs again?" The leader of this mental train is of course reason, which in human beings is an image of the deity's infinite wisdom. An earlier poem written late in 1771, "On Recollection," maintains that these ideas ranging licentiously and unboundedly accumulate as "ample treasure," providing a "pomp of images" that "to the high-raptur'd poet gives . . . aid." In these two poems, Wheatley engages the conscious struggle of developing a poetics that will permit license and freedom in her use of the words she requires. In "On Imagination" she succeeds in constructing a poetics of liberation that allows her to achieve freedom, if not in the real world, then certainly in the aesthetic. This poem's next stanza explains more fully the creative powers of her poetic controller.

"*Imagination!* who can sing thy force?" So the poet begins the passage in which she articulates the most dynamic expression of her theoretical aspirations—with a challenge! The remainder of the poem presents her response to that challenge. "Or who describe the swiftness of thy course?" she continues. As she has pointed out in "Thoughts on the Works of Providence," the force that she has not yet in that poem specifically identified as imagination can carry her mind from contemplation of "that mighty *Sol*" to man himself with astonishing immediacy:

And yet his radiance dazzles mortal sight
So far beneath—from him th' extended
   earth
Vigour derives, and ev'ry flow'ry birth . . .

The character of Wheatley's philosophic contemplation is precisely that which Ernest Tuveson identifies as a celebration of the natural sublime, wherein the celebrant, rather than turning inward in the tradition of medieval meditation, turns outward to focus on the heavenly bodies, the planets, and the stars, made worthy now of such mental activity by the new astronomy. As Tuveson puts it: "Behind this new sensibility was an *intellectus mundi,* an ideal of the fullest comprehension of the external world, which replaced the *contemptus mundi.*" Wheatley's determination to effect the illusion of rapid movement, however, anticipates Kant's description in the 1790 "Analytic of the Sublime" of an especially intense representation of what he calls the mathematical sublime: "The mind feels itself *moved* in the representation of the sublime in nature. . . . This movement may . . . be compared to a vibration, i.e., to a quickly alternating attraction toward, and repulsion from, the same object."

In "On Imagination," Wheatley's lines on the "swiftness of thy course? / Soaring through air to find the bright abode, / Th' empyreal palace of the thund'ring God" initiate a similar movement. With the force of imagination, the poet "on thy pinions can surpass the wind, / And leave the rolling universe behind." From this ethereal vantage point, the subordinate fancy can carry out its task of image gathering: "From star to star the mental optics rove, / Measure the skies, and range the realms above." But only imagination can enable her "in one view" to "grasp the mighty whole." Wheatley here represents the negative pleasure of the sublime, which Kant later analyzed in his *Analytic of the Sublime.* In the next line, she offers a provocative alternative; if one finds oneself repelled by the experience of contemplating the vast, the infinite, one may turn inward to the world of poetic creation: "Or with new worlds amaze th' unbounded soul." The mind, by employing the power of imagination, can thus instantaneously move from contemplation of the infinite heavens to focus on the interior world, no less infinite or "unbounded," of the poet. There are no "silken fetters" here, no wandering or roving; the very definite power of imagination—not the softly captivating agent of imagination, the fancy—brings about this sublime motion.

Then Wheatley does in fact "amaze" her readers, not by speculating about what Newtonian "mental optics" may achieve in wandering about the physical universe, but by demonstrating the power of her own mind to create an interior poetic world: "Though *Winter* frowns to *Fancy's* raptur'd eyes / The fields may flourish, and gay scenes arise." In moving immediately from theoretical discourse to allegorical narration, she ostensibly does violence to the thread of continuity, for there is no transition between the two stanzas. How can Wheatley, who is always so concerned with "bright . . . forms," so unreservedly breach the poem's structure? Before we can answer this question, we must identify the poem's genre. "On Imagination" is arranged into seven stanzas of irregular length: three initial quatrains followed by two stanzas of ten lines, a sixth of only eight and a final stanza of thirteen lines. This relatively indefinite pattern closely resembles that of the irregular ode. Although Wheatley was well acquainted with the wholly conventional couplet, hymn stanza, and blank verse of one poetic mentor, Mather Byles, she must have been equally acquainted with Cooper's two Horatian odes in the *Pietas* volume. Even so, the irregular stanzaic pattern of this poem, despite its use of couplets (Wheatley's favorite form), bespeaks the looser structure of the irregular ode. As Wheatley experimented with both the Horatian ode and the epyllion, she also experimented with the most lyric genre, the irregular ode.

This marked tendency toward experimentation in Wheatley all the more suggests the rebel rather than the alleged quiet, derivative imitator. The fact that she retains the regular rhythm of the couplet might be explained by her obvious preference for this verse form. Here, however, Wheatley simply requires a genre that will enable her to express her maturing poetics, and her search has led her to adapt the irregular ode to her couplets. What results is a stanzaic pattern that, certainly at this point in the poem, appears to do battle with the poem's content, thereby underscoring the tension the poet feels between neoclassical form (despite her facility) and what is becoming identifiable as Romantic content. We may even go so far as to say her use of ode here suggests she had both forms (with qualifications) and content in common with the Romantics.

Wheatley's creation of a transcendent world, however modest, heralds her affinity with the Romantics of the early nineteenth century. Even though winter and its "frozen deeps" prevail in the real world, the imagination can take one out of unpleasant reality and can build, with the aid of a fancy whose "raptur'd eyes" collect images, a pleasant, mythic world of fragrant flowers and verdant groves where "Fair *Flora*" spreads "her fragrant reign" and Sylvanus crowns the forest with leaves, and where

"Show'rs may descend, and dews their gems disclose, / And nectar sparkle on the blooming rose." Not satisfied that she has sufficiently explicated the power of imagination, Wheatley continues in the sixth stanza: "Such is thy pow'r, nor are thine orders vain, / O thou the leader of the mental train." Contrary to the fancy whose eyes are "raptur'd," imagination arranges "in full perfection all thy works." To this powerful faculty Wheatley attributes "the sceptre o'er the realms of thought." Such phrases as "leaders of the mental train," echoing Thomas Hobbes's *Leviathan*, and ruler over "the realms of thought" exalt the power of what most in the late seventeenth and eighteenth centuries called reason. Unlike Hobbes, however, whose "Trayne of thoughts" or imagination leads, without the check of reason, inevitably into error, Wheatley's imagination can even subject the passions, which in "Thoughts on the Works of Providence" are ever "lab'ring . . . for a vent": "Of subject-passions sov'reign ruler Thou." For this young slave poet (Wheatley had not yet been freed), her mighty imagination has but to command and "joy rushes on the heart."

Reluctant to leave her created world of ecstatic transcendence, Wheatley suggests in her final stanza that "*Fancy* might now her silken pinions try / To rise from earth, and sweep th' expanse on high." Once again she describes this faculty's function as before, with the delicate qualifier "silken"; fancy again lacks the overwhelming power of imagination. Fancy, nevertheless, discovers to the poet's imagination a vivid image of her mother's dawning sun, which Wheatley here calls Aurora: "Her cheeks all glowing . . . / While a pure stream of light o'erflows the skies." But after accomplishing a second, however brief, foray into an ideal world, Wheatley recognizes how limited is any poet's capacity to sustain indefinitely a poetic world; for as John Keats would later acknowledge of his immortal bird, she says, "But I reluctant leave the pleasing views, / Which *Fancy* dresses to delight the *Muse*." Rather than the dignified decorator that arranges all in pomp and "beauteous order," fancy is merely the dresser, not the organizer and creator. This couplet suggests that the distinction between fancy and imagination is, as has been implicit throughout the poem, one of degree, anticipating Samuel Taylor Coleridge's distinction between the primary imagination of all persons (that which, in Wheatley's terms, delights the muse) and the secondary creative power of the poet, which "dissolves, diffuses, dissipates, in order to re-create" (or in Wheatley's terms, which builds "new worlds [to] amaze th' unbounded soul").

It is winter's gelid reality that intrudes upon Wheatley's poetic world and "forbids *me* to aspire"; I add the italics here to emphasize that what the poet has been describing is her own intensely personal statement of release. "Northern tempests damp the rising fire," however, and "chill the tides of *Fancy's* flowing sea," causing the poet to close "the unequal lay." Bitter reality, however regrettably, must bring an inexorable end, even to the ecstatic energy of a flowing sea successively furnishing a flood of images to the creative imagination. Wheatley's song is unequal to the overpowering force of imagination simply because the force she describes is, finally, the poet's reason, not that of the real world. Reification must eventually yield to concrete reality. Wheatley nevertheless achieves in this poem an entirely fulfilling liberation, a temporary release from pain within a pastoral, Edenic realm of joy, ruled by a principal of order, wherein she can reside in safety—the product of her own creative imagination.

In this poem especially, this pre-Revolutionary War poet has recorded the primary motivation behind the struggle for American freedom. Her achievement is even more remarkable, however, when one observes that her imagination resonates with the same thought that brings Wordsworth, in the *Prelude*, to call this faculty "Reason in her most exalted mood"; when one recognizes in her lines the sublime celebration of nature; when one understands that, despite all her occasional elegies, she prefers the intimacy of the lyric; and when one discovers that she carries out experiments with that genre. Wheatley clearly participates in the thought that prefigures the Romantic movement. She even develops a theory of imagination, in 1773, that exceeds anything of the kind in the British Isles.

Not the white man's religion, not his politics, and not even his poetics, as learned by this brilliant, maturing poet, could answer her one overwhelming need—to be free. So, intelligent and sensitive artist that she was, Wheatley stubbornly hoped for political equality (though I doubt she would have found satisfying the Constitution ratified in 1789) but adapted the various religious elements known to her for her own needs; and, most significant for the course of American literary aesthetics, she developed a striking, new theory of poetry—one based on the more pliable promises offered by a poetry of imagination.

In America before 1773, both Cooper and Philip Freneau in his "Power of Fancy" had identified imagination in similar ways as wisdom and as "regent of the mind" (Freneau); and the British poet William Collins had called the power of fancy a divine gift. It was Wheatley, however, who for the first time, pressed by her predicament as a black woman slave, identified imagination as sublime mediator between man and God in the act of *poiesis*. For her, imagination is not merely the initiator of the meditative process leading toward absolute freedom; it is itself the very means to secure, even if only temporarily, release from a world "oppress'd with woes, a painful endless train." Nothing quite like this dynamic theory of imagination, so intimately commingled with and fired by the political struggle for American independence, was achieved in British poetics until the Romantic movement.

Breaking through the myth of the pseudo-Wheatley reveals that, contrary to conventional wisdom, this poet at the age of only nineteen or twenty had already developed a sophisticated theory of poetry that one may justifiably call a poetics of liberation. After her manumission, and with the prospect of freedom for black people that the gathering tides of the American Revolution *seemed* to promise, Wheatley came to speak out more directly regarding freedom for her black brothers and sisters. While Wheatley would have been chagrined by the Constitution of the United States (had she lived to see it), she nonetheless worked diligently with her pen to bolster the American pursuit of independence. For example, Wheatley's now-famous 1774 letter to Occom contains one of the most eloquent expressions of the quest for human freedom: "In every human Breast, God has implanted a Principle, which we call Love of Freedom; it is impatient of Oppression, and pants for Deliverance." This letter was reproduced more than than a dozen times in American newspapers before 1780.

Only a year and a half later, in 1775, we find Wheatley corresponding with the "Generalissimo of the armies of North America," George Washington, and penning "To His Excellency General Washington," which concludes with this often-quoted couplet, "A crown, a mansion, and a throne that shine, / With gold unfading, WASHINGTON! be thine." In Washington's reply to this personal encomium and paean to freedom, he invited the poet to visit him; according to Benson J. Lossing's *Field Book of the Revolution* (1860), Washington and Wheatley actually did meet at his Cambridge, Massachusetts, headquarters. Having passed along the poem to his former secretary, Colonal Joseph Reed, Washington, perhaps unwittingly, virtually assured that this poem would appear in several American publications during 1776.

Following the death in March 1778 of John Wheatley, her former master, the poet married John Peters on April 1. This move was in part an attempt to better her condition, as John Wheatley no longer supported her and apparently left no provision for her in his will. Peters had now acquired a reputation as an advocate before the courts, a shopkeeper, and a jack-of-all-trades, and must have seemed to Wheatley a likely provider. A possible reason her former master left her nothing was because both he and Nathaniel had remained in England since the summer of 1773. Contrary to another particle of conventional wisdom, Wheatley was not a loyalist but was instead a committed American patriot. Such a difference in political alignment must have provoked bad feeling between the poet, and John and his son, perhaps explaining why, though Wheatley was so care-

ful about commemorating persons she knew in elegies, there is no mention in her proposal for a new volume in 1779 of an elegy on the death of her former master. Despite her efforts to better her situation through marriage to Peters and owing to the vicissitudes brought on by the Revolutionary War, her decline apparently continued, for surely only some such desperation would have prompted her to appeal to the same audience in 1779 who had refused her in 1772— this later attempt exacerbated by the severe economic conditions prevailing during the heat of the Revolution.

As before, this attempt to elicit support from the Boston public failed. One of the few poems recovered from the thirty-three titles listed in the proposal attests her determination to contribute to the struggle for the manumission of all black people. Not recovered until 1980, "On the Death of General Wooster," with whose subject Wheatley had carried on a correspondence, includes an impassioned hope that the attainment of freedom from Britain will be accompanied by the granting of freedom for her black brothers and sisters. That the poet has doubts about whether that promise will prove true is strongly suggested by the obvious impatience of these lines that Wheatley, showing her flare for the dramatic, gives to the deceased Wooster speaking from his heavenly home:

> But how, presumptuous shall we hope to find
> Divine acceptance with th' Almighty mind—
> While yet (O deed Ungenerous!) they disgrace
> And hold in bondage Afric's blameless race?

The poet places this final plea in the mouth of one who has so recently given his life in battle (in July 1778) toward the achievement of what was to be, in Wheatley's mind, freedom for *all:* "Let Virtue reign—And thou accord our prayers / Be victory our's [*sic*], and generous freedom theirs."

The last year of Wheatley's life finds her still writing in the cause of freedom. Doubtlessly composed as a celebration of the Treaty of Paris of 1783 ending the Revolution and establishing America's independence, "Liberty and Peace" contains some of Wheatley's best lines. In phrases that find relevance today, Wheatley observes that "new-born *Rome*" has "to every Realm her Portals open'd wide" and still "receives from each [Realm] the full commercial Tide." She hopes the world will now see the end of "that Thirst of boundless Power, that drew, / On *Albion's* [England's] Head the Curse to Tyrants due." The following set of couplets articulates well the primary concerns of the poet:

> As for the East th' illustrious King of Day,
> With rising Radiance drives the Shades
>   away,
> So Freedom comes array'd with Charms
>   divine,
> And in her Train Commerce and Plenty
>   shine.

How appalled would this optimistic poet have been by the failure of freedom's promise for black people—how dashed her hopes! Alone, unattended, and preceded in death by her three children, Phillis Wheatley, once internationally celebrated, died on December 5, 1784, almost certainly from infection from the birth of her third child and from starvation. She deserved better then, and she deserves better now.

Selected Bibliography

PRIMARY WORKS

EARLY EDITIONS

Poems on Various Subjects, Religious and Moral. London: A. Bell, 1773.
Letters of Phillis Wheatley, The Negro-Slave Poet of Boston. Edited by Charles Deane. Boston: Privately printed by J. Wilson and Son, 1864.

RECENT EDITIONS

Mason, Julian D., Jr., ed. *The Poems of Phillis Wheatley.* Edited and with an introduction by Julian D. Mason Jr. Revised and enlarged edition. Chapel Hill: University of North Carolina Press, 1989.
Robinson, William H. *Phillis Wheatley and Her Writings.* New York: Garland, 1984. (Includes the memoir written by Margaretta Matilda Oddell of Jamaica

Plains that was appended to the 1834 Boston reprint of Wheatley's *Poems* as Appendix D. pp. 430–50.)
Shields, John C., ed. *The Collected Works of Phillis Wheatley.* Edited and with an essay by John C. Shields. New York: Oxford University Press, 1988.

SECONDARY WORKS

BIOGRAPHICAL AND CRITICAL STUDIES

Akers, Charles W. " 'Our Modern Egyptians': Phillis Wheatley and the Whig Campaign against Slavery in Revolutionary Boston." *Journal of Negro History* 60: 397–410 (July 1975).
Bassard, Katherine C. *Spiritual Interrogations: Culture, Gender, and Community in Early African American Women's Writing.* Princeton, N.J.: Princeton University Press, 1999. (With two important chapters on Wheatley.)
Bennett, Paula. "Phillis Wheatley's Vocation and the Paradox of the 'Afric Muse.' " *PMLA* 113, no. 1:64–76 (January 1998). (This issue features a special topic, ethnicity.)
Burke, Helen M. "The Rhetoric and Politics of Marginality: The Subject of Phillis Wheatley." *Tulsa Studies in Women's Literature* 10, no. 1:31–45 (Spring 1991).
Cavell, Anthony J. *Jackson State Review* 6 (Summer 1974). (Special issue reporting on the proceedings of and presenting papers delivered at the Phillis Wheatley Poetry Festival celebrating the bicentennial of the publication of Wheatley's *Poems*, November 4–7, 1973.)
Collins, Terrence. "Phillis Wheatley: The Dark Side of the Poetry." *Phylon* 36:78–88 (March 1975).
Dathorne, O. R. *The Black Mind: A History of African Literature.* Minneapolis: University of Minnesota Press, 1972.
Davis, Arthur P. "Personal Elements in the Poetry of Phillis Wheatley." *Phylon* 12, no. 2:191–98 (Second Quarter 1953). (Reprinted in William H. Robinson, ed. *Critical Essays on Phillis Wheatley.*)
Felker, Christopher D. " 'The Tongues of the learned are insufficient': Phillis Wheatley, Publishing Objectives, and Personal Liberty." *Resources for American Literary Study* 20, no. 2:149–79 (1994).
Finnegan, Ruth. *Oral Literature in Africa.* Nairobi: Oxford University Press, 1970.
Flanzbaum, Hilene. "Unprecedented Liberties: Re-reading Phillis Wheatley." *MELUS* 18, no. 3:71–80 (Fall 1993).
Foster, Frances Smith. *Written by Herself: Literary Production by African American Women, 1746–1892.* Bloomington, Ind.: Indiana University Press, 1993. (Pages 30–43 discuss Wheatley.)
Grimsted, David. "Anglo-American Racism and Phillis Wheatley's Sable Veil, 'Length'nd Chain,' and 'Knitted Heart.' " In *Women in the Age of the American Revolution.* Edited by Ronald Hoffman and Peter J. Albert. Charlottesville: University Press of Virginia, 1989. Pp. 338–444.

Isani, Mukhtar Ali. " 'Gambia on My Soul': Africa and the Africans in the Writings of Phillis Wheatley." *MELUS* 6, no. 1:64–72 (1979).

———. "The British Reception of Wheatley's *Poems on Various Subjects*." *Journal of Negro History* 66, no. 2:144–49 (Summer 1981).

———. "The Methodist Connection: New Variants of Some Phillis Wheatley Poems." *Early American Literature* 22:108–13 (Spring 1987).

Kendrick, Robert L. "Snatching a Laurel, Wearing a Mask: Phillis Wheatley's Literary Nationalism and the Problem of Style," *Style* 27, no. 2:222–51 (Summer 1993).

Levernier, James A., Jr. "Wheatley's ON BEING BROUGHT FROM AFRICA TO AMERICA." *Explicator* 40:25–26 (Fall 1981).

———. "Style as Protest in the Poetry of Phillis Wheatley." *Style* 27, no. 2:172–93 (Summer 1993).

Makouta-Mboukou, Jean-Pierre. *Black African Literature: An Introduction.* Translated by Alexandre Mboukou. Washington, D.C.: Black Orpheus Press, 1973.

Mason, Julian. " 'Ocean': A New Poem by Phillis Wheatley." *Early American Literature* 34, no. 1:78–83 (Winter 1999). (The poem "Ocean" appears on pages 78–80.)

Nott, Walt. "From 'uncultivated Barbarian' to 'Poetical Genius': The Public Presence of Phillis Wheatley." *MELUS* 18, no. 3:21–32 (Fall 1993).

Oddell, Margaretta M. *Memoir and Poems of Phillis Wheatley: A Native African and a Slave.* Boston: G. W. Light, 1834.

Okpewho, Isidore. *The Epic in Africa: Toward a Poetics of the Oral Performance.* New York: Columbia University Press, 1979.

O'Neale, Sondra A. "Phillis Wheatley." In *Dictionary of Literary Biography: American Colonial Writers, 1735–1781.* Vol. 31. Edited by Emory Elliott. Detroit: Gale Research, 1984. Pp. 260–67.

———. "A Slave's Subtle War: Phillis Wheatley's Use of Biblical Myth and Symbol." *Early American Literature* 21, no. 2:144–65 (Fall 1986).

Reising, Russell J. "Trafficking in White: Phillis Wheatley's Semiotics of Radical Representation." *Genre* 22, no. 3:231–61 (Fall 1989).

Richards, Phillip M. "Phillis Wheatley and Literary Americanization." *American Quarterly* 44, no. 2:163–91 (June 1992).

———. "Phillis Wheatley, Americanization, the Sublime, and the Romance of America," *Style* 27, no. 2:194–221 (Summer 1993).

Richmond, Merle A. *Bid the Vassal Soar: Interpretive Essays on the Life and Poetry of Phillis Wheatley (ca. 1753–1784) and George Moses Horton (ca. 1797–1883).* Washington, D.C.: Howard University Press, 1974.

Robinson, William H. "Phillis Wheatley: Colonial Quandary." *College Language Association Journal* 9:25–38 (September 1965).

———. *Phillis Wheatley in the Black American Beginnings.* Detroit: Broadside Press, 1975.

———. "Phillis Wheatley in London." *College Language Association Journal* 21:187–201 (December 1977).

———. *Black New England Letters: The Uses of Writing in Black New England.* Boston: Boston Public Library, 1977.

———, ed. *Critical Essays on Phillis Wheatley.* Boston: G. K. Hall, 1982.

Rogal, Samuel J. "Phillis Wheatley's Methodist Connection." *Black American Literature Forum* 21:85–95 (Spring–Summer 1987).

Shields, John C. "Phillis Wheatley and Mather Byles: A Study in Literary Relationship." *College Language Association Journal* 23:377–90 (June 1980).

———. "Phillis Wheatley's Struggle for Freedom in Her Poetry and Prose." In *The Collected Works of Phillis Wheatley.* Edited and with an essay by John C. Shields. New York: Oxford University Press, 1988. Pp. 229–70, 324–36.

———. "Phillis Wheatley's Subversion of Classical Stylistics," *Style* 27, no. 2:252–70 (Summer 1993).

———. "Phillis Wheatley's Subversive Pastoral." *Eighteenth-Century Studies* 27, no. 4 (Summer 1994), 631–47.

———, guest editor. *Style* 27, no. 2 (Summer 1993); special issue: *African-American Poetics.* (See the entries for the following individual authors for their essays on Wheatley included in this issue: Kendrick, Levernier, Richards, and Shields.)

Shipton, Clifford. *Sibley's Biographical Sketches of Those Who Attended Harvard College.* Vol. 11 (1741–1745). Cambridge, Mass.: Charles William Sever, University Bookstore, 1960

Silverman, Kenneth. "Four New Letters by Phillis Wheatley." *Early American Literature* 8, no. 3:257–71 (Winter 1974).

Smith, Cynthia J. " 'To Maecenas': Phillis Wheatley's Invocation of an Idealized Reader." *Black American Literature Forum* 23, no. 3:579–92 (Fall 1989).

Tuveson, Ernest. "Space, Deity, and the 'Natural Sublime.' " *Modern Language Quarterly* 12:20–38 (March 1951).

Zafar, Rafia. *We Wear the Mask: African Americans Write American Literature, 1760–1870.* New York: Columbia University Press, 1997. (Contains an important chapter covering Wheatley, pp. 15–39.)

MAJOR ARCHIVAL COLLECTIONS

First editions, letters, original manuscripts, and other Wheatleyana may be seen in collections at the Boston Public Library; Dartmouth College Library; Duke University Library; Massachusetts Historical Society; Historical Society of Pennsylvania; Library Company of Philadelphia; American Antiquarian Society; Harvard University's Houghton Library (including Wheatley's signed copy of Milton's *Paradise Lost*); New York City's Public Library: The Schomburg Center for Research in Black Culture (perhaps the most extensive holdings); the University of Illinois Rare Book Room (contains a copy of the 1773 *Poems* sewn together with a copy of Alexander Pope's *Essay on Man*); the University of North Carolina's Rare Book Room (Charlotte; houses all the volumes of Pope's *Works* owned and signed by Wheatley, obtained through the efforts of Julian Mason); Cornell University's Rare Book Room; Churchill College, Cambridge, England; The Scottish Record Office, Edinburgh; William Salt Library, Staffordshire, England; Cheshunt Foundation, Cambridge University; and the British Museum Library, London.

BIBLIOGRAPHICAL STUDY

Robinson, William H. *Phillis Wheatley: A Bio-Bibliography*. Boston: Hall, 1981.

—This article was written under the auspices of a National Endowment for the Humanities Summer Seminar Grant.

JOHN EDGAR WIDEMAN
(1941–   )

JAMES W. COLEMAN

DURING HIS EXTRAORDINARY career, John Edgar Wideman has admirably tried to carry out his responsibility as a writer. The evolution of this responsibility has increasingly moved him and his writing from more purely aesthetic concerns toward using his phenomenal artistry to address issues in black political and social life and to address exigencies in his own family life. His writing records both the satisfaction and the suffering consequent to his evolving quest. His scholarly and creative gifts were recognized early and won him international renown in 1963 when he became the second black student to win a Rhodes Scholarship, preceded in this honor only by Alain Locke over half a century earlier. In the years since, he has received numerous academic awards and grants and found an increasingly enthusiastic audience for his fiction, twice winning the P.E.N. Faulkner Award for Fiction, in 1984 for his novel *Sent for You Yesterday* and in 1990 for his novel *Philadelphia Fire*. He was also a MacArthur Foundation Fellowship recipient in 1993 for his creative work. His works also reflect family tragedy, however. His autobiographical books include *Brothers and Keepers* (1984), in which he discusses his relationship with his brother, who is serving a life sentence without parole for murder. And much of his major fictional and nonfictional work since 1989 reveals his own efforts to bond with his incarcerated

son Jake. The writing shows that the situation of his son and brother cannot be separated from the influence of race and racism on his larger family, on the black community of his hometown Pittsburgh, and on black people in America and Western society generally. In his fiction as well as his nonfiction, Wideman continues to revise and expand his role as a writer and intellectual who brings great artistry to bear on the political and personal.

Wideman was born on June 14, 1941, in Washington, D.C., to Edgar and Bette French Wideman, who were poor but self-sufficient, and he spent his early years in Homewood, a black section of Pittsburgh, Pennsylvania. He remembers Homewood fondly, and places much of his fiction there. After his family moved to Shadyside, a more prosperous and predominantly white section of Pittsburgh, Wideman attended the integrated Peabody High School. At Peabody, Wideman's interactions with the white student populace were eased by his athletic and scholastic skills: he starred on the basketball team, became senior class president, and earned valedictorian honors. His life became racially compartmentalized as he associated with white students in the classroom and the gym, and with black friends outside the academic setting.

This dichotomy was strengthened at the University of Pennsylvania (in Philadelphia), where Wideman received a Benjamin Franklin Scholarship for his achievements in academics and athletics, and majored first in psychology and then in English. He has described his university years as a theatrical performance—playing various roles that required a disorienting personal fragmentation. However uncomfortable his social life may have been, his Phi Beta Kappa academic performance won him a Rhodes Scholarship to study at Oxford University.

During his three years at Oxford, Wideman wrote a thesis on the eighteenth-century novel, led Oxford's team to capture England's amateur basketball championship, and married Judith Ann Goldman of Virginia. Returning to the United States with a bachelor of philosophy degree from Oxford in 1966, Wideman spent a year as a Kent Fellow at the University of Iowa's Creative Writing Workshop. He left Iowa to teach English at the University of Pennsylvania, where he became that university's first black tenured professor in 1974. Some of his black students requested that he teach a course in black literature, and, according to recollections recorded by Susan Fromberg Schaeffer, he remembers his reaction with chagrin:

> I gave them the jive reply that it wasn't my field. . . . I was one of the few black faculty members at Penn; they came to me for all kinds of soulful reasons, and I gave them the stock academic reply, which was true. But I felt so ashamed that I got back in touch with some of them, agreed to teach the course—and began my second education.

His only encounter with black literature at that point had been a perfunctory reading of Ralph Ellison. He began reading widely in this field and the course went well, but he was pained to discover how far he had drifted from black American culture, and especially from his family in Homewood. His efforts to bridge this gap led him to chair the University of Pennsylvania's first Afro-American studies program between 1970 and 1973, and radically altered his approach to his own writing.

A Glance Away

He published his first novel, *A Glance Away*, in 1967, when he was twenty-six. The main character in this novel, Robert Thurley, has reminded some readers of T. S. Eliot's J. Alfred Prufrock and Gerontion: much of the narrative delineates Thurley's frustration and despair in excruciatingly precise detail. Thurley is an ineffectual English professor who dissipates his energies in casual homosexual affairs with black men he picks up in bars. We better understand his self-destructive behavior after we see him in an involuntary ménage à trois, intimidated into bed with his domineering wife and his best friend, Al. Thurley is a victim of his own passivity.

Eddie Lawson, the novel's most important black character, is the best friend of one of Thurley's occasional sexual partners, the albino Brother Small. Eddie is a newly rehabilitated drug addict whose return home from a yearlong drug treatment program on Easter Sunday should signal his resurrection and rebirth. But his return to his family and community locks him into the same meaningless, absurd life that drove him to drugs in the first place. Eddie's mother, inconsolably mourning the death of her favorite and firstborn son, dies on Easter Sunday. Eddie and his sister Bette are paralyzed by this new loss: Bette's life in the shadow of her mother's cold, arid grief has not prepared her for self-directed action, and Eddie is crushed by depression. Thurley, improbably, becomes Eddie's only hope for change. As Eddie begins to turn back to drugs, Thurley breathes the fresh air of personal resurrection in a scene reminiscent of the final lines of T. S. Eliot's *The Waste Land*. Near the end of the novel, Eddie, Thurley, and Brother sit in the Bum's Forest at the edge of the black community as Thurley tries to share some of his newfound hope. Like the ending of *The Waste Land*, the close of *A Glance Away* is uncertain; the tenuous and fragile hope Thurley imparts cannot outweigh the pessimistic vision Wideman paints in the preceding pages.

Significantly, Wideman explores none of the black traditions that might lend meaningful content and coherence to Eddie's community. *A Glance Away* formally and thematically evokes comparisons with the works of Eliot, Joyce, Camus, and other white modernist masters. Although the book was favorably received by reviewers, its portrayal of black life is founded in the white modernist tradition of linguistic experimentation and literary allusion. Some reviewers praised the emotional power of the novel's language, but others remarked on Wideman's artistry, his originality, and his erudition rather than noting any convincing emotional investment in the racial identity of the characters.

While Wideman's critics may find the modernist techniques of *A Glance Away* inappropriately derivative of white aesthetic practices, Wideman's mastery of those techniques is nonetheless impressive. He builds upon and develops the narratological innovations of Joyce, Eliot, and Faulkner in his experiments with wordplay, stream of consciousness, surrealistic imagery, and multiple points of view. In Wideman's early novels, these experiments are detached from the rich African American arts and history that would make these works distinctly expressive of the black experience. Only in his later work does Wideman develop a vibrant black voice incorporating modernist techniques into the dominant chords of the black cultural tradition.

Hurry Home and *Lynchers*

His second novel, *Hurry Home* (1970), focuses on the struggle of a black intellectual alienated from the black community. The novel's obscure surrealism and occasionally impenetrable passages of stream-of-consciousness narration are again indebted—albeit less slavishly than in the first novel—to the literary masterpieces canonized by the white academic community. While *A Glance Away* accents the redemption of the white main character more than that of the black, relegating Eddie to the position of contrasting foil, Wideman chooses a black main character for *Hurry Home*. Cecil Braithwaite is irremediably black, despite his attempts to

John Edgar Wideman

avoid this realization, and the plot of the novel traces those efforts. Wideman shapes his modernist forms to accommodate the specific necessities of Cecil's estranged blackness, and *Hurry Home* provides one of the most intense and memorable portrayals of black alienation in American literature.

Cecil has symbolically escaped the ghetto when he graduates from law school; on graduation day, he tries physically to escape his origins by traveling to Spain and Africa. The novel centers on his inability to stay away, to sever the psychological and physical ties that pull him back to his wife, his community, and his assigned place in American society. His role as a black intellectual in the black community remains a very precarious one, fraught with problems Wideman does not resolve here, and must treat again in his next novel, *The Lynchers* (1973).

In *The Lynchers*, Wideman uses black vernacular dialect, black historical tradition, and black racial feeling to create a more powerful narrative. Despite its energy, the book remains problematic, as Wideman later recognized himself: it articulates a myth of the black community that emphasizes only pain, suffering, degradation, and hopelessness. In the introductory section, "Matter Prefatory," Wideman documents the injustices and atrocities of white oppression; these horrific historical anecdotes carry such force that the present seems overdetermined. The legacy of such a brutalizing history seems both unbearable and inescapable. Wideman chooses records of lynchings that scar in the very reading, such as the account that appeared in the Memphis *Press* of January 27, 1921:

> More than 500 persons stood by and looked on while the Negro was slowly burned to a crisp. A few women were scattered among the crowd of Arkansas planters. . . . Inch by inch the Negro was fairly cooked to death. Every few minutes fresh leaves were tossed on the funeral pyre until the blaze had passed the Negro's waist. (p. 15)

Wideman follows this appalling preface with the story of a contemporary attempt at vengeance, a failed black conspiracy to lynch one representative white policeman in symbolic reparation for the thousands of black lives lost to the lynching rituals of the preceding centuries.

In *Discipline and Punish* (1978), Michel Foucault describes two stages in the history of capital punishment: the spectacular, public display of dramatic power and the modern execution concealed and "civilized" behind discreet prison walls and a profusion of judicial and ancillary offices. Wideman anticipated Foucault in describing those two stages in *The Lynchers*. The lynching planned for the white policeman, modeled precisely on the barbaric murders it protests, is historically displaced in an era of more subtle persecution than that described in the "Matter Prefatory." Contemporary capital punishment reveals no identifiable hand torching the gasoline-soaked leaves, as Foucault tells us:

Punishment, then, will tend to become the most hidden part of the penal process. . . . As a result, justice no longer takes public responsibility for the violence that is bound up with its practice. . . . The apportioning of blame is redistributed. . . . justice is relieved of responsibility for [executing the penalty] by a bureaucratic concealment of the penalty itself.

In *The Lynchers*, the plan to lynch the policeman originates with Willie Hall ("Littleman"), a brilliant but uneducated ideologue. Of all the characters in *The Lynchers*, Littleman feels the weight of black history most intensely. He wants to galvanize the collective will of black people and to provoke a confrontation with the white authorities:

> What this town needs is a good old fashioned lynching. The real thing. With all the trimmings. It would be like going to church. Puts things in their proper perspective. Reminding everybody of who they are, where they stand. Divides the world simple and pure. Good or bad. Oppressors and oppressed. Black or white. Things tend to get a little fuzzy here in the big city. We need ritual. A spectacular.

Littleman is responding not only to the spectacular lynchings and burnings of the past, but also to the insidiously miasmic and amorphous nature of political suppression in the present. Modern forms of white domination cannot be traced to individual perpetrators. The oppressed blacks of Littleman's northern community are burdened with the memory of crimes against their race and yet disallowed repayment in kind for the carnival pageants of nineteenth- and early-twentieth-century southern lynchings. As Trudier Harris notes in her excellent analysis of this novel, Littleman's plan must fail, in part because there "is no repression immediate enough to mid-twentieth century Philadelphia to make the black men feel the wrongs committed against them as acutely as would a black community which had, say, witnessed a lynching in Mississippi around the same time." The history recounted in Wideman's "Matter Prefatory" has left its mark on the characters in the following story, but it has become abstract, mediated by time just as contemporary repression is mediated by a maze of bureaucratic agencies. Littleman's dream of revenge dies unrealized when, trying to incite a riot, he is beaten nearly to death by the police; as the novel ends, he is incarcerated in a hospital ward that he clearly will never leave.

Littleman's plan never reaches the black community, but he does share it with three other characters; all three fail to make Littleman's plan a reality, for various reasons. Thomas Wilkerson, more formally educated than Littleman, thinks too long about the plan and finds he cannot bring himself to kill according to Littleman's scenario. He becomes hopelessly tangled in intellectual paradoxes; before he can extricate himself, he is shot by Graham Rice, a suspicious and resentful co-conspirator. In the character of the fourth conspirator, Leonard Saunders, Wideman shows us the twisted product of modern white oppression. Through a childhood molded and marked by the intervention of various social and medical agencies, Saunders acquires a chilling detachment from his people. But, like Wilkerson, Saunders is ultimately foiled by his own conscience. Littleman's plan to kill the white policeman involved the preliminary murder of a black prostitute, and even Saunders' visceral rage is not enough to justify sacrificing yet another black victim. While Rice turns his aggression against Wilkerson, Saunders turns his against himself, drowning in his own "seas of blood, of bile and phlegm and sickly meandering whiskey." The historical oppression of ritualized murder has been completely internalized in Saunders, as in the other characters. As Littleman would have perpetuated the white ritual of lynching, the larger black community in *The Lynchers* is self-destructing in less shocking ways by perpetuating patterns that have afflicted it in the past.

The Homewood Trilogy: *Hiding Place, Damballah,* and *Sent for You Yesterday*

The Lynchers represented both a major literary achievement for Wideman and a crisis in his writing career. In 1973, he moved west with his family to teach English at the University of Wyoming at Laramie, and he published nothing more until 1981. During his "second education" teaching black literature at the University of Pennsylvania, he had reached a creative impasse, realizing that he did not have the tools to reconstruct the black world after it had broken apart in *The Lynchers.* In Wyoming, he continued reading nineteenth- and twentieth-century black writers, and wrote essays on their approaches to the problem of developing a legitimate black voice within a white literary tradition. Paradoxically, it was while living at a distance from his origins that he decided to mine more deeply the traditional materials of his Homewood community, which he had lightly touched in *A Glance Away.* The result was *Hiding Place* (1981), the first volume of what Wideman has called *The Homewood Trilogy.*

Wideman again wrestles with the problem of alienation in *Hiding Place,* and modernist techniques continue to be an influence on this work. However, he differentiates the novel from his earlier work by using the myths and traditions of his own family and the Homewood community to draw his characters out of their personal isolation. In an interview with Charles Rowell, Wideman describes the development of his craft between *The Lynchers* and *Hiding Place.*

> . . . In my first three books, the way I tried to assert continuity with tradition and my sense of tradition was quite different than my understanding of these matters in *Damballah, Hiding Place,* and *Sent for You Yesterday.* [In the first three books,] I was trying to hook [the modernist tradition] into what I thought was something that would give [black] people and situations a kind of literary resonance, legitimize that world by infusing echoes of T. S. Eliot, Henry James, Faulkner, English and Continental masters. . . . But as I grew and learned more about writing, I found . . . that what Bessie Smith did when she sang, what Clyde McFater did, what John Coltrane did, what Ralph Ellison did, what

Richard Wright did, what the anonymous slave composer and the people who spoke in the slave narratives did, what they were doing was drawing from a realm of experience, a common inheritance, that T. S. Eliot, Faulkner, Tolstoi, and Austen were also drawing from. I could take a direct route and get back to that essential mother lode of pain, love, grief, wonder, the basic human emotions that are the stuff of literature. I could get back to that mother lode through my own mother's voice. . . .

[This quotation comes from the Charles Rowell interview]

His mother's voice is part of the voice of his larger family and of the Homewood community. By drawing more directly on this voice, Wideman makes black culture more central in his work both thematically and formally.

The main character of *Hiding Place* is Tommy's relative Bess, who goes into seclusion after the deaths of her husband and son. She loses her faith in God, her family, and herself, and her vituperation makes her one of Wideman's most memorable characters. When Tommy comes to her hermetic cabin on Bruston Hill asking for help, she refuses, telling him he might as well go straight back down into Homewood and accept justice for the murder that he is accused of committing. Despite her genuine meanness, however, Bess's association with Tommy calls up positive memories of a time when she felt good about herself, her family, and her home. These recollections return Bess to the center of family and community life, reminding her that relatives and friends provide a supportive structure in the midst of suffering, poverty, and pain. She sees again that she wants and needs to be part of this community that takes care of its own. At the end of the novel, Bess prepares to leave Bruston Hill and move back into the heart of Homewood.

Bess acts as a griot, the repository and voice of the family's history. She places Tommy in that history: "You Lizabeth's son, Thomas. Your grandmother was my sister's girl. You wasn't even born when my sister Gert died. Freeda was her oldest. . . . You a Lawson now. You and your three brothers and your sister in the middle." Tommy has grown up in Homewood during the 1960s and carries a legacy of disillusionment from that decade when he squandered his life on dope and the fast, hip life. Having lost his wife and son, he has ended up on Bruston Hill, running from the police after taking part in a failed confidence game in which his friend killed a white man. He has never known the family history Bess is learning to value again. Through his association with her, Tommy learns to believe in himself and gains the courage to face what awaits him in Homewood. By developing a significant relationship with Bess, Tommy reasserts his claim to a nurturing family relationship that he has not had in a long time. Even if he goes to jail, the family will support him.

Throughout *The Homewood Trilogy*, Wideman explores the lives of his ancestors, parents, and contemporaries to portray a coherent nexus of family and community ties. Discussing Ernest J. Gaines's novel *Of Love and Dust* (1967) in a 1978 essay in *Callaloo*, Wideman notes that Gaines has developed Faulkner's modernist experiments with multiple points of view into something new:

The narrative method is less Faulknerian montage—the abutting or juxtaposing of varying, even contradictory perspectives—than it is mosaic, the gradual revelation of a design through the accretion of discrete fragments. . . . Viewpoints accumulate but their effect is the gradual revelation of a coherent perspective.

Wideman works to achieve just such an effect in *The Homewood Trilogy*, juxtaposing varying perspectives not to question the validity of objective perception so much as to enrich the panorama of the entire community and its history.

In the second volume of the trilogy, *Damballah* (1981), Wideman weaves together twelve separate short stories on a web of common thematic concerns, knitting together the tales as he would like to reknit his divided family. In a preface, Wideman addresses the collection to his brother Robby: "These stories are letters.

Long overdue letters from me to you. I wish they could tear down the walls. I wish they could snatch you away from where you are." Robby is serving a life sentence without parole. In his cell, he is separated from his brother by law; before his imprisonment, the brothers were separated by Wideman's physical and intellectual removal to the white academic worlds of the University of Pennsylvania and Oxford. In the dedication Wideman offers this collection of stories to Robby as both apology and explanation:

Stories are letters. Letters sent to anybody or everybody. But the best kind are meant to be read by a specific somebody. When you read that kind you know you are eavesdropping. . . . Remember. I think it was Geral I first heard call a watermelon a letter from home. After all these years I understand a little better what she meant. She was saying the melon is a letter addressed to us. A story for us from down home. Down Home being everywhere we've never been, the rural South, the old days, slavery, Africa. That juicy, striped message with red meat and seeds, which always looked like roaches to me, was blackness as cross and celebration, a history we could taste and chew. And it was meant for us. Addressed to us. We were meant to slit it open and take care of business. Consider all these stories as letters from home. I never liked watermelon as a kid. I think I remember you did. You weren't afraid of becoming instant nigger, of sitting barefoot and goggle-eyed and Day-Glo black and drippy-lipped on massa's fence if you took one bit of the forbidden fruit. I was too scared to enjoy watermelon. Too self-conscious. I let people rob me of a simple pleasure. Watermelon's still tainted for me. But I know better now. I can play with the idea even if I can't get down and have a natural ball eating a real one.

Wideman follows his address to Robby with an invocation to Damballah ("good serpent of the sky") and the other voodoo gods who provide their worshipers with " 'a sense of historical extension, of the ancient origin of the race. To invoke them today is to stretch one's hand back to that time and to gather up all history into a solid, contemporary ground beneath one's feet.' " This invocation precedes a family chronology and genealogical chart tracing Wideman's maternal line, all designed to help the reader connect the various narrative voices in the following stories. Wideman appears as himself in the story "The Chinaman," in which he practices telling stories to his wife in an attempt to capture the nuances of the black oral tradition. "The Chinaman" celebrates the creative, consolidating power of that heritage. May, Wideman's great-great-aunt and a dynamic storyteller, tells how she saved Wideman's grandmother, who was then an infant:

May's told the story a hundred times, but each time it's new and necessary. If she didn't tell the story right, there would be no baby shuddering to life in her arms when she runs through the crashing door. There would be no Lizabeth, none of us would be gathered in my grandmother's house on Finance Street listening to May tell how Geraldine came next.

Compared with May's gifted performance, Wideman's attempts to tell a story to his wife sound "stiff and incomplete." He remains the alienated intellectual, in but no longer of his family. But he persists in trying his own voice, and ends the story with an affirmative "amen."

In "Across the Wide Missouri," Wideman presents the most poignant account of the black intellectual's quest in *Damballah*. The narrator tells us he has tried to write this story before; like the narrator in "The Chinaman," he is practicing. The narrator is having difficulty telling a story about his father because he is trying to write through the impediments of his self-imposed isolation in Laramie, Wyoming, trying to write himself out of exile. Wideman movingly describes the writer-intellectual's realization of his distance from his father. He remains a precarious, marginal figure in the end, incarcerated beyond the Missouri River just as Robby is beyond the prison walls. But, recognizing something of both himself and his father in his own son, he understands better why he has placed himself at a distance from a painful past:

> He's the kind of kid who forgets lots of things but who remembers everything. He has the gift of feeling. Things don't touch him, they imprint. You can see it sometimes. And it hurts. He already knows he will suffer for whatever he knows. Maybe that's why he forgets so much.

The story "Tommy" depicts the dramatic encounter between John and his brother Tommy in Laramie, Wyoming, as Tommy flees west to escape the police in Homewood. This is the same Tommy who sought shelter in *Hiding Place,* and who reappears as Robby, Wideman's brother, in the autobiographical work *Brothers and Keepers.* Both "Tommy" and *Hiding Place* were inspired by Robby's stay with Wideman when he was trying to escape the law by hiding in Laramie. The story emphasizes the depth both of the brothers' estrangement and John's desire to bridge the distance between them.

In "The Beginning of Homewood," Wideman compares the story of his great-great-great-grandmother's life as a slave (a story passed on by May) and the story of Robby's flight and incarceration (the story Wideman tells over and over in *The Homewood Trilogy* and in his other books, inscribing it into the chronicle of his forebears and the extended family of Homewood):

> I was thinking the way Aunt May talks. I heard her laughter, her amens, and *can I get a witness,* her digressions within digressions, the webs she spins and brushes away with her hands. . . . What seems to ramble begins to cohere when the listener understands the process, understands that the voice seeks to recover everything, that the voice proclaims *nothing is lost,* that the listener is not passive but lives like everything else within the story.

Comparing himself to May, he contrasts his position as scribe with that of his enslaved great-great-great-grandmother, whose crime was merely running away, and Robby. After seeing Robby and his friend in chains in police custody, he asks himself,

> *why not me,* why is it the two of you skewered and displayed like she would have been if she hadn't kept running. Ask myself if I would have committed the crime of running away or if I would have stayed and tried to make the best of a hopeless situation. Ask . . . if anything had changed in the years between her crime and yours. Could you have run away without committing a crime?

The implied answer, of course, is no. The only way Robby could escape was through crime; the only real crime in Homewood is attempting to escape. Wideman, then, who ran away to distant universities, shares his brother's guilt.

While Wideman obviously identifies with the narrators of these stories, he has surpassed them in mastery of the techniques of the black oral tradition. In both *Hiding Place* and *Damballah,* Wideman accomplishes an original, distinctively black voicing of the modernist traditions that define American literature in the twentieth century. In a 1976 essay in *American Poetry Review,* he notes that

> black speech cannot escape entirely the frame of American literary language. . . . As long as the depiction of black reality was dependent for its verification on the conventions of another code (mainstream American literature) and the conventions of that code were not examined . . . the black voice in American fiction could never become a distinct, independent index to reality.

Striving to create a black literature independent of an external, authenticating code, Wideman applauds those authors who attack, in their fiction, the "literary frame which mediated between black speech and reality." Too often, he argues, that frame automatically invalidates black speech:

> Like Yeats or Joyce who felt the profound uneasiness of an Irish sensibility negotiating

within English, the language of their nation's conquerors, the relationship of the black American writer to the vehicle of his art is complex. Because of his African language and culture, the black man spoke English differently than the European. This difference was incorporated in colonial American literature as dialect, but Negro dialect was taken as a sign not simply of difference but inferiority. (p. 34)

In *Sent for You Yesterday* (1983), the third volume of *The Homewood Trilogy*, Wideman rejects the notion of closure and framing altogether. The novel begins with a brief conversation in heaven, where Brother Tate, a mute before he died, remembers his life on earth as a waking nightmare in which he was trapped in a boxcar, afraid to utter a sound for fear that his unleashed screaming would carry his soul away, to disappear into the atmosphere. After Brother tells his story, the novel begins, retelling Brother's story from other viewpoints. Freeda French, like Brother, lives in terror of people disappearing: her children, her husband, her own reflection in a soap bubble. The central event of her life occurred the day she saw through a window that someone was about to kill her husband in the alley outside. "John French about to die in the space framed by the window. Freeda's fist slams through the glass to shield him." In preventing his disappearance from her life, she slashes the flesh of her hand, and cherishes the scar as a memento of a successful aversion of ending, closure, and absence. This story, along with many others, is told and retold by various characters throughout the novel; none of the stories is ever completed because one retelling mandates another. The stories are never closed because each retelling involves the listener in reliving the tale. Wideman finds an analogue for contemporary white literary theory (the postmodernist doctrines asserting the interminable deferral of literary closure) in the oldest black oral traditions.

The main character, Doot, is a black intellectual who returns to Homewood to find his place there, conducting this search not from the periphery of Homewood society or from Lara-mie, Wyoming, but by living in the community. Doot takes as his goal the shaping of a myth of Homewood's history. This myth will ground him in the community and give him a reason to stay there and work; his grounding in Homewood will also allow him to serve the community. His myth centers on black music and musicians; his function as mythmaker is to reinterpret the traditional stories of his family and the Homewood community, altering them to reflect his own subjective experience of Homewood and its citizens. Again, Wideman is combining the black oral tradition with postmodernist literary precepts. Jacques Derrida tells us that two readings of the "same" book are inevitably different readings; so it is with the tale-tellings in *Sent for You Yesterday*. Doot asks his uncle's lover, Lucy, to tell him a story. She says, "There was the time I got you up to dance. But you've heard that before." Doot responds, "Never from you." Each retelling is different; Doot's mythifying interpolations and reshapings continue a tradition based on perpetual revision. He develops his own version of community and cultural tradition that will fulfill him intellectually and allow him to stay in the community and be a part of it.

Doot makes the two voices of his prefatory heavenly dialogue his heroes: Albert Wilkes, a legendary Homewood musician slain by the police, and Brother Tate, an albino mute who miraculously duplicates Wilkes's music. Music unifies, clarifies, and supports, offering the black community a bridge over its agony, suffering, and hardship. It translates the essence of the black past into the future and guarantees the continuance of black culture. As the novel closes, we see Doot preparing to take on the role Albert Wilkes and Brother Tate played: "I'm on my own feet. Learning to stand, to walk, learning to dance."

Brothers and Keepers and *Reuben*

In *Brothers and Keepers* Wideman shows us how his personal attitude toward black culture has paralleled the developments we have seen in his fictional characters. He tells the story of getting to know his imprisoned brother Robby after allowing their relationship to attenuate for years. As Wideman began removing himself from the black community in high school, he lost touch with his family as well. In *Brothers and Keepers* he recounts his struggle to accept fully his own black experience, and his discovery of his connections to his brother during that struggle. He takes full responsibility for seeking sanctuary in the white, Western academic community, and judges his flight more culpable than his brother's willingness to live among his people. He also considers the responsibilities of the black intellectual to make himself an accessible resource for the black community.

In his next novel, *Reuben* (1987), Wideman portrays a black intellectual who does not flee. Reuben, a black lawyer with a long record of helping impoverished black people, lives in a trailer in the heart of Homewood. Listening to Reuben talk to himself and watching him talk to his clients, the reader recognizes a discrepancy between Reuben's beliefs and his actions. Reuben believes that he cannot know an objective reality, that he can capture only an illusion of reality through fictions he tells himself, fictions that exert no influence over reality. On the other hand, Reuben takes legal action on behalf of members of the black community as if he were acting in a world of stable, fixed, intelligible facts and knowable, controllable things. He constructs fictions for black people (although they do not understand them as fictions) that give them the illusion of controlling their own lives. He suppresses his theoretical convictions in order to make himself effective in serving the practical needs of his black clients.

Reuben uses his fictions for self-defense as well. Whenever racist white society sets forth a nullifying, destructive fiction to control him, he critically counters it with a positive, empowering fiction of his own. On a larger scale, he also implicitly deconstructs the structure of negative black stereotypes, and replaces it with a fiction that achieves the dimensions of myth, of a rich, substantive, supportive black cultural tradition. Again, Reuben's deconstructing and

reconstructing fictions are actions that reshape reality when he, contradictorily, does not believe that he can both know and control it. A reshapable reality is a contradiction in terms.

Fever and *Philadelphia Fire*

Questions of agency, control, and self-determination figure largely in *Fever* (1989), a second collection of short stories. The title story grew out of Wideman's search for teaching materials. Richard Allen, a former slave, was a founder of the African Methodist Episcopal Church in Philadelphia. Reading Allen's 1794 narrative describing the yellow fever epidemic that devastated the city in 1793, Wideman became fascinated by his depiction of free blacks, despised and abused by white immigrants in cities like Philadelphia at the end of the eighteenth century. Despite their racial persecution, and at the risk of their own infection, Franz Gysin's notes in his essay on *Fever* that Allen and other members of the Philadelphia Free African Society "not only organized a small army of carters, grave diggers, and nurses, but they themselves received special training by [white abolitionist Dr. Benjamin] Rush and then worked along with him as auxiliary doctors, administering purges, bleeding patients, and making careful notes abut each case." The story came together for Wideman after the 1985 police firebombing of Philadelphia's MOVE headquaters. He revised an earlier draft to include among its narrators the voice of a mayor who speaks across the centuries to address both the plague and the fire. Wideman was beginning a process in his writing of linking past and present history to show that racism, perpetuated over the generations, produces equally horrible events in the past and present.

In the story "Fever," Allen attends a sick Jewish man who laments his own history of oppression and chides Allen for his service to those who oppress him. He even suggests that nothing Allen or anyone else does can redeem them, because God himself is the ultimate cruel author of human oppression: "He publishes one book—the book of suffering—over and over again. He disguises it between new boards, in different shapes and sizes, prints on varying papers, in many fonts, adds prefaces and postscripts to deceive the buyer, but it's always the same book." Thus, all devastating adversity is ultimately the same story, whether it's plague, fire, or institutionalized dehumanization in the form of slavery or police brutality. Some of the voices narrating the stories in this collection are identifiable individuals; others are strangely detached, distanced voices speaking from the perspective of the heavenly dialogue prefacing *Sent for You Yesterday*. One such anonymous voice in the title story tells us,

No one has asked my opinion. No one will. Yet I have seen this fever before, and though I can prescribe no cure, I could tell stories of other visitations, how it came and stayed and left us, the progress of disaster. . . . We have bred the affliction within our breasts. . . . Nothing is an accident. Fever grows in the secret places of our hearts, planted there when one of us decided to sell one of us to another.

Wideman quotes from autopsy reports recorded during the plague to argue against the rationale behind slavery: "When you open the dead, black or white, you find: Multiple sections through the pons, medulla oblongata and upper brain stem reveal normal gross anatomy. The cranial nerves are in their normal locations and unremarkable." In this and the other stories collected here, Wideman decries misleading surface appearances. All his characters—the white woman watching a black jogger in "The Statue of Liberty," the elderly Jewish man watching his black cleaning woman in "Valaida"—are at least initially deceived by the masks cloaking a common humanity. Whether these masks are God's fictions or man's, Wideman calls for their deconstruction and revision.

Following *Fever*, which at the end conflates the 1793 fever and the 1985 fire, Wideman "tell[s] the story of the fire" in his next novel *Philadelphia Fire* (1990). The novel's main plot portrays black writers' attempts to relate the fire to its underlying cause in *The Tempest*'s

story of Caliban. Caliban is a black man in the terms of the trope appropriated from the play to represent him. Miranda describes Caliban: "Abhorrèd slave, / Which any print of goodness wilt not take. . . . who hadst / Deserved more than prison." An oppressive legacy in the English language evolves from Miranda's words, and *Philadelphia Fire* portrays the black writers' efforts in Part 2 to rewrite *The Tempest* to change the legacy.

. . . this narrative is a sport of time, what it's about is stopping time, catching time. Watch how the play [*The Tempest*] works like an engine, a heart in the story's chest, churning, pumping, tying something to something else, that sign by which we know time's conspiring, expiring. . . .

. . . This is the central event. I assure you. I repeat. Whatever my assurance is worth. Being the fabulator. This is the central event, this production of *The Tempest* staged by Cudjoe in the late 1960s, outdoors, in a park in West Philly. Though it comes here, wandering like a Flying Dutchman in and out of the narrative, many places at once, *The Tempest* sits dead center, the storm in the eye of the storm, figure within a figure, play within play, it is the bounty and hub of all else written about the fire, though it comes here, where it is [in Part 2 of *Philadelphia Fire*], nearer the end than the beginning. . . .

Cudjoe and the fabulator, implicitly Wideman, who appears in the novel as a character, are writers whose personal lives make up subplots as they try to rewrite *The Tempest*. Even when the influence of the play's discourse is not tangible and not apparent in events such as the fire, it has a major role in black oppression. The fire is, paradoxically, the oppression that comes from the watery tempest, and it hides its source. This oppression is complex and insidious, and the writer's task of exposing its source and changing its course is difficult.

Part 1 of *Philadelphia Fire* mainly concerns the life of Cudjoe and his search to find the black boy Simba, missing in the fire, who is a "brother, son, a lost limb haunting him." Finding Simba and telling his story in Part 1 is similar to rewriting *The Tempest* in Part 2; it is a way of exposing the oppression behind the fire, changing Cudjoe's tragic sense of Simba's loss, and symbolically changing the fire's oppressive legacy. Returning from the Greek island where he has become an exile after deserting his wife and children, Cudjoe talks to Margaret Jones, a survivor of the fire, in an effort to find Simba, but largely because of his personal history, she does not fully trust him and his efforts fail. Cudjoe also renews acquaintances from his youth, and discovers that one of his friends, Darnell, is in jail, a victim of the same underlying oppression that caused the fire. Through his old friend Timbo, an attache for the black mayor who ordered the bombing that caused the fire, he examines the fire in the context of their 1960s activism. This activism has paradoxically led to Timbo's achieving his position and the mayor's attaining his and in turn to their apparently becoming complicity in the fire. As Part 1 ends, Cudjoe shares with Timbo his waking nightmare of the lynching of "me and every black boy I've ever seen. . . ." The lynching, the ultimate symbol of oppression, initiates Cudjoe's specific efforts to rewrite *The Tempest* in Part 2.

Cudjoe and Wideman become synonymous as characters as Part 2 depicts both Wideman's efforts to write a fiction that will empower him to connect with his imprisoned son and Cudjoe's efforts to rewrite *The Tempest*. The writers are trying to do the same thing because their goal is empowerment. A common oppressive discourse represented by *The Tempest* is behind the son's incarceration, the fire that destroys black lives, and black oppression generally. Both Wideman and the conflated writer Cudjoe struggle. Wideman, however, succeeds to a greater extent than Cudjoe. Wideman concludes his efforts to imagine a fiction that liberates his son with the following assertion: "We do have a chance to unfold our days one by one and piece together a story that shapes us. It's the only life anyone ever has. Hold on." Cudjoe rewrites but never stages *The Tempest*, because, ironically, it is rained out. However, the reason that he fails to stage it is greater than

this: "Prospero got that island sewed up tight as a turkey's butt on Thanksgiving. Play got to end the way it does. Prospero still the boss. Master of ceremonies. . . . And people can't wait to clap their hands and say thanks."

Part 3 portrays the life of a homeless black man named J. B. (James Brown), another victim of black oppression. The mysterious J. B. discovers an equally mysterious Book of Life whose life-generating codes have, like *The Tempest*, become the signs and symbols of oppression. J. B., like Cudjoe, has trouble telling the story of oppression that he finds in the book. But through his portrayal, Part 3 makes it clear that oppression has dire repercussions for everyone in Philadelphia and in America. The discourse that begins with *The Tempest* and creates a devastating tradition of oppression for black people also turns back on America in the form of the *Kiddy Korner* of violent little Calibans. The *Kiddy Korner* is the children who have been left alone by a society made callous by its own racism and oppression. They are the neglected black children and white children, all children, who *"have learned to hate us as much as we hate them."* Children such as this set J. B. on fire, and he burns alive as he runs to jump into Independence Square's empty fountain, a symbol of the missing source that is not apparent in the oppressive fire.

J. B.'s burning does not end the novel, however. The last ten pages focus on a rally for the fire victims that Cudjoe attends. In the midst of ominous sounds, Cudjoe does imagine the beginning of a potentially liberating fiction in the very last paragraph. He "hears footsteps behind him. A mob howling his name. . . . [and a] rumbling over the stones of Independence Square." But also, "Words come to him, cool him, stop him in his tracks. He'd known them all his life. *Never again. Never again.*"

One might conclude from Part 3 that the writer has a role in changing oppression, but maybe liberation also depends on readers. The sparse crowd for the rally in Independence Square would seem to indicate that the community is apathetic in the face of oppression. But still, the writers in this text have struggled to do a job. Although they have not rewritten

The Tempest and changed oppression, they have at least shown that oppression is a discursive construction, and not a "natural" reality. If it can be constructed through discourse, then discourse can deconstruct it—if readers will participate with writers in its deconstruction.

All Stories Are True

All Stories Are True (1992) is a third collection of short stories. Its stories, nine with American settings, and one with a South African setting, deal with the plight of incarcerated brothers and sons, black families and individuals in crisis, black communities infested by drugs and violence, and black South Africa ravaged by violence and suffering ("What He Saw"). This, too, is all the direct or indirect legacy of oppression. All the stories are true emotionally, psychologically, and realistically: some reconstruct reality in ways that clearly open up the possibility of hope; others give linguistic shape to that which is too horrible to face or too hard to understand, which is a way of coping with it after all.

The title story (the first) and "Welcome," (the last) take a hard look at family tragedies and agonizingly project hope. "All Stories Are True" begins in drug-infested Homewood, and moves to the prison where the narrator visits his brother. The brother tries to tell a story that sustains him in the face of parole boards that automatically deny parole and against the prison's constantly life-threatening atmosphere. He sees his hope symbolized through a leaf that blew over the prison walls the same day that his girlfriend visited to tell him that she was pregnant with his child. He ends the story with the admission that the "dumb [leaf] blew back in here again." But the brother has also concluded that "No matter how much I love Chance [Mandela] [my son] and Denise [my girlfriend] and Mom and youall, nothing, not all the love in the world can fill the hole that opens up when I get down, really down. Only way to save myself is to do it for me. I got to be the reason. I got to be worth saving. Can't live a

life for nobody else. Nobody can live one for me. . . ."

The brother, Tom, in "Welcome" explains his and his sister's pain and suffering and the overall predicament of all the people in *All Stories*: ". . . everybody I love in some kind of trouble that is past danger worse than danger a state I don't want to give a name to, can't say because I don't want to hear it." "Welcome" takes place at Christmas and is about the struggle of the sister (called "Mrs. Crawford" by a doctor) to deal with the death of her one-year-old daughter eleven years earlier and her brother's efforts to handle the loss of his young son to prison. The story ends with an episode in which the brother drives past a pitiful scene of a poorly dressed young father and his upset, crying young son waiting for a "bus that probably ain't coming for days this late on the weekend." He imagines the "whole dreary story line" of them freezing on the street. When he passes the scene again, however, the father is lifting and hugging the son, and the brother wishes that he could be that father. The scene and the sweet soprano singing of the waitress at Woodside Bar-B-Que, where he was going for a takeout dinner, make him cry and realize how much he is missing his own imprisoned son Will. But the story leaves the impression that this instance of catharsis and coming to terms with loss, in the context of black community and family empathy, is meaningful.

"Casa Grande," "Everybody Knew Bubba Riff," and "Newborn Thrown in Trash and Dies" are more open-ended stories that sustain and maintain by giving voice and form to chaos and unspeakable pain. Four-page "Casa Grande" is a father-son story that begins with a "story" the son wrote, "A Trip to Jupiter"; it ends with the father's journal entry that he wrote after a visit with his son, serving a life sentence at an Arizona prison, on his twenty-first birthday. The son's story seems to show how far away he is from everybody, including his parents. In the father's journal entry, he takes the word *hohokam* from the Pima Indians to reverse time and bring his son back to earth. Instead of meaning "those who are gone," it "could be a word of welcome, a whispered promise. That which is, soon goes away," and this could mean the son's condition. At the end, "time runs backwards . . . Great-time to Little-time, and oceans disappear down a drain no bigger than the pinhead upon which [the son] dances his angels, counts them as they exhaust themselves and one by one plummet back to earth."

"Casa Grande" is a fantastic fiction that copes with a horrible nightmare reality. One could say the same about "Newborn Thrown in Trash and Dies," the narrative of a newborn baby as she plummets down the trash opening to her death. The story is told in the baby's voice in the present, and her voice is also projected ahead to foresee what would be a life of abuse and violence. The story imagines the life of the child who has no voice to protest the unbelievable—that her mother would throw her down a trash shaft in the cold of winter.

"Everybody Knew Bubba Riff" expresses the chaos and craziness of Bubba's life through a stream of community voices that gives it an improvisational form of words. The story is about the life and death of the strong-armed street tough whom someone murdered, partly because his physical tactics no longer worked in a time when guns and drugs ruled the streets. "Everybody Knew Bubba" is a continuous riff that is one nine-page sentence from the beginning, ". . . Bubba here you are dead boy dead dead dead nigger with spooky Boris Karloff powder caked on your face . . . ," to the end, ". . . Big Bubba a dinosaur man wasn't even living in the right century man living by the wrong clock man he was Bubba all right your man Bubba Bubba Bubba everybody knew Bubba." The riff is voices like "a river you step in once and never again never the same," but it is a way of knowing Bubba.

Works of the 1990s: *Fatheralong, The Cattle Killing, Two Cities*

Wideman's next book is *Fatheralong: A Meditation on Fathers and Sons, Race and Society* (1994); it is an example of the impressive range of the author as a creative writer and thinker.

In keeping with its title, the text deals with both the concept of race as it functions in society and the way that race directly and indirectly affects the relationships between black fathers and sons. *Fatheralong* well defines what it means by race.

Though most of us have been conditioned to confuse race with culture, they are not synonymous. Race does not equal color, either. Nor is race the systematic description, classification, and analysis of what distinguishes one group from another. The concept of race, whose presence continues to poison our society, gradually evolved during the long European diaspora to every part of the globe. The word *race* evokes a paradigm, a systematic network or pattern of assumptions, relationships, a model of reality, of history and causation as complete, closed, and pervasive as a religion. Race is not a set of qualities inhering in some "other," it's the license to ascribe such qualities allied with the power to make them stick. . . ."

In the context of the insidious influence of race in American and Western societies, Wideman traces his own Southern family background to Promised Land, South Carolina, through his male progenitors, and in the process he also meditates on his relationship with his father and sons. The concept of race is the foundation of past and present oppression that separates black fathers and sons. Wideman speaks to his incarcerated son about the threat to them caused by race that is part of a tradition reaching back to the son's great-grandfather and his bothers: "The powers and principalities that originally restricted our access to the life free people naturally enjoy still rise like a shadow, a wall between my grandfathers and myself, my father and me, between the two of us, father and son, son and father." The only solution is to "speak these stories to one another" with "Love." As is true in the novel *Philadelphia Fire*, telling the story is life sustaining and liberating.

Critics and commentators have justifiably called *The Cattle Killing* (1996) Wideman's best novel, which is remarkable in an over-thirty-year career that has already produced seven novels and three collections of short stories of very high quality. Like *Fever*, *Cattle Killing* draws upon the 1793 yellow fever epidemic in Philadelphia for part of its primary historical background; the other part, as the title indicates, is the Xhosa cattle-killing movement in South Africa in 1856 and 1857. The text is reminiscent of *Philadelphia Fire* in that it shows that telling the story of oppression is liberating. But more than the earlier novel which exposes the powerful bonds of oppression as imposed by white, Western discourse, *Cattle Killing* focuses on black storytelling—black oral discourse—that connects the storytellers and sustains them over generations. It depicts an intersubjective connection among Africans and African Americans who tell the story of black oppression and transcend it through the ongoing process of narration itself. The most important thing is telling, listening, and telling again, on and on, "next and next. Always unknown. Always free." As long as the connecting stories do not stop, the tellers of the stories will remain spiritually free beyond the physical confines of white oppression. From the perspective of the novel as a written text, as Kathie Birat very perceptively points out, "the very power of storytelling lies in its capacity to embrace the endless movement of language itself, 'writing,' if not necessarily 'righting,' the wrongs of an 'upside-down' world."

The story told in *Cattle Killing* is the narrative of many people that moves back and forth, forth and back, in Africa and America, in the eighteenth, nineteenth, and twentieth centuries. It begins in Part 1 with the contemporary writer attending the conference in his hometown of Philadelphia and going to read to his father from his book. He talks about the reckless black boys killing each other in Philadelphia, and connects this to the heedless self-destruction of the Xhosas in 1850s South Africa when they killed their cattle, the source of their lives. The writer conflates this with the main story of a narrator during the 1793 Philadelphia yellow fever outbreak. This narrator accesses the reality of the South African cattle killing through the stories of Liam, an African he meets, and tells Liam's story of his oppression in England as he listens to it. And he meets and becomes synonymous with Bishop Richard Allen, whose story of the fever he tells, also. These stories are interwoven with stories the narrator tells to bond with and heal a mysterious sick woman, who is a victim of oppression and synchronously related to other women in his stories with whom he bonds. The contemporary writer wonders about the story he is writing: *"Was it a lie, a coverup to say [all these characters in different times have] looked into the same sky, walked the same earth and thus share a world, a condition. Even so, given the benefit of the doubt, what kind of world is it. Why is it not weeping for everything lost. And why is he afraid of dying. And who is he anyway, interchangeable with these others, porous, them running through him, him leaking, bleeding into them, in the fiction he's trying to write."* In the final analysis, the fiction the writer tries to write is John Wideman's and his son Dan's, too, because they appear in the epilogue.

Throughout Part 1, the nineteenth century narrator, a preacher in Philadelphia at the time of the fever, tells the story of his struggles with racism during the epidemic and his interaction with Liam, enslaved in England, now living in the vicinity of Philadelphia with his white wife. The narrator actually enters Liam's Africa through his stories: "I knew I must be in the Africa of Liam's stories. I was the boy he'd been before he was snatched away forever. His country big enough to hold England in its palm, his old world dwarfing even the immensity of this raw new one to which he'd run with his dreams, his flame-haired white woman." While in Liam's Africa, the African girl Nongquawse visits him in his dreams to tell him the story of how she related the evil prophecy of the cattle killing to a country already besieged by white people, and thus assured their doom. She warns him against her own prophecy—that killing the cattle, the very existence of the people, will somehow restore their life. She promises to return to him in a new dream, "a happier dream in a new land where the cattle are not dying,

. . ." Only our enemies dead in the new dream. . . ." But the narrator awakens to the American nightmare of whites burning Liam and his wife alive in their house. Part 1 ends with a horrific image of oppression: "Circles within circles. . . . a circle without and within, the monstrous python swallowing itself, birthing its tail."

Part 2 begins with the narrator's conversation with the mysterious woman. Speaking to the woman about her story and telling his story is also telling the story of Bishop Allen: "Just as I sit beside you on this bed, speaking to you, the dead speak to me. I feel them as the song says drawing me on, drawing me on. I . . . fought the fever. Met Richard Allen. Old Bishop Allen, dead now, but I see him, he sits on his bed, head bowed, wondering if God will follow him and Absalom Jones and their flock of dark sheep into the church they are building." Telling their common story of black oppression becomes too much when it includes Allen's sermon asserting faith that black orphans of the fever, segregated in a cellar and burned alive in a fire caused by their careless, pipe-smoking white watchman, will be an example of hope for black people. The narrator cannot believe that Allen "dared say those words." The horror of black oppression in his story finally makes the narrator stutter, and the "language [comes] apart in [his] hands." The woman comforts and tries to save him with the assurance that "it's fine . . . As long as you tried your best, baby. Fine. Fine. Fine." At the end of Part 2, he leaves open the possibility that the storytelling will continue and will bond and save him and the woman: "Tell me, finally, what is a man. What is a woman. Aren't we lovers first, spirits sharing an uncharted space, a space our stories tell, a space chanted, written upon again and again, yet one story never quite erased by the next, each story saving the space, saving itself, saving us. If someone is listening."

In the epilogue, Dan Wideman is the one who has been reading-listening to his father's story, and he uses his research in the British Museum's African archives for his own book to supplement and carry on his father's story in *Cattle Killing*. Dan finds "real" letters about a real relationship between brothers that corresponds to his father's account in the novel of the narrator's relationship to his brother, presumably lost on a voyage to Africa. In the letters, the real brother jumps ship to avoid being sold into slavery, makes it to South Africa, and helps the South Africans in their predicament caused by the cattle killing and white oppression. The last sentence of the real brother's letter concludes the text.

This note, the others I intend to write, may never reach you, yet I am sure a time will come when we shall be together again.
Hold on, Your Brother

It seems that the text's fiction and the real stories told outside that fiction can keep the process of the narrative going.

Two Cities (1998) is a novel about a woman named Kassima, Robert Jones, her lover, and Mr. Mallory, her tenant. What connects the characters' lives, the two cities of the title (Pittsburgh and Philadelphia) and approximately fifty years of African American history is the memories and photographs of old Mr. Mallory. Mr. Mallory remembers World War II, in which white soldiers murdered his friend Gus and tried to murder him because of their tryst with two white women; the murder of his friend and MOVE leader John Africa in the 1985 Philadelphia fire; and his desertion of his own family. He has taken boxes of photographs, most of them undeveloped, of what he has seen living in Philadelphia and Pittsburgh. His experience in the former city has driven him to the latter in his old age, where he finds self-destructive black youth gang violence. Kassima takes him in as her tenant to fill the void after losing her husband and two sons to the violence of Pittsburgh, and he dies in her house after she has started and then tried to end a relationship with Robert Jones. Mr. Mallory's death brings her and Robert Jones back together, and near the end of *Two Cities*, Kassima uses Mr. Mallory's photographs and negatives to stop a horrible black youth ritual at the funeral home. A gang that has murdered a black boy whose body is at the funeral home invades the home to desecrate the body, and in the process they throw Mr.

Mallory's body partly out of his casket into the street, also. Kassima throws the pictures and negatives into the street before the gang members: "Look. Look what you've done to him. Look what you've done to yourselves. Look. Look." The pictures symbolize Mr. Mallory's memories, the black history of two cities, and all that he has experienced. The gang members lives are a violent, self-destructive legacy of what Mr. Mallory's life and the pictures encompass. The boys stop and look at the pictures, but "who knows what they were seeing. What they said. Who knows what they thought. . . ."

In an interview conducted by Jacqueline Berben-Masi, Wideman gives his own assessment of the significance of Mr. Mallory's character that well describes what he actually accomplishes in the novel through Mallory's portrayal and the symbolism of the photographs.

. . . [Mr. Mallory is] like Reuben: his experience opens up great time, the past that's always present. And not only has he traversed spiritually that immense distance and stayed connected [to the African American experience], but he has the means to communicate that journey and some of the places he's been to other people. So, yes, he possesses a spirit bundle. The photos are literally a spirit bundle. That's why so many are undeveloped pictures. A sheaf of already finished photos would be almost contradictory. He prints, at the end of his life, some actual photos, because its time to touch Kassima, and touch Robert Jones, and touch the contemporary world of Homewood. He's like a prophet who can only speak at a given time and at a given occasion to usher in a new day or end an epic. As long as the photos are undeveloped, they are multiple, not reducible. Martin Mallory's bringing the authority of his experience, the authority of his unique witness to bear.

Like Wideman himself and the writers and artists in his novels who create fictions, Mr. Mallory is another artist who uses his art form to put stories of African American life and African American oppression together over "great time." The "multiple" stories that Mr. Mallory

can tell through his pictures could break an old pattern and be prophetic of a "new day" in Homewood when self-destructive black youth violence will end. *Two Cities* is another powerful text in the very impressive development of Wideman's fiction and of his career. Given the total context, which now includes *Two Cities*, it becomes clear that his writing and his career, among other things, have redefined the activist's role to include himself, a writer who does not work from the forefront or from a position of leadership.

Addressing a question about his activism in the 1960s, Wideman has said to Rowell that besides being out of the country from 1963–67, he did not participate in the Black Arts Movement because "I've always been sort of a loner, and very suspicious of groups and organizations and movements, and suspicious and not really at ease in that kind of situation." Given his consuming devotion to his craft and his distrust of organized groups, Wideman will never be an activist in the black community in the terms defined by 1960s activists. But his fictions portray black artists whose works tell stories from potentially liberating black perspectives, and the fictions concomitantly refute white, Western racism that insidiously resides in the very language that we speak, thus infecting our total sense of reality. He has also focused his nonfiction toward racial concerns. His non-fiction in the 1990s has critiqued race and racism from the opposite poles of the plight of endangered black youth and black men generally and the cultural consumption of black sports figures such as Michael Jordan and Dennis Rodman. Further, during the 1990s, he has supported national and individual liberation struggles through his own actions. When Nelson Mandela gave his first speech in South Africa after his release from prison in 1990, calling for an end to apartheid, Wideman stood with him on the stage, and he has since then participated in the movement to free death row inmate Mumia Abu-Jamal in the United States. Wideman has struggled to make his writing serve black political needs, and to reclaim his place in the black community by supporting black causes. One could say that this is activism redefined from the viewpoint of Wideman's writing and life. His own personal and artistic evolution is as fascinating as any story he has written.

Selected Bibliography

PRIMARY WORKS

NOVELS

A Glance Away. Chatham, N.J.: Chatham Bookseller, and New York: Harcourt, Brace & World, 1967.
Hurry Home. New York: Harcourt, Brace & World, 1970.
The Lynchers. New York: Harcourt, Brace, 1973.
Hiding Place. New York: Avon, 1981.
Sent for You Yesterday. New York: Avon, 1983.
Reuben. New York: Henry Holt, 1987.
Philadelphia Fire. New York: Henry Holt, 1990.
The Cattle Killing. Boston: Houghton Mifflin, 1996.
Two Cities. Boston: Houghton Mifflin, 1998.

SHORT STORIES

Damballah. New York: Avon, 1981.
Fever: Twelve Stories. New York: Henry Holt, 1989.
All Stories Are True. New York: Pantheon Books, 1992.

AUTOBIOGRAPHICAL WORKS

Brothers and Keepers. New York: Holt, Rinehart & Winston, 1984.
Fatheralong: A Meditation on Fathers and Sons, Race and Society. New York: Pantheon Books, 1994.

COLLECTIONS

The Homewood Books. Pittsburg: University of Pittsburg Press, 1992. (Contains *Damballah, Hiding Place,* and *Sent for You Yesterday.*)
The Short Stories of John Edgar Wideman. New York: Pantheon, 1992. (This collection arranges the collections *All Stories Are True, Fever,* and *Damballah* in reverse chronological order.)
Identities: Three Novels. New York: Henry Holt, 1994. (Contains *A Glance Away, Hurry Home,* and *Lynchers.*)

ESSAYS

"Frame and Dialect: The Evolution of the Black Voice in Fiction." *American Poetry Review* 5, no. 5:34–37 (September–October 1976).
"Defining the Black Voice in Fiction." *Black American Literature Forum* 11, no. 3: 79–82 (Fall 1977).
"*Of Love and Dust:* A Reconsideration." *Callaloo* 1, no. 1:76–84 (May 1978).
"*Stomping the Blues:* Ritual in Black Music and Speech." *American Poetry Review* 7, no. 4:42–45 (July–August 1978).
"Michael Jordan Leaps the Great Divide." *Esquire,* November 1990, pp. 138–45, 210–316.

"The Architectonics of Fiction." *Callaloo* 13, no. 1:42–46 (Winter 1990).
"Dead Black Men and Other Fallouts from the American Dream." *Esquire,* September 1992, pp. 149–56.
Introduction to *Live From Death Row.* By Mumia Abu-Jamal. Reading, Mass.: Addison Wesley, 1995. Pp. xxiii–xxxvii.
"Doing Time, Marking Race." *The Nation,* October 30, 1995, p. 503. Reprinted in *In Defense of Mumia.* Edited by S. E. Anderson and Tony Medina. New York: Writers and Readers, 1996. Pp. 126–30.
"Playing Dennis Rodman." *The New Yorker,* April 29–May 6, 1996, pp. 94–95.
"The Killing of Black Boys." *Essence,* November 1997, pp. 122–24, 126, 184, 187–89.
"In Praise of Silence." *Book World,* November 29, 1998, pp. 1–3. Reprinted in *Callaloo* 22, no. 3: 547–50 (Summer 1999.)

SECONDARY WORKS

BIOGRAPHICAL AND CRITICAL STUDIES

Bell, Bernard W. *The Afro-American Novel and Its Tradition.* Amherst: University of Massachusetts Press, 1987.
Berben-Masi, Jacqueline. "From *Brothers and Keepers* to *Two Cities:* Social and Cultural Consciousness, Art and Imagination: An Interview with John Wideman." *Callaloo* 22, no. 3:568–84 (1999).
Birat, Kathie. " 'All Stories Are True': Prophecy, History and Story in *The Cattle Killing.*" *Callaloo* 22, no. 3:629–43 (1999).
Byerman, Keith. *John Edgar Wideman: A Study of the Short Fiction.* New York: Twayne, 1998.
Coleman, James W. *Blackness and Modernism: The Literary Career of John Edgar Wideman.* Jackson: University Press of Mississippi, 1989.
Cooke, Michael G. *Afro-American Literature in the Twentieth Century: The Achievement of Intimacy.* New Haven: Yale University Press, 1984.
Foucault, Michel. *Discipline and Punish: The Birth of the Prison.* Translated by Alan Sheridan. New York: Pantheon, 1978.
Frazier, Kermit. "The Novels of John Wideman." *Black World* 24, no. 8:18–35 (1975).
Grandjeat, Yves-Charles. "Brother Figures: The Rift and Riff in John E. Wideman's Fiction." *Callaloo* 22, no. 3:615–22 (1999).
Gysin, Fritz. " 'Do not fall asleep in your enemy's dream': John Edgar Wideman and the Predicaments of Prophecy." *Callaloo* 22, no. 3: 623–28 (1999).
———. "John Edgar Wideman's *Fever.*" *Callaloo* 22, no. 3: 715–26 (1999).
Harris, Trudier. *Exorcising Blackness: Historical and Literary Lynching and Burning Rituals.* Bloomington: Indiana University Press, 1984. Pp. 129–47.
Mbalia, Doreatha Drummond. *John Edgar Wideman: Reclaiming the African Personality.* Selinsgrove: Susquehana University Press, 1995.
O'Brien, John, ed. *Interviews with Black Writers.* New

York: Liveright, 1973.

Rovell, Charles. "An Interview with John Edgar Wideman." *Callaloo* 13, no. 1:47–61 (Winter 1990).

Samuels, Wilfred D. "Going Home: A Conversation with John Edgar Wideman." *Callaloo* 6, no. 1:40–59 (February 1983).

———. "John Edgar Wideman." In *Dictionary of Literary Biography*. Vol. 33, *Afro-American Fiction Writers after 1955*. Detroit: Gale, 1984. Pp. 271–78.

Schaeffer, Susan Fromberg. "*Fever:* We Are Neighbors, We Are Strangers." *New York Times Book Review*, December 10, 1989, pp. 1, 30, 31.

Weets, Tatiana. "The Negotiation of Remembrance in 'Across the Wide Missouri.' " *Callaloo* 22, no. 3:727–39 (1999).

BIBLIOGRAPHY

Richard, Jean-Pierre. "John Edgar Wideman: A Bibliography of Primary and Secondary Sources." *Callaloo* 22, no. 3:750–57 (1999).

JOHN A. WILLIAMS
(1925–)

HERMAN BEAVERS

JOHN A. WILLIAMS has contributed to American letters as a novelist, journalist, and teacher for nearly fifty years. As the author of twelve novels and countless pieces of journalism and nonfiction, he has demonstrated a propensity for revealing America as a site of emotional and political intricacy. His writing works from the standpoint that in spite of its claims to equality and opportunity, America has often stood as a total contradiction for African Americans. However, it would be misguided to see Williams as an artist motivated simply by matters of racial inequality. Though he can count writers of the Black Arts movement as contemporaries, his work is not driven by separatist ideology. Moving through Williams' novels, readers see that he is quite capable of creating characters of various backgrounds with depth and texture. And as a man who has traveled around the world, Williams' ability to evoke the qualities of a particular landscape—whether it be the southern United States or southern Italy, complete with its smells, flavors, and panoramas—is peerless. Indeed, it is not unreasonable to suggest that he is vastly underrated as a literary portraitist, working in the linguistic equivalents of pastels and merged pigments using very precise strokes rather than painting character and place in broad strokes and bold colors.

Despite the fact that many black writers eschewed the literary establishment in the sixties, opting to create poetry and drama that spoke directly to the need for black liberation, Williams has remained steadfast in his desire to reach as wide an audience as possible. Thus Williams is not prone to didacticism, instead placing his characters in situations where the human costs are revealed with clarity and complexity. The reader sees characters like Max Reddick in *The Man Who Cried I Am*, Ralph Joplin in *Sissie* and *The Junior Bachelor Society*, or Abraham Blackman in *Captain Blackman* pausing to wrestle with moral issues because they have the capacity to recognize that their actions affect others beyond their own immediate sphere of influence. At the same time, Williams' fiction insists that our humanity is most worth pursuing when we have the ability to live on our own terms. Characters who yield their autonomy to others or whose excessive appetites overwhelm them do not fare well in Williams' fictions. Ike Plunkett in *!Click Song*, Corporal Barnes in *The Man Who Cried I Am*, or Moon in *The Junior Bachelor Society* help readers of Williams' fiction come to understand men who discard their moral compass in favor of emotional crutches that provide them the illusion of control. In the case of Plunkett, heroin addiction helps him avoid his failure as a writer; for Barnes, it takes the form of a confusion between violence and sexual conquest; and for Moon it is the cynicism that grows in the absence of fraternity and trust. However, the characters who survive in Williams' stories, even if the cost is large, manage to do so because they see that the most essential tool for survival is some form of human connection.

Beginnings

John Alfred Williams was born on December 5, 1925, in a town just outside of Jackson, Mississippi. His parents, Ola and John Henry Williams, had met in Syracuse, New York, where they later returned to raise their family. As the oldest of four children, young John Williams grew up during the depression in Syracuse's Fifteenth Ward, which contained a mixture of German, Irish, Jewish, and Italian immigrants. In this setting, Williams was relatively sheltered from the racial animosity to be found in more polarized environments. Perhaps because of the ways that the depression leveled distinctions, Williams grew up much more aware of the fact that he was poor, feeling shame at the necessity for his family to be on relief. But overall, Williams experienced a childhood that was filled with learning how to play sports at the local Boy's Club, discovering a love for reading, and getting into as much trouble as he could find.

After his parents' separation when he was fifteen and entering Central High School, John fell into a pattern of dropping out of school, reenrolling for a time only to drop out again in order to help the family financially. Though he resented seeing his classmates continue through high school and leave him behind, he labored on a garbage truck, worked for a messenger service, and took any other job he could do to make money. When he was able to attend school, he hovered between the desire to engage in mischief with his buddies and apply himself academically. As his bitterness increased, so too did his desire to leave Syracuse, to find a way to escape the stricture of having to be a provider.

It was not until he reached the age of eighteen, when he enlisted in the U.S. Navy during World War II and was sent overseas early in 1944, that Williams discovered how deeply racial prejudice could run. As a hospital corpsman, Williams made his way through the South Pacific, where he witnessed race riots between black and white soldiers, had his letters home censored by superior officers, and spent time in the marine brig.

After his discharge from the navy in 1946, Williams returned to Syracuse, where he completed high school and then took advantage of the GI Bill to attend Syracuse University. Majoring in English and journalism, Williams had not, at this point, decided upon a career in writing. Though he was able to publish some of his pieces in black publications, including the *Chicago Defender*, Williams did not believe that writing would sustain him. He married Carolyn Clapton in 1947, graduated from Syracuse in 1950, attended graduate school for a time, then dropped out when he decided to take a job to support his wife and son Gregory, born in 1948.

Because it was difficult for him to find a job in journalism or radio, Williams opted to work first in a foundry, then as a vegetable clerk at a supermarket, and finally as a welfare caseworker in Onondaga County, a job he held for four years. He had managed, during this time, to publish small pieces in periodicals and to work as a local correspondent for *Jet* magazine. And since his return from the war, he had written poetry. Several of his poems were published in small literary publications. Using his own money, Williams published a book of his poems, many of which dealt with his work experiences or his family life. By 1953, two years after the birth of his second son, Dennis, Williams was feeling increasingly driven to write, despite the fact that it interfered with his ability to provide a steady paycheck.

The following year, Williams, having separated from his wife, joined his family in Los Angeles (his mother, brother, and sisters had moved there in 1948), where he lived with his brother and worked for a variety of employers, including NBC and CBS and a black-owned insurance company. But he soon discovered that

California could not provide him with the sort of artistic nourishment that he required and he moved back to New York, where he began to write fiction seriously. Living in Greenwich Village, Williams continued to work for a number of odd employers, including a vanity press (Comet Press) and the publisher Abelard-Schumann. By 1956, he had immersed himself in the work that would become his first novel *(The Angry Ones)*, drawn largely from his experiences searching for a career in which he could be happy.

The greatest tension of this time, Williams would discover, revolved around his needs to be an artist and to make money. He and his wife had divorced in 1957, Williams intimates, for reasons that stemmed from economic difficulty. Readers can see the recurrence of this theme in his fiction, most notably in *The Man Who Cried I Am* (1967) and *!Click Song* (1982). In the former, Max Reddick, in need of employment, tries to find a job in New York as a journalist with no success until circumstances force him to finish his novel and live on meager savings. In the latter, Cato Calswell Douglass discovers that his books have never sold well and that none of his publishers have worked very hard to sell them. He struggles to maintain his integrity, even as he sees friends and rivals alike succumb to despair or disillusionment. In many ways, both characters' experiences represent instances that Williams has taken from his own life. He suggests that a writer's identity is the product of his or her artistic talents along with how he or she deals with the hazards that arise while trying to make a set of observations about what it means to be human. Both characters are confronted with individuals of all races who either cannot fathom the importance of writing or who, recognizing its importance, seek to silence the writer's ability to tell the truth. What is also touching in the later novel is the way that Williams depicts the writer's struggle to form a deep and lasting bond with his children, to raise them in a society that is neither just nor prepared to become so. The warm relationship between Williams and his sons, Gregory and Dennis (who is also a novelist), is reflected in *!Click Song*.

John A. Williams

John A. Williams: Novelist

Many of Williams' novels depict masculine competition. In his best works, he suggests that the most difficult struggle is to prevent cruelty from becoming synonymous with manhood; his characters must work to maintain their humanity, often under tremendous duress. Though his male characters are in conflict about a wide variety of issues, one thing that arises repeatedly in Williams' fiction is their desire to live uninhibited lives, to be who they are on their own terms, despite the pressures of racism. If the male characters' lives fall into a state of acrimony, they do so because there are individuals—if not groups—who make it their business to harass the protagonist because he has something those individuals desire. Looking at Williams' career as a novelist, we can see how this conflict plays itself out, with Williams working on successively larger conceptual frames. Ultimately, the epic struggles he chronicles point us toward questions of humanity, not simple racial issues. Aware of the challenges their racial identity furnishes, his characters simply wish to live a life that is free of illusion. Unfortunately, life cannot guarantee them security in the face of other people's delusions; therefore Williams places as much importance on depicting conflict from within the black community as from outside it. He harbors no illusion about the fact that blacks, in seeking to improve their lot, can operate purely for their own self-interest; there are blacks just as willing to exploit their fellows as whites. Further, he does not shy away from representing the pitfalls of cultural nationalism; though he creates characters who hope to make things better for the black community, Williams' protagonists display a profound distrust of static racial polarities. And because so many of his characters are middle class and upwardly mobile, what is at issue is always a dualistic dilemma: how will his characters fare in the white world and what strategies will they use to maintain their ties in the black world? Williams' fiction is so compelling because his characters cannot always find satisfying answers; their motives can easily be misunderstood. They can reach a state of such numbing consternation that they give up trying to build lasting bridges. Or, if pushed, they can resort to violence because they feel there are no other strategies worth pursuing.

Williams' first novel, *The Angry Ones* (originally titled *One for New York*), which he completed in 1956 but did not see in print until 1960, can be viewed as a book that anticipates the widespread interest in writing by black authors. The novel deals with the life of Steven Hill, a bright and ambitious black man who simply wants to make a life in New York City the traditional way: marriage, children, satisfactory employment. *The Angry Ones* opens with Steve being dropped off in Philadelphia after driving cross-country with a friend from California. Williams' decision to open the story in Philadelphia intimates that his novel concerns the struggle for freedom. Though brief, Steve's presence in Philadelphia, the "birthplace of American Democracy," establishes the fact that he will grapple with how to liberate himself from the self-doubt and exploitation that will

bring down his closest friends, just as Americans liberated themselves from British rule.

The novel displays concerns about writing and writers that will appear in Williams' later fiction, most notably the difficulty black writers have of making anything resembling a lucrative salary, the ways that black newspapers are "a weapon rather than a medium," and the fact that Steve knows that the black press puts writers in the position of writing "reams of copy for pennies and [having] to wait six months to collect them." It also uses a convention that Williams will exploit with greater success and to deeper effect in his later novels: competition between two male writers.

Steve's best friends are Linton Mason and Obediah Robertson, men he has known since his college days. Williams uses the friendship among the three men as a way to chart what the city of New York, where the three eventually end up, can do to an individual's self-worth. As a place where it is difficult to "make it," New York unfolds for Steve, Lint, and Obie during "the season of impatience" when they confront the question, over and over, "Where [are] the better things?"

Making matters more complicated is Steve's decision to rekindle his relationship with an ex-lover, Grace, who is now his brother Grant's widow following Grant's death in the Korean War. Their relationship resumes despite the fact that Grace desires security over risk, the reason for their initial breakup. When she asks Steve what he wants out of life he replies, "A little money, Grace. Enough so I don't have to sit around a couple of days waiting for Friday to roll around. . . . Most of all, I'd like to see the end of the day come, knowing I'd done something worthwhile and not merely existed for that twenty-four hours." Though it is clear that he and Grace are in love, her desire to have middle-class respectability clashes with Steve's insistence that having dreams is the most important aspect of a good life. Because the novel is set in the fifties, it takes place at a time when Steve can observe the subtle changes in opportunity for blacks who have some education. In an interview at NBC, for example, a personnel officer tells him, "Our policy is to hire people on their ability—we don't care what the color of a man's skin is."

However, Steve becomes quickly aware of the fact that New York's allure is so powerful that it makes one forget how damaging it can be to the psyche. For example, when he tries to find an apartment, he is faced with discrimination by the superintendents in nice buildings who refuse to rent to blacks, and he sees the squalid buildings of those who will. At the same time, Lint points him to a job at Rocket Publishing, a vanity press. Roland Culver, the press's editor, specializes in the manipulation and exploitation of his staff, which, except for Steve, is all female. Though he finds this situation more "curious" than uncomfortable, Steve is slow to comprehend that his hard work in setting up promotional campaigns for the authors whose books Rocket will publish is mere window dressing. "One thing surprised me, later," he relates after starting the job, "was that most of the manuscripts I'd given poor reports on eventually showed up in production."

What appears to be a reputable enterprise is simply, Steve discovers, an illusion. Indeed, the novel is principally concerned with the necessity of discovering the difference between what is real and what is illusory. Those who buy into New York's illusions often fall into dangerous circumstances. As it turns out, none of Steve's friends are immune to bad turns of fortune. Lint, who earlier in the novel is likened to a brother by Steve, accuses him of having an affair with his wife, Bobbie. The fact that Lint is white and that he so quickly falls into a state of racial animosity, though slightly implausible, shows how the quest for masculine dignity often jeopardizes relationships between black and white men. In the novel's climax, Lint and Steve have a fistfight, which only ends when Steve receives a phone call informing him that Obie, despondent over his own difficult job situation, has shot himself in the head and died. With his relationships with his two best friends over and only the prospect of a life with Grace as a certainty, Steve quits his job at Rocket and calls a man at an employment agency he had

visited some weeks earlier. The novel ends with a cautious optimism—Steve emphasizes his integrity by quitting an unacceptable job and beginning to search for the security of another, which emphasizes integrity over middle-class respectability.

Night Song

In Williams' second novel, the critically acclaimed *Night Song*, we find him once again depicting the lives of two men—one black, the other white—to make the point that men from all backgrounds are subject to failure and decline. What Williams makes clear, however, is that race can determine whether a fallen man gets an opportunity at redemption. The two men in the novel, Richie "Eagle" Stokes and David Hillary, are from different walks of life: Eagle is a renowned black jazz musician, Hillary is a white academic. Both are substance abusers: Eagle is a heroin addict, Hillary is an alcoholic. Based on the life of Charlie Parker, Eagle's story unfolds in the novel as one headed for a final, tragic end. Hillary's life, on the other hand, takes a turn for the better after a time, and the novel ends with his having received an offer to teach at an upstate New York college. Though Eagle has befriended him and brought Hillary into his circle, Hillary nonetheless does not intervene when a cop beats Eagle.

The novel's moral fulcrum does not come from either Eagle or Hillary, however. Rather, it comes from Keel Robinson, a black former preacher trained at Harvard Seminary. He runs a small coffee house, where he becomes Eagle's patron and offers Hillary a job and a chance to right his life. He is consumed for most of the novel with trying to grasp what role he might play in bettering the lives of others, especially in his relationship with Della, a white woman. This aspect of the novel—the interracial relationship—is not gratuitous; rather, Williams uses it as a way to articulate the need to love in the face of human frailty. By novel's end, Keel and Della have begun to work toward a more fulfilling relationship, but this is cast against the backdrop of Eagle's death and Hillary's escape back into respectability.

One other note about *Night Song* is its relationship to a failed book project on Charlie Parker. In an article on Parker published in 1960, Williams wrote, "By choosing to fight [discrimination], Bird automatically becomes a martyr; he is spoken of in these tones today. There is a strong suspicion Bird's personality helped change the role of the Negro jazzman. The Negro no longer had to conceal the fact that he had a mind." In many ways, both *Night Song* and the article on Parker gave Williams an opportunity to think about how hard it was for black artists to create lasting art and the obstacles white artists did not have to consider when they sat down to do their work.

Williams' love of Parker and jazz music come through very clearly in *Night Song* and in later novels as well; the music and the men who play it provide an important source of atmospheric content in his work. They also help him to round out his characters by giving them a lens through which to understand their lives as black Americans. Early on in *Night Song*, Eagle gives voice to the energies animating the blues: "I guess I was damned near gone last night. . . . Any night will do. I'm tired. I'm tired of things in this land: kids tryin' to go to school, shysters all over you, phonies ass-hole deep— . . . I'm tired of so many things, but goddam if I'll quit." What Eagle articulates here is the paradoxical nature of the blues; he characterizes all the obstructions in his life as drains on his artistic energy but he simultaneously implies that without these impediments his artistic endeavor would lack vitality and purpose. Like Parker, who died at the age of thirty-four, Eagle's life finally does come down to spiritual exhaustion and he eventually succumbs. But his demise is juxtaposed against David Hillary's false sense of renewal. Though Hillary actually despises Eagle, he nonetheless plans, upon returning to a job in an English department, to show Eagle off to his colleagues, as if to demonstrate his humanity. What Williams suggests here is the tenuous relationship between jazz and its audience, the ways that whites who claim a love for the black jazzman can, away from the jazz club, just as quickly fall back into racist disdain that ignores musical genius.

Sissie

The last novel of what could be referred to as Williams' "first phase" is *Sissie*, published in 1963. Unlike the first two novels, which juxtaposed the lives of two men striving for some form of success, Williams explores the dynamics of a black family in which the matriarch, Sissie, leaves a legacy of insecurity and self-doubt in her two surviving children, Ralph and Iris Joplin. When the novel begins, Iris is just returning from Europe, where she has become a well-known jazz singer. Her brother Ralph has become a successful playwright with a play on Broadway.

Set in a town that resembles Williams' native Syracuse, the novel begins with Sissie, married for a second time and living on the West Coast, near death. As Iris and Ralph prepare to fly across the country to see their mother before she dies, they reminiscence about the events that have led them to their respective crossroads. For Ralph, there is the rage and bitterness he feels because Sissie abandoned him in a foster home and left for Chicago to find work. He feels a hatred for his mother, which abates only when he finds love with his psychiatrist's receptionist. In writing that is noteworthy for its subtle probing of the transaction that unfolds between a psychiatrist and his patient, Williams allows Ralph to flash back to his first marriage, the birth of his daughter, and his halfhearted attempts to forge a relationship with his father. Talking to Dr. Bluman, Ralph describes his life so that we get events both from his point of view and from an omniscient narrator. The reader discovers that Ralph has become adept at minimizing the difficulty of his life with Sissie, even as he works to understand his family's plight in the face of racial prejudice and discrimination. This ability proves very difficult to reconcile, however, in light of Ralph's attempt to complete and sell his first play. Interestingly, he never tells Bluman about Doughnut, the white man he killed during the war and whose face he still sees in a recurring nightmare. The only person he has told about the murder is Iris.

But Iris is not without her demons, either. Sissie stands as the great judge of her life. When Iris marries an army lieutenant and moves to Germany, she does so having decided to give up her real love: singing, a talent she has inherited from her father. Perhaps because of this talent, Sissie insists that Iris' biggest aspiration should be to have children and make Harry, her new husband, happy. This is difficult advice for Iris to follow, if only because she realizes that what is most lacking in her life is using her voice. In what stands as remarkably candid writing for the time period, especially as it concerns black female sexuality, Williams chronicles Harry's inadequacy as a lover and includes a scene that foreshadows the breakup of the marriage. "She felt him moving away and when that lovely paralysis ebbed, she looked at him with hard eyes and a defiant smile that showed only around her lips. His eyes filled with hatred. Her eyes laughed him down. Wordlessly, he rose and went off." Though Williams is not generally described as championing women in any particular way, Iris is characterized as determined and dedicated. When she joins Time Curry's band, first as an accompanying vocalist and then later as the band's headliner, she must confront her inability to love, a trait she believes she has acquired directly from her mother.

The novel thus presents a family that has done whatever was necessary to survive hard times. Though the family has not remained intact—three of the five Joplin children die, Iris and Ralph's father abandons them—the novel's message is that people must figure out the best contingencies for making it through difficult times. But it also poses deep questions as to whether the ends justify the means, whether black children are not deserving of the same kind of unequivocal love and concern that other children receive. Moreover, Sissie, with her propensity to acknowledge her own desires (even if she acts on them only sporadically), anticipates a character like Toni Morrison's Eva Peace in *Sula*, who endures some of the same indignities but possesses more in the way of

tragic resourcefulness. She eventually wends her way into the middle-class lifestyle she desires, but only at the cost of her children's love. At novel's end, she begs Iris' forgiveness but dies before the daughter relents.

In many ways, Williams' decision to tackle such a multifaceted theme as the black family marked a growing maturity in his work. Moving swiftly away from the singular predicaments of the first two novels, Williams was beginning to develop characters whose complexity drives the novel's plot, rather than the plot's dominating the reader's attention. Moreover, he is clearly as comfortable writing about settings in Europe as he is writing about New York. With *Sissie*, Williams began to wrest more complexity from the raw material of his own experience, setting the stage for what many consider his finest work.

The Man Who Cried I Am

Williams published the novel for which he is best known, *The Man Who Cried I Am*, in 1967. Though it can be characterized in a variety of ways, it is perhaps best thought of as a roman à clef. The novel chronicles the exploits of Max Reddick from the beginning of his career to the end, but the novel's depiction of the King Alfred Plan (a contingency plan directed at the black community in the event of a coordinated racial rebellion) also allows us to describe this work as a "spy thriller" as well. Williams manages, however, to avoid making the novel into a "potboiler," a story whose plot overwhelms the attempt to portray human relationships. Beginning the novel in Leiden, the Netherlands, Williams moves backward and forward through time, in the process making Max Reddick into one of the most memorable characters in American fiction. Because he ruminates on his role in the cataclysm that is history, Max is both witness and survivor, wizened by his life as a writer but diminished by it as well. Of greatest importance, Williams suggests, is that Max has loved and lost more than once, but somehow kept his integrity intact.

A real turning point in Max's life comes when he falls in love with Lillian Patch, a schoolteacher he meets after returning to New York from World War II. Though she loves him, Lillian insists that Max find a job to support them, rather than relying on his writing. When she asks the question "Could we live on your writing?" Max realizes that he cannot answer with any certainty. Though he has experience as a journalist with a black newspaper, he is hesitant to return to that life, wanting instead to continue writing his novel. Things reach an impasse when Max discovers Lillian is pregnant. Though he has decided to seek employment, all his efforts to find a newspaper job are futile. Seeing this, Lillian decides to get an abortion, suffers a sudden hemorrhage, and dies. Symbolically speaking, what has killed Lillian was her adherence to black middle-class notions of the American Dream. And though Max achieves success as a prizewinning journalist and novelist after her death, eventually making the kind of money that would have satisfied Lillian's desire to live a middle-class life, his sense of outrage and cynicism remain. It takes the form of an interior voice Williams calls "Saminone," who talks to Max as if to remind him that in spite of his achievements, he is still a nigger.

What this suggests is that Williams' novel is as much about the assaults on black male identity as it is about race relations. Indeed, perhaps the most important thing about *The Man Who Cried I Am* is that it manages to balance these impulses against a rumination about the middle third of the twentieth century, from the 1930s to the 1960s. Once again, Williams sets up the relationship—some supportive, others antagonistic—between characters who share the same profession. In this instance, he uses two characters: Harry Ames, who bears a close resemblance to Richard Wright, and Kermit Shea, who, like Max, is a graduate of Western Reserve, Class of '37, but whose white skin provides him with all the advantages he needs to outpace Max.

Williams details the way that Ames and Max become friends in the 1930s, as their respective careers as writers take shape. Ames, as the older writer, is beginning to enjoy great success (having published the book meant to stand as the equivalent to Wright's *Native Son*). Max, younger and more unsure of himself, has, when the two meet, just published a novel and is discovering that the life of a black writer is made difficult by the people who are threatened by the very category itself.

Though this novel is valuable on any number of fronts, its chief significance is its deep rumination on what it means to be a black writer in America in the mid-twentieth century. As Williams creates him, Harry Ames understands the function of the black writer to be to incite rebellion. "When my name is mentioned," Harry tells Max early in the novel, "I want people to jerk up and look for trouble; I want trouble to be my middle name when I write about America." Williams succeeds in raising the stakes on Ames's words. As the novelist is depicted in *The Man Who Cried I Am*, it is clear Williams wishes to suggest that writers are never far from politics, that their work in fact makes them important figures in the political world (which is borne out at least partially when we look at Wright's life in international politics).

The novel also raises male rivalry to a higher pitch. As a well-connected journalist at a major magazine, Max knows exactly what to do with the materials in the briefcase that Ames has left for him prior to his death in Paris, and requests he place into capable hands. As he reads the files from the briefcase, Max realizes that the real reason Ames had chosen to do this has more to do with his desire to see Max dead, for Ames knows that the contents of the briefcase represent certain death. Earlier in the novel, before Ames leaves for the States, Max has a brief sexual liaison with Ames's wife, Charlotte, and Ames has decided that Max must die for his betrayal. As the novel begins, the reader comes to understand that Max is dying of rectal cancer and so he can view Harry's act through a clarity produced by his impending death. Taken on a symbolic level, the struggle on the part of artists to go places in the human mind and heart where few can bear to explore is finally what makes *The Man Who Cried I Am* such a compelling novel. Max's rectal cancer, thought of allegorically, has a great deal to do with the fact that his devotion to telling the truth literally leads to his being eaten from the inside out. That Williams makes it rectal cancer is also not to be dismissed as capricious or coincidence; rather, he wants to suggest that a black man (or woman) who elects to write represents a pain in America's proverbial backside. The King Alfred Plan can be understood, then, as Williams' attempt to assert that a body politic that has not endeavored to enforce equality among its citizens will, ironically, work to rid itself of them rather than make the necessary changes. Hence the Plan is a purification rite: blacks, as the novel's later chapters insist, are the "cancer" eating America from the inside out, and thus they must be contained and, most likely, exterminated.

Racism as a Systemic Problem

Unlike Williams' first three novels, which "trace the problems facing blacks in a white society," *The Man Who Cried I Am, Sons of Darkness, Sons of Light* (1969), and *Captain Blackman* (1972) work to view these problems as systemic, not the result of individuals' inability to resist prejudice. Writing at a time when mainstream publishers wanted anything dealing with the "race problem," Williams had to fight to resist the temptation to compromise his standards. He was not totally successful.

In an interview with Earl A. Cash, Williams describes *Sons of Darkness* as his least favorite book, referring to it as "one of my worst novels," concluding that it was a book he wrote "comparatively quickly," to make money.

In *Sons of Darkness*, Eugene Browning, a college professor turned activist, working for an NAACP-like organization called the Institute for Racial Justice, decides that nonviolent resistance is no longer a viable solution, particularly after a white cop kills an unarmed young black man. Rather that simply engage in rhetoric, however, Browning decides to hire a hit man to kill the racist cop. After turning to an old friend with Mafia connections, Browning uses his skills as an organizational fund-raiser to raise the necessary money to pay for the hit.

Though it would be easy to dismiss this novel as being simply a novel of the moment, reflective of the militant racial politics of the late sixties, a look at how hard Williams works to develop Itzhak Hod, the Israeli hit man, argues that this novel offers more than the usual thriller. Though it does have, per Williams' own criticism of the book, a linear plot progression, Browning's ambivalence about whether he has done the right thing, his strained relationship with his wife and eldest daughter, as well as his depiction of the Mafia don as both sympathetic and complex make this book, subtitled *A Novel of Some Probability*, an engaging piece of Williams' oeuvre.

Williams' next move was to turn back toward historical fiction, to explore something that had been part of *The Man Who Cried I Am* and that Williams himself had experienced during World War II: the racism to be found in the American armed forces, particularly the army. In *Captain Blackman* (1972), Williams examines the history of African American participation in each of America's wars, starting with the Revolution and ending with the Vietnam War. Abraham Blackman is an Army captain who, while out on patrol with his men, recognizes an ambush and, upon warning his men, is severely wounded. What unfolds occurs within Blackman's traumatized psyche, when he finds himself, still dressed in his fatigues, among men wearing eighteenth-century dress about to fight their first battle in the American Revolution.

Like *The Man Who Cried I Am*, this novel has at its core a deep concern with restoring the broken thread of history. Indeed, both novels share the notion that to be without history is to live a life of delusion. Further, the novel argues that black soldiers have participated in America's armed conflicts with distinction, but that participation has always been marked by unequal pay, lack of opportunity, and a dearth of basic respect from their fellow white soldiers. Published just a few years before the end of the Vietnam War, *Captain Blackman* brought into public discussion the racial unrest that had been rumored to be part of the American military presence in Vietnam, especially after Martin Luther King's death in 1968. Though it might have been politically correct to do so, the novel does not resort to antiwar commentary, opting instead to present the military experience as one that, for many black soldiers, is unavoidable due to their lower status in the racial hierarchy.

Williams does an excellent job of presenting the double-edged nature of military service. On the one hand, it allows us to see the difference between the respect accorded black troops by French commanders during World War I and on the other, the disrespect and dishonor visited upon them by American officers. Using a series of interchapters referred to as "Drumtaps" and "Cadences," Williams presents the historical overview of the military conflict in which Abe Blackman finds himself. For example, chapter 7 of the novel begins:

> The General answered smartly: "Yes, sir, those are the niggers. Gentleman, taking the lesson from our British cousins, we're merely employing one group of natives, the niggers, to fight another group of natives, the Indians. The strategy has met with marked success in the British dominions; we would be seriously amiss if we failed to use the same method."

What Williams communicates here, with but a simple swerve of the plot, is that black soldiers have historically been used as fodder by the U.S. armed forces. But their exploitation is merely part of a larger, more insidious design, one that ensures America's survival as a white supremacist illusion. The point, Williams suggests, is that we need to understand Abraham Blackman as a figure who is moving forward through history, from one military conflict to the next, but because of the military's racial prejudice he must not follow Army policy; he must march to a beat of his own devising or death will be the certain result.

Though the novel deals with each historical period with great detail, working to depict the conditions under which black men in the military labored, Williams' novel cannot be said to be a direct transposition of his own experiences in the navy. Indeed, by opting to make Abraham

Blackman a soldier in the army rather than the navy, Williams maintains some level of distance from his material. Though Abraham Blackman loses his leg in a Vietcong ambush, he decides that he will have his revenge by using black men who can pass for white to take over the military. The end of the novel is a bit implausible; however, it reflects Williams' frustration with the United States and his desire to depict moments where radical changes result because blacks take matters into their own hands. As the third novel in trilogy of works that explore the obstacles to blacks enjoying the full measure of American citizenship, *Captain Blackman* points to what appears to be Williams' sense of pessimism toward America and his use of fantasy and speculation to explore what lies on the other side.

Williams on Middle Age

In looking at the novels that appear after Williams' major phase, one sees Williams trying to ruminate upon the vagaries of middle age. In novels like *!Click Song* (1982), *Mothersill and the Foxes* (1975), *The Junior Bachelor Society* (published in 1976 and made into a miniseries by NBC in 1981), and *Jacob's Ladder* (1987), Williams presents us with protagonists who can understand their lives only by grappling with the realization of their own mortality.

As Gilbert H. Muller has described *Mothersill*, it represents a send-up of the myth of black male sexual prowess. The hero, Odell Mothersill, is described as "well-educated, urbane, professional. He is a man with a social conscience. He is warm and humane but ultimately narcissistic, unable to transcend egotism." In one particularly raucous scene, Mothersill makes love repeatedly to Elizabeth Cohen, as his downstairs neighbor, seventy-year-old Mrs. Brady, listens so intently that she must gratify herself with hot dogs. Though Williams appears to be trying to debunk the myth, the difficulty here is finding the correct vehicle to persuade the reader of his seriousness, which he never succeeds in doing. It can be seen, however, as a precursor to novels by Ishmael Reed, Al Young, and, later, Trey Ellis.

The Junior Bachelor Society deals with the intertwining lives of seven black men who have grown up together in the same neighborhood but whose lives have taken radically different turns. Bubbles and Cudjo have remained in town, working in a foundry, satisfied to show their athletic prowess in games of weekend football. D'Artagnan Foxx is a concert singer who lives as a bisexual in Europe. Clarence Henderson is a college professor, having been an all-American at Morris Brown College. Ralph Joplin, from Williams' earlier novel, *Sissie*, is resurrected as one of the Bachelors. And the group is rounded out by Ezzard Jackson, an unhappy executive, and Moon, the best athlete of the group who, ironically, makes a living as a pimp in California.

The plot centers on the reunion of the men, now in middle age, to honor the man who has shepherded each of them into manhood, Coach Chappie Davis. As members of *The Junior Bachelor Society*, these men have been imbued with the sense that life, like sports, has rules that must not be broken. As the former coach of a special group of young men, Chappie is beloved. However, Williams, himself entering middle age, uses the novel as a way to ponder the ways that time and circumstance are the enemy of even the most scrupulous of men, laying waste to discipline and an adherence to fair play. This is what makes Moon so compelling as a character, for even as Williams is ambivalent about him, he also knows that Moon's life is beset by violence that means he lives a difficult life. Moon's violence is distinguished from that which results from police corruption of institutional power. The other men, by contrast, live lives characterized by the need for stability: the higher they climb, the less likely they seem able to sustain it. The lesson of the novel is that, in the face of mounting predicaments, human connection is the most important aspect of life. Though we are not sure how each of the Bachelors will resolve the issues in their respective lives, the end of the novel speaks to the value of communitas; even as the Moons of the world go unpunished for their crimes, they, too, require a place among their fellows.

Six years after *The Junior Bachelor Society* (and its reworking into a television production), Williams ended a hiatus from novel writing with the publication of *!Click Song*. Also during this time, Williams left his position as a Distinguished Writer at City College of New York and joined the faculty of Rutgers University as the Paul Robeson Distinguished Professor of English, a post from which he retired in 1998. In *!Click Song* Williams ruminates upon the publishing industry and the writing profession as interdependent wholes and finds both of them to be corrupt. Though the novel could be read as the sour grapes of a "minor" novelist, *!Click Song* is distinguished by its unflinching honesty about the publishing industry and the ways it diminishes literary art. Williams' skill at creating a changing global landscape is impressive. Even as the novel occasionally lapses into sentimentality, it does suggest that the black novelist, poet, dramatist, and editor lead lives that can be characterized as degrading. It also intimates that the lives of white writers, while they can be equally demoralized, are made better by a sign system that validates their existence.

!Click Song begins with news of the suicide of Paul Kaminsky Cummings, a Jewish writer who is the friend and rival of the novel's protagonist, Cato Douglass, a black novelist who, while he is in many ways just as ambitious and talented as Cummings, does not enjoy the same level of notoriety. Through a series of flashbacks, Williams traces the development of both men's literary careers. Though Douglass enjoys success earlier than Cummings, publishing several books before the latter finishes his first full-blown novel, it is ultimately Cummings who acquires the greater star power. But it is not without its costs, for Cummings must accept his background. Having denied his Jewishness and invented a past for himself as the son of a labor organizer, Cummings provides Williams with a way to demonstrate that with all the self-delusions black writers may embrace—drugs, self-aggrandizement, self-hatred, or jealous rage—they cannot escape from the vagaries of race, especially as it pertains to skin color. In some of his most candid writing, Williams'

Cato Douglass must confront the obstacles that are meant to prevent him from achieving true greatness as an American writer. His decision to marry a white woman (which reflects Williams' own decision to marry a second time to a white woman, Lorrain Isaac, whom he married in 1965), is an excellent vehicle through which to explore Douglass' attempt to transcend racial limitations.

Of further interest is Williams' decision to place figures who surely represent Norman Mailer, Ralph Ellison, Richard Wright, and James Baldwin (among a number of lesser-known writers), as if he feels the need to set the record straight with regard to literary politics. *!Click Song* depicts both Ellison and Baldwin as operating at a relative remove from other black writers' efforts to become successful. Indeed, Williams cannot resist the impulse to chastise Ellison for what many termed his disinterest or distance from other black writers during the sixties and seventies.

But the novel's pivotal moment is juxtaposed against a reading he has given, as a novelist with a "fraying reputation," where only ten students show up to a reading sponsored by a black studies department at a university in Colorado. After he has read from his latest novel for nearly an hour and a half, a young woman asks Douglass to talk about the responsibilities of the black writer to black people. His reply is, in the context of both the novel and Williams' career, very important to consider. "They are . . . in exact proportion to the responsibilities the black community has to its writers, regardless of all obstacles, real or imagined. If the people they have none, then they cannot expect the writer to have them." Though *!Click Song* was by no means Williams' swan song as a novelist (he has since published three more novels), it was, perhaps, an opportunity to unburden himself in ways he had not previously done.

The novel does parallel many aspects of Williams' career as a novelist. And it is interesting to note that he has, in ways that mirror many of the writers from his generation, written movingly about what it means for black men to be involved with white women. Williams remar-

ried in the sixties and the reader can observe that his wife, Lori, is the person to whom he dedicates his books. Though it might not be considered politically correct, in the wake of the emergence of black female writers, Williams' novels have not shied away from representing the difficulties that accompany interracial marriage. Cato Douglass' relationship with his second wife, Allis, who is Jewish, is marked by attempts by her family to undermine the relationship. But the marriage is also tempered by the political upheavals of the sixties, when it is clear that Cato and Allis must work to transcend racial difference to forge a bond that can withstand the pressures.

Though on first glance it would seem that Williams' fiction includes interracial romance in order to take advantage of the sensationalism that often accompanied black writing during the sixties, as if it were meant to depict black men's (and white women's) hidden sexual desire, such a conclusion would be simplistic and inaccurate. Williams' goal, in looking at novels as varied as *The Man Who Cried I Am*, *!Click Song*, *Night Song*, and *The Junior Bachelor Society*, is always to depict the struggle to become and remain human, for his characters to rise above the false distinctions that separate human beings. Though his male characters are often trapped in circumstances that leave them angry and demoralized, the reader comes to understand the complexity of these men as Williams moves them through a variety of emotional states. And to his credit, his white female characters are never rendered as passive stereotypes, rather they are depicted as women who, whether or not they fully understand the impact of racism on the lives of the men they love, are singularly devoted to them. Indeed, in *The Man Who Cried I Am*, Max meets Margit Westoever and sees her as a white version of his dead lover, Lillian.

Inevitably, Williams' fiction, along with that of James Baldwin and William Marvin Kelley, can be viewed as some of the earliest ruminations on masculinity in African American fiction. Though he emphasizes this discussion in a racial context, he nonetheless works to provide us with characters—like Kermit Shea in

The Man Who Cried I Am—who illuminate men's sexual and social anxieties. Because of his own marriage, Williams' fiction presents an optimistic turn, suggesting that even as America fails to live up to its democratic promise, hope is to be found in the prospects of two individuals who discover one another in spite of America's horrible racial legacy and together build a relationship strong enough to resist its influence.

Clifford's Blues

Though Williams is himself skeptical of what critics have to say about black writing, opting instead to live by his own set of standards, it could be that in *Clifford's Blues* we find him taking risks not seen prior to this moment in African American writing. Published in 1999, when Williams had reached the age of seventy-five, the novel deals with a gay black man who is held as a prisoner of war in a concentration camp. Like *Captain Blackman*, the book has been meticulously researched, a process Williams began after driving through Germany with his wife. *Clifford's Blues* completes a trilogy of historical fiction that, along with *The Man Who Cried I Am* and *Captain Blackman*, "explor[es] the hidden aspects of the African American experience." Rather than depicting that experience in monolithic terms, Williams, by taking a character who is thrice marginal—the black who is an artist who is also gay—forces the reader to understand the great lengths to which the character must go to retain his faith in a higher being. But more than this, there is still the fact that as in *Captain Blackman*, Williams has undertaken to write a previously untold story that required telling.

Though he began the novel with the impulse to move back and forth across time, between Clifford's experiences in Dachau and a black family in the present, Williams eventually opted to render Clifford's experiences in diary form. He uses an exchange of letters between two friends, one of whom has acquired the diary from an old German whose life was spared by black American GIs, to frame the story. Beginning in 1933, the diary chronicles Clifford's travails. He opens an early passage:

> My name's Clifford Pepperidge and I am in trouble. I'm an American Negro and I play piano, sometimes, and I'm a vocalist, too. I shouldn't be here, but they brought me. Didn't listen when I was in Berlin, either. I am in Protective Custody, they call it. They've said I'll be out as soon as they finish their investigation. I hope so. God, I hate this place. . . . Damn. I'd even go back South to get out of here.

Though he suffers, his life is made easier by the fact that he is a singer and so he entertains the camp commandant in exchange for privileges and survival. What makes the novel's movement credible is that Pepperidge continually uses the American South as a way to create analogies for his suffering. Though it was life in the South that drove him away from the States, it is likewise the South that serves as a way to understand the Nazi's intentions. Further, because Clifford Pepperidge understands what it means to be invisible, he is able to empathize with the camp's other victims.

The fact that the diary begins in the years between World Wars I and II—when isolationism reached its peak in the United States; when the depression gripped the nation, turning its gaze inward—points to Williams' attempt to avoid sensationalizing events in Dachau. By working to create a novelistic rhythm where a decade's atrocities are broken down into disruptions of the camp's numbing routine and backbreaking labor, Williams heightens the reader's sense that Dachau's horrors are such that long after the camps are liberated, memories of its inhabitants and what they endured will linger. And by using the two letters framing the book as a way to raise the diary to the level of historical tract, Williams intimates that the horrors Clifford Pepperidge endures cannot be contained in polite circles, but neither are they easily translated into "history." Unlike fiction, which is an authorial invention, history demands verification and the patience to transform loose ends into logical conclusions. But the book ends with Dr. Jayson Jones, a historian, noting that "no one is going to be eager to hear Clifford play *these* blues," as if to suggest that he cannot, in the early stages of the project, imagine how the history will fit into what we think we know of a place like Dachau. As he does in novels like *The Man Who Cried I Am*, *Captain Blackman*, and *!Click Song*, Williams leaves the reader with the sense that one can never trust "history." There is always something left out, always some essential part of the story that is omitted. That Dr. Jones recognizes that there are those who may not wish to hear Clifford Pepperidge's cry of loneliness and despair is endemic, Williams suggests, of how race ritual prevents us from reaching across boundaries to address the suffering of the other. The blues Clifford sings, like all blues, are about disrupting those stories we think we know, about the calculus of suffering.

John A. Williams: Journalist

Any discussion of Williams would be incomplete were we not to make mention of his career as a journalist and writer of nonfiction works. Indeed, his work in this area makes him literary kin to figures as diverse as W. E. B. DuBois, Sterling A. Brown, Langston Hughes, and more recently, James Baldwin. As Gilbert Muller suggests, Williams' nonfiction and journalism bear a strong relationship to some of the themes to be found in his fiction. It is especially important to note that Williams' work as a journalist and nonfiction writer allows him the space to ruminate upon America as "a nation at war with itself." This perspective allows him to be equally critical of the sorts of obtuse conclusions and ill-conceived strategies formulated on both sides of the color line.

In 1963, Williams published an article in *Ebony* magazine entitled "The Negro in Literature Today." There he wrote, "If the Negro has nothing else . . . he has had the truth of American hypocrisy in the marrow of his bones." He goes on to chronicle the difficulties black writers face, not only in publishing their work but also in getting it taken seriously once it is pub-

lished. The article hearkens back to several articles published by Sterling A. Brown, including "Negro Characters as Seen by White Authors" and "Our Literary Audience." In the former, Brown seeks to lay out the stereotypes that black writers must confront in the works of white writers. In the latter, he notes, "Without great audiences we cannot have great poets." Williams advances some of Brown's observations, noting that there are a number of themes, such as interracial relationships, which are more warmly received in the works of white writers like Norman Mailer, John Updike, Bernard Malamud, and Jack Kerouac than in those by black writers. In works by black writers those themes can be dismissed within the realm of black revenge toward the white man or as the most serious indicator of how explosive race relations can become when sexuality is made part of that discussion.

Using nonfiction and journalism as spaces in which he could develop a deeper, more profound sense of what it means to be an American, Williams produced a number of pieces that illuminate the postwar United States. For example, in his book *The King God Couldn't Save* (1970), Williams depicts the failed quest of Martin Luther King. In work that anticipates the reckoning of historians and commentators on the shortcomings of the Civil Rights movement, Williams challenges the conventional view of King as visionary hero, instead positing him as the product of a number of contradictory forces that shaped him, including his class background and religious and ethical leanings. The picture that emerges is one that leads to the conclusion that King was nothing more than a creation of the dominant imagination, a figure who could assuage the fears of a white population who wished to maintain its superiority and status, while involved with advancing the illusion of racial progress.

There are very strong relationships to be drawn between Williams' "meditation" on King in this book and the character meant to stand for King in *The Man Who Cried I Am*, Reverend Paul Durrell. The novel's publication date, some three years before the nonfiction work, suggests that Williams had long been thinking about King as a public figure worth critique. Indeed, in an exchange between Max Reddick and Durrell, Williams has Reddick inform Durrell of his belief that he is "dangerous," noting that the entirety of the Civil Rights movement is tied to him, meaning that once he becomes a threat to the status quo, the movement will die with him. Such prescience, it is clear, is the result of Williams' travels as a journalist, which led him from one end of the country to another, trying to discern what, exactly, it means to be an American.

The result of such mobility is to be found in Williams' book *This Is My Country Too*, which was published in 1964, after he had been commissioned to write a two-part article by *Holiday* in 1963. He begins the book by noting, "I set out in search of an old dream, one that faded, came back into focus, and faded again." Beginning his travels in his native Syracuse and then heading North, Williams visits Vermont and New Hampshire by car, then switching to plane travel heads to Boston and Detroit, then by car again southward to Louisville, Nashville, Atlanta, Birmingham, New Orleans, and points in between. In many ways, the southern portion of the trip is reminiscent of the trip Albert Murray takes much later in his book *South to a Very Old Place* (1971). Williams ends his trip, fittingly, in Washington, D.C., where he can ponder the paradox of being an American, concluding, "America has yet to sing its greatest songs."

Conclusions

Though it would seem that John A. Williams' best-known novels might easily be dismissed as the works of a minor writer, such a conclusion would be wrong indeed. Williams' approach to writing is mirrored in Cato Calswell Douglass' rejection of black cultural nationalism; he has insisted on emphasizing craft over politics, depth over surfaces, and steady progress over the attraction of fads. His work, though it has not been explored sufficiently, offers the opportunity for scholars to examine the middle portion of the twentieth century through the eyes of a writer who has looked at America and its contradictions with unflinching honesty.

Selected Bibliography

PRIMARY WORKS

NOVELS

The Angry Ones. New York: Norton, 1960. Reprint, 1996.

Night Song. New York: Farrar, Straus and Cudahy, 1961.

Sissie. New York: Farrar, Straus and Cudahy, 1963.

This is My Country, Too. New York: American Library, 1965.

The Man Who Cried I Am. New York: Thunder's Mouth Press, 1967. Reprint, 1985.

Sons of Darkness, Sons of Light: A Novel of Some Probability. Boston: Little, Brown, and Company, 1969.

The King God Didn't Save: Reflections on the Life of Martin Luther King, Jr. New York: Coward-McCann, 1970.

Captain Blackman. New York: Thunder's Mouth Press, 1972. Reprint, 1988.

Mothersill and the Foxes. Garden City, N.Y.: Doubleday & Company, 1975.

The Junior Bachelor Society. Garden City, NY: Doubleday and Company, 1976.

!Click Song. New York: Thunder's Mouth Press, 1982. Reprint, 1987.

Jacob's Ladder. New York, Thunder's Mouth Press, 1987.

Clifford's Blues. Minneapolis: Coffee House Press, 1999.

NONFICTION

Flashbacks: A Twenty Year Diary of Article Writing. Garden City, N.Y.: Anchor Press Doubleday, 1972.

If I Stop I'll Die: The Comedy and Tragedy of Richard Pryor. With Dennis A. Williams. New York: Thunder's Mouth Press, 1991.

SECONDARY WORKS

BIOGRAPHICAL AND CRITICAL STUDIES

Blaine, Michael, Raymond Bowen, and Gilbert Muller. "*Clifford's Blues*: A Conversation with John A. Williams." *New York Stories*, Winter 2000, pp. 19–26.

Burke, William M. "The Resistance of John A. Williams: *The Man Who Cried I Am*." *Critique: Studies in Modern Fiction* 15, no. 3:5–14.

Cash, Earl A. *John A. Williams: The Evolution of a Black Writer*. New York: The Third Press, 1975.

Fleming, Robert E. "The Nightmare Level of *The Man Who Cried I Am*." *Contemporary Literature* 14:186–96.

Karrer, Wolfgang. "Multiperspective and the Hazards of Integration: John Williams' *Night Song*." In *The*

Afro-American Novel Since 1960. Edited by Peter Bruck and Wolfgang Karrer. Amsterdam: Gruner, 1982. Pp. 75–101.

Klotman, Phyllis R. "An Examination of the Black Confidence Man in Two Black Novels: *The Man Who Cried I Am* and *dem.*" *American Literature* 44:596–611.

Muller, Gilbert H. *John A. Williams.* Boston: Twayne, 1984.

Reckley, Ralph, Sr. "John A. Williams' *Sissie:* A Study of the Black Male and His Family." *Mawa Review* 5, no. 1:15–19 (June 1990).

Reilly, John M. "Thinking History in *The Man Who Cried I Am.*" *Black American Literature Forum* 21, nos. 1–2:25–42 (Spring–Summer 1987).

Smith, Anneliese H. "A Pain in the Ass: Metaphor in John A. Williams' *The Man Who Cried I Am.*" *Studies in Black Literature* 3, no. 3:25–27.

Smith, Virginia Whatley. "Sorcery, Double-Consciousness, and Warring Souls: An Intertextual Reading of *Middle Passage* and *Captain Blackman.*" *African American Review* 30, no. 4: 659–74 (Winter 1996).

Walcott, Ronald. "*The Man Who Cried I Am:* Crying in the Dark." *Studies in Black Literature* 3, no. 1:24–32.

SHERLEY ANNE WILLIAMS
(1944–1999)

FARAH JASMINE GRIFFIN

To READ ANYTHING by Sherley Anne Williams is to enter a world filled with black music and peopled by ordinary black women who speak in the cadences of the spirituals and the blues. In a 1988 interview with Claudia Tate, Williams stated that twentieth-century black women writers write about "black people trying to work out their own destinies, given this white backdrop . . ." and they are concerned with "what are we going to do about the here and now, me and you?" Williams' creative writing tends to center around relationships: between men and women, mothers and children, and women. Her critical writing attempts to explicate the relationship between oral and literary forms as well as to articulate a mode of reading that draws from sentiments that are indigenous to black American communities.

By focusing on the mundane, the everyday lives of ordinary black people—their relationships to each other and the ways white society influences those relationships—Williams gives voice to women who had long been ignored in American literature. Because she didn't see the experiences of "lower income black women, in any literature, they were always incidental to a larger story," she set out to create a body of work that explores their material, psychic, and existential lives. In so doing she recreates conversations that black women have amongst themselves in the language and rhythm in which they speak.

One of four girls, Sherley Anne Williams was born on August 24, 1944, to Jessie Winson and Lena Silver Williams in Bakersfield, California. An avid reader, Williams spent much of her childhood in search of familiar images and stories in the books she read. They were not to be found. Though she appreciated the realist fiction of Richard Wright, it was in the poetry of Langston Hughes and Sterling Brown, who would later serve as her mentor, that she felt most at home. She recognized Hughes's world of the urban poor and Brown's sharecroppers and farmers. She also learned from them how the blues as form provides inspiration for black poetry and could be used to give voice to black women.

For stories about women, Williams turned to the autobiographies of entertainers such as Eartha Kitt, Katherine Dunham, and Ethel Waters. In them she caught glimpses of her own environment. In an autobiographical essay published in Mary Helen Washington's *Midnight Birds* (1980), Williams wrote: "The material circumstances of their childhood were so much worse than mine; they too had had to cope with early and forced sex and sexuality, with mothers who could not express love in the terms that they desperately needed. Yet they had risen above this, turned their difference into something that was respected in the world beyond their homes. I in the free North, could do no less than endure." Williams did not read the work of black women writers until she was an adult. In her foreword to the 1978 edition of Zora Neale Hurston's *Their Eyes Were Watching God*, she writes that she did not encounter Hurston until graduate school. After reading it she "became Zora Neale's for life." In the language of the novel she "heard [her] own country voice and saw in the heroine something of my own country self." The truth of the language as well as the beauty of Janie's love story would later inspire Williams' own fiction.

After her mother's death when she was sixteen, Williams went to live with her elder sister Ruise in California. Although Ruise was a young single mother who worked as a live-in domestic, she managed to provide her younger sister with love, affirmation, and guidance. They lived off of her meager salary, what she received for Sherley's care, and what they got from occasionally picking cotton and grapes. As a senior in high school Williams received prize money from a story published by *Scholastic*, a newsmagazine for schoolchildren, and this added to their meager income. It also encouraged the young woman to continue writing. Williams credited Ruise and her young friends with providing her "with a community, with models, both real life and literary."

"Tell Martha Not to Moan"

These women became the inspiration for Williams' first professional story, "Tell Martha Not to Moan," first published in 1967 in the *Massachusetts Review* and then reissued in the influential anthology *The Black Woman* edited by Toni Cade Bambara in 1970. A showcase for a new generation of black women poets, critics, essayists, scholars, and novelists, the collection announced the dawn of the renaissance of black women's writing that followed the Black Power and feminist movements. As poet, critic, short-story writer, and novelist, Williams became one of the important voices of this movement.

"Tell Martha Not to Moan" exhibits many of the qualities that characterize Williams' later work. The central character, Martha, is a single welfare mother; her lover is a jazz musician. Ordinarily invisible to novelists, politicians, and the mainstream public, or viewed only as a sexual being who is dependent on the tax dollars of the middle class, in this story Martha is the protagonist. While she is not the first working-class or working poor woman to appear in black fiction she is unique. Unlike Ann Petry's working-class heroine Lutie Johnson in *The Street* (1946), for example, Martha is not an ambitious, noble, and chaste member of the "deserving poor." Unlike Annie Allen of Gwendolyn Brooks's collection of poetry of the same title or Maud Martha in Brooks's eponymous novel, Williams' Martha does not speak in the poetic language of the Western literary tradition. Martha is a sensual young woman who has a child out of wedlock and who chooses to live with her lover outside of marriage as well. She is funny and she lacks self-confidence. Her language is the eloquent black English that Williams grew up hearing. "My mamma is a big woman, tall and stout, and men like her cause she soft and fluffy-looking . . . Since I had Larry things ain't been too good between us. But— that's my mamma and I know she gon be there when I need her . . . Her eyes looking all ove me and I know it coming." Without lapsing into stereotypical dialect, Williams presents black urban speech in much the way that Zora Neale Hurston did with the black southern language of Janie in *Their Eyes Were Watching God*.

Williams provides her readers with insight into Martha's inner self, her limitations as well as her aspirations. Her lover, the piano player Time, is the complex intellectual—a frustrated black artist in a racist society. In her critical work *Give Birth to Brightness* (1972), Williams devotes an entire chapter, "The Black Musician: The Light Bearer," to the figure of the black musician in black American literature. In the brief time that he is in Martha's life, Time does bring light. He is an affirming presence naming her black skin beautiful: "What's the matter, you shamed of being Black? Ain't nobody told you black is pretty?" He also encourages her to think of her future; yet he cannot envision a future for them that includes her young son. By story's end he has abandoned Martha, who is pregnant with yet another child. While the first-person narrative is told in Martha's voice, mobility and music belong to the man, Time.

"Meditations on History"

If Martha is denied music and mobility, Odessa, the heroine of another of Williams' novellas, "Meditations on History" (1980), possesses both. "Meditations on History" is the story of Dessa, a runaway slave who twice escapes slavery. Dessa attempts to murder her master after he kills her beloved husband, Kaine, another musician (he plays the banjo). Dessa is first beaten and then sold on a coffel of slaves from which she escapes with two fellow slaves. Dessa and Kaine's is one of the most beautiful love stories to be found in American literature. In the opening pages, Dessa—imprisoned in a holding cell—retreats to her memory of her husband Kaine as a means of sustaining herself. Just as Time affirms Martha's black beauty so too does Kaine affirm Dessa's. She dreams of a day when after a long day's work in the fields, they return to their cabin to make love.

Feeling the coarse dirtiness of her clothing and her head rag, she tries to clean up before making love with Kaine.

> Holding her closer and pulling the dirty, sweaty rag from her head. . . . He stood with one leg pressed lightly between her thighs, his lips nibbling the curve of her neck. "I got to clean up a little." . . . He ran the tip of his tongue down the side of her neck. . . . His fingers caught in her short kinky hair, his palms rested gently on her high cheekbones. . . . He kissed her closed lids, his hands sliding down her neck to her shoulders and back, his fingers kneading the flesh under her tow sack dress and she wanted him to touch all of her. . . . He pulled up her dress and his hands were inside her long drawers. "I sho like this behind." His hands cupped her buttocks. . . .

This was love talk that made her feel almost as beautiful as the way he touched her.

Kaine affirms every part of her body that white standards of beauty deem unseemly: the kink in her hair, the curve and size of her buttocks, the dirt from working in the fields. His expression of love for her restores her femininity. Remembering this moment in her holding cell, Dessa feels, "It was gone as suddenly as it had come, the memory so strong, so clear it was like being with him all over again. Muscles contracted painfully deep inside her and she could feel the warm moistness oozing between her thighs." The rest of the story is told in a series of journal entries by Adam Nehemiah, a northern white intellectual writing an advice book for slave masters, *The Roots of Rebellion and the Means of Eradicating Them.* His interviews with Dessa reveal little that he wants to hear; consequently, throughout the story he asserts her stupidity and animality, referring to her as a virago or a stupid wench. After days of silence, when finally Dessa does speak, she does so in long circuitous narratives that frustrate him. But more often than not she sings "an absurd, monotonous little tune in a minor key, the melody of which she repeated over and over." As Nehemiah describes it: "Each morning we are awakened by the singing of the darkies and they often startle one by breaking into song at odd times during the day." So intent on getting his linear, straightforward confession, Nehemiah remains ignorant to the messages in the slaves' songs. Dessa sings:

> Lawd, gimme wings like Noah's dove
> Lawd, gimme wings like Noah's dove
> I'd fly cross these fields to the ones I loves.

Although the song and its hidden sentiment are based on the spirituals, in form it is a blues song with the two repeated lines and the third resolution line. A reader familiar with black music will know to look for the song's meaning and significance in that last line. Throughout the story Dessa and the plantation slaves sing such songs to each other as a means of planning her escape. She sings:

Tell me, sista, tell me brotha how long will
  it be
Tell me, brotha tell me sista how long will
  it be
That a poor sinner got to suffer, suffer here?

Another voice responds:

Oh it won't be long. Say it won't be long
Poor sinner got to suffer here
Soul's going to heav'n soul's gon ride that
  heav'nly train
Cause the Lawd have called us home.

Then a chorus of voices:

Good news, Lawd, Lawd, good news
My brotha got a seat and I so glad.
I hearda from heav'n today.

By daybreak on July 4, Dessa has escaped
with the assistance of the plantation slaves and
a community of Maroons, some of whom also
escaped from the coffel with her. Unlike Martha, she has music and mobility and there is
resistance and self-creation in both.

Williams opens the story with an extensive
quotation from Angela Davis' article "Reflections on the Woman's Role in the Community
of Slaves." The essay, written by Davis while
she was in prison, is one of the first scholarly
essays to document the role enslaved black
women played in resistance and rebellion as
well as their importance in maintaining the
community's well-being. Davis was inspired to
write the essay by the assertion of some Black
Power activists that women ought to play traditional conventional roles of mother and supportive wife in revolutionary struggle. Dessa is
the literary counterpart to the historical figures
about whom Davis writes. Williams shared Davis' frustration with the patriarchal turn taken
by many advocates of Black Power and black
nationalism. She wrote, "My disenchantment
with the exponents of Black Power began in
1967 while a graduate student at Howard University." There she encountered prescriptions
insisting that black writing should emulate the
harsh political realism of Richard Wright and
restrictive notions of gender relationships between black men and women. While not characteristic of all forms of black nationalism,
many of the emerging black nationalist philos-
ophies insisted upon conventional gender roles
for revolutionary black men and women in order to strengthen a black nation. The writings
of Amiri Baraka or Maulana Karenga are but
two examples of this type of thinking.

Williams' Education and Criticism

After completing her undergraduate degree at
California State, Fresno, in 1966 and a stint at
the historically black Howard University in
Washington, D.C., Williams went to Brown
University, where she completed a master's degree in American literature. She decided not to
pursue the Ph.D. because she "didn't want to
spend the rest of [her] life poring over other people's work and trying to explain the world thru
their eyes. Rather, what I gain from books and
it is often a great deal . . . must be melded with,
refracted through my experiences and what I
know of my contemporaries, my ancestors, my
hopes for my descendants."

Although she did abandon the Ph.D. program, she did not abandon the academy. Williams taught African American literature at
several universities including the University of
Ghana, University of Southern California, and
Cornell University. Upon her death, she was a
former chair and well-respected professor of the
department of literature at the University of
California at San Diego. Nor did she abandon
literary criticism. In a series of important essays and one scholarly monograph she sought
to explicate "the re-creation of a new tradition
built on a synthesis of black oral traditions and
Western literate forms."

Her critical book *Give Birth to Brightness: A
Thematic Study in Neo-Black Literature* was
published in 1972 and focused on works by
Amiri Baraka, James Baldwin, and Ernest Gaines.
Dedicated to her son Malcolm, the book concentrates on male writers and very masculinist
folk forms, figures, and themes. Williams' chapters explore types of African Americans found

in the literature, including rebels, street men, middle-class heroes, and musicians. Her central argument is that black writers have created a brilliant literature that provides "a vision of Black life" and explores "Black existence and life from the inside as life experiences which have significance in and of themselves rather than as a culturally deprived heritage which take its significance and meaning from the fact that it has been a source of irritation and embarrassment for white America."

Blues and Poetry

Williams found this same tendency important and attractive in the blues. For her the blues provided not only a vision of black life but also an inspiration for other black art forms, especially poetry. In her now classic essay "Blues Roots of Contemporary African American Poetry," first published in 1977, Williams wrote:

> The spirituals, play and work songs, cakewalks and hoedowns, and the blues are the first recorded artifacts to grow out of the complex relationship between Africans and Europeans on the North American continent. Afro-American oral tradition, of which these lyric forms are a part, combines with white American literature whose traditions are rooted more in the literate cultures of the West than in the oral traditions, either indigenous or transplanted, of the New World. Afro-American literature is thus created within the framework of multiple relationships, and the tension between the white literary and the black oral traditions informs and influences the best contemporary Afro-American poetry at the level of structure as well as theme.

For Williams, no oral form has been as influential as the blues. In a 1988 interview with Claudia Tate she asserts: "Until we know the blues intimately and analytically, we will not know ourselves." As with many black writers (including two who greatly influenced her— Sterling Brown and Langston Hughes), Williams finds in the blues a way of philosophi-

cally understanding a people. The earliest blues are about the relationships between men and women. The primary focus is on intimate relationships. In her two collections of poetry, *The Peacock Poems* (1975) and *Some One Sweet Angel Child* (1982), she moves beyond theorizing the relationship between poetry and the blues to actually create a series of blues poems in the voices of black women.

In *The Peacock Poems*, which was nominated for the National Book Award and the Pulitzer Prize, poetry is interspersed with William' own autobiographical prose as well as definitions of key terms and events. These are poems of a woman's wandering across the United States with her newborn son, John. In fact, many of the poems are based on episodes in her young son's life. In this collection she begins her successful experimentation with the blues form. There are two poems titled "Any Woman's Blues." In the first, which opens the collection, she writes:

> My bed one-sided
>   from me sleepin alone so mucha the
>   time.
> My bed one-sided, now,
>   cause I'm alone so mucha the time.
> But the fact that it's empty
>   show how this man is messin with my
>   mind.

Here is a blues as it might have been sung by one of the classic blues singers, Bessie Smith or Ma Rainey. It meets our expectations of such singers by starting the story and painting a first-person portrait of a woman in an empty bed. The last line suggests she will go on in other verses to explain to us how he is "messin' " with her mind. However, the poem ends there.

About one-third of the way into the collection, Williams returns to "Any Woman's Blues." The first lines read:

> Soft lamp shinin
>   and me alone in the night.
> Soft lamp is shinin
>   and me alone in the night.
> Can't take no one beside me

need mo'n jest some man to set me
right.

Although we have been led to believe that
this will be a song about a woman's lost love,
the first verse is spoken in the voice of a woman
lonely not for a man but for a sense of direction
and purpose. Such is the case with most of the
poems and the prose pieces in this collection.
The autobiographical persona is a woman who
prematurely gives birth to a son, wishes for the
child's father to want them, and takes on the
responsibility of caring for her infant child
while trying to find her own sense of self and
voice.

In *Some One Sweet Angel Chile* Williams
elaborates upon the blues forms and themes of
the earlier volume. *Some One* differs from *Peacock
Poems* in that it is divided into three major
sections. The first section contains "Letters
from a New England Negro," a series of poems
set in the nineteenth century and structured
like letters from a young black New England
teacher who goes South to teach the freedmen
and women. In one of the poems/letters, the
persona writes to her friend Edward, explaining
how the freedmen rename her.

Edward dearest,

They persist in calling me
Patient though I have tried to
Make it clear that neither
Emancipation nor Patience
is part of my given name . . .

Tonight my
Old devil tongue slipped from
Me after weeks of careful
Holding. I answered roughly
Some harmless question, My name
Is Hannah. Hannah. There is
No Patience to it.

"Hannah
our name for the sun," Stokes said
in the silence that followed
my remark. "You warm us like
she do, but you more patient
wid us when we come to learn."

There to educate them, she is educated by
them and through their insistence she does become
patient. The black New England schoolmarm
is a voice that is new to poetry and fiction
but not to the diaries, journals, and letters
of many black women who went South to
teach. Among these, Frances Ellen Watkins
Harper, Charlotte Forten, and Rebecca Primus
all left letters and/or diaries documenting their
experiences. By focusing once again on the kind
of woman left out of history books, Williams
gives voice to a silenced but not silent community
of women.

The second section of the collection, "Regular
Reefer," includes blues poems inspired by
the life of Williams' muse and model, Bessie
Smith. In "The Hard Time Blues" she writes:

This is what you get for sparkle and shine
This what you get for sparkle and shine
A two-bit husband and a bitch ain worth a
    time.

Poems based on Smith's life and music present
a richly complex, spoken voice of a black
woman. As a poet, Williams initiates a group of
black women poets and critics (such as Alice
Walker, Deborah McDowell, Gayl Jones, and
Hazel Carby) who will find models of protofeminist
strength, independence, and sexuality in
blueswomen.

The third section of the work is titled "The
Songs of the Grown" and appears to be closer
to the autobiographical poems of Williams' earlier
collection; similarly, she does continue
many of the allusions to black music and history.
Some One Sweet Angel Chile was nominated
for a National Book Award and a television
performance based upon it won an Emmy.

One of the major characteristics of Williams'
poetry and her criticism is her use of different
"voices," through which she speaks. "I am the
woman I speak of in my stories and poems," she
writes in *Midnight Birds*. "I was a 'man' in *Give
Birth to Brightness* and a sexual voice in 'The
Blues Roots of Contemporary African American
Poetry,' both critical works, and each of
these disguises has helped me come into my
own voice, clarified my own vision."

Williams' Feminism

Toward the end of her career, Williams' vision was more and more influenced by feminism, or "womanism," Alice Walker's term for black feminists who are as committed to liberating people from racial and class-based oppression as they are to eradicating sexism. Her critical essay "Some Implications of Womanist Theory" (1990) and the novel *Dessa Rose* (1986) are the outgrowths of this vision. Ironically, while Williams advocates a womanist theory of reading and while she praises the rise in critical works of black feminism by scholars such as Barbara Smith and Deborah McDowell, she nonetheless focuses her attention on writings by black men. She writes, "Womanist inquiry, on the other hand, assumes that it can talk both effectively and productively about men. This is a necessary assumption because the negative, stereotyped images of black women are only a part of the problem of phallocentric writings by black males. In order to understand that problem more fully, we must turn to what black men have written about themselves." This is certainly an ironic stance to take in an essay devoted to womanist theory, especially at a time when most black feminist critics were trying to bring attention to the works of black women writers.

Dessa Rose

If in her criticism Williams continued to focus on black male writers, in her fiction she turned to the solidarity between women across lines of race. *Dessa Rose: A Riveting Story of the South During Slavery* (1986) continues the story of Dessa from "Meditations on History." In the novel, Dessa joins a community of Maroons who set up in a dilapidated plantation house owned by a delusional raven-haired white woman, Ruth, who believes the fugitives to be her servants. The blacks play the charade in order to appease her when in fact they are in control of the house, its resources, and its land.

The story takes an odd turn when Dessa walks in on Ruth nursing her child. It is a reversal of a scene we have come to expect where the black wet nurse feeds her white charge at the expense of her own children. Not only does Ruth nurse the black baby; she also has an affair with one of the black men. Both instances infuriate Dessa. When she walks in on one of her comrades making love to Ruth, Dessa is forced to question her own desirability as a black woman. Focusing on Ruth's white skin and long, wavy locks, she constantly asks herself, "Is that what [black men] want?" When she expresses her disappointment, pain, anger, and betrayal, another fugitive, Ned, tells her, "Yo all just jealous cause he not diddling you. . . . Don't nobody want no old mule like you." Ned confirms the "validity" of the white supremacist link between black women and animals. One is here reminded of the words of Zora Neale Hurston's Nanny in *Their Eyes Were Watching God*: "De nigger woman is de mule uh de world so fur as Ah can see." The angry Dessa asks herself, "Had [Kaine] really wanted me to be like Mistress . . . that doughy skin and slippery hair?" She begins to remember her body and features as well as those of herself and other slave women. "My heels was so rough they snagged a tear in them sheets up to the House. Janet had that kind of skin remind you of hickory—red-brown and tough." However, by novel's end she has found love with another fugitive and she and Ruth, bound by their oppression from white southern patriarchal society, become sisters and friends who save each other. She saves Ruth from rape, and Ruth saves her from being returned to slavery. It is an interracial feminist utopia that rings untrue to many readers but nonetheless does allow us to imagine possibilities not provided by history.

Dessa Rose is especially significant for its open portrayal of a black woman's sexuality in a nonstereotypical way and in its role as one of the founding texts of a new genre—the neoslave narrative—that includes works such as Toni Morrison's *Beloved*, Caryl Phillips' *Cambridge*, Octavia Butler's *Kindred*, and Charles Johnson's *Middle Passage*. Shortly after its publication there was talk of turning the novel into a film, though that has not happened; it has also been the subject of numerous critical essays, book chapters, and dissertations.

At the end of her career, Williams continued to write. She published two books for children, *Working Cotton* (1992) and *Girls Together* (1999); she also staged the play "Letters from a New England Negro," part of her poetry collection, *Some One Sweet Angel Chile*. The play was shown at the Chicago International Theater Festival in 1992. *Working Cotton* draws on her own experiences of picking cotton as a young girl. Told in the voice of a young girl speaking in Black English, the book narrates her day working in the cotton field. As was the case with her first short story, "Tell Martha Not to Moan," *Working Cotton* also portrays Williams' feelings toward her family and herself as well as a range of emotions from pride and fatigue to hope and love. The book won the prestigious American Library Association Caldecott Award. *Girls Together* follows several young girlfriends who spend Saturday morning looking for fun and adventure in their housing project and the surrounding middle-class neighborhood. Both books are autobiographical and in both instances there are characters named for Williams' beloved older sister Ruise.

In May 1998, Williams' colleague black feminist critic Ann Du Cille organized a conference in recognition of the twelfth anniversary of the publication of *Dessa Rose*. Scholars and writers gathered to celebrate, discuss, and debate Williams' work—a tribute rarely made during a writer's lifetime. Sherley Anne Williams died in the summer of 1999 in San Diego.

Selected Bibliography

PRIMARY WORKS

CREATIVE

"Tell Martha Not to Moan." In *The Black Woman*. Edited by Toni Cade Bambara. New York: New American Library, 1970. Pp. 42–55.

The Peacock Poems. Middletown, Conn.: Wesleyan University Press, 1975.

Foreword to *Their Eyes Were Watching God*, by Zora Neale Hurston. Urbana: University of Illinois Press, 1978. Pp. v–xv.

"Meditations on History." In *Midnight Birds*. Edited by Mary Helen Washington. New York: Anchor, 1980. Pp. 200–48.

"Sherley Anne Williams." In *Midnight Birds*. Edited by Mary Helen Washington. New York: Anchor, 1980. Pp. 195–99.

Some One Sweet Angel Chile. New York: William Morrow, 1982.

Dessa Rose: A Riveting Story of the South During Slavery. New York: William Morrow, 1986.

Working Cotton. San Diego: Harcourt Brace Jovanovich, 1992.

Girls Together. San Diego: Harcourt Brace, 1996.

CRITICAL

Give Birth to Brightness: A Thematic Study in Neo-Black Literature. New York: Dial Press, 1972.

"Anonymous in America." *Boundary 2: A Journal of Postmodern Literature* 6:435–42 (1978).

"The Blues Roots of Contemporary Afro-American Poetry." In *Afro-American Literature: The Reconstruction of Instruction*. Edited by Dexter Fisher and Robert B. Stepto. New York: Modern Language Association, 1979. Pp. 72–87.

"Papa Dick and Sister-Woman: Reflections on Women in the Fiction of Richard Wright Hall." In *American Novelists Revisited: Essays in Feminist Criticism*. Edited by Fritz Fleischmann. Boston: G. K. Hall, 1982. Pp. 394–415.

"Langston Hughes and the Negro Renaissance: 'Harlem Literati in the Twenties' (1940); 'The Twenties: Harlem and Its Negritude' (1966)." *The Langston Hughes Review* 4, no. 1:37–39 (Spring 1985).

"Some Implications of Feminist Theory." *Griot: Official Journal of the Southern Conference on Afro-American Studies, Inc.* 6, no. 2:40–45 (Summer 1987).

"Remembering Prof. Sterling A. Brown, 1901–1989." *Black American Literature Forum* 23, no. 1:106–8 (Spring 1989).

"The Lion's History: The Ghetto Writes Back." *Soundings* 76, nos. 2–3:245–59 (Summer–Fall 1993).

"Some Implications of Womanist Theory." In *Within the Circle: An Anthology of African American Literary Criticism from the Harlem Renaissance to the Present*. Edited by Angelyn Mitchell. Durham, N.C.: Duke University Press, 1994. Pp. 515–21.

"Telling the Teller: Memoir and Story." In *The Seductions of Biography*. Edited by Mary Rhiel. New York: Routledge, 1996. Pp. 179–84.

SECONDARY WORKS

CRITICAL AND BIOGRAPHICAL STUDIES

DeLancey, Dayle B. "The Self's Own Kind: Literary Resistance in Sherley Anne Williams' Dessa Rose." *Mawa Review* 5, no. 2:59–62 (December 1990).

Diedrich, Maria. "Sherley Anne Williams: Meditations on History (1980)." In *The African American Short Story 1970–1990*. Edited by Wolfgang Karrer and Barbara Puschmann-Nalenz. Trier: Wissenschaftlicher, 1993. Pp. 133–44.

Holmes, Kristine. " 'This Is Flesh I'm Talking about Here': Embodiment in Toni Morrison's *Beloved* and Sherley Anne Williams' *Dessa Rose*." *Literature Interpretation Theory* 6, nos. 1–2:133–48 (April 1995).

Kekeh, Andree-Anne. "Sherley Anne Williams' *Dessa Rose:* History and the Disruptive Power of Memory." In *History and Memory in African-American Culture.* Edited by Genevieve Fabre and Robert O'Meally. New York: Oxford University Press, 1994. Pp. 219–27.

Rushdy, Ashraf H. "Reading Mammy: The Subject of Relation in Sherley Anne Williams' *Dessa Rose*." *African American Review* 27, no. 3:365–89 (Fall 1993).

Sanchez, Marta E. "The Estrangement Effect in Sherley Anne Williams' *Dessa Rose*." *Genders* 15:21–36 (Winter 1992).

Tate, Claudia. "Sherley Anne Williams" *In Black Women Writers at Work.* Edited by Claudia Tate. New York: Continuum, 1988. Pp. 205–13.

AUGUST WILSON
(1945–)

HARRY J. ELAM JR.

Somewhere along the way it dawned on me that I was writing one play for each decade. Once I became conscious of that, I realized I was trying to focus on what I felt were the important issues confronting Black Americans for that decade, so ultimately they could stand as a record of Black experience over the past hundred years presented in the form of dramatic literature.

August Wilson

WITH TWO PULITZER Prizes, two Tony awards, and numerous other accolades, August Wilson stands out as one of the most pre-eminent playwrights, if not the pre-eminent playwright, in the contemporary American theater. As noted in the quote above from an interview with Kim Powers, Wilson's self-imposed dramatic project is to review African American history in the twentieth century by writing a play for each decade. With each work, he re-creates and re-evaluates the choices that blacks have made in the past by refracting them through the lens of the present. Wilson focuses on the experiences and daily lives of ordinary black people within particular historical circumstances. Carefully situating each play at critical junctures in African American history, Wilson explores the pain and perseverance, the determination and dignity in these black lives.

In his early playwriting career Wilson did write works that are not part of this cycle: *Recycle* (1973); *The Homecoming* (1976); *Black Bart and the Sacred Hills*, a musical satire (1977); *The Coldest Day of the Year* (1977); *How the Coyote Got His Special Power and Used It to Help the People* (1978); and *Fullerton Street* (1980). Most of these works were produced, but all remain unpublished. Thus his recognition and renown as a playwright came as a result of his twentieth-century cycle. Although not written in chronological order, Wilson has completed plays on the 1910s, *Joe Turner's Come and Gone*; the 1920s, *Ma Rainey's Black Bottom*; the 1930s, *The Piano Lesson*; the 1940s, *Seven Guitars*; the 1950s, *Fences*; the 1960s, *Two Trains Running*; the 1970s, *Jitney!*; and the 1980s, *King Hedley II*. *King Hedley II*, like all of Wilson's dramas with the exception of *Ma Rainey*, is set in Wilson's childhood home, the Hill district of Pittsburgh, Pennsylvania. It even premiered in Pittsburgh, at the newly renovated Pittsburgh Theatre Center on December 15, 1999. *King Hedley*, however, is his first work to feature characters from an earlier play, *Seven Guitars*, which was first performed in January 1995. Ruby, who is young and pregnant in *Seven Guitars*, is now sixty years old and a mother of an adult son, King Hedley II. As with the earlier plays, Wilson brilliantly blends blues music, poetic dialogue, and rich complex characterizations together as he creates images of America's past from a decidedly African American perspective. At the start of the twenty-first century, Wilson was working on plays of the 1900s and 1990s that would complete his cycle. With these works, Wilson stated in an interview with Chris Jones:

> I can build an umbrella under which the rest of the plays can sit. My relating the zero to the '90s play should provide a bridge. The subject matter of these two plays is going to be very similar and connected thematically, meaning that the other eight will be part and parcel to these two. You should be able to see how they all fit inside these last two plays.

Central to each play in Wilson's historical cycle is the concept that the events of the past can and do have a powerful impact on the present. For Wilson's characters, past events have a commanding influence on their present dreams and aspirations. Their personal stories are inextricably linked to the history of African American struggle and survival in this country.

Repeatedly in these plays, Wilson creates black characters who are displaced and disconnected from their history, from their individual identity, and who are in search of spiritual resurrection and cultural reconnection. In *Joe Turner's Come and Gone* (1988), the central character, Herald Loomis, after seven debilitating years of coerced servitude, fights to recover a lost sense of self. Loomis, like other Wilson characters, has unfinished business—unresolved issues with the past and with his history. As a result, he and other Wilson characters must go backwards in order to move forward.

Wilson's dramatic cycle then demonstrates the impact of the past on the present. Ethics and aesthetics conjoin as the personal dynamics of his characters' lives have profound political consequences. As noted by Sandra Shannon in *Memory and Cultural Politics*, Wilson termed his project, "a 400 year old autobiography, which is the black experience." As an African American "autobiography," Wilson's work links African American collective memory with Wilson's own memories and with his activist racial agenda. His family background and own life experiences are evident in this project.

Early Life

August Wilson was born August Frederick Kittel on April 27, 1945. He was the fourth of six children. His father Frederick Kittel, a German baker, never lived with the family. His mother, Daisy Wilson, worked as a cleaning woman and later married David Bedford, a black ex-convict and former high-school football star. Wilson's troubled and troubling relationships with these two men figure in his plays and their depictions of masculinity and race. As signaled by his decision to change his surname from Kittel to his mother's surname, Wilson, August Wilson has never identified with his white father, but strictly with his African American heritage. According to Wilson, in a keynote address that was published in *American Theatre* in September 1996, "I stand myself and my art squarely on the self-defining ground of the slave quarters, and find the ground to be hallowed and made fertile by the blood and bones of the men and women who can be described as warriors on the cultural battlefield that affirmed their self-worth." Wilson believes his identity as an African American artist is inherently linked to the legacy of African American struggle and survival. Only after Bedford died in 1969 did the then twenty-four-year-old Wilson realize that his stepfather had cared about him. Bedford became the model for Troy Maxson, the towering central character of *Fences*. Like Bedford, Troy is a former athlete, a star in the Negro Baseball League. Corresponding to the twenty-three years Bedford spent in prison for a murder that occurred in an attempted robbery, Troy also has killed a man in a botched robbery and serves fifteen years in the penitentiary. After prison David Bedford found a job with the Pittsburgh Sewer Department and Troy Maxson works as a City of Pittsburgh garbage man. Troy's relationship with his son Cory is fraught with tension and misunderstanding. With these two men and other characters within his dramaturgy, Wilson considers questions of inheritance and history both personal and racial.

Wilson learned an early racial lesson in ninth grade, when a white teacher accused him of plagiarizing a twenty-five-page paper he had rigorously researched on Napoléon Bonaparte. The teacher, Mr. Biggs, maintained that this black child could not have produced such high-quality work and gave him an F for his efforts. Bruised by this false assault on his character, Wilson dropped out of school in 1960. While this affair ended his formal education, it did not deter his thirst for knowledge. A voracious reader, Wilson spent considerable time in the public library devouring the books in the "Negro Section." Reading the works of Ralph Ellison and James Baldwin, Wilson determined that he too wanted to be a writer. In a March 1987 article in the *New York Times Magazine,* Wilson told Samuel G. Freeman: "Just the idea black people would write books. I wanted my book up there too." His desire to be a writer led him first to poetry. In 1965 he helped to organize the Center Avenue Poets Theatre Workshop. That same year, at age nineteen, he moved out of his mother's house and rented a basement apartment in Pittsburgh's Hill district, where he fraternized with writers and painters. He took on part-time odd jobs and would write for hours. More importantly, he studied the characters and haunts of his neighborhood. He studied their vernacular, their signifyin' or vernacular word games, and their verbal boasts. Their language, style, and cultural politics would later become the stuff of his drama and an important source for his dramaturgy.

Influences

Wilson describes his poetry as largely "imitative." He found his own true voice as a dramatist as the decade of the 1960s drew to a close. Affected by the urgencies around black cultural nationalism of the late 1960s, Wilson, along with his friend Rob Penny, cofounded Pittsburgh's

August Wilson

Black Horizons Theater, a revolutionary-minded black theater. With his work at Black Horizons, Wilson encountered one of the so-called "4Bs" that continue to shape his dramas, the fiery playwright and poet Amiri Baraka, the leading theater practitioner of the black revolutionary theater movement of the late 1960s and early 1970s. Wilson staged Baraka's work and read his essays, including his famous black arts manifesto, "The Revolutionary Theater." Wilson maintained that Baraka's words and cultural politics inspired his own desire to use drama as a means to social ends.

In and around this same time frame, Wilson would also discover the other three Bs of influence: Julius Borges, Romare Bearden, and the blues. Argentinean short-story writer Julius Borges became significant to Wilson because of Borges' ability to blend the metaphysical and the mystical within his complex plot lines. Borges, with his skillful use of narration, blends the fantastical and the spiritual as his characters follow difficult and convoluted pathways.

According to Wilson, quoted in *"I Ain't Sorry for Nothin' I Done": August Wilson's Process of Playwriting*, by Joan Herrington,

> Borges will tell you what's going to happen. In one story, I can't remember the name of it, he wrote: "That Rodrigo would become the leader of an outlaw gang and end up with a bullet in his head would have been, at the outset, a very unlikely scenario. He was born in this town," and such and such. Then he places this guy as far away as he can from being a leader of an outlaw gang and right away, you're intrigued, because you know what's going to happen. The intrigue is how this happened. I thought it would be a great way to write a play.

Wilson used this Borgesian method in *Seven Guitars*, as he begins the play with the funeral of the character Floyd "Schoolboy" Barton. Within his other plays, such as *Fences, Joe Turner's Come and Gone*, and *The Piano Lesson*, and their incorporation of the supernatural and metaphysical, the influence of Borges can be seen as well.

Wilson discovered the work of artist Romare Bearden, a fellow Pittsburgh resident, in 1977 when his friend Charles Purdy purchased a copy of Bearden's collage, *The Prevalence of Ritual* (1964). Viewing this artwork had a profound effect on Wilson. In an essay that appeared in *May All Your Fences Have Gates: Essays on the Drama of August Wilson*, author Joan Fishman quoted Wilson as saying, "My response was visceral. I was looking at myself in ways I hadn't thought of before and have never ceased to think of since. In Bearden I found my artistic mentor and sought, and still aspire to make my plays the equal of his canvases." Wilson appreciated that Bearden's work was at once immediate and specific and profound and complex. He has sought to express this duality in his own work. Bearden's collages *Mill Hands Lunch Bucket* (1978) and *The Piano Lesson* (1984) were the direct inspiration for Wilson's plays, *Joe Turner* and *Piano Lesson*, respectively. Bearden's formula for collage, his use of

found objects and his blending of past and present parallel Wilson's pastiche style of playwriting and his interest in the impact of history upon the present. Within the artistry of both men the metaphorical and ritualistic coexist with the everyday experiences of African Americans. The two men never met, but Wilson wrote of Bearden in the foreword to *Romare Bearden: His Life and Art*:

> I never had the privilege of meeting Romare Bearden. Once I stood outside 357 Canal Street in silent homage, daring myself to knock on his door. I am sorry I didn't, for I have never looked back from the moment when I first encountered his art. He showed me a doorway. A rod marked with signposts, with sharp and sure direction, charting a path through what D. H. Lawrence called the "dark forest of the soul."

Wilson suggests that Bearden's art changed his own artistic creation and direction as a still unsure "young" playwright in 1977 at age thirty-two.

Despite the impact of Bearden, Borges, and Baraka on Wilson and his work, the most significant and most transformative of the four Bs of influence is the blues. Twelve years prior to encountering Bearden in 1965, Wilson discovered the blues while listening to an old recording of Bessie Smith's "Nobody in Town Can Bake a Sweet Jellyroll Like Mine." This recording transformed his life and his cultural ideology. The blues not only became a guiding force in his writing but the foundation he established for African American expressive culture and for what he believes is a distinctly African American way of "being." According to Wilson, the cultural, social, political, and spiritual all interact within the blues. Forged in and from the economics of slavery as a method of mediating the pains and dehumanization of that experience, the blues are purposefully duplicitous, containing a matrix of meanings. In *Ma Rainey's Black Bottom*, Ma reminds her bandleader and guitar player, Cutler, "The blues always been here." The blues for Wilson continue to offer a methodology for negotiating the difficult spaces of African American existence and achieving African American survival.

Structurally Wilson's "bluesology" acts as an aesthetic and cultural intervention that disrupts the conventional frame of realism. Rather than plot or action, character and the lyrical music of the dialogue drive the plays. Wilson, who was a poet before he became a playwright, celebrates the poetic power contained in the speech of poor and uneducated peoples. Wilson allows his characters to voice their history in the spoken equivalent of musical solos. Troy Maxson, an illiterate garbageman and central figure in *Fences*, fashions himself through bold expressive tales. Like the ancient city of Troy, he is an epic force, impregnable and larger than life. During one storytelling riff, Troy describes a wrestling match he had with Death. Later, he relates how the Devil came to his house offering furniture on credit. Rose, his wife, interjects a practical perspective that contradicts the veracity of Troy's tales, "Troy lying. We got that furniture from Mr. Glickman." Yet, the truth of the stories is not as significant as the power of the African and African American oral traditions that Wilson celebrates and asserts through Troy's performance. Troy's stories expand the realistic canvas of the play. They reach beyond the conventional temporal and spatial limits.

In his essay "Blues People" from *The Shadow and the Act* Ralph Ellison calls the blues a unique combination of the tragic and the comic, of poetry and ritual. Repeatedly Wilson's plays embody this blues formula. In each of the plays, Wilson's characters engage in a series of vernacular games, the dozens and signifyin'. All of these cultural activities are extensions of the blues or variations on a blues theme. Wilson sets his works in sites that enable such communal engagement, verbal jousting, and oral transmission of culture. He places the band interaction in *Ma Rainey* in the band room downstairs, separated from the recording studio above. The band room represents what American educator Houston A. Baker termed in his *Blues, Ideology and Afro-Amercan Literature* a "blues matrix." Baker envisioned the blues matrix as a "point of ceaseless input and output, a web of intersecting, crisscrossing im-

pulses always in productive transit." For Baker the prototypical site of the blues matrix is a railroad crossing, "the juncture of multidirectionality," a place "betwixt and between." Situated at the blues matrix, the blues singer through blues song transcends spatial and sociohistorical limitations. The band room as blues matrix is equally a site of power and potential. The band room is a space of unfinished business, where the band must rehearse its songs and await the arrival of Ma Rainey. It is a metaphorical space where the band members enact rituals and tales of survival that replicate the patterns of black experiences in America.

Similarly, Seth's boardinghouse in *Joe Turner's Come and Gone*, and Memphis' restaurant in *Two Trains Running*, the respective settings for these two dramas, are liminal spaces, blues matrixes, "betwixt and between." The boardinghouse serves as a way station for African Americans during the great migration from the South heading north to find work. Seth remarks, "word get out they need men to work in the mill and put in these road . . . and niggers drop everything and head North look for freedom." The characters come to Seth's boardinghouse in search of a new life, a new sense of self. Or as Wilson notes, "they search for ways to reconnect, to reassemble, to give clear and luminous meaning to the song." Memphis' restaurant also serves as a way station for its regular customers. As the play opens the restaurant is threatened by the advent of Urban Renewal and the impeding reality that it soon will be torn down. Thus its liminality is confirmed. The restaurant exists between its past glory and its uncertain future. Memphis laments, "At one time you couldn't get a seat in here. Had the jukebox working and everything. Time somebody get up somebody sit down before they could get out the door." The liminality of the spaces makes them locations of great creative and destructive potential. They are sites in which Wilson employs the "productive transit" of the blues.

Bolstered by the blues and these other influences, Wilson set out to become a playwright. At his friend Charles Purdy's instigation, he moved to St. Paul, Minnesota, in 1978 and wrote plays, including *Black Bart and the Sacred Hills*, for Purdy to direct with his company. In order to subsidize his income, Wilson also worked as a scriptwriter for the Science Museum of Minnesota. While in St. Paul, Purdy's wife introduced Wilson to his future second wife, Judy Oliver, a social worker. They married in 1981. His first marriage to Brenda Burton, a Black Muslim, produced a daughter, Sakina Ansari, in 1970, but ended in divorce in 1972. His second marriage would also end in divorce. He later married a third time, to Constanza Romero, who was the costume designer for *The Piano Lesson* in 1990. While in St. Paul, with the assistance of Purdy and writing for the Black Horizons Theater, Wilson honed his craft. He moved from writing more experimental, nonrealistic plays, such as *The Coldest Day*, in 1976, to the first version of *Jitney!*, written in 1979.

Wilson's career, his renown, and his destiny changed forever in 1982 when he submitted an early draft of his play, *Ma Rainey's Black Bottom*, to the Eugene O'Neill Playwrights Workshop in Waterford, Connecticut, and it was accepted. He had tried the previous year with *Fullerton Street* but was turned down. At the O'Neill, he met Lloyd Richards, the director of the O'Neill Playwrights Workshop and the Yale Drama School, and the first black director ever on Broadway (*A Raisin in the Sun*, 1959). Richards and Wilson began a friendship and collaboration that would lead to the production of six of Wilson's cycle plays at regional theaters across the country and on Broadway.

Ma Rainey's Black Bottom

Ma Rainey's Black Bottom premiered in 1984. Wilson's first critically acclaimed play and the most musical of his plays, it established a foundation for Wilson's blues theology that he articulated further with each of his later plays. In *Ma Rainey* the significance of finding one's cultural and spiritual regeneration through the blues song plays out principally through the conflicting views of the title character, Ma Rainey, and the spirited young trumpet player,

Levee, the pivotal character. Levee fails to understand his relationship to the music, and never realizes his blues song. Ma Rainey, on the other hand, recognizes that the blues can become both a self-accentuating song and a declaration of the collective, cultural memory of African Americans.

In *Ma Rainey*, as in Wilson's subsequent works, the dominant culture seeks to suppress, to control, and to commodify the black blues song. *Ma Rainey* opens with two white characters, Ma Rainey's manager, Irvin, and Sturdyvant, the recording studio owner and a producer of "race records," on the stage. Together Irvin and Sturdyvant strategize on their plan for the recording session and for capturing Ma Rainey's blues voice. Sturdyvant reminds Irvin, "I just want to get her in here . . . record the songs on the list . . . and get her out. Just like clock work, huh?" Wilson juxtaposes Irvin and Sturdyvant's plan to commercialize Ma Rainey's blues song with Ma's own resolve to protect the integrity of herself and her music. Ma testifies to Wilson's contention that the blues are a uniquely black voice that whites desire, but can not understand, "White folks don't understand about the blues. They hear it come out, but they don't know how it got there."

Wilson's blues improvisations not only infuse the content of his plays, but his form and structure as well. Ralph Ellison called the blues a unique combination of the tragic and the comic, of poetry and ritual. The structure of *Ma Rainey* embodies this blues formula. The events that transpire—from Ma's nephew Sylvester's stuttering rendition of the introduction to the recorded version of "Ma Rainey's Black Bottom," to Toledo's unfortunate death—combine the comic and the tragic, the poetic and the ritualistic. *Ma Rainey* plays out as an extended series of blues riffs providing each member of the band the opportunity to solo. Down in the band room, the band members engage in a series of vernacular games, the dozens, and signifyin'. All are extensions of the blues, variations on a blues theme. Wilson adds, through the voice of Toledo, that these forms of blues games are also examples of African retentions. When the bass player, Slow Drag, signifies on

Cutler in order to extract a reefer from him, Toledo explains that what he has performed is "an African conceptualization. That's when you name the gods or call on the ancestors to achieve whatever your desires are." Correspondingly, in the climactic moment of *The Piano Lesson*, Wilson extends this blues riff and the concept of African conceptualizations through the actions of Berniece. In a moment of desperation and urgency, Berniece sits at the piano to play and purposefully employs what Toledo would term "an African conceptualization." As her brother, Boy Willie, struggles upstairs with the ghost of the white landowner, Sutter, Berniece at the piano calls on the power of her ancestors to exorcise the ghost and save her brother.

Toledo's declarations of the need for African Americans to recognize their connections to Africa represent an important element of Wilson's blues theology. Wilson believes that in order for African Americans to be able to sing their own song, to feel truly liberated in the American context, they must rediscover their "African-ness." "One of the things I'm trying to say in my writing is that we can never begin to make a contribution to the society except as Africans," Wilson remarked in an interview with David Savran. Toledo, accordingly, reprimands the band and himself for not being "African" and for being "imitation white men."

To further the blues mood in *Ma Rainey*, Wilson composes his blues musician characters to correspond with the instruments that they play. Slow Drag, the bass player, maintains the bass line in the play. He is a slow and deliberate voice, who reinforces the action around him. Cutler, the bandleader and guitar player, strikes a practical tone. He is not one to improvise but has the power to embellish a theme, as when he tells the involved story of Reverend Gates. Toledo, the piano player, is the only member the group who can read. He is a philosopher who engages in monologues and storytelling riffs that are analogous to virtuoso, improvised piano solos. Toledo preaches a doctrine of Afrocentric nationalism. "As long as the colored man look to white folks to put a crown on what he say . . . as long as he looks to white folks for approval . . . then he ain't never gonna find out

who he is and what he's about." Toledo agitates for black nationalist consciousness. In the plays of the Black Arts Movement of the 1960s and 1970s, Toledo would have been the most prominent voice in the play. Toledo's voice in Wilson's drama, however, is muted. He is part of the ensemble, one instrument blending with the other blues sounds emanating from the blues matrix band room.

Levee, the youngest member of the band, presents himself with a boldness that the others lack. His self-importance is both stubborn naïveté and camouflage. Levee desires to fit in with the band, to be accepted, to achieve within a world that devalues African American spirit and accomplishment. Like a trumpet, Levee blares onto the stage. According to Wilson, in *In Their Own Words:*

> With the trumpet you have to force yourself out through the horn. Half-consciously I tried to make Levee's voice a trumpet. . . . Levee is a brassy voice.

Levee with his brassy voice represents the forces of modernity in conflict with tradition. Significantly, Wilson set the play in 1927, at a time when the country blues of Ma Rainey were fading in the taste of the black consuming public and being replaced by the more upbeat, danceable blues of Bessie Smith and the jazz sounds emerging from urban cities. Levee symbolizes this modern, urban blues landscape. Levee rejects and ridicules the "jug band" circus-style songs of Ma Rainey. He desires to play music that makes people move and that he can "lay down in the people's lap." Yet, Levee does not recognize nor understand that his new urban blues sound and jazz beats are deeply indebted to earlier African and African American sounds and sociocultural traditions. One of the most significant and repeated messages in Wilson's historical project is that modernity cannot erase but must embrace tradition; that the past constantly and continually impacts on the present.

Tragically individualistic, Levee speaks of personal ownership and individual achievement. He wants to play "his" music, write "his" songs, and form "his" band. He is unable to heed Toledo's warning to embrace communality and to think collectively:

> It ain't just me, fool! It's everybody! What you think . . . I'm gonna solve the colored man's problems by myself? I said, we. You understand that? We. That's every living colored man in the world got to do his share.

Levee does not think in terms of "we," but rather, isolates and alienates himself from the other band members and systems of African American communal empowerment. Rejecting communality, Levee believes that he is on a mission to sing his song. Yet, he does not understand the technologies of capitalism and white racism that constrict him and prevent such self-actualization.

In contrast to Levee, Ma Rainey, the title character, realizes her blues song and understands her relationship to the music. Based on the legendary blues singer, Gertrude "Ma" Rainey, Wilson's Ma Rainey recognizes the power of the music to move through her. "You don't sing to feel better. . . . You sing 'cause it's a way of understanding life." Ma explains that singing the blues is not simply therapy but rather an engagement with a complex and enabling force that acts to understand and even to transform and to transcend life. Ma remains a fiercely independent woman throughout the action of the play. Her interaction with all the men in the play is analogous to Houston Baker's reading of the blues musician at the crossroads; she situates herself inventively and uses the resources she has at her disposal to control and mediate the world around her. Ma demonstrates a practical understanding of the material hierarchy of the record industry and her place within it. Recognizing that the purpose of the recording session is to record her voice and her music, Ma does not allow herself to be objectified but uses her position as a desired musical commodity to legitimize her authority. She reminds Irvin, "What band? The band work for me! I say what goes!" After the recording session, Ma exercises her blues voice in one final act of defiance. She leaves the studio without signing the release forms that legally grant Irvin and Sturdyvant control over her recorded music. Through this act, she asserts the power of the blues singer to transcend and overcome material limitations. She retains her artistic autonomy and rebuts the usurpations of others who wish to claim her song. In his interview with Savran, Wilson said of the blues,

> The music is ours, since it contains our soul, so to speak—it contains all our ideas and responses to the world. We need it to help us claim the African-ness and we would be a stronger people for it. It's presently in the hands of someone else who sits over it as custodian, without even allowing us its source.

Still, Ma, a woman, is not the primary subject of Wilson's *Ma Rainey*. The play does not end with Ma's defiant exit from the recording studio, but escalates into tragedy in the band room below. The ending of *Ma Rainey* is a complex and confounding blues moment. It stands in stark contrast to the endings of Wilson's later dramas in which characters reach moments of spiritual fulfillment, acknowledge their relationships to the African American past, and perform actions of self-actualization, self-determination, and collective communion. Present in the final scene of *Ma Rainey* is the ironic anguish of the blues wail. After being exploited by the white studio owner Sturdyvant, Levee transfers and vents his anger against the unfortunate Toledo, who steps on Levee's shoes. Levee's stabbing of Toledo, like all acts of black-on-black violence, strikes out against African American collectivity and cultural unity. The murder of Toledo represents a performance of tragic, unfulfilled promise, a loss of the black self that must reclaimed through the triumph of the blues voice. The death of Toledo stands as a lesson that African Americans must learn from and that Wilson builds upon in his later plays.

Fences

In an interview with Hilary DeVries, Wilson claimed that he "started *Fences*" (1986), his first Pulitzer Prize–winning play, "with the image of a man standing in his yard with a baby in his arms." Beginning with this image, Wilson sought to subvert the dominant culture's representations of African American men as irresponsible, absentee fathers. Wilson creates Troy Maxson, a larger-than-life figure, who feels an overwhelming sense of duty and responsibility to his family. In fact, it is around his concepts of duty and responsibility that the character of Troy is problematized. Troy's worldview is myopic. With an impenetrable resolve, he perceives familial values from only his perspective. Troy's self-involved concept of familial duty and responsibility prevents him from seeing the harm he causes, the pain his decisions inflict on other family members.

Even before the text for *Fences* begins, Wilson situates its events culturally and historically through an introductory prologue. The prologue juxtaposes the historical reception of European immigrants to the northeastern United States with the relocation experiences of African American migrants from the South. While the northern cities, Wilson writes in the prologue, "nourished and offered each [European] man a partnership limited only by his talent, his guile and his willingness and capacity for hard work," these cities offered "the descendants of African slaves no such welcome or participation." Within these historical circumstances, and within the calendar year 1957, Wilson locates the particular plight of Troy Maxson and his family.

Then, in the play text, through a series of retrospective stories performed by Troy, Wilson reveals Troy's victimization by and resentment of the forces of social and economic oppression. Wilson also uses these moments to disclose the influence that Troy's prior relationship with his father now exacts on his relationship with his own son Cory. Physically beaten by his father, Troy was forced to strike out on his own. During the course of the play, Cory must undergo a similar right of passage. Repeating the family history, Cory physically confronts his father, is beaten by Troy and forced to leave his father's house. The repetition of behavior patterns by father and son underscores Wilson's conviction

that history plays an important role in determining contemporary identity. Only by literally confronting the embodiment of the past, one's father or "forefathers," can one gain entrance into the future or ascend into adulthood. Equally significant, Troy's storytelling is a ritualistic intervention in which performative aspects of African and African American culture are enacted. In these moments, Troy functions as an African griot or folk raconteur. Troy's stories expand the realistic canvas of the play. They reach beyond the conventional temporal and spatial limits. The resonance is both African and mythic.

In the play's second act, Troy's adultery provides the catalyst that propels his wife, Rose, to reassess her position, to gain a greater self-awareness, and to change. Rose blooms. Although Rose spiritually distances herself from Troy, she does not leave the marriage. Her final assessment of their marriage, delivered to her son Cory in the last scene, functions to reconcile father and son and emphasizes Rose's own resignation to "what life offered [her] in terms of being a woman." At the end of *Fences*, Cory is able to reconcile himself with his father and to accept the continued "presence" of his father in his life. This acceptance comes after Cory returns home from the Marines and announces to Rose his intent to boycott his father's funeral. Wilson juxtaposes Cory's return with the entrance of a new character, Troy's seven-year-old daughter from his affair, Raynell, Cory's half-sister. The intrusion of a new character during the play's denouement is a deliberate breach of the acknowledged and accepted covenants of realistic play construction. Wilson uses Raynell as a critical element in his redemptive strategy. Raynell visually represents the inextricable connection between past and present. Not only is she the manifestation of Troy's past infidelities but the signifier of his redemption. Her appearance enables both the audience and Cory to understand better the importance of inheritance, the perpetuation and veneration of history. In addition, here as in other Wilson works, the child, Raynell, symbolizes the hope for the family's future. Significantly, her entrance into the action not only occurs on the day of Troy's funeral, but in the year 1965, in the midst of the civil rights era, a period of intense struggle and new opportunity for African Americans.

The most significant redemptive act and transgression of realism in *Fences* is the final transcendent act of Gabriel, Troy's brother. Gabriel suffered a traumatic head injury during World War II and now has a metal plate in his head and functions at a diminished mental capacity. He believes he is the Archangel Gabriel and thus represents the earthly embodiments of heavenly power. At the end of the play, Gabriel summons his special faith to literally and symbolically open Heaven's gates for his brother Troy on the day of Troy's funeral. His actions proclaim a new day for Troy and the Maxson family. In addition, Gabriel's ritualistic and spiritual enactment is an exhibit of a syncretic cosmology, the presence of African tradition within New World religious practice. Prior to opening Heaven's gates, Wilson writes that Gabriel endures "a trauma that a sane and normal mind would be unable to withstand." Because Gabriel wholeheartedly believes he is the Archangel Gabriel, his will is resolute. Gabriel invokes a racial memory, an African inheritance. His actions again reinforce the impact of the past on the present as the family's African heritage provides a benediction for their African American present. Wilson's later works, *Joe Turner's Come and Gone*, *The Piano Lesson*, and *King Hedley II*, also feature rituals of religious syncretism. Consequently, this moment in *Fences* should be viewed as part of Wilson's continuing project to critique the African American experience of Christianity and to define and structure a particularly *African* American cosmology.

Joe Turner's Come and Gone

Joe Turner's Come and Gone, which premiered in 1987, remains August Wilson's most nonrealistic, nonlinear, and ritualistic work. Rhythms, symbols, and spirituality propel this work. The action does not evolve directly out of cause-and-effect linear progression. The events set this play within a world of liminality, betwixt and between. The year is 1911, a time on the cusp of the "great migration" from the South to the North. The liminality of the environment allows Wilson to foreground the spiritual nature of the acts that take place within this space. The play as a whole operates as ritual conveying blessings on the audience as a gathered congregation. Wilson set the work in 1911 because of the palpable and direct relationship of African Americans at that time to their African roots. Within this work perhaps more visibly than the others, Wilson asserts the African in African American experience.

The central character, Herald Loomis, comes to Seth's Pittsburgh boardinghouse as a character who is spiritually and psychologically dislocated. He comes in search of his wife, Martha, whom he was separated from some eleven years ago, when he was captured and kept in servitude for seven years by Joe Turner. Along with his daughter, Zonia, he has been on the road moving constantly, searching for Martha for four years. For Loomis the contradiction between his constant movement and the lack of movement within the direction of his life is most acute. Loomis realizes that his forward motion depends on going back and settling his unfinished business with his wife. "Got to find my wife. That be my starting place." His arrival at the boardinghouse, to the distress of its owner, Seth, interrupts the behavior and life of all the inhabitants.

Eleven years earlier, while acting as an agent of the church and warning men about the evils of gambling, Loomis was picked up on a Memphis street corner along with these other black men by Joe Turner, the brother of the governor of Tennessee. Turner kept Loomis and the other men in virtual servitude for a period of seven years. That period of bondage has severely damaged Herald Loomis and he is still recovering from its ramifications and wearing the scars. Wilson appropriated the title of the play from a blues song written by W. C. Handy, the "father of the blues." According to legend and Handy's account, black women sang this lament after their men were taken into servitude by Joe *Turney*, the brother of Pete Turney, the twenty-ninth governor of the state of Tennessee (1883–1897). "He come with forty links of chain, Oh Lady! Got my man and gone." The blues song served as a cultural response of women to a "world not of their making." This song is of historical, cultural, and theatrical significance. Wilson conflates these diverse modalities within the theatrical space and metaphor. History becomes theatrical as the theater becomes history. It was their reaction to the servitude that Joe Turner imposed upon their black husbands and brothers.

While Loomis wears the pain of his alienation on his face, the scars run much deeper and are hidden behind his facade until Bynum, a "conjure" man and resident of the boardinghouse, goads his revelation through song. Bynum provokes him into revealing his servitude by singing a song, "They Tell Me Joe Turner's Come and Gone." When Loomis hears the song, he reacts vehemently; he tells Bynum, "I don't like you singing that song, mister!" Clearly the song has political and social implications. It acts as a powerful medium for change. It compels Loomis to reveal that he is indeed marked as "one of Joe Turner's Niggers."

With the assistance of the mysterious and powerful Bynum, Loomis comes to understand his search as a spiritual and practical quest to find his "song," a connection to a past lost while enslaved by Turner. He journeys toward self-knowledge, spiritual and psychological liberation. Wilson believes that black Americans must rediscover "their song," their connection with their African heritage. In the play's final scene, Loomis draws a knife and cuts his own chest. He shouts, "I don't need anyone to bleed for me. I can bleed for myself." He bleeds for himself, but he also symbolically bleeds for black America in search of its collective song. Unshackled from the painful psychological burdens of servitude, Loomis rediscovers his song, his identity, and shines. His personal transcendence "heralds" to black Americans that they must regain their African past and reorient themselves in the future.

Loomis' bloodletting is a symbolic inversion of the Christian sacrifice where Christ bleeds for the sins of his followers. Loomis bleeds for himself. In a demonstration of self-determination, Wilson in his twentieth-century cycle rejects the passive restraints placed on blacks by Christianity. His young, fiery, tormented black male protagonists—Levee in *Ma Rainey*, Boy Willie in *Piano Lesson*, and Loomis in *Joe Turner*—all lash out against conventional Christianity and its failure within their own experience. Significantly, Joe Turner captured Herald Loomis while he was attempting to spread the Christian gospel as a deacon in the Abundant Life Church. His years of bondage have turned him away from Christianity. Prior to his self-scarification, his just-discovered wife Martha calls out to him to return to the church and give his soul to the Lord. "You got to look to Jesus. Even if you done fell away from the church you can be saved." His response to her rejects that validity of Christian salvation and the inherent racism with the dogma of Christianity. "Great big old white man . . . you Mr. Jesus Christ." In this powerful and passionately ritualistic scene, Martha and Loomis engage in a call-and-response interchange that challenges the authority of the Holy Ghost and the traditional rituals of prayer practices within Christian religion. Through this visual, aural, and spiritual moment, Wilson infuses the Christian with the African. He creates a blues moment in which the cultural becomes the mechanism for expressing the sociopolitical. Loomis comes to find his sense of self and new sense of spirituality and, as Bynum notes, he exits the scene "shining! You shining like new money!"

The Piano Lesson

In his second Pulitzer Prize–winning play, *The Piano Lesson* (1990), as in his first Pulitzer Prize winner, *Fences*, August Wilson appropriates and expands the traditions of American family drama in order to examine issues of inheritance. At the center of the family conflict in the play is a piano. According to Wilson, in his 1987 interview with DeVries, "The real issue is the piano, the legacy. How are you going to use it?" Boy Willie intends to sell the piano in order to buy land where his father worked as a share-

A Playbill for Wilson's *The Piano Lesson*.

cropper and his grandfather as a slave. His sister Berniece, on the other hand, believes that this piano, for which her father gave his life, must be kept in the family and can never be sold. The argument between brother and sister plays out as a dialectical debate for which the audience must construct a synthesis. Wilson creates convincing and rational arguments on both sides of the divide. The ideological separation of Boy Willie, the southern brother, from Berniece, the northern sister, becomes the site for a practical, spiritual, and ontological reconnection. On another level, the play is a ghost story concerned with the "real" threat represented by the ghost of the recently deceased white landowner, Sutter, who returns to haunt the family in his search for the piano. Ultimately Wilson suggests in *The Piano Lesson*, as he does in his other works, that African American survival in

the United States depends on the celebration of that spirit, that cultural memory that is particularly African.

While Boy Willie acknowledges the legacy of his father as a critical motivating force, Berniece pays homage to her mother. She presses Boy Willie to recognize their mother's role in the tragic history of the piano, "You always talking about your daddy, but you ain't looked to see what his foolishness cost your mother." Berniece, as she reflects on her mother, represents and defends the world and worth of women. Her perspective is decidedly "womanist," reflective of the differing meanings that social, cultural, and sexual relations hold for men and women. Berniece believes the value of women's suffering and sacrifice have been devalued in the traditions and rituals of the patriarchy. Berniece admonishes Boy Willie and her other male relatives, "I look at you and you all the same. You. Papa Charles. Winning Boy. Doaker, Crawley . . . you're all alike. And what it lead to? More killing and more thieving. I ain't never seen it come to nothing." She blames the violent and irrational male order for her pain, suffering, and loss.

Berniece, the sister who has migrated north, is a figure of conflict and contradiction. She both acknowledges and attempts to ignore the impact of the past on the present. Berniece controls the piano in *The Piano Lesson*. It rests in her house and she has determined to keep it there. In her rational and persuasive arguments for keeping the piano—and thwarting Boy Willie's efforts to sell it—Berniece relies upon the history, the legacy of familial sacrifice, both maternal and paternal, that have carried the piano to its current resting place. For Berniece, selling the piano would desecrate her parents' memories. Their uncle, Doaker, explains, "that why we say Berniece ain't gonna sell that piano. Cause her daddy died over it." At the same time, however, Berniece seeks to avoid the memories of the past. She is fragmented and dislocated from her southern roots and wants to maintain this dislocation. As a result, she neglects her duties as cultural progenitor. It is this position that Wilson seeks to critique in *The Piano Lesson*, as he told Savran in 1998, "the question was, 'Can one acquire a sense of self-worth by denying one's past?' "

As a symbol, the piano is complex and multilayered, its meanings are both personal and political. The socio-history of the piano is inextricably linked to the socio-history of the Charles family. Early in the first act, in a long and detailed monologue, Uncle Doaker Charles reveals to the audience the history of the piano. Doaker relates how Robert Sutter, the original slave owner of Willie Boy Charles, the grandfather of Doaker and the great-grandfather of Boy Willie and Berniece, wanted to purchase the piano from a Mr. Nolander. "Only thing with him [Robert Sutter] . . . he ain't had no money. But he had some niggers. So he asked Mr. Nolander to see if maybe he could trade off some of his niggers for that piano. Told him he would give him one and a half niggers for it." The "one and a half niggers" were Berniece Charles and her son, the great-grandmother and grandfather of Boy Willie and Berniece. Thus, the value of the piano was literally equated with that of the family. Both the family and the piano constituted property. Sutter's wife, Miss Ophelia, was distraught at losing her favorite slaves. So, Willie Boy, at the behest of Sutter, carves the portraits of the Charles family onto the legs of the piano. Yet, Willie Boy subversively exceeds Sutter's request. He personalizes the piano and creates "a new semantic field" by carving into the piano the history of the various members of the Charles family. Purposefully, Wilson's introductory description notes that the legs of the piano are "carved in the manner of African sculpture" with the "mask-like figures resembling totems." Willie Boy's carvings transform the piano into a contoured or relief family album. Through the artistic process he redefines the family's relationship to the piano and the semantics of ownership and property. In this way, he *re-members* his family and undermines the request of the slave-master Sutter. Through this act, the piano and its "songs" become the property of the Charles family.

Doaker goes on to describe the joy that Sutter's wife, Miss Ophelia, feels when she discovers the Charles family portraits that Willie Boy carves into the piano. "When Miss Ophelia seen [the carved piano] . . . she got excited. Now she had her piano and her niggers too." The carved wooden representation of the Charles family was enough to satisfy Miss Ophelia's desire. The wooden image replaced the real slave body. Accordingly, for Miss Ophelia, the carving equaled the real slave because neither was perceived as human. Thus, both the piano and the "niggers" remained her property.

Doaker in his continuing narrative reveals that years later, after slavery, Papa Boy Charles, Berniece and Boy Willie's father, remained obsessed with the thought of reclaiming the piano from Sutter family. "He talking about taking it out of Sutter's house. Say it was the story of our whole family and as long as Sutter had it . . . he had us. Say we was still in slavery." As the narrative explains, Sutter's possession of the piano constitutes a form of enslavement. The Charles' "liberation" of the piano from the white landowner Sutter, whose family held the Charles family as slaves, constitutes a symbolic declaration of self-determination. Ominously in the background of *The Piano Lesson* is an invisible white figure who is "going around to all the *colored* people's houses looking to buy up musical instruments." For Wilson, such sales represent a betrayal and regressive return of African Americans to the dominant culture's hegemony.

While Berniece keeps the piano, she does not play it. Her neglect of the piano, her unwillingness to confront the ghosts of her past threatens the current stability of the Charles family and allows the ghost of Sutter to return and contest them for ownership of the piano and the possession of their "songs." Thus, it is only at the conclusion of the play, when Berniece returns to the piano, that the ghost of Sutter can be exorcised. In the Broadway version and the final published edition of *The Piano Lesson*, Berniece, drawn to the piano by the confrontation between Boy Willie and Sutter's ghost, plays a song that explicitly calls on the ancestral spirits for assistance, "Mama Ola, I want you to help me." Wilson describes Berniece's offering to the ancestral spirits as, "*an old urge to song that is both a commandment and a plea. With each repetition it gains strength. It is intended as an exorcism and a dressing for battle. A rustle of* wind blowing across two continents." Inherent, then, in Berniece's calling on her ancestors is the African tradition of ancestral worship. Her act symbolically unites her with her earlier ancestors in Africa. This moment is significant in Wilson's pre-eminent project to recuperate the African-ness in African American experience. In this climactic moment of *The Piano Lesson*, Wilson extends this blues riff and the concept of African conceptualizations through the actions of Berniece. In a moment of desperation and urgency, Berniece sits at the piano to play and purposefully employs what Toledo in *Ma Rainey* would term "an African conceptualization." As her brother, Boy Willie, struggles upstairs with the ghost of the white landowner, Sutter, Berniece at the piano calls on the power of her ancestors to exorcise the ghost and to save her brother. Thus when Berniece returns to the piano and plays, she reconnects with the past. She calls on her ancestors and, thus, acknowledges the importance of the ancestral spirits and the power of these "ghosts." Berniece's invocation of the ancestors in conjunction with Boy Willie's call to battle exorcises the ghosts of the past that threaten the present. Her actions re-member the family and reaffirm the African in African American experience.

Two Trains Running

As with his other historical dramas, August Wilson sets *Two Trains Running*, which premiered in March 1990, in a time of transition, the year 1969, the final year of a decade that has come to symbolize resistance, irreverence, anarchy, and upheaval in America. African Americans turned from the nonviolence of the civil rights movement toward the fiery revolutionary politics of the black power movement. Wilson locates *Two Trains Running* in a small Pittsburgh restaurant that is at once within as well as outside of the pressing urgencies of those times. The shop must be torn down as part of the process of urban renewal. Outside its confines, a funeral for the deceased Prophet Samuel and a rally for the slain black leader Malcolm X are held. Inside the shop, the back-

ground characters confront issues of identity and black power, gender and self-determination. The play is at once timely and timeless, operating within a specific historical context and at the same time commenting on contemporary African American culture. Wilson writes about the black idealism and cultural nationalism of the 1960s with the historical distance of the 1990s. Like the character Hambone in this play, Wilson wants audiences to leave *Two Trains Running* chanting "I want my Ham!" In Wilson's play, "Ham" acts as metaphor for self-determination and revolutionary agency.

Before the action, the one female character, Risa the waitress, has engaged in a radical and intensely personal protest against the objectification of women. Frustrated by men who deny her humanity by observing her body as a sex object, Risa takes a razor and scars her legs, seven scars on one leg, eight on the other. Risa's revolt against objectification appears irrational but also lends itself to feminist interpretation. Recent feminist theory and theatrical criticism have reacted against traditional gender categories and questioned the construction of women on stage. No longer is she viewed simply as a sexual object or a possession for "some man to lay up with." Her scarification and the corresponding reaction by men emphasize the interlocking systems of women's oppression and objectification.

The plot of the play revolves around the regulars who frequent the restaurant and an interloper, Sterling, a young man recently released from prison. Sterling enters the restaurant early in the first act in search of direction. At issue in the play is the relationship between capitalism and spirituality. Set at a time filled with the rhetoric of black nationalism and the 1960s' paradigms of black liberation, Wilson bemoans the lack of black investment in the black community. Holloway, a wizened old regular at Memphis' restaurant, reports, "That's all you got around here is niggers with somebody else's money in their pocket. And they don't do nothing but trade it off on each other, I got it today and you got it tomorrow. Until sooner or later as sure as the sun shine . . . somebody gonna take it and give it to the white man. Money go from you to me to you and then—bingo, it's gone." The spiritual center of the play is Aunt Esther, an offstage mystic who at 349 years old is as old as the black presence in the United States. When spoken, her name, "Aunt Esther," sounds purposefully like the word "ancestor." Symbolically through her, Wilson links past to present and underscores the African in the African American traditions. She dispenses wisdom and advice. Then, in a manner not unlike African traditions for honoring river goddesses, asks her visitors to pay tribute by throwing twenty dollars into the river. "Say she get it."

While Holloway, Sterling, and Memphis all eventually honor Aunt Esther in this way, Mr. West, another regular at the restaurant does not. He refuses to "throw his money away" in this fashion. West, the owner of the local funeral parlor and the richest man in town, is spiritually bereft. He does not recognize the need for African American economic strategy that connects the acquisition of wealth to the maintenance of spiritual and social well being within the black community. Wilson contrasts West with the character Hambone. Hambone's mental condition has deteriorated to where he can only repeat two phrases and he repeats them over and over again: "He gonna give me my ham!" and "I want my ham!" Nine and one-half years before the play begins, Hambone painted a fence for the white butcher, Lutz. Lutz explained to him that he would pay him a ham if he did a good job or a chicken if the job was just adequate. After completing the work and expecting a ham, Lutz offered Hambone only a chicken. Hambone refused to accept it, believing he deserved the ham. Every morning, then, for nine and one-half years, he stands in front of Lutz' Meat Market and demands his ham. Lutz defers and repeats his offer of the chicken. Hambone, like Gabriel in *Fences* and Hedley in *Seven Guitars*, is another of Wilson's characters who, seemingly due to their diminished mental capacity, have little social value. These characters, however, have special powers and a unique understanding of the world. Holloway says of Hambone, "I say he might have more sense than me and you. Cause he ain't

willing to accept whatever the white man throw at him." Symbolically Hambone represents both the forgotten promise of forty acres and a mule due to black people, as well as the obsessed determination to get proper payment for the debt of slavery. When Hambone dies, West reveals that his body was scarred from head to toe. He literally wears the scars of slavery and is a monument to the black past.

The story, along with that of Memphis, the restaurant owner, reinforces Wilson's theme that one must go back in order to truly move forward. Prior to the action of the play, Memphis had been abused and run off his land by a group of white men. After seeing his mule killed, his land burned, and his deed to his land denied by a white judge, Memphis decided to leave Jackson, Mississippi, to call "it a draw" and to head north for Pittsburgh. Consequently, he too has unfinished business that he must settle. Faced with Urban Renewal and the plans for the demolition of his restaurant, Memphis refuses to accept the amount offered him by the city government for his property. After returning from his first trip to the courthouse, angered and insulted by the city's paltry offer of $15,000, Memphis relates the story of his mother's death and subsequent funeral. The loss of his mother served as a catalyzing moment for Memphis: "The last person I owed anything was gone. . . . I come and said 'Everybody better get out of my way.' You couldn't hold me down. It look like then I had somewhere to go fast. I didn't know where, but I damn sure was going there. That's the way I feel now. . . . I'll get off the canvas if I have to. They can carry me out feet first . . . but my clause say . . . they got to meet my price." Like a blues player improvising on a theme, creatively negotiating the pain of white oppression, Memphis determines to beat the city government at its own game and hires a white lawyer to plead his case. The result, after a visit to Aunt Esther and the hiring of a new lawyer, is a settlement for $35,000. At the end of the play, Memphis, with a new awareness of his "blues voice" and his power to determine his own destiny, decides to return south, "to go back and pick up the ball" and reclaim his land.

Seven Guitars

First performed in January 1995, *Seven Guitars* was Wilson's sixth play to reach Broadway. In *Seven Guitars* the blues infuse both form and content. Set in the 1940s, the play opens just after the funeral for the misguided bluesman Floyd Barton. The other characters gather in the backyard of Floyd's former girlfriend, Vera, to drink and commiserate. Floyd was a promising blues singer with a hit record to his credit. Over the course of the play, the plot reveals the circumstances that surrounded Barton's death. The main action of the play evolves through flashbacks to times when Barton was still alive. Consequently, the real movement of the play has already occurred, back in the past, before the opening scene. The play literally progresses forward by going back.

Floyd "Schoolboy" Barton's story unfolds like a blues riff with passion and pathos. His story is reminiscent of the tragic myths and legends of larger-than-life black bluesmen such as Buddy Bolden and Robert Johnson. Fiercely, Floyd believes that his future success depends on a new record deal with Mr. T. L. Hall, a white producer and agent. In *Seven Guitars* and his earlier plays, Wilson conceives of the oppression of African Americans in musical metaphors. Through the invisible presence and symbolic activities of offstage white characters, who attempt to seize or possess black music, Wilson suggests that the dominant culture subjugates African American humanity and suppresses the power and ability of African Americans to sing their song of perseverance. Correspondingly, Floyd Barton has written a hit record but as his sideman, Canewell, points out, he has "no hit-record money." Mr. T. L. Hall has exploited the illiterate Barton and the white-controlled record industry. The ability to control one's own song is for Wilson critical to being able to define oneself and to determine one's own destiny. In contrast, Floyd's myopic, self-obsessed desire for fame and fortune in Chicago results in his betrayal of the redemptive power of the blues and values of community. His capitulation with the forces of white hegemony is symbolized by his pawning his guitar, the instrument of his cultural potency. His demise is inevitable.

The music of the blues also finds expression in the language and banter of the seven characters, the "seven guitars." The characters engage in series of vernacular games, the dozens and signifyin'. All are extensions of the blues or variations on a blues theme. As in the earlier *Ma Rainey's Black Bottom*, Wilson creates characters whose vocal rhythms correspond to the blues. With *Seven Guitars*, each of the characters again functions as musical instruments, with each allowed moments of solo virtuosity. Featured more prominently than in any of Wilson's previous dramas are women, and their solos are among the play's most powerful moments. The poetic journey of dialogue is as important as the development of the plot. Like a bluesman, Wilson improvises upon, repeats, and revises earlier themes. His plays do not conform to the rules of conventional realism structure but instead rely on the dynamics of character and the lyrical music of the dialogue.

Paradoxically, in Wilson's works it is the characters who appear mentally impaired, besieged by madness, unable to grasp the reality of the world around them, who represent a connection to a lost "song" of self-determination and to a legacy of black social activism. The most recent manifestation of this black figure of madness is Hedley in *Seven Guitars*. The West Indian Hedley rants and raves about black social action. He rages against the white power structure, but his cries go unheeded by the other characters. Wilson, however, wants the audience to recognize the truth, power, and prophesy in Hedley's words. Hedley's obsession, his singular focus, enables him to connect with the suppressed and oppressed African American song of freedom in ways "a normal or sane mind" could not.

Throughout the play, Floyd and Hedley play a game around a lyric to the song "I Thought I Heard Buddy Bolden Say," or "Buddy Bolden's Blues." This song was based on Bolden's own classic jazz dance tune, "Funky Butt," and was recorded by Jelly Roll Morton in 1939, nine years before the date in which Wilson sets *Seven Guitars*. It soon became a jazz staple. Bolden, a builder and part-time barber, cornet player, and bandleader in New Orleans, has been called the first man of jazz. In keeping with Bolden's improvisatory conventions, Jelly Roll Morton and others constantly improvised the lyrics to the song in performance. Floyd and Hedley's disagreement over the lyric reflects back on the improvisational nature of the song and its oral transmission through time. It also symbolizes Floyd's and Hedley's divergent ideologies. While Floyd imagines Bolden as a self-serving fellow musician demanding payment, Hedley envisions him as a redemptive figure bearing monetary gifts and offering salvation. Within the drama of *Seven Guitars*, Wilson considers the cultural, social, and spiritual power of music and musicians. Art and ethics unite and art can function as a force for social change.

Jitney!

With *Jitney!*, Wilson again explores how the past shapes present action. Here the impact is both personal and political. Wilson first wrote *Jitney!* back in 1979. He then revised it from 1997 through 1999. It reached Broadway in 2000. Set in early fall 1977, at a gypsy cab station in Pittsburgh, it repeats and revises themes from Wilson's other plays. Yet, since this play is at once an early play as well as a recent addition to his cycle, it also reveals the antecedents for characters and questions that surface within the later plays. Becker's gypsy cab station, like the band room in *Ma Rainey*, Seth's boardinghouse in *Joe Turner*, and Memphis' restaurant in *Two Trains*, is a blues matrix, a place betwixt and between that allows for the free flow and congregation of the characters. As with these other environments, this is largely a malecentric world in which black men confront each other, themselves, and their position in the world.

At issue for all the men within this world is responsibility: what is their responsibility to themselves, to their families, to their people? The question of black men and their responsibility to family is vital to Wilson. *Jitney!* features generations of black men old and young. As with Wilson's other dramas, these are men who have been disenfranchised and disillusioned by the forces of American racism. Still, they are survivors. The older men, Turnbo, Fielding, Doub, and Becker, the owner of the cab station and the figure at the center of the play's action, are perhaps not as fully developed as those of Wilson's other plays and yet they have certain similarities to other Wilson men. Becker, like Memphis in *Two Trains*, must determine what course of action to take in the face of the threatened foreclosure of his business. From the outset of *Jitney!*, urban redevelopment threatens the livelihood of Becker and his men. The jitney cab station is to be torn down and replaced by housing units. Our historical distance in the twenty-first century from Urban Renewal projects of the 1960s and 1970s has shown us that while these projects proposed to change the urban landscape for the better, they often did significant damage by fragmenting black communities and destroying existing businesses and foundations for community linkages. Eventually in *Jitney!*, Becker and the others determine to take a collective stand against the forces of redevelopment and to fight the closure of the cab station. Becker comes to this decision only after he confronts his past through a character that is also simultaneously the symbolic embodiment of his future, his son Booster. In the first act of the play, Booster returns after twenty years in prison for shooting his white former girlfriend after she lied to her father and the authorities about their relationship. The tensions between father and son in this work bear similarities to that of Troy and Cory in *Fences*, as well as to the difficulties between Wilson and the real father figures in his life. Believing that Booster's actions destroyed his own hopes for the future, Becker never visited his son in prison and disowns him on his return. Yet, the scenes of confrontation between father and son—as each reviews his perspective of the past and the death of the son's mother—determine in Becker a new resolve. While Becker felt that he could not fight the forces of white hegemony in the past because of his obligations to his family, he now decides that he can no longer be passive but must take action to save his jitney cab station. "I'm through making excuses for anybody . . . including myself. I ain't gonna pass it on, I say we stay here."

Booster confesses to his father that he resented his father's inaction in the face of white racism and abuse. He justified killing his white girlfriend, Susan McKnight, who falsely accused him of rape, as revenge for his father's passivity. "I wanted them to remember my name. . . . I wanted to deal with the world in ways that you wanted to and couldn't or didn't or wished you had." Booster's action, however, is clearly a misguided revolutionary act. The murder does not change white/black racial dynamics but only lands him in jail, covers Becker in shame, and hastens the death of Booster's mother. Booster, similar to Levee in *Ma Rainey* and Sterling in *Two Trains*, is a warrior, but a misdirected one who has not yet found the proper channel for his fiery antiestablishment energy or developed a truly radical consciousness. Booster's relationship with Susan McKnight is Wilson's only foray into interracial desire in his cycle plays thus far. Interracial desire has the power to disrupt racial categories and threaten the sanctity of the borders between black and white. Wilson, however, thwarts this disruption and restores the status quo as Susan asserts her white privilege and black difference by crying rape.

Wilson juxtaposes Booster's warrior spirit and sense of responsibility in the play with that of Youngblood, the other young black man in the play. Like Booster, Youngblood has been institutionalized. He voluntarily completed his tour of duty and service in Vietnam. Unlike Booster, Youngblood believes in the American Dream and that society will do right by him. He uses money from the GI Bill to help him make a down payment on a house. He saves money from his job at the jitney cab station and is determined to somehow make a living and provide for his girlfriend Rena and their baby. Youngblood exhibits a decidedly different understanding of responsibility and response to the inequities of white racism than does Booster. While Booster revolts against the system, Youngblood has conformed within it. Yet, Wilson suggests that neither approach is without problems. Youngblood must deal with the forced closure of the jitney cab station and the indignities faced by Vietnam veterans on their return. Wilson seeks a methodology in which both revolutionary fervor and personal, civic, and cultural responsibilities can come together.

King Hedley II

Set in the crime-ridden 1980s, *King Hedley II* confronts issues of black-on-black violence. Wilson explores the roots of the rage, homicides, and drive-by shootings that consumed black communities in the 1980s. With *King Hedley II*, Wilson plunges characters and themes from *Seven Guitars* forty years into the future. Ruby, the youngest figure in *Seven Guitars*, is now a woman in her sixties with an adult son, King Hedley II. Ruby has named him after the man she slept with in *Seven Guitars*, when young and pregnant by another man. King, like Levee of *Ma Rainey* and Sterling of *Two Trains Running*, is another one of Wilson's misguided young warriors—an innocent and alienated product of lessons learned, the sins of the father reaped upon the son. The concluding moment of *King Hedley II* serves as both an ending and a beginning as King dies at the hands of his own mother. This murder, unlike those that take place earlier in the play, cannot provoke or compel retribution as it is carried out by King's own mother, the person that brought him into this world. It thus signals an end to the continuum of bloodshed, revenge, and violence. While this play premiered in Wilson's hometown, Pittsburgh, on December 15, 1999, it is still in process. As with his other works, Wilson will revise the play repeatedly on its journey to Broadway.

Even as Wilson works on this play and maps out plans for the final two plays in his cycle, his own life continues to link art and activism.

Aligning himself with the African American history of struggle and survival as well as the black tradition of a functional art of protest, Wilson delivered a powerful call for a new black theater movement at the Theatre Communications Group 1996 National Convention. Spurred on by the vociferous response to this speech, Wilson helped to organize the National Black Theatre Summit at Dartmouth College in March 1997. Over three hundred black theater scholars, theater practitioners, economic entrepreneurs, and community activists all came together to discuss the future of black theater. Significantly, the summit led to the creation of a new national black theater organization, the African Grove Institute, named after the very first documented black theater in the United States, Mr. Brown's African Grove Company (1821–1823).

Selected Bibliography

PRIMARY WORKS

DRAMA

Ma Rainey's Black Bottom. New York: New American Library, 1985.
Fences. New York: New American Library, 1987.
Joe Turner's Come and Gone. New York: New American Library, 1988.
The Piano Lesson. New York: Plume, 1990.
Testimonies. In *Antaeus* 66:474–79 (Spring 1991).
Three Plays. Pittsburgh: University of Pittsburgh Press, 1991. (Contains *Ma Rainey's Black Bottom, Fences,* and *Joe Turner's Come and Gone.*)
Two Trains Running. New York: Plume, 1992.
Seven Guitars. New York: Dutton, 1996.
The Janitor. In *Literature and Its Writers: An Introduction.* By Ann Charters and Samuel Charters. Boston: Bedford, 1997. Pp. 1901–1902.

ESSAYS

Foreword to *Romare Bearden: His Life and Art.* Edited by Myron Schwartzman. New York: Harry N. Abrams, 1990. p. 9.
"How to Write a Play Like August Wilson." *New York Times,* March 10, 1991, sec. 2, pp. 5, 17.
Preface to *Three Plays.* Pittsburgh: University of Pittsburgh Press, 1991. Pp. vii–xiv.
"The Legacy of Malcolm X." *Life,* December 1992, pp. 84–94.
"I Want a Black Director." In *May All Your Fences Have Gates.* Edited by Alan Nadel. Iowa City: University of Iowa Press, 1994. Pp. 200–204.

"Living on Mother's Prayer." *New York Times,* May 12, 1996, sec. IV, p. 13.
"The Ground on Which I Stand." *American Theatre,* September 1996, pp. 14–17, 71–74. (Reprint of the author's keynote address to the Theatre Communications Group, June 26, 1996.)
"August Wilson Responds." *American Theatre,* October 1996, pp. 105–107.

SECONDARY WORKS

BIOGRAPHICAL AND CRITICAL STUDIES

Adell, Sandra. "Speaking of Ma Rainey/Talking about the Blues." In *May All Your Fences Have Gates.* Edited by Alan Nadel. Iowa City: University of Iowa Press, 1994. Pp. 50–66.
Ambush, Benny Sato. "Culture Wars." *African American Review* 31:579–86 (Winter 1997).
Anderson, Douglas. "Saying Goodbye to the Past: Self-Empowerment and History in *Joe Turner's Come and Gone.*" *College Language Association Journal* 40:432–57 (June 1997).
Arthur, Thomas H. "Looking for My Relatives: The Political Implications of 'Family' in Selected Work of Athol Fugard and August Wilson." *South African Theatre* 6:5–16 (September 1992).
Awkward, Michael. "The Crookeds and the Straights: *Fences,* Race, and the Politics of Adaptation." In *May All Your Fences Have Gates.* Edited by Alan Nadel. Iowa City: University of Iowa Press, 1994. Pp. 204–29.
Barbour, David. "August Wilson's Here to Stay." *Theater Week,* April 18–25, 1988, pp. 8–14.
Bellamy, Lou. "The Colonization of Black Theatre." *African American Review* 31:587–594 (Winter 1997).
Bergesen, Eric, and William Demastes. "The Limits of African-American Political Realism: Baraka's *Dutchman* and Wilson's *Ma Rainey's Black Bottom.*" In *Realism and the American Dramatic Tradition.* Edited by William Demastes. Tuscaloosa: University of Alabama Press, 1996. Pp. 218–34.
Bernstein Richard. "August Wilson's Voices from the Past." *New York Times,* March 27, 1988, sec. 2, pp. 1, 34.
Birdwell, Christine. "Death as a Fastball on the Outside Corner: *Fences'* Troy Maxson and the American Dream." *Aethlon: The Journal of Sport Literature* 8:87–96 (Fall 1990).
Bissiri, Amadou. "Aspects of Africanness in August Wilson's Drama: Reading *The Piano Lesson* through Wole Soyinka's Drama." *African American Review* 30:99–113 (Spring 1996).
Blumenthal, Anna S. "*Joe Turner's Come and Gone:* Sacrificial Rites and Rebirth of the Self." *Postscript: Publication of the Philological Association of the Carolinas* 15:53–65 (1998).
Boan, Devon. "Call-and-Response: Parallel 'Slave Narrative' in August Wilson's *The Piano Lesson.*" *African American Review* 32:263–71 (Summer 1998).
Bogumil, Mary L. " 'Tomorrow Never Comes': Songs of

Cultural Identity in August Wilson's *Joe Turner's Come and Gone.*" *Theatre Journal* 46:463–76 (December 1994).

———. *Understanding August Wilson.* Columbia: University of South Carolina Press, 1999.

Brantley, Ben. "The World that Created August Wilson." *New York Times,* March 27, 1988, sec. 2, pp. 1, 5.

Brown, Chip. "The Light in August." *Esquire,* April 1989, pp. 116–25.

Ching, Mei-Lei. "Wrestling against History." *Theater* 20:70–71 (Summer–Fall 1988).

Crawford, Eileen. "The Bb Burden: The Invisibility of *Ma Rainey's Black Bottom.*" In *August Wilson: A Casebook.* Edited by Marilyn Elkins. New York: Garland, 1994. Pp. 31–48.

Dworkin, Norine. "Blood on the Tracks." *American Theatre,* May 1990, p. 8.

Elam, Harry J. "August Wilson's Women." In *May All Your Fences Have Gates.* Edited by Alan Nadel. Iowa City: University of Iowa Press, 1994.

———. "Of Angels and Transcendence: A Cross-Cultural Analysis of *Fences* by August Wilson and *Roosters* by Milcha Sanchez-Scott." In *Staging Difference: Cultural Pluralism in American Theatre and Drama.* Edited by Marc Maufort. New York: Peter Lang, 1995. Pp. 287–300.

———. "*Ma Rainey's Black Bottom:* Singing Wilson's Blues." *American Drama* 5:76–99 (Spring 1996).

———. "The Dialectics of August Wilson's *Piano Lesson.*" *Theatre Journal,* October 2000.

Elkins, Marilyn, ed. *August Wilson: A Casebook.* New York: Garland, 1994.

Fishman, Joan. "Developing His Song: August Wilson's *Fences.*" In *August Wilson: A Casebook.* Edited by Marilyn Elkins. New York: Garland, 1994. Pp. 161–81.

———. "Romare Bearden and August Wilson, and the Traditions of African Performance." In *May All Your Fences Have Gates.* Edited by Alan Nadel. Iowa City: University of Iowa Press, 1994. Pp. 133–49.

Fleche, Anne. "The History Lesson: Authenticity and Anachronism in August Wilson's Plays." In *May All Your Fences Have Gates.* Edited by Alan Nadel. Iowa City: University of Iowa Press, 1994. Pp. 9–20.

Freedman, Samuel G. "A Voice from the Streets." *New York Times Magazine,* March 15, 1987, pp. 36, 40, 49, 50.

Gantt, Patricia. "Ghosts from 'Down There': The Southernness of August Wilson." In *August Wilson: A Casebook.* Edited by Marilyn Elkins. New York: Garland, 1994. Pp. 69–88.

Glover, Margaret E. "Two Notes on August Wilson: The Songs of a Marked Man." *Theater* 19, no. 3:69–70 (1988).

Goldberger, Paul. "From Page to Stage: Race and the Theater." *New York Times,* January 22, 1997, sec. C, pp. 11, 14.

Gordon, Joanne. "Wilson and Fugard." In *August Wilson: A Casebook.* Edited by Marilyn Elkins. New York: Garland, 1994. Pp. 17–29.

Harris, Trudier. "August Wilson's Folk Traditions." In *August Wilson: A Casebook.* Edited by Marilyn Elkins. New York: Garland, 1994. Pp. 49–67.

Harrison, Paul Carter. "August Wilson's Blues Poetics." In *Three Plays.* Written by August Wilson. Pittsburgh: University of Pittsburgh Press, 1991. Pp. 291–318.

———. "The Crisis of Black Theatre Identity." *African American Review* 31:567–78 (Winter 1997).

Harrison, Paul Carter, et al., eds. "August Wilson's Call." *African American Review* 31 (Winter 1997).

Herrington, Joan. *"I Ain't Sorry for Nothin' I Done": August Wilson's Process of Playwriting.* New York: Limelight Editions, 1998.

———. "On August Wilson's *Jitney!*" *American Drama* 8:122–44 (Fall 1998).

———. " 'Responsibility in Our Own Hands.' " *Journal of Dramatic Theory and Criticism* 13:87–99 (Fall 1998).

Ivison, Douglas. "The Use and Abuse of History: A Naturalist Reading of August Wilson's *The Piano Lesson.*" *Excavatio* 10:9–20 (1997).

Joseph, May. "Alliances across the Margins." *African American Review* 31:595–99 (Winter 1997).

Kester, Gunilla Theander. "Approaches to Africa: The Poetics of Memory and the Body in Two August Wilson Plays." In *August Wilson: A Casebook.* Edited by Marilyn Elkins. New York: Garland, 1994. Pp. 105–21.

Kroll, Jack. "August Wilson's Come to Stay." *Newsweek,* April 11, 1988, p. 82.

Kubitschek, Missy Dean. "August Wilson's Gender Lesson." In *May All Your Fences Have Gates.* Edited by Alan Nadel. Iowa City: University of Iowa Press, 1994. Pp. 183–99.

Leverett, James, et al. "Beyond Black and White: 'Cultural Power': 13 Commentaries." *American Theatre* 14, no. 5:14–15, 53–56 (1997).

Marra, Kim. "Ma Rainey and the Boyz: Gender Ideology in August Wilson's Broadway Canon." In *August Wilson: A Casebook.* Edited by Marilyn Elkins. New York: Garland, 1994. Pp. 123–60.

McDonough, Carla J. *Staging Masculinity: Male Identity in Contemporary American Drama.* Jefferson, N.C.: McFarland, 1997.

Mills, Alice. "The Walking Blues: An Anthropological Approach to the Theater of August Wilson." *Black Scholar* 25:30–35 (Spring 1995).

Monaco, Pamela Jean. "Father, Son, and Holy Ghost: From the Local to the Mythical in August Wilson." In *August Wilson: A Casebook.* Edited by Marilyn Elkins. New York: Garland, 1994. Pp. 89–104.

Morales, Michael. "Ghosts on the Piano: August Wilson and the Representation of Black American History." In *May All Your Fences Have Gates.* Edited by Alan Nadel. Iowa City: University of Iowa Press, 1994. Pp. 105–15.

Nadel, Alan. "Boundaries, Logistics, and Identity: The

Property of Metaphor in *Fences* and *Joe Turner's Come and Gone*." In *May All Your Fences Have Gates*. Edited by Alan Nadel. Iowa City: University of Iowa Press, 1994. Pp. 86–104.

———, ed. *May All Your Fences Have Gates: Essays on the Drama of August Wilson*. Iowa City: University of Iowa Press, 1994.

Pereira, Kim. *August Wilson and the African-American Odyssey*. Urbana: University of Illinois Press, 1995.

Plum, Jay. "Blues, History, and the Dramaturgy of August Wilson." *African American Review* 27:561–67 (Winter 1993).

Reed, Ishmael. "In Search of August Wilson: A Shy Genius Transforms the American Theater." *Connoisseur* 217:92–97 (March 1987).

Rocha, Mark William. "Black Madness in August Wilson's 'Down the Line' Cycle." In *Madness in Drama*. Edited by James Redmond. Cambridge: Cambridge University Press, 1993. Pp. 191–201.

———. "American History as 'Loud Talking' in *Two Trains Running*." In *May All Your Fences Have Gates*. Edited by Alan Nadel. Iowa City: University of Iowa Press, 1994. Pp. 116–32.

———. "August Wilson and the Four B's: Influences." In *August Wilson: A Casebook*. Edited by Marilyn Elkins. New York: Garland, 1994. Pp. 3–16.

Saunders, James Robert. "Essential Ambiguities in the Plays of August Wilson." *Hollins Critic* 32:1–12 (December 1995).

Shafer, Yvonne. "Breaking Barriers: August Wilson." In *Staging Difference: Cultural Pluralism in American Theatre and Drama*. Edited by Marc Maufort. New York: Peter Lang, 1995. Pp. 267–85.

———. "August Wilson and the Contemporary Theatre." *Journal of Dramatic Theory and Criticism* 12:23–38 (Fall 1997).

———. *August Wilson: A Research and Production Sourcebook*. Westport, Conn.: Greenwood, 1998.

Shannon, Sandra G. "The Good Christian's Come and Gone: The Shifting Role of Christianity in August Wilson's Plays." *Melus* 16, no. 3:127–42 (1989).

———. "Conversing with the Past: *Joe Turner's Come and Gone* and *The Piano Lesson*." *CEA Magazine: A Journal of the College English Association* 4, no. 1: 33–42 (1991).

———. "The Long Wait: August Wilson's *Ma Rainey's Black Bottom*." *Black American Literature Forum* 25:151–62 (Spring 1991).

———. "Subtle Impositions: The Lloyd Richards–August Wilson Formula." In *August Wilson: A Casebook*. Edited by Marilyn Elkins. New York: Garland, 1994. Pp. 183–98.

———. *The Dramatic Vision of August Wilson*. Washington, D.C.: Howard University Press, 1995.

———. "August Wilson's Autobiography." In *Memory and Cultural Politics: New Approaches to American Ethnic Literatures*. Edited by Amritjit Singh, Joseph T. Skerret Jr., and Robert E. Hogan. Boston: Northeastern University Press, 1996. Pp. 179–80.

———. "A Transplant that Did Not Take: August Wilson's Views on the Great Migration." *African American Review* 31:659–66 (Winter 1997).

Smith, Philip E., II. "*Ma Rainey's Black Bottom*: Playing the Blues as Equipment for Living." In *Within the Dramatic Spectrum*. Vol. 6. Edited by Karelisa V. Hartigan. Lanham, Md.: University Press of America, 1986. Pp. 177–86.

Taylor, Regina. "That's Why They Call It the Blues." *American Theatre*, April 1996, pp. 18–23.

Timpane, John. "Filling the Time: Reading History in the Drama of August Wilson." In *May All Your Fences Have Gates*. Edited by Alan Nadel. Iowa City: University of Iowa Press, 1994. Pp. 67–85.

Wallach, Allan. "Fenced In by a Lifetime of Resentments." *New York Theatre Critic Reviews*, March 27, 1987, p. 319.

Wang, Qun. "Towards the Poetization of the 'Field of Manners.'" *African American Review* 29:605–613 (Winter 1995).

Werner, Craig. "August Wilson's Burden: The Function of Neoclassical Jazz." In *May All Your Fences Have Gates*. Edited by Alan Nadel. Iowa City: University of Iowa Press, 1994. Pp. 21–50.

Wessling, Joseph H. "Wilson's *Fences*." *Explicator* 57:123–27 (Winter 1999).

Wilde, Lisa. "Reclaiming the Past: Narrative and Memory in August Wilson's *Two Trains Running*." *Theater* 22, no. 1:73–74 (1990).

Williams, Dana A. "A Review Essay of Scholarly Criticism on the Drama of August Wilson." *Bonner Beitrage* 55:53–62 (June 1998).

———. "Making the Bones Live Again: A Look at the 'Bones People' in August Wilson's *Joe Turner's Come and Gone* and Henry Dumas's 'Ark of Bones.'" *College Language Association Journal* 42:309–19 (March 1999).

Wolfe, Peter. *August Wilson*. New York: Twayne, 1999.

INTERVIEWS

DeVries, Hilary. "August Wilson: A New Voice for Black American Theater." *Christian Science Monitor*, October 18, 1984, pp. 51–54.

———. "A Song in Search of Itself." *American Theatre*, January 1987, p. 25.

Di Gaetani, John L. "August Wilson." In his *A Search for a Postmodern Theater: Interviews with Contemporary Playwrights*. New York: Greenwood, 1991. Pp. 275–84.

Grant, Nathan L. "Men, Women, and Culture: A Conversation with August Wilson." *American Drama* 5:100–22 (Spring 1996).

Jones, Chris. "Homeward Bound: August Wilson." *American Theatre*, November 1999, p. 16.

Lyons, Bonnie. "An Interview with August Wilson." *Contemporary Literature* 40, no. 1:1–21 (Spring 1999).

Moyers, Bill. "August Wilson: Playwright." In his *A*

World of Ideas. New York: Doubleday, 1989. Pp. 167–80.

Pettengill, Richard. "The Historical Perspective." In *August Wilson: A Casebook.* Edited by Marilyn Elkins. New York: Garland, 1994. Pp. 207–26.

Powers, Kim. "An Interview with August Wilson." *Theater* 16:50–55 (Fall–Winter 1984).

Rocha, Mark William. "A Conversation with August Wilson." *Diversity* 1:24–42 (Fall 1992).

Savran, David. "August Wilson." In his *In Their Own Words: Contemporary American Playwrights.* New York: Theatre Communications Group, 1998. Pp. 288–305.

Shafer, Yvonne. "An Interview with August Wilson." *Journal of Dramatic Theory and Criticism* 4:161–73 (Fall 1989).

Shannon, Sandra G. "August Wilson Explains His Dramatic Vision: An Interview." In her *The Dramatic Vision of August Wilson.* Washington, D.C.: Howard University Press, 1995. Pp. 201–35.

Watlington, Dennis. "Hurdling Fences." *Vanity Fair,* April 1989, pp. 102–13.

JAY WRIGHT
(1934?–   )

VERA M. KUTZINSKI

JAY WRIGHT WAS born twice in the same place, in the city of Albuquerque, New Mexico, a location he revisits in so many of his poems. Official records mark his birthday as May 25, 1934, but Wright's father favored 1935 as the more appropriate birth year. Such discord between historical documents and personal remembrance may not surprise anyone familiar with the vagaries of nineteenth-century African American history, yet its persistence well into the twentieth century is a bit of an oddity. Such an imaginative doubling of one's person, with the glorious imperfections and the "numinous inexactitudes" it creates (to borrow a phrase from Guyanese novelist Wilson Harris), is as important to a narrative of Jay Wright's life as it is to any critical account of his poetry, plays, and essays. All his writings speak imprecisely and insistently from within the liminal spaces that exist between the lines of officially inscribed personal and cultural history. Wright's poetry, as much as his life, confounds any insistence on immutable historical "fact" by refusing to limit readers' imaginations to a one-dimensional perspective on history; for Wright, poetry is an exploration of multiple *Dimensions of History*, as the title of his second published book-length poem advertises. Trying on the various, and varied, formal ways in which human acts and historical events can, and do, exist is, for Wright's texts, not a matter of op-

posing writing to orality and, as readers have, rather unreasonably, come to expect from African American writers, privileging the latter as more authentic. On the contrary, writing poetry, and plays, is a matter of making available for imaginative scrutiny, and for intellectual enjoyment, modes of orality as well as of writing.

If dates are fluid, then so are other signs, such as proper names. If we grant that, we can easily accept the transformation of George Murphy, the construction worker, jitney driver, and handy man who was Jay Wright's father, into one Mercer Murphy Wright, of African, Cherokee, and Irish descent (Wright was the name of his adoptive mother). As Mercer Wright, he has a son with Leona Dailey, a Virginian of African and Native American ancestry, whose maternal commitments prove uncertain at best. Although she stays in Albuquerque, Leona returns the child to his father at age three. Mercer, then on his way from New Mexico to California, finds a place for his boy with an African American couple in Albuquerque, the cook Frankie Faucett and his wife, Daisy. A woman of strong religious fervor, Daisy Faucett initiates the young Wright into the rituals of the African American church with an intensity that some of Wright's early poems tempt one to translate back into scenes of religious education from James Baldwin's novel *Go Tell It on the Mountain.* In his early teens, Jay Wright leaves the Faucetts and goes to live in San Pedro, California, with his father and, later, his stepmother, Billie. Having played baseball since boyhood, Wright becomes a minor-league catcher for the San Diego Padres, the Fresno Cardinals, and the Aguilars of Mexicali in the 1950s. In addition to playing professional baseball in those days, Wright also discovers his talent for music and learns to play the bass, a passion he still actively pursues. His baseball career ends when, in 1954, he joins the U.S. Army and serves in the medical corps in Germany for the better part of three years. This also gives him the first of several opportunities to travel throughout Europe.

Upon his return to the United States, Wright enrolls in the University of California at Berkeley under the GI Bill. He devises his own major in comparative literature, graduates in 1961 after only three years, and moves on to Union Theological Seminary in New York on a Rockefeller Brothers Theological Fellowship. After one semester, however, he decides to return to literary studies instead of pursuing theology and leaves Union to enroll in a doctoral program at Rutgers University. In 1964, Wright interrupts his graduate studies to spend a year teaching English and Medieval History at the Butler Institute in Guadalajara, Mexico, a country to which he will return often, in body and in mind. Back at Rutgers again, Wright spends the next three years completing the requirements for the doctoral degree, all but the dissertation. While studying in New Jersey, where he meets fellow poet Henry Dumas, Wright lives and works part-time in Harlem, where he comes into contact with a number of other African American writers associated with the Black Arts Movement, notably, Larry Neal and LeRoi Jones. But, as a 1978 essay on Jones's poem "Hymn for Lanie Poo" shows, Wright is rather skeptical of the emergent Black Aesthetic, and his own poetry strikes chords more lyrical and meditative than militant. Wright's interest as a writer is more in "the act of the poem" than in a poetry of ideas, that is, poetry as political statement, or social critique.

He leaves New York City in the late sixties, just before the heyday of the movement that inspires LeRoi Jones to become Amiri Baraka and embrace black nationalism as political posture and personal credo. Though Wright may be said to share some of Baraka's internationalism, he has a rather different sense of the task of the black poet and the purpose of black poetry, as well as of what diasporic kinship and community might mean to an African American poet. Wright wants to create poems out of history rather than fetishize the past, be it European or African; in this sense, his poems, like Wallace Stevens', comprise an "invented world." Although some of Wright's poems are initially included in important new anthologies of African American poetry, such as LeRoi Jones and Larry Neal's *Black Fire* (1971), Abraham Chapman's *New Black Voices* (1972), and Stephen Henderson's *Understanding the New Black Poetry* (1972), he quickly becomes a marginal figure, invisible to Black Arts and Black Power supporters, including prominent publishers of Black Arts writing such as Morrow, Dutton, Random House, and Grove. Relocating to Mexico at a time when the Black Arts movement is picking up steam is not likely to have helped Wright's popularity. Wright and his wife, Lois Silber— they married in 1968—stay in Mexico for several years, first, briefly, in Guadalajara and then in Xalapa. Much of Wright's poetry is at home, or at rest, within these and other Mexican (and New Mexican) settings; they are important local geographies with associations at once historical and mundanely personal. William Carlos Williams comes to mind here as a poet with similar affinities for Hispanic America; so does Robert Hayden.

During his three years south of the border, Wright returns to the United States periodically to spend brief periods as Writer-in-Residence at Tougaloo and Talladega Colleges in Mississippi and Alabama and at Texas Southern University. There are also several months as a Hodder Fellow at Princeton University, where he does research and works on his early plays. In September 1971, the Wrights leave the Mexico they love, and to which they will return subsequently for only fairly short periods of time, for the Scotland of Hugh MacDiarmid and Wright's paternal ancestors. During Wright's tenure as Joseph Compton Creative Writing Fellow at Dundee University, among other things, he completes *Explications/Interpretations* (1984); he and his wife live in the town of Penicuik outside Edinburgh. Upon their return to the United States in 1973, the Wrights settle in the Northeast, first in Warner and Piermont, New Hampshire, then in Bradford, Vermont, which is still their residence. With this often inhospitable Frostian location as a home base, Wright continues to travel extensively, especially but not exclusively throughout the Americas. For instance, he first visits Asia in 1988, as part of a group of writers who visits the People's Republic of China under the auspices of the University of California, Los Angeles. He gives readings just about everywhere in the continental United States and, starting in 1969, has taught either full- or part-time at Yale, the universities of Utah, Kentucky, North Carolina at Chapel Hill, and Dartmouth College, Washington University, Brandeis University, and the University of Cincinnati.

Recognition has been slow in coming since Wright received his first creative writing fellowship in 1963, which has much to do with the perceived difficulty and inaccessibility of a poetry that has remained aloof from popularized representations of blackness and that practices a poetics of interculturation instead of advocating ideas of cultural authenticity. Wright's textual politics are typically frustrating and troubling to audiences reared on the idea that all African American writers are, or should be, cultural nationalists of either the militant or the sentimental persuasion. Since Wright's vision of African American expressive art has consistently challenged reductive narratives of racially or ethnically bounded cultural origins, his poetry, with its air of aesthetic autonomy, has tended to elicit more favorable responses from academics such as Harold Bloom and John Hollander, who read him as a descendant of canonical modernists such as T. S. Eliot, Ezra Pound, Wallace Stevens, and Hart Crane, than of black nationalist writers. And such readings are sensible, as C. K. Doreski confirms, for

Wright's poems brim with references and allusions to high-modernist poetry. But that is not the whole story, for we can hardly disregard the strange turns of his tropes, the characteristic restlessness, instability, and uncertainty that pulsate underneath the seemingly calm of familiar poetic surfaces. Such disjunctions are particularly noticeable in his early poems, whose surfaces tend more comfortably toward personal anecdote than do the energetic abstractions of his longer excursions into ritual and epic.

Wright has received a number of prestigious academic and literary awards during the course of the past thirty years, among them an Ingram Merrill Foundation Award and a Guggenheim Fellowship in 1974; an American Academy and Institute of Arts and Letters Literature Award in 1981; an Oscar Williams and Gene Derwood Writing Award in 1985; a MacArthur Fellowship in 1986; the 62nd Fellowship of the Academy of American Poets in 1996, and an honorary doctorate from St. Lawrence University in 1997. He has also been a member of the American Academy of Arts and Sciences since 1995. Yet he remains at the margins of the American literary establishment, as seems to be the fate of those African American writers who have resisted the imposition of a marketable cultural identity. The increased popularity of concepts such as cultural hybridity and the growing attention to diaspora studies facilitated in part by Paul Gilroy's Black Atlantic paradigm may change some of these biases and allow academic readerships to think through and appreciate the political implications of Wright's insistently cross-cultural poetic voice and what Doreski has labeled his "transcultural diasporic aesthetic." "For me," Wright explains in a 1983 interview in *Callaloo*, "multi-cultural is the fundamental process of human history."

In its sense of African American culture as hemispheric, polyvocal, and inevitably hybrid, Wright's poetry is closer to the sensibilities and theories of many Caribbean writers than it is to cultural nationalism that tends to be more characteristic of his African American colleagues from the United States. Notable in this respect are particularly Edouard Glissant, and his concept of a "poetics of Relation," and Wilson Harris' idea of processes of "cross-cultural imagination" at work in the Americas. Indeed, Wright has repeatedly acknowledged Harris' novelistic explorations of the twentieth-century possibilities of allegory and of epic as influences on his own verse. A belated version of the figure of the romantic poet, Wright's persona is an exile and a nomad who, searching for "lost relations," sets out on difficult journeys into uncharted territories where familiar temporal, political, and linguistic categories unravel and are rewoven into the fabric of strangely immediate and unstable poetic constructs. In many of Wright's poems, we find ourselves face-to-face with the "now" and the "here"—as in "And I'm walking, now" from the poem "First Principles"—even as the poetic narrative paradoxically pulls the reader ever deeper into the past. Particularly jarring in their refusal of temporal distinctions are lines such as "Now, I have searched the texts . . ." from "Benjamin Banneker Helps to Build a City." Due to the fact that the human body, for Wright, has multiple locations in space and in time, life and death cannot be regarded as separable states of existence. Wright's poetry shares this perception with Wilson Harris' novels, and it affects the language both writers use by producing unexpected metaphoric combinations, such as "static flux," "moving still," and "unfamiliar home." Meditations about the nature of temporality and about the fluid states of life-in-death, death-in-life—or, as Wright would have it, the responsibilities with which the dead "charge" the living—further complicate questions about cultural identity and about a possible "home." This "home" is conceived of as a temporary resting place for the world-weary "homecoming singer," which is also the title of Wright's first collection of poems.

Early Poems:
The Homecoming Singer

The Homecoming Singer (1971) was preceded in 1967 by a chapbook of fifteen poems in twenty-two unnumbered pages, titled *Death as History*; most of these poems are reprinted in *The Selected Poems* (1987). Like all of Wright's verse, *The Homecoming Singer* uses personal anecdote, but it does so more overtly, with the effect that it makes the poems seem more accessible. "A Non-Birthday Poem for My Father" is a good example:

And then into the New Mexico Hills,
. . .
Drinking and rolling drunk in the snow
with heavy women who could be Indian,
or at least bragged that they were.
Having one son by a woman who had nine,
and leaving them both,
not really deserting them,
but not really knowing what to do
with either one of them.

Such anecdotes are always, in Wright, catalysts for his speculations about the possible shape of a diasporic artistic tradition. Thus, in "A Non-Birthday Poem for My Father," "Origins," "First Principles," and "The Hunting-Trip Cook," memories of his two fathers become occasions for examining the responsibilities sons have toward fathers, whose choices they "must understand." Other figures from Wright's past are considerably more shadowy, including those of his alcoholic stepmother, in "Billie's Blues," and of Daisy Faucett, whose religious zeal resounds throughout "Wednesday Night Prayer Meeting," "The Baptism," and "Collection Time." But all those private ghosts share the space of this volume with the likes of Crispus Attucks and W. E. B. Du Bois in what is possibly a gesture of "intense communal daring" on the poet's part. "The tongues of the exiled dead" do indeed "live in the tongues of the living" ("First Principles").

Wright's daring also extends to fellow poet LeRoi Jones/Amiri Baraka, on whose "Poem for Willie Best" Wright improvises, and improves, brilliantly in "The Player at the Crossroads" and "Variations on a Theme by LeRoi Jones." But, however painful, the absence of "myths to scale your life upon," which Wright's early poems pointedly attribute to the African American church's failure to provide its members with adequate spiritual resources, and "the senseless, weightless,/ time-denying feeling of not being there" (in "Reflections Before the Charity Hospital"), does not lead to despair and violence, as they do in "Willie Best" where "The face sings, alone." As Wright puts in "The Dead," a poem from *Soothsayers and Omens* (1976): "it is not enough/ to sip the knowledge/ of our failings." Instead, this knowledge must heighten the poet's awareness of his need to construct "new categories for the soul/ of those I want to keep" ("Destination: Accomplished"). In "A Nuer Sacrifice" and "Death As History," this need directs Wright's "aching prodigal," from "Beginning Again," to West Africa, a spiritual landscape that is more fully explored in Section IV of *Soothsayers and Omens* and particularly in the quasi-ritualistic poem *The Double Invention of Komo* (1980).

The Homecoming Singer also acquaints the reader with a host of other actual and symbolic geographies that remain important to Wright throughout his poetic career: the imperiously capitalized American South; Mexico, which is of course even further south; and, perhaps incongruously, New England. In "An Invitation to Madison County," the American South offers unexpected memories and visions of community to the displaced poet whose journey retraces that of countless other African American writers, from Du Bois and Jean Toomer to Toni Morrison, Ernest Gaines, and Octavia Butler. The Southwest, often along with California, is a different place of origin, a gateway to Mexico in poems such as "Morning: Leaving Calle Gigantes," "Chapultepec Castle," "Jalapeña Gypsies," and "Bosques de Chapultepec." "A Month in the Country" offers the first glimpse of "New England reticence," a subject to which Wright returns in *Boleros* (1991).

The First Poetic Cycle: Different Beginnings

"Beginning Again," the poem that closes *The Homecoming Singer*, is an effective prelude to *Soothsayers and Omens* (1976), which declares, plainly: "The bridge is open." Like its prede-cessor, *Soothsayers* is a four-part poem and the first text in a four-volume poetic cycle that, according to Wright, continues with *Explications/Interpretations* (not published until 1984), moves on to *Dimensions of History* (1976), and culminates in *The Double Invention of Komo* (1980). Each of these book-length poetic sequences is part of a carefully constructed dramatic movement, almost a play in four acts. We may take this as a reminder that performance is a concept integral to what one may call Wright poetics of "movement," which incorporates elements from music as well as from drama. For the latter genre, in fact, Wright has often expressed a passionate preference. He has written some twenty plays, only a few of which have been published; even fewer have actually been staged.

In *Soothsayers*, voice fragments from a range of historical periods and cultural traditions, going all the way back to pre-Columbian times, emerge to guide the poet (and the reader) through dense mazes of mythological references and allusions as if to affirm, time and again, Wright's conviction that no African American "can have escaped grounding in other cultures." In this poetic environment, the cultural traditions of the so-called West are dynamically supplemented by other cosmologies, be they West African or American. Even Asia becomes part of the diaspora in the later poems, notably in *Boleros*. Wright's extensive research in Medieval and Renaissance literatures, world music, anthropology, the history of religions, and the history of science undergirds all his work. The Notes in *Explications/Interpretations*, *Dimensions of History*, and especially *The Double Invention of Komo*, all of which were appended in grudging compliance with request from publishers and have been excluded from *Transfigurations, Colleted Poems* (2000), showcase some of the principal holdings of Wright's interior archives. Some of the most important texts behind his poems include *The Akan Doctrine of God*, by Ghanaian politician and philosopher J. B. Danquah, and the multivolume studies of Dogon and Bambara traditional societies in Sudan and Mali which were conducted in the 1920s and 1930s by a team of French anthropologists headed initially by Marcel Griaule. Of particular importance to Wright's poems are Griaule's *Conversations with Ogotemmêli: An Introduction to Dogon Religious Ideas* (1948) and his collaboration with Germaine Dieterlen, translated as *The Pale Fox* (1965). Wright draws on these and other source books to attempt to restore to African American literature a sense of the kinds of spiritual resources the artist can cull from rigorous intellectual engagements with history. Writing poetry is his way of recovering, in the sense of reinventing, eclipsed connections between cultural traditions believed by many to have developed separately. Wright's poetry grows out of speculating on the possibilities for "understanding" and for "love" that may emerge when one beholds disparate things together and tries to articulate the "small movement" between them. As he puts it in "The Ritual Tuning," a poem from *Explications/Interpretations*:

> Love is to enter another's house
> a creature coined from vision's deepest
>   pain.

The hope is that such articulations, be they in the form of lyrics whose fast-moving lines and abrupt enjambments recall William Carlos Williams' clipped modernist verse, or stretched out into epic song, just might contradict death in its purported finality.

The poem that opens the first of *Soothsayers'* four parts is significantly titled "The Charge." Reminiscent of Wright's homages to paternal figures in *The Homecoming Singer*, this poetic sequence focuses even more on fathers and sons "gathered in the miracle/ of our own memories," with the poet in the role of the initiate who has accepted the charge to reconstruct neglected and severed ties. Even a poem such as "The Appearance of a Lost Goddess" does not disrupt *Soothsayers'* patriarchal (in)vestments. Wright's poetic reconstructions in this case take the initial shape of six short poems entitled "Sources," which inaugurate the systematic inquiry into African cosmologies as spiritual resources. "Sources," in fact, draws heavily on both West African and pre-Columbian myth,

which are happily intertwined in the lyric structures of a collective memory. Two longer poems follow and slow the first part's pace: "Benjamin Banneker Helps to Build a City" and "Benjamin Banneker Sends His 'Almanac' to Thomas Jefferson" are poems that weave elements of Dogon theology into and around quotations from the letters of the eighteenth-century African American astronomer, an "uneasy" stranger in his own land who laments his world's "lost harmony," partly due to the injustices of slavery. And the reader wonders, along with the poet: "Free. Free. How will the lines fall/ into that configuration?"

Interactions between fathers and sons intensify *Soothsayers'* Part IV, whose title, "Second Conversations with Ogotemmêli," invoke Marcel Griaule's "first" conversations with the Dogon sage. But the exchanges in Wright's "Conversations" are notably different from those that obtain between anthropologist and informer; so is their tone. For Wright's persona, Ogotemmêli, much like Banneker, is a spiritual guide (or "nani") who "will lead me into the darkness" and whose silences promise the speech of redemption with which to mend "the crack in the universe." These are all poems of spiritual apprenticeship whose goal is to articulate "a plan of transformations" in the midst of "turbulence" ("Homecoming"). For that purpose, they delve into the tales that make up Dogon cosmology, particularly stories about the different stages of the creation of universe, which are represented by Nommo, water spirit and creator of the First Word (that is, language), and his twin, Amma. Other revered and feared deities are Lébé, guardian of the dead, and the Pale Fox, or jackal, the agent of chaos. The terms and trajectory of Wright's journey into a heart of darkness, a reverse Middle Passage back to West Africa, are grafted complexly onto the matrix of Dante's allegorical poetry, whose sojourn into the underworld parallels that of Wright's persona to an extent, though their guides are rather different. Wright's homage to Dante is most explicit in "Homecoming," a poem laced with untranslated lines from the *Commedia*. The languages Wright incorporates in his poems are not limited to Italian, German, Spanish, and occasional instances of African American vernacular; they also come to include Dogon and Bambara ideograms, especially in *Dimensions of History* and *The Double Invention of Komo*, which gives these two epic poems a texture reminiscent of Pound's *Cantos*. This linguistic admixture becomes so dense, so insistently unfamiliar at times, that to call it "English" seems wholly inadequate.

But contrary to what Isidore Okpewho has suggested in his comments on *Double Invention*, West Africa is not this poet's "home." While *Soothsayers* has a clear affinity for African mythologies, its most significant residences on Earth are still Mexico and New Mexico. These geographies are already implicit in the opening poem's pre-Columbian references, such as the "quetzal feathers" that adorn the messenger in "Sources (1)," and are foregrounded in some of the transitional poems in the volume's middle sections, most notably in "The Albuquerque Graveyard," a prose version of which appears in the 1987 play *Daughters of the Water* as part of Paul Dawkins' lines. The play is set in San Pedro, California, "now."

> My life seems to revolve around gold and cemeteries. I wake up one morning in Albuquerque, New Mexico. It is Memorial Day, 1950. I have no flowers, but I go to the cemetery, to that part set aside for black souls. Through the grounds, I pick flowers, one here, one there, from graves and gardens, and when I arrive at my mound, I have a bouquet of dead things. There is no memory in a stolen flower or a stolen life.

In the poem, Wright's persona returns to the same place to worry his dead, who "lie here/ in a hierarchy of small defeats." The following four lines articulate a sense of purpose not retained in the above passage from the play:

> I am going back
> to the Black limbo,
> an unwritten history
> of our own tensions.

The poet's purpose is, in fact, dual: both to articulate a history that has not yet been written and to unwrite a history that has largely eclipsed the parts Africans and African Americans played in the founding of Western civilization. Particular attention is drawn to the United States by the fact that, as Doreski notes, both *Soothsayers* and *Dimensions of History* were published in the bicentennial year of 1976. Clearly, Wright's intent is not to found another nation but to remember "founding fathers" across existing national boundaries. It is in this sense that his poetry offers what Doreski calls a "postnational narrative" that emerges uneasily from the verse's ability, as he puts it in "Family Reunion," "to coax/ the speaker into echoes of himself, his selves,/ his forgotten voices, voices he has never heard."

If *Soothsayers* is the first four-part step toward the articulation of an alternative spiritual order, *Explications/Interpretations*, which is dedicated doubly, to poet Robert Hayden and literary critic Harold Bloom, marks the next stage in what Wright calls his "African-Hellenic-Judaic discourse." This volume introduces a new cast of characters, notably in "MacIntyre, The Captain, and the Saints," a dramatic poem that inaugurates Wright's rather eccentric use of personal ideograms in the context of his genealogical ties with Scotland. MacIntyre, the Irish/Scottish clan to which the names Murphy and Wright can be traced, is Wright's understudy in this poem. Rather than journeying to Sudan and meeting with the Dogon sage Ogotemmêli, the composite figure of MacIntyre converses with David Hume, Hugh MacDiarmid, and Captain Rattray about religion, ethics, and the possible intersections of astronomy, poetry, and colonial anthropology. So Hume, who supposedly understands only "quantity and number," comes to wonders near the end of the poem: "Can the facts grow from vision?/ Can a new star arise to figure/ a new constellation?" But dramatic poetry is not the only emphasis in *Explications*, which is at least equally attentive to the formal possibilities of African American music, especially the blues. The titles of *Explications'* three parts, "Polarity's Trio," "Harmony's Trio," and "Love's Dozen," reflect Wright's interest in music, rhythm, and number. "Tensions and Resolutions," which functions as a poetic prologue, suggestively links doubleness, or twinning, to one's placement within time:

> Each act caresses
> the moment it remembers,
> and the moment it desires.

The rhythms of such double directionality are the formal articulations of the poet's selfhood, his being-in-time. The principle of doubling underlies the arrangement of the poems in groups of three, six, and twelve (plus one), framed by a prologue and an epilogue of sorts, which already conveys a movement from a slow to a faster rhythm.

This sense of the rigors of musical form is strongest in "The Twenty-Two Tremblings of the Postulant," an excellent example of Wright's blues poetry, which is parenthetically subtitled "Improvisations Surrounding the Body." In this poem, the compositional principle is derived not primarily from the call-and-response structure of the blues lyrics, as it is in the blues poetry of Langston Hughes, though responsoriality, always along with and connected to responsibility, remains a vital thematic concern for Wright. Rather, the poem's shape is determined by an arrangement of twenty-two short poems across a sequences of chords. Each short poem corresponds not only to a different part of the human body, but also to a musical bar that belongs to a specific chord, I, IV, or V. In this poetic anatomy, we move from "1 (arm)" to "22 (eye)," passing "4 (fingers)" and Albert Ayler along the way, until we arrive at the last two bars, which are "tacit." The poem thus extends across a total of twenty-four bars, whose musical equivalent is a doubled blues line. These spatially represented sounds of flesh and bone make up the poem's, and the poet's, "grammar of being." As *Explications* improvises on the "measures" of the basic blues line, Wright's emphasis on the human body as a site of both knowledge and action yields the trope of the dance, of the body's "turning" in "Love Plumbs to the Center of the Earth."

> Left. Right.
> Turn. And counterturn.

I would have my foundation stone.
And so I carefully turn my words
about your longing.

Dance, as "Inscrutability," the volume's final poem, tells us, is the "body's speech," which is tuned "star-high" and thus "enhanced"; as the body *turns*, it *tunes* the spirit's words to the pitch of other "resonant" bodies. Mind and body, the spiritual and its material ground, are no more separate in these poems than male is from female; they are all necessary "twins." This is most compellingly rendered in "The Continuing City: Spirit and Body" and "The Body."

Although Wright, in his Notes to the poem, identifies *Explications* as an attempt "to claim this knowledge as part of the continuing creative life of the Americas," the Americas come into fuller view in *Dimensions of History*, written after *Explications* but published seven years before it. While dedicated to the late Francis Ferguson, with whom Wright studied at Rutgers, *Dimensions* owes its most significant debt to Wilson Harris and his idea of "vision as historical dimension." In this third volume of Wright's poetic cycle, the tripartite structure of *Explications* comes to be associated with the states of separation, transition, and (re)incorporation, the three stages of traditional initiation rituals. Part One, entitled "The Second Eye of the World. The Dimension of Rites and Acts," alerts us to these symbolic investments not only by being itself divided into three sections, but also by reproducing a Dogon ideogram that, according to Griaule and Dieterlen, represents the separation of the female from the male twins at the moment of circumcision. One historical dimension of such a separation is, of course, the condition of exile forced by the African slave trade. *Dimensions* begins a process of revaluing this historical condition of loss by turning it into an opportunity for a "special kinship." The persona's other selves are the dead to whose realm he descends and whose claims he seeks to understand in a spiritually barren land from which the gods have retreated. Among these dead are once again Du Bois and Crispus Attucks, now joined by Frederick Douglass, St. Augustine, the Haitian insurrectionists

Mackandal and Toussaint L'Ouverture, and the black explorer Esteban who accompanied the conquistador Cabeza de Vaca to the North American continent. Even Ogotemmêli returns in the figure of the blind sage at the beginning of the second poem in Part One, "The Key That Unlocks Performance. Vision as Historical Dimension." His appearance becomes a catalyst for the healing that occupies the textual space between "Anochecí enfermo" and "amanecí bueno" (I went to bed sick, I woke up well), a formulation that changes to the collective "Still, anochecimos enfermo Amanecimos bueno." At the end of this section, the persona embraces his vocation and names himself "a dark and dutiful dyēli," a historian/poet, or "scholar of the living event," who searches "for the understanding of his deeds."

Dimensions' Part Two, titled "Modulations," shifts to history's "Aesthetic Dimension" and begins with an offering of fourteen shorter poems under the heading "Rhythms, Charts and Changes." Each poem features a particular musical or poetic form, or an instrument, associated with the Caribbean, Spain, or Latin America, such as the Cuban *son*, the Arawak *areito*, and a fifteen-string Colombian guitar known as *bandola*. These musical forms, much like Wright's previous applications of the blues, contribute to defamiliarizing the cadences of English verse, to make English responsive to the "grammars" and metrics of other languages and artistic forms. The most intriguing of these formal hybrids are "Bandola 'a,' " which pays tribute to the dancer Teodora Ginés as legendary originator of the *son*, and "Villancico," whose modified iambic pentameter and elegantly end-rhymed lines evoke the distant cadences of Sor Juana's colonial Mexico:

Faithful one, you come, wind before the
    rain.
Bean-bred, corn fed, lady of the bead chain,
you hold an axe above your own domain,
where no ram dare plough, seed, or shake
    his mane.

The next section, "The Body Adorned and Bare," recalls the meditations on the body in *Explications/Interpretations*, to which it adds the trope of weaving (for instance, in "The Craft of Beating Cloth"), which will assume yet greater importance in *The Double Invention of Komo*. The four portraits of holy figures such as "El Cristo Negro" and "Mater Dolorosa" in Part Two, Section III, named "Retablos," or votive paintings, lead up to the "Log Book of Judgments," a series of poetic statements that translate historical experience into aesthetic and moral abstractions. "What Is Good," "What Is True," and "What Is Beautiful" culminate in "Meta-A and the A of Absolutes," where motion and the knowledge of one's moving are elevated to the status of moral principle, perhaps moral imperative.

I am good when I am in motion,
when I think of myself at rest
in the knowledge of my moving,
. . . ,
and walk from boundary to boundary,
unarmed and unafraid of another's
    speech.

Dimensions closes precisely with such walking "from boundary to boundary" in "Landscapes. The Physical Dimension." Perhaps the most immediately noticeable formal aspect of this final part are the encyclopedic block passages that list the vital statistics of five American nations: Venezuela, Colombia, Panama, Mexico, and the United States. The interstitial spaces between these massive building blocks are filled with Wright's enchanted mortar, a phrase that translates the Náhua, or Aztec, idiom "cal y canto," which literally means "mortar and song." "Cal y canto," an instance of linguistic syncretism in which we can see clearly the effects of Wright's cross-cultural theme on the architecture of his poems, is a rhizome whose roots extend to the work of Latin American poets like Pablo Neruda, Octavio Paz, and José María Arguedas; it is one of Wright's "emblems of the ecstatic connection." His poet's wanderings pause at the Great Gate of the ancient Mayan city of Labná on a wall that is both "a gateway to the beautiful" and "the image of our lives among ourselves" in a "star land, a

869

golden land." This is El Dorado transformed into a veritable city of gods.

The Double Invention of Komo, dedicated to the memory of Marcel Griaule, goes beyond *Dimensions* by risking "ritual's arrogance," as Wright admits in his afterword. It might be called the most African of Wright's poems, if it were not for the fact that it remains deeply attached to New World landscapes. *Double Invention* is Wright's most sustained and ambitious effort in the genre of dramatic poetry, for which "MacIntyre and the Captain" can be seen as a starting point. It is a poetic reenactment of the initiation ceremonies performed by the male Komo society among the Bambara, whose highly formalized rites are detailed in Germaine Dieterlen and Youssouf Tata Cissé's *Les fondements de la société d'initiation du Komo* (1972). The purpose of these ceremonies is conservative, that is, they maintain the Bambara men's traditional intellectual, religious, and social values. Wright takes the specifics of this ritual process as points of departure for his African American poetics of kinship. Of special importance to this poetic project are the 266 Great Signs that organize Bambara cosmology and are known as the Sigui. Each sign, or ideogram, inscribes a different "name," or aspect, of the god and thus binds him to the material objects and substances associated with Komo's altars, as in "*Makárí*–pity / compassion–wood." Some of these signs are drawn on posters and carried onto the stage during interludes in some of Wright's plays, notably in *Daughters of the Water*, an Afro-Cuban play Wright wrote in honor of Cuba's late poet laureate Nicolás Guillén. As is evident from "The Initiate Takes His First Six Signs, the Design of His Name," naming is a complex process in which one is joined to oneself as well as to others, in which the self is paradoxically "pierced with the joy" of being made whole. What Wright is after, here and elsewhere in the poem, is the sacred "grammar" of names on the basis of which he invents a secular "alphabet" of creation.

Double Invention is quite explicitly and self-consciously a poem about the relation of written signs to voice, which accounts for much of its difficulty. One preoccupation of *Double Invention* is how to achieve self-knowledge through writing, how to fashion a language that would redress loss and dispossession, and that would turn us from the inscriptions of radical difference with which the poem opens "to the clarity of being strange," In this new state, we can "extend [our] clan's walls" and "unfold the limits" of our bodies, be they singular or collective. Here are the poem's vexing opening lines.

> This is the language of desire.
>   baná yírí kọrọ
>   baná ba yírí kọrọ
>   dyigini yírí kọrọ
>   yẹlẹni yírí kọrọ
> Through this you will be fulfilled.

Michael Manson rightly calls these "harsh words," initially intimidating in their self-assuredness and in their foreignness. Yet, by the end of the poem, he argues, such fear has given way to a surprising sense of intimacy with the language of Komo, which comes to articulate our own complexities.

Double Invention is concerned with the dynamics of both speech and writing, and the difficult relations that obtain between them. Writing, in this poem, is apprehended as a process of simultaneous dismemberment and reassembly of meanings and communities. The written word has a double life as both "scalpel" and "suture"; it excises, and it circumcises. Like the ritual scars on the body of the Komo initiate, poetic writing confers knowledge of traditional values and, with it, kinship; though kinship, for Wright, is limited neither to one group nor to one gender. It is as if the poet's pen were a ritual knife "cutting" the initiate (and the reader) into kinship, marking him (and possibly her) as a member of a special, diasporic community; his loneliness is "cut away." It is in this way that the Middle Passage can be reimagined a *rite* of passage that compensates for the trauma of psychic dismemberment and geographical dispersal: "I have learned/ that there is a blessing/ in my body's disrupted blood." Wright's key metaphor here, the limbo, refers once again to Wilson Harris, who regards this dance, created on the crowded slave ships, as a form of silent collective resistance to enslavement and who understands transoceanic memory as the reconstruction of a "phantom limb." It is on such phantom limbs that Wright's persona "traverse[s] love's dispersal" as he moves from Africa to Albuquerque, to Berlin, to Bad Nauheim, to Florence, to Venice, and finally to Mexico City, the places that different stages of the Komo ritual evoke. For Wright's pilgrim, then, traveling is a way of expressing "my body's written correlations."

As the initiate becomes a "delegate," earlier statements on poetics and ethics, notably from *Dimension*'s "Meta-A and the A of Absolutes," undergo partial reformulation. Boundaries are now envisioned as scars, as tangible traces of an incision and its "instructive radiance."

> Now, may your necessary injury
> guide me to what is true.
> What is true is the incision.
> What is true is the desire for the incision,
> and the sign's flaming in the wound.

Yet, the immediacy of voice, of "what can be spoken," remains an issue in this "exile's scriptorium," a text in which being always speaks "with the tight voice of becoming" and which defines ignorance as "inattention" to voice, or voices. The poem is punctuated with instances of "I turn," "I continue," and "I speak" as if to remind us that claims to presence, no matter how arrogant, create a strange, but effective, intimacy between poetic persona and reader. Convinced, finally, of our own presence and stake in the poem, we mouth *Double Invention*'s closing lines as if they were our own:

> You present to me sacred things.
> I am reborn into a new life.
> My eyes open to Komo.

Later Poetry: *Elaine's Book* and *Boleros*

If reading *Double Invention* feeds hopes for continued intimacy with this poetic voice,

Wright's more distant tone in subsequent poems rather frustrates such expectations. One might say that the persona's feelings in both *Elaine's Book* (1988) and *Boleros* (1991) are distinctly more formal, and that despite the fact that *Boleros* may well be read as a collection of love poems. What surprises most in *Elaine's Books*, whose title dedicates it to Wright's sister-in-law, is the focus on female voices, which are usually silent in his earlier, more patriarchal paradigms, which flash briefly in "Zapata and the Egúngún Mask." While femininity is hardly ever entirely absent from Wright's poetry, this is the first book in which women assume some measure of historical significance, rather than remaining "twins" or muses shrouded in mythology. Still, myth is the most common garb that female voices wear in *Elaine's Book*; the difference is that these are myths from all corners of the world. There is, for instance, Yemanjá, the Yoruba/Afro-Cuban goddess of the waters, situated right next to the Virgin Mary; and Egypt's Hathor, along with ancient Greece's Aphrodite, shares textual space with the Virgin of Guadalupe, whom Wright links with the Aztec fertility goddess Tonantzin. Once time enters, verse turns startlingly to prose. The twenty-three poems in this volume are interspersed, at uneven intervals, by eleven prose vignettes, each of which is marked as "Confrontation" in the table of contents. Most of these passages are short quotations from epistolary sources or memoirs; some of these fragments are signed and dated, others remain unidentified. The latter is the case with passages from the writings of the astrophysicist Cecilia Payne-Gaposchkin, the first woman to become a full professor at Harvard in 1956. British-born Payne-Gaposchkin, whose presence in the poem recalls that of Benjamin Banneker, professes "disappointment because I received absolutely no recognition, either official or private, from Harvard University or Radcliffe College; I cannot appear in the catalogues; I do give lectures but they are not announced in the catalogues, and I am paid for (I believe) as 'equipment'; certainly, I have no official position such as instructor." Payne-Gaposchkin's humiliating objectification as "equipment" resonates with the "sins" committed against Phillis Wheatley, Judith Cocks, and Louisa Alexander, all former slaves. These "Confrontations" take center stage in *Elaine's Book*, and, like the lines from Octavio Paz, Paul Celan, and Hölderlin, they become part of a "city" as a figure for the poem itself. This "city" displaces the space of the "nation" by raising it "from the will of its forgetfulness."

A sequence of forty-two numbered, otherwise untitled poems, *Boleros* continues *Elaine's Book*'s parade of mythic female guides in poems dedicated to Erato, Calliope, Euterpe, Thalia, Polyhymnia, Clio, Terpsichore, and Urania. But these muses' familiar Greek names are doubled and destabilized by Egyptian counterparts, with the effect that Greek mythology is Africanized by being wedded to *The Egyptian Book of the Dead*: for instance, "(Erato ↔ Khat)" (#13) or "(Urania ↔ Ren)" (#21). The relation between each set of two names, signified by a double-pointed arrow, is one transculturation. Each of these poems acknowledges the cross-cultural possibilities Herodotus opened up when he claimed that the names of almost all the Greek gods came from Egypt, and hence from Africa. It makes good sense, then, that the Akan deity Odomankoma "guides Urania's hand," and that Clio converses both with the Dogon god Nommo and with the African American pianist Art Tatum as she weaves the "cloth of the Word." Following in the philological and political footsteps of Martin Bernal's *Black Athena: The Afro-Asiatic Roots of Classical Civilization* (1987), Wright's syncretic muses assert the very likely historical existence of Egyptian, African, and Semitic influences on ancient Greece, which Romantic scholarship discredited vociferously. Bernal points out that the rise of the transatlantic slave trade and scientific racism made the very idea of such cultural contamination at the heart of Western civilization increasingly intolerable to an academic establishment embroiled in nationalist politics.

Wright dedicates *Boleros* to his wife, Lois, "loved source of my new words," and many of these poems are splendid love lyrics in the tradition of "Meeting Her in Chapultepec" from *Soothsayers*. But even the poem's dedication is already complicated by a phonetic representation of one of the 266 Great Signs of Dogon and Bambara cosmology: "dyẹẹ—la connaissance de l'étoile" recalls the golden "star land" from the end of *Dimensions* and "the arrow turn[ed] inward from my bow," as this sign for union is described in *Double Invention*. In addition to signaling Wright's continuing interest in traditional African societies and their theologies, this particular ideogram calls attention to the multiple inscriptions of names throughout *Boleros*. That a poet who has two birth dates and can lay claim to two surnames should have an ongoing fascination with the processes of naming is hardly a surprise. In *Boleros*, Wright seeks to imagine the events that lead to names, be they the names of Greek muses, of saints' days, or of places.

All names are invocations, or curses.
One must imagine the fictive event that
    leads to
He-Who-Shoots-Porcupines-By-Night,
or Andrew Golightly, or Theodore, or Sally.
    (#5)

Such "fictive events" point not only to the tales of his own ancestry Wright was accustomed to hearing from his father; they extend to the entire history of the West with "All these silences, all these intimations/ of something still to be constructed" (#14). What, for instance, are the "invocations" or "curses" hidden in the names of the nine Greek muses in the first part of *Boleros*? What kinds of events might have inspired the names of the twelve "Saints' Days" adorned with "graces and the seasons" to which the poem turns next? And what stories lie buried in the place names scattered throughout the book, especially names of cities such as San Pedro, St. Augustine, Santa Fe, Oaxaca, and Xalapa, or Jalapa—"Halapa, Chalapa, Shalapa (ever what you call it") (#8)? But names, we know now, are always more than their history; they are also prophetic in that they elicit, or caress, "acts" in the future. In the twelve poems that comprise "Saints' Days" and progress from January to December, the poet moves from his "ancient theater" to "a new world" to gather together yet other voices. "Santa Bárbara (December 4th)," for instance, brings together the Greek Hera and the Akan Oya with the former slave Jarena Lee and her religious autobiographies. Perhaps the most powerful poem in this sequence is "Nuestra Señora de los Remedios (September 24th)," a dramatic meditation on racial violence and redemption that turns on the word *remedios*, salvation.

Boleros moves swiftly between historical and geographic locations, many of which are by now familiar places, intimate even. The sudden shifts from Guadalajara to Glasgow, from eastern Canada to Santa Fe, New Mexico, from Salt Lake City to Piermont, New Hampshire, to Egypt, and to West Africa are at times disorienting, almost dizzying. The poet also takes up several new residences, most notable among them St. Augustine, Florida, the first city the Spanish founded on the North American continent, and the city of Benares, or Banāres, in Uttar Pradesh. Known as Varanasi in the Hindi of modern India, Benares is a world of caste systems, of death, and of spiritual depth in which the socially dead can also be the most holy ones. The still peaceful shores of the river Ganges, famous from ancient Buddhist scripture, serve as an appropriate resting place for the poet/pilgrim who assures us, in lines that echo Langston Hughes' famous "The Negro Speaks of Rivers," that

> Black spirits such as mine will always
>   come
> to a crossroads such as this, where the
>   water moves
> with enabling force.

The poet's travels here, as always, are also explorations of poetic form. Most striking in this regard are the two trios of poems that follow the hushed, wintry "New England Days" to make up *Boleros'* fourth and fifth sections. Most of these fairly brief poems open with lines from popular Latin American tunes, such as "Un siglo de ausencia," whose rhythms of loss and desire insinuate themselves into Wright's English until "corazón" slings its vowels through "known" and "alone," and "forgive" embraces

the strangely enjambed "deliv-/erance," wreaking delightful havoc with expected stress patterns by transforming them slyly into syllabic meter, which is much more at home is Spanish popular verse than in English lyrics.

> Dime en donde encontrar-
> te, disposable heart, red star
> by which I set my course and flow,
> a vessel marked by the dim glow
> of pride. I am a song that cleaves
> to its Guinea way, stops, deceives
> itself, falls through a lowered tone
> and returns, enhanced by its own
> failure, to the key it sustains. (#39)

Such virtuoso performances, which "pick the composer's pocket" in the spirit of Art Tatum (#19), situate Wright's work at the American crossroads of poetry and music, and they show him at his very best.

Much has been written about modern and contemporary African American poetry's distinctive musical idiom, but the question of what improvisation could really mean to poetic practice has rarely been tackled beyond impressionistic commentary. Wright's poems show that improvisation is neither a form of imitation nor of spontaneous composition. To Wright, an accomplished bass player who has also tried his hand at jazz lyrics, successful improvisation—what he often thinks of as "the bird's flight" into meaning—is always grounded in detailed knowledge of, and loving respect for, sets of formal rules, even as those rules are stretched, bent, and broken. In other words, improvisation is a principle of poetic performance that requires not casual looseness but a most precise sense of limits. It is characteristic of Wright's poems, old and new, that spiritual possibilities, "the healing music of the head,/ my soul's improvisation," emerge from intellectual and emotional discipline combined with an exacting sense of artistic form. The poems in *Boleros* succeed in doing for contemporary African American poetry what the musical innovations of Charlie Parker, John Coltrane, and others achieved for bebop in the mid twentieth century.

"Confident,/ cocky,/ still uncomforted" (*Boleros* #7) after all these years, Jay Wright continues to insist that boundaries need not separate peoples; they are in fact places where communication and communities have and will yet again become possible, once the contemporary manifestations of nationalism wane. Part of this postnationalistic projection is the hope that more readers of African American poetry come to see, and demand, the intellectual challenges and pleasures that reside within beautiful shapes such as Wright's poems instead of being content with art as ideological consolation. Meanwhile, this poet/player stubbornly sits at the crossroads, and there he will remain, drenched to the bone, until someone, anyone, calls out his name and calls him home.

Selected Bibliography

PRIMARY WORKS

POETRY

Death as History. Millbrook, N.Y.: Kriya Press, 1967.
The Homecoming Singer. New York: Corinth Books, 1971.
Soothsayers and Omens. New York: Seven Woods Press, 1976.
Dimensions of History. Santa Cruz, Calif.: Kayak, 1976.
The Double Invention of Komo. Austin: University of Texas Press, 1980.
Explications/Interpretations. Charlottesville, Va., and Lexington, Ky.: Callaloo Poetry Series, 1984.
Selected Poems. Edited by Robert B. Stepto. Princeton, N.J.: Princeton University Press, 1987.
Elaine's Book. Charlottesville: University Press of Virginia, 1988.
Boleros. Princeton, N.J.: Princeton University Press, 1991.
Transfigurations. Collected Poems. Baton Rouge, La.: Louisiana State University Press, 2000.

PLAYS

Love's Equations. A Play. Callaloo 6, no. 3:39–75 (1983).
The Death and Return of Paul Batuta. A Play in One Act. Hambone 4:61–110 (1984).
The Adoration of Fire. Southern Review, Summer 1985.
A Sacred Impurity: The Dead's First Invention. Hambone 7:11–49 (1987).
Daughters of the Water. Callaloo 10, no. 2:215–81 (1987).

The Delights of Memory, 2: Doss. Callaloo 14, no. 1:157–80 (1991).
The Delights of Memory, 3: Leroy. Hambone 9:155–68 (1991).
The Delights of Memory, 1: Lily. Chicago: Bailiwick Theatre, October 6, 1994.

ESSAYS

"A Diamond-Bright Art Form." *Sports Illustrated,* Summer 1969.
"Introduction to Henry Dumas." *Poetry for My People.* Carbondale: Southern Illinois University Press, 1970.
"Myth and Discovery." In *The Rarer Action: Essays in Honor of Francis Ferguson.* Edited by Alan Cheuse and Richard Koffler. New Brunswick, N.J.: Rutgers University Press, 1970. Pp. 340–52.
"Love's Emblem Lost: LeRoi Jones' 'Hymn for Lanie Poo.' " *Boundary 2* 6:415–34 (1978).
"Desire's Design, Vision's Resonance: Black Poetry's Ritual and Historical Voice." *Callaloo* 10, no. 1:13–28 (1987)

SECONDARY WORKS

BIOGRAPHICAL AND CRITICAL STUDIES

Benston, Kimberly W. " 'I Yam What I Am': The Topos of (Un)naming in Afro-American Literature." In *Black Literature and Literary Theory.* Edited by Henry Louis Gates Jr. New York: Methuen, 1984. Pp. 151–72.
Callaloo. Jay Wright: A Special Issue. 6, no. 3 (1983).
Doreski, Carole. *Writing American Black. Race Rhetoric in the Public Sphere.* New York: Cambridge University Press, 1998.
Harris, Wilson. *The Womb of Space: The Cross-Cultural Imagination.* Westport, Conn.: Greenwood Press, 1983.
Kutzinski, Vera M. *Against the American Grain: Myth and History in William Carlos Williams, Jay Wright, and Nicolás Guillén.* Baltimore: Johns Hopkins University Press, 1987.
Manson, Michael T. "The Clarity of Being Strange: Jay Wright's *The Double Invention of Komo.*" *Black American Literature Forum* 24, no. 3:473–89 (1990).
Okpewho, Isidore. "From a Goat Path in Africa: An Approach to the Poetry of Jay Wright." *Callaloo* 14, no. 3:692–726 (1991).
Pinckney, Darryl. "You're in the Army Now." *Parnassus: Poetry in Review* 9, no. 1:306–14 (1981).
Stepto, Robert B. "After Modernism, After Hibernation: Michael Harper, Robert Hayden, and Jay Wright." In *Chant of Saints: A Gathering of Afro-American Literature, Arts, and Scholarship.* Edited by Michael S. Harper and Robert B. Stepto. Urbana: University of Illinois Press, 1979. Pp. 470–86.
Welburn, Ron. "Jay Wright's Poetics: An Appreciation." *MELUS* 18, no. 3:51–70 (1993).

RICHARD WRIGHT
(1908–1960)

JOYCE ANN JOYCE

IN HIS ESSAY "The Literature of the Negro in the United States," Richard Wright makes a comment that clearly exemplifies his own life and illuminates the progression of his physical movements as well as the development of his intellect: "For the development of Negro expression—as well as the whole of Negro life in America—hovers always somewhere between the rise of man from his ancient, rural way of life to the complex, industrial life of our time." Born on 4 September 1908, in an impoverished, rural environment in Natchez, Mississippi, Wright developed from an uneducated, lonely Southerner to become one of the most cosmopolitan, Continental, well-read, and politically active writers in American literary history. Poet, novelist, essayist, journalist, playwright, Communist, agnostic, and existentialist, he is now well known as the father of African American literature.

This recognition comes in response to the diversity of his talents, but primarily because his courage and honesty in challenging the literary stereotypes attributed to African American letters changed the entire course of African American fiction. In Wright's essay "Blueprint for Negro Writing," originally published in *New Challenge* in 1937, he outlines his criteria for the role of African American literature and the responsibility of the black artist. He says that white America failed to offer the black writer

serious criticism because it was astonished that a black person could write at all. Thus white America had no interest in the role African American writing could play in shaping American culture. He adds, "At best, Negro writing has been something external to the lives of educated Negroes themselves. That the productions of their [Negro] writers should have been something of a guide in their daily living is a matter which seems never to have been raised seriously." The publication of *Native Son* on 1 March 1940 demanded that white America look at African American fiction more seriously than it had previously done since the publication of the first black novel by William Wells Brown in 1853. The fact that Harper Brothers sold 200,000 copies of *Native Son* in thirty days was a sign of the indefatigable interest white America would have in Wright's works in the years to come. On the surface, the central issue of Wright's oeuvre is the relationship between blacks and whites. Yet a deeper reading goes beyond this sensationalized approach and explains why Wright's works have become essential representations of the American literary canon.

Voluminous studies treat the influence of Marxist ideology and existential philosophy on Wright's fiction and fail to detect those qualities in his art which make it peculiarly American and human. From his home environment to his experiences in Memphis, Chicago, New York, and Paris, Wright's position as an outsider instilled in him the ability and courage to analyze human behavior objectively and perspicaciously. This is reflected in a scene that Wright relates in *American Hunger* (1977), the second volume of his autobiography, concerning his ultimate break with the Communist party. Wright was feared by the party insofar as he was unable to submit emotionally and intellectually to its demands. *American Hunger* ends with a description of how the Communists forcibly ejected Wright from their ranks at a May Day parade. This painful and humiliating incident forced him to survey his past and to accept that the road to self-affirmation is lonely and arduous. The scene capsulizes Wright's understanding of human nature and his motive for writing:

> Yes, the whites were as miserable as their black victims, I thought. If this country can't find its way to a human path, if it can't inform conduct with a deep sense of life, then all of us, black as well as white, are going down the same drain. . . .
>
> I picked up a pencil and held it over a sheet of white paper, but my feeling stood in the way of my words. Well, I would wait, day and night, until I knew what to say. Humbly now, with no vaulting dream of achieving a vast unity, I wanted to try to build a bridge of words between me and that world outside, that world which was so distant and elusive that it seemed unreal.
>
> I would hurl words into this darkness and wait for an echo, and if an echo sounded, no matter how faintly, I would send other words to tell, to march, to fight, to create a sense of the hunger for life that gnaws in us all, to keep alive in our hearts a sense of the inexpressibly human. (p. 135)

Wright's childhood in the rural South instilled in him the deep yearning to know, the desire to explore the meaning of his experiences, and the boldness to express his knowledge. When Wright died on 28 November 1960, his exploration of the "inexpressibly human" had

taken him a long way from Natchez, Mississippi.

From his own accounts of his life, Wright was clearly different from the other members of his family. His very religious mother, Ella Wilson, met his father, Nathan Wright, at a party at the Cranfield Methodist Church. They were married in Natchez in 1907. Ella was a school-teacher; her husband, an illiterate sharecropper. Consequently her family considered their marriage to be a step down for her. In 1910 his mother gave birth to second son, Leon, who grew to be very different from Richard. When Nathan abandoned farming to become an itinerant worker in 1911, Ella and the two boys left their farm in the village of Roxie to live with her family in Natchez. Thus the family began to drift apart. While Richard's father left Mississippi altogether and moved to Memphis, Ella, Richard, and Leon remained with her mother, Margaret Bolden Wilson, a tyrannical, religious Seventh-Day Adventist mulatto. At an early age Richard began his rebellion against his grandmother and her religion. After years of trying, she gave up attempting to force him to attend church on Saturday.

Because of a lack of job opportunities for blacks in rural Mississippi, Ella decided to go to Memphis to join Nathan, who had found a job as a night porter in a drugstore. Ella was away most of the day, working in the homes of whites, and Nathan had both stopped providing for the family and coming home. As a result, Richard and his brother spent a great deal of time in the streets of Memphis.

In the winter of 1915 Ella Wright became ill, and Richard had to care for her and his brother until his grandmother arrived. Since she was unable to care for her sons, Ella sent them to Settlement House, a Methodist orphanage. After a short time Richard ran away because of the sexual advances of Miss Simon, the head of the orphanage. Wright's experiences with her were compounded by hunger and the pain of being separated from his mother. Found by a policeman and beaten by Miss Simon for his disobedience, Richard remained at Settlement House until the summer of 1916, when his mother gathered enough money to take her

Richard Wright

consciousness the hostility and danger the white world posed for him. His description of this revelation in *Black Boy* suggests how he refused to accept anything that diminished human dignity:

> We, figuratively, had fallen on our faces to avoid looking into that white-hot face of terror that we knew loomed somewhere above us. This was as close as white terror had ever come to me and my mind reeled. Why had we not fought back, I asked my mother, and the fear that was in her made her slap me into silence.
> (p. 48)

Like her tyrannical mother (though she was in no way as harsh), Ella was unable to frighten or indoctrinate her son into docility. Ella, Maggie, and the boys remained in Jackson only three months before moving back to West Helena. While their mother and aunt worked during the day, Richard and Leon roamed the streets. During this period, another incident occurred that impressed upon Richard the reality of racism and the way in which blacks continued to respond to that reality. Maggie's lover, "Professor" Matthews, robbed a white woman and set fire to her house, mainly because the woman refused to release him from the relationship. Maggie moved to Detroit with the "Professor."

When Ella again fell ill, Grandmother Wilson went to Arkansas and brought Ella and her sons back to Jackson. Because of his mother's illness, Leon was sent to Detroit to live with Maggie while Richard went to live with his uncle Clark in Greenwood, Mississippi. Continually sleepwalking and harassed by nightmares, Richard was very unhappy in his new environment. Although school took his mind off his unhappiness about Clark's home and harsh personality, he did not feel good again until he was reunited with his mother.

Not only did Wright have to deal with his mother's continued illness, but he also found that he could not accept his grandmother's religion—to have done so would have meant denouncing all the joys of life: she burned the books he brought into her home, forbade him

sons to stay at her parents' home in Jackson, Mississippi, where they had moved. Subsequently they went to Elaine, Arkansas, to live with her sister Maggie and her brother-in-law, Silas Hoskins.

Having been hungry much of his life, Richard was quite happy living in Elaine, eating as much as he wanted and enjoying the attention he received from his aunt and uncle. This happiness, however, was short-lived. Silas owned a thriving saloon frequented by the many black workers who labored in the nearby sawmills. Despite the fact that he often spent the night in his saloon armed with a gun, Silas was killed by whites who wanted to seize his valuable property. Richard, Leon, Ella, and Maggie quickly moved to West Helena and remained there for a short time before going back to Jackson. Because his grandmother was light skinned enough to pass for white, the young Richard had not given very much thought to racial differences. But the incident in Elaine and the reaction of his mother and aunt to it impressed upon his to listen to the radio, and refused to permit him to work on Saturday until he threatened to leave home. After numerous part-time jobs and interruptions from school, Wright entered the ninth grade and graduated valedictorian of his class at Smith-Robinson High School in Jackson in 1929. Again he was forced to assert his individuality. Because the black graduation class was to use the municipal party room on Congress Street for the first time, the principal attempted to coerce Wright into reading the speech he had prepared rather than the one Wright had written. Wright's speech, titled "The Attributes of Life," addressed how the educational system of the South deprived blacks of intellectual life and human dignity. Although he refused to accept the principal's speech, Wright did agree to cut certain passages that he felt might offend whites and some blacks.

At age seventeen Wright left Jackson to find work in Memphis. Although for years he had been reading all the magazines he could find, and despite the fact that he had published a story entitled "The Voodoo of Hell's Half Acre" in the *Southern Register* in 1924, it was in Memphis that a new world began to take shape for him. He read *Harper's Magazine, Atlantic Monthly,* and *American Mercury,* where he discovered H. L. Mencken. Reading Mencken's *A Book of Prefaces* and one volume of his *Prejudices* changed the course of Wright's life. In that single act he began his move from a rural way of life to an international one. In *Black Boy,* Wright explains how Mencken's use of words as weapons showed him that it was indeed possible to send words "to tell, to march, to fight, to create a sense of hunger for life that gnaws in us":

> I was jarred and shocked by the style, the clear, clean, sweeping sentences. Why did he write like that? And how did one write like that? I pictured the man as a raging demon, slashing with his pen, consumed with hate, denouncing everything American, extolling everything European or German, laughing at the weaknesses of people, mocking God, authority. . . . Could words be weapons? Well,

yes, for here they were. Then, maybe, perhaps, I could use them as a weapon? No. It frightened me. I read on and what amazed me was not what he said, but how on earth anybody had the courage to say it.

> (paperback ed., pp. 271–272)

Armed with the mortar for his literary arsenal, Wright left Memphis for Chicago in December 1927.

His artistic personality firmly set, at age nineteen Wright began the journey that later took him to New York and Paris. Detailed accounts of his life experiences are numerous. No other black American writer has attracted as much biographical attention as Richard Wright, most likely because of the strong interconnection between his life and works. At the same time that he mastered the craft of writing fiction, essays, and haiku poetry, he was equally successful at infusing his works with political messages that defied American and international societal conventions. On top of these accomplishments he still managed with indefatigable energy to be active in the Chicago John Reed Club, to attend the first American Writers' Congress, to attend the congress of the League of American Writers in New York, to work as coeditor of *Left Front* and editor of the Harlem Bureau of the *Daily Worker,* to act in a film production of *Native Son,* to organize the first Congress of Negro Writers and Artists, to attend the Bandung Conference (on Third World affairs), and to travel to Spain and Africa. His marriages to two white women accentuated his individuality by further alienating him from both black and white communities.

The purpose here is not to provide a detailed account of Wright's life, but to use the preceding commentary as example of those elements which make up his artistic sensibility and to show how that sensibility manifests itself in the diverse issues he addresses in his major works. Wright's literary career proper began in Chicago with the publication of poetry that demonstrated his early faith in communism. In *American Hunger* he explains that his interest in communism had nothing to do with economics, the great power of trade unions, or the excitement of underground politics. His interest was "caught by the similarity of the experiences of workers in other lands, by the possibility of uniting scattered but kindred peoples into a whole." Thus infused with the passion of wanting to improve the quality of people's lives and thinking the Communist party offered intellectual (as well as political) camaraderie to blacks, he joined the John Reed Club, a literary organ of the Communists. Though his affiliation with the party was short-lived and very disturbing, his initial enthusiasm for it inspired his first pieces of poetry.

Characteristic of much of Wright's poetry published between 1935 and 1940 and reflective of his early enthusiasm for communism, "I Have Seen Black Hands" is written in free verse. The line "I am black and I have seen black hands, millions and millions of them" begins the first three of the poem's four stanzas and thus becomes the refrain that captures the perspective from which the poet chooses to speak. The first three stanzas progress through images that describe the physical, sociological, economic, and political conditions of blacks, who, when they strike out in defense against oppression, end up in prison, hanged, or burned. The final stanza of the poem demonstrates what Wright felt the Communist party could do for mankind. It ends with images that, in his own words, "linked white life with black, merged two streams of common experience":

I am black and I have seen black hands
Raised in fists of revolt, side by side with
  the
    white fists of white workers,
And some day—and it is only this which
    sustains me—
Some day there shall be millions and
    millions
  of them,
On some red day in a burst of fists on a
    new
  horizon!
                    (*Richard Wright Reader*, p. 246)

Although Wright's interest in poetry waned (until he began writing haiku) after the publi-

cation of his first short-story collection, *Uncle Tom's Children*, in 1938, he published more poetry between 1933 and 1939 than most students of literature are aware. While poems such as "Rest for the Weary," "A Red Love Note," "Everywhere Burning Waters Rise," "Rise and Love," "I Have Seen Black Hands," "Red Clay Blues, "Red Leaves of Red Books," "I Am a Red Slogan," "Between the World and Me," and "Transcontinental" exemplify the diverse influence of writers such as Walt Whitman, T. S. Eliot, Langston Hughes, and Carl Sandburg, they also suggest that Wright's poetry served as precursor to the poetry of the black arts movement of the 1960s.

Like the poets associated with the black arts movement, Wright used words as weapons to build bridges between people. His most sustained poem is the striking piece "Transcontinental," dedicated to Louis Aragon in praise of his poem "Red Front." In an ironic, lightly satiric, mocking tone, "Transcontinental" castigates capitalism in its various aspects as it manifests itself throughout the United States, resulting in extreme wealth and poverty. Identifying with the underclass, the narrator hitchhikes across the United States. As he stands by the roadside in the heat, he sees the cool green of golf courses with long red awnings to protect the rich from the rain and sunshine. Swaying hammocks are slung between trees, indicating the time the rich have for rest and leisure. And he hears the tinkle of ice in tall glasses and the "silvery crescendos of laughter" as he and his companions, lost, hitchhike along highways in the heat, trying to get home.

Using the realistic descriptions that are characteristic of all his poetry, Wright surveys poverty, politics, and human suffering all across America. The word *America* rhythmically appears throughout the poem, suggesting the hypocrisy and corruption ironically antithetical to the self-image the United States attempts to propagate.

The typography of Wright's poetry (particularly "Transcontinental") shares a close affinity to that of the young black poets who were to follow him. Because Wright frequently spoke of the white writers who influenced him, critics tend to compare his works with those writers and thus overlook his connection to the African American literary tradition, especially in the case of his poetry. A more detailed study of Wright's poetry, Michel Fabre's "From Revolutionary Poetry to Haiku," collected in his *World of Richard Wright*, notes Wright's collaboration with Langston Hughes in "Red Clay Blues." And, of course, the influence of Hughes on such poems as "FB Eye Blues" and "Ah Feels It in Mah Bones" is evident. Yet while Wright's poetry looks back to Whitman and at the same time reflects the influence of Eliot and Sandburg, it also anticipates the black revolutionary poetry of the 1960s. Just as writers such as Sonia Sanchez, Haki Madhubuti, and Amiri Baraka based the structure of their poetry on black speech and music, in "Transcontinental" Wright created a poem rooted in an oral tradition with a strong narrative voice. Defying white middle-class notions of form, black poets of the 1960s used the same techniques that Wright employs for emphasis: no punctuation, excessive capitalization, the linking of several words and phrases together, the repetition of several letters in a word, and the use of profanity. These characteristics taken as a whole give the poem the quality of a song. It cannot be read with the same inflections as a lyric poem. It demands dramatization.

In order for a writer to "inform conduct with a deep sense of life," and in order to achieve the objectivity that prevents feeling from getting in the way of words, as Wright says he wishes to do, he must be able to feel and envision the connection between himself and those in the outside world. "Between the World and Me," Wright's most powerful poem from this early period, emerges as the poetic representation of his artistic credo, the raison d'être of his art. Published in the July–August 1935 issue of *Partisan Review*, the poem begins with a narrator who, while walking in the woods one morning, "stumbled suddenly upon the thing." Wright does not immediately identify the thing. The poem progresses through a narrative in which the reader experiences the details of the scene as the narrator experiences them.

Although the reader is aware that the narrator has stumbled upon the aftermath of a lynching, the poem's power comes from the way in which Wright has the narrator gradually describe the scene and develop it with sharp, realistic details. As he sees "a design of white bones slumbering forgottenly / upon a cushion of ashes," "a charred stump of a sapling pointing a blunt / finger accusingly at the sky," other details emerge: torn tree limbs, the remains of burnt leaves, a scorched coil of greasy hemp, a shoe, a tie, a ripped shirt, a hat, a pair of trousers stiff with blood, buttons, the butts of cigars and cigarettes, peanut shells, a drained gin flask, traces of tar, feathers, and a stony skull. Seeing these objects, the narrator is so overwhelmed with pity that he identifies totally with the spirit of the lost human life. Quite deftly without any awkwardness in transition, the narrator becomes the man who was lynched and burned:

> The ground gripped my feet and my heart
>   was
>   circled by icy walls of fear—
> The sun dried in the sky; a night wind
>   muttered in the grass and fumbled the
>   leaves in the trees; the woods poured
>   forth
>   the hungry yelping of hounds;
>   the darkness screamed with thirsty
>   voices;
>   and the witnesses rose and
>   lived:
> The dry bones stirred, rattled, lifted,
>   melting
>   themselves into my bones.
>   (Fabre, p. 239)

All of the materials (the gin flask, cigarettes, and the whore's lipstick, for example) become functional as they are used by the whites in their "lynching picnic." Tarred, feathered, and burned, the narrator completes his identification with the stony skull. The last lines of the poem—"Now I am dry bones and my face a stony skull staring in / yellow surprise at the sun"—complete the meaning of the last line of the prologue, "And the sooty details of the scene rose, thrusting themselves between the world / and me." The sooty scene has changed the narrator's perspective on life. This experience has stood between him and the world and altered his attitude toward his place in that world. Yet his staring in yellow surprise at the sun indicates that though the knowledge he now has fills him with anguish (also indicated by the blunt finger pointing accusingly at the sky), the sunshine pouring through the skull suggests that this knowledge has its positive side. What becomes important is how the narrator uses this knowledge of his place in the world. Analogously, just as the sooty scene stood between the narrator and the world, so racial oppression and the corruption associated with capitalism and imperialism thrust themselves between Wright and the world. His art is his means of challenging that corruption and lack of moral order.

The poignant, realistic details, totally devoid of overt moral statement, make "Between the World and Me" different from many of Wright's other poems and the short stories in *Uncle Tom's Children*. Although the original edition contained only four stories, subsequent editions included the autobiographical sketch "The Ethics of Living Jim Crow" and the story "Bright and Morning Star." The first story, "Big Boy Leaves Home," dramatizes how racism makes it impossible for young black boys to experience adolescence naturally. The story begins with a scene that terrifyingly moves Big Boy and his friends from innocence to experience. While he, Bobo, and two others decide to skinny-dip in a swimming hole located on the land of a white man known for his hatred of blacks, a white woman stumbles upon them, and the course of all of their lives is changed. When the woman cries out, she is joined by her fiancé the son of the owner of the land, who shoots and kills Big Boy's and Bobo's friends. When Bobo jumps on the man's back from behind, he flings Bobo to the ground and begins to hit him with his fists. Big Boy picks up the gun. Because racism has instilled in the white man the idea that he is superior to blacks, he walks toward Big Boy and demands that Big Boy give the gun to him. When the man continues to advance and refuses to stop, Big Boy nerv-

ously shoots him, and he and Bobo flee. While hiding in a hole, Big Boy witnesses Bobo's torture at the hands of a white mob; later, aided by his parents and the entire black community, he catches a ride north on a truck.

The next story in the collection, "Down by the Riverside," deserves far more critical attention than it has so far received. It opens with Mann (whose name is indeed symbolic), a black farmer, attempting to get his pregnant wife to a hospital during a flood. Unable to secure a boat any other way, Mann's brother, Bob, steals the postman's boat. When the postman discovers the theft, Mann kills him. Though he struggles against impossible odds, he succeeds in getting his wife to the hospital, but she is dead when they arrive. After his son and his wife's mother have been taken to high ground, Mann is forced to work on the rescue squad. When he takes a boat and goes with Brinkley, the young black man who volunteered to steer the boat, to save the Heartfields, he discovers that this is the family of the postman he killed. Unable to kill them when he has a chance, Mann saves their lives even as they recognize him. When he flees to avoid death once his guilt is established, he is shot in the back. A white soldier takes the butt of his rifle and pushes Mann's body near the edge of the water. His body "rolled heavily down the wet slope and stopped about a foot from the water's edge; one black palm sprawled limply outward and upward, trailing in the brown current. . . ." This last line evidences the subtlety characteristic of the entire story. The reader is reminded of Lulu, Mann's wife, whose "left arm fell from the table and hung limp" as the doctor pronounced her dead. Thus the black palm that sprawls limply outward and upward, trailing in the current, could be that of Mann's dead wife.

"Down by the Riverside" presents a disturbing portrait of a world in which racism has inverted the natural order of man's life. Mann, who is of high moral caliber and determined to provide for his family, refuses to accept the boat offered by the government, hoping that the predicted flood will not occur. Along with nature, numerous incidents thwart his determination to save his family: he stays in the house too long; Lulu has serious complications with her pregnancy; Bob steals a boat from a white man; Mann kills the postman Heartfield; he is forced to help evacuate the hospital; he goes to rescue a family, unaware of their identity; and he is unable to kill Heartfield's wife and children in order to save himself. The tragedy of the story is that Mann's courage and moral fiber are of no value in a world where the welfare of blacks is completely subordinate to the needs and whims of whites.

"Long Black Song" also portrays how racism inverts the natural order of human lives. When the story opens, Sarah, a young farmer's wife, is sitting on her front porch, watching her baby and wondering when her husband, Silas, who has gone to town to sell his cotton and purchase more land, is going to return. Stimulated by the beautiful summer day, Sarah muses about Tom, her one true love, who has not returned from the war. While Sarah is sexually aroused by her thoughts of Tom, a young white gramophone salesman arrives. After a brief conversation, he follows Sarah into her home and rapes her. Because he, like the fiancé in "Big Boy Leaves Home," sees blacks as inferior, he leaves the gramophone, which Sarah has not agreed to purchase, and tells her that he will reduce the price and return the following day to collect the money from her husband.

Despite the fact that Silas has just sold his cotton for 250 dollars, bought ten acres of land, and decided to hire a hand to help with next year's crop, Sarah's having been raped by a white man forces Silas to accept the fact that whites control his life. When the young salesman returns with a friend, Silas kills one of them; the other escapes, then returns to the farm with a mob. Very aware of the meaning of his actions and their consequences, Silas forces Sarah to leave the house with the baby. After killing as many of the mob as he can, Silas dies in the house when it is set on fire and burns to the ground. Sarah emerges as the moral consciousness through which we understand how racism inverts the natural order of things. When the salesman forces his will on Sarah, she is not strong enough to fight off his advances because she is sexually aroused. The

salesman is not aware of Sarah's mental state. His only recognition is that she is black and he is white. He completely denies her humanity. While Silas dies in order to preserve his dignity, he would not have reacted with as much outrage if the salesman had been black— he is more upset that the salesman is white than he is that his wife was raped. Having worked to acquire the same comforts as those enjoyed by whites and had some degree of success, Silas feels totally betrayed by Sarah's violation.

Two of the four stories in the collection evince Wright's faith in the power of communism to join poor black and white people in a struggle against the economic forces that oppress them. In "Fire and Cloud" and "Bright and Morning Star," Wright, presaging his attitude toward religion in his later works, shows how Christianity fails to meet the realistic needs of the black community. In "Fire and Cloud," Reverend Taylor is the voice of the black community; thus it is within his power to prevent a protest demonstration that is being planned. While the mayor and other leading whites attempt to coerce Reverend Taylor to stop the demonstration, the Communists are depending on him to support it. The whites make the mistake of taking Taylor to the woods to beat him into submission. Rather than making him submissive, the painful thrashing emboldens him and convinces him that *Freedom belongs to the strong!* At the end of the story he delivers a brief baptismal sermon about the fire that burned his back and steps out to join the marchers.

To a lesser degree, revolutionary consciousness replaces religious awareness in "Bright and Morning Star." Aunt Sue has one of her sons in prison because of his political involvement with the Communist party. She is worried about the welfare of her younger son, Johnny Boy, who is continuing his brother's activities and is involved with a white girl, also working with the Communists. In their search for Communists the sheriff and his men arrest Johnny Boy and take him into the woods to torture him, demanding that he reveal the names of his comrades. Before they find Johnny Boy, how-

Richard Wright at his typewriter.

ever, they look for him at his mother's house. As the sheriff and his men are about to leave, Aunt Sue feels a strong desire "to make them feel the intensity of her pride and freedom." Thus she shouts to the sheriff, "Yuh didnt git whut yuh wanted! N yuh ain gonna nevah git it!" When the sheriff tells her not to speak again, she boldly repeats her comments with more fervor. The sheriff then slaps her, knocks her to the floor, and kicks her in the temple and stomach. Weak and confused when the informer Booker later comes to visit her, she unwittingly reveals the names of the comrades to him. After Booker leaves and she realizes what she has done—and that he is on his way to the woods where the sheriff is holding her son—she wraps a gun in a sheet and takes the shortcut into the woods. When Booker arrives, she shoots him before he can reveal the names and, in turn, is shot. Before dying, Aunt Sue feels the need to assert herself one last time: "Yuh didnt git whut yuh wanted! N yuh ain gonna nevah git it! Yuh didnt kill me; Ah come here by mah-

sef. . . ." Unlike her sons, Aunt Sue's rebellion is not rooted in her faith in Communist ideology but in a desire, like Silas's, to preserve her dignity and make amends for the betrayal of her son.

Aunt Sue and the protagonists of the other stories collected in *Uncle Tom's Children* provide a contrast to the stereotypes and submissive characters represented in Harriet Beecher Stowe's *Uncle Tom's Cabin.* These defiant characters are dramatizations of how Wright wished he had been able to respond to the experiences he describes in "The Ethics of Living Jim Crow," the autobiographical sketch later added as prologue to the volume. Reactions to the collection were varied. Leftist journals such as *New Masses, Daily Worker, Partisan Review,* and the *New Republic* gave it ambivalently favorable reviews; papers such as the *New York Times* and the *New York Book Review* lambasted the work for what they saw as its depiction of racial hatred. Compared with the vehement response that followed the publication of *Native Son,* the reviews of *Uncle Tom's Children* were mild.

At the same time that Harper Brothers accepted *Uncle Tom's Children* for publication, they gave Wright a contract for *Native Son.* When the novel was published two years later, it was a Book of the Month Club selection and appeared on the best-seller list longer than any other book in African American literary history. With its publication Wright was suddenly famous. Because *Native Son* addresses the psychological, political, and economic issues of racism so boldly, this powerful novel has been both praised and criticized. At the same time that it is the best-known novel in the African American canon, a fair number of critics have asserted that it is flawed because of its heavy sociological emphasis. But such a view is possible only if one fails to appreciate the way in which Wright perfectly balances his creative vision and political commitment.

Native Son reflects the diversity of Wright's reading in sociology, psychology, history, and literature. It also serves as a model for the literary credo he had earlier outlined in "Blueprint for Negro Writing," where he discussed the interrelationship between literature and politics. Most of Wright's students and critics focus on the Black Nationalist theme and his Marxist ideology in "Blueprint" and ignore the important emphasis he gives to craft and form. While *Native Son* reflects the influence of Dostoevsky and Theodore Dreiser and explores the destructive effect of racism on human consciousness (both black and white), its artistic beauty attests to the value Wright placed on craftsmanship from the very beginning of his career. While addressing social and political issues, Wright displays keen insight into the interrelationship between art and reality:

> The relationship between reality and the artistic image is not always direct and simple. The imaginative conception of a historical period will not be a carbon copy of reality. Image and emotion possess a logic of their own. A vulgarized simplicity constitutes the greatest danger in tracing the reciprocal interplay between the writer and his environment.

Writing has its professional autonomy; it should complement other professions, but it should not supplant them or be swamped by them.

> ("Blueprint for Negro Writing,"
> in *Richard Wright Reader,* p. 48)

Wright understood that powerful art was something more than a sociological, historical document. He intended *Native Son* and the rest of his creative works to be something more than carbon copies of the interaction between blacks and whites. Wright saw the writer as a man in the world, involved in the affairs of that world. Simultaneously, though, the writer must maintain a commitment to his own aesthetic responsibility.

In the novel, the aspects of language—characterization, setting, structure, imagery, symbol, and point of view—all form an intricately woven net of linguistic threads that make manifest Bigger Thomas's consciousness. Divided into three parts, each charting the changes in Bigger's mind, the novel begins with a description of his home environment. His family's one-room apartment with rat-infested kitchenette contrasts sharply with the well-manicured lawn and plush environment of the Daltons, the rich white family for whom Bigger works as chauffeur. Mr. and Mrs. Dalton are philanthropists; their daughter, Mary, rebels against their upper-middle-class standards by dating Jan, a Communist. Totally unaware of how racism has shaped their consciousness and Bigger's, Jan and Mary invite him to eat with them in a South Side restaurant, where they purchase rum. After Bigger drops Jan off to catch the train, Mary continues to drink and is far too drunk to walk when Bigger gets her home. Afraid of losing the most comfortable job he has ever had and thinking quite irrationally, Bigger carries Mary upstairs to her bedroom. He is overcome with frenzy and fear when Mary's blind mother enters the room. To prevent Mary from making a sound, he presses a pillow over her face, suffocating her.

Because he knows that the white world will say that he raped her and will never accept that her death was an accident, he decapitates Mary so that he can get her body into the furnace and burn it. When he goes home to sleep, rest, and think about his actions, he begins to see his family from a new perspective. He realizes that they have let life defeat them and are blind to the role they play in that defeat. When he goes back to the Dalton home, the family's questions show him that the whites also are blind. So he responds to their questions, giving them answers that will convince them Mary took the train to Detroit. Feeling in control of his life for the first time, he decides to challenge the Daltons, and thus white society, by writing a ransom note. This decision is significant in Wright's characterization of his hero, for Bigger at this point is not known to be implicated in Mary's death and could have escaped. But that is not the novel Wright chose to write. Bigger does not ask for money because he wants to get rich or to use it to get away; he does so to test his power.

Realizing that the Daltons are blind to his humanity, Bigger is able to use their weakness to manipulate their thoughts. His fear of whites, however, which was responsible for Mary's death, also accounts for the mistake he makes that precipitates the discovery of Mary's bones and his identification as the killer. Because he is afraid to clean the furnace in the presence of the white reporters who lurk about the basement, he permits the ashes to back up and the house to get cool. Peggy, the housekeeper, then tells him to clean the furnace, and he has no choice but to obey the command given by a white woman. Not to do so would draw attention to the rebelliousness that he has masterfully managed to conceal. He is so afraid to remove the ashes in the presence of the white reporters that he performs the job quite badly, causing such a mess that smoke fills the basement. A reporter takes the shovel from Bigger. When the reporters find an earring in the ashes, they examine them more carefully and discover pieces of Mary's bones. Bigger jumps out a window and runs until he is captured.

Having spent his entire life up to this point hiding behind a wall of sullenness, Bigger is forced now to fight in an emotional arena. The questions that Max, the lawyer the Communist party appoints to defend him, asks Bigger about himself, coupled with the long ordeal of the trial, incite in him the need to reach out to make a connection between himself and another human being for the first time in his life. He had realized soon after Mary's death that the whites and the blacks around him are blind, but at first he is unable to acknowledge his own blindness. Thinking initially that the lawyer will understand him, Bigger attempts to explain to Max the meaning of his life and his revelation. Despite Max's eloquent speech, in which he asserts that Bigger's causing Mary's death was an act of creation, Max is unable to accept the reality of Bigger's life when Bigger says, "... what I killed for, I am! It must've been pretty deep in me to make me Kill! I must have felt it awful hard to murder." Like numerous critics of the novel, Max is unable to identify with Bigger's acceptance of violence. The sullen, fearful, and violent Bigger is transformed from innocence to experience, and from ignorance to knowledge. He comes to realize that blacks like himself must take control of their own lives, regardless of the price. Perhaps the most important passage in the novel is the one in which Bigger demonstrates his spiritual growth by explaining his connection to the rest of humanity. Referring to Mary's death Bigger says to Max:

> Mr. Max, I sort of saw myself after that night. And I sort of saw other people, too. . . . Well, it's sort of funny, Mr. Max. I ain't trying to dodge what's coming to me. . . . I know I'm going to get it. I'm going to die. Well, that's all right now. But really I never wanted to hurt nobody. That's the truth. . . . I hurt folks cause I felt I had to; that's all. They were crowding me too close; they wouldn't give me no room. Lots of times I tried to forget 'em, but I couldn't. They wouldn't let me. . . . Mr. Max, I didn't mean to do what I did. I was trying to do something else. But it seems like I never could. I was always wanting something and I was feeling that nobody would let me have it. So I fought 'em. I thought they was hard and I acted hard. . . . But I ain't hard, Mr. Max. I ain't hard even a

little bit. . . . But I—I won't be crying none when they take me to that chair. But I'll b-b-be feeling inside of me like I was crying. . . . I'll be feeling and thinking that they didn't see me and I didn't see them.

(paperback ed., p. 388)

His spiritual growth complete, Bigger now sees that he has been as blind as the whites. He understands that despite the entrapments of racism, blacks and whites have a shared human consciousness, and it is the black individual's responsibility not to succumb to the psychological pitfalls of racial oppression. By focusing on Bigger's consciousness, Wright encourages the reader to empathize with his character, an empathy that challenges the denunciations of both blacks and whites.

Max's characterization suggests that by the time of the publication of *Native Son* in 1940 the seeds of Wright's disillusionment with the Communist party had begun to sprout. The reader, like Bigger, initially expects that Max is capable of understanding his client. When he fails to do so, we gradually come to understand that his impressive speech was totally aimed at saving the image of the Communist party, which Bigger had implicated in Mary's alleged kidnapping. In *American Hunger*, Wright makes a comment about his Communist comrades that perfectly describes Max and his speech. When Wright's mother failed to grasp the symbolism of a "lurid May Day" cartoon in *New Masses*, Wright became sharply aware of the Communists' inability to reach the masses of black people. He thinks of the role he could play in rectifying this problem:

Here, then, was something I could do, reveal say. The Communists, I felt, had oversimplified the experience of those whom they sought to lead. In their efforts to recruit masses, they missed the meaning of the lives of the masses, had conceived of people in too abstract a manner. . . . I would tell Communists how common people felt, and I would tell common people of the self-sacrifice of Communists who strove for unity among them.

(paperback ed., pp. 65–66)

Wright soon realized that the Communists were not interested in how black people felt. He was disliked by the party because he could not be intimidated and was determined to live his life the way he thought it should be lived.

While working on *Native Son* in August 1939, Wright, who was living in New York, married Dhimah Rose Meadman, a Russian-Jewish ballet dancer. Tired of the confusion and hectic schedule of life in New York, he decided to take his bride to Mexico. She, however, decided to bring along her son, her mother, and a guest. Wright soon discovered that he and Dhimah were not at all suited to each other. They were divorced in 1940, their marriage having lasted less than a year. On 12 March 1941 Wright married Ellen Poplar, with whom he had been in love before marrying Dhimah, but whose hesitation in agreeing to marry him he had misunderstood. Also in 1941 his first daughter, Julia, was born, and Viking Press published *Twelve Million Black Voices*.

Subtitled *A Folk History of the Negro in the United States*, *Twelve Million Black Voices* is a pictorial analysis of the life of blacks in the United States from the rural South to the more urban North.

Demonstrating careful research into the sociological, economic, political, and cultural aspects of black history, *Twelve Million Black Voices* focuses on the issues of employment, food, debts, religion, education, and music in the rural South. The work then shows how during and after the great migration these same elements became manifest in the black ghettos of the North. The book's major contribution lies in Wright's ability to evoke through description and detail both the tragedy and the strength embodied in blacks' psychological reactions to their condition. A part of the power of the book comes from the perfect juxtaposition of commentary with devastating photographs that prevent neutrality on the part of any reader.

Twelve Million Black Voices is not a typical book for a contemporary American writer. It attests to the diversity of Wright's artistic interests and to the level of his political commitment. The first volume of his autobiography, published four years later, takes him even further in his determination to challenge the denial of human dignity and the accepted codes of racial oppression. Invited by Professor Charles S. Johnson, renowned chair of the sociology department, to speak at Fisk University, Wright rode in a segregated train to Nashville, Tennessee. The interaction between blacks and whites on the train and the self-effacement he saw in the blacks substantiated Wright's belief that the personalities and habits of blacks were affected by their involvement with whites. Speaking to a large crowd of both whites and blacks, he related his life experiences as a black man to the audience. The audience's uneasiness about the subject of racism convinced him that he needed to dig deeper into what it means to be black in America. After his speech he "resolved that night that [he] would stop writing [his] novel and string [his] autobiographical notes, thoughts and memories together into a running narrative. [He] did. After much hesitation, [he] called the book 'Black Boy.' "

A Book of the Month Club selection for February 1945, *Black Boy* brought Wright immediate, increased fame. It provoked varying views from black and white critics alike. In the tradition of the slave autobiography, *Black Boy* provides details of Wright's life from early childhood to his arrival in Chicago. It is a realistic and poetic account of the hunger Wright endured as a child, his closeness to his mother, the effect of his mother's illness, his problems with his father, his father's desertion, the violence he experienced from his mother's relatives, his love of words and books, his discovery of racism and his developing racial consciousness, his fight against his mother's and grandmother's religion, his scanty education, the instability of his family, and the development of his individuality.

By using the elements of his life as the specific example of what he presents from a general perspective in *Twelve Million Black Voices*, Wright merges literary expression with the need for social and political change in *Black Boy*. The poignancy of his expression elicited quite a number of vehemently negative reviews. Interestingly, Wright's sequel to this first volume of his autobiography, *American Hun-*

ger, published seventeen years after his death, was well received by the critics. Despite the fact that Wright had originally conceived these two volumes as a single piece, *American Hunger* is distinctly different from *Black Boy*. *Black Boy* emerges as an almost gothic exploration of what it means to be a black child in the rural South. *American Hunger* is light in tone, progressing through anecdotes and humorous, loosely connected episodes. While *Black Boy* is lyrically poetic, *American Hunger* is realistically prosaic.

In 1947, between the publication of *Black Boy* and Wright's next major work, *The Outsider*, he and Ellen moved to France. They settled in Paris, where their second daughter, Rachel, was born in 1949. Wright's move to France began the fifth stage of his life. Having come from a small rural town in Mississippi, he was now an internationally known American writer. The film *Native Son* premiered on 4 November 1950, with Wright playing the part of Bigger. His intellectual interests were stimulated and broadened by contact with the French writers Simone de Beauvoir, Jean-Paul Sartre, André Gide, René Martin, and André Malraux. Shortly after he arrived in Paris, he read Albert Camus's *The Stranger*. The book, rooted in existential philosophy, along with the many talks he had with his friends Sartre and de Beauvoir (in which they frequently discussed the individual's relationship to freedom), fueled his efforts to complete the novel he had begun before leaving America.

In April 1953 Chester Himes brought with him to Paris Wright's copies of *The Outsider*, published a month earlier by Harper & Brothers. Having said earlier that he did not expect Americans to like or accept the book, Wright was prepared for the numerous negative reviews the book received in America. Mistakenly believing that Wright was no longer aware of the realities of black life in America, some of his critics failed to see how *The Outsider* reflects the natural progression of Wright's development as a creative writer and political thinker, not to mention his understanding of what it means to be an "outsider."

The Outsider explores the idea of a man in

the modern world whose nihilistic attitude toward life and whose alienation from the rest of mankind diminish his dignity and cause his destruction. Cross Damon, the protagonist, is married to a woman he does not love, is emotionally tied to a mother about whom he has ambivalent feelings, and has a mistress who attempts to force him into marrying her. Burdened by the demands of these three people and totally dissatisfied with his life, he takes advantage of a chance to begin a totally new existence. When a train on which he is riding crashes, he leaves his wallet and overcoat near another man's body so that the man will be mistaken for him. After killing an old acquaintance who recognizes him, Cross goes to New York, assumes a new name, and attracts the interest of the Communist party. Because the party is trying to force Herndon, the owner of a building, to rent to blacks, two party members, Gil and Eva Blount, rent Cross an apartment. When Herndon finds out that Cross is living in the building, he and Gil Blount have an argument that ends in a gruesome battle. Finding them almost unconscious from fighting, Cross kills both of them, rationalizing that he hates them because they are tyrannical and fascist.

Since he and Cross share an interest in questioning the nature of freedom, Eli Houston, the district attorney whom Cross had met on the train en route to New York, deduces that Cross is the murderer. Houston says that he and Cross are lawless men, governed by lawless drives, living in a society that requires them to restrain themselves for the common good of society. Rather than putting Cross in jail, he allows him to remain free, realizing that society would not understand Cross's motives. He also intuits that Cross himself will suffer when he discovers that real freedom requires each individual to accept his connection to the rest of mankind. Threatened by Cross because of his intellectual and emotional independence, members of the Communist party kill him. Just before Cross dies, he realizes that "alone man is nothing. . . . Man is a promise that he must never break. . . . I wish I had some way to give the meaning of my life to others. . . . To make a bridge from man to man."

Cross Damon's words echo Wright's comment in *American Hunger* that he wanted to use his art to "attempt to build a bridge of words between himself and the outside world." In *The Outsider*, Cross emerges as the fictional representation of what Wright implied in the poem "Between the World and Me." When communism failed him, he understood that his works were his best means of giving meaning to his life. Cross Damon, though, is not Richard Wright. In *The Outsider* Wright uses his art to curb that welter of intense emotions seething inside his consciousness and offers it to the rest of us as a means of investigating the anxiety and fragmentation caused by our descent into the abyss of industrialization and technology.

Wright's next book, *Savage Holiday* (1954), also explores (though from a strikingly different perspective) the dangers of repressed impulses and feelings; like *The Outsider*, it demonstrates Wright's interest in those areas of human consciousness which do not directly involve racial issues. Erskine Fowler, a white, middle-aged insurance executive, has spent his entire life repressing the anger, love, and sexual desire he feels for his mother, whose promiscuity excited the young Erskine's jealousy and outrage. The events in the novel chart the consequences of that repression. When he is forced to resign from the Longevity Life Insurance Company so that his boss's son can replace him, he is overwhelmed by despair. In this emotionally weakened state, he is accidentally locked, naked, outside his apartment one Sunday morning as he reaches for the newspaper. When he goes to the balcony in a desperate attempt to crawl through his bathroom window, little Tony, the son of the prostitute next door, is frightened by Erskine's nakedness and falls ten stories to the ground. Because he feels guilty about Tony's death, Erskine decides to marry Mable Blake, Tony's mother.

Erskine's obsession with Mable stimulates a welter of feelings he has repressed for years. His peculiar behavior prompts Mable, who remembers seeing a set of feet climbing into Erskine's window the morning her son died, to attempt to determine if he is responsible for her son's death. Because he substitutes Mable for his mother, whom he both hated and loved, and because he desires Mable's body and hates her for stimulating his passionate desire, Erskine is unable to control the flood of his feelings: he takes a butcher knife and plunges it repeatedly into her stomach until the blood begins to spurt and run over the floor.

Although *Savage Holiday* has been neglected because of the violence in this last scene and because the all-white characters do not satisfy stereotypical notions of Wright's fiction, the work testifies to the diversity of his creative abilities and is consistent with his investigation of the human psyche, the "inexpressibly human." A captivating and psychologically realistic portrayal of how dormant, unresolved childhood traumas easily erupt in violence toward the self or others, *Savage Holiday*, like all of Wright's fiction, raises the question of the place violence holds in man's attempt to grapple with the meaning of his existence.

While the critics at home were clamoring over *The Outsider* and *Savage Holiday*, Wright had entered a new phase of his literary career with an enormous amount of energy. Between 1953 and 1957 he traveled to Spain, Indonesia, and Africa, and completed work on four political, sociological treatises. The first of these, *Black Power* (1954), is the result of Wright's trip in the summer of 1953 to what was then referred to as the Gold Coast (present-day Ghana). Kwame Nkrumah, head of the Convention People's party and a leader of African struggle for independence, was about to win his country's independence from the British. *Black Power* is an account of Wright's experiences. The essential value of the book lies in Wright's conclusions. He calls on Nkrumah to put Africa into the mainstream of twentieth-century economic developments. He asserts that in order for the African to make his national freedom secure and compete in a changing world, he must move beyond primitivism to achieve economic stability. The Gold Coast must be freed from its fetish past as much as from the colonial regime. In order for these things to be accomplished, the white man, including the missionaries who conditioned the African to adjust

psychologically to colonialism, must leave Africa. The book, of course, received mixed reviews.

His subsequent publication, *The Color Curtain* (1956), is a record of the Bandung Conference, the first meeting of twenty-nine newly independent nations of Asia and Africa. Held in April 1955 at Bandung, Indonesia, this international conference brought together national leaders, as well as writers, from Asia and Africa. They called for economic cooperation, the end of colonialism, and the revitalization of Asian and African cultures and religions. The book is quite valuable for the insight it provides into the problems Asia and Africa face in their relationship with the West.

Wright's last two literary, sociopolitical travel books, *Pagan Spain* and *White Man, Listen!*, were published in 1956. An exploration of those aspects of Spanish life Wright felt had gone unexamined, *Pagan Spain* is perhaps the more vivid of these pieces. He intrigues the reader with many descriptive scenes of Spanish cultural life as he travels through Madrid, Granada, Barcelona, Seville, Guadalajara, and Toledo. His interviews with flamenco dancers, bullfighters, professionals, intellectuals, prostitutes, peasants, bartenders, royalty, and priests omit no stratum of Spanish cultural life. Wright deduces that Spain's Catholicism is more pagan than Christian, that a wide chasm exists between Spain's pretense at morality and the reality of poverty and prostitution that governs the Spanish people's way of life. Wright's probing interest in the irrationality and violence that lie beneath the veneer of Christianity in Spanish culture echoes his depiction of the veneer of genteel civility and Christian morality that shields the violence of his Southern background.

Three of the four essays in his final nonfiction work, *White Man, Listen!*, a collection of lectures given in Europe between 1950 and 1956, capsulize what Wright had already said in *Black Power* and *The Color Curtain*. The new essay in this collection, "The Literature of the Negro in the United States," written before his travels to Asia and Africa, is important reading for any student or teacher of African American literary history. Presenting a historical overview of African American literature from its beginning to the 1940s, he illustrates that literature is culture bound. He explains that writers such as Alexander Pushkin, a black Russian, and Alexander Dumas, a black Frenchman, did not write about race because they were integrated into the mainstreams of their cultures; they were at one with their cultures. Because she did not live a life characteristic of a slave, Phillis Wheatley did not focus essentially on aspects of race. Having received the kind of education given to white girls, she felt integrated into the culture around her. In the nineteenth century, when the harshness of slavery had begun to escalate, black writers such as George Moses Horton and James Whitfield wrote out of a sense of the psychological distance between them and the land in which they lived.

Tracing this tendency of blacks to depict themselves at odds with the environment in which they lived to writers such as Paul Laurence Dunbar, Claude McKay, Melvin B. Tolson, and Margaret Walker, he concludes that "expression springs out of environment, and events modify what is written by molding consciousness." Thus black literature will change, he adds, when the political and sociological conditions for the black change. This prophetic essay challenges those who hold that Wright's stay abroad separated him emotionally from the realities of black life in America. He was friendly with and helped a number of black writers who were writing in America when he wrote in France. If Wright is correct in his assertion that a people's literature is conditioned by the elements of their environment—and African American literary history clearly substantiates his assertion—then it is essential to note that despite his travels throughout the world and residence in France, he continued to identify with the plight of oppressed blacks in America. But Wright also extended that identification to oppressed peoples in Third World countries. Just as one manifestation of oppression in the South was replaced by another in the North, so Wright's travel books show that the same elements of capitalism that oppress blacks in America could be found in the colonial regimes of Africa and Asia. Thus his experiences with Third World writers, his continued harassment by the American and French secret services, and his knowledge of the universality of racial oppression made it impossible for him to overcome the psychological reaction to racism that had long shaped his character.

Referring to his last novel, *The Long Dream* (1958), Wright said in a letter to his Dutch translator, Margrit de Sablonière, that it was the first novel of a trilogy conceived to "demonstrate the extent to which 'racial conditioning' remained strong among blacks even after they had left the environment that engendered it." Analogously, Wright's interest in this subject attests to the extent to which he, too, remained psychologically conditioned by racial oppression.

Rather than manifesting Wright's failure to deal with a wider scope of African American expression, as some critics hold, *The Long Dream* exemplifies his intellectual and artistic maturity. He was cognizant of the changing political and social currents not only in Asia and Africa but also in America. Completed after the Supreme Court's *Brown v. Board of Education* decision in 1954 (to which Wright refers in *White Man, Listen!*), *The Long Dream* portrays the improvements in the life-style of blacks in Mississippi. On another level, however, it treats the ironies embodied in those improvements.

Unlike all of Wright's previous novels, *The Long Dream* focuses on the lives of a middle-class black family in Clintonville, Mississippi. Tyree Tucker owns a funeral home and a brothel that he maintains through the bribes he pays Hadley, the chief of police. Because he successfully plays the role of Uncle Tom, Tyree enjoys a powerful and comfortable position in the black community. His goal is that his son, Fishbelly, will take over his establishments after his death. Fishbelly, however, emotionally different from his father, is unable to maintain his father's legacy. When the brothel burns down, killing many people, the chief of police requests Tyree's canceled checks in order to avoid implication in an investigation. Tyree has already given some of the checks to his mistress. Unconvinced that Tyree does not know where the checks are, Hadley has Tyree killed. Because Fishbelly is unable play the role of Tom as his father did, Hadley frames him by having a white woman accuse him of rape. Fishbelly is put in jail but will not reveal the whereabouts of the missing checks. He is eventually released and forced to leave town. The novel ends with Fishbelly en route to Europe. The still unpublished "Islands of Hallucinations," the second book in the trilogy, treats Fishbelly's experiences in France.

While the sole tension in Wright's other novels comes from blacks' interactions with whites, here the relationship between Fishbelly and his father plays a primary role. The reader experiences Fishbelly's changing response to his environment through his relationship with his father, his mother, and the black and white communities. Depicting Fishbelly's life from early childhood to young adulthood, the novel describes the total chronological and emotional life of its hero.

The Long Dream is the last of Wright's works that he submitted for publication. Both *Eight Men*, his second collection of short stories (1961), and the novel *Lawd Today* (1963), were submitted by his wife. *Eight Men* shows that Wright was conditioned by racial stimuli and at the same time imbued with the intellectual currents of his day on the Continent. Each of the eight stories probes the meaning of life from varying perspectives. The first story, "The Man Who Was Almost a Man," is reminiscent of the earlier "Big Boy Leaves Home" in its treatment of a young black male's innocence in a hostile Southern environment and his move northward at the end of the story. "The Man Who lived Underground" is much like *The Outsider* in its search for the meaning of life and the protagonist's alienation, and "The Man Who Killed a Shadow" picks up the theme of the violence that ensues from repressed fears and desires depicted in *Savage Holiday*. Two of the stories, "Man of All Work" and "Big Black Good Man," evince a humorous sensibility totally atypical of Wright's other works. Although Wright completed *Eight Men* eight years before his death, it is uncertain whether he would have been

completely satisfied with *Lawd Today*. Originally entitled "Cesspool," and completed and rejected many times before the publication of *Native Son, Lawd Today* emerges as the least powerful of Wright's works. Influenced to some degree by James Joyce's *Ulysses*, Wright's novel portrays one day in Jake Jackson's life in the Black Belt of Chicago. Though the novel is by no means as captivating as Wright's other fiction, a part of its value lies in the way it presages his adroit use of descriptive detail, his realistic characterizations, and his vivid descriptions of the activities of life in the Black Belt.

The dominant characteristic of Wright's works—his poetry, short stories, novels, travel books, sociopolitical treatises, and autobiographies—is the power that forbids neutrality on the part of any reader. His desire "to keep alive in our hearts a sense of the inexpressibly human" demanded that he destroy the illusions and hypocrisy modern society has contrived to conceal its debilitating moral corruption. While still a young man in the 1930s, Wright realized that the most prominent example of modern society's degradation lay in racial oppression. The historical details he outlines in *Twelve Million Black Voices* and his characterization of Bigger Thomas symbolically present the idea he states straightforwardly in *White Man, Listen!* approximately seventeen years later: the concept that the history of black people in America is the history of America. Through his experiences in Europe, Asia, and Africa, he expanded his vision to include the interconnections between the low quality of life for people of color all over the world and the industrial, technological advancements of the western hemisphere.

Wright is the father of African American literature not only because his bold attack on racism gave the black writers who followed him the courage to express their visions truthfully, but also because to date no one writer has surpassed him in the diversity of creative accomplishments or in the ability to synthesize politics and art. When he died on 28 November 1960, in the Clinique Eugène Gibez, apparently of a heart attack, he left a legacy of haiku poetry, plays, interviews, book reviews, commentaries, lectures, and unpublished works to add to the list of well-known publications that bear the mark of his iconoclastic creative temper.

Selected Bibliography

PRIMARY WORKS

POETRY

"Child of the Dead and Forgotten Gods." *Anvil*, no. 5:30 (March–April 1934).
"Everywhere Burning Waters Rise." *Left Front*, no. 4:9 (May–June 1934).
"I Have Seen Black Hands." *New Masses* 11:16 (June 26, 1934).
"A Red Love Note." *Left Front*, no. 3:3 (January–February 1934).
"Rest for the Weary." *Left Front*, no. 3:3 (January–February 1934).
"Strength." *Anvil*, no. 5:20 (March–April 1934).
"Ah Feels It in Mah Bones." *International Literature*, no. 80:4 (April 1935).
"Red Leaves of Red Books." *New Masses* 16:6 (April 30, 1935).
"Between the World and Me." *Partisan Review* 2, no. 8:18–19 (July–August 1935).
"Spread Your Sunrise." *New Masses* 16:26 (July 2, 1935).
"Hearst Headline Blues." *New Masses* 19:14 (May 12, 1936).
"Old Habit and New Love." *New Masses* 21:29 (December 15, 1936).
"Transcontinental." *International Literature*, no. 1:52–57 (1936).
"We of the Streets." *New Masses* 23:14 (April 13, 1937).
"Red Clay Blues." *New Masses* 32:14 (April 1, 1939). (With Langston Hughes.)
Haiku, This Other World. Edited by Yoshinobu and Robert L. Tener. New York: Arcade Publishing, 1998.

SHORT STORY COLLECTIONS

Uncle Tom's Children: Four Novellas. New York: Harper & Brothers, 1938.
Eight Men. Cleveland: World, 1961.

NOVELS

Native Son. New York: Harper & Brothers, 1940.
The Outsider. New York: Harper & Brothers, 1953.
Savage Holiday. New York: Avon, 1954.
The Long Dream. Garden City, N.Y.: Doubleday, 1958.
Lawd Today. New York: Walker, 1963.
Rite of Passage. New York: HarperCollins, 1994

AUTOBIOGRAPHIES

Black Boy: A Record of Childhood and Youth. New York: Harper & Brothers, 1945. Paperbook, New York: Harper & Row, 1966.

American Hunger. New York: Harper & Row, 1977.

NONFICTION

Twelve Million Black Voices: A Folk History of the Negro in the United States. Photo direction by Edwin Rosskam. New York: Viking Press, 1941.
Black Power: A Record of Reactions in a Land of Pathos. New York: Harper & Brothers, 1954.
The Color Curtain: A Report on the Bandung Conference. Cleveland: World, 1956.
Pagan Spain. New York: Harper & Brothers, 1956.
White Man, Listen! Garden City, N.Y.: Doubleday, 1957.

ESSAYS

"Blueprint for Negro Writing." *New Challenge* 2:53–65 (Fall 1937). Reprinted in *Richard Wright Reader*.
"How 'Bigger' was Born." *Saturday Review* 22:4–5, 17 (June 1, 1940).
"I Tried To Be A Communist." *Atlantic Monthly*, no. 159:61–70 (August 1944).
"A World View of the American Negro." *Twice a Year*, no. 14–15:346–348 (Fall 1946–Winter 1947).

COLLECTED WORKS

Early Works: Lawd Today!, Uncle Tom's Children, Native Son. Vol. 1 of *Works*. New York: Library of America, 1991.
Later Works: Black Boy (American Hunger), The Outsider. Vol. 2 of *Works*. New York: Library of America, 1991.

MANUSCRIPTS AND PAPERS

Wright's papers are housed in the Beinecke Rare Book and Manuscript Library at Yale University. Some of his letters are in the Schomberg Collection at the New York Public Library and at Princeton University.

SECONDARY WORKS

BIOGRAPHICAL AND CRITICAL STUDIES

Algeo, Ann M. *The Courtroom as Forum: Homicide Trials by Dreiser, Wright, Capote, and Mailer*. New York: Peter Lang, 1996.
Bloom Harold, ed. *Richard Wright's "Native Son": Modern Critical Interpretations*. New York: Chelsea House, 1988.
Brignano, Russel C. *Richard Wright: An Introduction to the Man and His Works*. Pittsburgh: University of Pittsburgh Press, 1970.
Burgum, Edwin B. "The Art of Richard Wright's Short Stories." In his *The Novel and the World's Dilemma*. New York: Russell and Russell, 1963.
Butler, Robert J., ed. *The Critical Response to Richard Wright*. Westport, Conn.: Greenwood Press, 1995.
Callaloo 28 (Summer 1986). Special Wright issue edited by Maryemma Graham.
Campbell, James. *Paris Interzone: Richard Wright, Lol-*

ita, *Boris Vian and Others on the Left Bank, 1946–1960*. London: Secker & Warburg, 1994.

CLA Journal 12 (June 1969). Special Wright issue.

Cripps, Thomas. "*Native Son* in the Movies." *New Letters* 38:49–63 (Winter 1971).

Delmar, P. Jay. "Tragic Patterns in Richard Wright's *Uncle Tom's Children*." *Negro American Literature Forum* 10:3–12 (Spring 1976).

Ellison, Ralph. "Richard Wright's Blues." *Antioch Review* 5:198–211 (1945).

Fabre, Michel. *The Unfinished Quest of Richard Wright*. Translated by Isabel Barzun. New York: William Morrow, 1973.

————. *The World of Richard Wright*. Jackson: University of Mississippi Press, 1985.

————. *Richard Wright: Books & Writers*. Jackson: University of Mississippi Press, 1990.

Fabre, Michel, and Ellen Wright, eds. *Richard Wright Reader*. New York: Harper & Row, 1978.

Farnsworth, Robert, ed. *The Life and Work of Richard Wright*. Kansas City, Mo.: University of Missouri–Kansas City, 1971.

Farnsworth, Robert, and Ray Davis, eds. *Richard Wright: Impressions and Perspectives*. Ann Arbor: University of Michigan Press, 1971.

Felgar, Robert. *Richard Wright*. Boston: Twayne, 1980.

Fishburn, Katherine. *Richard Wright's Hero: The Faces of a Rebel-Victim*. Metuchen, N.J.: Scarecrow Press, 1977.

French, Warren. "The Lost Potential of Richard Wright." In *The Black American Writer*. Vol. 1. Edited by C. W. E. Bigsby. Deland, Fla.: Everett/Edwards, 1969.

Gayle, Addison. *Richard Wright: Ordeal of a Native Son*. Garden City, N.Y.: Doubleday, 1980.

Gibson, Donald. "Existentialism in *The Outsider*." *Four Quarters* 7:17–26 (1958).

Gounard, Jean-François. *The Racial Problem in the Works of Richard Wright and James Baldwin*. Translated by Joseph J. Rodgers Jr. Westport, Conn.: Greenwood Press, 1992.

Hakutani, Yoshinobu, ed. *Critical Essays on Richard Wright*. Boston: G. K. Hall, 1982.

Hodges, John O. "An Apprenticeship to Life and Art: Narrative Design in Wright's *Black Boy*." *CLA Journal* 28:415–33 (1985).

Joyce, Joyce Ann. *Richard Wright's Art of Tragedy*. Iowa City: University of Iowa Press, 1986.

Keady, Sylvia H. "Richard Wright's Women Characters and Inequality." *Black American Literature Forum* 10:124–28 (Winter 1976).

Kearns, Edward. "The 'Fate' Section of *Native Son*." *Contemporary Literature* 12:146–155 (Spring 1971).

Kent, George E. "Richard Wright: Blackness and the Adventure of Western Culture." *CLA Journal* 12:322–43 (1969).

Kinnamon, Keneth. *The Emergence of Richard Wright*. Urbana: University of Illinois Press, 1972.

Lawson, Lewis. "Cross Damon: Kierkegaardian Man of Dread." *CLA Journal* 14:298–316 (1971).

Macksey, Richard, and Frank E. Moorer, eds. *Richard Wright: A Collection of Critical Essays*. Englewood Cliffs, N.J.: Prentice-Hall, 1984.

Margolies, Edward. *The Art of Richard Wright*. Carbondale: Southern Illinois University Press, 1969.

McCall, Dan. *The Example of Richard Wright*. New York: Harcourt Brace, & World, 1969.

Miller, Eugene. *Voice of a Native Son: The Poetics of Richard Wright*. Jackson: University of Mississippi Press, 1990.

Reilly, John M. "*Lawd Today*: Richard Wright's Experiment in Naturalism." *Studies in Black Literature* 2:14–17 (Autumn 1971).

————. "Richard Wright's Curious Thriller, *Savage Holiday*." *CLA Journal* 21:218–23 (1977).

————, ed. *Richard Wright: The Critical Reception*. New York: Burt Franklin, 1978.

Smith, Valerie. "Alienation and Creativity in the Fiction of Richard Wright." In her *Self-Discovery and Authority in Afro-American Narrative*. Cambridge, Mass.: Harvard University Press, 1987. Pp. 65–87.

Sprandel, Katherine. "*The Long Dream*." *New Letters* 38:88–96 (Winter 1971).

Trotman, C. James, ed. *Richard Wright: Myths and Realities*. New York: Garland, 1988.

Turner, Darwin T. "*The Outsider*: Revision of an Idea." *CLA Journal* 12:310–21 (1969).

Urban, Joan. *Richard Wright*. New York: Chelsea House Publishers, 1989.

Walker, Ian. "Black Nightmare: The Fiction of Richard Wright." In *Black Fiction: New Studies in the Afro-American Novel Since 1945*. Edited by A. Robert Lee. London: Vision Press, 1980.

Walker, Margaret. *Richard Wright: Daemonic Genius*. New York: Warner Books, 1988.

Webb, Constance. *Richard Wright: A Biography*. New York: Putnam's, 1968.

Williams, John A. *The Most Native of Sons*. Garden City, N.Y.: Doubleday, 1970.

BIBLIOGRAPHIES

Brignano, Russel C. "Richard Wright: A Bibliography of Secondary Sources." *Studies in Black Literature* 2:19–25 (Summer 1971).

Davis, Charles T, and Michel Fabre. *Richard Wright: A Primary Bibliography*. Boston: G. K. Hall, 1982. (Contains a list of Wright's unpublished manuscripts.)

Inge, Thomas, Maurice Duke, and Jackson R. Byer, eds. *Black American Writers: Bibliographical Essays*. 2 vols. New York: St. Martin's Press, 1978.

Kinnamon, Keneth, Joseph Benson, Michel Fabre, and Craig Werner. *A Richard Wright Bibliography: Fifty Years of Criticism and Commentary, 1933–1982*. Westport, Conn.: Greenwood Press, 1988.

AUDIO RECORDINGS

Black Boy. Prince Frederick, Md.: Recorded Books, 1998.

Literature of the Black Experience. Washington, D. C.: National Public Radio, 1981.

VIDEO RECORDINGS

I'll Make Me a World: The Dream Keepers. Directed by Tracey Heather Strain. New York: WNET-TV, 1999.

Native Son. Presented by Walter Gould. Chicago: Facets Video, 1994.

Richard Wright, Black Boy. Written, directed, and produced by Madison Davis Lacy. San Francisco: California Newsreel, 1994.

Richard Wright: Writing His Weapon. Directed by Rex Barnett. Atlanta, Ga.: History on Video, 1995.

FILM

Three Black Writers. New York: WCBS and Columbia University, 1969.

ACKNOWLEDGMENTS

Acknowledgment is gratefully made to those publishers and individuals who have permitted the use of the following material in copyright.

Williams Andrews, excerpts from *To Tell a Free Story: The First Century of Afro-American Autobiography, 1760–1865*. Copyright © 1986 by William Andrews. Reprinted with the permission of the author and the University of Illinois Press.

Toni Cade Bambara, excerpts from "What It Is I Think I'm Doing Anyhow" from *The Writer On Her Work*, edited by Janet Sternberg. Copyright © 1980 by Janet Sternberg. Reprinted with the permission of W. W. Norton & Company, Inc.

Amiri Baraka, excerpts from "Philistinism and the Negro Writer" from *Anger and Beyond: The Negro Writer in the United States*, edited by Herbert Hill (New York: Harper, 1966). Copyright © 1968 by Amiri Baraka. Excerpts from *The Autobiography of LeRoi Jones/Amiri Baraka*. Copyright © 1984 by Amiri Baraka. Excerpts from "Preface to a Twenty Volume Suicide Note," "In Memory of Radio," "Look for You Yesterday, Here You Come Today," and "Notes for a Speech" from *Preface to a Twenty Volume Suicide Note*. Copyright © 1961 by Amiri Baraka. Excerpts from "An Agony. As Now," "BLACK DADA NIHILISMUS," and "Rhythm & Blues" from *The Dead Lecturer* (New York: Grove Press, 1964). Copyright © 1964 by Amiri Baraka. Excerpts from "Dutchman" from *Dutchman and The Slave* (New York: William Morrow, 1964). Copyright © 1964 by Amiri Baraka. Excerpts from "A Poem Some People Have to Understand," "A Poem for Black Hearts," "Black Art," and "The World Is Full of Remarkable Things" from *Black Magic* (Indianapolis: The Bobbs-Merrill Company, 1969). Copyright © 1969 by Amiri Baraka. "Y The Link

Will Not Always Be Missing #40" from *Wise, Why's Y's* (Chicago: Third World Press, 1995). Copyright © 1995 by Amiri Baraka. Excerpt from "Monk's World" from *Funk Lore* (Los Angeles: Littoral Books, 1996). Copyright © 1996 by Amiri Baraka. "Ka' Ba" from *Black Magic* (Indianapolis: The Bobbs-Merrill Company, 1969). Copyright © 1969 by Amiri Baraka. All reprinted with the permission of Sterling Lord Literistic, Inc.

Stephen Vincent Benét, excerpt from *John Brown's Body* (New York: Doubleday, 1928). Copyright 1927, 1928 by Stephen Vincent Benét. Reprinted with the permission of Brandt & Brandt Literary Agents, Inc.

Jacqueline Berben-Masai, excerpt from "From *Brother and Keepers* to *Two Cities*: Social and Cultural Consciousness, Art and Imagination: An Interview with John Edgar Wideman" from *Callaloo* 22.3 (1999). Copyright © 1999 by Charles H. Rowell. Reprinted with the permission of The Johns Hopkins University Press.

Gwendolyn Brooks, excerpts from "Gay Chaps at the Bar," "The Bean Eaters," "A Bronzeville Mother," "The Last Quatrain," "Mrs. Small," "Jessie Mitchell's Mother," "The Ballad of Rudolph Reed," "The Anniad," and "In the Mecca" from *Blacks* (Chicago: Third World Press, 1991). Copyright © 1991 by Gwendolyn Brooks. Reprinted with the permission of the author.

Sterling A. Brown, excerpts from "The Odyssey of Big Boy" and "Southern Road" from *The Collected Poems of Sterling A. Brown*, edited by Michael S. Harper. Copyright © 1980 by Sterling A.

Leon Forrest, excerpts from "The Light of the Lightness Transformed" from *The Furious Voice for Freedom: Essays on Life*. Copyright © 1994 by Leon Forrest. Reprinted with the permission of Asphodel Press.

Ernest J. Gaines, excerpt from "A Conversation with Ernest Gaines," edited by Ruth Laney, in *South Review* 10 (Winter 1974). Copyright © 1974 by Ernest J. Gaines. Reprinted with the permission of the author. Excerpt from "Miss Jane and I" from *Callaloo* 3 (May 1978). Copyright © 1978 by Charles H. Rowell. Reprinted with the permission of The Johns Hopkins University Press. Excerpts from *A Lesson Before Dying*. Copyright © 1993 by Ernest J. Gaines. Reprinted with the permission of Alfred A. Knopf, a division of Random House, Inc.

Nikki Giovanni, "The True Import of Present Dialogue Black vs. Negro" from *Black Feeling, Black Talk/Black Judgement*. Copyright © 1968, 1970 by Nikki Giovanni. Reprinted with the permission of HarperCollins Publishers, Inc.

Vince Gotera, excerpts from " 'Lines of Tempered Steel': An Interview with Yusef Komunyakaa" in *Callaloo* 13, no. 2 (1990). Copyright © 1990 by Charles H. Rowell. Reprinted with the permission of The Johns Hopkins University Press.

Michael S. Harper, excerpts from "American History," "Brother John," "Strange Song," "Deathwatch," "We Assume: On the Death of Our Son, Reuben Masai Harper," and "Dear John, Dear Coltrane" from *Dear John, Dear Coltrane* (Pittsburgh: University of Pittsburgh Press, 1970). Copyright © 1970 by Michael S. Harper. Reprinted with the permission of the author. "Love Medley: Patrice Cuchulain" from *History Is Your Own Heartbeat: Poems* (Urbana: University of Illinois Press, 1971). Copyright © 1971 by Michael S. Harper. Reprinted with the permission of the author and the University of Illinois Press. Excerpts from "High Modes: Vision as Ritual: Confirmation" from *Images of Kin*. Copyright © 1977 by Michael S. Harper. Reprinted with the permission of the author and the University of Illinois Press. Excerpts from "Song: I Want a Witness" and "Homage to the New World" from *Song: I Want a Witness* (Pittsburgh: University of Pittsburgh Press, 1972). Copyright © 1972 by Michael S. Harper. Reprinted with the permission of the author. Excerpt from "History as Apple Tree" from *Photographs: Negatives: History as Apple Tree* (San Francisco: Scarab Press, 1972). Copyright © 1972 by Michael S. Harper. Reprinted with the permission of the author. Excerpt from "A White Friend Flies in from the Coast" from *Debridement* (Garden City: Doubleday, 1973). Copyright © 1972 by Michael S. Harper. Reprinted with the permission of the author. Excerpt from "Br'er Sterling and the Rocker" from *The Collected Poems of Sterling A. Brown*, edited by Michael S. Harper. Copyright © 1980 by Michael S. Harper. Reprinted with the permission of HarperCollins Publishers, Inc. Excerpt from "Alice" from *Nightmare Begins Responsibility*. Copyright © 1977 by Michael S. Harper. Reprinted with the permission of the author and the University of Illinois Press. Excerpts from "The Drowning of the Facts of Life" from *Healing Song for Inner Ear*. Copyright © 1985 by Michael S. Harper. Reprinted with the permission of the author and the University of Illinois Press. Epigraph and excerpts from "Study Windows" and "Homage to the Brown Bomber" from *Honorable Amendments*. Copyright © 1995 by Michael S. Harper. Reprinted with the permission of the author and the University of Illinois Press.

Robert Hayden, all poetry is from *Collected Poems of Robert Hayden*, edited by Frederick Glaysher. Copyright © 1962, 1966, 1970, 1972, 1975 by Robert Hayden. Copyright © 1985 by Emma Hayden. Reprinted with the permission of Liveright Publishing Corporation.

Langston Hughes, all poetry from *The Collected Poems of Langston Hughes*, edited by Arnold Rampersad and David Roessel. Copyright © 1994 by the Estate of Langston Hughes. Reprinted with the permission of Alfred A. Knopf, a division of Random House, Inc.

Zora Neal Hurston, excerpts from *Their Eyes Were Watching God*. Copyright 1937 by Harper & Row, Publishers, Inc., renewed © 1965 by John C. Hurston and Joel Hurston. Reprinted with the permission of HarperCollins Publishers, Inc.

Kennedy in One Act. Copyright © 1988 by Adrienne Kennedy. Reprinted with the permission of University of Minnesota Press.

Keorapetse Kgositsile, excerpt from "When Brown Is Black." Reprinted with the permission of the author.

Jamaica Kincaid, excerpts from *Annie John.* Copyright © 1983 by Jamaica Kincaid. Excerpts from *Autobiography of My Mother.* Copyright © 1994 by Jamaica Kincaid. Excerpts from *My Brother.* Copyright © 1997 by Jamaica Kincaid. Reprinted with the permission of Farrar, Straus & Giroux, LLC.

Yusef Komunyakaa, excerpts from "Returning the Borrowed Road" from *Dedications and Other Dark Horses* (Laramie, Wyo.: Rocky Mountain Creative Arts Journal, 1977). Copyright © 1977 by Yusef Komunyakaa. Excerpts from "Pushing In All the Buttons," and "Following the Floorplan" from *Lost in the Bone-wheel Factory* (Amherst, Mass.: Lynx House Press, 1979). Copyright © 1979 by Yusef Komunyakaa. Excerpts from "Nothing Big" from *Toys in a Field* (Black River Press, 1986). Copyright © 1986 by Yusef Komunyakaa. Excerpts from "The Man Who Carries the Desert Around Inside Himself: For Wally," "Gerry's Jazz," and "Blue Light Lounge Sutra for the Performance Poets at Harold Park Hotel" from *February in Sydney*, Matchbook #17 (Unionville, Ind.: Matchbooks, 1989). Copyright © 1989 by Yusef Komunyakaa. All reprinted with the permission of the author. Excerpts from "The Tongue Is," "Songs for My Father," and "Changes, or Reveries at a Window Overlooking a Country Road, with Two Women Talking Blues in the Kitchen" from *Neon Vernacular: New and Selected Poems* (Middletown, Conn.: Wesleyan University Press, 1993). Copyright © 1993 by Yusef Komunyakaa. Reprinted with the permission of the University Press of New England. Excerpts from *Copacetic* (Middletown, Conn.: Wesleyan University Press, 1984). Copyright © 1984 by Yusef Komunyakaa. Reprinted with the permission of University Press of New England. Excerpts from *I Apologize for the Eyes in My Head* (Middletown, Conn.: Wesleyan University Press, 1986). Copyright © 1986 by Yusef Komunyakaa. Reprinted with

the permission of University Press of New England. Excerpts from *Dien Cai Dau* (Middletown, Conn.: Wesleyan University Press, 1988). Copyright © 1988 by Yusef Komunyakaa. Reprinted with the permission of University Press of New England. Excerpts from "Losses" from *Indiana Review* 10, nos. 1–2 (1987). Copyright © 1987 by Yusef Komunyakaa. Reprinted with the permission of *Indiana Review.* Yusef Komunyakaa, excerpts from "Ode to a Drum," "Testimony," and "Anodyne" from *Thieves of Paradise* (Middletown, Conn.: Wesleyan University Press, 1998). Copyright © 1998 by Yusef Komunyakaa. Reprinted with the permission of University Press of New England.

Audre Lorde, excerpts from "Uses of the Erotic: The Erotic as Power"; an interview with Adrienne Rich; "Eye to Eye: Black Women, Hatred and Anger"; and "The House of Yemanjá" from *Sister Outsider.* Copyright © 1984 by Audre Lorde. Reprinted with the permission of The Crossing Press. Excerpts from "125th Street and Abomey," "The Black Unicorn," "Fog Report," and "Recreation" from *The Black Unicorn.* Copyright © 1978 by Audre Lorde. Reprinted with the permission of W. W. Norton & Company, Inc. Excerpts from *Zami: A New Spelling of My Name.* Copyright © 1982 by Audre Lorde. Reprinted with the permission of The Crossing Press. Excerpts from "Love Poem" and "Afterimages" from *Chosen Poems, Old and New.* Copyright © 1982, 1976, 1974, 1973, 1970, 1968 by Audre Lorde. Reprinted with the permission of W. W. Norton & Company, Inc. Excerpt from "On My Way Out I Passed Over You and the Verrazano Bridge" from *Our Dead Behind Us.* Copyright © 1986 by Audre Lorde. Reprinted with the permission of W. W. Norton & Company, Inc. "Learning to Write" from *Collected Poems.* Copyright © 1997 by the Estate of Audre Lorde. Reprinted with the permission of W. W. Norton & Company, Inc.

Clarence Major, excerpt from "Self-Interview" in *The Dark and the Feeling: Black American Writers and Their Work* (New York: Third Press, 1974). Copyright © 1974 by Clarence Major. Reprinted with the permission of the author. Excerpts from *All-Night Visitors,* unexpurgated edition. Copyright © 1969, 1998

Saga. Copyright © 1991 by Ntozake Shange. Reprinted with the permission of St. Martin's Press, LLC.

Karl Shapiro, excerpt from the introduction to Melvin Tolson, *Harlem Gallery: Book I, The Curator.* Copyright © 1965 by Karl Shapiro. Reprinted with the permission of Twayne Publishers, a division of Simon & Schuster, Inc.

James Edward Smethurst, excerpts from *The New Red Negro: The Literary Left and African American Poetry, 1930–1946,* edited by John Callahan Copyright © 1999 by Oxford University Press, Inc. Reprinted with the permission of the publishers.

A. B. Spellman, excerpt from "The Beautiful Day #9." Reprinted with the permission of the author.

Melvin Tolson, excerpts from "Psi" and "Alpha" from *Harlem Gallery: Book I, The Curator* (New York: Twayne, 1965). Copyright © 1965 by Melvin Tolson. Excerpt from *Caviar and Cabbage,* edited by Robert Farnsworth. Copyright © 1982 by Melvin Tolson. Excerpt from "Odyssey of a Manuscript" from *New Letters* 48 (Fall 1981). Copyright © 1981 by Melvin Tolson. Melvin Tolson, excerpt from opening poem and "The Underdog" from *A Gallery of Harlem Portraits,* edited by Robert Farnsworth (Columbia: University of Missouri Press, 1979). Copyright © 1979 by Melvin Tolson. Melvin Tolson, excerpts from "Dark Symphony" from *Rendezvous With America* (New York: Dodd, Mean, 1944). Excerpts from *Libretto for the Republic of Liberia.* Copyright 1953 by Melvin Tolson. All reprinted with the permission of Melvin B. Tolson, Jr.

Jean Toomer, excerpts from "Karintha," and "Song" from *Cane.* Copyright 1923 by Boni & Liveright, renewed 1951 by Jean Toomer. Reprinted with the permission of Liveright Publishing Corporation.

Margaret Walker, excerpts from "I Want to Write," "For My People," "Dark Blood," "We Have Been Believers," "Farish Street," "I Hear a Rumbling," and "On Youth and Age" from *This Is My Century: New and Collected Poems.* Copyright © 1989 by Margaret Walker Alexander. Reprinted with the permission of The University of Georgia Press.

John Edgar Wideman, excerpts from the preface, and from "The Beginning of Homewood" from *Damballah.* Copyright © 1988 by John Edgar Wideman. Reprinted with the permission of Vintage Books, a division of Random House, Inc. Excerpts from "Frame and Dialect: The Evolution of the Black Voice in Fiction," *American Poetry Review* 5 (1976). Copyright © 1976 by John Edgar Wideman. Reprinted with the permission of the author. Excerpts from *Philadelphia Fire.* Copyright © 1990 by John Edgar Wideman. Reprinted with the permission of Henry Holt and Company, LLC. Excerpts from *The Cattle Killing.* Copyright © 1996 by John Edgar Wideman. Reprinted with the permission of Houghton Mifflin Company. All rights reserved.

Sherley Anne Williams, "Any Woman's Blues" [2 poems] from *The Peacock Poems* (Middletown, Conn.: Wesleyan University Press, 1975). Copyright © 1975 by Sherley Anne Williams. Reprinted with the permission of University Press of New England. Excerpts from "Letters from a New England Negro" and "the hard time Blues" from *Some One Sweet Angel Chile* (New York: William Morrow, 1982). Copyright © 1982 by Sherley Anne Williams. Reprinted with the permission of the author c/o the Sandra Dijkstra Literary Agency.

August Wilson, excerpts from *Ma Rainey's Black Bottom.* Copyright © 1985 by August Wilson. Excerpts from *Two Trains Running.* Copyright © 1993 by August Wilson. Excerpts from *The Piano Lesson.* Copyright © 1990 by August Wilson. All reprinted with the permission of Penguin, a division of Penguin Putnam Inc.

Jay Wright, excerpts from "A Non-Birthday Poem for My Father," "Destination: Accomplished," "Family Reunion," from *Selected Poems of Jay Wright* (Princeton: Princeton University Press, 1987). Copyright © 1987 by Jay Wright. Excerpt from "The Dead" and excerpt from an untitled poem from *Soothsayers and Omens* (New York: Seven Winds Press, 1976). Copyright © 1976 by Jay Wright. Excerpts from "MacIntyre, the Captain, and the Saints," "Tensions and Resolutions," "Love Plumbs to the Center of the Earth," and "The Body Adorned and Bare" from *Explications/Interpre-*

Photographs and Illustrations

Frances Ellen Watkins Harper. Source unknown.

Michael Harper. Photograph by Rachel M. Harper. Used by permission of the University of Illinois Press.

Robert Hayden. Fisk University Library. Reproduced by permission.

Chester Himes. Fisk University Library. Reproduced by permission.

Langston Hughes. The Bettmann Archive/ Newsphotos, Inc./Corbis-Bettmann. Reproduced by permission.

Zora Neale Hurston. AP/Wide World Photos. Reproduced by permission.

Charles Johnson. Photograph by Jerry Bauer. © Jerry Bauer. Reproduced by permission.

James Weldon Johnson. Fisk University Library. Reproduced by permission. James Weldon Johnson, Bob Cole, and Rosamond Johnson. Source unknown.

June Jordan. AP/Wide World Photos. Reproduced by permission.

Jamaica Kincaid. Photograph by Jerry Bauer. © Jerry Bauer. Reproduced by permission.

Yusef Komunyakaa. Photograph by Ted Rosenberg. Reproduced by permission.

Nella Larsen. The Beinecke Rare Book and Manuscript Library. Reproduced by the Yale Collection of American Literature, Beinecke Rare Book and Manuscript Library. Reproduced by permission. Nella Larsen receiving the Harmon. UPI/Corbis-Bettmann. Reproduced by permission.

Audre Lorde. The Library of Congress.

Paule Marshall. AP/Wide World Photos. Reproduced by permission.

Claude McKay. The Library of Congress.

Toni Morrison. AP/Wide World Photos. Reproduced by permission. Accepting the Nobel Prize, 1993. AP/Wide World Photos, Inc. Reproduced by permission.

Gloria Naylor. AP/Wide World Photos. Reproduced by permission.

Bishop Daniel A. Payne. Fisk University Library. Reproduced by permission.

Ann Petry. AP/Wide World Photos. Reproduced by permission.

Ishmael Reed. AP/Wide World Photos. Reproduced by permission.

Sonia Sanchez. The Granger Collection, New York. Reproduced by permission.

Ntozake Shange. AP/Wide World Photos. Reproduced by permission. Ntozake Shange and Laurie Carlos. UPI/Bettmann. Reproduced by permission.

Slave narrative poster, 1851. Courtesy of The Library of Congress. Slave narrative poster, 1769. Mason I. Lowance, Jr. Reproduced by permission.

Melvin B. Tolson. The Library of Congress.

Jean Toomer. Source unknown.

Alice Walker. AP/Wide World Photos. Reproduced by permission. Whoopi Goldberg and Margaret Avery in a scene from *The Color Purple*. Archive Photos/Warner Bros. Reproduced by permission.

Phillis Wheatley. The Bettmann Archive. Reproduced by permission.

John Edgar Wideman. Photograph by Jerry Bauer. © Jerry Bauer. Reproduced by permission.

John A. Williams. AP/Wide World Photos. Reproduced by permission.

August Wilson. AP/Wide World Photos. Reproduced by permission. The July 1970 Playbill for Athol Fugard's *Boesman and Lena*. Directed by John Berry. PLAYBILL is a registered trademark of Playbill Incorporated, N.Y.C. All rights reserved. Reproduced by permission.

Richard Wright. Archive Photos. Reproduced by permission. Richard Wright seated at his typewriter. Corbis-Bettman. Reproduced by permission.

Malcolm X. Corbis-Bettmann. Reproduced by permission.

CONTRIBUTORS

William L. Andrews. E. Maynard Adams Professor of English, University of North Carolina, Chapel Hill. Chair of the Department of English. Author of *The Literary Career of Charles W. Chesnutt* and *To Tell a Free Story: The First Century of Afro-American Autobiography, 1760–1865.* Co-editor *of The Norton Anthology of African American Literature* and *The Oxford Companion to African American Literature.* CHARLES W. CHESNUTT

Katherine Clay Bassard. Associate Professor of English, Virginia Commonwealth University. Author of *Spiritual Interrogations: Culture, Gender and Community in Early African American Women's Writing.* SPIRITUAL AUTOBIOGRAPHY

Herman Beavers. Associate Professor with the Department of English and Director of the Afro-American Studies Program at the University of Pennsylvania. Author of *A Neighborhood of Feeling; Wrestling Angels into Song: The Fictions of Ernest J. Gaines and James Alan McPherson,* and the forthcoming *Prodigal Allegories* and *Still Life with Guitar.* JOHN A. WILLIAMS

Daphne A. Brooks. Assistant Professor of Literature, University of California, San Diego. Published articles on black feminist theory, performance, and nineteenth-century literature. Author of the forthcoming *Bodies in Dissent: Performing Race, Gender, and Nation in the Trans-Atlantic Imaginary.* PAULINE HOPKINS

Jane Campbell. Professor of English, Purdue University, Calumet. Author of *Mythic Black Fiction: The Transformation of History.* Her work has appeared in *Callaloo: A Journal of African and African American Arts and Letters; Obsidian; Black Women in America; Oxford Companion to Women's Writing in the United States; Dictionary of Literary Biography; Heath Anthology of American Literature; Belles Lettres,* and *U.S. Media and the Middle East: Image and Perception.* MARGARET WALKER

Barbara T. Christian. Professor in the African American Studies Department at the University of California, Berkeley, where she helped found the doctoral program in African Diasporic Studies. Author of *Black Women Novelists: The Development of a Tradition* and *Black Feminist Criticism,* editor of the contemporary section of the first *Norton Anthology of African American Literature,* and co-editor of a feminist collection entitled *Female Subjects in Black and White: Psychoanalysis, Race, and Feminism* with Elizabeth Abel and Helene Moglen. PAULE MARSHALL

James W. Coleman. Associate Professor of English, University of North Carolina, Chapel Hill. Author of *Blackness and Modernism: The Literary Career of John Edgar Wideman;* numerous essays in literary journals, and a forthcoming book on African American male writers. JOHN EDGAR WIDEMAN

Wayne F. Cooper. Historian, writer, and editor. Author of *Claude McKay: Rebel Sojourner in the Harlem Renaissance.* Editor of *The Passion of Claude McKay: Selected Poetry and Prose, 1912–1948.* CLAUDE MCKAY

George P. Cunningham. Professor with the African Studies department at Brooklyn College (CUNY). Author of *Langston Hughes and the Discourse of the Harlem Renaissance.* Co-editor, with Marcellus Blout, of *Representing Black Men.* W. E. B. DU BOIS

Thadious M. Davis. G. C. Vanderbilt Professor of English at Vanderbilt University. Her publications in African American and Southern literatures include *Nella Larsen, Novelist of the Harlem Renaissance* and *Faulkner's "Negro": Art and the Southern Context.* ERNEST J. GAINES

Elin Diamond. Professor of English, Rutgers University. Editor of *Performance and Cultural Politics.* Author of *Unmaking Mimesis: Essays on Feminism and Theater; Pinter's Comic Play,* and numerous essays on performance and feminist theory. ADRIENNE KENNEDY

Madhu Dubey. Associate Professor of English and Afro-American Studies, Brown University. Author of *Black Women Novelists and the Nationalist Aesthetic* and of essays on twentieth-century African American fiction. TONI CADE BAMBARA

Brent Hayes Edwards. Assistant Professor of English, Rutgers University. Author of the upcoming book, *The Practice of Diaspora*. CLARENCE MAJOR

Harry J. Elam Jr. Christensen Professor for the Humanities, Director of the Introduction to the Humanities Program, Director of Graduate Studies for Drama, and Director of the Committee on Black Performing Arts at Stanford University. Author of *Taking It to the Streets: The Social Protest Theater of Luis Valdez and Amiri Baraka*, co-editor of *Colored Contradictions: An Anthology of Contemporary African American Drama*, co-editor of *A Critical Reader on African American Performance and Theatre History*, and author of *(W)Righting History: The Past as Present in the Drama of August Wilson* (forthcoming). His articles have appeared in *American Drama, Theatre Journal, Text and Performance Quarterly*, as well as in several critical anthologies. AUGUST WILSON

Frances Smith Foster. Charles Howard Candler Professor of English and Women's Studies, Emory University. Director of the Institute for Women's Studies, Emory University. Editor of *A Brighter Coming Day: A Frances Ellen Watkins Harper Reader* and *Minnie's Sacrifice, Trial and Triumph, and Sowing and Reaping: Three Rediscovered Novels by Frances E. W. Harper*. FRANCES ELLEN WATKINS HARPER

Carla Freccero. Professor of Literature and Women's Studies, University of California, Santa Cruz. Co-editor of *Premodern Sexualities and Popular Culture: An Introduction*. JUNE JORDAN

Lisbeth Gant-Britton. Marlene Crandell Francis Professor of the Humanities, Kalamazoo College. Author of *African-American History: Heroes in Hardship*. Published in *Camera Obscura* and the University of California, Los Angeles's *Paroles Gelees*. Contributor to *Peering into Darkness: Race and Color in the Fantastic* and *Women of Other Worlds: Excursions Through Science Fiction and Feminism*. Winner of the Los Angeles Mayor's Office Special Commendation for contribution to racial understanding through education. OCTAVIA BUTLER

Henry Louis Gates Jr. Author of *Figures in Black: Words, Signs and the Racial Self; The Signifying Monkey: Towards a Theory of Afro-American Literary Criticism;* and numerous journal articles, essays, and book reviews. Editor of the *Norton Anthology of Afro-American Literature*, among others.

Winner of the American Book Award, 1989. ISHMAEL REED

Vince Gotera. Editor of *North American Review*. Teaches creative writing and multicultural literature at the University of Northern Iowa. YUSEF KOMUNYAKAA

Nathan Grant. Assistant Professor of English, State University of New York at Buffalo. He has published several articles, in *American Drama, Callaloo*, and *African American Review* on African American literature, art, theater and film, and is currently at work on a book on Jean Toomer, Zora Neale Hurston, masculinity, and contemporary black writing. COUNTEE CULLEN

Robert M. Greenberg. Associate Professor of American Studies, Temple University. Author of *Splintered Worlds: Fragmentation and the Ideal of Diversity in the Work of Emerson, Melville, Whitman, and Dickinson*. ROBERT HAYDEN

Farah Jasmine Griffin. Associate Professor of English, University of Pennsylvania. Author of *Who Set You Flowin'?: The African American Migration Narrative* and *If You Can't Be Free Be a Mystery: In Search of Billie Holiday*. Editor of *Beloved Sisters and Loving Friends: Letters from Addie Brown of Hartford and Rebecca Primus of Royal Oak, Maryland*. Co-editor of *Stranger in the Village: Two Centuries of African American Travel Writing*. SHERLEY ANNE WILLIAMS

Eric L. Haralson. GLORIA NAYLOR

William J. Harris. Author of *The Poetry and Poetics of Amiri Baraka: The Jazz Aesthetic*. Editor of *The Leroi Jones/Amiri Baraka Reader*. Co-editor of *Call & Response: The Riverside Anthology of the African Literary Tradition*. Teaches American and African American literature and creative writing at Pennsylvania State University. AMIRI BARAKA

Stephen E. Henderson. Professor of Afro-American Studies, Howard University. Editor of *Understanding the New Black Poetry*. Co-author, with Mercer Cook, of *The Militant Black Writer*. Author of numerous articles on black American culture and poetry. Former director of the Institute for the Arts and Humanities, Howard University. STERLING BROWN

Marianne Hirsch. JAMAICA KINCAID

Margaret Homans. Author of *Women Writers and Poetic Identity; Bearing the Word: Language and Female Experience in Nineteenth-Century Women's Writing;* and articles on Toni Morrison, Alice Walker, and Gloria Naylor. AUDRE LORDE

Dianne Johnson. Associate Professor of English, University of South Carolina. Researches on the history of African American children's literature. As Dinah Johnson, author of four picture books. LUCILLE CLIFTON

Norman W. Jones. Doctoral candidate at the University of California, Los Angeles. RALPH ELLISON

Joyce Ann Joyce. Professor and Chair of the African American Studies Department, Temple University. Author of *Warriors, Conjurers, and Priests: Defining African-Centered Literary Criticism; Richard Wright's Art of Tragedy*, and *Sonia Sanchez and the African Poetic Tradition*. Co-editor of *The New Cavalcade: African American Writing from 1760 to the Present*. Author of numerous articles on the works of African American writers and novelists. RICHARD WRIGHT

Vera M. Kutzinski. Professor of English, African American Studies, and American Studies, Yale University. Author *of Against the American Grain* and *Sugar's Secrets*. Currently writing a book on contemporary Caribbean fiction. JAY WRIGHT

Alycee J. Lane. Assistant Professor of English at the University of California, Santa Barbara. Publications include *Black Bodies/Gay Bodies: The Politics of Race in the Gay/Military Battle;* "Black Power Movement" in *Gay Histories and Cultures: An Encyclopedia of Lesbian and Gay Histories;* and the foreword to *Loving Her*. GAYL JONES

James K. Lee. Assistant Professor of English and Asian American Studies, University of Texas, Austin. Postdoctoral fellow, University of California, San Diego. Published in *Literary Studies: East and West; Korean Culture*, and other critical collections. ISHMAEL REED

Lois Leveen. Visiting Assistant Professor of English and Humanities, Reed College. Published articles in *MELUS, Women's Studies*, and *African American Review*. JESSIE REDMON FAUSET

Arthur L. Little Jr. Associate Professor of English, University of California, Los Angeles. Author of *Shakespeare Jungle Fever: National-Imperial Revisions of Race, Rape, and Sacrifice*. Published articles on William Shakespeare and other early modern dramatists. SAMUEL R. DELANY

Mason Lowance Jr. Professor of English, University of Massachusetts, Amherst. Former Guggenheim Fellow and Fellow of the National Humanities Institute, Yale University, and a member of the American Antiquarian Society. Author of *Increase Mather; Massachusetts Broadsides of the American Revolution; The Language of Canaan; The Typological Writings of Jonathan Edwards; The Stowe Debate;* and *Against Slavery: An Abolitionist Reader*. THE SLAVE NARRATIVE IN AMERICAN LITERATURE

Wahneema Lubiano. Teaches in the Literature Program and African and African American Studies Program, Duke University. Author of the forthcoming *Like Being Mugged by a Metaphor*. TONI MORRISON

Nellie Y. McKay. Professor of American and African American Literature, University of Wisconsin, Madison. Publications include *Jean Toomer, Artist: A Study of His Literary Life and Work*. Editor of *Critical Essays on Toni Morrison*. General co-editor of the *Norton Anthology of African American Literature*, and co-editor of *Approaches to Teaching the Novels of Toni Morrison* and *Beloved, A Casebook*. Has published many essays and articles on African American and American fiction and autobiography. JEAN TOOMER

Marilyn Mobley McKenzie. Associate Professor of English and African American Studies, George Mason University. Author of *Folk Roots and Mythic Wings in Sarah Orne Jewett and Toni Morrison: The Cultural Function of Narrative;* the forthcoming *Spaces for the Reader: Toni Morrison, Black Studies, and the Praxis of Cultural Studies*, and numerous articles and reviews about Toni Morrison, Black women writers, and African American life and culture. ANN PETRY

Jacquelyn McLendon. Associate Professor and Associate Chair of English, Director of Black Studies, College of William and Mary. Author of *The Politics of Color in the Fiction of Jessie Fauset and Nella Larsen*, and numerous articles in the field of African American literature. GWENDOLYN BROOKS; NELLA LARSEN

James A. Miller. Professor of English and American Studies and Director of Africana Studies, The George Washington University. Editor of *Harlem: The Vision of Marvin and Morgan Smith* and *Approaches to Teaching Wright's "Native Son."* LEON FORREST

Keidra Morris. Doctoral student in the English department at the University of California, Los Angeles, specializing in Afro-American and Caribbean literature with an emphasis in transnational migration. PAUL LAURENCE DUNBAR; MELVIN TOLSON

Harryette Mullen. Associate Professor of English and African American Studies, University of California, Los Angeles. Published on topics regarding African American literature and culture. Author of four books of poetry, including *Muse & Drudge*, and the forthcoming *Sleeping with the Dictionary*. THE BLACK ARTS MOVEMENT

Robert G. O'Meally. Zora Neale Hurston Professor of English and Comparative Literature and Director of the Center for Jazz Studies, Columbia University. Author of *The Craft of Ralph Ellison and Lady Day: The Many Faces of Billie Holiday* and editor *of Living with Music: The Jazz Writings of Ralph Ellison* (forthcoming). RALPH ELLISON

Arnold Rampersad. Sara Hart Kimball Professor in the Department of English, Stanford University. Author of *The Life of Langston Hughes.* LANGSTON HUGHES

Esther Nettles Rauch. Author of articles in such publications as *College Composition and Communication* and *Puckerbrush Press.* PAUL LAURENCE DUNBAR

Sonnet Retman. Teaches at University of California, Los Angeles and Occidental College. Currently working on a book tracing the construction of race, region, and nation in documentary texts of the 1930s. CHARLES JOHNSON

Mary Margaret Richards. Associate Professor of English, Wofford College. Author of articles on Alice Walker, Anne Tyler, T. S. Eliot, and William Shakespeare. ALICE WALKER

Sandra L. Richards. Professor with the Department of African American Studies and Department of Theatre at Northwestern University. Author of *Ancient Songs Set Ablaze: The Theatre of Femi Osofisan* and of articles on African American and Nigerian playwrights. NTOZAKE SHANGE

Mark A. Sanders. Associate Professor of English, Director of African American Studies, Emory University. Editor of *A Son's Return: Selected Essays of Sterling A. Brown.* Author of *Afro-Modernist Aesthetics and the Poetry of Sterling A. Brown.* STERLING BROWN

Scott Saul. Teaches American cultural history, University of Virginia. Published articles and reviews in *Boston Review, TLS, Theater,* and other publications. Author of the forthcoming book, *Freedom Is and Freedom Ain't: Hard Bop and the Movement of American Culture.* MICHAEL S. HARPER

Ivy Schweitzer. Associate Professor of English, Dartmouth College. Author of *The Work of Self-Representation: Lyric Poetry in Colonial New England.* Co-editor of *The Literatures of Colonial America: An Anthology.* Early period editor of the *Heath Anthology of American Literature.* JAMAICA KINCAID

John C. Shields. Professor of English, Illinois State University. Author of *The American Aeneas: Classical Origins of the American Self* (forthcoming); *Eighteenth-Century American Poetry, an Anthology;* and numerous articles and essays. Editor of *The Collected Works of Phillis Wheatley.* PHILLIS WHEATLEY

J. T. Skerrett Jr. Professor of English, University of Massachusetts, Amherst. Author of critical articles on James Weldon Johnson, Richard Wright, Paule Marshall, Toni Morrison, and others. Co-editor of *Memory, Narrative and Identity: New Essays in Ethnic American Literatures* and *Memory and Cultural Politics: New Approaches to American Ethnic Literatures.* From 1987 to 1999, editor of *MELUS,* the journal of the Society for the Study of the Multi-Ethnic Literature of the United States. JAMES WELDON JOHNSON

Cynthia J. Smith. GAYL JONES

Suzette A. Spencer. Ph.D. candidate in the African Diaspora Studies Program at the University of California, Berkeley, where she studies African American and Caribbean literatures. PAULE MARSHALL

David Van Leer. Professor of English, University of California, Davis. Author of *Emerson's Epistemology: The Argument of the Essays; The Queening of America: Gay Culture in Straight Society;* the upcoming *Reconcilable Differences: Studies in Classic American Sexuality,* and articles on American culture for *The New Republic* and *The Times Literary Supplement.* JAMES BALDWIN

Alan M. Wald. Director of the Program in American Culture, Professor of English, University of Michigan. Author of five scholarly books on the U.S. literary left. Editor of "The Radical Novel Reconsidered" series at the University of Illinois Press. Serves on the editorial boards of *American Literature, Science & Society,* and *Against the Current.* CHESTER HIMES

Cheryl A. Wall. Professor of English, Rutgers University. Author of *Women of the Harlem Renaissance.* Editor of several volumes of and about Zora Neale Hurston. ZORA NEALE HURSTON

Margaret B. Wilkerson. Director of Media, Arts and Culture, Ford Foundation. Professor-on-Leave, African Studies, University of California, Berkeley. Author of *Nine Plays by Black Women.* Author of numerous articles on African American theatre and is completing a biography on Lorraine Hansberry. LORRAINE HANSBERRY

Wilburn Williams. Author of *The Desolate Servitude of Language: The Poetry of Melvin B. Tolson.* MELVIN TOLSON

INDEX

Numbers in boldface refer to extended treatment of a subject.

M

X

Y

Z